Media Sociology

Media Sociology

A READER

edited by

Jeremy Tunstall

University of Illinois Press
Urbana, Chicago, London

Originally published in Great Britain in 1970
by Constable and Co Ltd
Published simultaneously in the United States
by the University of Illinois Press
Introductory material copyright © 1970 by Jeremy Tunstall
American edition printed in Great Britain

Library of Congress Catalog Card No. 77-125598
252 00126 5

Acknowledgements

The publishers wish to thank the following for permission to use the undermentioned material: Roger L. Brown for 'Approaches to the Historical Development of Mass Media Studies'; Winston Fletcher for 'Britain's National Media Pattern'; Andrew Tudor for 'Film, Communication and Content'; James Curran for 'The Impact of Television on the Audience for Newspapers, 1945–68'; Aleksander Matejko for 'Newspaper Staff as a Social System'; Oliver Boyd-Barrett for 'Journalism Recruitment and Training: Problems in Professionalization'; Philip Elliott for 'Selection and Communication in a Television Production'; Michael Lane for 'Books and their Publishers'; Peter H. Mann for 'Books, Book Readers and Bookshops'; Johan Galtung and Mari Holmboe Ruge, and the *Journal of International Peace Research*, Oslo, for 'The Structure of Foreign News'; Jay G. Blumler and Denis McQuail, Univ. of Chicago Press, and Associated Book Publishers (Methuen) for 'The Audience for Election Television', extracts of which were taken from their book, *Television in Politics* (1968), and from *Television and the Political Image* (1961) by Denis McQuail and Joseph Trenaman; Denis McQuail for 'The Audience for Television Plays'; Jay G. Blumler and the Editor of *The Sociological Review* Monograph (1969) for 'Producers' Attitudes Towards Television Coverage of an Election Campaign'; the Editor of *The Sociological Review* Monograph (1969) for 'Public Service and Private World' by Tom Burns; *Social Forces* for 'Mass Communication and Social Change' by Melvin L. DeFleur, and 'The Mass Media and Egyptian Village Life' by Ibrahim Abu-Lughod; Joseph Bensman and Crowell, Collier and Macmillan Inc. for 'The Advertising Agency Man in New York' which is taken from *Dollars and Sense* (1967); *Public Opinion Quarterly* for 'Developments in Soviet Radio and Television News Reporting' by Gayle D. Hollander, and 'The Spiegel Affair and the West German Press' by Ronald F. Bunn; BBC Publications for 'Reflections on the Impact of Broadcasting' by Robert Silvey; *Revista Española de la Opinion Publica* for 'The Effects of Media Portrayal of

v

Violence and Aggression' by James Halloran; *Television Quarterly* for 'Decision-Making in Network Television News' by Malcolm Warner; Leicester University Press and the Television Research Committee for 'Social and Personality Factors Associated with Children's Tastes in TV Viewing' by D. Harper, Joan Munro and Hilde T. Himmelweit which is taken from their publication: *Second Progress Report and Recommendations* (1969); the Royal Statistical Society and B. P. Emmett for 'The Design of Investigations into the Effects of Radio and TV Programmes and Other Mass Communications'; and St. Martin's Press, Inc. for 'The National Press and Partisan Change' by David Butler and Donald Stokes which is taken from *Political Change in Britain: Forces Reshaping Electoral Choice* (1969).

Contents

vii

Introduction

Donald Hansen and Herschel Parsons, the American compilers of a research bibliography called *Mass Communication*, thought that of 10,000 separate items on the subject published between 1945 and 1967 less than 3,000 were worth inclusion. It has been said that most 'mass media' research compares unfavourably with the low standards of some other social science areas. Certainly the boundaries of mass media research are at least as unclear as those of some other proliferating fields of social science. The media are of concern not only to sociology, psychology, political science, history, international relations and other social sciences but also to linguistics, literary criticism, and those engineering and technology disciplines which have transformed and will continue to transform them. The media are also of sufficient interest to many commercial marketing organizations and to some governments to ensure that much media research is not published.

This Reader is called *Media Sociology*, partly to avoid words like 'mass' and 'communication', and partly to emphasize that it concentrates less than is usually the case upon audiences. 'Sociology' is intended in a fairly broad sense, and the book is meant for students taking introductory social science courses dealing with the media. In the introduction I will avoid summarizing each of the articles in the volume; instead I will deliberately concentrate on those areas of media sociology which are least well covered by research. These introductory remarks will, therefore, be of a speculative nature.

The volume contains only a few American pieces; although a Reader consisting primarily of British articles will be of more interest to British students, I hope that it may be of use also to some American students and researchers. American understanding of the British media – and, probably even more so, the media of most other countries – has often been rather imperfect.

Media research has long been dominated by American social scientists. Rather than attempt the impossible task of including even a selection of the American classics in this field, I have assumed that the reader of this volume also has access to at least one of the following:

Bernard Berelson and Morris Janowitz (eds.), *Reader in Public Opinion and Communication* (New York: Free Press. London: Collier-Macmillan), 1966 edition. 788 pp.
Lewis Anthony Dexter and David Manning White (eds.), *People, Society and Mass Communication* (New York: Free Press. London: Collier-Macmillan), 1964. 595 pp.
Wilbur Schramm (ed.), *Mass Communications* (Urbana: University of Illinois Press), 1960. 695 pp.

1. *The media: a value-laden subject**

Politics can never be far removed from those media which, in any country, enable few to speak to many. But in formal education, organized religion, culture, entertainment and leisure, the media are also widely regarded as being of central importance. A good deal of ordinary family life focuses upon the use of television, newspapers, magazines, radio and records. Moreover the media provide much of the material which members of one nation use to form images of other nations. All of these are spheres of human society where emotions tend to run high, attitudes are often forcefully expressed, and ideology is seldom absent. The nature and quality of the media play a part in the quality of our lives. To say that media issues are value-laden is, then, to understate. The media are saturated with social values of every conceivable kind.

Ideology, indeed, is present in the very terms with which social scientists have tried to describe the field – terms like 'propaganda', 'public opinion' and 'mass communication'. Propaganda, having derived its meaning from the *propagation* of the Roman Catholic faith, has since acquired overtones of political extremism and some dubious implicit assumptions about neutrality. 'Public opinion' also assumes certain values. 'Communication', often used to indicate merely interaction or behaviour, may seem a relatively value-free term, but it also carries value implications. Who is against 'better communication'? And 'mass media' or 'mass society' are the most value-laden terms of

* These headings broadly follow the order of articles. Exactly the same subheadings will be found in the introduction to the Selected Bibliography, at the end of this volume – pp. 545-6. Notes and Sources begin on p. 499.

all; Leon Bramson has shown in *The Political Context of Sociology* (1961) that the term 'mass' carries a double burden of both extreme left and extreme right ideology.

The term 'media', of course, is also neither clearly defined nor free of values; obviously 'media' places emphasis on the production and engineering apparatus – which may have ideological implications. For the moment I merely intend to say that 'media' for me means newspapers, magazines, radio, records, television and books operating on a fairly large scale.

The more serious difficulty, however, lies not in labelling the wide field of enquiry, but in some of the main categories within the field. 'Information', 'education', and 'entertainment' are not mutually exclusive and do not distinguish between the intentions of those who produce and the gratifications of those who receive. In Britain before 1855 one of the practical difficulties in taxing newspapers lay in defining what a 'newspaper' was. The distinction between a 'newspaper', a 'magazine' and a 'book' has grown no easier since. This labelling problem provides endless opportunities for dispute as to the proportion of 'serious' matter put out by broadcasting organizations. James Halloran's article in this volume (see p. 319) shows that children do not necessarily find 'violent' programmes the most violent. There is another finding by Harper, Munro and Himmelweit (pp. 366-8) that children also do not necessarily find 'children's' programmes the most childish. This same labelling problem presents appalling difficulties for 'content analysis' researchers in choosing their categories before they start counting.

2. History of media research

The first article in this volume, one by Roger Brown about the history of media studies, indicates there are various ways in which this huge body of research material might be approached. Interest in the media has had strongly *political* overtones. By the second world war this developed into a practical attempt at discovering what refinements should be added to first world war experience in order to use the media effectively against the enemy. Much media research could be classified on an *Against Whom?* basis. In the 1930s it had been against Nazi persecution; in the 1940s it was against the German and Japanese war efforts. Later much research became strongly anti-communist in tone, including much of the work on media in the poor nations. A continuing theme has been opposition to the goals of media proprietors – for instance the political goals of newspaper owners, or the commercial goals adopted in television programming.

Another historical approach could be in terms of the *financing* of media research. Commercial market research on media has, at least since the 1930s, been overwhelmingly predominant in terms of total sums of money spent. In Britain large national surveys of media audiences began in the 1930s; these are discussed in the Political and Economic Planning Report on the *British Press* (1938). Some of this money has spilled over into more academic kinds of research. The American Federal government has been a major source of finance, and so has the American Jewish Committee. After 1945 an ever-increasing quantity of research came from American Schools of Journalism and Communications, research conducted by men teaching vocational university degree courses in journalism and related subjects. Especially in recent years some of this has been of a high standard. But even if fashionable jeering about American Professors of Journalism has become less well founded, it was more justified during the 1950s.

The 1940s was a decade in which many of the most prominent American social scientists conducted research about the media. By about 1950 some of them were drifting away to other areas of interest – partly because research was suggesting that the media were less potent than previously supposed, and partly perhaps because the new anti-communist, rather than anti-Nazi, sources of research funds were less attractive intellectually.

During the 1950s large numbers of 'content analysis' studies were undertaken. But perhaps even more characteristic of the period was the conception of a *flow of communication*. Some research assumed that the *content*, such as a politically persuasive advertisement, produced 'effects', such as changed voting intentions. This kind of Communicator→ Recipient model has been called the 'hypodermic' model.

Improbable assumptions about the inevitable success of jabs of communication were replaced by a predominant model of flow. Newspaper journalists were seen as 'gatekeepers' selecting perhaps 10% of material from the available flow of newsagency copy. The concept of opinion leader – first reported in 1944 by Lazarsfeld for the 1940 Presidential Election – was shown by Katz and Lazarsfeld in

Personal Influence (1955) to apply to non-political information as well. 'Opinion leaders' are friends, relatives or other people who to some extent control the flow of messages from the media to the individual audience member.

A flow was also assumed by Harold Lasswell who wrote in 1948: 'A convenient way to describe an act of communication is to answer the following questions:

> Who
> Says What
> In Which Channel
> To Whom
> With What Effect?'

Lasswell went on to describe the five fields of study with which these five questions dealt as:

> Control Analysis
> Content Analysis
> Media Analysis
> Audience Analysis
> Effect Analysis

During the 1950s this formula became an extremely influential one in American media research. Unfortunately, it appeared at a time when some of the ablest and most creative research workers were moving out of the field, and many inexperienced people were moving in.

The flow approach in general and Lasswell's model in particular seem too often to have functioned to provide a rather superficial appearance of scientific rigour. Lasswell's formula and categories constitute a useful shorthand system of classification; but if too rigidly or literally interpreted some dubious assumptions can be read into what Lasswell wrote. One such dubious assumption is that the discovery of some kind of measurable 'effect' on the audience is the ultimate purpose of media research. The flow model narrows down the field in many ways which makes any general findings – or any contribution to theory – improbable. The flow is in one direction only, with no feedback from the audience; it emphasizes single types of 'acts' of communication; it suggests short-term studies. Perhaps the most naïve question is the first one – Who? – which reveals a lack of concern with media organizations. Above all the flow model tends to deny some of the outstanding characteristics of the media – the large scale of operations, the quantity of output and intake, the huge variety, the continuation over long periods of time, and the point that short-term 'effects' are often no more probable than that smoking a single cigarette should cause advanced lung cancer.

I do not intend to reject the notion of a *flow* of communication from media organizations, past gatekeeping communicators, out via broadcast network or newspaper printing press and distribution system to small primary groups – such as families – complete with their own gatekeeping opinion leaders. Indeed the pieces in the present volume are placed roughly in this kind of flow order. But I would like to suggest the use of terms such as 'Performer' and to distinguish between different types of media organization. Rather than a single flow we might think of a *flood* of communication – or of a tidal river delta with many kinds of flow moving over different routes and at different speeds towards an audience which itself sometimes floods back up the delta. The important point, however, is to remember that models should be an aid to, not a substitute for, thought.

3. Historical study of the media

Social science research on the media has tended to concentrate on questionnaire surveys, content analysis and experiments. It has been not only a-theoretical but also a-historical. In the United States many Professors of Journalism appear to have seen the writing of biographies and histories of newspapers as an escape from the social science invasion. Working journalists and other communicators have produced a huge autobiographical literature. While there is a much larger number of scholarly historical works in the US, the relatively small number in Britain – some written by Americans – are often of higher quality. Stanley Morison's 'anonymous' *History of The Times* (5 vols.) is of unusually high quality but marred by the official history's characteristic weaknesses of self-congratulation, a preponderant concern with the details of editorial policy and excessive reliance on rigid chronology.

No British work – even Asa Briggs' excellent work on broadcasting and the BBC – could be accurately described as historical sociology. One of the problems confronting systematic work is the vast body of material represented by the back numbers of publications. But sampling can be used once hypotheses have been developed. A study of similar quality to Neil Smelser's *Social Change in the Industrial Revolution* (1959) but dealing with the 'Northcliffe Revolution' of a hundred years later would be most welcome. The central event was Northcliffe's launching of the *Daily Mail* in 1896. It is already clear that the picture of Northcliffe as an original newspaper genius contains a good deal of mythology. My own hypothesis would be that the so-called 'Northcliffe Revolution' was but one step in the American Revolution in world media; the editorial and business ideas were mostly American and so were some of the men (such as R. D. Blumenfeld, editor of the *Daily Express* 1902–29). British broadcasting can also be seen in terms of a long – and not entirely successful – struggle to resist American influences. The *Daily Mirror* began its climb to become Britain's biggest selling daily newspaper, after being re-modelled in 1934 on the lines of the New York tabloids by the American owned J. Walter Thompson advertising agency.

During the 'Northcliffe Revolution' the modern journalist and the modern advertising agent developed side by side. This has also been the pattern in other areas of post-1945 American media influence, such as West Germany and Japan. The connection between (1) the establishment of a 15% advertising agency commission, (2) a press not owned by political parties or major industrial interests, (3) a high level of advertising expenditure and (4) a high sale of daily newspapers per population should be investigated – perhaps comparing France and Italy with the countries under more American influence. Such an investigation might show that the modern advertising agency is, after all, a necessary condition of a relatively independent newspaper press.

4. Cross media patterns

Melvin DeFleur's article (p. 58) contains some important historical material. Although he is primarily concerned with the diffusion of the media in American society, the article also suggests how remunerative comparative studies across the media can be. The cinema film industry was badly hit by television. But James Curran's article (p. 104) shows that, despite the very large amount of work on the topic, there is little reliable evidence to show that television has damaged newspapers. Television, it seems, is a functional alternative for cinema films, but not for (at least British national) newspapers.

The mixture of media to which individuals expose themselves varies with their age and education. Cinema films, for instance, have an audience predominantly of adolescents and young childless adults. After marriage cinema attendance declines, and daily newspaper purchase rises sharply. Data from many western countries reveal that the more educated watch somewhat less TV. But the type of satisfaction provided, rather than the character of the media, seems most important.

Unfortunately research on the 'declining' medium of film is rather sparse – as Andrew Tudor points out (p. 92). One consequence of the appearance of television on a large scale around 1950 was that research interest swung away from films; the same is true of radio and comics. But perhaps the most glaring cross-media weakness is the small amount of attention given to advertising in relation to other media content.

How many people read newspapers primarily for the classified advertisements? Do many viewers – as some research suggests – not know which channel their TV set is switched to? Do people notice that both press and broadcast advertisements are usually more 'polished' than the non-advertising content? These are merely a few specific questions at the audience/content level. There is also the general question of how much influence advertising has on media content of various kinds – a question which has received surprisingly little research. Countries like Britain with 'mixed' broadcast systems might make the most suitable research sites.

5. Organizational goals

The large social science literature on organizations includes extremely little research on media organizations. Certainly these organizations present many problems to the research worker. One problem is to decide: when is a media organization an organization? Should a broadcast network or a chain of newspapers be regarded as one organization or a federation of numerous organizations? Should the over 200 publications of a company like the International Publishing Corporation

(IPC) be regarded as separate organizations, or would its divisions – each dealing with a specialized type of product such as newspapers, books, printing, consumer magazines, business magazines – be the more realistic organizational units? Another problem is presented by the many jointly owned subsidiaries – some publications are owned 50/50 by two large media groups.

Much of the popular debate on the media concerns the *goals* of organizations. Organizations in the media are criticized for having *commercial* rather than *educational* goals; the same organizations are defended with the argument that their major goal is to provide popular *entertainment* rather than unpopular *cultural* fare. As in many arguments about the media there is a tendency for concepts to be confused and for both sides to adopt somewhat over-simplified positions. Most larger media organizations do not have one simple type of goal; few large organizations in any industry, indeed, have a 100% profit goal. But compared with organizations of similar size, those in the media have an unusually broad *mixture of goals*. At least in most western countries, few media organizations have purely partisan *political* goals; the pursuit of such a goal is usually not popular with the audience and thus requires a political subsidy – which was common in Britain and America 100 years ago, and is still common in, for instance, Italy. Few large organizations in the media adopt a purely commercial goal of *maximizing profit*; too vigorous pursuit of profit goals tends to be counter-productive, risks the loss of legitimacy in the society – including the threat of political or commercial sanctions. And although the pursuit of educational or cultural goals may meet an effective demand sufficient to support a small organization, no large media organization can pursue without major subsidy a purely *educational* goal.

The BBC is one example of a large media organization which pursues a mixture of goals. The BBC's official goal is to provide information, education and entertainment (Tom Burns, p. 135); disputes as to how this mixture should be interpreted do not alter the general acceptance that some such mixture of goals is inevitable.

Various bases have been suggested by sociologists, such as Talcott Parsons, Amitai Etzioni and Peter Blau, for classifying the goals of organizations, but they have not been successfully applied to media organizations. This may be partly due to the importance of advertising revenue, which gives most organizations in the media two separate sets of customers – advertisers and ultimate audience – whose interests sometimes coincide and sometimes conflict. Most media organizations can be seen as having a mixture of three types of goal:

(1) an *audience* goal, which stresses raising the sales or total attending audience size;
(2) an *advertising* goal, which stresses raising advertising revenue;
(3) a *non-economic* goal, which may stress political partisan, educational, cultural or merely general prestige objectives.

Conflict between the audience and advertising goals may occur on a daily newspaper, for instance, because most advertising is directed at women and hence the advertising goal stresses editorial features aimed at women; but more men than women buy and read newspapers, and editorial matter – such as sport – which will attract men will not attract advertisers. The non-economic goal also partly coincides with, but partly conflicts with, the other two goals. Some prestige goal element may attract wealthier audience members, thus justifying higher advertising rates; younger age-groups are more volatile, but also better educated, so the non-economic goal may coincide with the audience goal. Non-economic goal emphasis may also ensure that broadcasting organizations get their licences renewed; but too much such emphasis may result in economic loss and ultimate takeover. In practice a *coalition goal* appears to develop which stresses not maximizing audience levels, but maintaining or increasing audience levels.

Most smaller and more specialized organizations (often subsidiaries or divisions of larger groups or chains) have a somewhat more uniform type of goal. Some book publishing companies have a predominantly non-economic goal as Michael Lane shows (p. 239). Further along a continuum from non-economic to economic goal would come many national news organizations (newspapers, news magazines, and national news departments of broadcast networks) – many news operations try to balance an appeal to a fairly large audience with the performance of a prestige or 'flagship' function within a larger media organization. A more vigorously economic goal is pursued by 'entertainment' sectors of broadcast organizations, by many magazines (especially of the 'consumer' or 'technical' type) and by many monopoly local newspaper groups (which operate at high profit levels in the great majority of provincial cities in America, Britain and other western countries). The most uniformly economic goal is to be found in advertising agencies where the relentlessly commercial intentions of the 'clients' – the advertisers – predominate, as Joseph Bensman's article indicates (p. 202).

6. *Media organizations, communications organizations*

How can we discuss organizations in the media without distinguishing between the large diversified national media corporations and the small local or specialized operation manned by two or three people? I suggest two polar types of organization:

(1) *the media organization*, the prime distinguishing characteristic being the deployment of large scale *production* machinery (printing presses or broadcast studios and engineering apparatus) serviced by a large labour force of technicians.
(2) *the communications organization*, a usually much smaller and more specialized editorial or creative department which employs a staff of 'communicators' oriented towards an ultimate audience of readers, viewers or listeners and towards 'performers'.

The media organization typically contains within it a number of communications organizations, such as several editorial departments or programme-making departments. But the major concern and major costs of the overall media organization are tied up in buying, manning and supplying the production facilities, the printing presses, TV studios and engineering departments; the great majority of a media organization's employees perform technical, administrative, commercial and clerical functions. Only a small minority of a media organization's employees work within its constituent communications organizations as communicators (journalists, producers, editors). A media organization is usually diversified. There are two main types of media organization – (a) The *regional* media organization, and (b) The *national* media organization.

The *regional media organization* typically owns one or more daily newspapers with a regional monopoly, other publications (such as weekly papers in the surrounding area) and interests in television or other media. It usually has connections or involvement with non-media commercial activities in the region.

The *national media organization* often contains within it a number of regional media organizations. It is also typically spread over a variety of different media. In most western countries there are a few dominant national media organizations. Among the most controversial are the Axel Springer group in West Germany, the Hachette *(France-Soir)* group in France, and the *Time-Life* magazine, book and TV group in the United States. In some countries national media organizations own major broadcasting interests. Moreover, the major broadcasting organizations themselves have most of the characteristics of national media organizations. In all countries broadcasting organizations are dependent on government licensing, which in itself makes them highly controversial. Moreover the resulting insecurity leads to another source of controversy: government licensed broadcasting organizations are often extremely eager to diversify into other areas – to become more like the other national media organizations. Even the BBC is heavily involved in publishing. Major commercial broadcasting organizations in Britain and elsewhere are involved in a wide range of activities – such as film-making, TV set manufacture and electronics generally.

That the national media organizations are more dominant in Britain than elsewhere (with the possible exception of Japan) results from a combination of special factors. These include the pattern of national media dominated from London – illustrated in Winston Fletcher's article (p. 79); the fact that most *regional* dailies are also owned by London-based groups; the concentration of broadcasting in London since the founding of the BBC; the London dominated 'regional' structure of commercial TV in which film, entertainment, TV set and newspaper interests were deliberately allowed to acquire major control. In consequence several major national media organizations hold a predominant or monopoly share in at least one area:

(1) British Broadcasting Corporation (BBC) – Radio (local, national, overseas).
(2) Electrical and Musical Industries (EMI) – Popular music.
(3) International Publishing Corporation (IPC) –
    (a) Labour inclined national newspapers.
    (b) Consumer magazines.
    (c) Technical magazines.
(4) S. Pearson – Financial press.
(5) Thomson Organisation – Daily regional newspapers in large areas of Scotland, Wales and Northern Ireland.

Social scientists have taken extremely little notice of the development in many countries of these national media organizations. They have emerged primarily since 1950 with commercial television, the disappearance of direct daily newspaper competition in most provincial cities, and an organizational urge to diversify away from unstable advertising-related sources of revenue. This last factor has led the media organizations into book publishing where a previously non-economic orientation made acquisition easy. The media organizations have also moved into the new electronic areas with considerable vigour. It is noticeable that since 1960 most of the more technically advanced innovation has been conducted by the national media organizations.

Three of the commonest criticisms of national media organizations are that –

(1) They are aggressively expansionist and competitive – 'driving weaker brethren to the wall'.
(2) They are monopolistic in certain areas.
(3) Their size, commercial ramifications, and political importance makes them partners with governments.

The seriousness and the apparent inconsistencies of such criticisms suggest that systematic study of these organizations is required. Such studies pose problems which cut across several types of social science expertise; an inter-disciplinary approach – perhaps including not only economic, sociological and political science, but also accountancy skills – may be necessary.

A rare study actually concerned with a whole national media organization is that of Tom Burns (p. 135) who conducted interviews in 1963 with middle level and senior people in four widely different sections of the BBC.

The other organizational studies in this Reader deal with what I have called *Communications organizations*. One type of communications organization is the news organization; there are many similarities between the news organizations studied by Malcolm Warner (p. 158) and Aleksander Matejko (p. 168) even though the first are TV news departments in New York and the second type are newspapers in Warsaw and Cracow. In both cases there is a similarly ambivalent attitude towards the audience. In both cases personal relations are warm and informal; in both cases these relations contrast with the rigid time-tabling required by deadlines – for transmission and printing. In both cases journalists have a fair amount of personal autonomy within a set of shared occupational values. In both New York and Warsaw there is a great deal of contact, at the top, with the political 'authorities'.

Another type of communications organization is the book publishing firms studied by Michael Lane. Here again we find an organization concerned with editorial activities, cut off from physical or engineering production work, and staffed by another group of communicators with strong occupational values. The editorial personnel in publishing, as well, are oriented towards the ultimate audience, to whom they have rather ambivalent attitudes; editorial personnel in publishing are also oriented towards 'performers' – book authors in their case.

Yet another type of communication organization are the advertising agencies studied by Joseph Bensman. Unlike the media organizations they do not pump programmes through a network or produce millions of inky newspapers in basement production plants. The advertising agencies – like other communications organizations – are concerned primarily with paper-shuffling activities. Advertising agencies are, however, a somewhat deviant type of communications organization in that their structural position is unusually weak. The strongly commercial goal gives advertising agency personnel few defences against feedback from the audience; audience research is taken very much more seriously in advertising agencies than in any other kind of communications organization. But the even more important difference in advertising agencies is that organizational control is largely located outside the organization altogether – in the hands of the 'client', usually an advertising manager or director in a consumer goods manufacturing company. Contrary to some popular mythology communicators elsewhere are accorded substantial security of tenure and tactical autonomy within a set mixture of goals; but in advertising agencies there is considerable (at least psychological) insecurity and a relative lack of autonomy even in matters of small detail. Advertising agencies began as freelance agencies working for newspapers, and although they now work for advertisers the 'freelance' relationship continues – represented by the advertiser's freedom simply to take the account (and all the work) elsewhere. The location of much of the effective organizational power outside the organization is one factor leading to a high level of internal conflict within advertising agencies – since advertising 'clients' in effect compete against each other for the agency's services and executive time. Much of what happens inside advertising agencies can probably only be captured by direct observation and – as one who has also studied advertising agencies – Joseph Bensman's study seems to me a participant observation classic.

The distinction between media organizations and communications organizations which I have suggested focuses on the *production* orientation of the media organization and the audience-and-performer orientation of the communications organization. The work of social scientists concerned with innovation and technology, such as Tom Burns, Joan Woodward, Chris Argyris and Charles Perrow, is applicable here. But a more organization-oriented view of the media in general seems essential if we are not to perpetuate the predominant view in which the media messages sometimes appear to be reaching the audience members' eyes and ears as if from heaven above or (in some perspectives) hell below.

7. *Communicators*

'Communicators' can be defined as non-clerical workers within communications organizations – people who work on the selecting, shaping and packaging of programmes, 'stories' and other messages for transmission to the ultimate audience. Communicators, then, include journalists, advertising agency personnel, producers and directors in broadcasting, editorial personnel in book publishing. Whereas the overall media organization can to a great extent be 'programmed' by a proprietor in financial terms, the work of communicators cannot be easily prescribed. In Charles Perrow's terminology the number of exceptional cases is high and 'search procedures' cannot be logically analyzed or routinized. As in other lines of non-routine work, such as social casework, no logical or routinized 'search' is possible; a communicator's work is 'creative', requires 'flair' and 'personal contacts'.

Communicators become highly absorbed in their tasks – as several articles in this volume report – and they work to 'deadlines' which vary according to the frequency of publication or transmission. Philip Elliott reports (p. 221) that in a television series the main sources of material were (1) daily newspapers, (2) associations and organizations which appeared relevant to the subject matter, and (3) personal contacts of the communicators themselves. This is probably fairly representative of 'search procedures' in 'factual' and journalistic media output.

But the work carried out by communicators is extremely specialized and varied. 'Journalists' may be national editors, knitting specialists, photographers, sports sub-editors, or foreign correspondents. Advertising agency personnel may be artists, media buyers or public relations men. There are also major differences between communicators' work at the national, regional and local levels. In keeping with this wide variety of work activities the public's image of communicators is unclear. Communicators are uncertain of the social status of their occupation and unclear as to what role they play, or should play, in relation to audiences. There is a widespread sense among communicators of a sharp contrast between organizational power and individual powerlessness.

Many communicators enter communications occupations with motives of a literary, artistic or creative kind. Oliver Boyd-Barrett's article, for instance, shows that the majority of journalism recruits want to write books (p. 196). Communicators are looking for satisfactions of a personal and creative kind. Much activity derives from personal relationships rather than from impersonal procedures or methods of assessment. The individualistic predispositions of many communicators are strengthened by the definition of work roles in terms of establishing 'personal contact' with such performers as sportsmen, actors, politicians, authors. Occupational values stress verbal facility and much of the occupational value system is contained within a strongly oral and anecdotal tradition. This is often accompanied by a largely mythological picture of the occupation's past – a golden age (Michael Lane, pp. 249-51) when editors really were editors, publishers really were publishers, etc. News values and dramatic values stress personalization and conflict as techniques for communicating with audiences. The tendency to stress the importance of already famous 'names' is accompanied by a warmness for the underdog; Anglo-Saxon foreign correspondents, for instance, tend to prefer minorities – for instance Turks rather than Greeks in Cyprus (see Galtung and Ruge, p. 279).

Typically placed in a complex set of roles, communicators often manage by playing off one role partner against another to extend their autonomy. This autonomy can be most extensive or most restricted at the *national* rather than local level. The ideology of the occupation encourages them often to equate their own autonomy with the public good and to resist what they see as the narrowly self-interested preferences of organizational superiors and prominent performers; Jay Blumler describes BBC producers resisting the pressure of the government party during an election (p. 411).

Communicators, despite their stress on personal contacts (and office politics), tend to concentrate their personal acquaintance within the employing organization to a fairly small departmental span. Rather than *vertical* ties within the employing organization their occupational contact networks tend to stretch *horizontally* outside the organization, to include not only performers but people engaged in the same speciality in competing organizations. These 'competitors' are often also regarded as 'colleagues'. Communications organizations typically bulge at the middle and have few senior posts. Specialized careers are confronted by vertical blocks. The communications occupation is frequently a bridging career into some other line of work – such as public relations or administration. Many careers involve moves between organizations – and this is a major basis for unease about organizational mergers.

The very wide range in status, size of audience, and pay, within communications occupations leads to widely differing types of career pattern. The non-graduate journalism recruits discussed by Oliver Boyd-Barrett represented the majority entry pattern in the late 1960s. But there has long been in British journalism an élite career pattern; one version leads from Oxford after a fairly short initiation into a foreign correspondent's post. And the BBC is not the only media organization in which men with foreign news experience play leading parts.

But very little systematic knowledge exists in Britain about any kind of communicator. Nor are there any studies of communicators' Trade Unions; it might be interesting to compare the performance of the National Union of Journalists with that of the printing unions. In the United States there are many studies of small or specialized segments of communications occupations. But even there few adequate studies exist of the overall national picture. The size of the United States and its very de-centralized media pattern present special difficulties. But despite a great deal of writing about the Washington press corps, and some interesting studies by political scientists of certain specialized aspects, the only attempt at a broad systematic study of the whole Washington press corps is Leo Rosten's admirable *The Washington Correspondents* (1937). If little systematic knowledge exists at the *national* level about American journalists, even less is known about communicators in American entertainment.

8. *Performers and stars*

'Performers' are, on my definition, the people whose faces, movements, words (or words which script or speech writers have written for them) appear in the output of the media. Performers may be actresses, sportsmen, politicians, 'experts', singers, authors. Many performers are not 'well known'; some are deliberately chosen by communicators – for instance in TV 'vox pop' street interviews – for being unknown. Many other performers are frequent, but not star performers – part-time politicians, minor sportsmen, authors who are not 'names'. All types of media content – education, sport, politics, literature – use the device of personalization. But in each case there is concentration on relatively few stars among the many performers. Some media require stars more than do others. The *daily* frequency media, and especially daily newspapers, need stars less because customers have daily habits of attendance. The low frequency, or one-shot, types of output – notably films and books – need stars the most, because each time the customer must be enticed to *contract in* to something which is otherwise unfamiliar, but which a star author's or actress's name can fill with familiar promise.

The star performers are one more cross-media phenomenon. The star actress appears in films, TV plays, radio interviews, fan magazines, soap advertisements. The star sportsman appears not only in televised matches, but in daily newspapers, sports magazines, and 'as told to' books.

Leo Lowenthal showed in 1944 that biographies of popular American magazines had switched from 'heroes of production' to 'heroes of consumption'; there has also been some interesting work done on the film hero. But we do not know enough about the various types of star performer. We do not yet understand the phenomenon of the political leader who has a popularity rating markedly different from that of his party. Nor do we know enough about the process by which lesser performers become media stars, or the other process by which stars fall from media stardom.

Obviously the rise of a politician, or any other performer, to stardom is a complex process – and not dependent upon media performances alone. But the communicators are clearly one group whose support will assist the rising performer. There seem to be discernible patterns – including a rising flood of ecstatic coverage, a more balanced 'mature' stage of stardom, and a declining phase, often marked by savage criticism when 'now it can be revealed' details are much in evidence.

One possible approach to this rise and fall of media performers may lie through the work situation and careers of communicators. Communicators may shield certain facets of the star performer from the public while establishing 'personal contacts' for future use. In the rising phase of stardom the performer and communicators engage in mutual support and protection; but these common interests decline when the performer's star future begins to tarnish. Moreover some communicators themselves become performers and others wish to. Philip Elliott's TV presenter is one example of a communicator-performer (pp. 232-7); another type is the TV newscaster reported by Malcolm Warner (p. 163).

9. Media content: culture, news, violence

The Hansen and Parsons bibliography lists over 400 'content analysis' studies and these are only a selection. One of the most quoted definitions was produced in 1952 by Bernard Berelson:

> Content analysis is a research technique for the objective, systematic and quantitative description of the manifest content of communication.

This admirably clear definition points to some of the strengths of content analysis – the content analyst (or his assistants) actually sits down with the newspapers (or whatever the material may be) and counts words, paragraphs and square inches. But the adjective, *manifest* content, also points to some of the weaknesses of content analysis. Is it the *manifest* content that gets across to the audience? What about the message 'between the lines', what about such subtleties as humour? What about visual material – film, close-ups, movements, colour?

Many content studies produce impressively precise quantitative findings – that more references to certain kinds of political symbol appeared in one newspaper rather than another, the precise numbers of deaths, beatings and shootings seen on TV during the peak hours of children's viewing. But some such studies also invite the comment that 'the methodology is impressive – but so what?' Other studies, however, do demonstrate that content analysis techniques can be used to produce findings of broader public or theoretical interest. Bernard Berelson himself set out to discover how much time Americans spend 'in the presence of culture', using a fairly rigorous definition (only 15% of book reading time, 1% of newspaper reading, 1% of radio listening, and one-fifth of Broadway plays in 1963 qualified as 'culture'). He concluded that the average American adult spent four hours a month 'in the presence of culture' – with commercial TV as the most important single media source of culture, followed by magazines, books, radio and records.

Much content analysis has concerned 'news'; a good deal of this work has focused on 'bias' in political coverage but not many studies have added substantially to Walter Lippmann's *Public Opinion* or Robert Park's article 'The natural history of the newspaper' – published in 1922 and 1923 respectively. One of the few exceptions to this generalization is the article, reprinted in this present volume, by Johan Galtung and Mari Holmboe Ruge (p. 259) which promises to become a classic social science answer to the question – 'what is news?' Other articles in the present volume which deal with 'news values' include those by Malcolm Warner (p. 158) and Ronald Bunn (p. 439). Some of the news values which emerge in American coverage of the Vietnam war or German coverage of the Spiegel Affair – conflict, personalization, sudden 'negative events' – are not entirely absent in the Soviet Union. Gayle Hollander reports (p. 252) that competition with foreign broadcasts has produced some changes in the previous Soviet preference for 'positive' and rather slow news. Soviet news has become more competitive, faster and somewhat more negative.

James Halloran comments (p. 314) that in discussions of media violence and its impact on children, the focus of concern is usually on fictional violence, not violence in the 'factual' news bulletins. This raises the broad question of whether 'news values' differ from 'dramatic values', 'cultural values' or perhaps merely human values?

Personalization and conflict are to be found not only in factual and fictional crime, but in humour, sport, art and politics. Many of the factors which Galtung and Ruge find as predisposing foreign events to become news – élite persons, negative events, unexpectedness-within-predictability, cultural proximity – are also to be found in Shakespeare's plays. 'News' indeed existed before either newspapers or the earlier newsbooks. The word 'news' occurs frequently in Shakespeare meaning information. This usually word-of-mouth 'news' already had the familiar negative connotations. A contemporary of Shakespeare, Michael Drayton, wrote:

> Ill news has wings, and with the wind doth go,
> Comfort's a cripple and comes ever slow.

10. *Audiences*

All who have had any interest in media research – the military, foreign ministries, political parties, advertisers, psychologists, sociologists, political scientists, and columnist critics – have wanted to know what the media do to audiences. Hansen and Parsons list over 700 studies in this area since 1945; Wilbur Schramm in preparing a UNESCO bibliography in 1964 on *The Effects of Television on Children and Adolescents*, even after throwing out the chaff, found 165 studies worthy of further attention.

The second world war saw a great deal of 'propaganda' directed by governments at their own and each other's populations. Nor did the large quantities of research which accompanied this expensive activity indicate that all the effort was wasted. Carl Hovland and other researchers working for the US War Department reported that particular indoctrination films could produce substantial changes in conscripts' attitudes. The Shils and Janowitz study (1948) of German soldiers captured in late 1944 and early 1945 showed, however, the severe limitations of some propaganda – especially in relation to primary group ties – and played a part in the 'rediscovery of the primary group'. The high point of this rediscovery came in the mid-1950s with *Personal Influence*, although Paul Lazarsfeld was one social scientist who never lost sight of the obvious point that people's values are grounded in family, work and other primary groups.

That Lazarsfeld had had longstanding connections with market research was probably significant; anyone with the most superficial knowledge of advertising knows that media campaigns cannot sell any product to anyone. On the contrary, failure to demonstrate any un-ambiguous connection between what advertising campaigns say and what housewives buy has long been a source of anxiety and insecurity in advertising agencies (see Joseph Bensman, pp. 206-9).

Robert Silvey's article (p. 301) includes some interesting material on German broadcasting to Britain in 1939–40; Silvey deftly summarizes much of the existing 'media effects' knowledge. His successor as head of BBC audience research, B. P. Emmett (p. 372), discusses re-search evidence on the failure of several informational programmes to provide the intended 'effect'. Further findings of an apparently negative kind are reported in Denis McQuail's study of the audience for British TV plays (p. 335); the educated middle class and the un-educated working class watch much the same TV plays. Research on the impact of the media during election campaigns has continued to show that, despite the appearance of TV, the media seldom have a dramatic effect in shifting votes from left to right or vice-versa. The article by Jay Blumler and Denis McQuail on the Leeds election studies (p. 452) provides British evidence along the lines of some American data.

Perhaps the single outstanding investigation in this area is the Himmelweit, Oppenheim and Vince study, *Television and the Child* (1958), conducted in Britain in the mid 1950s at a time when children with TV could be matched with children from non-TV homes. This study reported that most of the fears – and hopes – about TV were unfounded. Such findings contributed towards a kind of negative con-ventional wisdom. A sentence from Joseph Klapper's *The Effects of Mass Communication* (1960) was much quoted:

> Communications research strongly indicates that persuasive mass communication is in general more likely to reinforce the existing opinions of its audience than it is to change such opinions.

But Klapper said much else. Moreover, media-related changes have been shown in many studies – including those in the present volume.

These are sometimes not the expected changes – Emmett shows that BBC producers have sometimes had the opposite 'effect' to that intended. The findings on the very uniform response of the British public to TV plays can be regarded, McQuail suggests, as indicating either uniform mediocrity or the 'effect' of bringing diverse social classes and educational levels into a democratically shared experience. Harold Wilensky also produced in his article on media use in Detroit, 'Mass Society and Mass Culture', remarkable evidence on a 'middle mass' – which could scarcely be dismissed as negative findings.

As with many traditional research questions it has become increasingly concluded that 'What effects do the media have on audiences?' may be the wrong question. It makes discovering whether cigarettes cause lung cancer look, by comparison, a simple task. Rather than the old question, 'What do the media do to people?', some researchers see a more relevant question as being: 'What do people do with the media?' Much research now talks of uses, gratifications, functions and interaction – rather than 'effects'.

A great deal of research has been conducted on captive audiences – students in psychology laboratories and children in classrooms; surveys of randomly selected national samples of the general population have also isolated respondents and cut them off artificially from the family groups where most – but not all – media consumption occurs. We need more broad-ranging research which studies the media within the family/socialization/domestic context and within the work/leisure/relaxation/life-style context. In these and other areas – for instance violence and conflict – media research must adopt theoretical perspectives from other relevant social science areas. Laboratory experiments and randomly selected samples of the general population should be recognized as only two of the possible methodological approaches.

11. *Audience research by the media*

The simplest kind of feedback from the audience to the media organizations occurs in the case of the rising or falling sale of a publication. But media organizations also conduct a large amount of audience research. In Britain in 1969 at least one million separate interviews were conducted, and something like £3 million spent (James Halloran has estimated) on specifically audience research. There were three major continuing audience research operations:

(1) The BBC's *'Survey of Listening and viewing'*. This involved a national quota sample of 2,250 interviews each and every day – i.e., over 800,000 interviews a year. The main object of this exercise was to estimate the total number of *individuals* in the audience for each BBC radio and TV programme each day. This form of BBC enquiry began in 1939.

(2) *Television Ratings* organized by JICTAR – a Committee which included the advertising agencies, the ITV companies and the advertisers. This service which used meters attached to TV sets in 2,650 *households* where 7,700 individuals lived, was aimed at providing a continuing index, for commercials and programmes, of the percentage of *sets switched on*, in each ITV region. This form of service began in 1957.

(3) *The National Readership Survey* organized by JICNARS – a Committee including the advertising agencies, the national newspapers and periodicals, and the advertisers. This survey involved a national random sample of 30,000 *individuals* a year. It was designed primarily to show the socio-economic characteristics and consumer habits of the readership (as opposed to the circulation) of all the national daily and Sunday newspapers, 60 national magazines, and some regional daily newspapers. This form of survey began in 1953.

Other continuing surveys are conducted. For instance the BBC has Audience Reaction panels. The commercial TV Rating research is accompanied by a system of diary research.

In addition to these centrally conducted and continuing surveys much other research is done by the individual media organizations – especially in the largest organizations' audience research findings are one kind of evidence used in most major decisions about launching new publications and programmes, and 'facelifting' or 'killing' old ones.

Audience research is taken most seriously in advertising agencies – where commissioning, carrying out and reporting on various kinds of 'audience', 'product' and 'advertising' research is a major function; another major function within an agency – planning and buying media insertions – operates to a large extent on research results. After advertising agencies, audience research is taken most seriously in broadcasting organizations. Even in the BBC as Tom Burns describes (pp. 155-6) an audience figure can have a major impact on the morale of people making a programme. If audience figures continue to decline the future of a programme must be in doubt.

In newspapers day-to-day or week-to-week research is less important. There is an overall circulation figure and set page positions in the paper – which in the *short-term* are constant to an extent not found in broadcasting – with its more varied contents and volatile switch-flicking audience. But even among many press journalists the broad pattern of research findings is known. In questioning national specialist journalists in London in 1968 I found that a large minority had seen audience research reports; among correspondents from some organizations – including BBC news and the *Daily Mirror* – over half had seen such reports. The great majority of British journalists in senior executive positions on national newspapers see research findings regularly.

The lowest prevalence of research within communications organizations is likely to be within those with the lowest total audience and the lowest frequency (or most one-shot type) of output. These will include book publishers, film and record makers.

Academic studies on the media make relatively little reference to such research; sometimes it is briefly stated that this internal research is not available to academics. However, the article by James Curran (p. 104) is partly based on such material. But the important task for media sociology lies in discovering, not what these audience surveys say, but how the results are used within communications and media organizations. Not until we have studies of the use of audience research – and of other sorts of audience response such as letters and telephone calls – within the organizations, will we begin to understand the feedback from the audience. And until we understand this feedback our knowledge of the part audiences play in the media will be inadequate.

12. The media and politics

The notion that a communicator could, from his newspaper office or broadcast studio, push his hypodermic into the distant voter and fill him up with red-blooded or blue-blooded voting intentions was long ago shown to be absurd. Lazarsfeld and his colleagues in *The People's Choice* (1944) started a tradition of voting research studies which have shown that most voters selectively expose themselves to agreeable political media output and that the opportunities for outright conversion by the media during an election campaign are limited. Even when the voters are confronted with political opponents in one package – as in the Kennedy–Nixon debates of 1960 – the 'effects' are not necessarily clear. The popular belief that Kennedy decisively 'won' the debates is not unambiguously supported by the empirical studies in *The Great Debates*, edited by Sidney Kraus. Such research findings have led some people – including some social scientists – to say that after all the evidence shows the media to have little political impact. This, however, is like saying that the evidence shows advertising campaigns to have little effect on soap sales. The huge number of variables makes any completely clearcut 'effect' of specific media outputs on specific audience behaviour (such as voting or purchasing soap) improbable. The more relevant questions, then, are: 'What part does advertising play in soap marketing and purchasing?' and 'What part do the media play in the political system and political behaviour?' That the answer to either question should be 'None' is highly improbable and we should demand strong evidence of those who give such an answer.

Most of the evidence which is deployed on this question is taken from random sample surveys of the electorate. The weaknesses of such surveys in relation to the media audience in general also apply in the specific case of politics. In these questionnaire surveys several kinds of artificial *narrowing* down take place; for instance in some election campaign surveys adults are asked questions like, 'How many election campaign programmes have you watched on television?' Some of the limitations here are obvious:

(1) Only the weeks of the campaign, rather than the years between campaigns, are included.
(2) The definition of what is political content rules out any material which is not very explicitly 'political'.
(3) These questions assume that people remember accurately from which media output they receive certain information – although much market research evidence and research on survey methodology suggests that these assumptions may be false.

Two further examples of this narrowing down may be quoted. Although some survey data has shown *magazines* to be an important source of political and other information, magazines are given low emphasis in many discussions about the media and politics; the vast variety of magazines presents severe problems for survey research. But *Reader's Digest* is surely not the only 'non-political' magazine which carries political values. Another example is *humour*; political humour in cartoons has for over a century been regarded as an important political weapon, but it seems at least possible that political jokes – for instance in 'comedy' programmes on television – are no less important. *That Was The Week That Was* was surely not the only 'comedy' programme to carry political values.

Blumler and McQuail (p. 452) and Butler and Stokes (p. 479), show – as other researchers have shown – that there *are* some interesting changes of a media-related kind in election voting intentions; just because the media cannot be shown to shunt large blocks of Republican voters into the Democratic column or Conservative voters into the Labour column (or vice-versa), this does not prevent such studies showing important changes. Studies included in the present volume show at least four important ways in which the media operate within the political system and upon political behaviour:

(a) Even during the election campaign itself some apparently media-related changes do occur – for instance the substantial increase in Liberal support during the British election campaign in 1964 (pp. 472-6).

(b) That much political persuasion through the media reaches only the already favourably inclined does not exclude media-related shifts of opinion within the 'already converted' group. This can take the form of *repulsion* or *attraction*. Repulsion is illustrated by the Leeds finding that, in the 1959 British Election, Conservative newspapers repelled some Conservative supporters (p. 456). Both repulsion and attraction are illustrated by the Butler and Stokes finding that before the 1964 Election some Conservative readers of Conservative newspapers drifted away from their loyalty – in line with these newspapers' criticisms of the Conservative Government – and drifted back again, as the papers returned to support the Government in the immediate pre-election period (p. 479).

(c) Jay Blumler's study of the TV producers of BBC election programmes during the 1966 campaign shows that these producers vigorously resisted attempts by the political parties to dictate the shape of coverage; there is even some indication that such attempts may harden the determination of communicators (p. 422). If this can happen during an election campaign, in a sensitive sector of a 'neutral' media organization, and within a set of agreed rules for 'balanced' coverage – it seems probable that in other more fluid circumstances political communicators do have a considerable degree of latitude in deciding at least the form in which political disputes are presented.

(d) Ronald Bunn's study of German press coverage of the Spiegel Affair of 1962 also illustrates the extent to which the press can influence the presentation of political events (p. 439). Blanket coverage by the press, and the commitment of a substantial proportion of independent and normally pro-government German newspapers against the government's actions *preceded* the government resignations. The *speed* of media involvement is another aspect of the Spiegel Affair which is an important characteristic of the part the media play in politics generally. Both in the *presentation* of policies and in the *timing* of decisions the functioning of the media impinge on political events.

It might be argued that the Spiegel Affair was a special case – in that it involved a government attack upon the professional position of a journalist. But given the importance which democratic governments attach to presenting their policies before 'public opinion', and given the role which communicators play in this process, as well as in defining what a political crisis is, it seems likely that in many 'major political crises' the role of political communicators – or at least the political functions of the media – will be one controversial aspect of the 'political crisis'.

Instead of the usual 'further research is necessary' plea it might be more accurate to say that research on the part the media play in politics has hardly begun. For this reason the lack of adequately comprehensive evidence on Washington journalism is especially serious – although the work of political scientists such as Bernard Cohen and Dan Nimmo constitutes an important beginning. I suggest that the following are among the areas on which we need research:

The overall relationship between the political system and the media structure, for instance the London dominated pattern of both politics and media in Britain and the more de-centralized pattern in the United States and West Germany.

The political decision makers. How much of their intake of information comes from the media and how much of their activity is directed towards getting things into (or keeping things out of) the media content?

The 'proprietors', 'publishers' and others in executive charge of media organizations – what are the political implications of their political or 'non-political' stances?

Media Organizations collectively as a type of interest group are of some importance.

Communications Organizations. The political activities which go on within TV departments are of some interest – as Warner and Blumler show in this volume; but much more needs to be learnt about them.

Communicators at the national level in politics have not been adequately studied. One of many historical topics on which much has been said, but on which little systematic is known, is the role of journalists in the United States and Europe in launching the Marshall Plan. I myself have looked at the British Lobby correspondents. Another obvious area for research is the role of financial journalism in national politics.

Performer–Communicator relationships. What part do these play in the often noticed phenomenon of the President or Prime Minister whose 'honeymoon' period is followed by press criticism and subsequent decline on the opinion polls?

The content of political news. As the Galtung and Ruge article in this volume indicates, well designed studies of foreign news can be extremely instructive. This subject seems especially important for the study of international relations – since Bernard Cohen's study suggests that in the US State Department the foreign policy-makers themselves get much of their broad picture of world events from the press and news-agency tickers – rather than from the slower and less convenient diplomatic sources (*The Press and Foreign Policy*, pp. 135–46). If this is the case in Washington, it is probably even more the case in some small capitals elsewhere in the world.

The political media behaviour of the audience-electorate has been inadequately studied; this is especially so within *families* where many political attitudes appear to be formed and where most media consumption takes place. For instance, the different political loyalties of

men and women have been more often noted than political opinions and
media exposure within marriage have been studied. On the general
question of political exposure within the broad pattern of media exposure and style of life Harold Wilensky's 1964 article 'Mass Society
and Mass Culture' is again instructive.

1.3. American media dominance

Very little attention has been paid by media researchers to a world-
wide phenomenon, the extraordinary extent of both the direct presence
and indirect influence of American media. I have already suggested
that the 'Northcliffe Revolution' in the British press around 1900 can
be seen as a largely American revolution. But the impact of American
popular journalism within Britain goes back to 1800 – the year when
William Cobbett, who under the name of Peter Porcupine had learnt
in Philadelphia the new trade of people's journalism, returned to
Britain where he became the first *popular* journalist of national importance and notoriety. The larger newspaper market in an America without newspaper taxes already meant that popular innovations almost
inevitably started in the United States.

The rise of the great American-owned international news agencies to
challenge the British Reuters and the other European agencies has been
well documented; but the post-1945 world leadership of the American
AP and UPI, the French AFP, and Reuters has received less attention
from social scientists than it deserves. American dominance has now
gone far beyond the provision of international news. American influence on the whole internal media structure of some major nations has
been profound – especially in such nations as Canada, Australia,
Mexico, Britain, South Africa, West Germany, Japan, India, Brazil,
Argentina and Venezuela.

The pattern of Hollywood domination of the world film industry
has often been described. With costs of production covered by the
domestic US market, Hollywood was able to charge relatively low
prices to meet the ravenous demand of film audiences around the
world. This domination included the use of non-American stars and
the US financing of films made in Europe. By the late 1960s over three-
quarters of films made in Britain were American financed. The use
of American programmes in British TV has been more rigorously

controlled. But the Hollywood film pattern has been closely followed by American commercial TV in large tracts of the world, including Latin America, Africa, and some parts of Asia.

Obviously this pattern is related to American world-wide general commercial strength and strength in such fields as toiletries, food, cars and electronics in particular. Connected with this marketing phenomenon is the dominance of American advertising methods and of a few major American 'international' advertising agencies.

Since 1945 American world-wide media dominance appears to have grown at a quicker pace. Two important developments in the mid-1950s in Britain were: (1) the appearance of commercial TV, which inevitably drew on the American experience; (2) the removal of news-print rationing, which had been in operation since 1939, and the emergence of the British press from 15 years of deep-freeze. In the subsequent period of rapid change many 'innovations' were adapted from US journalism. On the business side the most important single event was the arrival in Edinburgh in 1954 of Roy (later Lord) Thomson – who brought with him the business practices of a major chain of small newspapers in Canada and the United States.

During the 1960s the world-wide American communications domination has been consolidated. Three factors in this process are well known.

(1) The appearance of many small new nations, with a huge demand for cheap media material – especially film and broad-cast material.

(2) The increased importance of advertising following from the importance of *commercial* TV on the world scene. In Britain, whereas in 1960 under half the leading advertising agencies were American controlled, by the end of the 1960s nearly all were American controlled.

(3) The American lead in electronics, telecommunications, space, and satellites. This was symbolised by the setting up in 1964 of INTELSAT in which (at first) 61% of the shares were US owned (through COMSAT) with the American company, AT and T, as the largest single shareholder.

Somewhat less familiar is the argument put forward by Herbert I. Schiller in *Mass Communication and American Empire* (1969) that the inevitable heavy involvement of the US Federal Government in this world-wide process is controlled largely through the Department of Defense, and not through the Federal Communications Commission (FCC). This comes about *directly*, according to Schiller, because the allocation of frequencies and the making of national telecommunications policy (which in Britain are the responsibility of the Telecommunications Minister) are under the control of the National Communications System of which the Executive Agent is the US Secretary of Defense. Schiller argues that further *indirect* control is exercised by the Department of Defense because major electronics companies – like RCA, which controls the NBC national TV/Radio network – are holders of major defence contracts. For Schiller, therefore, the American 'communications empire' is part of the 'military industrial complex' and the significance of the world-wide US media dominance is that its policies stem directly from US military and foreign policy.

My own suspicion is that the US dominance in world media includes both desirable and undesirable influences. But the issues raised seem of sufficient importance – for both public policy and social research in many countries – to warrant a good deal of further investigation.

14. American media research dominance

American dominance on the world media scene is as nothing compared with American dominance on the media research scene. A very high proportion of all media research studies – and probably an even higher proportion of the best ones – have been carried out by American social scientists. But this media research nevertheless reflects rather too much the vices and rather too little the virtues of American social science in general. Too many American studies are about the magazine reading habits of 50 pig farmers in S.W. Iowa, and too few exhibit the kind of qualities to be found in Harold Wilensky's 'Mass Society and Mass Culture' – virtues such as the creative use of both social theory and research methods and the selection of a research problem of some sociological importance and public concern.

Despite such an excellent interdisciplinary journal as the *Public Opinion Quarterly* too much American research is marked by disciplinary provincialism. Despite the presence of major centres of media research in a number of great universities in the North-East United States, there is an odd lack of evidence on the workings of the national media in New York and Washington. Despite the liberal values of the media researchers there is a surprising reluctance to tackle with vigour such topics as the media and the Negro, or for that matter the equally important topic of the media and the Jew. Despite the excellence of some American research on the media and development in the poor nations, there has been a disturbing propensity of other researchers to ally themselves with rather dubious diplomatic and military activities in places like South-East Asia.

There are social scientists in the developing nations quite capable of producing research about their own national media which is as good as most American research – or rather better to judge from Ibrahim Abu-Lughod's article in this volume (p. 322). But in the developing world – and in Europe also – there is a tendency to become too involved in the minor intricacies of the local media system. Some media phenomena – satellite TV seems one obvious example – must be studied cross-nationally. In any case the American media industry has so greatly over-spilled the borders of the United States that one can ask: What do they know of American media, who know them only within the continental United States?

15. Public media policy and social research

Despite frequently voiced warnings against 'government interference' in the free press, and regardless of the formal constitutional position, all governments do 'interfere' directly in the affairs of the media. Whereas anyone may be allowed to start up a printing press, anyone cannot be allowed to start broadcasting – this was (fairly) soon discovered even in the United States; the allocation of broadcast frequencies has to be controlled – and the national government in all countries becomes involved. (In Europe the regulation has to be particularly severe because of the interference problem from neighbouring countries.) Governments also have to take into account other telecommunications requirements – telephones, police, military and civil aviation communications and overseas broadcasting.

This central question of frequency allocation is a major difference between broadcasting and the press. But even the newspaper press – whose traditions are strongly marked by nineteenth-century *laissez-faire* values – is deeply involved with governments. This is especially the case in the many countries whose press is heavily dependent on imported newsprint, and printing machinery; newspapers, because of the great perishability of the product, are also very vulnerable to the policies of regional and local government – for planning and building permissions as well as in all aspects of traffic and transportation.

The low frequency media – such as books and films – are at least equally subject to government influence. Governments are themselves often producers of books and films on a substantial scale; books, as in Britain, are often given special financial exemptions. And films – as in France and Britain for many years – can be dominated by various types of subsidy and taxation.

The whole issue of government subsidy and taxation of the media – although much debated in detail – has never received the comprehensive study or international comparison, which the importance of the topic might seem to justify. In the United States there is a long history of newspapers receiving special treatment – on such issues as the legal status of children delivering newspapers and through special cheap postage rates. In some European countries there are numerous special *subsidies* from governments for newsprint, ink, machinery, film and book production, and special financial privileges for journalists; in Britain and other European countries the media also benefit from various import-saving, unemployment-saving and regional planning financial inducements. The media, like other businesses, also suffer from *taxation* – and of course try to use their political influence to minimize taxation. In some countries – such as Italy – there are general advertising taxes; in Britain there has been an important levy on commercial TV advertising, which was steadily increased during the 1960s.

Despite continuing national and international concern over the finances and control of the media, the many official investigations almost invariably concentrate upon only limited aspects of one medium, for instance the national or the regional newspapers, and consequently no comprehensive picture of the full plus and minus (subsidy and taxation) picture is available. This is especially serious since some of the major policy questions can only be answered by cross-national comparison. For example it is sometimes argued that newsprint and other subsidies produce a government controlled press; but France has huge subsidies and a press with a reputation for some political independence. Any comprehensive account of media-government financial relations would also, of course, need to look at two especially important areas: (1) advertising revenue and the extent to which this performs the function of subsidy; (2) broadcasting licences and the way in which these are allocated and can be withdrawn.

During the 1960s most major western nations had public enquiries on the question of media control, finance, competition and monopoly. A common theme in these enquiries was the closure of specific newspapers or a specific kind of monopoly threat. These enquiries, however, seldom confronted the problems very systematically. Typically, for instance, rather dubious assumptions were made on the question of 'Is television killing off newspapers?' (a subject which James Curran's article in this volume shows to have generated more heat than light).

Between Britain and the United States there is a curious tendency to admiration of the other country's procedures for public enquiries and public policy making. In the United States there is an admiration for such 'typically British' institutions as the Press Council – an institution which, like some other 'typically British' institutions, was borrowed from Scandinavia without much acknowledgement, and plays a rather minor part in British journalism. American admiration frequently extends to include the British Royal Commission type of enquiry; enquiries such as the Shawcross Royal Commission on the Press and the Pilkington Committee on Broadcasting, both of which reported in 1962, offer very little that can satisfy a social scientist – or for that matter anyone who prefers to see decisions made on the basis of at least some systematic evidence. (Both reports were compared unfavourably with the Robbins Committee on Higher Education which reported in the following year and conducted a major programme of research.) In Britain there tends to be great admiration for investigations conducted by Committees of the us Congress. An example of such an enquiry was the hearings of the us Senate Anti-Trust and Monopoly sub-committee (of the Judiciary Committee) on *The Failing Newspaper Act* – hearings which took place in Washington in 1967 and 1968 on a major piece of proposed legislation affecting the monopoly-competition issue in a number of states and large cities; most of the voluminous published evidence consists of the self-justifications of the interested parties and rather little of the 'evidence' put forward is of a sophisticated or systematic kind. The part played by evidence from academics is slightly higher than in the British enquiries, but this evidence does not always compare favourably with that of the directly interested parties.

One is left with the conclusion that in both the US and UK great decisions are being taken about the future of the media which will influence politics, education, leisure, commerce and other aspects of society in many important ways. But these decisions seem to be made in an oddly accidental manner – with most politicians, media owners, communicators and social scientists showing concern only with one small sector of the media and demoralized by the scale and complexity of the overall issues.

16. *Theory, ideology, methods*

I have already suggested that media research should *first* more frequently adopt a cross-media comparative approach; *secondly* pay more attention to the media organizations; and *thirdly* look at the overall communications flow – from media organization to ultimate audience member and back again – rather than focusing on studies of only one stage in the flow. All of this amounts to a plea for somewhat less micro-sociology and somewhat more macro-sociology. Perhaps I should quote further examples of studies which might advance our knowledge of the media –

(a) Women and the media – which could include the role of girls and women in media content, women as communicators and women as audience for media output (including advertising).
(b) Working class and the media. Is there any substance in the contention that a nation like Britain gives rather a poor level of minimum education to its lower working class, and then through its national media (not only the BBC) emphasizes cultural values to an extent which is inconsistent with educational policies and expenditure?
(c) Elite values and the media.

Ideology and the media go so much hand in hand that the whole field seems a particularly promising one for social science exploration. The themes of 'neutrality', 'balance', 'impartiality' and the 'common-carrier' concept of the press are all topics of great public concern as well as social science interest. The mass media have, of course, already been looked at from the perspective of the sociology of knowledge. Whether a distinctive body of social theory dealing specifically with the media will emerge is itself a contentious question. Social scientists with differing views on this subject can, however, be grateful to Melvin DeFleur for his *Theories of Mass Communication* (1966). There will also be fairly widespread agreement that social science studies of the media must pay more attention to theory – both in using, and contributing to, theory. In the past media research has benefited from importing theoretical perspectives from several neighbouring fields; this process should surely continue. Theoretical developments in a number of fields – such as organizational theory, symbolic interactionism, social psychiatry, exchange theory, conflict theory, linguistics, disengagement theory, collective behaviour – appear to have much to offer.

If media studies need the refreshing impact of new theoretical approaches, there is also a need for some changes in the most preferred methods of social research. The very broad range of media studies means that just as almost the entire range of social theory may be relevant at least at some point, so also nearly the whole range of research methods can be used. I have not intended to imply that laboratory experiments, content analysis, or random samples should cease; my contention is rather that they should continue – in combination with other, less used, methods. The strengths of random sample surveys – such as the sample of 2,500 US adults reported in Gary Steiner's *The People Look at Television* (1963) – are well known. However, the weaknesses of these methods are also quite well known, and it may be worth remembering that such 'hard' data studies will not automatically impress those natural scientists who originally devised sampling procedures for the study of plant and animal, not human, subjects.

The choice of methods depends not only upon the hypotheses and problems selected but in the finance available. Where largish research funds are available other sorts of research design than national random samples of *individuals* may be more sociologically remunerative. Such methods may include longitudinal studies – for instance following the media exposure of the same young people as they grow up. Another useful methodological approach would be a design which incorporates the advantages of the single detailed case study but reduces some of its disadvantages – for instance a design which involves a systematic comparison of a number of studies each of which uses direct observation or other 'intensive' techniques. Such studies might retain some of the flavour of the specific media but could also span: (1) communications organizations with differing types of goal; (2) different types of media, e.g. press and broadcast; (3) different types of audience gratification.

In this introduction I have tried to suggest that students of the media should not approach media sociology in an uncritical frame of mind. If some of my own criticisms seem exaggerated, or should they become quickly outdated by new research, so much the better. At the very least the pieces in this Reader – a third of them not previously published – surely indicate that media sociology is a field of considerable intrinsic fascination, social importance and intellectual challenge.

Jeremy Tunstall

The Open University
September 1969

PART ONE:

Cross Media Patterns and Media Research

1. Approaches to the Historical Development of Mass Media Studies*

Roger L. Brown

The full history of mass communications research still waits to be written. When the story comes to be told, however, there are a number of particular circumstances which the writer will need to pay attention to. For one thing, the mass media have always been much in the public eye, so that there has been a constant interplay between popular opinion about their performance and more considered intellectual assessments.

Indeed, critical attention has been paid to the mass media since their beginnings, and the volume of discussion has increased markedly since the latter years of the nineteenth century: yet the application of empirical research techniques to the mass communications field dates only from the 1930s. Thus one topic which any historical account must deal with is the impact of what we are now learning to call the 'behavioural sciences' on earlier forms of thinking about mass communication, realizing at the same time that earlier views were themselves heavily coloured by social scientific thinking of a more philosophical sort. Further, any full history of media research will, of course, have to pay considerable attention to the impetus given to such research by the media industries themselves, so that a second major focus of interest inevitably lies in the changing relationships between the sorts of research directly commissioned by the industries (and other clients) and the sorts of research conducted within universities and similar centres. Very little social scientific research conducted within universities, of course, can really be seen as 'pure' research, in the sense of its being conducted without any reference at all to the current concerns and problems of the larger society, and media research has

* Not previously published.

certainly been at least as sensitive as most fields to pressures of this kind. Hence a third topic which a history of mass communications research will need to cover is the nature and effectiveness of the general social pressures which have moulded academic endeavours.

What are regarded as the proper objectives for the future historian of media research should be made clear at the outset. In recounting the development of a branch of the social sciences, the sequence of events one is properly attempting to account for comprises the set of theoretical propositions which hold sway at particular periods. For it is the attempt to develop theories which distinguishes the social sciences from the work of social critics and lay commentators. Today we may think of theories about mass communications as involving essentially the statement of relationships between variables. For example, it has been suggested that there is a curvilinear relationship between the level of anxiety produced by fear-arousing messages and the consequent degree of attitude change; or, to take a more general proposition, it has been argued that the mass media are particularly effective in areas where there is little ego-involvement on the part of the audience. But if we turn back to what social psychologists wrote about mass communications in the early years of this century, we shall be far less likely to find correlational statements of this kind. And we shall find that the concepts employed were very different, too: writers made much of the idea of crowd behaviour, and speculated on the nature of the 'popular will'. So the historian needs to pay attention to changes in the general form and character of theoretical statements, as well as to their specific contents. And in the mass media field particularly it seems that attention needs to be given to the role which new methods of research have played in bringing about shifts in the kind of theory current at different times.

A fragmented field?

Given a research field that has to some considerable extent been the heir of pre-empirical approaches to its subject matter, and which has certainly been subjected to the pressures stemming from the prevalent concerns of particular publics and clients, it would not perhaps be surprising if the historical account of its emergence which finally came to be accepted dwelt on the fragmentary, non-cumulative nature of the undertaking, and emphasized uncompleted programmes and false starts rather than a purposive development towards greater understanding. Although this is not the view implicit here, the issue needs to be faced squarely, since some of the available historical accounts do paint this sort of picture.

Berelson's classic 'obituary' for mass media research in the United States represented one of the few attempts to sketch in the social scientific origins of the field and to assess what had been achieved up to that time.[1]* The writer was no doubt trying to be controversial and challenging, yet even so there are peculiarities in his presentation which can hardly be justified on these grounds. In the first place, Berelson appears to confuse the issue by heading his paper 'The State of *Communications* Research'. Although studies of the mass media have on occasion, particularly in the United States, been linked administratively (and sometimes in terms of curricula) with studies of such topics as small-group interaction and even with older disciplines such as descriptive linguistics, no very convincing intellectual arguments in favour of such arrangements are on record, and it is probably safe to say that the degree of academic interchange between some of these ill-sorted bedfellows has been minimal. Yet Berelson, for example, includes in his list of 'minor approaches' 'The mathematical approach: represented by Shannon and Weaver'. Although information theory has had a considerable impact on certain branches of experimental psychology, particularly in the field of cognitive processes, and has roused some interest among linguists, it seems to have had no lasting influence on the course of mass media studies. In short, by casting his net very wide, and by making reference to any line of enquiry that could be regarded as involving the study of communication, Berelson manages to give the impression of an extremely fragmented field. Yet the wide domain he marks out has never existed as an academic discipline and nobody has seriously claimed that it should. Hence it is important to note that Berelson is not confining himself to mass media studies, but is surveying a range of interests that are linked in some cases merely through the possession of a common verbal label.

Again, Berelson does not suggest the known ways in which particular theoretical advances made by the pioneers he names have occurred in historical sequence and contributed to a progressively

* Notes and sources begin on p. 499.

more refined synthesis. For example, although Lazarsfeld's *The People's Choice* is listed as a characteristic work by one of the four 'major figures' (Lasswell, Lewin and Hovland being the others),[2] no mention is made of the way in which the initial suggestions about opinion leadership and the two-step flow contained in the 1940 voting study were related to Lewin's small group researches as part of the process which Katz and Lazarsfeld later on referred to as the 'rediscovery of the primary group'.[3] Thus not only are essentially *un*related lines of enquiry listed as equal members of a field of study, the historical relations which *do* exist are also largely left untreated. And it is a study of the links between the theories and methodological approaches of such men as Lazarsfeld and Hovland which would constitute a major part of the historical account one has in mind. For such men as these belong to a mainstream tradition of media study.

It may seem strange to talk of a 'mainsteam' tradition in communications research at all, for academic enquiry into the media has been institutionalized on a multidisciplinary basis, particularly in the United States, though more recently in Europe also. Yet it is to an extent just because of this multidisciplinary organization that a central line of development can be traced. Thinking and research conducted independently by psychologists, sociologists and political scientists has on occasion thrown up parallel theories which have seemed to be in clear conflict with each other. However, insightful syntheses have sprung from these very difficulties.

It is worth noting that Berelson's real or feigned pessimism about the future of communications research was the aspect of his thesis which White questioned in a rejoinder written five years later, and not the mode of argument itself.[4] Indeed, White's digest of recent research does little to suggest that lines of enquiry determined by crucial theoretical questions might constitute the basic underpinning of the field. He presents a picture of even more chronic fragmentation than Berelson, and while this is in part due to the greater difficulty of bringing into sharp focus a wealth of empirical studies conducted in the very immediate past, it is still perhaps revealing that White organizes his material so far as possible along disciplinary lines, with separate sections devoted to work by psychologists, sociologists, political scientists and anthropologists, among others. Again, White follows Berelson in dealing with the 'journalism-communications school researchers' under a separate heading, here once more following an arrangement which mirrors the lines of *departmental* organization characteristic of many American universities, rather than the less tangible lines which link theoretical perplexity with its attempted solution. Thus White's paper, too, is in fact symptomatic perhaps of a view of mass media studies (and White does *not* deal with other types of 'communication' research) which sees them as progressing by the cumulation of essentially isolated studies of particular phenomena, rather than as being marked by a changing and hopefully evolving view of the role of media systems within societies.

As already suggested, the development of empirical communications research as we know it dates only from the 1930s, while the rise of the modern media predates this development by a number of years.[5] Some historians of the mass media have employed the term 'communications revolution' to refer to the emergence of the modern newspaper press, of the cinema and of radio. But of course these events themselves span a period of some thirty years, so that the revolution was in no sense an overnight event. In Great Britain, changes in the major sources of newspaper revenue dated from the 1890s. Cinemas became common in the years between 1910 and 1920. Broadcasting of music became common in the early 1920s and the British Broadcasting Corporation was set up in 1927. Yet newspaper readership studies were not common till the latter 1930s and the full development of academic research into the visual media has only begun in the post-war years. Thus between 1900 and 1935, roughly speaking, the mass media existed without mass communications research as we know it today.

Gesellschaft and propaganda

Thinking, however, about the mass media *was* of course heavily influenced by the prevailing views of sociologists and psychologists in the period prior to the development of those empirical research techniques with which we are now familiar. A sketch of what these theories were has been provided by both DeFleur[6] and Qualter,[7] and attempt need be made here to rehearse that early thinking about the supposed chronic susceptibility to persuasion of modern, particularly urban populations, which sprang from the sociology of Tönnies and Durkheim among others, and from the social psychology of writers such as Le Bon and McDougall. To provide one example of the sort of thinking to which social scientists and social critics of this period contributed, Shils' summary of a major sociological tradition provides a concise reminder:

> The main theme of nineteenth-century sociology, developing as it did from the philosophy of history, was the emergence and operation of the large-scale society, the 'great society', 'bourgeois' society. In their perception of the movement from 'status' to 'contract', from *Gemeinschaft* ('community') to *Gesellschaft* ('society'), from 'mechanical solidarity' to 'organic solidarity', sociologists saw modern society as impersonal, co-ordinated by actions based on expediential calculations, and highly individualistic.[8]

A whole chapter in the history of social thought is summarized here, but it was of course the concept of the isolated, unrestrained, atomized, possibly anomic individual which had the greatest impact on ideas about mass media. If societies were like this, then persuasion via the mass media was all too easy, since a person was restrained from accepting new ideas by very few social ties or traditional orientations.

The beliefs that the mass media were, for this sort of reason, agents of enormous potential power characterizes much of the period between the turn of the century and the second world war. And of course a number of events during these years served to provide apparent empirical support for this view. Again, space precludes a detailed listing and discussion of such events, and indeed here again a full narrative still waits to be written; but one or two illustrations of what is meant can be given.

During and after the first world war there was a widespread (and perhaps justified) belief in the power of propaganda, and numbers of books published during the 1920s provided *exposés* and criticisms of campaigns waged by the major powers.[9] With the rise to dominance of Stalin in the Soviet Union, and the takeover of Germany by the National Socialists, new fears arose. If totalitarian régimes found home propaganda so successful in persuading and controlling their populations, might not international propaganda be equally effective? And faith in the automatic power of the mass media was further strengthened by the success of consumer advertising, particularly with the development of commercial radio in the United States in the 1920s, while the newly developed public relations business made sweeping claims about its ability to engineer consent. However, the popular view which these events engendered was to be progressively challenged.

Empirical research

Indeed, in terms of general ideas about the effects of mass communication, the period since the late 1930s has been marked by an orientation quite different from that characteristic of the preceding decades. Instead of a very general set of assumptions about the automatic effectiveness of mass persuasion, the goal of much academic research has been to specify the precise conditions under which the media are likely to produce changes in information levels, attitudes and behaviour; and it should be admitted that the complexity of the picture which has emerged is at least partially responsible for the fact that the lines along which important research is moving are more difficult to trace than are those cruder assumptions which guided social criticism and social policy in an earlier era. Even so, several major lines of development are discernible.

Perhaps most important, the picture of the mass media audience as a mere set of isolated individuals has been replaced by one which stresses the structured nature of that audience, the channels of interpersonal communication within it, and the modifying influence which membership in face-to-face groups exerts over external efforts to modify shared beliefs. This major shift in the way the media audience is conceptualized has of course much to do with that 'rediscovery of the primary group' which Shils describes in the paper already quoted, and which Katz and Lazarsfeld also summarize in the historical preface to *Personal Influence*. But research on the structure and functioning of the primary group has been only one of the lines of enquiry leading to a more circumspect account of media effectiveness.

Many of the advances in our understanding of the variables which affect the ability of mass communicated messages to modify ideas and behaviour are associated with the methodology of the controlled experiment, and an historical account of the development of media studies needs to pay considerable attention to both the power and limitations of this mode of enquiry.[10] Although pieces of empirical research on comparative effectiveness can be found as far back as the late 1920s, it was only in the mid 'thirties that this kind of work commonly began to be undertaken. In the United States, the impetus given to experimental studies during the second world war is symbolized by the programme of research directed by Hovland, initially for the Research Branch of the army's Information and Education Division, and subsequently at Yale.[11] The fruits of this continuing programme are, of course, proof of the advantages which accrue from the conduct of a long-term and multifaceted assault on a particular research front, yet the very sophistication of the theories developed has itself introduced a considerable complexity into the field, and made the drawing of clear lessons about when the media will produce changes in real-life situations an extremely difficult task. Yet one generalization of a rather different sort can be made. Because of the nature of the experimental situation, and due to the aims of social psychological researchers (which commonly involve the study of differential, rather than absolute effectiveness), research employing controlled experiments does tend to suggest that effects can rather easily be produced. Thus, although the findings from laboratory experiments on the change-producing potential of mass media materials have led to increasingly sophisticated generalizations about the conditions under which *maximum* effects can be produced, the general tenor of the results tends to emphasize earlier beliefs in the power of mass persuasion.

Surveys of mass media audiences, and more particularly panel studies of media effectiveness, on the other hand, have served to suggest that the media are far less effective than was once thought, or at least that the lessons drawn from totalitarian or wartime conditions are not directly applicable to relatively stable, industrialized societies under peacetime prosperity.[12] Like the controlled experiment, the wide use of the sample survey came in only in the late 'thirties,[13] so that the findings from research employing this method of data collection have been published during roughly the same time period as those accruing from the Yale programme and similar work.

The fact that rather large changes of attitude are commonly produced in the laboratory under experimental conditions, while survey investigations commonly show a nil effect, has led some to suspect that one or other of the methodologies is at fault. But as Hovland himself has pointed out in a classic paper,[14] detailed scrutiny of these apparently conflicting bodies of findings does not in fact reveal any theoretical conflicts. It is equally clear though that lay interpreters of the social sciences are now provided with a golden opportunity of quoting empirical findings selectively to suit their current brief. Even so the theoretically fruitful synthesis of findings based on different methods may serve as one of the major justifications for that multidisciplinary label which media students have sometimes espoused. Certainly, the availability of two relevant methodologies has meant that extreme care has been needed to extrapolate from data collected under particular circumstances.

But if the last quarter-century has been marked by the emergence of a much more qualified account of the power of mass communication, as already suggested an equally important change has taken place in the characteristic mode of enquiry. The use of controlled experiments and sample surveys has increased enormously, and whole new cadres of researchers have arisen to make use of them, both inside and outside universities. But although the deployment of progressively more refined research techniques has meant that we now have a much truer picture of the impact of mass communications, and although a wealth of sophisticated theory has emerged from these endeavours, yet it is possible to argue that these developments have not all been for the good.[15]

Albig, a member of an older academic generation, has surveyed some of the American public opinion research carried out between 1936 and 1956.[16] He notes the rising proportion of quantitative studies carried out during these two decades, and admits that it was inevitable for older, more philosophical approaches to be supplanted. Yet he also expresses considerable regret that too little attention was paid during this period to the development of general theories of the public opinion process. Similar comments might be made about other branches of communications research, and it is worth enquiring about the relationships between methodological refinement and theoretical advance.

The inhibition of theory

In the first place, the availability of sophisticated empirical techniques can itself inhibit the development of theory. At one level, academics find that a secure reputation can be made on the basis of research which essentially involves the perfecting of methodological devices. Unfortunately, work of this sort may on occasion become an end in itself.

At another and more important level, reputations can be established on the basis of a sequence of small, self-contained and relatively *ad hoc* research projects, each of which is methodologically impeccable, but which do not as a whole knit together into a sequence designed to achieve real theoretical advance. And of course the manner in which universities have developed over the last few decades has encouraged many academic researchers to devote themselves to undertakings of these sorts. The expansion of higher education not only raises self doubts about academic performance at the bottom end of the league table, so that the security of a list of publications is eagerly sought for, the threat of professional anonymity posed by expansion also encourages production of the quickly executed piece designed to catch a current fashion. And laboratory experiments and small-scale surveys lend themselves readily enough to meeting pressures of this sort. This account, of course, would apply quite generally to the behavioural sciences (and perhaps to other academic fields); however, there are additional reasons why many recent empirical studies of the media have been less than fully relevant to the development of general theory.

Academic mass media research has some of its roots in applied research in the same field, and the link has remained a close one for a variety of reasons. But while some applied research has stimulated theoretical development, the general trend seems to have been in the other direction.

In Great Britain, the so-called 'Northcliffe revolution' represented a switch in the basic economics of the newspaper industry. The proportion of their revenue which national dailies drew from advertisers increased sharply, and the accompanying changes in the way in which these newspapers competed against each other had its consequences for the type of research in which the media industries were first interested. Advertising rates, then as now, were computed in terms of the absolute size of the readership and its demographic composition, and newspaper managements needed to be able to provide advertisers and advertising agents with reliable facts and figures. Although exaggerated and ill-founded claims were often made in the early years, continued reliance on advertising revenue made it certain that each new advance in research methodology would soon be applied to the task of providing ever-more refined data of the required sort. Although the net sales of any particular edition of a paper or magazine provide a crude yardstick of audience size, the resulting figures tell one nothing about the sex or social class of purchasers, or about how many individuals actually 'read' a particular copy, while it is just these details in which advertisers are particularly interested. Sample surveys of the general population or of the readership of a particular journal can provide information on these topics, and it is to this technique that the publishers of newspapers and magazines have increasingly turned over the last thirty years or so.

But of course the mere collection of readership data (or of comparable data about radio and television audiences) is not in itself likely to stimulate theoretical advance, and it can indeed be argued that the media's main call has been for ever firmer assurances that the data supplied to them should be highly valid and highly reliable. In lucrative product fields where there is fierce competition between competing firms, winning a marginally larger share of the market may represent a major victory. Under these conditions, very precise information about the relative effectiveness of different advertising media is vital. Thus so far as academic researchers have been involved in meeting the needs of the media industries, emphasis has once again tended to be placed on the refinement of method rather than on the search for explanatory concepts. And rapid social change, particularly in terms of the growth and distribution of real income since the second world war, has meant that the collection and sifting of up-to-date fact has been of additional importance.

It can be argued, however, that the media have more recently become interested in theories of a certain sort, and it is perhaps important to recognize the nature of these propositions and distinguish them from social-scientific theories proper. So far as they exist on advertising revenue, the print and broadcasting media must seek to show that there is a positive relationship between exposure to their messages and stipulated types of purchasing behaviour, and the development of sophisticated statistical methods has made it possible to express such relationships very precisely in terms of multiple correlations or regression equations. But while the resulting mathematical formulations do essentially involve propositions about relationships between variables, nothing about *why* these relationships hold, or about the processes that link exposure with purchasing behaviour, needs to be said for the findings to have high relevance for policy formulation by media institutions and advertisers. Although more advanced mathematics are enjoying a current vogue in the behavioural sciences, little of general theoretical importance seems so far to have emerged from those types of media equation which have the greatest commercial value.[17]

It may perhaps be asked why so much attention is given to commercial communications research in a discussion devoted primarily to the development of academic theory. For the answer, one must turn to the way mass media studies have been institutionalized within universities in the United States. In the State universities, departments of journalism date from the turn of the century, and these have continued to serve as training centres for aspiring reporters and editors. It was natural that in many cases they should be extended to acommodate those social scientists who became interested in media questions. This juxtaposition of teachers of craft skills – many with practical media experience – and research workers has served to keep the latter group in close touch with the practical problems actually faced by the media, while the incorporation of departments of advertising and public relations in larger units bearing the 'communications' label has served to intensify such links. Not unnaturally, the fact that the media have often been ready with funds for commissioned research has itself served to draw academic social scientists into a range of applied fields. It need hardly be added that it is to the much vaster body of American research that workers in Europe will often turn for the first clues to some problem in which they become interested. In recent years too, the social scientist's yearning for added deference has been linked with an attempt to import into his work the methodological rigour perceived as characteristic of the physical sciences.

But if methodological advance, the structure of academic life and the interests of the media themselves serve to account for the emphasis on valid data and for the relative paucity of attention given to general theories of mass communication, it must still be stressed that the years since 1940 have yielded a rich harvest of theoretically relevant findings, particularly at the social psychological level. And the historical account will not be complete unless attention is directed to the academic response to this situation.

Synthesis or dogma?

Klapper, in a number of publications culminating in his book *The Effects of Mass Communication*,[18] has attempted to prepare a theoretically coherent digest of the bulk of the significant empirical studies of effectiveness which have appeared over the past thirty years. While it would be hard to deny the utility of Klapper's work, what is of particular interest in the present context are the reasons for its warm reception and continued high status over the last few years as a source of organizing concepts. For these things are in themselves indications of the apparently meaningless complexity which had developed, and of the desire felt by many for a formulation which would produce pattern out of apparent chaos. But while such a synthesis has various sorts of utility, and clearly represents a more sophisticated general view of mass persuasion than might have been produced in, say, 1935, the dangers and limitations inherent in a propositionalized schema such as Klapper's must also be recognized.

In a field in which methodological (and theoretical) advance has led to an accumulation of insufficiently digested findings, the danger may be that any comprehensible synthesis will itself become dogma and itself provide the starting points for further research, sometimes to the neglect of the original, underlying studies. Again, no single empirical investigation is likely to undermine the general orientation of such a synthesis, so that again an unnaturally long life may be given to propositions that themselves deserve considerable scrutiny. And academic researchers may well find themselves relying heavily on the available generalizations, since the continued demands of alarmed (and sometimes alarmist) pressure groups that they be told what the professionals know about the effects – the effects of aggressive media content, for example – may lead such researchers to respond with a set of statements which can be used to suggest that relatively firm 'answers' have been arrived at. Perhaps it is true that more emphasis has been given to the first of Klapper's propositions ('Mass communication *ordinarily* does not serve as a necessary and sufficient cause of audience effects . . .') than to those later ones which state quite plainly that there *are* conditions under which the media may be almost as powerful as they were once believed to be when public concern was directed towards totalitarian propaganda; and if this is the case, it may be due equally to the selective use of such generalizations by media spokesmen themselves, and to academics' desire to be rid of the irritant demands of PTAS or moralizing housewives.

The second of Klapper's propositions states that '[The] mediating factors are such that they typically render mass communication a contributory agent, but not the sole cause, in a process of reinforcing the existing conditions.' The norm-reinforcing, integrative, functional view of the mass media which this apothegm suggests has itself provided the starting point for some interesting re-thinking of our view of mass communications.[19] To some extent this has perhaps represented merely another swing of the pendulum away from the belief in media power current in the 'twenties and 'thirties, a phase subsequent to the more qualified beliefs about effectiveness stemming from the application of empirical methodology. But it is illuminating to give further consideration to why this sort of view has only quite recently begun to form a framework for empirical research and theory development.

If the first impetus to non-academic communications research arose from the media's need to have accurate information about their audiences, a second and perhaps more important one stemmed from their wanting to know whether or not the advertisements they carried did in fact produce the effects intended. And advertisers' concern about the effectiveness of their messages was paralleled by similar concern on the part of party and government propagandists, military establishments and educationalists. Thus the second major focus of applied communications research involved the measurement of changes in information, attitudes and behaviour; and the main tool employed was, of course, the experiment or quasi-experiment.

While techniques for conducting valid and reliable controlled experiments have now been systematized at a high level, even so there is one set of circumstances which is still liable to baffle the research worker. If, at the end of the experiment, there is no statistically significant difference between the experimental and control groups (to adopt the terminology applicable to the simplest type of situation), then there is a lack of certainty about how this finding is to be interpreted. Assuming the design to be valid, there is still no way of telling whether the necessary acceptance of the null hypothesis is due to no change having been produced by the message, or whether the measuring instruments employed have just not been sensitive enough, or sufficiently 'on target', to measure marginal changes which have in fact occurred. Thus in experimental research attempts are commonly made to maximise the between-groups variance so that the results can be unambiguously interpreted. Given methodological motivations of this sort, it is possible to argue that the application of the controlled experiment to mass media research was unlikely to lead to a view of the media as stabilizing agents. Indeed, quite other methodologies have been employed to substantiate perspectives of this nature.'[20]

Functional analysis

Even so, there has recently been something of a vogue for the use of Merton's paradigm of functional analysis in the mass media field.[21] Yet the model has been followed somewhat mechanically, there has been a considerable over-emphasis on functional integration, particularly at the personality level, and as Klapper himself points out, the studies of the gratifications which audience members derive from the media have seldom in fact achieved the full status of functional analyses.[22] It could indeed be argued that mass communication researchers have on the whole been ignorant of, or ignored, the debate about functionalist terminology and theory which has been conducted amongst sociologists. This may in itself furnish evidence of the separation of media studies from the mainstream of sociological thinking, and it is worth speculating, finally, why this should have been the case. Although mass communications studies may have been slow to gain full academic respectability, partly perhaps due to close ties with allied applied fields, and partly to the manner of their institutionalization within universities, this has not prevented recent social psychological theories (such as that of cognitive dissonance) from having a considerable impact on considerations of audience behaviour at the appropriate level. Perhaps it is that since about 1940 the field has been identified with, and to an extent monopolized by, work following the paradigm of the Yale school. Certainly, the lack of general theories about mass communications seems to have something to do with the attention paid (and not only by the lay public) to a *guru* such as McLuhan. Perhaps, in due course, ideas drawn from fields where sociological thinking has been turned to media problems will be re-applied in the context of fully industrialized societies (work on the developing countries furnishes the obvious case in point). We need to know far more about the links between susceptibility to, and usage of, the mass media and the age and class structures of total societies. At the moment, however, one has to recognize the recent dominance of social-psychological approaches.

Merton sought to relate the methodological characteristics of American communications and public opinion research to the typical organizational problems of teamwork, and brought out his point by a whole series of insightful contrasts with the work done by members of the German 'sociology of knowledge' school.[23] But of course the kind of empirical findings under discussion here, and the characteristic orientations of the research practitioners, are themselves inviting subjects of study for the sociologist of 'knowledge'. And it is not merely a matter of some topics having been studied to the neglect of others (though the relative lack of attention paid to the communicators themselves may be an indication of an historically important constraint on research), it is basically a question of the manner in which cultural and political assumptions are reflected in the types of data and theory which have come to be highly regarded. For example, the idea put forward above that mass media research has been centrally concerned with the refinement of theoretical propositions stating relationships between variables is itself a notion which can become the object of historical and sociological scrutiny. Further, although the suggestion that the development of thought about the media has been merely fragmentary has already been challenged, Merton himself makes a still valid point about the fragmentary nature of the 'knowledge' characteristically studied in communications research. Thus although the atomized view of the audience may now be a dead letter, an atomized view of what is transmitted *to* and known *by* that audience is still inherent in much of our thinking. Again, this could be related to data collection techniques such as the structured questionnaire and the various kinds of attitude scale now in current use: but the more important point to be stressed is that a distanced inspection of the *sorts* of 'knowledge' we assume the media to be transmitting can add further depth to our historical understanding.

In studying the mass media, as in other academic domains, the everyday pressures of academic life and the excitements of current research suggest clearly enough the functions which a considered historical view of the field can serve. And of course the development of such a view can in itself be a worthwhile research undertaking. But to reiterate the warning given at the start, much historical delving into the pre-empirical phases of media study still waits to be done, while we are in many respects too close to recent developments to see them in full perspective. Yet the consciousness that one is working in a tradition, or striving to emancipate one's views from the limitations imposed by past situations, is something which can provide a discipline supplementary to, and perhaps corrective of, the disciplines imposed both by whatever reality one assigns to the objective social world and by the currently received techniques of investigation.

2. Mass Communication and Social Change*

Melvin L. DeFleur

Excellent histories of each of our principal mass media have been available for some time. These have extensively documented the dates, contributions of individuals, invention of technical devices and other details which have played significant parts in the development of each major form of mass communication. Almost uniformly, these histories have been prepared by writers specialized in the study of some particular medium (journalists, students of the cinema, educators in broadcasting, etc.).[1] Sociologists and other social scientists have paid relatively little attention to the patterns of growth of the media in terms of their broader implications for the study of social change. Although themselves often intimately involved in the process by which new cultural traits become accepted into society, the mass media may be viewed in their own right as cultural innovations. In recent years, substantial advances have been made in understanding the processes by which new items of culture spread through a social system, achieving widespread adoption by the members of its population. Such 'diffusion studies' of the 'adoption of innovation' promise to provide the foundation for the eventual development of an analytical, quantitative and empirically-based theory of social change.[2] It is the intent of the present paper to clarify a number of concepts which will enter such a theory, to suggest points where they can be linked to broader sociological theory, and then to present data which illustrate the potential utility of the conceptual framework.

* This article was first published in *Social Forces*, 44 (1966) pp. 314–26, and is an outgrowth of a paper presented at the annual meeting of the American Sociological Association, Montreal, Canada, 1964. The writer is indebted to Elaine C. El-Assal for her many contributions to both works.

58

The illustrative sets of data are the *diffusion curves* which four major mass media of communication have followed during their respective periods of acceptance by American households. These curves are related to a background of classical studies of the adoption of innovation, and are compared with each other in terms of similarities and differences from one medium to another. The major social, political, and economic events which appear to have influenced these quantitative growth patterns are brought out for each medium. While most studies of mass communication attempt to unravel ways in which the media influence society, the present analysis tries to bring out ways in which society has influenced the media.

Towards a clarification of basic terms and a convergence with more general theory

The terminology of the growing body of literature reporting on the diffusion of items through populations is characterized by a considerable lack of uniformity in the use of terms.[3] For this reason, more rigorous efforts need to be directed towards standardization of the *meaning* of concepts, and towards *consistency* in their use from one writer to another. Such standardization needs to be based upon definitional principles *which also underlie more general sociological theory* so that an emerging empirical theory of social change which rests in part upon contributions from the diffusion studies can eventually converge with broader conceptual schemes. Two obvious requirements along these lines are: (1) that the variables to be included in an empirical theory of social change must be *measurable*, and (2) that theoretical concepts related to the diffusion process must be defined in such a way that their social action or behavioural *referents* are clear.

Elementary as they may seem, the two requirements noted above have not been adequately met in the past, and this has been a source of substantial confusion. For example, in the sociological literature, even the word 'innovation' itself is used in a bewildering variety of ways. It sometimes means newly invented items of *technology* such as hybrid seed corn.[4] It also means the act of working out some new *deviant form of behaviour* which will aid the individual in achieving a culturally approved goal (by illegitimate means).[5] For other writers, the term refers to a *cultural modification*, such as the development within a group of a new code of approved conduct.[6] For still others, it has meant the psychological and overt actions associated with the *acquisition* of some new procedure, belief, device, etc., including the reaching of a decision to adopt and also the overt act of adopting.[7] Other terms (invention, diffusion, etc.) used widely in research related to the study of innovation have shown equal degrees of confusion in definition and meaning.

The present discussion is not intended as a suggestion that such heterogeneous classes of events are unimportant objects of study. But when such a variety of referents are all denoted by the same symbol, thought and communication are severely hampered. A standardized terminology has become an indispensable and urgent prerequisite for the further development of a systematic approach to social change *via* the quantitative study of diffusion and related phenomena.

A second urgent prerequisite is the linking of theoretical concepts from diffusion studies and the study of innovation to concepts from more general sociological theory. One of the reasons why this has not been done extensively in the past is undoubtedly explainable by the fact that sociologists have not yet developed very much in the way of validated general theory about which widespread consensus exists.

The work of Talcott Parsons, among contemporary American sociologists, makes a claim to being directed towards this goal. There is no complete agreement as to how well this goal is being reached by his particular efforts, but there is at least one aspect of Parsons' 'theories of systems' that seems to provide linkage points for potential convergence with an empirical and analytical theory of social change.[8] This key aspect is Parsons' approach to the conceptualization of social action by treating it within three broad systems:

First, the orientation of action of *any one* given actor and its attendant motivational processes becomes a differentiated and integrated system. This system will be called the *personality*, and we will define it as the organized system of the orientation and motivation of action of one individual *actor*. Secondly, the action of a plurality of actors in a common situation is a process of interaction, the properties of which are to a definite but limited extent independent of any prior culture. This interaction also becomes differentiated and integrated and as such forms a social system. Personality and a social system are very intimately related, but they are neither identical with one another nor explicable by one another; the social system is not a plurality of personalities.

Finally, systems of culture have their own forms and problems of integration which are not reducible to those of either personality or social systems or both together.[9]

Even at the time the general theory of action was formulated, these divisions were neither new nor unique; they were simply introduced as focal points around which the details of the theory were then elaborated. But for present purposes, it can be shown that certain explanations and theories concerned with diffusion and innovation have been formulated at one or the other of these levels, and thus fall within (or are special cases of) one of the three systems of action in the sense implied above.

Illustrations are provided by the attempts of diffusion theorists to explain diffusion curves. For example, an early study by Pemberton showed that when plotted over time on a cumulative basis, the typical diffusion curve usually assumes an 'S' shape. The finding that such curves frequently assume this particular form has been attributed by Rogers,[10] Sheppard,[11] and others to 'interpersonal influence', that is to interactional mechanisms within the *social system*.[12] According to this approach to conceptualizing the diffusion of innovation, actors in a social system who have already adopted a particular item 'expose' or otherwise influence those who have not. Adoption, under this view, is role interaction between a user of the item and one or more non-users which results in alterations of the roles of the latter in such a way that usage of the item becomes part of their roles. If one such actor influences (say) two others, who in turn influence two others, and so on, the curve of adoption will follow a cumulative binomial expansion, much as is the case in an unchecked infectious epidemic. Given sufficient time, the available roles in the system will be altered. That is, saturation will be approached and the curve will tend to level off. The end result of this interactional process, which we can call the 'epidemiological' theory of diffusion (and which we have oversimplified here), is the classic S-shaped diffusion curve, sometimes called the 'logistic curve of adoption'. This approach to the study of social change, through the analysis of the adoption of particular new combinations of culture traits and through interactional events within the social system, appears (when stated in the above terms) to be easily subsumable under the general theory of action as laid out by Parsons and his colleagues.

The data to be presented in the present paper have an important bearing upon the potential validity of the epidemiological theory of diffusion as a *general* model of the adoption of innovation. Such an explanation requires that the actors in the relevant social system be available to each other through time so that the required interactions can take place. If a diffusion curve is found which stretches over a century or so, so that early adopters are long dead before the later adopters acquire the item, then the observed process would not fit well with required underlying assumptions concerning stability in the system of action through time. Such a diffusion curve is in fact clearly in evidence for one of the mass media under study (newspapers).

This suggests that a more adequate explanation of this pattern must be sought within the *cultural* system of the society into which the new item was introduced. New items are adopted by members of groups, communities, or societies who have institutionalized ways of relating themselves to each other. The traditions, group values, social norms, level of technological accumulation and other variations in cultural conditions can serve as prerequisites to (or barriers to) social change. The rate of adoption or degree of penetration of a given new item will be significantly influenced by such factors. A substantial literature has accumulated with respect to this problem.[13]

Another widely used approach to the study of diffusion has focused attention more heavily upon events within the *personality* system. This is well illustrated in the work of Rogers, who defines the 'adoption process' as, 'the mental process through which an individual passes from the first learning about an innovation to final adoption'.[14] The adoption process is broken down into five stages: *awareness, interest, evaluation, trial* and (permanent) *adoption*. Insofar as such action may be thought of as contributing to the maintenance of the personality system, or as aiding the system in achieving some form of equilibrium, there appears to be no barrier whatever regarding convergence of this formulation with more general theory. In particular, the Parsons *et al* treatise on 'Personality as a System of Action' provides a sophisticated set of concepts and propositions which appears to be more than adequate for handling the 'adoption process' as a special case of orientation, motivation and performance of a given actor.[15] In any case, this conceptualization sees the new item moving through a group or community as the result of the separate actions of individuals as they pass through their decision-making series. This approach also appears to be somewhat limited as a *general* model of the adoption process because it rests upon assumptions of systematic rationality and deliberated decisions on the part of all adopters. Perhaps more important, it tends to ignore events which occur in the other systems mentioned. Its articulation with such systems remains to be made clear.

These varied approaches to understanding the diffusion of innovations have resulted from the broad interdisciplinary attacks which have been made on this problem. The twin needs for conceptual standardization and for providing linkages with more general theory have become more and more urgent as the body of research reports has grown richer. It is towards these needs that the following attempt at conceptual clarification of basic terms is addressed. The definitions given below do not purport to be either new, sophisticated, or particularly unique; the concepts defined are elementary. The definitions attempt, however, to provide clear *action referents* for these simple terms (so as to permit convergence with theories of action), and to provide a reasonably standardized framework for approaching data concerning the spread of the mass media and for diffusion studies in general.

A *new item* will refer to some combination of culture traits, mechanical, symbolic, normative or other, which has not previously been widely incorporated into the cultural system of the relevant group or society. Such new items can come to the attention of the relevant group or society through borrowing or through invention.

Invention will refer to the *act* of forming some new combinations of culture traits, that is, some new item. This definition makes invention a behaviour pattern of an actor rather than an element of mechanical or other technology.

Innovation will indicate some *change in patterns of conduct or action* related to some culture trait or item (combination of traits). Such a definition is anchored in potentially observable events and focuses upon patterned action rather than upon new devices, psychological processes, or stages in an individual's acquisition of new habits. Innovation (as change in patterns of action) *may* take place through the adoption of new items brought to the attention of the group or society, but it may also come about because of changing modes or conduct towards items which already exist as part of the established cultural system. Such a definition frees the study of innovation from being simply the study of the adoption of newly borrowed or invented things and broadens it to include behavioural, that is normative, reorientations towards items concerning which a group already has some action pattern. Innovation is thus an event in the cultural system of a group or society.

Obsolescence can be defined as the abandoning of formerly institutionalized modes of conduct related to some established item. Defined thus, obsolescence is a *special case of innovation*, that is a *special case of change* in patterns of action related to some culture trait or item (combination of traits).

Diffusion curve refers to a quantitative function describing the proportion or number of members of a group or society who have acquired a given new item or who have changed their action patterns with respect to it over some period of time. Obsolescence should show a kind of 'reverse' diffusion curve. Its form should be opposite to the familiar S-shaped curve describing adoption. There should be a 'curve of abandonment' for once-institutionalized behaviour forms that are dropping out of the social or cultural system of a given group or society. Diffusion curves may or may not be reliable indices to the patterns of action which the members engage in with respect to the item. An actor may possess an item but not use it; use it but not possess it, etc. They do, however, reveal important data on the degree to which an item has been accepted, rejected or abandoned by a group or society.

Institutionalization will refer to the stabilizing of widespread patterns of action related to some cultural trait or combination of traits. In this sense institutionalization is the end product of innovation and represents *equilibrium* in a system rather than change. If behaviour patterns related to a particular item have been institutionalized, it can be postulated that such an item fulfils some *functional need* in the social system in question. The diffusion curve for an item whose relevant behaviours have become institutionalized should show a distinct 'levelling off' to a relatively long-term 'plateau'.

These six definitions (and the meanings given or implied for the several auxiliary terms contained within them), provide a simple conceptual framework for the comparative analysis of quantitative data on the patterns of innovation and obsolescence related to the

TABLE I

THE GROWTH OF DAILY NEWSPAPERS
IN THE UNITED STATES, 1850–1957

Year	Total circulation of daily newspapers (excluding Sunday)	Total number of households	Circulation per household
1850	758,000	3,598,240	·21
1860	1,478,000	5,210,934	·28
1870	2,602,000	7,579,363	·34
1880	3,566,000	9,945,916	·36
1890	8,387,000	12,690,152	·66
1900	15,102,000	15,992,000	·94
1904	19,633,000	17,521,000	1·12
1909	24,212,000	19,734,000	1·23
1914	28,777,000	22,110,000	1·30
1919	33,029,000	23,873,000	1·38
1920	27,790,656	24,467,000	1·13
1925	33,739,369	27,540,000	1·22
1930	39,589,172	29,997,000	1·32
1935	38,155,540	31,892,000	1·20
1940	41,131,611	35,153,000	1·17
1945	48,384,188	37,503,000	1·29
1950	53,829,072	43,554,000	1·23
1955	56,147,359	47,788,000	1·17
1957	57,805,445	49,543,000	1·17

Sources:
US Bureau of Census, *Historical Statistics of the United States, Colonial Times to 1957*, Series R-176 (Washington, D.C.: US Government Printing Office, 1960), p. 500.

US Bureau of Census, *Historical Statistics of the United States, Colonial Times to 1957*, Series R-169 (Washington, D.C.: US Government Printing Office, 1960), p. 500.

US Bureau of Census, *Historical Statistics of the United States, Colonial Times to 1957*, Series 255 (Washington, D.C.: US Government Printing Office, 1960), p. 96.

media of mass communication as they have appeared in the American society.

In the sections which follow, the diffusion curves of each of the four major media (newspapers, movies, radio, and television) have been charted and these have been related to temporal patterns and to concomitant variations in social, economic or other cultural conditions in the society. The ways in which the suggested definitions given above can aid in understanding these quantitative patterns and can clarify patterns of development in one medium as related to another, are brought out.

Newspapers

Table I presents the basic data for newspapers in terms of circulation figures for daily papers over approximately a century. Data are also presented on the number of households in the United States during the same period. The household is used as a meaningful unit of adoption within the social system of the American society. The diffusion curve of daily newspapers *per household* is shown graphically in Figure I. Obviously, this curve can be only an approximation. Some newspapers are purchased by adoption units other than households. Nevertheless, the graph shows with some clarity the general pattern of the spread of the newspaper through the American population during more than a century. The most significant feature of this curve is that it resembles the classic S-shaped temporal diffusion pattern very well. (A smooth curve of logistic form has been drawn through the observed data.)

The history of journalism shows very clearly that the diffusion curve of the daily newspaper is closely related to the occurrence of such broad social and cultural changes as the spread of education, the development of press technology, the growth of cooperative newsgathering, news-distributing agencies, and the increasing urbanization of the American society. These significant concomitant trends have undoubtedly been of substantial importance as major influences on the shape of the diffusion curve for newspapers. The general curve in terms of its overall pattern seems to have been relatively unaffected by war, political change or even economic fluctuation (although these would undoubtedly be related to more minor variations in the actual circulation figures around the general pattern).

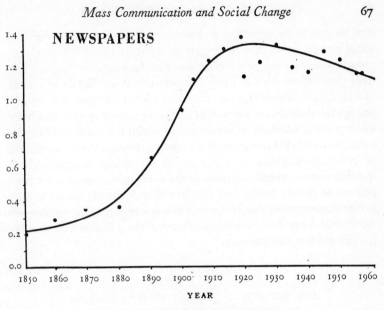

FIGURE I

The Diffusion Curve for Newspapers: Number of Subscriptions to Daily
Newspapers per Household

The period of most rapid growth was from about 1880 to about
1905. This corresponds very closely to the infamous episodes of
'yellow journalism', when the great metropolitan newspaper empires
of the late nineteenth century were locked in bitter competition for
increased circulation. The spur which this vigorous promotion gave to
circulation probably had a considerable influence on the adoption
curve (although such an ex post facto interpretation would be difficult
to demonstrate conclusively).

Interpersonal activities within the social system may have played
some part in generating this diffusion curve. A given person perhaps
influenced others to subscribe to a paper. But an explanatory theory
based solely upon such considerations would appear to have severe
limitations for this type of diffusion data. Furthermore, while the
diffusion curve shown in Figure I indicates that the daily newspaper
reached virtual saturation as a new item in the American society
shortly after the turn of the century, subscriptions per household have
declined somewhat since. It would be very difficult to account for this

turn of events by appealing to interactional mechanisms within the social system, other than to suggest the unlikely possibility that individuals were exerting personal influence on each other to stop reading daily newspapers. A more likely interpretation is that the development of additional media during the several decades of the twentieth century has provided *functional alternatives within the cultural system*, which are making modest inroads in the degree to which the society satisfies its collective needs for communication content through the consumption of newspapers. However, the complex of various institutionalized social processes related to the use of the newspaper in our society have become so deeply established that it will undoubtedly be some time before these modest trends towards obsolescence become accelerated. Additional research is needed to bring out the influences responsible for this modest obsolescence.

TABLE II

THE GROWTH OF WEEKLY MOTION PICTURE
ATTENDANCE IN THE UNITED STATES,
1922–1955

Year	Average weekly movie attendance	Total number of households	Weekly attendance per household
1922	40,000,000	25,687,000	1·56
1925	46,000,000	27,540,000	1·67
1930	90,000,000	29,997,000	3·00
1935	80,000,000	31,892,000	2·51
1940	80,000,000	35,153,000	2·28
1945	85,000,000	37,503,000	2·27
1950	60,000,000	43,554,000	1·38
1955	46,000,000	47,788,000	·96

Sources:
us Bureau of Census, *Historical Statistics of the United States, Colonial Times to 1957*, Series H. 522 (Washington, D.C.: us Government Printing Office, 1960), p. 225.
us Bureau of Census, *Historical Statistics of the United States, Colonial Times to 1957*, Series A. 242–244 (Washington, D.C.: us Government Printing Office, 1960, p. 15.

The diffusion curve for newspapers actually reveals very little of the behavioural alterations which took place in our society because of their introduction. Subscribing is obviously only one of many forms of action that can be related to this particular item. Newspaper readership has been studied in considerable depth, and it is known to vary markedly from one segment of the population to another. Thus, the diffusion curve provides only a very inadequate index to *innovation* (as defined earlier), revealing only the fact that newspapers were purchased. Whether they were skimmed, read with care, used as a basis for forming political opinion, or merely used to wrap garbage cannot be determined from the curve. The development of an adequate understanding of the actual innovations in conduct related to such an item requires increasing attention to empirical research on *every aspect of newspaper usage* and related forms of action among those who consume them.[16]

Motion pictures

The motion picture had an early development and subsequent growth, which, in terms of historical detail, showed little correspondence to that of the newspaper. However, Table II showing average weekly movie attendance *per household*, indicates that motion pictures followed a rough S-shaped curve of growth during much of their adoption period. Figure II presents the same data graphically.

The data show both considerable variability and what may appear as a substantial departure from the classical S-shaped curve. The latter is due primarily to the severe drop in weekly movie attendance per household which occurred in the postwar period. This drop had become so pronounced by 1955 that weekly attendance at motion picture theatres had been reduced to half of the peak which this medium had achieved before the second world war. It should be noted that 'weekly attendance' at a motion picture theatre is a form of social action. For this reason, this diffusion curve reveals actual innovation (as defined) more accurately than a curve based upon the possession or acquisition of the motion picture as a technical item – as might be the case for a curve based, say, upon the number of motion picture theatres per household over a given span of time.

Because of this closer correspondence between diffusion curve and innovation, the S-shaped diffusion curve can be seen in this case to have a reverse counterpart, namely a pattern of *obsolescence*, by which certain forms of social action associated with movies, once deeply institutionalized, now are fading out of the American society.[17] If this trend continues, then periodic attendance at a motion picture theatre may join the buffalo hunt, barn-raising, and the bare-knuckle boxing match as extinct forms of social activity. Such curves of obsolescence, and the factors associated with them have received far less research attention than adoption curves, although from a theoretical point of view they are equally important for the study of social change.

While it is true that attendance at public theatres is disappearing, the motion picture as a technical item is not. Probably more people actually *see* movies now than ever before, but *via* their TV set. Thus, while the film and associated technical items (projector, screen, etc.) have not changed very much, there has been a great modification in associated forms of action. This situation provides an excellent example of innovation and obsolescence with respect to an item already established in the technological culture, an item which in itself has changed but little, but with respect to which substantial alterations in social action have occurred. A diffusion curve based upon social action data more faithfully reveals actual patterns of innovation.

The major fluctuations around the general pattern of per household movie attendance have been closely related to economic, political, and other cultural events within the larger society. Such attendance plunged sharply downwards during the depression years (Figure II) but recovered as war approached. The second world war, which disrupted normal family activities in many ways, had a decidedly limiting effect on weekly movie attendance. The shape of this curve thus appears to be governed both by interactional events in the social systems and by trends in the cultural system.

The overall declining trend in motion picture attendance is obviously inversely correlated with the growth of the electronic media. Radio and television both appear to have made inroads on motion pictures. While it may be true that 'movies are better than ever', they appear to be losing ground sharply as their pattern of obsolescence has developed. This trend, of course, raises the issue as to why the forms of action surrounding one medium remain as established institutions and those of another are threatened by oblivion. The answer would appear to lie in the social and psychological needs (in the functional sense) to

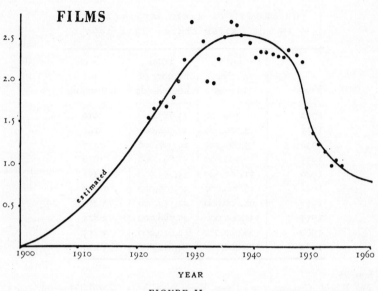

FIGURE II

The Diffusion Curve for Films: Weekly attendance at Motion Pictures
per Household

which the medium relates itself, and in the types of concomitant
cultural and technological changes which develop within the society.
The American society is apparently 'gratifying its needs' as a system in
ways other than by going to the movies, and the time formerly devoted
to this pastime is now being given over to other activities which serve
as functional alternatives.

Radio

Radio's history has been brief, but in terms of set ownership it has become the most massive of our mass media. Table III shows that there
are now more than three radio sets per household on the average in the
United States. This adds up to nearly *180 million* sets!

Figure III shows graphically that radio in its brief life span
achieved saturation adoption in a period of only about 40 years (1922-

TABLE III

THE GROWTH OF RADIO SET OWNERSHIP
IN THE UNITED STATES, 1922–1962

Year	Total number of sets	Total number of households	Sets per household
1922	400,000	25,687,000	·016
1925	4,000,000	27,540,000	·145
1930	13,000,000	29,997,000	·433
1935	30,500,000	31,892,000	·956
1940	51,000,000	35,153,000	1·451
1945	56,000,000	37,503,000	1·493
1950	98,000,000	43,554,000	2·250
1955	135,000,000	47,788,000	2·825
1960	166,000,000	52,610,000	3·155
1962	176,000,000	54,652,000	3·220

Sources:
The World Almanac, 1963 (New York: New York World-Telegram, 1963),
p. 761.

US Bureau of Census, *Historical Statistics of the United States, Colonial Times
to 1957*, Series A 242–244 (Washington, D.C.: US Government Printing Office,
1960), p. 15.

US Bureau of Census, *Current Population Reports: Population Characteristics*,
Series P–20, No. 106 (Washington, D.C.: US Government Printing Office, 1951),
p. 11.

US Bureau of Census, *Current Population Reports: Population Characteristics*,
Series P–20, No. 119 (Washington, D.C.: US Government Printing Office, 1962),
p. 4.

1962), as compared to about 75 years for newspapers. Movies also
required about four decades to reach their peak.

An interesting feature of the S-shaped diffusion curve for radio is the
plateau which occurred during the second world war period (see
Figure III). This, of course, was due to restrictions on the manufacture
of radio receivers for the consumer market during the national
emergency. However, the most striking feature of radio's adoption
curve is the 'recovery' that it made following the war years, even when
faced with competition from television. Thus, radio's curve of diffusion was little influenced by either the Depression, which occurred

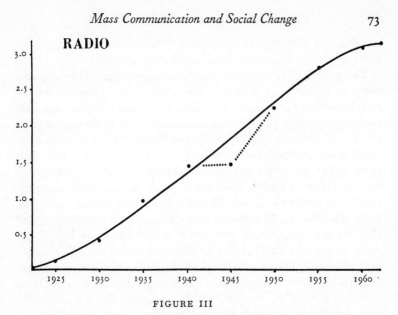

FIGURE III

The Diffusion Curve for Radio: Number of Sets per Household

shortly after it started to be adopted, or by the impact of wartime restrictions. But in spite of its spectacular numbers, radio in many ways has shown unmistakable patterns of obsolescence at least on the part of its mature adult audience. At one time, the behaviour patterns of the American family with respect to their livingroom radio were deeply institutionalized. Radio listening occupied the evening hours of millions of people. But with the arrival of television, radio was forced out of the livingroom and out of the attentions of most families during the important evening period. In the face of the functional alternative offered by TV, which took over the fulfilment of needs which radio formerly served, the latter resorted to *alternative audiences* and *alternative needs* which could be appealed to at the beach, in the kitchen, or in the automobile. The current affluence of the American society has placed millions of transistorized sets in the hands of children and teenagers. Radio's programming has increasingly been tailored to appeal to this immature audience. The diffusion curve of radio, developed from set ownership, may be an accurate record of the acquisition of sets. However, such a curve provides no hint of the actual patterns of innovation and obsolescence that have occurred as forms of social action with respect to this item (which itself has changed but little, other than to become smaller and more portable).

The growth of radio, then, must be understood not only against a series of political and economic conditions which characterized the cultural system but against competitive functional alternatives, a shift to new technology (transistors), a successful shift to alternative audiences with different needs to fulfil, and broad changes in patterns of social action associated with receiving sets. Unlike movies, with their cumbersome public theatres, radio emerged as a medium capable of making far more flexible adjustments in the face of these changing conditions in the social and cultural systems than was the case with films. Finally, the patterns of innovation, institutionalization and obsolescence as forms of observable action which lie behind the diffusion curve of radio cannot be fully understood through attempts to explain such curves with 'epidemiological' reasoning, or with the 'adoption process' conceptualized solely in psychological terms. More complex models are needed, which take into account important variables from the personality *and* social systems, as well as the impact of functional alternatives or other conditions of the *cultural* system.

Television

Television's introduction into the American society was beset with difficulties. First, the second world war stopped its technical development completely for several years. Then there was the postwar 'freeze' on new station licences imposed by the FCC for the purpose of achieving a workable frequency allotment plan. In spite of these setbacks, television's growth has been extremely rapid. It can be contrasted with that of newspapers, which required three-quarters of a century to become a common household item. Television required only a decade to reach virtual saturation. Table IV shows that there is now more than one TV set per household in the United States. The graph shown in Figure IV indicates that TV's growth followed a somewhat accelerated S-shaped diffusion curve of the general classical pattern. It is little wonder that social scientists have not as yet been able to make definitive statements concerning television's impact on modern society or upon human personality.

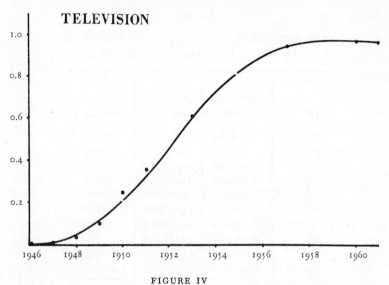

FIGURE IV

The Diffusion Curve for Television: Numbers of Sets owned per Household

The social and cultural conditions which facilitated the growth of television were several. The society had achieved a level of technology which permitted mass manufacture of receiving equipment at a price within the means of the ordinary citizen. Established cultural practices concerning broadcasting, including the role of the federal government and the relationship of news services to broadcasters, had already been institutionalized. A huge pool of entertainment talent was available from films, radio and the stage. The profit goal and its financial base (from advertising revenue) was copied from radio. Network programming had already been widely used and awaited only adequate electronic technology suitable for TV. The population had for more than two decades become accustomed to the moving picture image complete with sound. The set was also a natural baby sitter, aiding with a nagging problem in some families. Thus, television was a new item which 'fitted' remarkably well within the personality, social and cultural systems of the society to which it was presented. Finally, no political or economic upheaval prevented its rapid acquisition.

We need not assume that television is the final medium. It is still largely chained to the AC outlet by its power supply cord; it is chained

TABLE IV

THE GROWTH OF TELEVISION SET OWNERSHIP
IN THE UNITED STATES, 1946–1961

Year	Total sets in use	Total number of households	Sets per household
1946	8,000	38,370,000	·0002
1947	250,000	39,107,000	·0064
1948	1,000,000	40,523,000	·0247
1949	4,000,000	42,182,000	·0948
1950	10,500,000	43,554,000	·2411
1951	15,750,000	44,656,000	·3527
1953	28,000,000	46,334,000	·6043
1957	47,200,000	49,543,000	·9527
1960	54,000,000	52,610,000	1·0264
1961	56,900,000	53,291,000	1·0677

Sources:
US Bureau of Census, *Historical Statistics of the United States, Colonial Times to 1957*, Series 242–244 (Washington, D.C.: US Government Printing Office, 1960), p. 15.

US Bureau of Census, *Current Population Reports, Population Characteristics*, Series P–20, No. 106 (Washington, D.C.: US Government Printing Office, 1961), p. 11.

US Bureau of Census, *Current Population Reports, Population Characteristics*, Series P–20, No. 119 (Washingon, D.C.: US Government Printing Office, 1962), p. 4.

to the transmitting station by its frequency band; and it is in many ways chained to the cultural tastes of its mass audience who *still* prefer the 'horse opera' to the Metropolitan Opera.[18] A more sophisticated medium would be one which permitted an almost unlimited range in programme selection (in the form of tapes or records), an independent power supply, natural colour, complete portability and high quality reproduction. Thus a more sophisticated medium may combine the best qualities of stage, concert hall, movie theatre, stereo records, books, and newspapers in a completely portable device. Our present television sets will probably one day appear as obsolescent as the crystal set.

By plotting the curves for each of the present media on a single

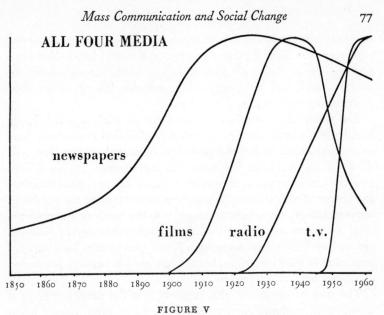

ALL FOUR MEDIA

newspapers

films / radio / t.v.

1850 1860 1870 1880 1890 1900 1910 1920 1930 1940 1950 1960

FIGURE V

The Diffusion Curves for all four Media with ordinate standardized

graph in Figure V (with the units of each 'standardized' so as to reach their peak at the same level on the ordinate axis), the general patterns of diffusion of each of these four cultural items can be compared. The long slow growth of newspapers stands out against the quick rise of television. In spite of these differences, each is a reasonable approximation of the classic S-shaped diffusion curve.

Conclusions

The study of the media within this broad perspective cannot reveal the nuances of interaction which occurred within individual households when decisions were made to adopt or not to adopt each medium as part of the family's routines. Such a perspective does show that the spread of the media occurred according to patterns followed by other invented items. The S-shaped curves for the radio receiving set, the daily newspaper, and household television appear to have followed the same general regularities in their spread through the population as such unrelated items as hybrid seed corn, instant coffee, hair spray, and oral contraceptives. Motion picture theatres, on the other hand, show signs that they are headed in the same directions as the kerosene lamp, the straight razor, and the buggy whip, and due largely to the same theoretical principles of social change.

The present discussion has suggested that the study of social change based upon examination of quantitative diffusion curves can have severe limitations. Such curves provide a beginning point for an analytic theory of social change. But when diffusion concepts are not defined in social action terms (as they need to be), it becomes clear that they can obscure drastic changes in behaviour, revealing only the number of some technical item which has passed into the hands of a population. This by no means implies that the quantitative study of diffusion curves based upon item acquisition is not worthwhile. Such data are important in their own right, but the relationship between possession and usage may remain unclear.

The present discussion also suggests that the development of a quantitative, analytical, and empirical theory of social change based upon diffusion data will require a great deal of prerequisite effort directed towards conceptual clarification. Such clarification will depend in large part upon the standardization of the meaning of terms through the use of behavioural or action referents. Only by this means can students of social change build the foundation for the theoretical structures which will eventually link their efforts at explanation with a more general theory of social action. The definitions of diffusion concepts presented earlier in this paper have indicated some of the points where such linkages are possible.

As for the mass media themselves, viewing them within the perspectives of the present paper has perhaps revealed few startling or new insights into the factors which 'caused' them to emerge and spread through society; nor does it permit new generalizations concerning their 'effect' on the population which has altered their daily lives around them. It does, however, place them within a context of more general processes of social change and social action. This should aid in the formulation of hypotheses concerning their growth, saturation or decline. While such theoretical explorations tell us little of the ways in which the mass media influence society, they do help reveal some of the complex ways in which society has influenced the mass media.

3. Britain's National Media Pattern*

Winston Fletcher

Great Britain is a comparatively small country. It has a high density of population and a fairly fast and cheap system of internal transportation. Express trains travel from South to North in a few hours. The great majority of Britons (and for the purposes of this article we shall exclude Northern Ireland) live within 100 miles of either London or Manchester.

As a direct result, regional media of communication are comparatively unimportant. The average Briton gets his news from a national newspaper, his entertainment from nationally networked television programmes; his wife listens to national radio while she's doing the washing and gets her recipes from nationally published women's magazines. When they both go out to the cinema – which they now do very rarely – they see a nationally distributed film.

Most countries have a national system of film distribution, many countries have national radio networks, most countries have at least a few national magazines. But in no other major western country are *all* main communications media so predominantly national, with local and regional media so relatively unimportant.

Newspapers

Table I gives a breakdown of the daily and Sunday newspapers in Britain.

It will be seen that, although there are a large number of local papers, their circulations total only just over half that of the nationals – even including with the provincials the two London evening newspapers and the major Scottish dailies (which often describe themselves as

* Not previously published.

79

TABLE I

NATIONAL AND NON-NATIONAL NEWSPAPER CIRCULATIONS

	No. of newspapers	Total circulation April 1969 (millions)
National dailies	9	14·9
Scottish editions of national dailies	2	1·1
Total national dailies	11	16·0
London evenings	2	1·7
Provincial dailies and evenings	71	6·4*
Welsh dailies and evenings	4	0·3
Scottish dailies and evenings	10	1·2
Total non-national dailies	87	9·6
Total national Sundays	7	23·8
Scottish Sundays	2	1·7
Provincial Sundays	3	0·5
Total non-national Sundays	5	2·2

* Four of the smallest provincial dailies do not publish circulation figures, but in total these would not exceed 150,000.

national since a proportion of their circulations are distributed nationally).

The situation on Sundays is even more extreme. National Sunday papers completely dominate the scene – the average British household buying approximately 1½ of them per week. The Glasgow *Sunday Post*, with a circulation of over 1 million, is the only major non-national Sunday paper published.

Moreover, the national newspapers are read fairly evenly throughout the country. The advertising industry as a whole sponsors a continuing readership survey, to discover how many people read – as against buy – all the major newspapers and magazines in Britain. The survey, known as the JICNARS National Readership Survey, contains data on the demographic and other characteristics of the readers of each of the media it covers: their age, class, sex, where they live, whether they own a car, whether they have a bank account, how much time they spend watching television, etc. 15,000 individuals are interviewed every six months, so that exceptionally accurate and up-to-date information is available to publishers and advertisers, showing exactly how many and what kind of people read each major magazine and newspaper. Probably, this kind of survey can only be carried out economically *because* most people in Britain read national rather than local papers.

TABLE II

PERCENTAGE OF ALL ADULTS (16+) IN EACH AREA
READING THE LISTED NEWSPAPERS
(FEBRUARY–JUNE 1968)

	UK	London & SE	Wales & SW	Midlands	N. West	North & NE	Scotland
Daily Mirror*	42	45	40	47	36	35	43
Daily Express	27	25	24	23	33	22	50
Daily Mail	14	15	13	16	20	13	7
Sun	9	9	9	10	13	11	1
Daily Sketch	9	13	9	14	5	5	0
Daily Telegraph	9	15	10	6	5	4	2
The Times	3	5	3	3	2	2	1
The Guardian	2	2	2	1	3	2	0
Financial Times	2	2	1	2	1	1	1
News of the World	41	42	43	44	45	42	20
People	40	36	41	43	51	47	20
Sunday Mirror	36	43	40	42	29	32	9
Sunday Express	27	29	29	23	31	21	28
Sunday Times	10	12	12	8	10	8	7
Observer	7	9	6	5	7	5	5
Sunday Telegraph	5	8	6	3	3	3	1
Glasgow Sunday Post	11	1	0	2	6	16	82

* Includes *Daily Record* in Scotland.

The JICNARS National Readership Survey reports the regional pattern of readership for the main national newspapers to be as in Table II.

There are of course some regional differences. Most of the national media are weak in Scotland, mainly because of the strength of the *Sunday Post* and the Scottish edition of the *Daily Express*. The *Daily* and *Sunday Telegraph* are strongest in London and the South East and they get progressively weaker the further away one gets from that area. But overall it is surprising how evenly the national newspapers cover the country.

Of course, this does not mean that the other characteristics of the people who read different newspapers are so similar. The class profiles of the various media are particularly different, as Table III shows.

TABLE III

PERCENTAGE OF ALL ADULTS (16+) IN EACH
SOCIAL GRADE* READING THE LISTED
NEWSPAPERS (JICNARS SURVEY,
FEBRUARY–JUNE, 1968)

	AB	C1	C2	DE
Daily Mirror	16	28	49	42
Sun	3	7	12	11
Daily Telegraph	29	15	4	3
Times	11	5	2	1
News of the World	15	28	50	49
People	18	33	47	44
Sunday Times	32	16	6	3
Observer	18	11	4	2

* Social grade is based on the occupation of the head of the household.

Age and sex are also important factors in readership habits – though less so than class. Other factors, such as car ownership or intensity of television viewing, which appear to correlate with readership habits probably do so only indirectly, i.e., wealthier people tend to read the *Daily Telegraph* and wealthier people tend to own more cars, therefore car owners tend to read the *Daily Telegraph*. (Though a chicken and egg relationship enters here: the *Daily Telegraph* knowing that most of its readers have cars, will aim to have particularly good car articles – thus appealing to more car owners, who tend to be wealthier, and so on.)

In addition to the national and local daily and Sunday papers there are several hundred small local weekly papers – which fall somewhere between newspapers and magazines, though their format, paper and printing are visually similar to newspapers. These weekly publications have very small circulations – very few of them exceed 50,000 per week – and almost nothing is known about their readership. However, even within their own areas their penetration must be rather low.

What is the explanation for the strength of the national newspapers? It is probably that London has always been both the centre of government *and* easily the largest centre of population and industry in the country – so that most news emanated from London. Whereas in many other countries the seat of government is *not* the largest industrial town. Additionally, the development of the railways made it possible to deliver newspapers quickly and cheaply, usually overnight, throughout the country. (Excluding Scotland, all the provincial newspapers which do have worthwhile circulations are *evening* newspapers.) London dailies dominate the North of England largely through editions printed in Manchester.

Magazines

Britain has no major general interest pictorial magazine. There is no *Life*, no *Paris Match* – nor even a *Time* or *Der Spiegel*. Attempts have been made to launch a general interest magazine – the last major try was Hulton's *Picture Post* – but they have always failed. There are probably two reasons for this. The first is the strength of the national papers: the British read more newspapers every day than are read in other countries, and many of these newspapers – in at least features and photographic coverage – are arguably better than most foreign papers. There may thus be no underlying demand or need for an additional general interest magazine.

The second reason probably lies in the importance of the British women's weekly magazines. There are four massive circulation national weekly magazines in Britain, as Table IV shows.

These magazines are extremely cheap, because they carry a very great deal of advertising. And they carry a great deal of advertising because they are read by so many women; most display advertising is, of course, primarily directed towards women.

A general interest magazine must, therefore, compete with a highly

TABLE IV

BRITISH WEEKLY WOMEN'S MAGAZINES

	Circulation (April 1969)	No. of readers (JICNARS Feb.–June 1968)
	('000)	('000)
Woman	2,526	7,763 (37% of all women)
Woman's Own	1,978	6,965 (33%)
Woman's Realm	1,174	4,641 (22%)
Woman's Weekly	1,676	3,592 (17%)

effective national press editorially, and with mass circulation womens' magazines for advertising revenue. It seems hardly surprising that no general interest magazine has survived in Britain for long.

Table V shows that the women's weekly magazines cover the country as evenly and thoroughly as the national newspapers. Not even the nationalistic Scottish ladies veer to any great extent from the national pattern, though in fact 31% of them also read a 5d. weekly called *People's Friend*, which is virtually unknown in the south.

TABLE V

PERCENTAGE OF ALL WOMEN (16+) IN EACH AREA READING THE WOMEN'S MAGAZINES (JICNARS FEB–JUNE 1968)

	UK	London & SE	Wales & SW	Midlands	N. West	North & NE	Scotland
Woman	37	39	34	36	37	37	32
Woman's Own	33	34	31	33	33	34	31
Woman's Realm	22	27	20	22	19	21	13
Woman's Weekly	17	18	18	18	14	16	18

Unlike those for the national newspapers, the readership profiles of the woman's weeklies do not vary much by social grade or age either, except that *Woman's Weekly* has a slightly older readership than the other three. Indeed it is often extremely difficult to see in exactly which ways the women's weekly magazines do differ from each other, and to understand by which criteria women choose to buy one rather than another.

Apart from the women's weekly magazines the only really mass circulation magazines in Britain are the radio and television programme publications: the *Radio Times* (BBC) and the *TV Times* (Independent Television), which are each read by approximately 28% of the population each week. These publications have aimed to broaden their appeal from that of simple programme timetables (the ubiquitous national press publishes all radio and television programmes daily). They include articles of general interest related, even if tenuously, to the week's programmes and to show business. However, it is doubtful whether many of their readers view them as real magazines. And, of course, they too are as national as radio and television.

There are four other groups of publication worth noting: the weekend 'leisure' magazines, the women's monthly magazines, the special interest magazines and the newspaper colour magazines. The weekend leisure magazines *(Reveille, Weekend, Tit Bits)* are printed on poor quality newsprint and have a primarily down-the-market readership; the women's monthly magazines are mostly printed on high quality art paper and have a primarily up-the-market readership. The special interest magazines, of which the most important are the motoring magazines, vary widely, of course, depending upon their form and readership, and upon the interest for which they are catering; and the newspaper colour magazines, which are given away free with their respective newspapers, necessarily have (almost) the same readership patterns as their newspapers. The perhaps amazing thing about these four disparate groups of publication is, once again, their even coverage of the country shown in Table VI.

There are, of course, a few regional variations. In addition to *People's Friend*, a magazine called *Weekly News* is read by 34% of the Scots but by almost no one anywhere else. There are just over 30 local magazines from the *Basildon Journal* to the *Tunbridge Wells Focus* – but these, like the local weekly newspapers have tiny circulations and low coverage even within their own areas. Overall the situation for the magazines is the same as for the newspapers: it doesn't matter where you live, you read the same old stuff.

TABLE VI

PERCENTAGE OF ALL ADULTS (16+) IN EACH AREA
READING THE LISTED MAGAZINES
(JICNARS FEB–JUNE 1968)

	UK	London & SE	Wales & SW	Midlands	N. West	North & NE	Scotland
Reveille	15	14	12	17	16	15	11
Weekend	14	14	11	15	13	16	12
Motor	4	5	4	4	4	3	3
Practical Motorist	8	8	8	8	9	6	6
Vogue	8	10	10	7	8	6	5
Good Housekeeping	8	9	9	7	6	6	5
Sunday Times Magazine	11	13	14	9	11	9	8
Daily Telegraph Magazine	10	16	12	6	7	5	2

Television

There are three television broadcasting channels in Britain: BBC1, BBC2, and ITV. The two BBC channels have been and are intended to be national networks. With the exception of a small number of local news programmes, transmitted regionally at off-peak times, almost all BBC television programmes are transmitted nationally.

Independent commercial television was set up by the 1954 Television Act. This Act was not only the basis of commercial television's existence, but it also set out in considerable detail the kind of system that was to be operated. The Act specifically stated that independent television should be developed regionally, and that, therefore, regional contractors should be appointed to produce and transmit programmes of particular relevance to their own areas.

As a result of this policy there are now 13 television programme companies covering the British mainland:

Anglia Television
ATV Network (Midlands)
Border Television (Southern Scotland and the Border counties)
Grampian Television (Northern Scotland)
Granada Television (Lancashire)
Harlech Television (Wales & West/Central England)
London Weekend Television
Scottish Television (Central Scotland)
Southern Independent Television
Thames Television (London mid-week)
Tyne-Tees Television (North-East)
Westward Television (South-West)
Yorkshire Television

The areas covered by these companies vary considerably in size, but the percentage of homes in each area which see independent television is fairly level throughout the country (Table VII). The total of the percentages of all UK homes in each area comes to more than 100% – it comes to 115·7% – because of overlap, 31·4% of homes being in areas served by more than one transmitter.

TABLE VII

ITV HOUSEHOLDS BY REGIONS

Station/area	% of all UK homes in each area	ITV houses as a % of all homes in the area
Anglia	7·7	70
ATV (Midlands)*	16·5	83
Border	1·0	84
Grampian	2·2	74
Granada (Lancashire)*	14·7	84
Harlech (Wales & West)	8·3	78
London*	27·2	82
Scottish	7·5	81
Southern	8·9	71
Tyne-Tees	5·1	87
Westward	3·0	74
Yorkshire*	13·6	71

* Networking centre.

M.S.—D

The fact that the five companies based in the four main centres – London, Midlands, Lancashire, Yorkshire – broadcast to more people than the others has meant that these companies can and do charge higher advertising rates than the others. With their greater income they can afford to produce more and better programmes for their own audiences, and to sell these programmes to the smaller companies who have neither the funds nor resources to produce many expensive programmes themselves. The small regional companies do produce programmes of local interest, but these are once again almost always transmitted at off-peak viewing hours and therefore achieve low viewing figures. Presumably, however, the small stations have in the past attempted to transmit local interest programmes at peak viewing hours, with unsatisfactory results.

A good deal is known about how many people watch each programme transmitted in every area. JICTAR, a sister body to JICNARS, runs through a research company called AGB a panel of 2,650 homes. In each of these homes a monitor is fixed to the television set, which records exactly when the set is switched on and off, and the station to which it is tuned.

Further market research is carried out continuously to discover how many people watch the set when it is on, who they are, how they vary from programme to programme and so on. In Britain, therefore, the audience for television is as thoroughly researched and documented as are the readers of the press.

The great uniformity of taste for TV programmes can be illustrated from Christmas week 1968. The three most popular TV programmes that week were: 1. *Till Death Us Do Part* (a comedy serial about a Cockney family); 2. *The Val Doonican Show*; 3. *Apollo 8*, a BBC programme on Friday 27th December about the first flight round the moon. Table VIII shows the proportion of sets switched to these programmes in the various regions.

In the same week an episode of *The Forsyte Saga* had the fifth biggest national audience in Britain. Moreover this episode – of a drama serial with some artistic pretensions – came in the top ten programmes of the week in regions where eight-tenths of the British population live. What figures such as those in Table VIII do show is the extraordinarily even national spread of popularity for TV programmes.

TABLE VIII

THE REGIONAL AUDIENCE FOR 3 TV PROGRAMMES,
WEEK ENDING 29TH DECEMBER, 1968

| | % of houses in area with TV sets switched to: | | |
Station/area	Till Death Us Do Part	The Val Doonican Show	Apollo 8
Anglia/East	44	47	43
Midlands	46	46	43
Border	—	50	48
Grampian/N.E. Scotland	48	45	55
Lancashire	45	44	38
Wales & West	50	42	43
London	49	46	41
Scotland, Central	47	49	48
Southern	49	46	45
North-East, Tyne-Tees	49	48	48
South-West, Westward	42	43	49
Yorkshire	41	40	43

Radio

The British Broadcasting Corporation was set up as a state-owned national broadcasting service. Largely for engineering and administrative reasons the country was divided up into six regions: North, Midlands, South and West, Scotland, Wales, and Northern Ireland.

These regional administrations have sponsored certain forms of cultural activities within their areas, e.g., the Northern and Scottish Symphony orchestras and the Northern Dance orchestra. They also broadcast regional news in addition to the national news broadcast from London. The great majority of all programmes, however, excluding the local news, are national. Even the local orchestras normally broadcast nationally, and were always intended to do so. When a new BBC regional structure was outlined in 1969, critics said that it would still further increase London domination.

Cinema

Since the advent of television, cinema audiences in Britain, as elsewhere in the world, have dwindled. In 1968, 46% of the population claimed to 'never go' to the cinema, and a further 36% go only 'infrequently'. Young people, however, as Table IX shows, go to the cinema far more than their elders.

TABLE IX

FREQUENCY OF CINEMA-GOING
(JICNARS SURVEY, FEBRUARY-JUNE, 1968)

Cinema going	All	16–24	25–34	35–44	45–54	55–64	65+
	%	%	%	%	%	%	%
Regularly	5	19	5	2	2	1	2
Occasionally	13	37	17	9	5	3	2
Infrequently	36	33	50	48	40	28	17
Never go	46	10	27	41	54	70	79

Compared with other communications media, the cinema is now comparatively unimportant. Whilst most Britons read a daily paper and watch television every night, very few go to the cinema even weekly. Cinema admission figures show that probably fewer than 5% of the population – i.e., those who claim to go 'regularly' – can be going to the cinema every week. Table X shows that people's lack of desire to go to the cinema is fairly uniform throughout the country.

No information is available on whether the same films are equally popular – or unpopular – throughout the country. (Obviously certain minority-interest foreign or art films are likely only to be popular in London and major city centres.) But approximately 700 of the 1,700 cinemas in the country are owned and run by the four major national circuits: Associated British Cinemas, Classic Cinemas, Essoldo Group, Rank Theatres.

TABLE X

CINEMA GOING (JICNARS SURVEY, FEBRUARY–JUNE, 1968)

	All	London	Midlands	North	Southern	Anglia	Wales & West	North East	Scotland
	%	%	%	%	%	%	%	%	%
Regularly	5	6	5	5	4	4	6	5	8
Occasionally	13	15	11	10	11	11	12	11	14
Infrequently	36	38	34	35	45	38	36	33	30
Never go	46	40	50	50	40	40	46	50	49

The national media pattern

The five major communications media, it would seem, cover the country fairly uniformly. The same media, and largely the same programmes and articles within media, appear to be more or less equally liked, or disliked from Land's End to John O'Groats. Perhaps this is not entirely surprising. Nobody expects Londoners to want different corn flakes from Lancastrians, nobody expects a Manchester housewife to want a different shampoo from her Bristol counterpart. There are *some* differences in regional tastes for media – and there are some for corn flakes and shampoo too. But the differences in tastes and habits that vary with age, sex, and socio-economic class are far more important. Britain has a *national* media pattern.

4. Film, Communication and Content*

Andrew Tudor

Film is one among many communications media prominent in contemporary society. This is a rather stronger statement than it might at first seem because it reflects one of the major assumptions underlying much media research. An implication of giving pride of place to the term *communication* in that it is the key common process of the phenomena under study. *Mass, primary, secondary,* are all familiar prefixes to the ubiquitous concept. But in both research and commentary we are time and again required to identify the basic characteristics of *communication*: what, how, and why?

Thus, although this paper is centrally concerned with film, much of the discussion relates to media studies in general. I have not chosen to give a lengthy survey of the sociological literature on the cinema partly because I do not find it especially impressive, but particularly because such analysis largely stands or falls in relation to the available work on more extensively researched media. In a general discussion such as this it is the common theoretical assumptions of media sociology which provide a point of departure.

Perspectives

Media studies exemplify the classic division into macro- and micro-analysis. As with any other complex social phenomena we can focus our attention on both macroscopic and microscopic aspects of their operation. The distinction is a conceptual one, and the two levels of analysis complement one another. But in much media research this conceptual distinction has been elevated almost to a defining factor; media studies are predominantly microscopic. Indeed, what we speak

* Not previously published.

of as the *sociology* of mass media is very often *social psychology* or *psychology*. The focus is on the individual or small group level of analysis even where terms like 'national character' are employed. Nor does this seem to be based on any general reductionist position of the form associated with the work of, for example, George Homans[1] the research seems simply to have gravitated in this direction. It may be that a pressure towards 'scientism' has assisted this process, but whatever the reasons the net result is a *relative* neglect of truly macroscopic phenomena. The concept of *mass society*, once intimately related to the field, was one attempt to introduce more strictly sociological concerns. The somewhat empty formulations of McLuhanism, are conceivably responses to this lack of macroscopic understanding, although in a rather extreme and polarised form. But there does not seem to be any fundamental necessity for this divorce of interests. Rather the opposite. The media are so much located in contemporary *society* that they are an ideal field for the crossing of disciplinary boundaries. Communication is a vital process at almost all levels of analysis, from the two person face-to-face situation up to the largest societal scale. And the basic perspectives applied in these analyses are not necessarily tied to the specific level in question. Indeed the logic of many approaches seems to be very much the same. Let me briefly illustrate.

The simplest perspective in communications research, one might almost say the theoretical lowest common denominator, is that incarnated in Lasswell's five question series: 'Who, Says What, In Which Channel, To Whom, With What Effect?'[2] This is an input-output chain running from communicator through medium to audience from whence emerges the output commonly termed *effects*. The model, if such it can be called, is one of uni-directional flow. The questions we are invited to ask of the process are basically descriptive in their import. Who are the communicators? What are the effects of the media? The answers are often rather *ad hoc*. Dependent on the specific disciplinary interests of the researcher the answer to 'Who?', for example, might be expressed in terms of personality characteristics, social background variables, or perhaps political preferences. Although this is not in itself necessarily bad, there is clearly a limited range of usefulness to such *ad hoc* description. Thus there is an understandable tendency for researchers to go beyond this and attempt to relate the various characteristics of the communication process one to the other.

Instead of simple description we find studies relating the *who* to the *says what*, or the *to whom* to the *with what effect*. The simple flow-model becomes more complex in the attempt to organize the discovered empirical relations between the different components. Thus:

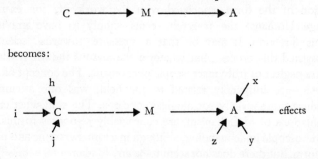

becomes:

where h, i, j . . . are the variables acting on the communicator(s) – motivation, organizational exigencies, economic factors, moral orientations, and so on. The second set, x, y, z . . ., refer to the variables affecting audience perception of and response to the communication message. Situation of consumption, personality characteristics, and cultural expectations would be some examples.

Various approaches can be based on such a model. It might be possible, for example, to relate h, i, j . . . to the ultimate category of *effects*, employing communicator, medium, and audience as intervening variables with x, y, z . . . as conditioning variables. This would be to treat the whole system from initial input to final output. But more frequently the explanatory chain is broken down in some way, most simply through separate consideration of two clusters: communicator-medium, and medium-audience-effects. Huaco, for example, finds it necessary to look at the social characteristics of the groups of film directors with whom he is concerned, and then relate this information – in a rather superficial way – to the ideology expressed in the films they make.[3] As he is fully aware these are not the only relevant variables. Organizational structure, distribution structure (as in the British duopoly of Rank and ABC), the roles of producer, production company, cast, writers, etc., will all impinge to various degrees on the finished product. The specification of these factors is a task for research but, most important from the present point of view, the *formal* intent is to establish the relation between communicator variables and medium content.

The other cluster is that involved in the study of effects and their relation to audience characteristics. Once given the film content, how does it relate to subsequent audience responses? A classic case is the Kendall-Wolfe study of selective perception. In a group of men shown a series of satirical anti-prejudice cartoons they found that those who were already prejudiced tended to interpret the films as supporting their position.[4] Predispositions are clearly of some importance in determining interpretation and effects of a medium. There is also evidence to suggest that certain situational variables such as darkness, restricted information sources, and other physical and psychological conditions act in a similar way.[5] Other researches indicate more general cultural factors. Hulett, for example, found that audience conceptions of the cinema did not attribute 'accuracy and seriousness of purpose' to commercial films with the result that the film under study – *Sister Kenny* – was an ineffectual propaganda instrument.[6] These examples are only meant to be indicative of the wide range of factors involved; there is an immense literature on media effects. But once more the formal intent seems to be relatively simple. To relate, on the one hand, media content and the many variables determinate upon the audience to, on the other hand, the blanket notion of effects.

A simple model of this type has its fair share of problems, not the least of which are methodological. How do we analyse content? On what basis can we construct suitable indicators of effects? How do we assess the causal 'weight' of the many factors impinging on the communication process?[7] These, and other such questions, have exercised the talents of media researchers for several decades. But there are also substantive problems in relation to the model itself. First, although this is not inherent, the model is often employed in a fundamentally microscopic way. The focus, as in much survey research, is on the individual. Where social background variables are used they are summarized in terms of statistical parameters based on aggregating individual characteristics. Of course there are partial exceptions. Analysis of the way in which the organizational structure of the medium influences film production would, of necessity, have to treat macroscopic organizational characteristics, while the extensions implied by the two-step flow hypothesis fill in some of the undefined edges.[8] Nevertheless, the communication model often exists in a sociological vacuum, the empty space of which is only filled by *ad hoc* description. The result is a proliferation of data, expressed in a wide range of terminology, and not especially amenable to comparative analysis or generalization.

A further problem of the model is its unidirectionality. This often invoked issue,[9] taken to its limits, would lead to an absurd picture of the world wherein media communicators held positions of virtually absolute control. There are undoubtedly many feedback processes operative in the communication situation. The crudest, and clearest, is the simple case of the decision to attend. The manifold economic importance of this 'box-office' issue makes it a powerful feedback source. But there are also rather more complex factors involved. The way in which the 'common culture' defines the reciprocal role-obligations of communicator and audience would be a case in point. Both groups will have their own expectations of what is an acceptable film, and the combinations and permutations of such patterns could be crucial in relation to the whole character and content of the medium. Again there seems to be a need to provide a more comprehensive social and cultural 'environment' for the communication model.

Finally, the model makes relatively little attempt to specify the nature and influence of the medium itself. Rectifying this does not necessarily mean, however, that we must go to the other extreme of 'media determinism'.[10] The problem is to find in what way a medium can 'alter' communicator input, rather than assuming some direct equation between medium and message. It may be that there are characteristics of specific media which are conducive to different degrees of distortion. Fully to approach this we need a much more advanced understanding of the different 'languages' of the media, and the various 'levels of meaning' involved in the process of communication.[11] Here again we are returned to the way in which the larger cultural environment impinges on particular communication processes. It is fundamental to the concept of 'language' in this context that there is a shared social and cultural conception of it external to specific acts of communication. These are the kinds of emergent macro-characteristics which the sociology of the media must find ways of elaborating.

Much of the impetus for media research has come from psychology, social psychology, and the relatively small scale empirical researches common in the USA during the 'thirties and 'forties. Macroscopic analysis has remained perhaps the least developed aspect of the field. The principal theme of what major studies there are has been that of 'mass society' in one or another form.[12] Regardless of some excellent work which has been carried out under this rubric, the mass society tradition has served to direct our attention away from certain important factors. The principal questions, although not the only ones, to be put by a macro-sociology of communications are those relating large scale social pressures to the nature and content of the media. The mass society approach tends to answer such questions in a monistic way. Drastically simplified, the argument is based on isolating the anonymous mass characteristics of contemporary media and relating them to similar characteristics in society at large. The implicit point of reference seems to be some pre-modern world of face-to-face communication. It is true that contemporary means of communication have played a vital part in the large-scale changes of the twentieth century, as we are frequently reminded by studies relating mass communication to modernization.[13] All this is involved if we take mass society as our point of reference. But if we lean too hard on such a concept we are unable to explore the manifold differences between and within societies and media. The 'mass' question is only one aspect of our phenomena.

Outside of the mass society studies the major impetus to macroscopic analysis has stemmed from the European sociological tradition. The sociology of knowledge as developed from Marx, Durkheim, and Mannheim; the relation between cultural and social factors classically analysed by Weber; and a sociological interest in art, are the seed-beds of this development. Given their different sources it is not entirely surprising that there is a cleavage between micro- and macro-media studies. The one has concentrated on 'sophisticated' methodologies and small-scale researches; the other on trying to show in what way given cultural configurations (in this case the style and content of the media) relate to certain characteristics of the societies in which they occur. Thus Wolfenstein and Leites explore the way in which the cinema reflects the psychological preoccupations of members of particular cultures; the cinema is a public world for acting out psychological fantasies. Huaco, employing a crude Marxist base/superstructure conception, tries to show how German expressionism, Soviet expressive realism, and Italian neo-realism relate to their various societies and eras. Siegfried Kracauer writes a 'psychological history of the German film' in terms of the social and psychological characteristics of German society between the wars. Herbert Gans argues for differential relations between class and culture in Britain and America.[14]

What these studies have in common, apart from any question of their virtues and faults, is an attempt to relate the content and style of the films to particular aspects of the societies in question. The films are seen as *reflecting* or, rather less often, *influencing* the societies in which they appear, but whichever is the case there is some form of one-to-one relation between society and medium. Expressed in more general theoretical terms, it assumes some form of one-to-one relation between social structure and culture.

This approach is far too simple. It directs our attention towards establishing correlations (not necessarily statistical) between cultural and social configurations, but since the specific components of each side of the equation are not clearly stipulated the case for particular relations has to be continually established in an *ad hoc* way. Clear theoretical statement of the components of both social and cultural systems is a prerequisite to rigorous analysis at this level. In addition, the straightforward assumption of reflection or influence is hardly sufficient. The relation between social and cultural systems is highly complex, as the work of Weber and Sorokin, to name but two, should remind us. In some branches of contemporary sociology the structure culture question has become increasingly important. Writers as diverse as Peter Berger and Talcott Parsons have devoted considerable energies to its exploration, but applications to particular cultural products are, as yet, relatively rare.[15]

Many of the issues raised in the past few pages can be summarized in terms of an amended communication model:

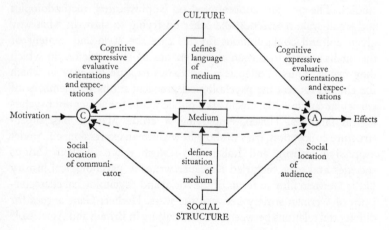

This diagram is mostly self-explanatory. Orientations and expectations are internalized from the culture by communicators and audiences, although the extent of such internalization and hence the extent of 'shared culture' is itself variable. They are broken down into three analytic categories partly because it has seemed useful to do so in other fields of sociology, and partly because similar breakdowns can be made into different 'levels of meaning' of communicated items.[16] If the theoretical language applied to a phenomenon is not uniform there is not much hope of piecing together any consistent picture. The distinction between culture and social culture is also analytically conceived, and their particular functions in defining 'language' and 'social location' of the medium separated out. Extensive microscopic knowledge of the way in which the communication process acts as a point of interpenetration between structure and culture would lead to a solution of some of the problems of macro-analysis. However, the culture/social structure relation may also be justifiably considered at the level of emergent properties. By this I mean that we can establish macroscopic relations between the two *without* necessarily knowing the microscopic detail of *how* they do in fact relate. In the long run we would ideally wish to know both since they are complementary elements in our understanding of social communication. It is my most general contention that media studies have now reached the point where they need to move in both directions if they are to move at all.

This formulation is not presented as a solution to the problems I have discussed; indeed the model raises still more. But it can be seen as a schematic outline of the type of conceptions and relationships which might bear further thought. There are a number of problem areas which emerge out of this formulation but, for the present, I would like to limit my attention to certain aspects of the medium itself. In particular, to discuss the 'language' of the medium and the related question of content.

Problems

The problem of the 'language' of a medium is important in two general respects. The degree to which communicator and audience share the same conception of 'meaning' is clearly an important determinant in the communication process. If there is full agreement on the 'language' then 'noise' will be minimized within the limits of the 'language' capacity; any lesser level of institutionalization will allow ambiguity and distortion. More generally, different media languages may be variously fitted to a range of tasks. It seems likely, for instance, that music is a much less effective conveyor of straightforward information than is the printed word. Such issues are of some importance if we are fully to analyse specific media, or compare one medium to another. The second respect in which the concept of 'language' is important is in relation to more macroscopic concerns. At this level the fundamental rules and practices of operation of a 'language' can provide us with a basis for characterizing given media. Socio-linguistics could be seen as a paradigm case of such a task. This information can then be employed as more a specific element in the structure/culture equation.

It can, of course, be argued that these questions, although interesting, are not really the meat of which media research is made. *De facto* this is true, but that does not make it any the more desirable. As I see it, the problem is broadly as follows. Most researchers – however rabidly empiricist – make use of some variation of the communicator-medium-audience model. And the central focus of this model is the medium itself. Yet our conceptions of such characteristics as medium language remain painfully undeveloped, particularly in media other than the written word. Is the cinema *inherently* a medium which leans heavily on an emotional-expressive form of communication? It is my *impression* that it is, cognitive and evaluative levels of communication playing a less direct part in the cinema than in certain other media. Is film language less open to communicating messages of an abstract nature because of the particular quality of the film image?[17] Does the admixture of visual images, narrative, and sound, structure audience response in radically different ways from that achieved by black print on white paper? Do technological factors, such as the Cinerama screen, lead to more or less, the same or different, forms of involvement than, say, the classical nineteenth-century novel? All such questions are intimately related to the study of the medium language and, perhaps unfortunately, may well be crucial for other aspects of media research. This arises from the peculiarly important position of content in understanding the communication process.

Whatever the initial area of interest in a medium, sooner or later we come up against the question of the 'message'. It is simply not possible to talk about the *effects* of a medium unless we can isolate input-from-medium from all the other inputs acting on an audience. By the same count we cannot talk about the way in which different factors influence communicators unless we are also able fully to comprehend the products of their principal goal – communication. Thus, *content analysis* figures prominently in the literature. At its most simple this methodology applies primarily to the written word, and operates on the basis of counting key words or measuring the number of column inches devoted to particular topics. Such methods as the Cloze procedure, contingency analysis, and the semantic differential are rather more developed versions, but still primarily applicable to the written word.[18] The spoken word adds an element of tone and expression thus requiring some form of judgmental technique. The combination of visual imagery (at more than one level), spoken word, written word, music and narrative structure, found in the cinema complicates the issue considerably. To say the least!

To take *only* the visual element. One of the first films ever made – perhaps *the* first – was the Lumière brothers' *A Train Coming into a Station*. Described in words it is exactly that: a train coming into a station. But the train is shot coming towards the camera making the film something more than that simple verbal statement; the illusion is created of a train coming out of the screen producing, at least in the unsophisticated audiences of the period, a sensation of fear. Slightly more complex is the question of camera angle and lighting. Figures shot and/or lit from above or below are made to seem weak or strong, powerful or powerless, sinister or honest. Welles' *Citizen Kane* is a classic, stylized, example. Film editing is another area where characteristics of content are lost in verbal description and yet extremely difficult to codify in the manner required for content analysis. Eisenstein's theory of 'emotional dynamization' and montage relies on the collision of different images and actions in a dialectical manner.[19] His justly famous Odessa Steps sequence in *Battleship Potemkin* could be simply described as 'the clearing of the Steps by the White Guard'. But the impact on the spectator and the strong identification with the people against the soldiers is a result of the choice, ordering, and timing of the images. And all these are the least complex of examples. Indeed Eisenstein may well be more open to formal analysis precisely because he operates with a very clearly structured editing style. But what also must be dealt with is the way in which style and treatment can alter the basic elements of a narrative, imbue it with different and sometimes contradictory meanings through extremely subtle techniques of lighting, composition, and the rest. The addition of sound and music simply adds layer upon layer to an already rich cake.

All these familiar cases, and the many more unmentioned, are part of what must be understood by the *language* of the cinema. Now content analysis developed particularly in relation to linguistic forms where there was already a considerable corpus of knowledge about the language in question. On the basis of this knowledge, categories could be set up and methodically applied. The procedure makes some sense because we are already aware, to some extent at least, of the units' structured relations, and techniques involved in the written word. We are far short of this mark in relation to media like film, TV and drama. Although at the purely technical level problems of sampling and sheer quantity may be rather less than in, say, newspapers, at the conceptual level we have no clear idea of the languages involved. Thus we are unable to do a competent job of 'objective' content analysis in the orthodox sense of the term. It comes, then, as something of a shock to find that Huaco relies on bald summaries of plots which he analyzes on the basis of 'objective' content analysis techniques.[20]

Part of the problem results from the remarkable empiricism which has historically characterized much of the media literature. We must use 'objective' techniques, even when inappropriate, because it is scientific to do so! There is evidently a time and place where highly developed methodologies should be employed; but to be obliged to apply them across the board is the sort of *scientism* which persistently sets us back. Before we can apply such methods, if we are able to at all, we need an understanding of the different languages of these complex media, and hence an ordered picture of them on which we can base our analyses. Semiology, touched on above, may provide one entry into the field. In trying to delineate the units of communication, the structured relations between them, and the nature of meaning, it could suggest the beginnings of a cinematic 'linguistics'. But it would be easy to fall into the trap of becoming *too* formal *too* soon. The application of the psychology of perception to art suggests an accumulating knowledge of various aspects of media languages.[21] And the contemporary sociological concern with the nature of culture and the sociology of knowledge could contribute to a macro-sociology through clarifying the general relationship between social structure and culture. But scientific pressure for the premature application of 'scientific' modes of analysis leads to a concentration on the areas most amenable to the prescribed methodological forms. Instead of opening up new frontiers such approaches tragically emasculate our subject matter.

Understanding the language of films seems, then, to be a vital long-term investment. But in the short term it is still important to study the cinema even with less than adequate tools. Given the centrality of the content problem, what can we do? Historically there have been various answers. Plot summaries are one possibility, but these will clearly have to be something more than simple narrative description. Another strategy involves adopting the methods of the critic as a mode of analysis, thus openly introducing an element of subjectivity. This is probably more applicable to macro-analysis if only because the requirements at such a level are more often summaries of thematic and moral clusters than close analysis of specific films. Yet another method is the use of judgment techniques on the assumption that *n* heads are better than one. This may well be debatable but it is rather beyond the scope of this paper to enter that particular arena. But whichever we choose it is clear that we cannot expect to occupy the same level of scientific 'respectability' as other more developed fields of media research. Complex problems are not amenable to automatic methodological solution.

I have deliberately tended to be rather strongly critical and paint a somewhat gloomy picture of this field of study. Those familiar with the work will know to what extent I may have exaggerated. To those who are not, I can only say that there *are* problems of the complexity suggested here, they should not be underestimated, but not all work has retreated before them. In the final analysis the problem, I think, is two fold. First, mass media studies have for many years engaged in haphazard 'fact capturing'. That they are not alone in this is hardly the point. This has served to direct attention away from certain of the important, and admittedly complex, issues. Secondly, the methodological process has become almost an end in itself. It is not just a turn of phrase to suggest that the history of mass media studies is also the history of sociological methodology. There is a considerable pressure on researchers, whatever the demands of the particular topic, to pay lip service to the gods of positivistic science. Scientific we must be but not, I think, necessarily in this monistic way. There are other perspectives in circulation and no reason at all blindly to accept the received word from the past.

5. The Impact of Television on the Audience for National Newspapers, 1945–68*

James Curran

Reading through the forty-odd studies on the effect of television viewing on the press is enough to cause the student of the media to lose faith in social research techniques, not to mention faith in his own intellectual ability to draw together what would appear to be bewilderingly contradictory evidence. The findings of these studies are so totally inconsistent that it would seem to be impossible to generalize about the variables influencing TV audience reaction to the press, let alone arrive at a firm conclusion about the overall effect of television on newspaper use.

Some studies suggest that television viewing has displaced the more traditional medium of the newspaper, causing a drop-out among newspaper readers, depressing newspaper sales, reducing the time spent reading newspapers and running down still further the already tarnished image of the press.

Other studies suggest that television viewing has had precisely the opposite effects on newspaper readership: it would seem that television has recruited new readers, inflated newspaper sales, increased the time spent reading newspapers, expanded reader interest in different types of newspaper feature and enhanced an already favourable image of the newspaper medium.

Inevitably, there are also studies which suggest that television viewing has had no discernible impact on newspaper reading at all.

The contradictory nature of the evidence raises serious doubts about its validity. Certain inconsistencies can be attributed to divergencies of

* Not previously published.

experience in different sampling areas, among different groups of people, at different points of time. Certain claims and counter-claims can be down-graded since they are made merely *sotto voce* or by implication. But many inconsistencies cannot be accounted for, and this inevitably calls into question the adequacy of conventional empirical survey methods which have been used to measure the influence of television on the press.

Empirical survey evidence

The least satisfactory of the standard research approaches adopted are the simple *retrospection* surveys. These studies merely report what people *think* the effect of the new medium has been on their newspaper reading habits and other leisure activities. The weakness of these studies is that the accuracy of the findings depends entirely upon fallible memory recall. It is unlikely that respondents are able to recall with any precision changes in their newspaper reading habits over a period of time. It is even less likely that respondents who had acquired a TV set some years previously would recall the changes in newspaper use with the same degree of accuracy as more recent TV owners.[2] More important, self-evaluation of the effect of television requires a logical isolation of the effect of television viewing from all other influences on newspaper reading habits. This problem of isolating the effect of TV has exercised two generations of media researchers; it is not a problem which is likely to be resolved by a spontaneous self-rating on the part of informants. Add to this the existence of social norms hostile to television,[3] causing people to provide highly misleading information about the use they make of television,[4] and it becomes quite clear that the thousands of dollars and thousands of pounds spent on restrospection surveys have yielded findings which are of limited value. The use of large samples does not make the findings any more accurate, although they may have succeeded in impressing individual media space buyers in advertising agencies.

More beguiling but no less misleading are the attitudinal studies on press and television. The temptation is to accept at face value professed statements about the media which prove, on close analysis, to be merely rationalisations of motives which respondents are unconscious of or which they are anxious to conceal. Any inferences drawn from such rationalisations are liable to be erroneous, however temptingly plausible they may at first sight appear to be.

For instance, a relatively high proportion of newspaper readers profess to be dissatisfied with the sensationalism, morbidity and triviality of the newspapers they read.[5] Does this criticism partly explain, as Dr Belson suggests, the decline in the number of popular newspapers purchased?[6] It is curious that those very items to which declining newspaper sales have been attributed also happen to be the items which readers tend to read most avidly. It is even more curious that the features which Dr Belson has recommended as an antidote to falling newspaper sales, in compliance with what his respondents professed to want, happen to be features which are very much less popular. Sex, crime, violence, scandal and gossip, the very topics deplored, regularly obtain high 'thorough readership' scores.[7] On the other hand, 'real news' items, allegedly so much in demand, normally obtain low 'thorough readership' scores in popular newspapers save in exceptional circumstances. Consider the representative findings of one 'reading and noting' study, an investigation into what was read in eighteen consecutive issues of five national dailies in 1963.[8] The most read news stories were human interest stories about ordinary people (with a tragic theme), human interest stories about celebrities, stories about ordinary people (sex, love and romance), stories about ordinary people (bizarre, humorous, non-serious), and stories about ordinary people (crime). The least read news stories, on average, were items about home politics, social problems, special news, war, international affairs, industrial news and city news. Apparently what people say they want during an interview is not what they actually read when the interview is over.

Without knowing a good deal more than we do about why people read newspapers and watch television, it is very difficult to assess the significance of professed attitudes towards the media, not less to assess how these attitudes might influence media use. The difficulty of assessing professed attitudes is further confounded by the tendency of what is said to be motivational information, as to why people read newspapers and watch television, to take the form of self-proving statements. Much of the research on audience motivations so-called is rooted in rationalistic assumptions about the functions performed by the press and television media, assumptions which are then fed into the questionnaire design itself – only to emerge, as empirical 'findings' derived from large, carefully constructed, and indubitably representative samples. The findings are the assumptions and *vice versa*. Any attempt to evaluate attitudinal evidence in the light of 'proven' motivations for newspaper reading is liable to lead to false conclusions.

For instance, in the detailed study undertaken by Dr Belson, thirteen motives for newspaper reading were listed and respondents were asked which statements explained why they read newspapers.[9] It emerged from the scaled responses to these statements that the simple desire to 'know exactly what is going on in the world' was the main motive for newspaper reading. In short, the newspaper's main appeal was to gratify the demand for news about current affairs.

Presumably this finding so-called enables us to evaluate additional attitudinal data on the media. A number of studies indicate, for instance, that television news has eclipsed the news service provided by the press. The most detailed of these, a study conducted by the BBC in 1962,[10] showed that television was considered by the majority of the public to be a more important, more authoritative and more interesting source of news than the press. 58% of respondents claimed to rely on television as the *main source of news* about what was going on in the world as compared with only 33% who claimed to rely principally on newspapers; 68% said that the television news service was the most *trustworthy*, while only 6% said the same for the press; 67% declared that television *makes the news most interesting* as compared with only 27% who gave the same rating to daily and Sunday newspapers. Thus it would seem that television has eroded the main appeal of the newspaper by usurping its function as the most trustworthy, most interesting and principal source of news about current affairs.

This seems a reasonable enough inference from the data but it does not stand up to detailed scrutiny in the light of additional empirical evidence. No survey covering the same ground as the 1962 investigation was conducted in the pre-television era. The only relevant survey is a BBC study conducted in 1957 during the transitional period from radio listening to television viewing.[11] While it does not reveal what attitudes were like before the introduction of television, it does throw light on the respective functions of the media.

It would appear that the press was *not* 'the main source of news about what is going on in the world' in the pre-television era. In this 1957 study, 24% of respondents said they relied principally on television, 31% on the press and 47% on the radio. Nor does the press emerge as the most authoritative source of news before the advent of television. 86% of informants said that radio news was 'more trust-worthy' than news in the press. Perhaps, even more surprising, the press does not seem to have been rated first among the media for making 'the news most interesting' before the introduction of tele-vision. For in the 1957 survey, 28% of the sample considered television to provide the most interesting news service, but the second largest group (26%) ranked the radio the most interesting source of news, followed by daily newspaper supporters (23%) and Sunday newspaper supporters (9%).

The fortuitous existence of the BBC survey splits wide open basic assumptions about the media. Whatever else people expect a news-paper to be, they have never, it would seem, expected it to rival media they can hear or see as a principal source of news or as a source that can compete with these rival media for interest and authority. These find-ings raise a fascinating question: what *do* people expect from newspapers if it isn't simply the news interestingly and authoritatively treated?

To this question we shall return. That it is necessary to pose such a fundamental question underlines the need for caution in accepting res-pondents' assessments of their own motives. It also underlines the difficulty of evaluating the real significance of the large accumulation of attitudinal data until such time as we know a great deal more about the gratifications derived from newspaper reading.

The third and probably the most important category of survey evidence consists of *comparative studies*. This approach takes a number of different forms but the guiding principle remains the same: the effect of television viewing can be measured by noting the difference in the reading habits of viewers and non-viewers. This approach, however, raises a number of serious methodological difficulties.

The first difficulty is that differences between viewers and non-viewers reflect inherent differences between these two groups. The first studies, as it has now been generally acknowledged, slipped up entirely by assuming that viewers and non-viewers were alike and that valid comparisons could be drawn by simply noting the differences in reading habits between these two groups. These studies made an obvious inference: any differences in reading habits between viewers and non-viewers could be attributed to television. The comparative method – and it is still favoured by a number of researchers – involves merely counting up the spots on two leopards, one exposed to tele-vision and the other not. The difference in the number of spots counted must *ipso facto* be attributed to the one environmental factor, television, which is being controlled.

The problem bedevilling such an approach is that early adopters of television sets are not typical of the population at large. Every major study has revealed that pioneer viewers differ substantially according to a number of demographic characteristics from people who subsequently acquired television sets.[12] In other words, this comparative technique amounts to no more than measuring the difference between early and late adopters of television sets, rather than measuring the effect of television. This confusion has led to a number of highly misleading claims. For instance, one study conducted in New York noted that viewers tended to spend more time reading newspapers than did non-viewers.[13] From this it was concluded that television viewing tended to increase the time spent reading newspapers. However, it appears that early adopters of TV sets in New York tended to be drawn from the higher income and more educated section of the community, precisely the people who tend to spend a large amount of time reading newspapers in any case.[14] The higher reading intensity noted among viewers is likely to have reflected the reading habits of the sort of people who became viewers rather than the effect of television viewing itself.

Comparison of the reading habits of people before and after they have acquired television sets does not evade this difficulty; indeed the 'before and after' survey approach merely multiplies the methodological difficulties. Newspaper reading habits are subject to a large number of random influences other than television. For instance, people in Britain tend to read more as they grow older;[15] marriage normally causes a radical adjustment in newspaper reading habits;[16] an increase in the cover price of newspapers encourages to some extent a reduction in the household intake of newspapers,[17] and so on. It is, therefore, highly misleading to attribute changes in newspaper reading habits to the phenomenon of television alone. To take but one example: a study relating to newspaper reading habits over a period of years purports to show that television viewing has increased newspaper readership.[18] The sample under consideration consisted exclusively of adolescents. Yet it would seem to be a universal phenomenon, and certainly as true of Canada and America as it is of the United Kingdom, that adolescents read more as they advance through the teens.[19] In short, the reported increase in reading intensity may reflect the effect of television viewing over time, but it may reflect the simple fact that adolescents read more as they grow older. The latter interpretation is the more plausible.

Attempts have been made to get around this difficulty of measuring a moving escalator by *also* measuring the changes in reading habits of non-viewers during the same period. Since both samples are moving at the same rate, any differences between the samples, it is reasoned, can only be attributed to the controlled factor, the influence of television. This procedure merely returns us to the methodological trap mentioned above: the assumption that viewers are of the same breed as non-viewers. If they are of a different breed – and, to repeat, the demographic evidence suggests that the actual differences between the groups are profound – then there is every reason to believe that they will *respond* differently to the same stimuli. The different response of viewers and non-viewers to identical stimuli is a point we shall take up again.

Some students of the media have tried to solve the problem of making viewers and non-viewers alike by making the two groups resemble each other, using a statistical weighting technique. For this procedure to be completely successful, it is necessary to insure that the matching of viewers and non-viewers is so perfect that all differences between the two groups, other than exposure to television, have been fully eliminated. In practice, the execution of match sampling techniques fell far short of this ideal. With one notable exception, samples of viewers and non-viewers were matched merely according to a handful of demographic characteristics. These characteristics were selected on the basis of guesswork without any systematic attempt to find out whether they were important or even relevant. The two groups of viewers and non-viewers were simply made to resemble one another according to an arbitrary selection of characteristics, and the rest was left to good faith.

The one notable exception is the now famous study conducted by Dr Belson in which the matched sampling technique was radically altered and improved. He not only recognized that different aspects of newspaper usage must be distinguished when matching viewers and non-viewers; he also recognized that extensive pilot work must replace armchair intuition in the selection of variables, if the samples of viewers and non-viewers are to be successfully matched.

The method used by Dr Belson was what he called the 'stable

correlate' technique.[20] By this method, respondents in both the proposed viewing and non-viewing samples are tested in advance to find behavioural variables which, while related to the use of the medium, stand independently of media use itself. There can be no question that this method of drawing up a matched sample eliminated some of the deficiencies which invalidated the findings of previous and, indeed, subsequent studies. Yet, despite its technical ingenuity and sophistication, it is nevertheless open to a criticism which casts serious doubts on the validity of the whole of Dr Belson's findings. The test scores relate always to *behavioural* variables; *psychological* and *attitudinal* variables are left entirely out of account.

Empirical evidence suggests that, by excluding psychological variables, Dr Belson failed to eliminate all non-television influences on newspaper reading habits. Two studies indicate that non-readership of newspapers is associated with anomic individuals who do not feel involved in the outside world and who generally take an inactive part in civic and social life.[21] To judge from these studies, therefore, Dr Belson failed to match viewers and non-viewers in terms of their propensity to read newspapers by omitting the variable of anomie. Unless it can be assumed that anomic people were equally distributed between the samples of viewers and non-viewers, this omission is likely to have prejudiced Dr Belson's findings on the effect of television viewing on newspaper readership. Thus, if anomic people had been concentrated among viewers, this would have distorted the results in a way which would suggest that television viewing had become a substitute for newspaper reading. On the other hand, if anomic people had been concentrated amongst non-viewers then this would have distorted the results in a way which would suggest that television viewing has recruited new readers to the newspaper medium.

To take another example, this one drawn from a series of studies on the *Daily Herald* conducted by Odhams in the late 1950s and early 1960s.[22] These investigations, while too rich and too complex in content to be summarized here, provide powerful support for one proposition; namely that the relationship between the content of a newspaper and the personality needs and attitudes of its readers is an important influence on newspaper reading habits. The prototype radical *Daily Herald* reader was unrepresentative of the popular national newspaper reading public. A large number of *Daily Herald* readers expressed strong resentment that they had been inadequately rewarded for the contribution they had made to the community, believed that their interests had been disregarded, and were highly critical of what they held to be the predominant values of society. But, then, the *Daily Herald* was itself an unusual popular daily newspaper. The official newspaper of the labour movement, and editorially tied to Trades Union Congress policy since 1922, the *Daily Herald* achieved a mass circulation in the 1930s. Its readership after 1945 dwindled and, despite the new editorial freedom it acquired in 1960, an exceptionally large number of its readers continued to be amongst the elderly and the lowest paid section of the community.

It emerged clearly from these studies that the *Daily Herald* fed back to its readers their own opinions and attitudes, structured reality in a way which confirmed their assumptions, and vindicated their sense of grievance. It is this symbiosis between newspaper content and the values and personality needs of its readers which partly explains why the *Daily Herald* had a more devoted and more loyal hard-core readership, measured according to a large number of different criteria, than any other popular daily newspaper. This loyalty to the *Daily Herald*, in turn, partly accounts for the high average level of reading intensity among its readers[23] despite the disproportionately large number of *Daily Herald* readers who were drawn from those who are generally light readers of daily papers – the poor with limited formal education.

Consider what happens when research leaves out of account this factor of the 'identity' relationship between the reader and his newspaper.[24] Even the sophisticated 'stable correlate' method, as applied by Dr Belson, failed to eliminate important and relevant differences between viewers and non-viewers – and once this point is granted, then it follows that what is measured is not the effect of television viewing *per se* but differences in the newspaper reading habits of viewers and non-viewers, differences which were built into the sample itself. Whether a matched sampling technique for measuring the effects of television in newspaper reading can ever be made to work is a moot point. What is clear is that the attempts tried so far have been unsuccessful and the conclusions drawn from such attempts lack authority.

Despite the contradictory evidence submitted by social researchers, journalists and public spokesmen for the press have not resisted the temptation to make pronunciamentos on how television will affect the future of the press. 'The great weakness of television,' writes William Rees-Mogg, Editor of *The Times* and a spokesman for the optimists, 'is the brevity of its current affairs and news coverage. . . . The brief vivid snapshot, the actual sight of the people involved, the headline news or the inconclusive five minute discussion, often make television coverage an aperitif for newspaper coverage in greater depth.'[25]

The majority view, however, is more pessimistic: 'Other time occupying interests such as television tend to reduce newspaper reading' is the collective verdict of the Newspaper Proprietors Association and this gloomy view is endorsed, sometimes in a more extreme form, by the majority of national newspaper publishers testifying to the 1961–62 Royal Commission.[26] Morale amongst the rank and file of journalists is no higher. Clive Irving, one of the many successful journalists to leave the press for television, compared his departure from newspapers to 'the casting off from a mistress who has gone to seed'.[27] Journalists will soon be 'reduced to writing on lavatory walls' is the only half-frivolous verdict of Maurice Richardson, the distinguished columnist for *The Observer*;[28] and Marshall McLuhan, probably the most famous of current prophets, goes so far as to foresee the death of the printed word. McLuhan claims only to be reading – or, shall we say, feeling – the writing on the wall: 'The classified ads (and stock market quotations) are the bedrock of the press. Should an alternative be found the press will fold. Radio and television can deal with sports, news, comics and pictures.'[29] By this line of reasoning, newspapers have little more function than their traditional one of wrapping up fish and chips. How such a dinosaur has managed to stay alive is a curious phenomenon. Is it really only the classified ads and the stock market quotations that have held its body and soul together?

Let us go back to the evidence – while first admitting that it has not been possible to discover the effects of television on newspaper reading by using matched samples. There is still one method left open. If it cannot establish the direct effects of television viewing, it can at least clinch an argument as to the future prospects of the press. We refer to the humble but neglected method of inspecting trends in newspaper consumption. These trends are remarkable – but not what they seem.

The evidence on newspaper consumption

At first glance, a recent analysis of viewing and reading trends in the United States would seem to be in line with the pessimistic view held by many press journalists themselves. On the basis of a correlational analysis of newspaper circulation, magazine subscription, cinema attendance and television ownership per household statistics Professor Melvin DeFleur concludes that the press in the United States has been partially displaced by other media. 'As far as the newspaper is concerned, the factors leading to a decline in circulation are not difficult to assess. Other mass media, meeting needs similar to those met by newspapers began to appear in American Society. . . . Each can serve as a potential *functional alternative* to the newspaper in some degree by supplying news, information and entertainment content.'[30]

The same pattern of declining newspaper circulation, *per capita*, coinciding with the growth of other media, in particular television, is also true of a number of countries outside the Soviet bloc.[31] But no country has experienced a more dramatic decline in newspaper sales during the period of increasing television ownership than the United Kingdom. In 1968, for instance, an estimated 762·8 million fewer national newspapers were bought than in 1951.[32]

Even more striking is that Table I appears to show a close connection between the diffusion curve of television ownership and the overall trend of newspaper sales and readership during the post-war period. Immediately after 1945 when television viewing was confined to a very small minority, newspaper sales and readership continued to rise. But when the number of television licences issued sharply increased during the 1950s there was a corresponding decline in newspaper sales and readership. The rate of decline only slowed down after the early 1960s when the rate of growth of television ownership also flagged.

That newspaper consumption should have declined so markedly in the United Kingdom during 'the age of television' and that this experience has been duplicated, if in a less dramatic form, in a number of other countries, might seem to give powerful support to the notion that television has displaced the press.

It is tempting to place heavy reliance on these correlations, because they seem so clear. Yet the correlational approach in studying trends

TABLE I

TV LICENCES AND ANNUAL NATIONAL NEWSPAPER TOTAL SALE

Year	Total annual net sales of national newspapers*	Number of combined radio & TV licences issued (year ending March 31st)†
1947	6,273,911,276	14,560
1951	6,807,218,051	763,941
1955	6,753,606,470	4,503,766
1959	6,515,986,604	9,255,422
1963	6,201,884,498	12,442,806
1968	6,044,449,626	13,068,079

* Wherever possible, figures have been taken from total monthly net sales returns of national newspapers registered in the archives of the Audit Bureau of Circulation (ABC). When ABC figures are unavailable, total annual net sales have been estimated by multiplying average circulation figures for January–June and July–December by the relevant number of publishing days, as reported in *Armstrong Warden's Press Analysis, Willing's Press Guide, Benn's Newspaper Directory* and *British Rate and Data* or as recorded in the Advertising, Circulation, Research or Record Offices of national newspaper publishers. Total annual net sales of each national newspaper have been weighted according to the modal number of publishing days during the post-war period (310 for dailies and 52 for Sunday papers) except in the case of newspapers which opened or folded during the year.
† British Broadcasting Corporation Audience Research Department.

in media use is open to precisely the same objection as the empirical survey techniques reviewed above: namely, the difficulty of isolating the influence of television viewing from all other influences on newspaper reading habits. Television is, after all, only one of a number of rival claimants to the press for the public's available leisure time. It cannot be concluded *ipso facto* that, because the development of television viewing has coincided with the fall in newspaper consumption, television is the causal factor in the decline. The decline may reflect an expansion in the range of recreational opportunities, an expansion that only *coincides* with the growth of television. For that matter, the decline may reflect a deterioration in the quality of the press or any number of other variables. The conclusion of Professor DeFleur's correlational analysis from a correlational analysis of some sophistication, must therefore be regarded as speculative.

This qualification may seem somewhat fastidious in view of the dramatic fall in newspaper consumption in this country. Certainly it is tempting to conclude that television viewing must be, if not wholly, then at least partly responsible for the slump in newspaper sales. But the correlational approach is open to a second and more serious objection. It is a deep-rooted statistical convention to regard circulation (that is, the number of newspapers sold per publishing day) as the overall index of public demand. The convention is based on the commonsense assumption that how many newspapers people buy reflects in rough and ready terms how much they read and how much they are prepared to spend. The assumption is a 'reasonable' one but its application is more questionable. Newspapers differ significantly in terms of content, size and price and these differences are increased by taking a period of years as a basis for comparison. No statistician would measure the demand for chocolates, for instance, by calibrating the number of boxes sold per annum. It is equally doubtful whether the convention of treating circulation as a standard unit of measurement provides a satisfactory basis for statistical analysis.

This is not to suggest that analyses using such rough criteria are themselves invalid, but merely to stress the limitations of such an approach. For these analyses to be more comprehensive two changes in procedure are required. For one, factors other than television must be considered in explaining trends in newspaper circulation. For another, a new criterion other than circulation must be developed as a measure of public demand. If these two changes in procedure are made we can at least discover the historical nature of the phenomenon which television is so often invoked to explain.

The experience in the United Kingdom is especially suitable for a detailed analysis of reading trends, because the fall in newspaper sales and readership has been more striking in this country than elsewhere. During the 1940s, the United Kingdom experienced the biggest boom in newspaper sales the country has ever known.[33] The war was probably responsible for increasing news interest as well as recruiting new readers to the national press;[34] and the restriction on leisure activities during the post-war years of austerity may have well have encouraged the sale of newspapers. Yet it is questionable whether these two factors alone account for the unprecedented increase in circulations. Another important factor has to do with the *size* of the newspapers read.

Newsprint rationing, imposed during 1939–45, was continued after the war because of the world-wide paper shortage and the country's balance of payments problem. Even in 1948 newspapers were only a third of their pre-war size.[35] This meant that a person who wished to obtain the same spread of newsprint in 1948 as before the war was forced to buy three times as many newspapers. The etiolated size of national newspapers during and immediately after the war would seem, then, to be one basic reason why newspaper duplication – the purchase and readership of more than one newspaper – was very much higher in the 1940s than in the 1930s.[36]

But with the relaxation of newsprint restriction in the 1950s, newspapers reverted back to their former size. And as newspapers became larger in size, so cover prices were increased. The average national daily and Sunday newspaper in 1968 was more than three times the size of the average daily and Sunday newspaper in 1945, and cost more than four times as much to buy (Table II).

The return to the large, economy size packaging of newspapers called for an adjustment in newspaper reading habits artificially distorted by the war and newsprint rationing. As newspapers became larger and more expensive, so newspaper duplication tended to decline (Table III).

This falling trend in newspaper duplication was intensified by the reduction in the number of newspapers available for purchase. No less than six national newspapers have folded since the war and this loss has been compensated only by the launch of one quality Sunday paper, the *Sunday Telegraph*.[37] The sharpest slumps in newspaper sales, not surprisingly, have occurred in the years when one or more national newspapers have been forced to close down. The closure of these six national newspapers represents a net loss of no less than 656·193 million newspapers sold per annum.

In theory a reduction in the number of newspapers available for purchase is not *necessarily* responsible for reducing the number of newspapers bought and read. The goodwill of a closed newspaper is normally purchased by another newspaper and the readers of the closed newspaper are acquired as part of the remaining assets. In practice, however, the forced conscription of readers of a closed newspaper does depress newspaper consumption. Firstly, a high proportion of readers of the deceased newspaper already read the newspaper which has incorporated it. The result is, normally, for some households to accept the *de facto* change and not to look for another newspaper to replace the one that died. Secondly, the shotgun marriage between two

TABLE II

NATIONAL NEWSPAPERS: AVERAGE PRICES AND PAGE NUMBERS

Year	National daily newspapers*‖			National Sunday newspapers‖		
	Average† cover price	Average‡ number of pages	Average§ editorial page load	Average† cover price	Average‡ number of pages	Average§ editorial page load
1945	1·45	6·229	4·450	2·00	9·426	7·110
1950	1·55	8·661	6·118	2·15	12·356	8·644
1955	2·175	12·587	8·039	2·653	15·572	9·714
1960	2·85	17·263	11·006	4·16	24·915	15·090
1965	3·98	20·842	13·345	6·30	33·402	19·993
1968	5·416	22·245	13·915	7·75	35·352	19·288

* Excluding *Daily Worker/Morning Star*.

† Based on the average cover price of each national newspaper over the whole year, taken to the nearest 0·25*d*, as reported in the *Royal Commission on the Press 1961–2* (HMSO Cmd. 1811–7) or as recorded in the advertising or research departments of national newspaper publishers.

‡ Calculated by dividing the total number of pages published in one edition (normally London edition) of each national newspaper, as recorded in the research or advertising departments of national newspaper publishers, by the relevant number of publishing days. Where necessary, less accurate estimates have been taken from W. A. Belson, *The British Press*, Part III (London Press Exchange Ltd, 1959), Marjorie Deane 'United Kingdom Publishing Statistics', *Journal of The Royal Statistical Society*, Vol. CXIV (1951), and *Survey of the National Newspaper Industry* (Economist Intelligence Unit Ltd, 1966).

§ Calculated from the total number of columns or column inches of advertising published in one addition of each national newspaper over the year, divided by the relevant average number of columns or column inches per page, and by the relevant number of publishing days. Data supplied by national newspaper publishers, advertising or research departments, or, when necessary, above mentioned sources, *Royal Commission on the Press 1947–49* (HMSO Cmd. 7700) and *The Advertiser's Weekly* (London 1950).

‖ Excluding colour supplement.

newspapers is not always to the liking of the readers concerned; for households which read a number of newspapers the temptation is simply to cancel the regular order for the newspaper now forced upon them. To take just one example, the incorporation of the *Empire News* by the *News of the World*. Table IV shows that 6·499 million readers of the *Empire News* were passed on as a legacy to the *News of the World*.

TABLE III

AVERAGE NUMBER OF NATIONAL NEWSPAPERS
READ PER ISSUE BY ADULTS (OVER THE AGE
OF 15) IN GREAT BRITAIN*

Year	National daily newspapers	National Sunday newspapers
1947†	1·411	2·319
1951†	1·555	2·627
1955†	1·434	2·386
1959‡	1·353	2·140
1963‡	1·286	1·818
1968§	1·160	1·789

* Estimates before 1959 have been weighted according to the percentage difference in the estimated number of newspapers read per issue for the same year, 1956, as reported by the Hulton and IPA Readership Surveys.
† The Hulton Readership Surveys. *The Financial Times* is not included.
‡ The Institute of Practitioners in Advertising (IPA) National Readership Surveys (January–December Reports). The *Daily Worker/Morning Star* is not included.
§ The Joint Industry Committee for National Readership Surveys (JICNARS) (February–December Report).

TABLE IV

THE DEATH OF THE EMPIRE NEWS

	Average readership per issue*		
	1959	1960	1961
	('000)	('000)	('000)
News of the World	17,717	17,472	18,132
Empire News	6,412	6,499	—

* The IPA National Readership Surveys (January-December Reports).

M.S.—E

Yet in the year that followed the closure of the *Empire News* the readership of the *News of the World* increased by only 660,000 readers.

One reason why the *News of the World* derived so little benefit from this acquisition was that no less than 54% of *Empire News* readers also read the *News of the World* during the period immediately before the closure of the *Empire News*.[38] The second explanation is that among the remaining 46% of *Empire News* readers there was a large number who simply didn't like the *News of the World*.

This reduction in the number of newspapers was caused by economic and competitive pressures within the newspaper industry rather than by a fall in real public demand. After 1945, there was a steady deterioration in the cost and revenue position of small popular newspapers caused by escalating fixed costs, retail price fixing by their competitors at an uneconomic level and, above all, by the declining attractiveness of small circulation popular papers to advertisers.[39] As a result, the *minimum* circulation required for small popular newspapers to survive was progressively increased at a time when circulations were depressed by falling newspaper duplication. This led inevitably to the closure of popular newspapers with the lowest sales and (in advertising terms) a nondescript readership.

That the contraction in the newspaper industry was the cause rather than the consequence of the catastrophic fall in newspaper sales is best illustrated by the record of the *News Chronicle* and *Empire News*. These two newspapers, commanding on their death-bed an average circulation of 1,162,194 and 2,084,397 respectively, can hardly be said to have collapsed because they failed to appeal to a significant audience. Even more remarkably, the *Empire News* actually *increased* its circulation by 5.97% during its last five years of publication life, whereas the average popular Sunday paper lost 7.14% of its circulation during the same period (Table V). Even the record of the *News Chronicle* with a modest 7.87% fall in circulation in its last five years compared not unfavourably with the average popular daily paper during the same period. No less surprisingly, both the *Empire News* and the *News Chronicle* actually increased their sales revenue by over 50% in their last five years. Sharply rising public expenditure provides startling confirmation, if it is required, that both papers satisfied important public needs. Yet both papers were forced to close down because advertisers were dissatisfied with the quality and quantity of their readership.

TABLE V

THE LAST FIVE YEARS OF A NATIONAL SUNDAY AND A NATIONAL DAILY NEWSPAPER: CIRCULATION AND SALES REVENUE

Year	Average annual net circulation*				Gross sales revenue†			
	Empire News	Average national popular Sunday newspaper	News Chronicle	Average‡ national popular daily newspaper	Empire News	Average national popular Sunday newspaper	News Chronicle	Average‡ national popular daily newspaper
					£	£	£	£
1954	1,977,655	4,529,763	1,309,778	2,714,912	1,069,938	2,453,622	2,537,660	5,370,574
1959	2,095,808	4,206,472	1,206,763	2,657,122	1,816,367	3,645,608	3,896,829	8,596,322
% change	+5·97%	−7·14%	−7·87%	−2·13%	+69·76%	+48·58%	+53·6%	+60·06%

*Audit Bureau of Circulation *inter al.* (see Table I).

†Calculated by multiplying the total annual net sales of each national newspaper by its average price. Price changes occurring during the year have been taken into account by multiplying the two average six monthly circulations of each newspaper by its cover price and the average number of publishing days before and after the price rise in each six month segment.

‡Average of all *surviving* national popular daily and Sunday papers, excluding the *Daily Worker/Morning Star* and the *Sunday Post.*

TABLE VI

ANNUAL SALES OF NATIONAL NEWSPAPERS: COPIES AND PAGES

Year	National daily newspapers†		National Sunday newspapers†		Total national newspapers†	
	Total annual net sales	Total number of pages sold annually*	Total annual net sales	Total number of pages sold annually*	Total annual net sales	Total number of pages sold annually*
1945	3,938,940,524	20,297,655,417	1,099,562,953	9,626,008,372	5,038,503,477	29,923,663,789
1950	5,259,706,917	42,973,076,854	1,710,993,877	19,620,455,593	6,970,700,794	62,593,532,447
1955	5,095,726,735	60,185,651,038	1,657,879,735	25,983,159,862	6,753,606,470	86,168,810,900
1960	5,053,381,352	90,492,246,616	1,484,931,475	36,245,862,290	6,538,312,827	126,738,108,906
1965	4,846,350,236	102,791,631,196	1,360,858,619	40,828,077,526	6,207,208,854	143,619,708,722
1968	4,674,205,933	100,125,630,592	1,370,243,693	39,950,727,876	6,044,449,626	140,076,358,468

*Calculated by multiplying the total annual net sales of each national newspaper by its annual average number of pages published per copy, taken to the nearest three decimal points. Colour supplements are excluded from the estimates.
†All estimates have been weighted according to the modal number of publishing days in the year.

In short, two factors were of critical importance in causing a fall in newspaper sales during the post-war period: the end of newsprint rationing and economic pressures causing a reduction in the number of newspapers available for purchase. It cannot be assumed, therefore, that television viewing was the principal agent responsible.

People cannot be said to be spending less on newspapers or buying less newsprint simply because they are buying fewer newspapers, especially when the newspapers in question are very much larger. Nor can they be said to be spending less when newspapers themselves are costing more. Clearly new categories of analysis are needed which take into account radical changes in the newspaper as a product, in order to obtain a meaningful index of gross newspaper consumption.

While total annual net sales of national newspapers declined by 926·251 millions during the period 1950–68, the total number of newspaper pages purchased increased by no less than 79,029·559 millions during the same period (Table VI). The misleading convention of treating newspapers as a standard unit of measurement has concealed the fact that newspaper page consumption has enormously increased during the period of development of television. Fewer boxes of chocolates are being sold but the boxes themselves have become very much bigger.

A very precise way of measuring gross newspaper consumption is to estimate the total average square inches of editorial text purchased per publishing day *per capita*. This measurement takes into account not merely changes in the average number of pages published in national newspapers but also differences in page size *between* different national newspapers. By this method, advertising space can also be successfully excluded from the analysis. As Table VII makes clear the editorial load purchased per publishing day by the average adult nearly doubled between 1950 and 1968.

Another meaningful index of consumption (as against circulation) is total expenditure on national newspapers as a proportion of overall consumer expenditure. During the same period, of course, public expenditure on a wide range of products and services has also increased. To take this factor into account, public expenditure on national newspapers has been calculated as a percentage of expenditure on comparable products and services.

Table VIII shows that expenditure on national newspapers has sharply increased as a percentage of discretionary expenditure on:

TABLE VII

AVERAGE SQUARE INCHES OF EDITORIAL TEXT
PURCHASED PER CAPITA (OVER AGE OF 20)
PER PUBLISHING DAY*

Year	National daily newspaper	National Sunday newspaper
1945	340·6	1069·7
1950	687·4	1838·8
1955	872·9	2055·9
1960	1241·1	2799·3
1965	1289·3	2868·6
1968	1211·9	2824·8

*Calculated by: (a) Estimating the annual average square inch area of editorial text published per copy of each newspaper. Changes in page or column size have been taken into account by estimating the total square inch area of editorial text published before and after the change(s) took place and by dividing the sum of these estimates by the relevant number of publishing days in that year; (b) Multiplying the average square inch area of editorial text of each newspaper by its average net circulation; (c) Dividing the total square-inch area of editorial text purchased by the number of persons over the age of 19 as reported in *Annual Abstracts of Statistics* (HMSO) and *Monthly Digest of Statistics* (March 1969). Colour supplements are excluded from the estimates.

(a) Print media as a whole.[40]
(b) Luxury products and services.[41]
(c) Inessential products and services.[42]

No less remarkable is the fact that public expenditure on national newspapers has also increased markedly as a percentage of total consumer expenditure.[43] This demonstrates that despite competitive pressures holding back newspaper price increases[44] (pressures which have, incidentally, caused British papers to be under-priced by comparison with comparable papers in America and on the Continent),[45] *people are spending more on national newspapers than ever before.*

There is further evidence to suggest that not only is more editorial matter being published but that more editorial matter is being read. Odhams and, subsequently its parent company, the International Publishing Corporation, conducted continuous monitoring research on what was read in national newspapers during the post-war period.

TABLE VIII

ANNUAL PUBLIC EXPENDITURE ON NATIONAL NEWSPAPERS* AS A PERCENTAGE OF
CONSUMER EXPENDITURE† (AT CURRENT MARKET PRICES)

Year	Total luxury expenditure		Total inessential expenditure		Total expenditure on the media		Total consumer expenditure	
	%	Index	%	Index	%	Index	%	Index
1945	0·94455	100·0	0·72119	100·0	28·99168	100·0	0·445146	100·0
1950	0·96357	102·0	0·70624	97·9	25·65897	88·6	0·398199	89·5
1955	0·99577	105·4	0·73134	101·4	29·66500	102·3	0·41661	93·6
1960	1·18311	125·3	0·86348	119·6	31·95861	110·2	0·46416	104·3
1965	1·21716	128·9	0·90362	125·3	34·09477	117·6	0·49255	108·3
1968	1·23974	133·6	0·91031	126·2	33·70455	116·3	0·50505	113·5

*Public expenditure on national newspapers has been calculated by aggregating the annual gross sales revenue of all national newspapers, except the *Sunday Post*, and weighted according to the modal number of publishing days in the year.
†All estimates for annual consumer expenditure have been taken from *National Income and Expenditure Reports* (HMSO) for 1952, 1964, 1968 and 1969.

The aim of these surveys, carried out at intervals during the post-war period, was to discover for the purposes of editorial policy what was read rather than how much was read. However, since there was a high degree of continuity in the items checked in terms of content, position and column length, and since the number of items checked was increased in proportion to the increased size of newspaper, this data does provide a rough estimate of reading intensity over a period of years.

Table IX shows that taking 1947 and 1967 as two points of comparison, there was an estimated increase of 676 square inches of editorial text read per average copy of popular national Sunday newspapers. Similarly, there was an estimated increase of 634 square inches read per average copy of popular daily newspapers during the period 1949–67.[46]

In order to take into account the reduction in the number of popular Sunday and daily newspapers read, the total area of editorial text read per average issue has also been estimated. Thus, comparing the years 1947 and 1967, the total estimated area of editorial read in popular Sunday newspapers increased by 32,993 million square inches and the total area of editorial text read in popular daily newspapers has increased by 23,453 million square inches.[47] It is not possible to estimate precisely the increase in the average area of editorial text read *per capita* during the post-war period since the sample of newspapers selected for the Odhams and IPC reading and noting studies has among its several omissions the whole of the quality press. The very growth of the quality press itself, however, would suggest that overall reading intensity has increased since quality newspaper readers are known to read more intensively than popular newspaper readers.[48]

Figures showing the total size of the reading public as a percentage of the adult population are perhaps the most revealing of all (Table X). The sheer size of the national newspaper audience is itself an eloquent testimony to the enduring appeal of the printed word. During the period, 1963–8, no less than 83% of the adult population read a national daily newspaper, 92% read a national Sunday newspaper, and 97% read either a national daily or Sunday newspaper.

No less remarkable is the success of the press in retaining the loyalty of the large number of readers, recruited during the artificial circumstances of the second world war. With the return to normal peacetime conditions, and with the increase in the number of rival attractions

TABLE IX

SQUARE INCHES OF EDITORIAL TEXT READ IN POPULAR NATIONAL NEWSPAPERS

Popular Sunday newspapers				Popular daily newspapers			
Year	Base no. of newspapers	Average square inch area of editorial text read per newspaper*	Estimated total millions of square inches area of editorial text read†	Year	Base no. of newspapers	Average square inch area of editorial text read per newspaper*	Estimated total millions of square inches area of editorial text read†
1947‡	(6)	665	41,435	1949§	(4)	421	15,107
1955	6	760	53,710	1960	4	940	37,014
1963	4	1,277	72,819	1963	4	1,018	36,522
1967	4	1,341	74,427	1967	4	1,055	38,361

*Calculated from *The People/Sunday Paper Readership Interest Surveys* and the *Daily Herald/Daily Paper Readership Interest Surveys* (International Publishing Corporation and Odhams).

†Estimated from the *Hulton Readership Surveys* (weighted estimates as in Table III) and IPA *National Readership Surveys*. Figures are per average issue.

‡Projected estimate from the average thorough readership of six Sunday papers in 1955 (22 issues checked) on the basis of the average thorough readership of *The People*, 1947–55 (46 issues checked).

§Projected estimate from the average thorough readership of four daily papers in 1960 (48 issues checked) on the basis of the average thorough readership of the *Daily Herald* and *Daily Mail* since 1949 (81 issues checked).

competing for the reader's time and attention, a reduction in the number of people reading newspapers was perhaps to be expected. In fact, the percentage of the adult population reading national newspapers has remained relatively constant throughout the post-war period, with variations so small as to fall well within the margin of error in national readership surveys. Penetration by the national press would seem to have reached saturation point in the 1940s and to have been maintained undisturbed by the growth of television.[49] (Table X.)

TABLE X

% OF THE POPULATION OVER THE AGE OF 15
READING NATIONAL NEWSPAPERS*

	National daily newspaper	National Sunday newspaper	National newspaper Sunday or daily
1947–50*	79·7%	92·1%	—
1952–5*	80·0%	93·1%	—
% difference	+0·3 pp	+1·0 pp	—
1956/7–61†	83·6%	92·6%	96·7%
1963–8†	82·9%	91·7%	96·7%
% difference	−0·7 pp	−0·9 pp	nil

* Hulton Readership Surveys; all national newspapers excluding the *Financial Times*.

†IPA/JICNAR National Readership Surveys: all national newspapers excluding *Morning Star/Daily Worker*. Estimates for the period 1965/7–61 have been taken from the IPC Group Readership Tables and, for the period 1963–8, are based on computer processing of IPA/JICNAR cards financed by the International Publishing Corporation. The computer cards for 1962 were damaged and this year has therefore been omitted.

The growth of television ownership would also appear to have reached near saturation level.[50] Over 99% of the population live in television transmission areas, and are able to receive television broadcasts.[51] During the four year period, 1965–8 inclusive, the percentage of the population with a TV set in their home[52] and the percentage of the population viewing television on an average day[53] has remained relatively static. It is therefore legitimate to compare the size of the audiences reached by the press and television media.

The figures are startling. In 1968, *81*% of the population read a national newspaper on an average day[54] while only 69% watched television.[55] Moreover, the difference between the size of the two audiences reached by the newspaper and television media is even greater than these figures suggest, since a significant percentage of the population read a provincial but no national newspaper.[56] Thus twenty-two years after the first post-war television broadcast was transmitted from Alexandra Palace, the press still appealed to a much larger audience than television.

Conclusion

In short, the notion that television viewing has displaced the press merely derives from a deep-rooted statistical fallacy about the significance of newspaper circulation statistics. The newspaper is not a standardized unit of measurement and should not be treated as such in analysing newspaper consumption trends.

In fact, gross newspaper consumption in the United Kingdom has risen very substantially during the age of television. The public is buying more pages of newsprint per head of the population. Public spending on national newspapers has increased significantly as a percentage of total consumer expenditure. The amount read in national newspapers also appears to have increased considerably. And while the national newspaper press has sustained the high level of readership achieved in the 1940s, the number of national newspaper readers has substantially increased. Yet all this has occurred at a time when economic forces within the press industry have artificially depressed newspaper consumption.

It should perhaps be pointed out that the findings for the United Kingdom may well apply to other countries where newspaper circulation *per capita* has fallen during the period of growth of television. Not merely are circulation statistics in themselves inadequate to measure the level of newspaper consumption, they may well also be misleading for the very same reasons that obtain in the United Kingdom. The trend towards larger and more expensive newspapers and the reduction in the number of newspaper publications is not unique to the British press,[57] and it would therefore seem reasonable to assume that the trend towards falling newspaper duplication, and therefore falling newspaper circulation, is not confined to the United Kingdom. Future studies which distinguish between changes in newspaper buying and reading habits and changes in the level of newspaper consumption, and which assemble supplementary evidence on the demand for newspapers, may well arrive at conclusions very different from those suggested by circulation and television ownership *per capita* trends.

The world trend in newspaper consumption requires clarification in the light of further research. What is clear, however, is that television has not displaced the press in the United Kingdom. Every meaningful index of demand for national newspapers registers the success of the press in retaining the interest and loyalty of the public during the age of television. There is nothing to justify the pessimism among journalists, induced by the economic insecurity of the press industry and steadily falling newspaper sales. Nor is there a shred of evidence to support Professor McLuhan's sweeping assertion that television viewing, by changing our sensory equipment, has eroded the need for the printed word.[58]

This is not to suggest, however, that television viewing has necessarily reinforced public demand for newspapers. A larger number of factors other than television viewing may explain the enduring appeal of the national newspaper press. Space does not permit a detailed correlational analysis between press and television media and the results of such an analysis must necessarily be inconclusive. It should be pointed out, however, that there appears to be very little connection between the growth in the size of the television audience and changes in the size of the newspaper audience. Nor does there appear to be a close connection between changes in the level of reading and viewing intensity. Nor does television viewing appear to have substantially influenced the type of features read in national newspapers. Indeed what is remarkable is how little the pattern of feature readership has changed not merely during the period of growth of television but since the pre-television era. What was read in national newspapers more than thirty years ago is remarkably similar to what is read today.[59]

In view of the apparent lack of connection between reading and viewing trends it is difficult to suppress the conclusion that the newspaper has an independent life and distinctive appeal of its own. Unfortunately, investigations using a matched sample technique are no longer possible in the United Kingdom since the pre-conditions of research, representative samples of viewers and non-viewers, no longer obtain. A new approach is needed to investigate the interrelationship between press and television; an approach, moreover, which conceives of the differences between press and television not merely in terms of information content or communication form, but, more important, in terms of *the relationship of the audience to the medium*. What is needed is not a rationalistic appraisal of the manifest functions fulfilled by press and television but an understanding of their *latent* functions – the needs satisfied by the two media and the gratifications derived from media use. A fund of insights are available in extensive and largely untapped research.[60] These provide a foundation from which it should be possible to explore the reasons for the enduring appeal of the press medium.

PART TWO:

Communications Organizations and Communicators

1. Public Service and Private World*[1]

Tom Burns

> The question of what the purpose or goal of a group is, and, conse-
> quently, what things will help or hinder the achievement of that
> purpose, is very often a political question. Factions within the
> group disagree, manœuvre to have their own definition of the
> group's function accepted. The function of the group or organiz-
> ation, then, is decided in political conflct, not given in the nature
> of the organization.[2]

It is difficult to think of any institution, public or private, with a
more explicit and precise definition of its purpose than the BBC's,
which is to operate a broadcasting service as a means of information,
education and entertainment. Yet the same definition could be, and
has been, claimed for the services provided by commercial television
companies; and public controversy about the aims of the BBC's services
is one of the stand-bys of press and publicists since its foundation.

The definition of its primary task given by society and voiced by
Parliament in the BBC's Charter therefore, is only a first step, essential
perhaps, but no more so than the injunction laid on a commercial company by its shareholders that it should make a profit, or on the State
itself that it should promote the welfare of its citizens and protect them
and their interests. The prescription itself immediately poses a number
of questions about the nature of the information, education and entertainment, about their quantity and quality, and about the proportion
which each should represent as well as about what will promote and
what will prevent their successful presentation. Indeed these questions
have formed the matter of the national debates, inside and outside
Parliament, and of the Committees of enquiry which have preceded

* First published in *The Sociology of Mass Media Communicators*, in *Sociological
Review Monograph*, No. 13 (1969).

the review and renewal of the BBC's Charter. The Corporation itself contributes to these debates, and in so doing claims the right to have a voice in the framing of the Government's prescription. The debates are inevitably reflected within the Corporation itself.

Dispute about current interpretations of the task of radio and television broadcasting seems to have mounted within the Corporation itself in recent years.

Three distinct views made themselves apparent. For many people, the 'pragmatists', the three purposes of informing, educating and entertaining the public seemed to be quite distinct but nevertheless compatible because there was in fact an explicit and general public demand for all three things. Others – the 'platonist' school – saw the BBC as an institution with a specific and now inalienable historic part to play in the life of the nation. Whether this role had been deliberately chosen and achieved or was the consequences of social forces which had operated through historical circumstances, the BBC's relationship with the nation was now normative. In international or national crises, it spoke in a real and important sense for the nation as well as to it. For the majority of people, the measure of the significance of any public issue was the weight the BBC gave to it. Moreover, while nobody is naïve or presumptuous enough to see the BBC as prescribing some national code of morals, it is believed that the normative function which it undoubtedly has discharged in politics is also attached to its observance of moral standards, in entertainment principally, but also in comment and criticism; so the programmes broadcast carry a special sanction in that they are what the BBC, the national broadcasting authority, sees as fit and proper to offer the nation. A third section of opinion – whose reported slogan 'television for television's sake' underrates the Aristotelian authority of their position – seems to regard this normative role either as undesirably arrogant, or played out, or as imposing irrelevant constraints on the development of broadcasting forms so as to mirror contemporary events, society and culture swiftly and forcibly.

While I believe that the only injustice done in this account to these three views lies in its brevity, it should be said that they are in fact inferences from the interviews and conversations rather than summaries of statements explicitly made; the most explicit statements tended to be about opinions imputed to others which were in conflict with the stand which could be assumed to be the speaker's.

There may, of course, be other views of the BBC's function, or purpose, or mission in society. All I have done is to present, in capsuled form, the three which make themselves evident to me in interviews with some 200 members of the Corporation's staff in the middle and higher ranks. The form and length of the present paper prohibit any discussion of the public debate itself. Indeed, the whole report of which this forms part, while it is about the BBC, is not about the BBC as a public institution. Varieties of policy and changes of policy, the extent and exercise of public control, the content and merit of programmes, the competence of producers and performers and the inevitable speculation and public interest aroused by an organization which probably absorbs more of the time of the people of the country than any other single institution – all these familiar and proper matters of discussion enter in only in so far as they represent the outer environment of the situations which have been the object of study.

But it would be wrong to omit any reference here to the case which has been argued from time to time in lectures, speeches and articles by the Director-General and other official and unofficial spokesmen of the Board of Governors and the Board of Management of the BBC. In fact, the best statement of this viewpoint has been made not by any of these, but by a former Controller of Programmes, Television, Mr Stuart Hood. He writes:

> The BBC functions on a system of devolution. A producer is given full powers in making a programme or series of programmes. On him rests the final judgment of what is right and seemly to present to his audience. His decisions may range over a wide field. They may concern a theme, a topic for discussion or debate; the choice of a film-clip; a dramatic situation; a camera-angle; the words of a song; a single word. If he is doubtful on any point he may refer his problem to his superior, who will either make a decision or refer the matter higher. The ultimate instance is the Director-General, who – before giving his ruling – may consult with the producer himself or with senior members of the staff. Judgments are not based on written laws – although there is a code of practice governing violence in children's television or 'that area of adult time when children are known to be viewing in substantial numbers'. In part, they are based on precedent and tradition; but precedents can be ignored and traditions questioned and modified. What they are based on can best be described as a programme ethos – a general view of what is fitting and seemly, of what is

admissible and not admissible, which is gradually absorbed by those persons involved in programme-making. It is intangible, undefined and baffling to newcomers and freelance producers or directors. One of the best definitions of it was provided by Sir Hugh Greene in an address delivered in Rome to the International Catholic Association for Radio and Television. One element in what he called 'the in-grained code' was 'the proper sensitivity of production staff to the world around them, so that they are concerned with a relationship to the audience which cannot exist if the language in which they are talking, and the assumptions they are making, seem to be too remote from the language and assumptions of the audience and of the times in which they are communicating'. This formula is both liberal and flexible.[3]

It will be noted that this prescription, liberal and flexible as it may be, is nevertheless concerned with negative sanctions – with the exercise of censorship, rather than with a positive formulation of purpose or function. If anything, it seems to square with the third view I have presented above, of 'broadcasting as a mirror of contemporary life' subject only to the two constraints of 'public opinion' (overwhelming pressure from outside organizations or articulate sections of the public) and 'programme ethos' (the individual producer's interpretation of both the function of broadcasting and of the constraints of 'public opinion'). But, in fact, it represents much more clearly the present stage of the 'liberal dissolution' of the Corporation ethos itself as it was created by Reith's generation.

The great merit of the conception of the role of radio broadcasting, developed in the formative decades, when Lord Reith was Director General, was that it had a clear view of the matter,[4] if a limited interpretation of the task which this imposed. If the function of broadcasting in society is construed as the provision of political, social and cultural navigation charts, the job Reith chose for the BBC to carry out was that of maintaining a kind of pilot service. Or, to shift the line of vision a little, the BBC developed as a kind of internal diplomatic service for the nation, representing the British – the best of the British – to the British. 'BBC culture', like the BBC's standard English vocabulary and pronunciation, was not peculiar to itself but an intellectual ambience composed of the values, standards, and beliefs of the professional middle class. Sports, music, and entertainments which appealed to the lower classes, were, of course, included in large measure in programmes, but the manner in which they were purveyed – the context of presentation – remained indomitably upper middle class; and there was, too, the point that they were only on the menu as ground bait.

But – and this is crucial – the pattern was deliberately worked out. Reith, in short, knew what he was doing. There is no sense in which a public broadcasting service for the nation can become a 'value-free', or neutral administration. 'It is an outstanding characteristic of the European liberal *idea* of the state that it is neutral, that it adopts a *neutral* position in internal values, such as the problem of what truth and justice are; it leaves the choice and judgment of all values of this sort to special social groups (for instance, to the Church) or to the conscience of the individual. The real basis of national sovereignty is a purely "formal" legal structure, divorced from all questions of internal value'.[5] But neutrality of this kind, even notionally, can even so only attach to the State. The rationale of the creation of a Broadcasting Corporation separate from the Government is that neutrality cannot be assumed in these regards. There is no culturally or morally neutral position to assume.

The monolithic structure of the Reithian ethos broke up during the 1950s. Oversimplifying, as one has to, one can point to three principal factors contributing to the change. The advent of television itself probably did most. Broadcasting was no longer *sui generis*. The cinema, television's model as well as competitor, had its own conventions, standards and mythology, and, more important, an entirely different relationship with its audience (i.e., it put a different construction on the social task of providing a navigation chart of the social and physical world). Commercial television, when it came, destroyed not only the monopoly of the BBC in the economic sense but also its special relationship with the nation of universal representation and total responsibility.

The breaking of the uniqueness and the unity of the link between broadcasting and the nation which first television itself, and then commercial television, accomplished, meant the intrusion of other renderings of Britishness and of rightmindedness and the consequent shrinking of BBC values to something sectional and questionable. So that while the social function of commercial television was, as before, to provide interpretations and models with the greatest acceptability, (but this time obviously and admittedly to provide ground bait, and for a very different kind of fishing), one considerable side-effect has been to put the whole BBC operation and policy into the framework of 'brand-image' making.

It is also arguable, of course, that changes in Britain's social structure which occurred, or became manifest, during the 'fifties brought into question the authority of the whole hierarchy of values on which the Reithian system depended. But arguments of this global sort quickly become circular; after all, the collapse of the old BBC ethos played no small part in the change in orientation of British society.

The BBC has not by any means turned its back on the Reithian ethos and purpose; many, indeed most, of its activities still faithfully reflect the traditional image. But there has been change, and it is change which is significant, as it is change of which we are most conscious. The breaking of the BBC monopoly was achieved by political manœuvres within one party, and however nobly the BBC strives to retain its reputation for political neutrality, it has been brought down from the heights of supra-political, almost supra-national, authority which it enjoyed during the sound broadcasting monopoly.

A consciously 'circulation-building' element has entered into the handling of news, and comment on news; successful presentation is related more and more to exclusive, sometimes sensational, interviews and reporting. Many programmes have appeared to make bids for popularity by disregarding the cautious (or responsible) standards associated with the earlier days of monopoly. The hauteur which governed Corporation attitudes and behaviour towards commercial television at first has given way to a more or less open acknowledgment of rivalry on the same terms, a rivalry which admits of the interchange or common employment of popular performers and producers and of the growth of a policy of short-term contracts – both of which must dilute any distinctively BBC style or approach, and reduce the public appreciation of differences of ethos and purpose between the Corporation and commercial television companies.

The Corporation has felt itself compelled to fight on two fronts; the old certainty of purpose has gone; and the clear challenge and opportunity has been replaced by a dilemma.

There is nothing particularly novel or distinctive about the three 'insider' views with which we began; they echo major sections of opinion outside the Corporation. But while the content of all the utterances which bore on this matter was what is vaguely called the relationship of the BBC to the public, the debate was carried on as an internal affair. The principals in the debate whose rehearsals were quoted by adherents and opponents were in strategic position within the Corporation. The three kinds of interpretation of the BBC's task were identified with them.

This is natural enough, since the main issues in the debate about interpretation have to be settled within the Corporation and as the result of the interplay of discussion and argument among its officials. Equally naturally, each view squared with the interest of such sections in either keeping its present standing or influence, or bettering it.

Thus the catholicity of the pragmatists was not illogically related to the suspicions of the staff in Light Entertainment and Schools Broadcasting, and of others who felt some affinity with them, that their contribution to the BBC's output was tolerated as an 'unfortunate necessity'. The slogan most frequently encountered was 'a balanced programme' – i.e., a total output in which Light Entertainment would have a rightful share.

There's some disquiet here because we see the top places in the Corporation all being filled by journalists. You see, when you had a few showmen up there, they'd take the view 'I didn't like this but it's a popular and – in the interests of a balanced programme – I'll put it in'. The journalists now will quite likely take the view that if they don't like a show and if it's not getting a *very* big audience, they can scrap it.

A 'balanced programme' policy would, in fact, serve as an insurance policy – something which would quieten the unexpectedly widespread feelings of insecurity about the future which turned up in many interviews in Light Entertainment and in Schools Broadcasting. Thus:

One has the feeling that the Corporation could well do without Light Entertainment. It has Light Entertainment because it has to – that although it did many good things even prior to the advent of commercial television, that if they could do without us they would. That is the feeling. It's only very recently, when things became competitive, let's face it – that audiences are wanted to keep the Corporation alive – that they really acknowledge that they had to have Light Entertainment, and there was no way out of it. Although, of course, there's always the feeling that if you can develop the big audience puller with 'Your Life in Their Hands' then probably they'd junk it. They'd let Light Entertainment go.

You're here as ground bait. All right, so stick to your job as ground bait, and don't think of Light Entertainment being a viable television commodity in its own right.

and again:

It's an unsafe world ... If we're talking of allies – which is the point you made – I don't think there are any allies. I think they're a bunch of hostile critics.

T.B. Has this feeling of it being an unsafe world grown in the last year or so?

Yes. Oh yes. Prior to Pilkington, there wasn't the feeling of quite so much insecurity as there's been since.

Obviously, there is no active, present fear that the Corporation will 'junk' Light Entertainment, or even that it wants to, but there remains the uncertain feeling that Light Entertainment is there to act as ground bait for the mass audience, that its first and only job is to attach the audience to the BBC channels, and that its existence depends on keeping mass audiences in a way that other output departments' existence does not. There is, beyond this, an awareness that over the past few years a critical ideological campaign has been fought and won in BBC television, the outcome of which has been to place Talks Department in the centre of the programmers' picture of television, with News and Current Affairs and Outside Broadcasts within the main frame. All these three departments observe the same canons of life immediacy, of the television screen acting as reflector of the 'real world' of people, happenings, things and ideas – a world which is real in so far as it is topical. Drama remains a datum of existence for television in its 'home cinema' function. Light Entertainment, equally, remains an 'unfortunate necessity', its marginal character inescapably perpetuated in the adjective tagged on to its very title. So,

It is very difficult, no matter what kind of prestige one attains in a good Light Entertainment show, to realise that prestige in comparison with other parts of our output. The cachet isn't there.

The visible direction of these observations shows that the belief that BBC policy should be guided by the actual and actively expressed public demand for a balanced variety of kinds of programme rests on apprehensions about the unwilling acceptance by 'The BBC' of the very existence of whole departments. The insecurity engendered by such apprehensions and the suspicion felt in such departments that they are victims of tacit demarcation rules about status or, at least, esteem within the Corporation both find a rational basis in the sweeping successes of people from Talks Department in gaining the dominant position in Television Service, and the striking contrast of the shrinking of influence or representation of other kinds of production experience in the higher ranks.

In both the television programme departments included in this study, there was a great deal of discussion of the paradoxical situation of there being far more insecurity prevailing in the Service now the BBC had entered on a new lease of secure existence.

As in other contexts, the goal of political conflict is to have the leaders of one or other party gain positions of power; thereafter, of course, they will administer in the interests of the community as a whole, and with strict justice and equity, but it is at this point of succession to positions of power that the political system and the careers system of organizations meet. The success of people from one section of the organization rather than others, must be seen as reflecting on the general level of ability and initiative in that section. The kind of talents and experience which that section requires and rewards is shown to be demonstrably relevant to the kind of talents and experience required by the organization as a whole. The success of individual members from a section suggests that the cases it has argued have been well argued by them in the past: more particularly, that their view of the Corporation's task and of the best way of discharging it has won over other views – that the career victory is also an ideological victory. The structure of working relationships and functions in the section from which they came, and the jobs of people who operate within it, are less likely to be adversely affected than those in other sections by the changes instituted by the new men who have appeared from that section, have gained by its existing structure and may perhaps have modelled it. While the experiences, expertise, and viewpoints the section now has in common with the man at the top may not be an unmixed advantage in the eyes of the members of the section, it seems to be so to others. And there is, lastly, the immediate benefit of the current of promotions set going by any displacement from the top positions in the section.

The outcome of competition for succession to senior posts in an organization tends therefore, to have repercussive effects throughout its membership, affecting far more, and far more people, than the small group of contestants for the positions.

> *T.B.   You used to have big names (from your side of things) around
>   the Corporation at one time?*
>
> Oh well, you've got the journalists in now. When —— was here you felt you had the ear of the bosses. But now he's gone, and because —— [his successor], I suppose, is a BBC man, let's put it, from way back – he's probably looked upon as such by the top brass – we've become much more of a 'department' than we used to be, just another limb of the Corporation, and feeling just a bit more remote.
>
> *T.B.   I see. So far from having your people fed up to the top, you're
>   having people fed into your top.*
>
> Yes. And I think this will probably go on. For instance what future is there for a producer here? I'm personally quite interested in administrative jobs and have done them in the past . . . but I don't really reckon there's a great deal of opportunity, unless I managed to get the ear of somebody somewhere, to make the jump from production to administration. You see, and there's this feeling – as was definitely stated when —— addressed us. One of the chaps said 'You don't want to finish up with a lot of producers who are fifty-five or sixty' and the answer was 'That's quite right'. So you see immediately one feels a little more remote, and cut off and wondering about the future . . .

It is this repercussive effect which links the legitimate self-interests of the members of a department or section in an organization to the actual and possible changes which occur in the occupancy of the senior posts at the top. The kind of consequences which are to be looked for from such changes are, for the general run of staff, legible in the attitudes taken in the general debate about policy by the new occupants. At the very outset of this study, the new appointments to the highest posts in the Engineering Division were discussed largely in terms of their meaning for career prospects, and the kind of qualifications or personal qualities or Corporation experience which might be most favoured; there was no apparent concern in other kinds of policy change which the new men might institute. More generally, such attitudes are related to alternative lines of action which are actually or possibly pursued by different sections.

Individual programmes now have greater freedom. People think in terms of this or that programme rather than of the BBC as a whole. The amount of control exercised over them centrally has slightly diminished. Individual programmes have more autonomy.

T.B. *This applies to matters of content – journalistic content, perhaps. Is there any other sense in which this greater freedom, or autonomy, is exercised?*

Yes, I think in its attitude to its audience. This applies much more to television – a feeling not so much that a programme is only justified by the audience that it gets but that, bearing in mind the cost of the service, and the physical limitations of it, you have to think very very hard before you put on a programme that is only of interest, say, to one million as against six million. I think there is a difference between this and saying; 'Oh, this is a programme which will bring in an audience of thirteen million and therefore we can charge a lot for the advertising.' I'm not sure, though, that the distinction is always made in that form. Sometimes the BBC attitude to justification by figures is just as blatant as the commercial companies'. It can be very honest and very democratic, this feeling, but it can be used as a stick to beat everything that doesn't command a large audience.

T.B. *There is a patchiness, then, partly because of the nature of television . . .?*

And partly because of history. I mean, Reith lives on at Broadcasting House and not at Television Centre . . .

The growth of the Television Service within the BBC, its success in the battle for audiences with commercial television, and the more recent emergence of a group of young and vigorous people into controlling positions within the service have all contributed to a greater autonomy in the administration of Television. The internal politics of this change are complicated, but nevertheless clear enough in the practical issues involved.

T.B. *If you are right in saying that the BBC is becoming more 'plural' – culturally, administratively, and in terms of policy aims – than it was, obviously the resistance must come from the Administration, which is going to be much more comfortable with a monolithic corporation than with a lot of groups who want to go their own sweet way.*

I must say this had not occurred to me. It is very easy to talk, isn't it, of 'The Administration' as an external body, without bothering to separate it into its various categories. Frankly, of some sections of the Administration that one comes into contact with – you know perfectly well that they would never have anything to do with deciding the character of the output . . . But may be if one looks at it from the point of view of Television Centre, one certainly gets the impression that in one respect, that is in staffing and recruitment – and I think it is a very widely held impression – that recruiting and staffing in Television is done far more according to the whim, or decision, of the heads – than elsewhere. Appointments Boards, and things like that have less meaning in Television Centre than they do at Broadcasting House.

T.B.   On the programme side?

Yes – on the programme side. I think it is felt that it is quite clear who will get the job because the man who runs the programme and his superiors have decided that they want him on the job. Now this may be a naked geographical thing. As you say, the Administration is at Broadcasting House. It is not there.

The broad division of opinion about the way in which the Corporation should interpret the definition of its primary task which has been imposed on it as a public institution represents more than a natural but impotent interest in issues which are really for the governing body to settle. The debate is ideological, in the sense in which a coherent system of ideas and principles may nevertheless be consonant with the self-interests of a group of people. This is not to say either that the ideas themselves are thereby invalidated or suspect, or indeed that people hold those opinions which will tend to their own advantage – 'for ideas and actions do *not* simply follow from the social positions of the individual'. They do, however, strengthen that particular position which he regards as important for his present and future hopes or chances in life. The kind of views about policy expressed by individuals, and imputed to others, are allied to their fears and interests, and serve also to codify and rationalize courses of action which protect or advance them.

There is nothing peculiar to the BBC in the development of a closed system of internal politics out of the variety of interpretations of its task which are publicly available. What was surprising, in so exceptionally articulate a working community, was the absence of discussion about the social functions or social consequences of broadcasting – outside, that is, the context of the issues of 'responsibility' which have already been touched on, and which are discussed below at greater length.

This may have been merely an aspect of what is supposedly a traditional British distaste for speculative discussion. Possibly it derives from a perception of the futility of the efforts made to trace direct causal connections between broadcasts and the conduct, attitudes, fears, or aspirations of the public, adult or child. It could, again, spring from a reluctance to disturb a complex of assumptions about the relationships of the BBC to its functions and to the public.

I am inclined to attach some importance to the last consideration. The lack of interest in the audience which was so evident can hardly be construed as a kind of schizoid withdrawal, which was the first construction I placed on it. Certainly, the functional relationship between the views of how the BBC should perform its institutional task, and interest-groups within the Corporation implies that the ideological systems so developed should be autonomous, and thus to some extent shielded from reality. Certainly, also, one encounters something of the 'insider' feeling characteristic of the cultural enclaves inhabited by the highly committed – such as professional musicians, scientific researchers, artists, and cult teenagers – although both the egalitarian principles within the enclave and the rejection of the totality of outsiders as 'square' lack the moral fervour of the archetypes.

There is a further general consideration.

Occupations which exist to provide direct services to customers, an audience or a clientele require an organization of effort or skill directed towards pleasing individuals. This carries with it a connotation of interest, attention or deference which, outside the context of paid or feed employment, would imply that one attached a special value to them and to their well-being. Service occupations therefore tend to carry with them a countervailing, and ordinarily concealed, posture of invidious hostility. This 'latent reversed role' manifests itself at times when the public is not present but is under discussion: in servants, waiters and the occupants of those manifold positions which are needed to lubricate the passage of a public into, through and out of shops, aeroplanes, ships, trains and buses, hotels, restaurants and theatres. There are also episodes when over-exigent demands for attention or deference or some transgression by members of the public license retribution. More important, in the more highly esteemed reaches of the service occupations, there is the evidence of the traditionally rigorous and irrelevant disciplinary codes prevailing for patients in hospitals and pupils in schools. In the occupations which serve a large and absent public – journalism, advertising and films – the compensatory reaction against the service relationship appears to waver between a cultivated indifference and contemptuous dismissal. It was a television dramatist who pictured the 'typical television audience' as 'mum sitting in the best armchair drinking cocoa with a teen-age son on the sofa trying to get his hand up his girl's skirts'. And a public of millions must, it seems, be envisaged as 'moronic'.

It would be easy to multiply quotations voicing the same sentiments as these last, but it would also be absurd to suggest that they are representative of opinion within the Corporation. What is significant about them is that they can be publicly uttered by anyone at all inside the Corporation. That they have been said is, I believe, partly because of the three defensive postures I have mentioned, but more directly the consequence of the incorporation of professionalism within a large, complex organization. When the relationship between broadcaster and public is enshrouded in a very large array of other relationships, each bearing responsibility, and themselves arranged in a hierarchy – so that relationships with one's equals are usually of less consequence than that with one's superior, and less still than with his superior – it tends inevitably to become not so much obscured or extinguished as 'taken care of'. It is taken care of not simply by unloading the burden of the relationship on to superiors, but by the growth of certain institutional forms which empty it of personal involvement. It was possible to discern three such institutional forms: The 'responsible attitude' traditional in the Corporation and the ethical constraints which are implicit in the tradition; secondly, the cultivation of 'professionalism' in the special sense in which it is used inside the Corporation, and thirdly, by a limited, controlled use of Audience Research to provide crude audience figures (measured in millions) and an Audience Response measure; procedures which reduce awareness of the public to the safe dimensions of a percentage.

The responsible attitude is familiar enough:

The fact that if you're doing an hour's drama you're playing around with eight or nine thousand pounds of somebody's money – a lot of money. Again, the viewing figures – one producer was saying that on the night his show was being transmitted he was driving through a Cotswold village which seemed pretty unchanged from what it had been perhaps two hundred years ago, but through all the front windows he could see a little blue screen, and it suddenly came home to him that these people – most of them – were watching something that he had conceived – in an office – in his own mind. The implications of this are considerable, I think.

T.B. *Yes. They're always with you, presumably, in some form or other, though perhaps not quite in that concrete form?*

They always should be with you.

T.B. *This is, I suppose, the basis of the weight of responsibility which builds up as one approaches the time of recording or transmission?*

Yes, especially with live transmissions, when you know that it only needs just one person to go berserk for say some fifteen million people to be influenced in some way . . . As Owen Reed said, if you show a hanging on a children's programme, the chances are that some of the children watching will have attempted to do the same, in imitation – which brings the responsibility home.

There seems, in fact, no way of attaining any direct relationship with an audience which will be more significant, or even realistic, than the 'viewing figures' or driving past the front windows of Cotswold cottages. 'Responsibility', for the broadcaster, is institutional. It has had to be generalized, turned into a routine of thought and behaviour, and, outside the context of occasions such as this interview, enclosed within the structure of the Corporation itself. Indeed, 'responsibility' was more easily and clearly registered among the engineers and others not directly concerned with programmes:

In our organization the pressures are not commercial but if I can . . . yes, I think this is a fairly sensible term – 'public service conscience'. It's not a nice thing to say, it sounds a bit uppity, but if you do have a conscience the pressures in an organization like this are tremendous.

Yet, like the other institutional forms of the relationship with the audience public, 'responsibility' has become subject to some ambiguity and manipulation. It can be dodged:

> The system in the organization is such that you could either work very hard, or you could live happily – and it doesn't make an awful lot of difference either way to the immediate situation.

Among producers, on the other hand, there is a feeling that 'responsibility' is somehow at odds with 'artistic integrity'; and that the moral restraints or censorship traditionally exercised implicitly by heads of programme departments are now a set of conventions which it is smart, or wise, to outmanœuvre: one reaction to *That Was The Week That Was* is said to have been the relaxation of self-censorship over the themes and language of 'situation comedy' series mounted by Light Entertainment.

> We've got a thing coming off now, a confidence trickster dressing up as a parson, and slipping into some Euston Road flophouse. Well this thing was billed for April 17th. We found that it's Good Friday, and we've altered the date! But that's as far as we're prepared to go.

Standards of responsibility were now perceived as varying between departments and even programmes:

> ... Partly because of the speed at which they have to work, there comes in a certain meretriciousness, a certain slickness, a tendency to do things in their programme, which, if the press did them, they'd despise, and almost a certain degree of hypocrisy. I can give you one very good example of that. When Bennie Paret, the boxer, was killed, there was a telerecording of the fight, and the final blows were considered so – vile – that it wasn't shown. But *Panorama*, in the course of a discussion about boxing, says, 'And now we will show you these ghastly thirty or forty seconds.' And you are shown this. And you come back, and then he says, 'Vile, disgusting, disgraceful, and now here is X, Y and Z to talk about this.

These, and other passages in interviews, refer to isolated instances and episodes. They are not seen as wholesale trends, even in individual output departments, certainly not as a deliberate policy change. Yet they reveal some unease, and point to the present as a period of testing out an ethical tradition which is proving hollow. This is not to suggest that a kind of Gresham's law operates in broadcasting, but that, within the Corporation, there is a widespread feeling not so much that the young lions are taking over but that the Corporation in this one respect has gone for a ride with a tiger.

The comment by one newcomer to the Corporation, if not wholly serious, was at least half serious:

> One of the interesting things to me about the BBC and what it does do and what it doesn't do, is that it has done everything except nudity. And since it has no real censorship from above, this is very strange. I remember that when they visited the Windmill, the girls put special clothes *on*. Well, if you're going to be politically uncensorable, and if you're going to have as much violence as you see on television it's strange that this hasn't been exploited. Because it's an audience puller, and if people care about viewing figures, I'd have half expected this. I think maybe there's a great opening there for somebody.

The word 'professional' has an extraordinarily wide currency in the Corporation. In the context of programme production, and of the BBC's relationship with its audience, it seems to have three separable, though not distinct, meanings. First, and most frequently, it means merely the opposite of 'amateur' – i.e., good of its kind, expert, finished; there seems to some people a danger of professionalism, in this sense, degenerating into 'slickness' or even 'journalistic slickness'. Secondly, there is the more conventional use of the word to mean 'qualified by prolonged and specialized training'. A professional engineer is obviously a professional in this sense, but so is a man who has become a producer after many years apprenticeship in the theatre or films, or a floor manager. Thirdly, there is the sense in which it indicates 'a code of behaviour where the first consideration is the need of the client and the quality of the work'.

This third sense involves the appraisal by the professional of what the needs of the client are, independently of the demands and wishes expressed by him, and the appraisal of the service he gives by standards other than appreciation or reward. The first direction of reference – to the client (i.e., the public) – was hardly ever invoked in discussion.

The second bulked very large, and relates to one's own sense of successful accomplishment, possibly unreliable, and to the regard of the head of one's department, one's fellows and, most constantly and evidently, the studio staff with whom one works.

The insistence on professionalism arises at least in part from the need to protect oneself from or shelve consideration of the unseen, unknown audience. Even in those output departments in which constant and patent reference was made to audience figures and Audience Response percentages, it was said with great firmness that what counted was judgment by fellow professionals of a programme's quality.

Yet, it was also apparent – and frequently enough said – that producers hardly saw anything of each other. Two producers claimed they hadn't done more than exchange hellos with other producers for months – seven months, one said. Producers tend to isolate themselves, or to get isolated, in the show.

> *T.B.   One of the impressive things about watching a production going on is the special relationship which obtains between producer and cast, floor managers, and crew, and so on – a very difficult relationship, but all balanced on the isolation of the producer and the insecurity which necessarily comes from that. When the thing's in rehearsal, it seemed to me, he's going down a long slide . . .*
>
> Yes.
>
> *T.B.   and he's got to end up at the bottom – safely, he hopes. He can't stop. The relaxation at the end, after the show, is very much a happy landing feeling. He's isolated because he's the steersman . . .*
>
> The isolation is the thing most producers are afraid of. They don't like it, they don't welcome it. That's why they stick so closely to the notion of the team. They're constantly referring to 'the team'.
>
> Particularly in this department, we're very much on our own. . . . On my own programme, very often I have to do things which I know if I asked my boss he'd say no. It would be right for my boss to say 'No, you mustn't do that'.

Even in the studios, or rather, in the gallery above the studios and sealed off from it, the producer is physically isolated. To retain control and the feeling of control, requires intense concentration:

When you're producing and you sit in the gallery, you see twenty people, all of whom are not merely expert – but incredibly slow. They seem to you to have a lot of inside knowledge, which you haven't got. But they seem at the same time not to be carrying out your instructions, because from the point of view of a producer speaking into a microphone, to get twenty people to do the right thing at any one moment is inevitably a long process, and it seems utterly endless. The producer must have a tremendous amount of patience to get anything done at all. Occasionally the patience cracks.

The utter absorption of the producer in his show – a commitment far more complete than I have encountered anywhere else – is the product of cumulative pressures. He may be, and often is, responsible for the original idea. The number of people involved, at least in television, is larger than any other form of presentation required. At the time of transmission he is responsible not for a film, which other people will market, or a performance which is now in the hands of the cast and the backstage workers, but for the output, at that time, of the BBC. More of the final product rests on his decisions than with other kinds of staged or filmed performance. And most important of all his responsibility remains throughout the performance, whether it is recorded or transmitted live.

This absorption demands emotional reinforcement and expressive demonstration. No kind of detachment is really permissible; commitment has to be – and be seen to be – deep, sincere and binding, although surface cynicism, in the right circumstances and in the right company, enters in, as it does with other professionals whose occupational values have nevertheless to be central to their lives – scientists, priests, doctors. For producers, this aspect of professionalism develops naturally from the conventions of the theatre. In rehearsal, the twentieth repetition of a joke line or a comic sequence will be greeted with the same appreciative laughter by the other members of the cast and the other 'professionals' (producer, stage manager, and aspirant juniors) as they gave at the first rehearsal. The producer, especially, must respond. He must, above all, it seems, 'believe in' his show.

T.B.   What has struck me is that the producer has got to feel that the show he is doing is really good, and that, moreover, he likes this kind of thing?

Yes, I think he must, even when he's offered an idea, and he takes it from this stage. It is rather like approaching a painting, for instance. One has to put as much of one's own personality into it as possible – but one has to rely on so many people around you. You have to work as a 'team'.

Subsequent discussion, too long to reproduce here, made it clear that there did not exist an alternative professional attitude of dealing competently and expertly, even imaginatively, with a show – *Compact* for example, or *Juke Box Jury* – that one did not regard as anything but unintelligent pop. Taking production responsibility, in these cases, would mean – if it were to be done *professionally* – remodelling the content and presentation so that it did represent one's own best, by any criterion.

The weight of commitments – of cast, studio crew, specialists, engineers and of the Corporation itself – which bear on the producer is met by a total commitment on his side. Given not only the special unreality of theatrical or even film productions, but the fact that the *Dunford Dialogues*, the *Billy Cotton Band Show*, *Today*, *Z Cars*, *Panorama*, *Saturday Night Theatre* and *Don Giovanni*, all represent quite different orders or species of unreality, the producer must immerse himself in the particular unreality in which his show exists, an immersion which demands involvement of a far more extreme kind than we accept under the ordinary dispensation of a 'willing suspension of disbeliefs'.

The professional role of television or radio producer requires him, therefore, to insulate himself, for the duration of the rehearsal and production period, from the worlds of other productions, both his own past efforts, and those proceeding concurrently. He must match his production: 'A square show needs a square producer', as one said, and, since this is not easy for people who live by being sophisticated, one must adjust one's perception of the outside world – including the public – so as to make it possible. So, if one is producing a show which I, as an outsider, suggest is very square indeed, the producer must reply, as one did, 'But this is the squarest country in the world'.

Insulation applies to audiences too. The relationship with the audience has to be reduced to the simplest possible terms. I found it difficult to discover whether any kind of reaction from the outside world had been regarded as relevant or worth attention in the days of monopoly broadcasting. Since competition – between sound and television, between the BBC and commercial television, between Third, Home and

Light programmes – had been instituted, a little more information about the response of audience had become admissible. But the response elicited – viewing or listening figures, and an Audience Response quotient – applies only to the competitive situation itself.

Beyond the restricted use of Audience Research figures to measure the size of audience and the volume of applause, a use related exclusively to competition between rival broadcasters inside and outside the Corporation, there was, as one comment put it, I think rightly, 'no evidence, to the people inside Television Centre, of people at the top of the Corporation knowing, or indeed caring, what the audience makes of the service it receives'.

The Audience Research Department was not one of the subjects of this study, and its activities are referred to here only in so far as they serve as a constant connection between the BBC and its public.

Audience Research did not attract much attention from the Pilkington Committee. From the Beveridge Committee, however, the service received a good deal of criticism. This criticism still holds good. It does so, I believe, not because of any deficiency in the department itself, but because of the constraints put on its role within the Corporation, constraints noted by the Beveridge Committee (paras. 234–5) and which called forth the comment 'To whom is the broadcaster responsible? If it is only to his own conscience, the decision might better be described as irresponsible.'

What I have tried to suggest is that there are reasons for the constraints put on Audience Research and that these are not the irresponsibility, or arrogance, of broadcasters. (The situation is not, therefore, one which can be met by a Public Representation Service, as the Beveridge Committee recommended.) The pressure on those responsible for programmes is such that fuller or deeper analysis of audience reactions would amount to an intolerable strain.

Even the information contained in an Audience Response (A.R.) index may have to be rejected. The shock of a reported A.R. figure of 63 for a programme in a series which had touched 75 was enough to disrupt the first hour or two of rehearsal of a subsequent production. Very little work was done. The atmosphere of dejection deepened with every new arrival. Clusters formed around the leading actors, the floor manager, and the assistant floor manager, with the producer circulating between them and the telephone. The whole assembly was, in fact, engaged in a more preoccupying task than rehearsal for the next show:

the search for a reassuring explanation. It was found eventually in the concurrence of a sports film on the commercial network.

'This,' it was explained to me, 'is what it's like on the morning when you've got a low audience figure'. For cast and production team, it was 'the figure'. Even after rehearsal began, the figure returned to the centre of the stage during waits: – '63 – and I thought it was such a bloody good show'.

For a sociologist, it was rather like watching the whole practice of medicine being reduced to the use of the thermometer. But its significance lay not so much in the importance attached to a statistical index as in the lack of curiosity about its meaning, the damage this particular return inflicted and the way in which the damage was repaired. The clear objective throughout was to restore the safe enclosure of the artistic world within which they could sustain the complex system of commitment and belief their work called for.

The world of autistic activity and belief which producers, programme departments, and broadcasting as a whole can create around itself is liable to be construed as complacency, as it was by the Beveridge Committee.

Entry into this closed world, with its private enthusiasms and its new absolutes based on the shortest of critical perspectives proved a disconcerting experience for newcomers used to the larger and slacker involvement of students or of writers and journalists, and led to some odd interpretations:

There was one other thing which I did feel very uncomfortable about when I joined, and still do. I've been on two courses and each time there seemed to be an attempt being made by somebody to do a job of brainwashing. I don't think it was a conscious attempt. It was just that everything to a lot of the senior lecturers seemed to be for the best of all possible worlds. You were left with two uncomfortable thoughts. (a) Why it was necessary to try and brainwash like this, and (b) well if everything is so grand, why aren't the programmes better? And 2X was a case in point – the first lecture on this course, about a man who'd travelled all over the world, and had come to the conclusion that home was the best and that we had nothing to learn from anyone. This, constantly repeated during both courses, generally from administrators or from people fairly high up in the Corporation, left a sort of uncomfortable taste in the mouth – that they considered there was some need for this.

These observations referred (by name, later) to heads of output departments ('administrators') who were regarded by producers as ruthlessly critical. 'Brainwashing' is an almost ludicrously inappropriate word in this context. But the fierceness of the reaction of this particular newcomer to the BBC jogs one into awareness of the almost deliberate and certainly perpetual effort made to domesticate the world the Corporation inhabits. Perspectives are drawn so that they terminate within the range of its control of influence, considerations are reduced to a common Gestalt, public issues translated into internal politics.

To repeat – there is nothing peculiar to the BBC, in the creation of a private world out of an occupational milieu. It is, in fact, a necessary corollary of becoming committed to a job and an organization. This withdrawal into a closed, isolated world of ideas, activity, involvement and resources is at its clearest and most intense in the producer's gallery of a studio. The elaborate provisions made to ensure that everything and everybody conceivably relevant to what is going on is available within the studio, and to physically exclude everybody and everything else – and the sheer necessity of these provisions for production to be achieved – afford a paradigm of the closed system which the Corporation creates for its members.

2. Decision-Making in Network Television News*

Malcolm Warner

Television news, because its compression of form imposes special editing and newsgathering requirements, is subject to much greater central control than is the case with the average newspaper. This makes for a small number of decision makers, and piles the responsibility on their shoulders. They are a *national* institution in a way that the various American newspapers are not, and this makes them a factor of major political importance.

This study of the central 'gatekeepers' in television network news did not deal with a *sample* of the decision makers; it covered *all* the important participants. Since under 50 people effectively shape the nation's TV news, and they are concentrated principally in the New York newsrooms of the three major TV networks, this was a reasonably accessible collection of individuals. Each of the three networks has a Vice-President or President in Charge of News, an Executive Producer, an Associate Producer, and so on. (Titles vary slightly from network to network.) Although not at the top of the administrative hierarchy, the Executive Producers have the specific responsibility, and in fact the power, to decide the form and content of the widely-viewed news shows of NBC, CBS, and ABC. Thus *three* men constitute the 'power élite' of the television news policy.

Our interviews with these television 'gatekeepers' have been treated so as to preserve anonymity, as that was one of the conditions given to the individuals involved. This enabled them to speak frankly and by-pass formal public relations channels. Quotations and descriptions presented below have been edited to remove material that would make

* This is part of an article first published as: Malcolm Warner, 'TV Coverage of International Affairs', *Television Quarterly*, VII (1968), pp. 60–75.

identification possible; in some cases they are amalgams of comments made by two or more individuals. This procedure does violence to the personalities involved, but since the selection of quotations is designed to focus attention on elements that are common to all three networks, personalities would not come through strongly in any case.

This observer was allowed to observe any part of the news operation in the three networks, and was excluded only from the most confidential conversations, which were very rare. In each network the following roles were studied: the Vice-President in charge of news, the Executive Producer, the Washington Bureau Chief, the Associate Producer (also known as Producer or Senior News Editor), the News Editor, the Newscaster/Commentator, the writers, the copy editors, and the reporters.

Since small numbers of people are involved in making decisions on news coverage at each network, they naturally develop a relatively homogenous point of view. With the exception of the reporters, they are in frequent, informal contact. On questions affecting the news show each one knows fairly well what the others are likely to think. As one copy editor phrased it: 'After working with the show for so long, you can tell what will and will not interest the writers, editors, and producers. It's a basic journalistic sense. . . .' An Executive Producer observed: 'The other guys here know what I'm after.' A news editor added: 'All of us think alike.'

Common approaches among all three networks are encouraged by the fact that each monitors the output of the others very carefully – and all keep a watchful eye on the *New York Times*. It is interesting to note that each network feels that the other two pay more attention to it than it pays to the others. In addition, many of the principal news personnel at the various organizations have known each other in various capacities for years; a large proportion of them came up through similar journalistic channels. This does not mean that each network does not have a unique style, but it does mean that the similarities in news judgment among the networks are more impressive than the differences.

The Vice-President in Charge of News: His main task is the overall direction of the news department and the delegation of specific production and editorial functions. Although he observes a general policy of non-interference, he is responsible for interpreting the organization's policy on news, and is concerned with such matters as levels of taste, how much controversy to get into, and so on. 'We let the people in the news show have their own views within bounds. These must be acceptable to the management of the news division and the company. They must be *overseen* by the company.'

The broad paternal influence of the Vice-President in setting the style for a news show may be inferred from the following comment made by one of them on a specific, to some possibly trivial, point.

A locution is gaining currency among news broadcasters (not only ours), which I find tasteless and repugnant. It is referring to the President of the United States merely as 'Lyndon Johnson'. He is, it must be clear, either 'President Johnson' or 'Mr Johnson'. Occasionally, if there is good reason, he is 'President Lyndon Johnson', especially when distinguishing him from 'President Andrew Johnson'.

While we're on names, saying 'French President de Gaulle' prevents confusion with 'Bulgarian President de Gaulle'; and I believe the proper non-sectarian usage is 'Cardinal Spellman', not 'Francis Cardinal Spellman'.

All Vice-Presidents are heavily concerned with relationships with the Federal Government. Here is a composite view:

I believe we are part of the Establishment, even if unconsciously. Journalists try to ingratiate themselves with their sources. I have to live with these people. The Washington staff also have to. Nothing occupies us more than the Vietnam war – that's the government. Space, that's the government. Elections, that's the government. How much does the government use us? Well, we are at the mercy of government officials and congressmen. There's the question of licence renewal that never worries newspaper editors. . . . The government could put us out of business if we lost the big local stations. The other reason is that the people who run the networks are part of the Establishment. . . .

The Executive Producer: If the Vice-President in Charge of News lays down the ground-rules for the news operation, the Executive Producer is charged with interpreting them. He is in control of the news selection process. He puts the show together and has the final word on the 'line-up'. This is the order in which the items of news are to be presented, how much time will go to each, how much film, and so on. While some decisions may be delegated to others, the final responsibility is his.

The Executive Producer is constantly dealing with news materials and the men who produce and handle them. People come into his office with messages, news tapes, scripts, and so forth all day long. The phone constantly interrupts his routine, especially to and from Washington. Many of the conversations are conducted in a jocular vein. Personal relations seem to be warm.

The Associate Executive Producer: Next in importance to the Executive Producer in day-to-day decision-making is his chief associate. The exact title of this official varies; he can be called Producer, Associate Producer, or Senior News Editor. He works very closely with the Executive Producer, often putting together the show in his absence. Indeed, in at least two of the three network shows the task of supervising day-to-day operations is largely delegated to this level of decision-making. According to one network executive, the role of the associate is also 'to worry about tomorrow's show', to see that film is coming in, that correspondents are sent off to certain areas, and so on.

The Washington Bureau Chief: While the ultimate decisions are made in New York, the Washington Bureau Chiefs have a great deal to say about what goes into the show, especially when Congress is in session and important news is breaking in the Capital. One described his activities as follows:

> I handle all the film and administrative responsibility. We have three writers who also act as reporters and editors. The commentator is very busy. We take all day, then in the afternoon talk. I know what is available. All the time we keep New York informed. Control is in New York, but it's no problem for us . . . they respect the opinion of people closer to the story.
>
> It's difficult to work in Washington, because so much news is what is *said*, ideas. You have to know *who* said it. Many social problems come out this way, via Congressional hearings, such as the problems of the American city. . . . The first day of the hearings on Vietnam – the beginning of the Congressional doubts – with Rusk, we had *nine* minutes of the show.
>
> All news is managed, isn't it? The Pentagon hasn't come out and said we have blundered. All released news is managed. Nobody tells me what I have to put on, *but* nobody says anything he doesn't want to. . . . If you don't know something, that's managed news. But in Vietnam, the guys [reporters] are all over the country and can go anywhere they want.

The News Editor: He keeps up with the progress of various stories constantly checking and re-checking, and is responsible for the details of the news, within the broad policy laid down by the executive producer. He may handle news reports, edit film or both. In at least one network he works most closely with the Associate rather than with the Executive Producer.

News editors cut out much of the blood and gore from Vietnam coverage, but have to work with so much filmed violence that they tend to become jaded and cynical. Whatever private feelings they have become smothered by the sheer quantity of war footage; to protect themselves they maintain a certain 'hard-boiled' atmosphere.

The Writer: The role of the writer is to translate the guidelines provided by the Executive Producer into narrative, working with raw inputs from the wire services and other sources. Writers are college graduates, usually majors in English Literature or Journalism, who formerly worked on leading newspapers. They may also report from the field, but are generally based in the newsroom. They provide the parts of the show that are read by the newscaster, although the latter may re-shape these items or write some of his own copy.

Writers are not primary decision-makers, but they can often, by a phrase, affect the flavour of a report. They adapt to the style and stance of the show as a whole, although they are held on a 'long' rather than a 'short' leash.

The Copy Editor: An important step in the selective process takes place at the point where the tape is taken off the wire service machines and distributed to those in the newsroom who use it to build the show. The copy editor, who is in charge of this function, is primarily responsible to the news editor, but has to maintain an overview of the total news flow in order to make an intelligent selection. He reads the *New York Times* carefully in the morning, and monitors radio and other TV networks as well as the wire services.

The Reporter: Since he works outside the newsroom, the reporter is not an integral part of the dynamics by which a show is produced. Nevertheless, in a sense he also is a decision-maker, since he controls the images that actually appear on film (in conjunction with the cameraman and possibly a field producer), and creates some of the copy. He is thus really an intermediary between the producers, who decide that he should be covering a particular area or problem, and the final editing process.

The Newscaster/Commentator: He is not the master of the news show, as it might appear to the viewer watching the home screen. A leading executive remarked: 'One of the myths of broadcast news is that the stars have the responsibility.' But neither is he a mere news reader. The role of the 'star' varies somewhat from network to network, but all of them participate in the formation of day-to-day policy. In addition, they write or re-write some of their own copy, they may choose to follow a particular story, or they may comment on the news by means of 'editorial eyebrows' – using their facial muscles to register a variety of reactions. A Washington Bureau Chief noted: 'The Executive Producer is boss, but if the commentator wants to do something, he can do it too.' While the commentator may garner more than his fair share of the glory, he also takes a disproportionate amount of the blame. When a mistake is made, fifteen people in the organization may be involved, but the public blames the star. To quote another executive: 'The man in camera is hung with it.'

Criteria for news selection

Criteria used in news selection are largely subjective; personnel in TV newsrooms have difficulty articulating them. The executive producers very frequently use the phrase 'it grabs' me' or 'it doesn't grab me'. This is a shorthand way of saying that it excites their news sense. It often happens, on Mondays, that nothing in fact 'grabs' them. As one put it: 'It seems like a light day . . . a quiet newsday, nothing special.' This suggests an absolute criterion, but the fact that a show must be put on leads to relative criteria – some items are less unsuitable than others. 'Some days we command the news, other days the news commands us. Judgment is based on instincts of 25 years in the business. The wire services and other gatekeepers decide something, but this has to be probed.'

When asked to define their criteria more precisely, TV news personnel mention a large number of factors, including importance to the domestic public, the number of people affected, audience interest, political balance, dramatic quality, and of course, 'freshness' and 'timeliness'. Again, there is frequent recourse to generalities.

Importance to the domestic public: One Vice-President felt that his organization looked for news that was 'of interest and importance to the American people – but considered more narrowly as of timeliness and immediacy; this means Vietnam, air pollution, medical developments, aviation safety, educational practices, American commitment to Southeast Asia, and 'failing support for us leadership in Europe.' There is an admitted bias toward domestic political news. An executive producer remarked: 'I'd count in the poverty programme, and Vietnam as an American political story . . . and every other year, you know, is a political year . . . elections.' (It is interesting to note that Vietnam was nearly always seen more as a domestic story than as foreign news.) A copy editor, likewise, said that he emphasized political news: 'I stress it very strongly. . . . People are concerned with what their government is doing. If there's a big story, it has national impact. . . . I treat the war as a special kind of news story. . . . People are dying there. Everybody is concerned whether they have a father or a son there.'

Number of people affected: This is a closely related criterion. In the words of an executive producer: 'Significance is the only criterion. My personal inclination is for a story that affects a lot of people.' A copy editor added: 'We figure the number of people it affects – the national and international interest, basic everyday interests.' Washington Bureau Chiefs were likely to stress the role of power and change: 'In Washington especially, you have to judge whether the man who says something will have some effect on it; do they have power in their position. In the case of Senators, for instance, you have to see what committees they sit on, what they can change. News boils down to significant change.'

Audience interest: Attitudes toward the audience are ambivalent. On the one hand, the tastes of the audience are seen as important, as a factor that must be taken into consideration. On the other, there seems to be considerable doubt as to what the audience really wants and a feeling that it is improper to play up to the audience too much. An executive producer states, 'We try to (create) . . . a programme for a national American audience based on the assumption they may not have read or heard any other news. We also assume that they are as literate and informed as we on the staff. We don't offend them, even if we simplify our approach. We are watched by millions of people, but that's an abstraction; I sometimes have the feeling nobody is watching. No conception of the audience, except on the smallest possible sampling, namely me, affects my news judgment.' Another executive suggested that there was some controversy about how much simplification should be attempted, when he observed: 'There's a long-standing argument about the mental age of the average TV viewer.' An associate producer specifically denied pandering to the audience: 'We don't know the audience and it doesn't matter; we don't tailor the show to the audience.' Some producers feel that perhaps audience tastes should be given more systematic consideration: 'We don't do enough research, that's our problem. The research department made a study three years ago – why people like the show – but that's all I know.'

Political balance: Judging from their observations on a wide range of subjects, the sympathies of decision-makers in TV news are overwhelmingly Democratic or Liberal Republican, but they try to keep their personal views in the background. 'In the area of politics we're extremely anxious to maintain a fair balance, although under the law we are not required to. But the public easily gets irritated about political questions.' Or again: 'We try to be fair. As long as we're accused of being too Republican *and* too Democrat then we know we're fair.'

Dramatic quality: This criterion also arouses some ambivalence. As a Washington Bureau Chief remarked: 'Imposed on the news gathering is the "show-biz" angle. The newsmen are stars in Hollywood terms; this affects the roles in the programme, the make-up of the programme and what they want. . . . You get into an area outside news.' But the same man remarked later: 'We try to cover what is significant – no pictures for pictures' sake, for example, parades.' A film editor who cut much of the gore from Vietnam coverage said that he left some in because 'violence was news'. Another observed that demonstrations were 'rather cliché these days – not much of interest unless they were violent'. An executive producer spoke of the need to give the illusion of speed. 'Last night we were very peppy – each item under two-and-one-half minutes.'

Foreign affairs coverage

Foreign affairs news is seen as secondary to domestic news unless, as in the case of Vietnam, it can be treated as a domestic story. 'Generally speaking,' said one executive producer, 'foreign news is not as popular as domestic news, but sometimes you can show foreign countries in relation to domestic topics. We have no great educating mission.' 'The biggest thing this week is China,' said another, 'but how to fit it in? Generally we have more material than we can use.'

Covering developing nations was seen as especially difficult, because cost considerations were added to questions of news judgment: 'The developing nations are an economic problem. We have *one* man in the whole of Africa to deal with it. . . . There's very little coverage of Latin America too. And we're only just involved in Southeast Asia. The reporters are often not to blame – the problem is with the editors back here. A legitimate question is to ask if coverage of such foreign news is the role of the evening show. We're interested in the day's news rather than trends – although we do some.'

Another executive producer agreed: 'After covering the main stories of the day and the Vietnam war and the Great Society, there's little space for anything else. . . . Trend stories like Latin America are difficult to communicate. . . . African coverage is largely of exotic and superficial crises. But we're good on domestic race questions.'

Most TV news decision-makers thought that the evening news shows would eventually go to one hour – actually 50 minutes, but it was not clear whether this development would be likely to lead to greater foreign affairs coverage. It is possible that the same considerations that result in curtailment of foreign news on half-hour shows would apply to the longer format. Also, doubt was expressed that an hour-long show could hold attention. 'I think we will go to a one-hour news programme,' observed a Vice-President. 'It will be a service. The set will be on, but people not necessarily watching.' The same doubts led an executive producer to oppose a one-hour show: 'I don't think the show will go to an hour. We can't keep people's attention for any more than a half-hour.' Some wondered whether there would really be enough good stories to fill a longer show. 'That is fine in a lush news, period, but it'll be difficult in the summer. We'll have to have seven or eight minute mini-documentaries. I think it could be made interesting for prime time.'

A Washington Bureau Chief assumed that the show would eventually be extended: 'When we go to an hour, we'll do more (on foreign affairs), probably fill it with interviews. We won't use experts – you can talk to them over the phone to get the facts. Here you get back to "show-biz", because experts are generally dull.'

The principal problem in connection with presentation of more international news on prime time television news shows thus seems to be seen as how to make the items conform to the demanding standards that are now applied. Already, with the half-an-hour shows, there is often a situation of poverty in the midst of plenty. That is, there is much more material than can be used, but there may not be enough that satisfies the news requirements of the executive producer and his associates. Some speak of 'anxiety where we feel or suspect that we couldn't fill it', even though such an extreme situation seems never to have arisen. For foreign affairs to play a larger part on evening television news, either new and more gripping methods of presentation will have to be found or the decision-makers in the networks will have to be persuaded to broaden their present criteria for selection.

3. Newspaper Staff as a Social System[*]

Aleksander Matejko

Human relationships in highly effective groups is a subject which is arousing more and more interest among sociologists and social psychologists. Research on groups of scientists,[1] engineers, and artists[2] of various kinds has been multiplying. It is hoped that as a result of this work the management of these highly qualified groups will be made more efficient, that the members of these groups will have better job motivation, and that the good atmosphere and team co-operation already found in them will be consolidated. For especially in the case of highly qualified work, which seldom lends itself to standardization, harmonious relationships are of paramount importance.[3]

It was thought that in this field it would be useful to make a structural-functional analysis[4] of a particular type of social system – in this case the staff of a daily or weekly paper. The staff of a paper offers a particularly attractive object of interest to sociologists, especially when it consists of a team of people with rather high ambitions in their job, who at the same time are closely connected with each other and form a crystallized group.

It should be pointed out that not only in Poland but in other parts of the world as well there have been comparatively few specifically sociological studies of this kind.[5] Mention should be made, however, of an interesting study by W. Breed on human relations in the American dailies of medium size.[6]

In Poland, sociological research on editorial staffs was begun in 1962 by making a descriptive survey of the staffs of two daily papers, one in Warsaw and one in Cracow and of two weekly papers, also one in Warsaw and one in Cracow. We deliberately chose papers excelling in quality and attractiveness, so as to be in a position to find out which

* First published in *The Polish Sociological Bulletin*, I (1967), pp. 58–68.

specific features of the paper's social system (the editorial staff) are connected with its pre-eminence.

The main source of information was the interview. Out of a total of 223 people on the staffs of these papers, 133 were interviewed. Although all categories of the employees came into the study, journalists (nearly all of whom were interviewed) formed the great majority of the respondents. The interviews were based on a questionnaire covering: personal data, type of job, details of career, type of present employment and conditions in it, description of the editorial staff, the respondent's place on the staff, the closeness of the respondent's links with his occupation, with his present job, his colleagues, superiors, with the prominent people on the editorial staff and with the staff as a whole, and the respondent's environment outside his work. The study was carried out as part of the research plan of the Cracow Press Research Centre.[7]

The aim of the study was to obtain a description of the human relationships characteristic of a rather compact and ambitious newspaper staff. A further aim was to show the influence of this system on the attitudes of the various members of the staff to their job. The third aim was to discover which factors affect this system most, and give it its present shape. A newspaper staff attracted our interest as a social system: (a) more or less conducive to the realization of the professional and personal aims of its various members, (b) more or less internally integrated and adjusted to its external environment, and (c) managed with greater or lesser efficiency.

If the social system of the particular newspaper staff is to retain its equilibrium, it must successfully fulfil its basic functions, which are connected with the existence and the growth of the paper as well as with the existence of editorial collectif. We shall examine here the following four functions: (i) the adoption and achievement of goals, (ii) adaption to the demands of the external environment, (iii) the maintenance and strengthening of internal cohesion, (iv) effective control of what is going on within the editorial collectif.

On all four papers we found that the staff members had very strong social and professional ambitions. They tended to look on journalism as a job calling for boldness, a job in which they should put forward and submit to public discussion such views of their own as would lead to wide controversy, and as would inspire other people and compel them to revise their stereotyped ways of thinking and acting.

It is not surprising, then, that on the papers in our study the dominating role in the social system (staff) belongs to the journalists (contributors). On both dailies they form the majority of the editorial staff, and on both weeklies much more than the majority. It is they who set the tone of the paper, it is their opinions that count, and their value and aspirations as journalists that count the most. As a result, all four papers are quality papers with high ambitions.

It often happens that the newspaperman's ambitions extend beyond journalism to the creative, literary sphere as well. This is because the journalists have many and wide contacts with other people in the creative arts and the professions, such as scientists, academics, artists, writers, engineers, physicians, etc.[8] The journalists want to raise their prestige to the level of those professions, and therefore try to make their work look as creative as possible. They specialize in various subjects, and try to secure a stable position not only in their own world of the press, but also in the particular environment – artistic, legal, political, or theatrical, etc. – in which they are professionally interested. Hence the tendency for journalists to keep introducing new subjects that will be of interest to the public, and that will bring public acclamation not only to the paper itself but also to the people working on it.

A number of circumstances, both external and internal, determine what new topics are brought up and whether or not they see the light of day. Many factors – the authorities' approval or disapproval of the ideas put forward by the paper, limitations of space, the editor's encouraging or discouraging attitude towards the ideas submitted by journalists, commendation or lack of commendation on the part of colleagues, the set habits of readers – all have an effect on the creative atmosphere in the newspaper office. In the case of the two weeklies in the survey, these factors on the whole had an inspiriting effect. The same was true of the two daily papers, although in them there was much less chance of development.

In all four cases, however, circumstances were not such as to warrant the high social and professional aspirations of the staff. The chances of finding space for their articles, of being able to execute their bold new plans, of finding access to attractive material (e.g., through foreign travel), of reporting an interesting subject, etc., were restricted, mostly by external considerations independent of the paper. Both the editors in charge and the journalists under them were well aware of the necessity for putting up with outside restrictions. What is more, this awareness was one of the strong bonds between them.

On the other hand the social and professional aspirations of the newspapermen were not restricted to any great extent by the relationships within the staff itself. It rarely happened that a journalist was held back in his professional ambitions by pressure from above or by the general atmosphere in the office. What is more, it would be true to say that both these factors – that is, the attitude of the editors and the atmosphere among colleagues – tended rather to provide inspiration, to arouse ambition, and to condemn the easy way out. In this respect the situation here was quite the opposite of that found on the American papers investigated by W. Breed, where the atmosphere in the office clearly discouraged the newspapermen from taking an interest in wider affairs, and encouraged them to pursue success in the narrow field of sensational or local news.[9]

It should be added that the staff of the papers in our survey did not complain to any great extent of their ambitions being frustrated by authoritarianism on the part of the editors, or by the unjust favouritism of one group over another, or by the low professional, intellectual or moral level of other members of the staff (and the editors in particular), or by bad human relations in the office. Complaints were, of course, sometimes made, but much less frequently than are met with among the staff of many other Polish or foreign papers.

Adaptation to external conditions

The fact that, as we have said before, the newspapermen in our survey have close links with other socio-occupational milieux, undoubtedly makes it easier for them to keep well informed of readers' tastes and of the best way to influence them. All four papers in our survey clearly cater for the educated classes. Since both writers and readers belong mostly to the intelligentsia, there is no difficulty in finding a common language. The occupational motivation of the newspapermen is based firmly on the wish to maintain the level of their paper and to keep raising it. They are usually sensitive to public opinion, which reaches them easily, especially through social contacts. Clearly they are anxious not to lose the confidence of their readers, but, on the contrary, to increase that confidence by taking up topics of special importance to the wider public.

As an important medium of mass communication, the paper, and in particular the daily paper, must fulfil a whole series of requirements of a political nature. Some of these matters are of a delicate nature. For instance, the paper is expected to show certain problems in a certain light, or to fulfil tasks of particular importance to the authorities. The editors, and especially the editor-in-chief, have the difficult task with regard to the staff, of passing on the authorities' suggestions, and of inducing the staff to follow the line postulated by the authorities. On the other hand, the editor-in-chief represents the staff in contacts with the authorities, and is the mouthpiece of their wishes. In both cases he must act as a cushion for the shocks that are inevitable in every change in the staff or in the profile of the paper, etc., changes which at the same time often have a very strong impact on the mood and professional morale of those writers who take their work seriously.

In all the papers in our survey, the editor-in-chief keeps his finger on the pulse of the situation in his contacts with the government and Party authorities. This usually takes up a great deal of his time. Since he has many duties outside the office, he is sometimes unable to act effectively as head of the paper, and be readily available to members of his staff who want his advice or decision. This is not very good for the paper, but on the other hand it is very important that the editor-in-chief makes a good job of his role as linkman with the authorities, as the entire staff knows well enough.

Internal cohesion

The standard of the paper depends on the talents and enthusiasm of its editorial staff. Hence the atmosphere of the office must be such as to promote the individual and collective initiative of the staff. In all the offices investigated in our survey, both the editors and the more humble employees alike are jointly interested in keeping up the level of the paper. This creates a bond of understanding between them, and does a great deal to maintain the friendly atmosphere among the staff. The editor usually gives his staff a great deal of freedom. He imposes only the minimum restrictions, and avoids bureaucratic methods entirely. 'You have to trust people,' remarked the editor of one of these papers. 'Let them assume full responsibility for their own work. . . . In running this paper I have learned the value of tolerance. I know that we have to do with a very sensitive organism.'

Emphasis is placed on careful selection of staff and on the encouragement of strong job motivation. As a rule there are few changes of staff. It is a great honour for a newspaperman to get into the staff of any of these papers. Nearly three-quarters of the newspapermen have been working for the same paper for more than 5 years. These are men with experience in their job. Nearly two-thirds have been working in this occupation for more than 10 years, and over 90% have been working as newspapermen for more than 5 years, but only 20% are aged 45 or over. One-quarter are women, this proportion being the same as the national average in this occupation. Four-fifths belong to the intelligentsia by background. As far as earnings are concerned, newspapermen exceed the national monthly average (3,175 zlotys, according to a 1960 survey), but there is a considerable difference between the élite, such as the journalists and editors, and the rest of the staff. Approximately three-fifths of the élite and about two-fifths of the rest have an income which provides over 2,000 zlotys per person in the family. More than two-fifths of the first group and only one-fifth of the second group assessed their own financial situation as better than average.

There is a very friendly atmosphere, although distance is respected between the principal journalists and the rest of the staff. The editors usually enjoy considerable authority among their staff, owing to the fact that they themselves are writers. In this study, we compared three different kinds of authority accorded by the whole staff to the editors: professional authority (as journalists), administrative authority (as bosses), and personal authority (as colleagues). In the majority of cases these various kinds of authority coincided (this is an important index of the functional value of the editors), which undoubtedly makes for stability of relationships on the paper's staff.

As a rule the formal organization of the office is simple, loose, and fairly elastic. Sometimes the various sections are not even clearly demarcated. The same can be said about the demarcation of responsibility. The organization is very pliable and the editor changes it as he goes along, as he thinks fit. This is possible because there is a distinctly crystallized informal organization in the office, welding people together and bringing order to the human relationships. This organization is obvious on all levels of the staff of these papers, but especially at the top, on the editorial level.

On these papers the editors have been a well-knit team for years back. They are not only colleagues during office hours but friends as well. In the case of the two weeklies, for example, the people at the top form a solid group. In both cases the editor-in-chief leaves the day-to-day running of the paper to his deputy and to the Editorial Secretary. He is a personal friend of both men. These three people are at the helm of the paper. Between the three the responsibilities are fairly clearly delineated.

As has been said above, the dominating group on these papers is comprised of the journalists (feature writers), who have been closely linked with each other for years. They come nearest to the editors, with whom they are closely connected both professionally and socially. Other categories of the staff (such as the people who work in the city section or the telegraphists working on the daily paper) form their own groups. These, however, are of much less significance. The correctors and office staff who are not journalists are really outsiders, although as a rule they are on polite terms with the newspapermen. The fact that people have worked together on one paper for a long time brings them closer together. But between the writers and the non-writers, between the famous names and the anonymous employees unknown to the general public, between the editors and the common or garden run of employee, the fundamental barriers remain.

It is worth stressing that the members of staff are very loyal to each other and ready to help. There is a marked feeling of solidarity between those who meet every day in the office. Help is always at hand for anyone in need, and in many cases there is a considerable amount of social life between members of the staff.

Internal control

For the good of the office, life there has to be regulated in some way. When the paper is due to come out, everything must run smoothly. Order of at least an elementary kind is imperative. Once a certain level has been achieved, it must be kept up, both as regards the quality of the paper and the quality of the human relations on the staff itself and with the world outside. Finally, the paper's reputation outside has to be maintained. It is much easier to achieve this when a specific sub-culture begins to emerge, that is, when the employees unhesitatingly accept rules of behaviour that safeguard the staff as a whole.

In the case of the papers in our survey, this kind of subculture is rather well developed. Even although there are no distinct prohibitions or punishments, or even formal organization in certain cases (hence the view sometimes encountered that confusion reigns in newspaper offices), the work of both individuals and groups goes ahead quite efficiently. There are no particular troubles, and people are relatively disciplined and happy.

On all the surveyed papers, there is division of responsibility. One person (the technical editor) looks after the everyday run of the work. Someone else looks after the financial side. One person is valued as a constant source of new ideas. Another is regarded by the others as an authority on moral questions, and his opinion is sought whenever there is a dispute. One person is known to be always ready to organize help in time of need. Another acts as the paper's conscience, and openly expresses opinions even if they are extremely displeasing to the authorities above. All these people are necessary if the social system on the paper is to function properly. They are all needed, since they help to lower tensions which might otherwise threaten the cohesion of the staff, and poison the atmosphere in the office.

The art of managing the staff of a paper largely boils down to co-ordinating the various social mechanisms that allow the system to function, manipulating them for the common good, and preventing conflict between the various elements of the system.

As far as the papers in our survey were concerned, it was obvious that the praxeological principle of minimum intervention was being applied: 'Meddle as little as possible with the course of events, achieve your ends by interfering as little as possible, and wherever possible without your own intervention.'[10] This principle is of particular significance when one is dealing with highly qualified people who know their jobs and each other. The confidence shown by a superior in his subordinates in such a case encourages the team still more to show collective initiative, and frees the man in charge from having to keep pushing, urging, and controlling. In such circumstances the team effectively controls itself, and itself produces creative energy to push it along.

The authority of the general editors is recognized and respected, since everyone realizes that the paper must appear, and it must be on a satisfactory level. As regards especially the technical editors, they are expected not so much to show tact as to show they really know their job, which is the best guarantee that the material prepared for the press is reliable and to be trusted.

The freedom found on the papers, in our survey, and the accompanying elasticity or organizational structure, are particularly conducive to the creative spirit, since they eliminate restrictions on it. At the same time the minimum of order is maintained to ensure that the work of the team goes on.

Newspapermen's evaluation of their job and of the paper's staff

In this study considerable weight was attached to finding out how the staff of the paper regarded their job and its institutional framework. The newspapermen were asked about the attractions and drawbacks of their job, and the following hierarchy of positive and negative traits was obtained (these traits are given in order of the frequency with which they were given first place):

attractions
of the job:

51%	(1) attractive in itself because it offers the opportunity for wide contacts and for seeing life,
24%	(2) it gives a large degree of personal freedom, much more than do other office occupations (with which the newspaperman often compares his own),
25%	(3) it gives the opportunity to do something useful for the community.

100%

drawbacks
of the job:

34%	(1) it is nerve-wracking, exhausting work involving constant tension,
20%	(2) neither the authorities nor the public really understand the character of newspaper work and its problems,
17%	(3) it is poorly paid compared with the effort and qualifications required,

14%	(4) it is marked by professional dilettantism as compared with the more specialized professions,
11%	(5) it achieves little effect,
4%	(6) it has no drawbacks.

100%

Of course in the newspaper world the various categories of employees assess their own occupational situation differently. The journalists have much more cause for satisfaction than the telegraphists, for example, some of whom treat this as a temporary stage, as an unpleasant but necessary stepping-stone to something better on the professional ladder. But even among the journalists, two-fifths said they had insufficient opportunities for creative expression, while more than two-thirds were dissatisfied with themselves (evidence of their tendency towards self-criticism). There is a general feeling of insecurity. This insecurity is heightened by insufficient specialist, professional training (hence a certain amount of jealousy with regard to, e.g., physicians and engineers), and by exaggerated ideas of respondents that the occupation of newspapermen enjoys low prestige among the public.[11]

The newspapermen have fairly high social and professional aspirations, and their job does not in itself offer them a field where they can find sufficient stability, where they can feel completely secure and enjoy the satisfaction of some permanent achievement. As with the actor, the newspaperman must always assert his position anew, by producing new effects which are very soon forgotten. Even the most effective article has a short life especially an article published in a daily. Consequently the more ambitious journalist often tries to publish a book. This, however, calls for quite a different approach – first and foremost concentration on a single subject, which is difficult for a man who is used to jumping from one subject to another. At any rate, the social model of the literary man is an attractive one, and one that is not too difficult for the newspaperman to achieve, as compared with the alternative roles of professor, politician, or social worker.

The newspaperman's very type of job compels him to write often, and on topics which are sometimes rather far apart from each other. The pressman is sometimes forced by the needs of the moment to choose certain topics and even to treat them in a certain way. Haste and the urgency of the moment do not always, of course, go hand in hand with maturity of knowledge. Neither do they have a good effect on the newspaperman's morale.

It is striking that among the newspapermen and especially among the journalists there was fairly considerable criticism of their own occupational group. Asked to mention the principal traits of newspapermen, the journalists mentioned negative traits above all: superficiality (one-third of the replies), conceit (a sixth of the replies), cynicism and opportunism (an eighth of the replies). On the other hand positive traits such as mental agility, sensitivity, and wide horizons were mentioned, it is true, but came further down the scale (all these positive traits taken together were mentioned in only a little more than a third of the replies). It is worth adding that the newspapermen took a rather pessimistic view of the prestige of their occupation both in the eyes of the public and in the eyes of the authorities.

This self-criticism should be interpreted in terms of the disproportion between the newspapermen's aspirations and their actual social and occupational situation. The élite of the newspaper staffs (the editors and journalists) think the essence of their job is above all to inform readers and to intervene in the public interest (28% of the replies to each of these points, making altogether 56%), and only to a lesser extent to form public opinion (26%) or to act as a link between the authorities and the public (10%). According to the journalists in our survey (100%), the traits desirable in journalists are: honesty and personal integrity (as many as 36% of the replies), a well-stocked mind and wideness of horizons (23%), and only further down the scale agility of mind, talent and professional skill, easy rapport with people and commitment on public issues (which altogether accounted for the remaining 41% of the replies).

According to the élite of the newspaper staff, external difficulties are responsible for the difficulty of achieving these ideals. When asked (100%) about conditions necessary for the exercise of the occupation of newspaperman *lege artis*, three-quarters of the replies mentioned external conditions: satisfactory working conditions and pay[12] (29%), freedom of expression (25%), good treatment by the authorities (8%), good atmosphere in the office (7%), public respect and understanding of the character of the job (5%); whereas only a quarter of the replies mentioned the intellectual level (17%) and moral level (9%) of the newspapermen themselves.

Conclusions

1. In his job the newspaperman is continually under stress of various kinds. He is subject to changes of mood. Sometimes he feels the lack of having someone on whose decision he can rely. Other people's opinions of his work are only relative, and besides not always convincing either to him or to others. The effects he achieves in his work are ephemeral. It is not surprising therefore, that the newspaperman's moods sometimes change from one extreme to another: from nonchalance that is irritating to the environment, to complete discouragement. This fluctuation of mood is very characteristic of the newspaper staff. Periods of great enthusiasm alternate with periods of apathy.

2. In these circumstances, a pleasant atmosphere among the staff, inspired by the tactful behaviour of the editors, is a matter of particular importance. The friendly atmosphere in the office is an effective antidote to moods of depression. The understanding and help of the people in the immediate environment (other people on the staff) neutralize the stresses caused by the very character of the job, and more or less successfully help to restore the nervous balance.

3. The confidence felt by the staff in the assessment of their work by their superiors, who enjoy all-round authority (professional, administrative, and personal), facilitates self-analysis and helps people to take a balanced view of their own achievements and shortcomings in their work. When a person is aware that what he says and does can have an effect on the situation in the office, this awareness helps him to find a firm foothold both on the paper and in this occupation as a whole. Freedom in the office encourages people to take an active attitude towards their work and to attach appropriate weight to its ethical side. This of course all has a great impact on the results of both the individual and the team.

4. There is fairly marked functional equilibrium in the social systems represented by the staffs of the four papers investigated here. This goes along with the fact that these papers are on a high level and that the newspapermen are on the whole satisfied with their present job. This is by no means typical of all Polish papers. It should be remembered that the papers in our survey were specially selected as being attractive, quality papers, the aim being to find out what was specific about their

social systems, and what probably affects the quality of the paper and the working atmosphere.

5. In all four cases it was found that relationships on the staff were very democratic, although at the same time the editors saw to it that all the principal functional mechanisms were working properly.[13] On the whole the newspapermen are given a free hand in their work, while at the same time efforts are made to see that the elementary functional needs of the social system are met in a regular and satisfactory manner.

6. Since as far as the press in the socialist countries is concerned the functional need for harmonious contact with the authorities is of fundamental importance, the editor-in-chief focuses his main effort on the role of intermediary between the paper and the authorities. Naturally this could be a drawback to the paper if the editor-in-chief was authoritative and anxious to make all the decisions alone, and if, being absorbed in his outside contacts, he had no time for matters within the paper itself and no understandings of these matters. In the case of the papers in our investigation, the editors-in-chief willingly and successfully delegate part of their responsibility to teams, and entrust their colleagues with their confidence, with the result that the danger referred to above is avoided.

7. It would be useful to make a comparative study of the staffs of papers in different countries with different social and political systems. If this were done, it would be advisable to use, as here, the method of structural-functional analysis. For the Polish case seems to show that, in contrast to some other countries, Polish newspapermen traditionally belong to the élite of the intelligentsia in their country and that, in their own eyes and especially in the eyes of wider circles of the intelligentsia, this imposes on them the duty of taking an active, creative attitude towards what they do. This gives rise to high ambitions, but at the same time leads to frustration, since they find it impossible to fulfil their plans as they would like.

8. This disproportion between growing aspirations and limited possibilities is noticeable in the social and occupational system of a newspaper office. It is all the more significant, then, whether and how far this dialectical friction of psycho-social opposites takes place within the framework of a social microsystem that is elastic enough and efficient enough to produce not frustration but socially useful creative energy.[14]

4. Journalism Recruitment and Training: Problems in Professionalization*

Oliver Boyd-Barrett

Two post-war Royal Commissions, which were established primarily to examine the finances of the British press, have made recommendations favouring in at least certain respects a degree of professionalization in journalism.[1] Both the Press Council, set up to exercise general surveillance over press affairs, and the National Council for the Training of Journalists, with which we will be largely concerned in this paper, are limited to those recommendations.

Control over the entry of new recruits to an occupation, and provision of formal training for them, are measures frequently recognized in the relevant literature as professional characteristics or as procedures associated with professionalization, though they are not sufficient ingredients of either.[2]

It can be argued that journalism as it exists does not constitute a profession, and that its structure does not allow for appreciable advance in professionalization.

Ernest Greenwood, for example, defines an occupation as a profession according to its possession or otherwise of five major attributes: (i) a systematic body of theory, (ii) professional authority, (iii) community sanction, (iv) ethical codes and (v) a professional culture.[3]

Applying this framework to journalism we find that these five attributes are either non-existent or exist only to a very limited degree. Thus, there is no system of abstract propositions to which new recruits are exposed and without which they cannot practise. This is in despite of the fact that in American schools of journalism for instance, great stress is placed on related fields such as mass communications

* Not previously published.

theory. Goode, in his discussion on librarians in a similar context, makes the following observation:

> While the general knowledge embodied in professional library curriculums is likely to be communications theory, the sociology or psychology of mass communications, or the psychology of learning as it applies to reading, most day-to-day professional work utilizes rather concrete, rule-of-thumb, local regulations and rules, and a major cataloguing system. The problems of selection and organization are dealt with on a highly empiricist basis, concretely, with little reference to general scientific principles. Moreover, little if any of the current research in librarianship attempts to develop general principles.[4]

Without such a systematic body of theory, the absolute necessity for a lengthy advanced period of training before practice, and the status concomitant with such training, is called into question.

Secondly, journalists do not maintain professional-client relationships in which the client is subordinate to the professional's monopoly of functionally specific knowledge and protected by professional norms of restraint. To a varying extent the service provided by journalists is tailored according to public demand, and this service is much more closely associated with commercial objectives than is usually the case, for example, in librarianship. Thirdly, the occupation has no power by law to license members or to confer a professional title. Fourthly, there is no single, universal, binding code of ethics. And, finally, there is little evidence of a formal professional culture characterized by institutional settings and professional meetings which stress rationality.

There are elements of these professional attributes in the occupation. Though there is no such principle as professional secrecy known to British Law, for example, there is a case for arguing that journalists in Britain are at least accorded a semi-professional status in this respect and with regard to protection of news-sources, but this is a status underlined more by a spectacular denial of it, as in the Vassall Tribunal, than by formal confirmation.[5]

The Press Council may be regarded as a source of normative regulation. Its deliberations are not, however, binding. Newspapers have voluntarily undertaken to publish Council judgments and few have failed to publish judgments that have gone against them. It may be argued that the Council has had a beneficial impact on journalism practice – in reducing the causes for complaint in cases of forced entry into private homes by reporters, for instance – but it is just as possible that such a reduction would have occurred in the absence of a Press Council, in response to reader reaction. A survey of over 200 specialist newsgathering journalists on national media[6] reveals that few journalists at this level are conscious of any major impact the Press Council may have had. 56% believed that the Council had 'no impact' on their field, 35% thought it had a 'little beneficial impact' and only 6% a 'very beneficial impact'. Crime correspondents were the only group to express general enthusiasm for it, probably because the type of judgments made by the Council concerning newsgathering behaviour are mainly relevant to a few fields only, of which crime is one. It is possible of course that over time the Council will construct a sound body of precedent which could form the basis of a future code of ethics, although the official history of the Council does not give this impression.[7] It is likely that the type of complaint that reaches the Council touches only on relatively superficial (visible to the public) or flagrantly deviant practices. We should note, however, that Millerson[8] in his comprehensive examination of the literature on professions and professionalization, argues that the presence or absence of a code of professional conduct does not signify professional or non-professional status, but rather that the need for a code depends upon the professional situation. As the Dutch Provos said of democracy, professionalism is as much related to feeling as it is to rules and regulations.[9]

British journalism does, finally, have a professional association of its own – the Institute of Journalists. This is a non-qualifying association concerned with standards of practice and status of practitioners, but with a very low rate of 'completeness' (about 2,000 members out of an approximate possible total of 20,000), whose membership is not representative of the occupation generally. In 1966 a 'trial marriage' took place between the Institute and the National Union of Journalists (NUJ) with a view to an eventual merger. The NUJ enjoys high 'completeness' (approximately 19,000 members in 1966), and ranks higher on Blackburn's 'unionateness' scale (which assesses the degree to which an organization is wholeheartedly a trade union, identifying with the labour movement and willing to use all the powers of the movement), than many white-collar trade unions. Blackburn's hypothesis that completeness varies inversely with unionateness would nevertheless hold true for journalism, which as we shall see, embraces many different types of organization and practitioner.[10] It remains the case that journalists have been traditionally easier to organize around 'class' issues of pay and work conditions, than around 'status' issues of professional control.[11]

The present issue is not so much whether journalism is or is not a profession as whether journalism is or is not susceptible to professionalization along any dimension. That it is, the above considerations would indicate, but whether professionalization is likely to advance further than this slight level remains the theme under discussion. Millerson, who argues in favour of the 'continuum' approach to professions, has defined a profession as a type of 'higher-grade, non-manual occupation, with both subjectively and objectively recognized occupational status, possessing a well-defined area of study or concern and providing a definite service, after advanced training and education'.[12]

Focusing on just one aspect of this definition at the moment, it follows that it is necessary for practitioners to experience the need for professionalization – to be concerned with its furtherance – and that the public should recognize this objective as legitimate.[13] Interview data with specialist newsgathering journalists attached to national media organizations, whose internal occupational status is high, reveal a lack of concern on their part for the issue of professionalization, or a belief that professionalization is impossible in an occupation so segmented and disorganized. This would indicate therefore an absence of subjective identification with professionalism amongst at least one major category of newsgathering journalist.[14]

It might be argued on the other hand that the existence of the National Council for the Training of Journalists (NCTJ), specifically concerned as it is with raising standards of practice through formal training and socialization, is likely to provide the conditions wherein subjective identification with professionalism can grow. Millerson has outlined certain factors which contribute to success in the process towards professionalization, which the NCTJ to a limited extent at least would seem to fulfil: (i) an ability to achieve a definable basis of background knowledge and practice, plus a crystallization of the activities composing the occupational task, (ii) opportunity to acquire knowledge and practice, (iii) development of self-consciousness by emerging professionals, and (iv) realization and recognition of the occupation as a profession by those outside the occupation.[15]

Outside recognition may be both cause of the preceding factors and a result of them. With regard to journalism it is not so much outside recognition which exists as a pressure on the occupation to professionalize, a desire on the part of various critics of the communications industry, Royal Commissioners included, that journalism should become a profession, articulated in recommendations that journalists should act and be seen to act 'responsibly'. These critics fear what they believe to be the possible misuse of the assumed power which journalists can exercise over public opinion, beliefs, attitudes and behaviour. They seek reassurance that such power is used democratically, in accordance with values highly rated by society, namely, objectivity and social responsibility, and by people adequately qualified to do so. Part of the disturbance felt by critics in this connection may plausibly arise from the discrepancy between the power attributed to communicators by society and the relatively low or ambiguous status which the majority of such communicators possess. Whether or not the term 'professionalization' is used, there appears to be a widespread opinion that the rules of operation governing the behaviour of communicators should be visible and should be characterized by the deeply-engraved norms of public service common to the traditional professions.

The National Council for the Training of Journalists

The survey upon which this study is based took place shortly before signs of structural reconsideration with regard to the position of the NCTJ occurred. The following account refers to the structure of the NCTJ as it operated in 1969. The limitations of this structure in relation to training objectives and professionalization and the value conflicts they represent and which are discussed below, were in part responsible for the reconsideration. Although the consequences of any reassessment cannot yet be predicted, the nature of the problems involved is unlikely to change for some considerable time.

The NCTJ has been operating in its present form since 1955. It is dependent for financial support upon the newspaper industry (and, now, indirectly, upon the Industrial Training Board), in particular upon the provincial newspaper industry. It organizes a wide variety of courses, some of them for highly experienced journalists. But its most important function is the provision of formal training for young journalists with only one or two years' experience, and more recently, for totally inexperienced recruits. This function was initially performed through day or weekend release systems, but since 1965 most of these have been substituted by lengthier 'block-release' courses. These are run from six centres, five of them Colleges of Technology, one of them a Polytechnic, by NCTJ approved lecturers who are all ex-journalists and some of whom do occasional journalistic work during vacations. Most of these courses are geared towards training in reporting or newsgathering, with very little emphasis given at this level to sub-editing. One centre specializes in training for newspaper photographers. Trainees on block-release courses are all attached to provincial or non-national newspapers. Under a recent agreement between the NUJ and the Newspaper Proprietors' Association (representing national newspapers), no national newspaper may now recruit staff who have not had three years' experience on non-national publications (two years for graduates), although exceptions are allowed for in certain fields of newsgathering.

A new recruit to a non-national newspaper works a probationary period of six months, after satisfactory completion of which he is indentured to that newspaper for three years (two years in the case of graduates). During that time, if he was recruited before the age of 24, he is required to take NCTJ courses – usually block-release courses on which he spends a period of two months in each of two years of his indentures. At the end of his final year of indentures he is encouraged to sit the Proficiency Certificate Test. Although possession of the Certificate entitles its holder to a higher salary, it can in no way be regarded as equivalent to the qualifying examinations of the established professions. The Certificate is not a necessary preliminary to fully-statused employment, nor is it given attention by all employers, least of all the national press.

In addition to the block release courses, the NCTJ has established one full-year course for students who have not, usually, had any experience at all in journalism. Some of these are sponsored largely by Local Authority public grants, and many are selected by the NCTJ rather than by individual newspaper editors as is normally the case. There are, finally, special block release courses for graduate entrants.

Information was collected by self-completed questionnaires in March, 1969, from 99 trainee journalists, representing a response rate of 73%, from the two largest training centres, Harlow Technical College, which is 20 miles north of London, and Sheffield Polytechnic in the centre of the major Lancashire-Yorkshire industrial concentration of the North of England. Thirty-four of the respondents were attending the one-year course for pre-entry trainees at Harlow. Twenty-nine were on first-year block-release courses, and 36 on second-year block-release courses. In addition to questionnaire data, further information was gathered by interview from the lecturers in charge of these courses, and informally, from trainees on a graduate block-release course at Sheffield in 1968.[16]

Over three-quarters of the sample were aged between 18 and 20 inclusively. There were exactly twice as many men as there were women, though amongst the pre-entries there were almost as many women as there were men. Well over half the students came from lower-middle and upper-middle white-collar backgrounds (Social Classes II and IIIi in the Registrar General's classification), and nine came from senior executive/managerial/professional backgrounds (Social Class I). 65% had completed schooling at age 17 or over. Over three-quarters had at least four 'O' levels, and over half had at least one 'A' level qualification. 45% had two or more 'A' levels (two 'A' levels also being the minimum university entrance qualification). Figures for the total intake into the training scheme in 1968 show that 17% had fewer than five 'O' levels, 33% had five or more 'O' levels, 35% had one or more 'A' levels and 15% were graduates.

Consequences of dependence

Millerson has argued that an occupation need not be organized in order to be professional.[17] Nevertheless, lack of organization in an occupation can create considerable difficulties in the professionalization process, as Reader has shown in his study of professionalization in nineteenth-century Britain.[18] This is particularly so in the case of journalism.

There are three considerations here: the looseness of the term 'journalism', the distribution of journalists geographically, and the unsystematic procedure of initial selection of new recruits.

Carr-Saunders and Wilson have pointed out that the scope of journalistic activities is so wide as to preclude, as they saw it, a common connecting link upon which training can be meaningfully based:

It has often proved difficult to describe the whole range of activities falling within the scope of a profession; more often than not they are many and various. But a connecting link can usually be found between them because it appears on analysis that these activities take the form of applying a particular technique in different spheres of practice. This cannot be said of journalists. They are employed in reporting, writing-up, interviewing, sub-editing, and though these are not jobs which any one can do without a considerable amount of experience, no specialized intellectual training is an indispensable preliminary.[19]

Ignoring the last point for the moment, it is apparent that journalism covers a wide range of activities which can be performed in an equally wide range of organizations: small provincial weekly newspapers, trade journals, specialist magazines, promotional publications, national newspapers, radio and television stations, etc. Although its objective is to embrace all recruits to editorial journalism, the NCTJ has focused particularly upon provincial newspapers in its training programme, largely because these have been the most cooperative. In doing so it has tapped the major staff recruiting ground of the national press which has traditionally depended upon the flow of experienced non-national journalists to London. But this still leaves open some important channels of entry: magazine entry for example, or the 'élite' channel by which some graduates enter straight into national newspaper journalism. Official NUJ figures for the period 1967–8 reveal a discrepancy between NUJ and NCTJ registrations of the order of 20%, indicating that this proportion of the total intake into the occupation evaded NCTJ training. In fact the proportion is probably somewhat lower than this due to certain inadequacies of the data and job definitions, but is nevertheless sizeable.

The national distribution of journalists also creates certain problems: the majority of Britain's 20,000 journalists work outside of London; only 3,000 work on national newspapers. This has made it impossible to combine a centralized recruiting scheme with the occupational preference for on-the-job training, and has necessitated regional distribution of training facilities.

Both these factors of distribution and disorganization have helped maintain the unsystematic process of initial selection which is still in operation. Although certain newspaper groups have from time to time[20] adopted their own recruitment system there has never been a standardized, unambiguous entry pattern for the entire occupation. The NCTJ has made an attempt to standardize formal training, which before had almost been non-existent, but its power over initial selection of candidates is limited. Because it is dependent upon the goodwill of newspaper editors and in particular of provincial newspaper editors (or proprietors, or group representatives), who are responsible for sponsoring their junior staff on NCTJ courses, the NCTJ has not attempted to wrest control over initial selection from them. This is a power jealously guarded by editors who, perhaps with some justification, believe they are the only people competent to decide what quality of candidate best meets the peculiar exigencies of their own organizations. And it has not been without some effort that the NCTJ has managed to persuade editors that formal training is beneficial. Its success in this respect is largely if not totally due to the fact that NCTJ training has become a condition of employment endorsed by the NUJ in negotiation with proprietors. As in the case of the Press Council, though not to the same extent, it should be remembered that the initial impetus for a standardized training scheme covering the whole industry came from outside the occupation itself.

Without systematic control over initial entry there can be no standardized criteria on which to base acceptance of candidates or even, as we shall see, to decide what constitutes 'merit'. It may be argued, and is argued by some editors, that the suitability of any candidate can be determined by the quality of his work after a given period of experience. But this is not true of journalism generally. Not only will individual editors differ in their expectations and requirements, but there is also tremendous possible variation both between different types of editorial organization and between different tasks within each organization. Given the absence of a formal career structure in journalism and the high rate of mobility between organizations and tasks by journalists, this is obviously an important consideration in the context of recruitment. It implies, in turn, that even with centralized and standardized recruitment and training by a body independent of individual employers, the common denominator of journalistic skills and qualifications to be taken into account is not likely to cover much ground.

The survey data show that of those employed by newspapers well over half the trainees (62%) obtained their first job by writing letters on their own initiative to one or several newspapers. A further quarter

(25%) answered job advertisements in the press. Whether or not a student found his first job with ease or with difficulty was usually dependent upon the number of newspapers or advertisements written or replied to, and the reception of an ultimately successful interview offer. These trainees generally sought work in the locality or region of their home. The likelihood of their finding a job was therefore partly dependent on the number of vacancies or even of newspapers in the area, rather than on their own merit alone. Thus, this system not only fails to ensure that the best applicants are selected, but also fails to ensure equitable distribution of candidates to those areas where there are vacancies.

The onus of entry is placed very much on the shoulders of the applicant – he must declare himself in face of the lack of systematic channels for such declaration, and the general absence of all publicity. Many practising journalists and editors regard this lack of system as an advantage. They believe that only a would-be entrant who really desires to be a journalist, and who can meet the requirements of the work will persevere in spite of the lack of system. Yet there is no evidence to show that this procedure does in fact select the most suitable candidates. High motivation does not necessarily correlate with high ability, and neither high motivation nor high ability necessarily reveal themselves before initial selection.

In a system in which the personal idiosyncrasies of individual newspaper editors might be expected to play a large part, the likelihood of entry through informal networks is greater than in a more impersonal system. The evidence here is indirect, but only 8% of the survey trainees reported a close family relationship with a journalist, whilst a quarter of the sample reported being significantly influenced by a personal contact in their decision to enter journalism. In not more than 15% of cases the influential person was a 'friend of the family', usually involved in newspapers, or a close relative, usually a journalist. The lowest proportion in any of the groups in the survey (8%) to report such an influential person is found amongst the pre-entry trainees – who are mostly selected by the NCTJ. This and other less direct evidence suggests that pre-entry students are more likely to be influenced in favour of entry by impersonal criteria – through careers literature for example – than other groups.[21]

In addition it was found that the proportion of women amongst pre-entry students was much higher than amongst the other groups. This indicates again that where selection is by a body independent of any particular employing organizations, the criteria used are more likely to be freer from occupational prejudices and personal preferences. Newspaper editors tend to be cautious in their employment of women, and several female respondents reported that they were employed as a last resort in the absence of any suitable male applicants.[22]

Thus, by and large the NCTJ has no control over initial selection of entrants directly, but where it does then the opportunity for selection by merit alone appears to be greater. It should also be noted that NCTJ publicizes its pre-entry course, therefore giving some indication to prospective candidates how they might enter into the occupation. Whereas for other groups such publicity was rarely available. Impressionistic evidence also suggests that the general absence of publicity material discourages school careers masters from recommending journalism as a career to those who express interest in it, and may help maintain public misconceptions concerning the nature of the occupation.

The educational dilemma

The NCTJ can exercise some control over the level of educational qualifications possessed by new entrants. This it has done. By imposing minimal educational qualifications for acceptance on to their courses, they influence editors to recruit entrants with these qualifications within the sector of journalism in which the NCTJ has most authority. (There is evidence to indicate that a few editors still appoint juniors who have not got the minimal qualifications and who escape attention by failing to register with the NUJ, possibly with the collusion of the editors concerned.) These minimal qualifications have been upgraded over recent years and now stand at the 'five "O" level' stage, or 'two "A" level' stage for pre-entry students. Although this will lead in time to a general upgrading of average qualifications for the occupation generally, this upgrading is unlikely to be any greater than for comparable white-collar occupations, and may not necessarily be keeping pace with national trends.

The importance of initial selection rests on the fact that, as we have seen, the national newspapers have traditionally taken their editorial staff from non-national newspapers in and outside of London. If entrants to these smaller newspapers are recruited on the basis of their apparent suitability to those newspapers it may not follow that they will also be suitable for national newspaper work.

Despite the fact that the NCTJ has taken steps to upgrade the educational qualifications of trainees in recent years, its attitude towards further upgrading has been ambiguous. This is more evident informally than formally. Several lecturers in journalism stress the fact that provincial newspapers are very dependent on juniors for general reporting work. In 1967, figures for all weekly newspapers show that amongst editorial staff there were 1·37 seniors to every junior only, compared with a ratio of 2·36 to 1 for all staff of all newspapers. Almost 30% of the total labour force of journalists (NUJ members) are aged between 16 and 23. Of these, almost half are aged 20 years or under. In raising educational qualifications further, they feel, the NCTJ would be imposing increased salary costs on the provincial press. Additionally, more highly educated trainees might be less willing to accept the type of work expected of them on such newspapers. It could therefore become more difficult to find staff, which would also affect salary costs. Or alternatively, it would be more difficult to persuade more highly educated staff to accept the long period of indentures which now exists as a concession by the NCTJ to provincial newspapers to persuade them to sponsor juniors on NCTJ courses by assuring them of a minimum period of service on the part of these juniors. In the case of pre-entry students, for whom the minimal qualifications are two 'A' levels – the same minimum as for university entrance – difficulties have arisen from the fact that some of these students have been 'lost' to universities after starting the full-year course. Such loss, if it increases, will be viewed as financial wastage, to be avoided where possible.

The doubt expressed in this connection by lecturers, whose attitude reflects that of a great number of practising journalists, some of whom are not convinced of the need for formal educational qualifications at all, is enhanced with regard to employment of graduates. Although block-release courses are provided at some centres for graduate training, there is a certain amount of hostility shown by lecturers towards graduates, and by graduates towards the training they receive. Few of the lecturers are themselves graduates. They, in common with many journalists, tend to associate graduates with academics, and believe that few graduates make satisfactory employees, particularly on the provincial press, for whose needs the NCTJ mostly caters. But they are also hostile towards the 'élite' channel of entry which some graduates make into national newspaper journalism straight from university. This attitude is largely supported by the NUJ which wishes to equalize opportunities for success in the occupation by avoiding discrimination in favour of graduates, and is confirmed by recent arrangements designed to eliminate, partially at least, such a channel.

The number of graduates who enter journalism each year is uncertain, and estimates have varied from 6 to 15% of the total intake.[23] A substantial though uncertain proportion of these do not enter the NCTJ scheme. Graduates represented 15% of the total number of registrations with the NCTJ in 1968. The NCTJ, in recognizing the particular problems associated with graduate training, had planned for a one-year post-graduate and university-based course. This has met with considerable difficulties. The cost of such a scheme tends to be prohibitive, since it is difficult to persuade newspapers to sponsor trainees on a graduate one-year course when they are not convinced of the suitability of graduate employees on non-national publications. In addition to which the Industrial Training Board is unwilling to underwrite the expense of such a scheme. Even if these difficulties were overcome there remains the further problem which was pointed out by one highly placed NCTJ informant that the present NCTJ training staff did not appear to be adequately qualified to run a university-based course.

This problem is related to that of objective recognition of journalism as a profession, or rather, the absence of such a recognition. British universities are cautious, bar a few exceptions, in their attitude towards vocational training on academic campuses. They are not convinced that in the case of journalism such training is even necessary vocationally, a view also held by many journalists. This caution is not peculiar to the universities. One training centre established at a Polytechnic (the status of which ranks between that of a university and a college of technology) has been required to dissociate itself from the institution on the grounds that its training standards are insufficiently academic.

The grounds for this criticism become apparent on inspection of the content of NCTJ courses. The subjects include press law, local government, English, shorthand, and specific journalistic skills. We have seen that in the literature on professionalization, Millerson included,[24] great stress is placed on the idea of a systematic body of theoretical knowledge as the basis for advanced training and education. Both the NCTJ and most journalists concerned with the issue have always been hostile towards the introduction of non-vocational elements in training. Yet they have not until recently assessed the degree to which this policy might damage the status of the occupation, and hence its chances of outside recognition as a profession. Even though, as Goode has pointed out[25] education in related fields of knowledge such as mass communications theory does not of itself make the occupational practitioner a professional, it does appear to aid in the development of professional recognition from outside bodies. In America and in several European countries, journalism training enjoys university status, and though that status has been low in comparison with other disciplines, it appears to be increasing. R. L. Jones reports that in America there is evidence of journalism faculty members being invited on to other faculties.[26] A survey report shows that 30% of members of the Association for the Education of Journalists (roughly equivalent to the NCTJ in Britain) hold doctorate degrees. 84% possess Master degrees, and 92% have Bachelor degrees. This association produces a quarterly publication, *Journalism Quarterly*, devoted to research reports in communications, communications history, and teaching developments in the field.[27] Another survey reveals that 58% of American daily newspapermen are college graduates, about half of whom majored in Journalism and half in liberal arts subjects other than journalism.[28] Limited survey data in Britain, on the other hand, show that only 30% of specialist Fleet Street newsgatherers are graduates – and these represent the élite amongst British newsgatherers.[29] It was highly improbable that more than 10% of Britain's 20,000 journalists in 1968 were graduates.

In America the very fact that the AEJ ranks highly on several professional dimensions, and is recognized as a professional body, might be expected to affect the public's perception of the occupation generally. Data exist, however, which reveal a similarity of status ranking of newspaper reporters in a number of industrial societies, including Britain and the USA.[30] The meaningfulness of the data is not entirely clear. But in considering the process of professionalization, the significant trends would be most visible at the top of the occupational structure, which the term 'newspaper reporter' does not represent (it ranks relatively low in the white-collar options given to respondents). But if journalism generally – and we have seen that the concept is a loose one embracing many different internal levels of status – ranks lowly in America despite the relatively high educational level of journalists, then the future status of British journalists at a time when educational levels are rising rapidly may fall unless occupational educational levels keep pace or grow faster. This is not to say that education is the only factor to consider, but that it is one of the most important factors to consider in connection with professionalization.

Even though journalism cannot produce a body of theoretical knowledge that is pertinent to the actual practice of journalism, it can nevertheless be argued that whatever the case may be objectively, the fact that journalists must be well acquainted with many different fields of knowledge in the course of their work, and yet, in the majority of cases have had no general education at graduate level, could weaken the possibilities of public recognition of the occupation as a profession, or indeed, as an occupation of high status.[31] Under such circumstances it can come as no surprise that in cases of critical conflict between communicators and public bodies, the confidence expressed by the public in the competence of communicators is often very low.

Thus, the activities of the NCTJ in raising the status of the occupation, and thereby helping to professionalize it, are limited to the degree of its dependence for finance on current arrangements with the newspaper industry, and in particular on the provincial newspaper industry for whose needs the contents of training courses are primarily geared; as well as by the consensus of values held between journalism lecturers and newspaper editors concerning the advantages of graduate entry; and the attitude of academic institutions towards journalism training.

It should be noted, however, that the climate of opinion in the NCTJ and NUJ in late 1969 had begun to turn towards the possibility, in at least one instance, of blending journalism-training with a general sandwich course in communications at a Polytechnic. The initiative for this idea came from outside both bodies, and the favourable reaction it received from them was occasioned by the perceived consequences of the establishment of the Industrial Training Board. In their more general considerations for the future of journalism training the NUJ appeared to favour a gentle expansion of the block-release system to include a little non-vocational education, whilst the NCTJ was slightly more ambitious.

Subjective identification with professionalism

It might be argued that the NCTJ, in providing a common experience of journalism through training for new recruits, in organizing together the basic skills required of journalists, and in attempting to structure early career patterns, is likely to produce the conditions for subjective identification with professionalism on the part of new recruits.

The survey data give only little support for this point of view.

Respondents were asked to state in an open-ended fashion the reasons why they had chosen journalism as a career. The replies fell into six broad categories: (i) Journalism seen as a non-routine, non-conventional, sociable occupation and therefore attractive – accounting for 35% of the respondents; (ii) Journalism seen as the most desirable occupation available or possible for the respondent – 29%; (iii) Journalism seen as a creative occupation – 16% (additional evidence here shows that well over three-quarters of the sample wished to write a book, a third of whom claimed to be writing one already. The type of book which the great majority were interested in writing was fictional); (iv) Journalism seen as self-educational – 5%; (v) Journalism as a 'bridging occupation', offering good prospects – 3%;[32] (vi) Journalism seen as a public service occupation – 1%.

The almost negligible number of respondents who viewed the occupation in the light of 'service' does not augur well for the possibilities of professionalization. This is not to say that individual professionals need be altruistic, but that so few should mention service, or some related professional orientation in their reasons for choice of occupation is surprising and would not be expected of entrants to already established professions.[33]

The stress given by respondents to the unstructured, non-conventional nature of the occupation is indicative of their hostility towards any form of organization. Though organization is not necessarily related to professionalism it may be argued that a deep commitment to freedom from control, to maximization of individuality, would make the establishment of professionalism more difficult than in occupations in which such values did not rank so highly. And indeed, these values are as much occupational values of journalism as they are of individual journalists.[34] Further evidence of the strength of these values is indicated in replies given to a question asking which occupation respondents would have entered if for some reason they could not have entered journalism: the occupations mentioned largely include characteristics that are also salient in the respondents' perception of journalism – occupations specifically concerned with people, in which performance and communication are important.

The motivations which led respondents to choose journalism appear to have been met in their actual experience of the work involved. Those who actually experienced journalism as a non-routine, non-conventional, and sociable occupation, for instance, accounted for 58% of the respondents.[35] No mention was made of anything resembling satisfaction with the occupation for its 'service' functions. Occupational disadvantages mentioned by respondents were fewer and less vehemently stressed. Although there is insufficient space to document the evidence at length here, it appears that trainees tended to overestimate certain occupational characteristics in their assessment of it, downgrading certain disadvantages which did not fit with their initial expectations. Analysis of time consumption would indicate a greater degree of routine and conventionality than the expectations of respondents alone. On average, the most important single category of work in terms of time consumed in desk work (25% of work time), or office work. Well over a third of all respondents spend between a quarter and a half of their time in the office (excluding pre-entries), and a further quarter spend between half and three-quarters of their employment in the office. The second largest single category of work is that of 'diary reporting', which involves coverage of fairly routine, predictable events. This is followed by coverage of court proceedings, council affairs, annual general meetings, dinners and so forth. Such work is likely to become quickly familiar to most trainees, tedious sometimes, predictable often, a shorthand exercise always. Feature writing accounts for only 10% of total time. One in five respondents attached to newspapers were dissatisfied with opportunities for initiative. A third reported that less than a quarter of the stories they wrote were the result of personal initiative entirely. However, two-thirds reported that over three-quarters of all stories written for any single issue of their newspaper actually appeared in print. A fairly high proportion reported experience of a 'fair amount' or a 'great deal' of pressure from advertisers, which would contradict their motivations to escape commercial or business work.[36]

Nevertheless, over three-quarters of the total sample regarded journalism as their probable full-time career and would recommend journalism as a career to a younger relative.

This degree of satisfaction with their choice of career, at a stage of that career which for most of them would be the least attractive objectively, indicates that trainees felt little dissatisfaction with the organization of the occupation and its uncertainties. Where expectations were not met, it appears that they were postponed, incorporated into their expectations concerning future career possibilities. Respondents' preferences for future types of work-role within journalism tend to be those in which opportunity for self-expression and initiative are highest: feature writing, general reporting, specialist writing. Sub-editing and/or managerial work aspirations account for only 10% of respondents, despite the fact that sub-editing is generally a more effective channel to executive/managerial positions than writing, and is also, along with executive/managerial work itself, one of the more structured tasks of editorial journalism, allowing greater objective opportunity for organization of journalists involved with it. More detailed data show that a substantial proportion of respondents (about a quarter) were oriented towards those fields of journalism explicitly concerned with entertainment functions (i.e., those fields most likely to follow public demand, least likely to approach anything resembling a professional-client relationship vis-à-vis readership). In the reasons given for their future aspirations, 15% gave what might be interpreted as 'professional' interests, concerning their short-term future (desire to improve their general journalistic ability), but only 4% gave such responses for long-term interests. The majority of reasons given for short- and long-term interests were related to the idea of opportunity for initiative, freedom and self-expression generally. Journalistic ideology, it is appropriate to say in this connection, places great stress on that which is 'new', and tends to underestimate the possibility of valid precedents upon which future behaviour can be based.

Data were collected to help assess the extent to which trainees favoured the present recruitment system, the training they received, and how far they had been influenced by such training.

More respondents were in favour of improving the present system of recruitment than those who were not (47% as opposed to 38%). But whereas those who did not wish to improve the entry process were all predisposed towards a non-professional system, by no means all who wished it to be improved were in favour of a more professional system. The reasons given by a third of those in favour of improvement may be interpreted as a protest against professional tendencies in the system: they wished to see less emphasis on paper qualifications, greater support for the present initial selection patterns and so forth. The proportion of anti-professional respondents in this connection was in fact greater than the pro-professional group. The majority of respondents, however, were favourably disposed towards the NCTJ and its present operation (including both its professional and anti-professional elements). The data would suggest that training does not rank highly on the list of priorities of work-assessment in the minds of trainees.

Information was sought to indicate to what extent trainees' perception of the journalist's role in society might demonstrate professional attitudes. Respondents were asked what they thought the role of a journalist in society should be and what in fact it tended to be in practice. Over a third of the sample found no discrepancy between these, and a further one in five found only a mild discrepancy.

The most frequently mentioned and emphasized component of a journalist's role in society as it should be, was that of the informant, almost always qualified with the words 'unbiased', 'impartial', and 'accurate', 'precise'. The informant role was stressed by 57% of the sample, 14% of whom interpret it morally as well to include the obligation to 'awaken' or 'enlighten' the public to certain types of information. Over a quarter of all respondents mentioned the entertainment function of a journalist's work, and a fifth saw their task as informant partly in the light of the 'watchdog' or protective sense of mediating between individuals and social institutions. The idea of opinion-formation appears in the replies of a fifth of the respondents. Only four believed it to be a journalist's function to follow rather than lead public opinion in this connection. Most of the discrepancies perceived between the ideal and the actual roles were connected with defaults in the enactment of the informant role – biased news, sensationalism, and inaccuracies.

There appears then to be general perceived consensus around one particular component of the journalist's normative role, which may be regarded as a basis for professional theory. But in fact the emphasis upon the *informant* role indicates an understanding of the occupations' objectives primarily through application of technique, a technique concerning collection and presentation of data which does not require any abstract body of knowledge or developing theory.

Whether the ingredients of that technique also invite consensus and support is a different question. The NCTJ for example regards short-hand as an essential tool. Only 15% of the sample directly repudiated this belief by saying that for them shorthand was 'not very important'. About half of those who answered regarded it as 'fairly important', and only a third as 'absolutely essential'.

Respondents appear to agree with the NCTJ's attempts to standardize initial career structure. Well over two-thirds (79%) would recommend a younger relative to start in journalism in provincial newspapers: as many as 37% specify a weekly provincial newspaper, and a further 12% simply suggest the 'bottom'.

Attitudes towards education amongst trainees are roughly in accord with NCTJ policy. The vast majority of respondents would recommend a younger relative to leave school at the 'A' level stage, almost regardless of their personal school-leaving age. Attitudes towards university are ambiguous: half (48%) would recommend against it as a preliminary to journalism, and a third (30%) in its favour. Pre-entry students account for half of those in favour of university-entrance, perhaps because some of them have not rejected university as a possibility for themselves.

The evidence then provides no one clear answer to the question of whether the NCTJ is helping to establish subjective identification with professionalism. However the fact that most trainees are highly satisfied with the occupation as they find it indicates acceptance by them of prevailing journalistic ideology, which by and large is not favourable towards professionalization. Few trainees are happy with professional tendencies in the recruitment process, although they have no major complaints against training, probably because they do not regard it as a salient influence on their lives. On-the-job experience would be much more conducive towards acceptance of prevailing ideology than pre-entry training and pre-entries in general are more favourable towards professional tendencies. When asked explicitly to state their perception of the journalist's role in society, most respondents do give 'service' related answers, but the role itself is perceived in a largely technical sense.

Although the NCTJ fulfils some of the objective conditions for success in professionalization, its function in this respect is hindered by a relative lack of independence from employing organizations, an alien occupational ideology and non-standardized occupational structure, its own perception of its role and the perception of those outside the occupation, and certain possible consequences of self-selection amongst its trainee recruits. It is possible but uncertain that in a training system which gave more emphasis to pre-entry training, cultivation of professional subjective identification would be more effective.[37]

5. The Advertising Agency Man in New York*

Joseph Bensman

Economic and structural characteristics of the advertising agency

Advertising is a labour-intensive and capital-extensive industry. The advertising agency makes no great investments in capital goods. Its major capital investments are in typewriters, calculating machines (and in a few large agencies the rental of computers), duplicating equipment, and office furniture. The rental of office space is the major fixed cost of an agency. By and large, labour costs – primarily salaries – are the single largest item in agency costs. Labour costs on an average constitute 70% of the annual operating costs of an advertising agency.

Because of the absence of an elaborate machine technology and the corresponding presence of labour-intensity, advertising is properly called a service industry. Advertising men emphasize this service feature of the agency until the truth becomes a cliché. The composite cliché is as follows: 'All we have to offer our clients is a service – our skill, our knowledge, our brains, our talent, our know-how, and our judgment. All we create are ideas, plans, slogans, and arrangements of words, pictures, sounds, and symbols. To the extent that we execute these functions well, and only to the extent that our clients have need for these functions, are we entitled to the high fees, commissions, and salaries we earn.'

---

* This article consists of short extracts from a much longer piece, which was first published under the pseudonym of Ian Lewis in Peter L. Berger (editor) *The Human Shape of Work* (New York, Macmillan, 1964). The same full-length piece was subsequently published under the author's own name in: Joseph Bensman, 'The Advertising Man and his work, its organization, Ethics, and Meaning' in *Dollars and Sense* (New York, Macmillan, 1967), pp. 9–68.

If an agency can succeed in convincing a prospective client that these claims are true (and they are claims until proved or disproved by subsequent actions), the agency can make a powerful case. For American business has a continuous need for 'brains', ideas, judgment, wisdom, counsel, and know-how. It is by now a truism that most major brands of consumer goods are not distinguishable from one another to the consumer when he tests them by means of blind-product tests. If this is true, the tremendous differences in the sales success of various competitive brands are primarily due to differences in the marketing effectiveness of the competitive manufacturers, including advertising.

In a number of industries the marketing organizations of the manufacturers (the sales and distribution organizations, the financial reserves, the dealer-relations programmes, merchandising and sales promotion programme) are considered to be at a parity. However, some companies have made tremendous sales successes with the introduction of new brands and the revitalizing of declining brands, while the equally well-marketed competitive brands (aside from advertising) have suffered declines or only moderate gains in sales.

Thus slogans like 'Winston tastes good like a cigarette should', or 'Be sociable, have a Pepsi', have been worth hundreds of millions of dollars to their respective manufacturing companies.

However, since the advertising agencies' claim for their value to business is based on the intangibles of skill, talent, knowledge, know-how, and so on, and not on objective technological processes, the client can at any time reject the claim, especially since every advertising agency makes substantially the same claim in attempting to seduce accounts from other agencies.

While we have stressed the fact that the operating income of agencies is relatively small, the number of persons engaged in advertising is still smaller. The labour-intensity of advertising thus consists of a relatively small number of highly paid specialized technicians and managerial officials.

A large-sized but not gigantic agency with billings of approximately $100 million will have an operating income of $15 million. If we allow all costs but labour costs and profits not to exceed $3·5 million, then direct and indirect payments to personnel will amount to $11·5 million. Such an agency, if well run, may employ from six hundred to seven hundred people. The average agency income available for profits and payments to personnel is thus in the neighbourhood of $16,000 to

$18,000 per employee. Since at least 60 per cent of the employees of an advertising agency are relatively low-paid clerical, bookkeeping, and stenographic help, the average amount of money available for the professional, creative, and managerial staff is estimated at (depending upon whether the agency employs six hundred or seven hundred persons in total) from $27,000 to $34,000 per professional employee. Since many agencies are owned by their professional, creative, and managerial staffs, salaries, profits, and profit-sharing funds can at times be considered as part of the same pool.

Salaries, *per se*, cover only part of the perquisites of the advertising man. Profit-sharing plans allow the agency official to accumulate a retirement fund or a separation allowance that may result in a yearly deferred income of up to 20 per cent of his annual income, which when collected is taxable at capital-gains rates.

Stock options and increases in the value of stock in the agency (whose prices are artificially pegged by the company) provide additional capital gains. The opportunity to acquire stock, however, is more than a capital gain, a way of evading taxes when one moves up the income ladder. Stock acquisition is a genuine method of becoming wealthy, based on talent alone as the agency defines talent. Since the advertising agency is a capital-extensive and labour-intensive industry, the physical assets of an agency do not constitute a limit to stock acquisition. One does not 'water' the stock (physical assets) by issuing more stock (equity shares), since the physical assets are of little value in themselves. The issuance of stock to an individual simply means that his 'services' represent an important part of the service that the agency sells to its actual or prospective clients. Of course, if an individual makes known to his bosses his estimate of his own worth, they are more likely to calculate the value of that individual's services in terms of the total matrix of the agency's total income-earning services, and reward him accordingly.

All of this means that valued individuals can easily acquire stock, and can do so at a very young age. Stock acquisition is made easy by issuance of new low-price issues, by options, and by deferred-payment plans. The ease of stock acquisition means that in advertising, the American dream of rags-to-riches can be realized in a sufficient number of cases to serve as goad and pull to thousands of young men in advertising who may be on the make.

Becoming a millionaire is thus the major promise that the myth of advertising offers to the able. It is not the only promise. To those who know they will be moderately successful but will not become wealthy the opportunity to live as if one were rich is almost as seductive. This is done through 'fringe benefits'.

Advertising men are the customers of the media representatives (television and radio networks and stations, newspapers, magazines, and outdoor advertising), of television and commercials production companies, of graphic-arts firms, of research firms, and of thousands of would-be suppliers of services. The standard way of selling one's services is to wine and dine the agency representative who is reputed to have even a minor voice in a 'buying decision'.

The other side of the wining-and-dining complex is almost equally attractive (if one is attracted). The agency man is the supplier for the advertiser or the client. As such, his job is to wine and dine the client. Everything that advertisers do for the agency man can be and is done for the client. There are some differences, however. The amount spent on entertainment is expected to be appropriate both to the position of the agency man and to the position of the entertainee in the client organization. One is not expected to take a 'clerk' to the Chauveron, nor is a 'clerk' expected to entertain the president or the advertising manager of the client firm. If he does, he appears to be arrogating the position of his bosses.

There are other differences. When entertained by the suppliers, a low-level agency official can be gay, carefree, and expansive, even to a high-ranking official in the supplier firm. When he entertains the client, a high-ranking agency man must, if necessary, pretend deference even to a low-ranking official in the client firm. Thus mobility in temperament becomes a role requirement for the advertising man.

The expense account thus becomes a major way for a man of modest income to live, during the day, as if he were rich. And this quality of life is far more important psychologically than any increment in income the agency man can gain by cheating on the expense account.

Whenever an agency loses an account, or whenever it is deemed necessary to cut operating expenses, the largest single pool of expenses is the pool available for salaries and wages (since over two-thirds of all agency expenses are in this category). Similarly, since the major concentration of labour costs is the high salaries offered to creative, technical, and managerial staffs, the major opportunities for cost-cutting are in this area. To state it differently, firing clerks and secretaries to cut costs is not particularly effective, since the salaries for these categories do not contribute much to costs.

This potential vulnerability of the upper management in the agency business is from time to time made an actuality when accounts shift. The agency that loses a major account (from $2 million to $25 million) finds itself in a cost-income squeeze. If the account lost represents a sizeable proportion of its billings, the other accounts cannot bear the burden of maintaining the salaries of the executives. Wholesale firings are likely to ensue. However, since many account personnel work on more than one account, if they are fired because of the loss of one account they are unavailable for work on other accounts. The clients of these other accounts may resent the loss of favoured copywriters, account executives, commercial producers, or media planners and take their accounts out of the agency. Thus the loss of one major account may start a vicious cycle that in a number of specific instances has resulted in the sudden demise of large and profitable agencies.

When such losses occur, the job market becomes flooded with applicants, including many individuals who have the same general qualifications. Whether such enforced mobility constitutes an asset or a liability to the career aspirations of an individual depends on the opportunities available at the time of loss of job. In advertising, the loss of job by competent, capable, and blameless men constitutes a major career obstacle.

The atmosphere of gambling that characterizes all aspects of the agency business is reinforced by the defencelessness of the agency and its personnel in the face of the whim, fancy, and even perhaps of the wisdom and ability of the client. This ambiguity is the opposite side of the coin from the confidence, assertiveness, and brazenness that advertising men exhibit in making a pitch, when they claim that advertising can do anything and everything.

The ambiguity that represents the greatest opportunity and menace for a specific agency is simply based upon the inability, in all but extreme situations (as previously specified), to measure the value, efficiency, and effectiveness of a specific advertising idea, advertisement, or campaign. Sales may go up fantastically, and sometimes both the agency and client may be in a frenzy to know why. This becomes a problem because, if one does not know what one is doing to make sales go up, any change may be disastrous. Second, if one's gains are thought to be due to chance, then chance can convert the gains to losses just as easily. Similarly, sales losses do occur even after it appears that every step taken by the agency and the client has been thought out carefully, planned, researched, and pretested, and when all concerned have been convinced they have a winner.

The 'irrationality' of the marketplace is a source of anxiety, despite the fact that every step may be taken to rule out chance. Research, surveys, pretesting, test markets, controlled experiments – all are attempts to eliminate this ambiguity and irrationality. But the failure to anticipate, to prevent one's 'best laid plans' from going astray, is part of the very structure of the market. So many things go into the marketing operation, of which advertising is only a small part, that it is almost impossible to isolate the contribution of a single commercial, slogan, campaign, piece of artwork, or media plan. One can specify all the factors that might conceivably lead to sales success, but one recognizes that each factor applies to one's own brand and one's own marketing operation (including advertising) and also applies to each of a dozen competing brands and to each of a dozen product classes that do not compete directly but do constitute substitute methods of consumer-income disposal. Thus, a brand of beer may compete with all other brands of beer in its sales area (though all brands do not compete uniformly throughout the entire sales areas), with whiskey (by brands and types), with other types of non-essentials, and with, as in the case of shoes, brands and types of necessities.

For each competitive situation, then, there may be several hundred factors that affect the success of the advertised brand. Several thousand factors, therefore, may affect sales success. As if this were not bad enough, it is almost impossible to isolate each factor as it operates in the marketplace. The marketing operation is so complex that each factor is simply one small element in a causal chain, but unusual success or failure in any one factor can affect the total chain.

A further complexity is introduced by the fact that it is extremely difficult to measure each factor separately or to measure two or more factors together in terms of a common scale of values. In the latter case, it is as difficult to measure the relative importance of each factor as it is to measure the factors themselves. Moreover, the factors involved in any 'marketing chain' are continuously changing. Each successful or unsuccessful attempt at measurement may become ancient history before the measurement is completed.

All research – marketing, sales, copy, product, package, consumer, motivational, media, merchandising, test-market, image, and operations research – represents attempts by the client or agency to narrow the ambiguity or to reduce the risk in making decisions. And all these methods must confront the difficulties of action in a complex 'irrational' and uncontrolled market for which there are limited and imprecise measures. Over $400 million is invested in marketing research in one year by agencies and by clients in their anxious attempts to overcome the irrationality of the marketplace.

The feeling of anxiety and powerlessness held by top executives in the face of the tremendous responsibilities placed upon them for sales and advertising success constitutes the largest single opportunity for both missionaries and charlatans in the field of advertising research. There is a cycle in research that begins when a 'charismatic' hero discovers a new approach – the large-scale sample survey, programme analysing, the store audit, image research, motivation research, operations research, semantic differential, scales, scaling research, computer simulation, or linear programming, to name a few. After each such 'discovery', there is an intensified assault on the sales resistance of top agency and client officials to prove conclusively that once the new method is adopted, rationality and 'science' will govern marketing. Many of the methods and services are 'bought', and the new crusade begins. After the results of such research are in, the method is either discarded or absorbed as a minor tool in the inventory of available methods for research. The method, when absorbed, develops its defenders, who now resist the claims of new crusaders who possess another final solution. The failure of such methods to allay the sense of powerlessness and anxiety in the face of an irrational market is attested by the fact that each new discovery is superseded by a newer one which, in time, will be superseded.

This does not mean that research methods are universally useless. It does mean that, in the light of the complexity of marketing, research works best when there is a clearly defined, specific problem which can be so stated that a specific research finding can, in advance, be interpreted as offering a solution to the problem. Thus small, undignified, and inelegant studies frequently are the most useful, simply because there was a reason for undertaking them. However, these small studies do not have the grandeur and the elegance of large, theoretical, highbrow studies that appear to solve all problems except the specific one that evoked the study in the first place. Advertising men, in and out of research, want to fly before they can walk.

The irrationality of the marketplace and the lack of ability to specify what is good or bad advertising constitute a major source of job insecurity for the advertising man. If sales are up, it can be claimed (by the client) that they should be even higher. If sales are down, it can be claimed (by the agency) that only the advertising kept them from going even lower. Since no one 'really knows', skill at persuasion, at use of pressure tactics, at politics, and at 'human relations' becomes as important in gaining and keeping an account as the 'objective reality'.

The organizational and personnel problem this presents is decisive. Since the client is the source of all benefits to the agency and its personnel, and since agency personnel are usually better paid than officials in corresponding positions in the client firm, the burden of proof of the agency's efficiency is placed on the agency.

It is unusual when client personnel do not resent the 'excessive salaries', the glamorous expense account, and the claims of infallibility that agencies make in their initial solicitation for an account. Their resentment is expressed in excessive demands upon the agency. Tight deadlines, impossible work loads, and unreasonable tasks are presented to the agency as a matter of course. This is often expressed in the phenomenon of the 'exercise'. The client will present a real or hypothetical marketing or advertising problem to the agency. A short deadline is given, and the implicit or explicit threat is made that retention of the account requires a satisfactory solution to the problem. The agency personnel are then compelled to work day and night, weekday and weekend, under fantastic costs of money, time, and energy to prove the agency worthy of keeping the account. After all the work is done and the agency has demonstrated its loyalty by dancing to the client's tune, the final report is frequently left unread for weeks or filed away without ever having been read. The agency has, for the time being, paid for the commissions it earns from the largesse of the lower-paid client. In rare instances agencies will resign accounts because of the physical or mental breakdown of key personnel (lower-ranking personnel count less) or because the excessive demands by one client prevent their giving full attention to other, more profitable or less demanding accounts.

The philosophy of the exercise and the attitudes it engenders in agency management are major determinants of relationships within the agency. This is precisely so because the anxiety, powerlessness, and pressure placed upon the agency and its personnel by clients are linked to the extremes of success and failure that are possible because of labour-intensity, the claims for infallibility, and the inability to measure successful advertising.

The occupational and skill structure of the agency

The agency, to repeat, is a service industry that provides intangible skills and counsel to a manufacturing or marketing company. Its product, advertising, is not a standardized product that is mass-produced and sold at low cost to a large number of widely distributed consumers. On the contrary, the final product of the agency – a radio or TV commercial, a print advertisement or a billboard – is made in somewhat the same way as any other piece of art. The difference between genuine art and advertising (as production and not as aesthetics) is that advertising art involves committee planning, consultation, strategy, research, and the coordination of a wide variety of artistic and non-artistic specialists. The former include writers, audio technicians, painters and graphic men, photographers, engravers, cameramen (cinematic or still), musicians, animators, film editors, TV directors, stage designers, and producers. Art in advertising thus may resemble art in architecture or art under a patronage system in which the patron and his minions determine a great deal of the content and execution of the final art product.

Perhaps the only routine and semi-automatic work in advertising is in typing, billing, and other clerical work. Production work in the sense of semi-skilled or unskilled factory work is almost entirely absent. As estimated earlier, almost 40% of total agency personnel are engaged in creative, administrative, professional, or high-level staff work. While it is true that there is a wide variety of higher skills assembled in one relatively small enterprise (six hundred to seven hundred people), it is also true that the number of people who professionally exercise any one skill is relatively small.

The account supervisor is a man whose major responsibility is to represent the agency to the client, to receive instructions from the client, to make agency recommendations to the client, to coordinate the efforts of the agency in preparing plans and advertising for the client. The account supervisor is in charge of over-all supervision of the account and is concerned with policy, while the account executive is placed in charge of administering the internal operation of the agency as it relates to a particular client.

Working for and with the account supervisor and executive is the account group. The account group consists of creative, technical, and staff specialists, media planners and buyers, researchers, merchandisers and sales-promotion men. Each account group thus is a miniature advertising agency that has a full range of specialists attached to it and is capable of rendering a complete servicing of the account. There are as many account groups in an agency as there are accounts. When the account is a large one, the staff assigned to that account may be employed exclusively on the account in question. When the account is a small one, members of an account group may divide their time between a number of accounts.

Thus the agency usually has a double organization. One set of 'bosses' consists of the account supervisor and executive. The other set consists of the heads of individual departments, that is, research director, copy chief or creative director, media director, art director, and so on. Each set of 'bosses' has the same employees, and each set has at times different vested interests in the distribution of its employees' time and efforts. The overall agency officers – the president and chairman of the board – are the referees when conflicts occur, and the board of directors offers the formal representation of the various vested interests of both types. Their meetings are the official stage where conflicts are acted out and, if possible, resolved.

Typical conflicts are as follows:

1. When account personnel work on more than one account, their account supervisors may feel that the 'part-time' help are spending too much time on other accounts. The account supervisors almost always feel that their account is understaffed. In terms of pressures on the account supervisor, this is probably true.

2. The 'part-time' staff usually feel that account supervisors are too demanding. Instead of having two, three, or four part-time jobs, they feel they have that many full-time jobs.

3. The account supervisors quite often feel, especially if their account is not a huge or major one, that the creative and technical staff assigned to them are the rejects, misfits, and incompetents who have been assigned to their account on the basis of lack of ability.

4. Most service personnel are technicians, artists, or specialists, while the account supervisor is either a 'business administrator', with no

specialized, creative knowledge, or an ex-specialist. As a result, the creative or technical specialist feels that nincompoops, politicians, and incompetents meddle unnecessarily in business they know nothing about. They tend to feel that incompetents among their own bosses and at the client's shop force them to do countless revisions of perfectly good work, or even force them to execute ideas that are so badly conceived or undefined that perfect execution only makes apparent the stupidity of the plans. Thus they feel that most of the work done is totally unnecessary.

5. The account supervisors, on the other hand, feel that the technical specialists are 'purists', academicians – temperamental, obstreperous, and difficult. Moreover, they resent the feeling that the technical and creative specialists communicate a sense of being superior and of treating the account executive as if he were a dope.

6. Department heads resent the account heads, frequently feeling that the latter make excessive demands for their accounts on departmental personnel. They tend to feel that account heads want to tell the service heads and personnel how to do the work that the latter are especially qualified for. They also feel that account heads, to save their own necks, will risk the necks of the service personnel by forcing them to do inferior, dishonest, or unnecessary work. They feel they are obliged to be cat's-paws, rescuing the chestnuts from the fire caused by the negligence and incompetence of account heads.

7. The account heads reciprocate this feeling, justifying their attitudes in terms of the jealousy and intransigence of the heads of the service departments.

8. All the above conflicts are expressed quite often in private gossip, in conflicts over salaries and over the amount and availability of agency stock. The account executive feels that he is the businessman whose job it is to deal with the client, keep him happy, and keep the account in the shop. He has to have tact, to lie, flatter, drink, eat, and live with stupid people in order to keep an account. He must do this by being self-effacing, polite, and deferential even under the pressures of the conscious and unconscious needling and resentment of the client. This entitles him to a lion's share of the rewards.

The technical or creative specialist feels that he does the actual job of planning, creating, and executing the final product (the advertisement) and/or its placement in a medium. Since this is the manifest job of the agency, the lion's share of the reward should be his.

9. In addition, each specialist group develops a special theory of advertising that just happens to make its function supreme. Copywriters insist that the slogan or apt phrase, the play on words, is the particular ingredient that sells a product. Art directors will stress the symbol and the mood as being especially creative of positive brand images that lead to sales. When images become passé, art directors may insist upon humorous animation. ('You can get across unprovable claims by exaggerating them so much that even if the viewer consciously disbelieves them, he unconsciously accepts them.')

Television producers sell 'realistic' and 'atmospheric' mood photography, montage effects, use of succession of still shots of puppets to produce 'animation' – all techniques designed to transport the viewer out of his normal, hardheaded buying attitude into a world that, because of the suspension of belief, is more 'real' than the real world, and within which buying the advertised brand is linked to the fulfilment of the viewer's idealized self-image. Thus the TV producer, too, can make a claim for greater salary and more stock on the basis of attainment of this ideal.

The research director knows no limits to his megalomania except those that he encounters in the resistances that all other departments offer to the inquisitive snooping of research. Research enables the research director to 'know' the audience, the customer, the sales personnel, and to 'know' the action that will lead to success. He can research everybody's area of competence except his own, and can thus tell everyone else how to do his work. Every other department is forced, in the face of the self-aggrandizing research director, either to limit the operations of research or to control them to serve the special purposes of that department.

Research *does*, however, sometimes provide answers to specific questions, *does* provide an aura of knowing for the agency as a whole, is useful to specialists in providing them with viable alternatives, and is helpful to the account supervisor in keeping an account and to top management in acquiring accounts. This utility constitutes the claim of the research director and his department for higher salaries and a greater share of profits.

Ethics in dealing with clients

The client is the advertising man's sole source of bread and butter.

In addition to being well aware of this fact, the advertising man has other images of the client, which include the following:

Most clients are stupid. If they weren't they'd be working in agencies where they'd get paid more.

Most clients are technically incompetent.

Most clients are sadistic, or resentful of the agency man because of the latter's ability and salary.

Most clients are unreasonable and overdemanding. They also stick their noses into business they are not equipped to handle.

Most clients are hungry, thirsty, and vain. They need constant attention, flattery, and fake deference.

Most clients are ingrates. They will switch accounts for petty reasons, especially after the agency has done a superhuman job.

Most clients want the credit for work well done, and will blame the agency for their own mistakes.

Some clients are gullible fools, but these are nice people.

All the above images are not applied to all clients. In fact, each agency will have one or more clients whose personal qualities, business acumen, and administrative ability set so high a standard that all other clients look feeble in comparison.

These images set the stage for the discussion of client-focused ethics. The fundamental strategy of the agency is to make convincing its claim for distinctive agency superiority and indispensability in meeting the client's needs. Once one acquires the account, the initial argument plus its proof must be continuously demonstrated, even in the face of falling sales ('They could, under other circumstances, fall even faster').

Ethics in relationship to the client are based on the norm: *'Don't ever tell a direct lie to the client.'* This may not even be an ethical norm, since it is based on the assumption that without the client's trust in one's basic honesty, no enduring client-agency relationship is possible. The norm is thus a pragmatic device to keep the account.

If we consider the rule as an ethical norm, however, another set of normative propositions follows. While one does not tell a lie to the client, one does not always have to tell the total truth. The agency's fundamental business requirement is to keep profitable accounts.

Therefore, agency communications to the client tend to conceal negative aspects of agency operations – inefficiency, indecision, or lack of attention to his account because major attention has been given to other accounts. It is assumed that clients are big boys and that it is their problem to discover the negative aspects of the client-agency relationship, not the duty of the agency to inform on itself.

When an account is secure, however, the agency may criticize its own advertising, volunteer research results that are negative, or otherwise criticize its own operation, especially if the agency is immediately prepared to take protective action. Such self-criticism builds trust and forestalls client-originated criticism.

The deviant individuals in client-agency ethics are of two types. The *schlemiel* who reveals agency difficulties to the client (either by accident or as an attempt to curry favour) is a menace who cannot be kept around. The moral leper, on the other hand, who tells the client lies that are too big, risks creating a basic mistrust by allowing himself and the agency to be exposed as 'defrauding' the client. He is the worse menace. Between these two extremes are the tough realists who know how and when to tell the truth.

The 'tough realist' client is respected but feared because there is less need to manipulate him and less danger of a sudden disenchantment. The tough realist expects more and less of the agency at the same time. He does not ask for miracles, but he does ask for hard, creative work. A good agency can provide this without the necessity for deception.

Conclusion

It is difficult to be overly critical of advertising because it is not so very different from most areas of upper-middle-class life. We have noted that advertising is different from other 'executive suite' life only insofar as it distils and concentrates the essence of the executive suite. Advertising pays the same material rewards that are central to the American dream. The rewards are greater than can usually be found in other businesses and are available to more individuals. It is perhaps only just that the risks – personal, professional, and psychological – are greater in advertising than in most other professions. If one wants to play for big stakes, one must be prepared to suffer big losses.

Moreover, simply because of the pressures, difficulties, and irrationalities that are central to its structure, advertising recruits, selects, and rewards those individuals who are psychologically attuned to its environment. In addition to material rewards, it offers deep-seated psychological rewards, a feeling of narcissistic well-being, to those who can meet the demands imposed on them by the nature of the work itself. It is unfortunate that many men discover only after having devoted half a career to advertising that they are not equipped to work in the field. This belated discovery occurs only because the demands and pressure placed upon a man increase with length of service and with responsibility. Moreover, failure in advertising is often more final than in other professions.

One way to evaluate advertising as a career or a profession is to ask the questions, 'Would you recommend advertising as a career to the son of a dear friend?' and, 'Under what conditions would you recommend it?'

The answer that this author would make constitutes his summary of this essay. If the son has genuine talent or creative ability in any field, advertising is the last place for him to be. A truly autonomous, creative person will find the pressures of committee politics and decision-making destructive of his creative talent. If he accepts his new assignments, he must experience guilt for having betrayed his original talent.

If the friend's son is kind, gentle, ethical or religious, and believes in spontaneous social relationships, advertising would be an incompatible profession. Advertising requires strong defences, toughness, nerve, the willingness to exploit oneself and others. Our young man might crack under the pressure or, worse, develop these characteristics necessary for occupational survival.

There are individuals for whom one could recommend advertising as a profession. If a young man had no great creative talent but was a good technician in an applicable field, he might be a prospect one could recommend. It he was fairly bright but had no talents, he might also be a prospect. In addition, he would need a healthy constitution, 'nerve' but no nerves, and the capacity for hard but not necessarily meaningful work. He would have to have the capacity for handling himself, tact, and the ability to enjoy superficial social relationships. He should be something of a show-off who could control the need to show off and, in doing so, be able to enjoy showing off to himself.

If he had all these qualities, and if monetary success or the sense of power was a sufficient motivation for his actions, he could be a successful and, perhaps, well-adjusted advertising man.

Obviously, advertising does attract the kind of men it needs to do a reasonably effective job of selling its clients' wares. In doing so, advertising as an industry fulfils the requirements placed upon it by other segments of the economy. Because it does so, it is difficult to say that advertising is better or worse than the society for which it is a cynosure. If advertising is to be condemned, much of our society is also to be condemned.

But as a place of work advertising leaves much to be desired. All work, but especially advertising, demands that the worker give much of his total personality, his total self, to the job. The very creative sources of a man are involved in what he gives to others through his work and what he receives from others by virtue of his work. The quality of one's work shapes, channels, and gives expression to one's creative energy. If the job demands the ability to exploit and manipulate others, both in personal and in impersonal relationships, the very self that provides the basic energy for these actions must of necessity be corroded by these actions. If one attempts to build walls against one's own exploitation and against attempted exploitation by others, a great deal of one's psychic energy is invested merely in self-protection. It is no wonder that the field is populated by would-be artists, novelists, scholars, and poets who rarely manage to fulfil the promise that gave meaning to their youth.

It is perhaps not demanding too much to ask of people to give to their work that which in themselves they value most highly – in abstract terms, love, creativity, authenticity. But these demands cannot be made of the vast majority of employed persons in our essentially materialistic society, since the demands made by their work are somewhat less than individuals at their best can give and, more often, are somewhat perverted versions of what individuals at their best have to offer.

Advertising simply accepts the world as it is, and then makes it even more so.

PART THREE:

Communicators, Performers and Content

1. Selection and Communication in a Television Production – A Case Study*

Philip Elliott

The research idea and method

The case study reported in this paper was designed as part of an exploratory project to fill a gap in mass communication research and theory.[1] The intention was to supplement a survey of audience reactions to a television documentary series, with an analysis of the way these programmes were produced. Most mass communication research has started with the output of the medium as given and then gone on to assess audience effect.[2] This study was designed to investigate the processes of selection and decision through which the programmes passed before they reached the viewer.

The programmes were a series of seven half-hour documentaries, titled 'The Nature of Prejudice', and originally transmitted on consecutive Sunday afternoons. The series was in production for just over fifteen weeks and throughout that time the activities of the production team were observed and recorded.[3] The observation was non-participant and loosely structured. Each day's notes were ordered into a prepared schedule summarizing the main activities and the part played by each member of the production team. Observation was guided by the general aim of the study. In summary this was to analyse the process of production to show the range of material included, the way this was shaped into programme form, the intentions of the different production personnel involved in this, and the way in which other factors, of a social, cultural or organizational nature, impinged upon the whole process.

There is a sense in which 'The Nature of Prejudice' series was both

---

* Not previously published.

'typical' and 'unique'. It was a typical documentary series in production. But each series has a different subject and a different production team. Rather than simply describe the work of the individuals who made up this team, attention has been directed towards factors in the situation which are likely to be similar for all productions. Nevertheless, allowance must be made for personal factors. In assessing the conclusions of this paper, it must be remembered that they are based on only one case. They are put forward as starting points rather than final assertions.

Although there has been considerable argument over the precise nature of the relationship, it has been a common assumption in sociology that literature and art 'reflect society'.[4] It is one of the aims of this paper to illustrate one aspect of the relationship for this programme series, by analysing the collection and selection of programme material. Because of the way these processes were organized, the eventual programme content may be described as a sample of the 'conventional wisdom' current in society on this particular subject.[5]

The second aim of this paper is to question a model of mass communication which is based on an analogy with interpersonal communication.[6] According to this model the relationship between television production and the audience is a circle of communication and feedback. The model is comparable to the two person interaction models of social psychology. In particular it stresses the communication intended by the production personnel as an important factor in programme production.[7] It is easy to show that one link in the model – the feedback from audience to production – is tenuous, except on the point of audience size.[8] This paper takes up the question of the other link – the communication from production to audience – and seeks to show that, in the case of these programmes at least, 'communication' – defined as the attempt to transmit particular knowledge and ideas – is not an appropriate term. In contrast, the model of television production suggested by this study is of a relatively self-contained process following established technical and occupational routines.

The production of the programmes

Diagram I shows, in summary form, the production stages through which the programmes passed. Each stage included different activities, but all were part of the same interdependent process. The diagram is only an analytic device. There was considerable temporal overlap between one stage and another, and the production personnel themselves used the technical names for their activities. These do not necessarily coincide with the names given to the analytic stages.

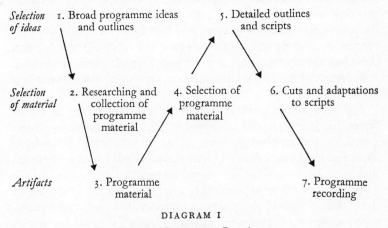

Selection of ideas	1. Broad programme ideas and outlines		5. Detailed outlines and scripts
Selection of material	2. Researching and collection of programme material	4. Selection of programme material	6. Cuts and adaptations to scripts
Artifacts	3. Programme material		7. Programme recording

DIAGRAM I

The Stages of Programme Broadcasting

The diagram shows the way in which the production process moved twice from the level of ideas to the level of actual programme material. Stages two, three and four were all dependent on the broad ideas for subject areas developed in the first stage. Further ideas were developed at stage five, but these depended heavily on the material collected in the previous stages. This is the aspect of the production process upon which this paper will concentrate. Some attention will also be given to the final stage because additional factors appeared at that point which further inhibited 'communication'.

Stage 1: Programme ideas and outlines

The idea for a series of programmes on prejudice had been under discussion in the television organization for some time. The associate head of the department dealing with documentary programmes eventually arranged transmission time for the series and he contracted a producer and a director to handle the production.[9] As executive producer, he had overall responsibility for the series within the organization. But the practice in this department was to leave the programme producer a relatively free hand. This was especially the case with 'The Nature of Prejudice', because the programme producer was a man of considerable experience and reputation, and well known to the executive producer. On appointment, the only direction on content which the programme producer received was that the series should not concentrate exclusively on problems of race and colour. It was felt that these had already been sufficiently covered on television, whereas an examination of the whole phenomenon of prejudice would break new ground.[10]

The programme producer actively disliked prejudice in all its forms.[11] However, he did not intend to make the programmes a direct assault on the problem by using either an emotional or a didactic approach. He thought the first better done through dramatic presentation in a play or a film. The second he regarded as a misuse of the medium because it would inevitably result in a decrease in the size of the audience. Instead the producer expressed his programme philosophy in terms of 'evidence' and 'conclusions'. He saw his task as collecting 'evidence' about the subject, from which both he, and the guests invited into the studio to appear on the programme, would be able to draw 'conclusions'. In the same way some of the audience might draw the same 'conclusions', or at least be inspired to think about the subject anew.

Thus two forms of direct 'communication', aiming at attitude change, were ruled out from the start.[12] Nevertheless the theory of 'evidence' and 'conclusions' did suggest that the programmes would arrive at a new statement about the phenomenon. The producer assumed that at least some of the audience would react to this statement in the same way that he did. The description of the programme materials as 'evidence' makes it especially important to analyse the methods and sources through which they were obtained.

In the first meetings of the production team, the producer outlined his general ideas for the programmes. The series was to move from an opening survey of the wide variety of prejudices to be found in society, to a concluding discussion, in which a panel of guests in the studio would be invited to sum up the phenomenon. In between, the programmes were to cover a number of different prejudices – race and colour, religious, social, inter-generational, inter-sexual, and national. Except the last, these all reflected the producer's assessment of the most important types of prejudice current in society.

Even at this stage, however, the producer wondered whether enough material could be found to make a series of programmes, each devoted to a prejudice of a particular type, without also making the programmes very repetitious. Drawing on the conversations he had had with a few academics and on some background reading,[13] the producer moved away from a topic-based, to a concept-based approach.

Most of the concepts which eventually provided the basis for different programmes in the series were explicitly mentioned in the early production discussions. These were the origins of prejudice, 'in-groups' and 'out-groups', stereotypes and methods of combating prejudice. These were partly the areas which the producer thought the most important, and partly areas suggested by the visual possibilities of programme ideas and material found in the researching stage (Stage 2).

Initially the topic-based approach ran side-by-side with the concept-based approach, but gradually the latter began to predominate in guiding the researching activities. Most of the researching was completed, however, before the producer finally decided how the concepts would divide up into individual programmes. Both the topics and the concepts mentioned above, functioned throughout the researching stage as general headings under which programme material was organized.

Stage 2: Researching for programme material

The process of researching may be conceptualized in terms of three separate chains. These chains represent both three separate ways through which programme ideas were generated, as well as describing the three necessary conditions which any programme material had to meet to qualify for inclusion.

The Subject Chain. The Subject Chain was an extension of the broad subject headings discussed in the previous section. The producer played a key part in deciding which of these headings would form the basis for the series. They derived from his own ideas and experience, supplemented by some background reading and two contacts with academics interested in the subject. These broad subject areas then themselves led on to specific ideas for illustrative programme material. For example, the heading of stereotyping was developed because it obviously lent itself to visual illustration. Nevertheless the fact that initially a criterion of importance played as great a part as a criterion of visual possibility, is shown by the example of social prejudice. The producer repeatedly referred to this, even though there was some doubt among the production team as to whether it was still applicable, and few ideas were forthcoming on how to make it visual. Thus little reference to social prejudice was included in the eventual programmes because it failed to satisfy the other two necessary conditions. The Subject Chain is illustrated in Diagram II.

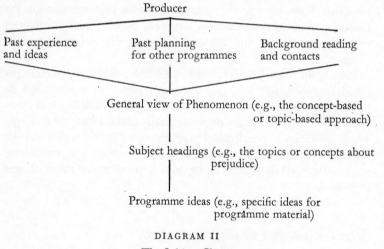

Producer

Past experience and ideas | Past planning for other programmes | Background reading and contacts

General view of Phenomenon (e.g., the concept-based or topic-based approach)

Subject headings (e.g., the topics or concepts about prejudice)

Programme ideas (e.g., specific ideas for programme material)

DIAGRAM II

The Subject Chain

The Presentation Chain. At the start of the production, the series was allocated a budget. This allocation provided one basis for the second chain – the Presentation Chain. The programmes were to be shown in an 'off-peak' time-slot. Attached to that time-slot there was a recognised 'normal' budget figure. Both time-slot and budget figure were associated with production in a particular style, involving little use of film and based on studio presentation.

In their intial discussion of the series the producer and director planned within this accepted production style. Much of the programme time was to be devoted to discussions in the studio between panels of expert guests. These would be led by a presenter, who would also link the other visual material which could be worked into the basic format. This consisted mainly of stills, a small amount of archive film and film specially shot for the series.[14]

Planning followed the accepted style, even though the budget figure initially suggested by the executive producer was considerably higher than the norm (by 25%), which suggests the importance of production routines accepted by those working in the medium. In this case plans for the series were not constrained or limited by the budget figure, but structured by the production style associated with budget and time-slot.

The one adjustment which was made by the producer when he found he was well within the budget figure, was to increase the amount allowed for original filming. The final budget estimate allowed for ten days' hire of film crew, instead of four. The power of the accepted production style is demonstrated again however by the fact that in the end only five of these days were used.

Nevertheless, for a combination of reasons, both the producer and the director thought it desirable to obtain original film for the series. Because film is the most expensive production technique, it has a scarcity value; its use marks a programme out from others. Film is a very flexible medium which can be cut and edited by producer and director to meet their requirements. It is easier to capture dramatic action on film than in a studio and so film is believed to have greater impact.

Most of the film eventually shot for 'The Nature of Prejudice' was of 'talking head' interviews. It is particularly interesting that the above arguments applied to the film material in this case. This was despite the fact that the content of the film was mainly 'talking heads', the usual content of studio production. For example, in deciding how to employ a film unit for the time available, one subject suggested was 'Vox Pop' interviews. These were justified on the grounds that they could be easily arranged to fill the film unit's time, and they would provide original film with 'actuality' impact.

These 'Vox Pop' sequences are one example of an idea thrown up by the Presentation Chain, shown in Diagram III. Programme ideas suggested themselves, or were confirmed, because they were particularly suitable for one of the methods of presentation within the accepted production style.

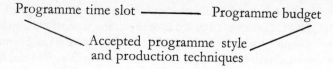

Programme ideas

DIAGRAM III

The Presentation Chain

The Contact Chain. The Contact Chain, shown in Diagram IV, is an elaboration of the very simple point that, to qualify for use, a subject had to be known to the production team. One example of the operation of this principle resulted in the inclusion not merely of a new programme idea, but also of another broad subject heading – national prejudice. The producer was put in touch with a psychologist who had recently completed a series of experiments investigating the development of national stereotypes in children. National prejudice was added to the list of subject areas because the techniques used in this experiment could be re-enacted on film. (Thus the idea was confirmed by the Presentation Chain.)

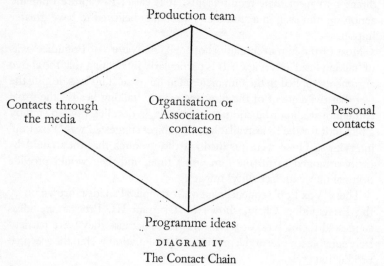

DIAGRAM IV

The Contact Chain

The Contact Chain was especially important during the first few weeks of researching. Indeed the role of the researcher can be seen as an attempt to institutionalize contact mechanisms within the production team.[15] The researcher's task was to search out programme material within guidelines laid down by the producer. To do this she needed a good knowledge of possible sources.

One of the first requirements was to find interview subjects for the film sessions. The producer wanted to recruit examples of both prejudiced people, who would be prepared to state their views on film, and of the victims of prejudice, who had their own case stories to tell. The interview subjects were eventually recruited from three main sources: first stories in the press published during the researching period, second organizations and associations representing people who were a likely target for prejudice, third contacts personally known to a member of the production team. These were the three basic contact mechanisms which applied to all forms of material, with the variation of course that other material involved other organizations, specializing in the relevant subject.

These mechanisms were relatively productive of examples of 'victims' of prejudice, but not of 'prejudiced' people.[16] The eventual lack of 'prejudiced' interviewees is a good example of the way the production team depended on the three mechanisms. Three 'prejudiced' interview subjects were thrown up by stories in the press, but two of these were vicars whose statements to camera were too theological to be very useful. In addition the producer asked the people he stopped in the street for the 'Vox Pop' interviews, to confess their prejudices. This method was also largely unsuccessful in obtaining statements of prejudice on film. Out of 40 'Vox Pop' interviewees, 32 denied having any prejudices themselves, and only four admitted feeling prejudiced on specific subjects.

Two of the other interviewees had recently completed research projects in an area of race relations. Again stories in the press were the contact mechanism which brought them to the attention of the production team. Two other pieces of research were re-enacted on film for inclusion in the programme. One of these was the investigation of the development of national stereotypes, mentioned above; the other was a study of the development of colour preferences among children. The producer was put in touch with both psychologists through personal contacts and, in both cases, he found that the research was eminently

suitable for film presentation. Apart from the guests invited into the
studio, discussed below, these four pieces of programme material were
all the academic research included in the programme. It can be seen
that this sample of research was drawn through the Contact Chain,
reinforced by the Presentation and Subject Chains.

Although the way the individual interviewees were recruited illustrates most points about the Contact Chain, the mechanism of personal
contact did play a more important part in the selection of some of the
other types of material. There were a number of reasons why the production team tried to use personal contacts wherever possible, especially
in preference to formal approaches through bureaucratic machinery.
Indeed put together with the personal basis of selection for employment within the organization, and the use made of personalized,
quasi-charismatic relationships at work, it appears as if personal, parti-
cularist relationships are uniquely important in the organizational
system of television production.[17]

The reasons for using personal contact mechanisms in researching
may be divided into four main groups. First, personal contacts were
believed to be more productive – the producer could detail his own requirements and short-circuit cumbersome formal procedures. For
example, permission to film in a multi-racial school was initially refused
by the local authority. Eventually qualified permission was obtained by
a direct approach to a member of the authority, known to the producer.

Second, personal contacts gave the producer greater control over the
source of the material – he was more likely to see the full range of
material and so was better able to assess its quality. For example, direct
approaches were made to the film librarians for archive film in the hope of
making full use of their personal knowledge of their libraries' contents.

Third, personal contact tended to result in greater co-operation
from the subjects. While recruiting the interview subjects, the researcher approached a social worker with whom she had previously
worked on another programme. This social worker provided not only
six examples of 'victims' of prejudice for interview, but also a location
in which the filming could take place.

Fourth, the ability to produce personal contacts at appropriate
moments reflected on the status and expertise of the production
personnel. The ability to produce such contacts was part of the formal
role requirements placed upon the researcher, but others in the team
also felt it incumbent upon them to suggest contacts. For example, in

the course of a vain pursuit of some American educational film, a telephone call was made to a contact in New York on the off-chance that it might prove fruitful.

These reasons all contributed to the stress on personal contact which, together with the press and the organization mechanisms, played an important part in structuring the range of material available to the producer at the next stage.

Discussion of the three chains

In introducing the three chains, it was mentioned that each was both capable of generating programme ideas, and a necessary condition which each programme idea had to satisfy. Thus programme ideas had to fall within one of the broadly defined subject areas – though as we saw in the case of national prejudice there was scope for re-alignment of the areas if an idea was strongly supported by the other two chains. Second, programme ideas had to be suitable for presentation by one of the accepted techniques. Third, programme ideas had to be visible to the production team through a narrow range of contact mechanisms.

In many ways the criteria which were missing at this point are as interesting as the three which were present. In particular there was very little reference to the substantive content or meaning of programme ideas. For example none of the four pieces of academic research was included primarily for its findings. The Subject Chain itself simply defined the broad headings under which programme material was to be collected. It did not suggest what should be said about any particular area. At this stage, programme material was collected through well-developed production routines and not as contributions to any particular 'communication'. Moreover, the range of material visible to the production team was very limited, especially by the action of the Contact Chain.

Stage 4: The selection of programme material
Stage 5: The writing of programme scripts

These two stages will be considered together. The producer preferred to write the scripts around the programme material once it had been collected. But after the material had passed two initial selection criteria, the variety available to the producer was limited, so that he had little scope in compiling the programmes.

Most of the programmes in the series were divided into two parts. In the first part the presenter linked together statements taken from the filmed interviews and occasionally other types of inserted material. The second part was usually devoted to a studio discussion between the presenter and one or more expert guests. The first, and the last two programmes, varied from this format. Programme 1 contained no studio discussion[18] while both the last two programmes were almost entirely produced in the studio.

The material from the individual interviewees could only be selected for its substantive content once it had already passed two initial tests. These were for coherence and authenticity. Interviewee statements had to be reasonably complete, coherent and concise, because any used had to stand alone in the programmes without support. The interviewer's questions, for example, were not included. This was a special problem with the 'victims' of prejudice. Several of these were taxed beyond the limits of their verbal skills by the interview situation.

The second criterion also affected the 'victims' more than any other group. Some asserted prejudice or discrimination against themselves without providing sufficient circumstantial evidence to convince the producer that their claims were completely authentic. Table I shows the number of complete interviews which were ruled out as unusable by these two criteria. These figures understate the ratio of unusable

TABLE I

THE USE OF THE FILMED INTERVIEWS

Type of interviewee	No. unusable	No. usable	Average no. of usages in series
'Victims'	6	10	2·2
'Prejudiced'	1	2	—*
'Experienced'	0	3	3·3
'Representatives'	0	3	4·7
'Researchers'	0	2	—*

* In both cases a mean figure would be misleading as one interviewee was used four times and the other only once.

material because they show only the rejection of complete interviews. Several interviews, counted as usable, only yielded one or two short statements.

Two types of interviewee, the 'representatives' and the 'experienced', were the most productive of coherent, authentic statements. This is suggested in the table by the figures for average use. The 'representatives' were three men who held leadership positions within different minority groups. The 'experienced' were people who worked in different multi-racial situations and who were invited to comment on their experiences. The use made of the 'representatives' seems an especially interesting point for future work to follow, particularly because organizations and associations were an important contact mechanism at the researching stage.[19]

In terms of the producer's original production philosophy, set out above, the interview statements, and the other material, went into the programmes as 'evidence'. But the list of different types of interviewees shows that there was some variation in the authority which they had for giving 'evidence'. One use made of the interviewee material was to provide statements of a series of different points of view. Little attempt, however, was made to differentiate between the different arguments contained in these statements, or to show the viewer their relative merits.

This point is well illustrated by the use made of some statements by one of the 'prejudiced' interviewees. It so happened that he was a lecturer in social psychology. In one statement, for example, he alleged that different coloured rats exterminated each other and concluded that such colour differences were biologically important. The producer regarded this as an inaccurate and prejudiced statement, but the only clue he provided for the viewer, to counteract the authoritative impression already given by the interviewee's caption – 'Lecturer in Social Psychology' – was the presenter's next words: 'Well, possibly. But there are surely a lot of flaws in that argument. Even if black and brown rats are as hostile to each other as is claimed, what about black and white and brown rabbits ?' This is a particularly good example of what appeared to be a general lack of concern with both the 'communicative' effect and the authoritative basis of the statements included in the programmes.

But although the interviewees varied in the authority they had for making their statements, they were all questioned in a similar way to elicit a series of personal opinions. This applied even to the 'researchers' and the 'experienced'. For example only one of the former was questioned directly on the findings of the research.

Thus the scripts, written around the results of the researching and selection stages, included simply a sample of the personal opinions current in society about the topic of prejudice. The statements were 'evidence' of the 'conventional wisdom' available in society. Nevertheless, according to the producer's production philosophy, the 'evidence' was to lead to 'conclusions', especially in the studio discussion sections of the programmes, analysed in the next section.

Stage 7: Programme recording

The very fact that the producer left the 'conclusions' to emerge from the expert guests in the studio discussions, meant that he could play less part in deciding their content. This was partly because the guests had expert status and so were expected to be responsible for their own opinions, and partly because this production stage involved another member of the production team, the presenter, who not only led the 'live' discussion, but also played an important part in deciding its content.

The guests themselves were selected through similar channels to the contact mechanisms described in the researching stage. One difference however was that, in place of the press, previous appearances on television not only brought different experts to the attention of the production team, but also enabled them to judge their televisual competence. What any given expert would say appeared to be a far less important selection criterion than his ability to say something in a presentable way. The producer did provide the guests with outlines of the programme material and of the part which he expected the studio discussion to play in the programme, but except for the first discussion, in Programme 2, the studio sections were not extensively prepared or rehearsed. This exception is examined more closely below because, on this occasion, the producer did start with the intention of 'communicating' particular ideas. He was largely prevented by the operation of other factors in the process.

One important intervening factor was the nature of the studio discussion itself. This was an uneasy compromise between two possible modes – a spontaneous conversation and an information channel. The ideal of a spontaneous conversation was most clearly expressed in planning for the final programme, which was to provide the 'conclusions' for the whole series. Conversational ability was the main criterion for selecting guests for that programme. They were to be 'global thinkers' who were able to 'get out of the box and into the living-room'.[20] That is they were expected to sustain a smooth and erudite conversation, in which the viewer would feel he was present.[21]

In contrast the producer's initial plans for the discussion in Programme 2, were for a series of exchanges which would contain the information – the 'conclusions' – which he wanted put across. These exchanges were planned and rehearsed with the two guests involved. The conversational ideal was present however in both the dress rehearsal and the final 'take'. It inhibited the use of the discussion as an information channel, particularly by the making of conversational points. For example one of the guests emphasized the influence of British colonial experience on racial attitudes. The presenter took this up by suggesting that physical differences must be more important because most people alive now had not participated in the Empire. While this was a perfectly good point to make, it does illustrate the way in which the format of the discussions tended to reproduce the series of contradictory statements and questions contained in the rest of the programme material. Conversational points tended to be of a contradictory or critical nature and often moved the discussion away from the main theme. An example of this occurred in the discussion of the findings of the second piece of research, recorded on film. The presenter questioned the psychologist about his use of the categories 'English/Not-English' instead of 'British/Not-British', in order to make the point that the research appeared prejudiced against the Welsh and the Scottish. The result was that no findings from the research were elicited by the discussion.

It will be apparent from these examples that the use of the conversational mode was to some extent a result of the style adopted by the presenter.[22] Other aspects of the presenter's role also inhibited the use of the discussions as information channels. Thus, in Programme 2, the producer particularly wanted to include a discussion of the theory of the 'authoritarian personality', and of the principles of sampling to justify scientific method. Both these were dropped, at the presenter's instigation, because he argued they would cause the viewer to lose interest by over-complicating the issue. It was particularly noticeable that in the discussions immediately prior to programme recording, the presenter would 'take the role of the viewer' and use such phrases as 'what I and the viewer want to see is . . .'.

His situation differed in important ways from that of the rest of the production team.[23] He was able to take an outsider's perspective because he came to the programme material fresh on the recording day, whereas the production team had been working with it for some weeks. Moreover he was the only member of the production team actually to appear on the screen. It was accepted that this made the series to some extent 'his', so far as the viewers were concerned.[24] He had originally been picked for the 'weight' of his public personality, and he knew that his future work opportunities depended on the public personality which he presented, or was believed to present, to the viewer. In this context it is important that one aspect of 'weight' was the ability to conduct and participate in conversations on any subject.

Thus the presenter had more reason than others in the production team to attend to the viewer's reactions. He did this largely by simplifying the material to what he believed was the viewer's level of interest, and occasionally by suggesting re-orderings of material for greater dramatic effect. In the studio discussions, the presenter's concern with simplification was reflected in his use of simple analogies and summaries to illustrate the guest's argument. As these were made, 'off the cuff', in the course of the conversation, it was not surprising that several were denied by the guests as inaccurate or misleading. Even those which were substantially correct further contributed to the impression of programme content as a series of bald statements of different points of view.

A third factor which contributed to the general inability to 'communicate' 'conclusions' through the guests in the studio, was the lack of preparation given to these sections after Programme 2. This lack of preparation was itself partly a deliberate policy, because the meticulous rehearsal of the discussions in Programme 2 had prevented the presenter from using some of his conversational points. Nevertheless one consequence was illustrated by the discussion in the following programme. The presenter's scripted introduction to the discussion ended with a series of questions, which it was implied the guest would answer. But the guest, struck by the statements made on film by the 'prejudiced' interviewee, the lecturer in social psychology, whom she had just heard for the first time, devoted her attention to demolishing his arguments. The fact that the lecturer in social psychology had been included simply as an example of prejudice, was not explained to the guest nor clear to her from an initial viewing of the programme.[25]

Thus situational factors in the final production stage further demonstrate the inapplicability of a 'communication' model. These factors even impeded the attempt, which the producer did make in the second programme, to 'communicate' specific ideas. Nevertheless the analysis of this stage does show references being made to the audience, especially by the presenter. These references were specifically concerned with audience *reaction*, however, and not with 'communication'. The question was how to keep the viewer interested, not how to ensure he assimilated, or even was presented with, particular items of information. This concern was mirrored at earlier stages in the process by, for example, the argument that film had impact for an audience.

This distinction between *reaction* and 'communication' or effect, is one of considerable importance, if only to prevent an extreme (and empirically unjustifiable) extension of the argument of this paper. This extension would be that the production team paid no attention at all to their potential audience. They did pay attention but largely in terms of *reaction*, not in terms of 'communication'. The production team's principal concern about their audience was to prevent them switching off by trying to hold their interest and attention. One accepted way of doing this was to keep the substance of the programme moving, which suggests another reason why the programme content consisted of a series of different, briefly developed, points of view.

Conclusion

This paper has attempted to show the way in which the processes of selection and decision behind a series of television documentaries, followed a number of accepted production routines, which resulted in a relatively fortuitous sample of what has been termed, 'conventional wisdom' appearing on the screen. Because of the influence of the conversational mode in the studio discussions, these sections of the programme also produced little more than 'conventional wisdom', albeit from people speaking with the authority of experts, unlike those whose views were recorded on film. Throughout, the producer, and others in the production team, attempted to allow for possible audience reactions, but not to 'communicate' specific ideas or information to the audience.

In the space of this paper it is not possible to do more than suggest some of the possible wider implications of these conclusions. Indeed the conclusions themselves cannot be said to have been substantiated on the basis of this single case study. Nevertheless, it is interesting to relate them to the structural situation of the broadcast media; especially the need to avoid control by sectional interests which has resulted in a stress on such policies as balance, fairness and the lack of an editorial view.[26]

Another structural feature of the broadcast media is the divorce from direct contact with their audience. McQuail has argued that this divorce, coupled with the need to know how to communicate with the audience, results in such adaptations as 'professionalization' and 'ritualism' within the production organizations.[27] These are akin to the accepted production routines outlined in this paper, but the suggestion of this study is that these routines are explicable without reference to attempts to 'communicate' with the audience.

2. Books and their Publishers*

Michael Lane

When one considers how important is the part that they play in an almost completely literate society, books and their publishers have received little attention from social scientists; certainly by comparison with the press. In one way this is inevitable: the total number of people directly involved in British publishing is very small, much smaller than the number of journalists. Moreover, the glamour traditionally associated with publishing has recently faded greatly by comparison with the newer media of communication, such as television.[1] On the other hand, despite technological changes in information storage and retrieval books still play a major role in conserving and transmitting skills and cultural values. Rightly or wrongly they tend to be perceived as less transient than the newer media, and are afforded a perhaps exaggerated respect. It is illuminating that only books have so far survived the passage through the Restrictive Practices Court and have their selling price fixed.

In order to go some way towards remedying this defect, I want here to propose a tentative framework for the study of books and more particularly publishers, since it is they who provide the institutional and organizational framework for the production and dissemination of books. I shall start by looking at books; then at publishers' 'lists' (i.e., their catalogues, which reflect the range of books they publish); finally at the structural position of the publisher – his relations with the forces operating on him, for example, printers, authors, authors' agents, other media and, not least, his public. Without consideration of these essentially factual and descriptive questions, it is not possible to go on to the critical, sociological problems. First, publishers mediate between an author and his audience in that they provide the

* Not previously published.

mechanism by which the one reaches the other. Their position is that of the classical entrepreneur, linking the makers (author or printer) with the consumer. Further, the heterogeneity of the product makes it inevitable that the publisher and the consuming public will tend to attach labels to books, to place them in categories. These two factors raise certain important issues. First, to what extent and on what criteria do publishers positively determine what books they will produce? Second, to what extent do the labels of the publisher and the labels of the public coincide? Third, to what extent does the label attached by a publisher to a book determine the audience it will reach? In effect, the central sociological question is the extent to which publishers manage and control values and knowledge rather than simply purvey.

Types of books

Men habitually discriminate between books and especially between types of books. Our response to Milton's poems, for example, is totally different from our response to a technical manual for a car. Nor are the distinctions we make always simple ones. If we were to take 'Imaginative Literature' as one very broad category as opposed to 'Technical (or Factual) Literature' on the other hand (rather as Public Libraries classify books as either 'Fiction' or 'Non-Fiction', and issue tickets for use accordingly), we would still want to make some significant subdivisions.

A passage in Jane Austen's *Northanger Abbey* conveys the sort of distinction I am interested in:

'I am no novel reader – I seldom look into novels – Do not imagine that I often read novels – It is really very well for a novel.' Such is the common cant. 'And what are you reading Miss . . .?' 'Oh! It is only a novel!' replies the young lady; while she lays down on her book with affected indifference, or moment-ary shame. 'It is only Cecilia, or Camilla, or Belinda; . . .' Now had the same young lady been engaged with a volume of the Spectator, instead of such a work, how proudly would she have produced the book, and told its name. . . .'

In the same way someone nowadays found with a paperback thriller might well be embarrassed and attempt to pass it off as 'just something I bought to read on the train'. As against this Shakespeare's plays or Henry Fielding's novels (or Jane Austen's for that matter) are accorded a special respect: they are, in some way, both signs of, and repositories of, core values of our cultural system, in its widest sense.

This type of distinction might seem, at first sight, to be rather far away from the everyday business of publishing. I believe that, on the contrary, it is an absolute, fundamental one, explicitly recognized by publishers themselves, for we would expect a distinction of this importance to be echoed, at the very least, among the organizations that produce books. One way in which we might approach this is via Amitai Etzioni's framework for the analysis of organizations in terms of the goals they pursue.[2] Two from his list of types concern us here: first, the organization having a 'cultural goal', that is, one whose aim is the transmission of certain beliefs and values; second, the organization having an 'economic goal', that is, one whose aim is to gain material returns from its activity. If we are meaningfully to classify books, we need to take into account the beliefs that publishers hold about the profit potential of different types of titles, and this is intimately related to perceptions of their cultural value. In practice within the book trade, we can distinguish five broad categories. (These are not to be confused with subject categories based on a book's content.) They are:

1. General
2. Fiction
3. Literature and Belles Lettres
4. Educational and Technical
5. Academic

These categories are far from easily characterized, not least because a book may be first published as simply 'Fiction', but over time become transmuted into 'Literature and Belles Lettres'. Moreover, what one publisher considers 'Academic' books may be defined by another as 'General'.

General list books normally include all non-fiction works that the publisher (or in some cases, the author) sees as written for, or at least readily accessible to, a non-specialist audience – biography, popular history, non-technical natural history and science, books on the arts, on travel, and so on. In this, as in the succeeding classes, the relativity of the labelling process is very much to the point. A publisher on whose list highly specialized academic books predominate, may define a book as of general interest that a publisher with a very 'popular' list would consider 'academic' beyond doubt. Those whom the publisher defines as his expected public (a question to which I shall return) provide a critical determinant. If a publisher aims his books at a public of university lecturers, then one that he feels will be of interest and accessible to a school teacher is, relatively, 'general'. If, on the other hand, he aims his books at an audience of manual workers, one potentially of interest to a school teacher is, relatively, 'academic'. The problem is given a further complication by changes in subject fashions. For example, during the anniversary of the first world war there was a fashion for highly specialized military and diplomatic histories of the period. The social sciences seem currently to be enjoying a similar vogue. On the whole, general books are seen as being steadily, if rarely spectacularly, profitable. Though I have presented fiction as a single category, the folk-lore of publishing would warrant dividing it. On the one hand, first novels and 'quality' novels – the epithet is quite indefinable – are thought to be absolutely certain economic failures, except in the case of 'quality' novels whose authors have a well-established following. In this event, the danger is that though a book may sell well (more than 10,000 copies, say), the advance on royalties that the publisher has paid to the author may take a very considerable period to recoup and money may be tied up that could be more profitably employed elsewhere. Here publishers somewhat resemble film-producers; for both the 'opportunity costs', to use an economists' term, on capital committed to a project whose returns are large but delayed, may be unacceptably high. When and whether the costs are accepted relates to the question of the goals of publishing, to which I shall return later. The other half of fiction – 'popular' or 'light' fiction – is believed to be profitable. It includes historical novels, war stories, detective and thriller stories and romances.

The substance of the next category, Literature and Belles Lettres, is self-evident: drama, poetry, literary criticism. The majority of reprints of classic literature are included here, except for those whose textual or critical apparatus would justify their inclusion in the 'academic' category, and those specifically designed for use in educational institutions. Classic reprints apart, books in this category are considered economic poison in the trade. A Betjeman occurs once in a publishing life-time (and even he, before his success had produced several volumes of verse that did little, if any, better than the average). As a consequence, it is rare to find a print order for a volume of poetry, or a play, greater than 1,500 copies. (First novels, considered an almost equal risk, usually print around 3,000.) Since the production overheads, which remain more or less constant regardless of the size of the print order, are roughly the same for a novel by a popular author and a book by an unknown poet, this has the added effect of making many of the works in this category relatively expensive.

'Educational and technical books' are again a fairly straightforward group, though they form a unique one as far as sales are concerned. Not only are publishers the sole body so far to have been allowed to continue to impose a fixed retail price, but also books may only be distributed through booksellers who are members of the Booksellers Association. Though some loopholes, such as book clubs, have long existed where the public may obtain reprints at a lower price (and more loopholes are being discovered and exploited) there is no general way in which books may be bought at a discount, with a single exception. Publishers divide their product into two types for sales purposes, 'net' and 'non-net'. Many educational and technical books are 'non-net' and may be (1) bought in bulk at a discount and (2) supplied other than through a bookseller. Moreover, there is an important distinction between books in this category and those in the three I have already discussed, in that it is, at least theoretically, possible to create a book for a specific market (designed in terms of the school curriculum or the examination syllabus), to produce it in a quantity to meet a predictable demand, and to price it within a range that is known in advance will be acceptable. Given these three characteristics and the national (and, where some firms operating internationally are concerned, global) expansion of education and thirst for the acquisition of skills, it is not surprising that this is (rightly) considered to be an extremely profitable category of books to publish.

Finally, 'academic' books are those whose content or approach directs them primarily at a specialized, professional audience of a level somewhat above those in the previous category. They differ, too, in that the material they present is usually original in some respect, and in that they are not primarily designed to meet examination-style requirements (though they may indeed be so used). They are directed at an audience of university or equivalent level and above. Interestingly, the changes that have taken place in university curricula and the whole structure of higher education seem to be leading to a hybrid category somewhere between this and the previous one.

Publishers' 'ideal-types'

Just as we can classify books so, to a lesser extent, can we characterize publishers according to the books they produce. However, I am not going to present an exhaustive classification. Rather, I want to describe some 'ideal-type' publishers, in Weber's sense of the word.[3] That is, we should not, necessarily, expect to find any publishing house actually existing with quite the purity of characteristics of the conceptual type. In constructing these ideal-types, I want to take two factors into account: first, publishers' beliefs about the profitability or otherwise of different kinds of books; second, the constitution of publishers' lists. These consist of two components. On the one hand, they include current titles, that is, books published recently and still (with the exception of certain bestsellers) in stock from the first printing: on the other hand, they include the 'back-list', that is, books published some time previously and kept available by reprinting. (The process Compton Mackenzie describes in his memoirs whereby the presses were stopped after a very short run, and restarted in order to give a book the sales cachet of having reached a second printing, seems to have fallen into abeyance.) The first ideal-typical publisher corresponds to what is probably the public definition of the profession. His current list is composed of general books and fiction (mostly, but not entirely, 'quality' fiction), with a sprinkling of literature and belles lettres. Many of the best-known and longest established houses come very close to this picture. Given the beliefs that are held (on good grounds for the most part) about profitability, the economic situation of houses of this type would seem, at best, marginal. Indeed, my own research suggests that a 5 per cent return on capital is common; in other words, the current lists of these publishers are simply not economically viable. I shall return to the question of why this should be the case later. However, the back-list of this type of publisher will provide a large proportion both of the total list of books he has available, and of the house's income.

The second ideal type, the house that produces academic books, is closely approached by the great university presses, and one or two others. Here the economic picture is somewhat obscure. Though the market may not be gauged with anything like the precision that is theoretically possible for educational books it is, nevertheless, very much more predictable than that for general books and fiction. As against this, academic books are often expensive to produce, and tend to have a low rate of turnover. Despite recent advances in reprinting techniques which have, to some extent, obviated against the need for massive stockholding the amount of capital that may have to be tied up in an academic book, remains relatively high. For this reason, university presses must either be extremely well established, as with the Oxford and Cambridge University Presses, and be able to draw on the returns from past capital invested, or receive large grants-in-aid, as with many American university presses. Generally speaking, with academic books, the distinction between current and back-list titles is a nominal one.

The third type, the educational and technical publisher, bears a much closer resemblance to production industries at large. Of necessity, the product is geared to market demands. New titles will be produced to meet a new demand, and old titles kept in print solely on condition that a sufficient demand continues. In view of the way in which school syllabuses and educational purchasing operate, this tends to mean that titles remain profitably in print for a considerable time. Teachers tend to become accustomed to a course set around a particular text; it is cheaper to replace a few copies a year rather than the whole stock. The proven popularity and profitability of titles using a particular substance and style make publishers very wary of taking on, developing and producing new materials.

The final type I would call the 'genre', or 'formula' publishers. Here the content is less important than the market, in that the house, using the technique of 'variations on a theme' designs and produces books geared to a specific audience demand. Though these are usually light fiction – romances,[4] westerns, detective stories – some large, illustrated works (on art, objets d'art, natural history, travel) are coming to be produced in this way, at relatively low prices for a mass market, to meet a new type of demand. Based on criteria of low unit profit and high, rapid turnover, this style of publishing offers high profit at relatively high risk. The product is essentially a luxury consumer goods, subject like others in its class to the vagaries of public taste and dependent (in view of its mass market) upon general prosperity.

Clearly publishers' beliefs about the profitability of different categories of books provide us with a clue to the goals at which they aim.

The role of the publisher

Though I have concentrated my attention up to now on books, I have touched on some of the complex of forces operating on the publisher. I want now to consider some of these more directly. Standing, in a sense, midway between an author and his audience, publishers may choose to focus their concerns on one or the other or (though rarely) on both. Those who focus on the author see themselves as playing a rather passive role: their task, as they view it, is to provide expert, technical skills that will enable a manuscript to be turned into the finished product, available in the bookshop. If, in addition, they define the goal of their organization as primarily a cultural one, concerned with the transmission of values, there are certain obvious questions we have to ask. What values do these publishers have? How are these values reflected in a particular house's output? What mechanisms operate within a publishing house to control and achieve its cultural goal? More immediately, how do publishers reconcile the need to remain economically viable with the fact that imaginative literature of excellence, where those values are typically seen as located, is believed to be (for the most part, justifiably) likely to lose money? After all, publishers must stay above a minimum financial threshold if they are to survive. The first questions need extensive empirical data, of which we have little. My own preliminary investigations are suggestive, at least on the initial point. Publishers are, even by the standards of other élite occupational groups, disproportionately drawn from families high in the social scale. Furthermore, rates of self-recruitment (i.e., the proportion of sons following fathers' occupations) compare with the highest mentioned in David Glass's *Social Mobility in Britain*.[5] Finally, they are very highly academically qualified as a group. Of the sample of publishing managers I surveyed, 65 per cent were good honours graduates, or better. We would expect the values of publishers then, in view of these factors, to show some signs of their élite, academic origins. In Britain one of the core values of this group, to be seen in educational philosophies and elsewhere, has typically been, for want of a better description, gentlemanly excellence, usually coupled with an aversion to commercial values – what our more snobbish Victorian forefathers called 'trade'. Yet publishing, as I have said, is perforce trade and members of the profession frequently refer to the activity as a whole as 'the book trade'. We might rephrase the last question I put earlier then, in terms of this apparent paradox. General publishers of the type I am considering have a policy of publishing anything 'good' that they are offered, provided only that it is within their sphere of competence. (On the whole, they tend to avoid non-literary special-ist, academic books since they feel themselves unable to judge them.) However, since they believe their own values to embody the 'good', or at the very least to provide a touchstone for detecting it, this means that they will only publish those things that are consonant with their own values. Again, since it takes time to reach positions of authority within a firm, there is an inherent tendency towards conservatism in values. Included in this notion of 'the good' is a belief in the notion of spontaneous creativity. Hence, publishers of this type rarely, if ever, explicitly commission a work from an author. At the opposite pole, the bulk of educational and technical works are written to a specific, often detailed, commission. Only in this way can a market demand be met. To a very limited extent, the process is spreading to the general pub-lisher, except that he would normally commission something from an author, rather than a work from someone, and the difference in emphasis is significant.

The reasons for and resolution of the paradox and problem I posed earlier is complex. In the first place, publishing of this type is only possible where some other sector of organization than the current general-cum-fiction list is producing reasonable profits. This can come about in either or both of two ways. On the one hand, the back-list may be extremely profitable. On the other, a profit-creating sideline may be developed to provide, effectively a subsidy. This will usually be concerned – hardly surprisingly – with education in some way or another. Where this is the case, the 'sideline' will have very low status, and not be regarded as 'real publishing'. These facts do not explain *why* publishers go on producing books that will lose money, only how it is possible for them to do so. The answer to the 'why?' question is two-fold. On the one hand, it is culturally determined and lies in the value-system of the publisher; on the other hand, it is economically determined and lies in the need to create a back-list for the future. Very few of the back-list books that now keep their publishers solvent made money at their time of publication. Moreover, picking the 'classics' of the future is somewhat akin to picking Derby winners with a pin, the difference being that picking a Derby winner is hardly likely to be a matter of individual survival, whilst picking future classics may well affect the ultimate survival of a publishing house. Hence, there tends to develop an endless balancing act between current losers that may make good, and the back-list profits. When the balancing act fails, the house has two options: to be taken over by someone who has capital (and, perhaps, expertise) to inject – this has become increasingly common in recent years; or to cease publishing new books for a period in order to recover, which is less common, since it involves a considerable loss of reputation, not to mention the obvious risk of mortgaging the future.

We have seen something of the part that the public plays as an economic force interacting with the publisher. Of its other parts, probably the most important it plays is at a remove, in the mind of the publisher. (Though for the publisher whose involvement in books is primarily for a profit, this part is effectively subsumed in its first role.) General-cum-quality fiction publishers tend to see the public as cast actually or potentially in their own image. Like them, it is deeply concerned with the house's image and wary of any activity that might prejudice its cultural prestige and values. The extent to which the traditional publisher deludes himself that his reputation and imprint are essential in sustaining sales borders on megalomania. What little research is available shows that, with the exception of one or two houses (notably Penguin, for obvious and special reasons) the public pays singularly little attention to imprints. Indeed, Dr Mann's survey of bookshop use[6] suggests that an over-emphasis on the imprint as opposed to the content may be counter-productive. Further, tendencies towards conservatism are enhanced by the (in all likelihood, mistaken) belief that the public has certain expectations which should not be too emphatically controverted. It is this image of the public which reinforces the low key publicity presentation which characterizes publishers of this type. The role of advertising in book sales is controversial and little known. It may well be that while large-scale, widespread publicity for a book has little effect on hard-cover sales, it has considerable impact on the subsidiary rights (paperback, films, serialization and so on) on which publishers have become increasingly dependent, financially. Earlier I spoke of the 'labels' that are attached to books. A strong case could be made that the whole process of categorizing books as respectable, somewhat staid – even dull – has acted as a continuing brake on the growth of general publishing in an age of increased literacy and leisure. Recent surveys have shown that book-reading, let alone book-buying habits remain typically middle-class.

Just as publishers take pains not to disconcert their public by producing books that are out of key with their list as they see it, so they are equally careful not to give offence to actual or possible authors. The quality of the list and the house-style, in the broadest sense, are thought to be greater attractions to good authors than would be sales efficiency, say. It is characteristic, too, that as much as possible is done to conceal the cash nexus between author and publisher. The growth of the literary agent can be seen in this light, in a period when fewer and fewer authors have private incomes or sinecures, and when the rewards of successful authorship can be immense. Few authors have more than this negatively constraining role which the publisher attributes to them. Only where (and the cases are extremely rare) a house is effectively a 'one author firm' can that one author play a direct and positive role by threatening to move to another house if his desires are not met. Literary agents – a phenomenon of the last thirty or forty years – tend to have rather more power, since the number of large agents is smaller than the number of publishing houses, and the majority of authors use agents. This is strengthened by the tendency of authors to feel more loyalty to their agent than to their publisher. Strategies for handling problems of this kind are relatively easily solved by the publisher whose goal is economic; he can calculate the probable profit or loss of a course of action and behave accordingly. For the publisher with a cultural goal such straightforward financial calculations will not be applicable. A parallel process is believed by publishers to have taken place amongst themselves. Just as part of the mythology of the trade now is that in 'the good old days' authors were loyal to their publishers, so it is believed that publishers used to be loyal to one another. The practice of 'poaching' authors (i.e., persuading them to change publishers) is seen as an unfortunate post-war phenomenon. Anyone who has read memoirs or biographies concerned with an earlier era of publishing will know that this is far from the case. In technical terms, the publisher's role vis-à-vis the author is, on the whole, a passive one. In Britain, unlike America, it is rare for a house to have its own style, in the limited sense. That is, there is little attempt to impose a particular mode of language usage, or to insist on any form of 'party line' towards issues, at least not explicitly; the values to which I referred earlier may play an analogous role, circumscribed by norms of individualistic creativity and a strong commitment to the right of free expression.

Towards other media, publishers display a profound ambivalence. They depend, increasingly, as I have said, on the sale of subsidiary rights if they are to make sufficient profits to survive. In addition, films, television, and newspapers provide essential publicity. On the other hand, their brashness offends publishing notions of decorum and the threat they offer to leisure reading is more frequently noticed than the fillip that can be given to book-buying by such things as the television presentation of the *Forsyte Saga*. There is a belief too (sometimes reflected in book reviews) that the pure metal of literature is being debased by an alloy of books only intended as the basis for film scripts. The tardiness of English publishers in bringing out books on the film until the public had started to desert the cinemas reflects both the ambivalence and the conservatism of the trade.

In discussing the beliefs of publishers I have touched at several points on a complex of attitudes that, together, constitute a sort of 'Golden Age' mythology. The overall make-up of publishers' lists today differs surprisingly little from that of lists of fifty or sixty years ago, and with the exception of the paperback revolution, as it has been called, styles of production and presentation have scarcely altered. Indeed, mass literacy and its consequences seem to have stimulated conservatism rather than change. Why this should be the case would require a study of its own, and I can only sketch in the briefest of explanations. For hundreds of years its élite quality has been a defining characteristic of culture (in its restricted sense), and literacy a symbol of élite membership. At the same time culture has been accorded an almost magical potency. As gatekeepers of the magic power, publishers are threatened when the main tool in its manipulation becomes suddenly spread beyond the ritually pure, and hence *safe*, hands of the élite group. Perhaps one of the most dramatic pieces of evidence for this is the prosecuting counsel's submission, in the *Lady Chatterley* trial, that though the book was fit for the members of the jury, none of them would surely like their servants to read it.

How is the conservatism to be seen? Most noticeably visual styling and public presentation as a whole, with very few exceptions, reflect little of the changes in taste that are evinced in other fields. Many publishers, I have suggested, are subject to strains arising out of the inherent conflict between economic and cultural goals. This is exacerbated, on the one hand by major social changes (such as the spread of literacy and the steady, if sometimes slow, growth of leisure), which have extensive implications for book publishing; on the other, by a deepening in the cleavage that has always existed between the public and artists on the criteria of creative worth. Where the great publishers of the past saw their role as the creation of public taste, publishers today generally tend to respond to the cross pressures either by directing their attention to fulfilling market demands, or by trying to sustain or recreate what they believe to be the consensual values of the past. Though the facts it asserts may be wrong, the myth of the Golden Age serves both to help explain the passive, but nevertheless, positive, role that publishers exert, and, from their point of view, to legitimate it.

The paucity of the material available precludes any kind of conclusive answer to the questions I posed at the start. Nevertheless, this paper may serve to set out in more detail the context to those questions, and to illuminate the areas in which answers may be found.

3. Developments in Soviet Radio and Television News Reporting*

Gayle Durham Hollander

In the thirteen years since Stalin's death, the Soviet radio and television systems have greatly expanded.[1] This growth has been linked with important political developments of the sort most commonly described by the overly simple label 'liberalization'. Earlier, reliance on *Pravda* to set the line for other media had resulted in a slow news-handling process that could not compete with news broadcasting systems of the Western type. By the late 'fifties, access to foreign radio had increased to such an extent that Soviet news disseminators had to release news faster on their own domestic media.[2] Soviet officials today are continuing to try to contain this new, faster reporting within the confines of the traditional Soviet policy of controlled news, but this has produced strains on the theory and practice of mass communications in the USSR.

Theory and practice of mass communications

In 1960, *Partiinaya Zhizn (Party Life)* indicated the following major change in procedure:

> The central radio stations in Moscow must first of all ensure timely broadcasts of important political information, effective commentary on domestic and foreign events, the organization of various artistic programmes. . . . Because radio should give the population the important news before the newspapers do, TASS has been instructed to transmit news immediately to central and local stations.[3]

* First published in *Public Opinion Quarterly*, 31 (1967), pp. 359–65.

A handbook for radio journalists published three years later reiterated this directive: 'Radio should communicate all important news to the population earlier than do the newspapers.'[4]

The transferral to broadcasting media of primacy in news reporting was not accompanied by any changes in the basic orientation of news broadcasting, however. All mass media are still viewed as means of socializing the Soviet citizen; they are instruments of indoctrination in Communist values and ideology as interpreted by the Party leadership at any given time. Further, the media are pledged to act as agents of agitation for implementing Party economic, political, or social policies, which represent attempts to translate its ideology into reality. News, whether transmitted by printed or oral media, is viewed as the illustration of positive trends in the process of creating the Communist society: 'Events are regarded as being news only in so far as they can be meaningfully related to that process.'[5] Thus, human interest as understood in the West is still almost completely absent in Soviet news reporting; humans have significance only as symbols of social and historical processes. Similarly, reports of accidents and crime are infrequent; such happenings do not represent positive developments, and therefore are insignificant. A recently published handbook for those preparing 'Latest News' broadcasts on radio outlined the journalist's task of selecting news events so that the world appears as ideology has already described it. 'Latest News' broadcasts should be:

> Information in editions – not the impartial photographing of that which occurs in our enterprises and construction sites, in scientific and higher educational institutions. It is a question of the purposeful, directed selection of those facts and events which represent the broadest social interest, which graphically and convincingly propagandize the policy of our Party, mobilize the people for the successful construction of the Communist society.[6]

Those acquainted with Soviet literature will recognize the elements of 'socialist realist' thinking here – the representation of the present as one would like the future to be.

The political orientation of Soviet news coverage is evident in the order of news sources to be used. According to official instruction,[7] Party and government bodies are to be the prime sources of news items; following them in priority are economic councils, trade-union organs, and Komsomol (Young Communist League) bodies. While this official hierarchy may be circumvented in practice, its existence is nevertheless an indication of measures taken to ensure that 'correct' news is broadcast; content cannot but be dominated by Party and economic affairs under such a system. Foreign news comes largely from the wires of TASS or NOVOSTI, the official Soviet press agencies.

Other ways of influencing news content are not unique to broadcasting, but are important and currently effective. On the national level, a Party or government decree, which may be covert or published, can determine general propaganda campaigns (in which news reporting is included), organization of the broadcasting and journalism professions, or the treatment of a specific news item. On the local level, Party organs are responsible for supervising all enterprises, among them the broadcasting media. While such formal means of control are significant, it would be an error to attribute the still rather monolithic character of news broadcasting to their effect alone. Probably the most continuous control mechanism is self-censorship on the part of persons handling the news. Although this process exists to some degree everywhere, it is distinguished in the Soviet Union by the high sensitivity to political and ideological acceptability of material that is necessary. This sensitivity has become increasingly important in the past decade, when heavy-handed means of control have been largely replaced by more prophylactic means, the basis of which is the internalization of political expectations. Any Soviet news-writer or broadcaster should know how to handle a news item; indeed, he owes his position in part to that ability.

News content and scheduling

Since it is the general historical trend and not the isolated event that is important in Soviet news, topicality has not been a prime issue. A Party congress, for example, may occupy almost the entire news time for the duration of its proceedings. Other occurrences during this period are summarized only after the more historically significant event (such as the Party congress) is terminated. Domestic news is still heavily overweighted with the publicizing of economic achievements and Party and government affairs.

The absence of reportage on crime and accidents has become rather embarrassing for officials, since people learn of these happenings from other sources. The increase of foreign visitors to the Soviet Union has opened up one information channel; another was expanded with the lifting of jamming on foreign broadcasts to the Soviet Union in June of 1963. This loss of a monopoly over information has necessitated various changes in news reportage and broadcasting. Soviet journalists have openly discussed this development as a current problem of the profession:

> We must respond promptly to various, perhaps unfavourable, phenomena and incidents that occur in our life. Or else it turns out that while we keep silent, the people learn about them from foreign radio broadcasts and, furthermore, learn about them in incorrect and distorted interpretations. We still consider ourselves to have a monopoly in the field of information. But this isn't so. After all, by lagging in information, we sometimes involuntarily orient people to foreign radio, and once any false version begins it is difficult to stamp it out.[8]

Indications are that news broadcasts rank among the most listened-to programmes on Soviet radio. In interviews with recent Soviet émigrés,[9] 38 out of 43 reported that radio brings the news most quickly as compared with other Soviet channels. In 87 interviews, there were 58 mentions of some type of news programme as 'my favourite programme'. Most of the interviewees mentioned listening to news at least once a day. The prime listening times were early morning, evening (6 to 10 p.m.) and late night (after 10 p.m.), or some combination of these three times.

By virtue of their frequency, news broadcasts form a sort of framework for the broadcasting day. Although straight reportage remains the predominant form of presentation, attempts have been made to introduce greater variety in format. A television news programme called 'Television Accusation' contrasts good phenomena in Soviet life with bad, accusing those responsible and attempting to induce some change. Interviews, guest appearances, *feuilletons*, short commentaries, and chronicles are other common types of news programmes.

The bulk of radio news is broadcast over Programmes One and Two, from Moscow Central. Programme One, the national network station, is the backbone of foreign and non-local domestic news broadcasting; from it the local stations take the bulk of their news materials. The second programme, *Mayak* (or *Beacon*), was instituted in its present form in the summer of 1964. It represents one attempt to compete with popular foreign stations in the absence of jamming. Broadcasting on some of the same frequencies as foreign stations, *Mayak* is a composite of light music and hourly news – a response to the demands of listeners who prefer variety and up-to-date news broadcasts of foreign stations to the characteristically monotonous Soviet stations. Various republics have created their own *Beacon* programmes for local audiences: *Promin* in the Ukraine, *Araz* in Azerbaidzhan, and *Fakel* in the Sverdlovsk area. Moscow's Third Programme is musical and literary, with no significant amount of newscasting. A Fourth Programme broadcasts to the Far Eastern sections of the country, using news from Programme One. Table I summarizes the frequency and total time per day of radio news broadcasts.

TABLE I

FREQUENCY AND TOTAL TIME PER DAY OF SOVIET RADIO
NEWS BROADCASTS, JUNE, JULY, 1965

Station	Straight News		Press Review		Commentary	
	Times per day	Total minutes	Times per day	Total minutes	Times per day	Total minutes
Moscow:						
Programme One	8	120	2	25	1	20
Mayak	25	305	8	80	6	45
Programme Four (Siberia)	8	120	4	50	0	0
Kiev:						
Programme One	5	60	3	30	0	0
Promin	3	20	0	0	5	45

Sources: Radio Liberty Monitoring Reports: *Radio Moscow* (June–July, 1965); *Radio Kiev* (June–July, 1965).

Until the institution of the third television channel in Moscow during the spring of 1965, there were two major television programmes. One of these was oriented towards the European sector of the country, the other was national. There are now two main channels in most large cities, both of which broadcast news. Table II summarizes television news broadcast frequency in several cities in late 1964. Because of shorter broadcasting hours (usually at noon for two to three hours and in the evening from about 4 to 11 p.m.) and the less repetitious nature of television programming, news broadcasts on television are far less frequent than on radio.

TABLE II

TOTAL NUMBER AND MINUTES OF TELEVISION NEWS
BROADCASTS PER WEEK IN SELECTED SOVIET CITIES, 1964

City	Programme One		Programme Two	
	Total times	Total minutes	Total times	Total minutes
Leningrad, Aug. 24–30	11	235	13	190
Moscow, Dec. 7–13	14	260	7	190
Kiev, Oct. 6–11	12	280	no news scheduled	
Odessa, Oct. 6–11	12	265	no second programme	
Lugansk, Oct. 6–11	11	215	no second programme	

Sources: Leningrad: *Radio i televideniye*, August 22nd, 1964. Moscow: *Tsentralnoye televideniye*, December 17th, 1964. Other cities: *Govorit Kiyev*, October 2nd, 1964.

One problem of television news reporting has been to avoid simple repetition or rehashing of radio broadcasts and to impart a distinctive character to television news. The most explicit statement attempting to define the function of television in news broadcasting appeared in a *Pravda* editorial in August 1965:

Television viewers are interested in all the various events taking place in the country and abroad. Of course, Soviet people know about these events through reading newspapers and magazines and listening to the radio. From television they expect additional information, lively and clear commentaries, expanding their horizons, and helping them to understand better the events taking place. . . . Television, as distinguished from radio, has a full opportunity with its visual means (film clips, photos) to disclose more convincingly and sensibly to the viewer the meaning of any particular fact and show it to him visually.[10]

Conclusion

The recent developments in Soviet radio and television news reporting that we have been discussing may be viewed as a crystallization of possibly inherent problems in the traditional Soviet news-handling system. During Lenin's time, the newspaper was the most developed news medium. His experience with the underground press during the revolution made him cognizant of the tremendous power of the press in transmitting information to the population and forming public opinion. Censorship was a relatively effective device in the suppression of undesirable news. Since that time, however, media with radically different qualities, like radio and television, have gained prominence in the world, and the newspaper has had to yield some of its functions to them in the interests of expediency. The perfection and spread of radio and television have made necessary a revamping in use of communications media in the Soviet Union, as elsewhere. One aspect of this process in Soviety society is the re-ranking of domestic media to give radio and television their just priority in the rapid transmission of information. A second effect has been the injection of variety into the format of news presentation, and the inclusion of news items about accidents and other undesirable events about which information could previously be had only through foreign radio or word of mouth. A third aspect is the present attempt to delineate separate functions for the news media, so that they complement, not compete with, one another. Kharlamov and Mesyatsev, the last two Chairmen of the State Committee on Radio and Television, USSR, have clearly made significant attempts to respond realistically to these challenges of modern technology and the demands of their own developing society.

4. The Structure of Foreign News

The Presentation of the Congo, Cuba and Cyprus
Crises in Four Foreign Newspapers*

Johan Galtung and Mari Holmboe Ruge

1. *Introduction*

In this article the general problem of factors influencing the flow of
news from abroad will be discussed, following the kind of reasoning
given by Östgaard in his article,[1] but in a somewhat different way.
A systematic presentation of factors that seem to be particularly important will be followed by a simple theory and the deduction of some
hypotheses from them. No claim is made for completeness in the list of
factors or 'deductions'. Some of these hypotheses will then be tested
on data relating to the presentation in four Norwegian newspapers of
three particular and recent crises abroad. Gaps in our present knowledge will be indicated and some possible policy implications drawn.

The point of departure is our world as a geographic structure
divided roughly into 160 territories, most of which are called nations
and are 'autonomous'. The international community of nations is
structured by a number of variables and highly stratified into 'topdog'
and 'underdog' nations so that the world is geography on which are
superimposed two relatively similar levels of human organization: the
inter-individual and the international. The two levels are not independent of each other and the more they are linked (the more population
and leadership in any nation are interdependent), and the more nations
are interdependent because of increasing efficiency of communication
and military action,[2] the more valid is the old sociological slogan about
'everything's relevance for everything else'.

* First published in *Journal of International Peace Research*, 1 (1965) pp. 64–90.

Thus, the world consists of individual and national actors, and since it is axiomatic that action is based on the actor's image of reality, international action will be based on the image of international reality. This image is not shaped by the news media (press, radio, TV, newsreels) alone; personal impressions and contacts, professional relations abroad, diplomatic dispatches, etc., count too – whether less, equally much or more, we do not know. But the regularity, ubiquity and perseverence of news media will in any case make them first-rate competitors for the number-one position as international image-former. Since the adequacy of an action is often, but by no means always, positively related to the adequacy of the image on which it is based,[3] research into the adequacy of the image the news media give of the world is of primary importance.

At the interpersonal level the relationship between the *events*, the *perception* with all the selective and distorting factors that are operative under different circumstances, and the final *image* is relatively well explored. At the level of collective perception, where perception is made on behalf of others to be relayed to these others later, the situation is much more complicated. From world events to personal image we have the chain of communication presented in Figure I.

Figure I. *The chain of news communication*

world events → media   → media → personal   → personal
                perception ↑ image   perception ↑ image
                        selection   selection
                        distortion   distortion

We are concerned with the first half of this chain, from world events to news image, or, to be more specific, to the printed page in the newspaper since our data refer to that. In other words: *how do 'events' become 'news'?* This does not mean that the second half is unimportant – on the contrary, it is the personal image, not the newspaper that counts, but this will be discussed in a later article. In analysing the first half we shall treat the news media as non-personal indivisible entities and not distinguish between the journalist in the field in the news-sending country, the local press agency bureau, the district bureau, the central bureau of the press agency, the district bureau on the receiving end, the local bureau in the news-receiving country, the news editor in the receiving newspaper, the layout man, and what not – to indicate a chain with some seven or eight steps in it.[4] The chain may of course be much shorter if the newspaper has a correspondent; it may then be reduced to event-correspondent-editor, which involves two steps only. Östgaard has indicated many of the problems along this chain,[5] and detailed analysis here is certainly important for future research, but our analysis will treat news media *in abstracto* and limit itself to some reasoning from first principles.

2. *The theory*

To do this a metaphor with sufficient heuristic power to offer insights (but certainly not proofs) is useful. One such metaphor is as follows. Imagine that the world can be likened to an enormous set of broadcasting stations, each one emitting its signal or its programme at its proper wavelength. (Another metaphor might be of a set of atoms of different kinds emitting waves corresponding to their condition.) The emission is continuous, corresponding to the truism that something is always happening to any person in the world. Even if he sleeps quietly, sleep is 'happening'[6] – what we choose to consider an 'event' is culturally determined. The set of world events, then, is like the cacophony of sound one gets by scanning the dial of one's radio receiver, and particularly confusing if this is done quickly on the medium-wave or short-wave dials. Obviously this cacophony does not make sense, it may become meaningful only if one station is tuned in and listened to for some time before one switches on to the next one.

Since we cannot register everything, we have to select, and the question is what will strike our attention. This is a problem in the psychology of perception and the following is a short list of some obvious implications of this metaphor:

F_1: *If the frequency of the signal is outside the dial it will not be recorded.*

F_2: *The stronger the signal, the greater the amplitude, the more probable that it will be recorded as worth listening to.*

F_3: *The more clear and unambiguous the signal (the less noise there is), the more probable that it will be recorded as worth listening to.*

F_4: *The more meaningful the signal, the more probable that it will be recorded as worth listening to.*

F_5: *The more consonant the signal is with the mental image of what one expects to find, the more probable that it will be recorded as worth listening to.*

F_6: *The more unexpected the signal, the more probable that it will be recorded as worth listening to.*

F_7: *If one signal has been tuned in to the more likely it will continue to be tuned in to as worth listening to.*

F_8: *The more a signal has been tuned in to, the more probable that a very different kind of signal will be recorded as worth listening to next time.*

Some comments on these factors are in order. They are nothing but common-sense perception psychology translated into radio-scanning and event-scanning activities. The proper thing to do in order to test their validity would be to observe journalists at work or radio listeners operating with the dial – and we have no such data. For want of this the factors should be anchored in general reasoning and social science findings (but references to the latter will be given in the notes only since they are not essential to our reasoning).

The first factor is trivial when applied to radio sets, less so when applied to events in general. Since this is a metaphor and not a model we shall be liberal in our interpretation of frequency and proceed as follows. By the 'frequency' of an event we refer to the time-span needed for the event to unfold itself and acquire meaning. For a soldier to die during a battle this time-span is very short; for a development process in a country to take place the time-span may be very long. Just as the radio dial has its limitation with regard to electro-magnetic waves, so will the newspaper have its limitations, and the thesis is that *the more similiar the frequency of the event is to the frequency of the news medium, the more probable that it will be recorded as news by that news medium.* A murder takes little time and the event takes place between the publication of two successive issues of a daily, which means that a meaningful story can be told from one day to the next. But to single out one murder during a battle where there is one person killed every minute would make little sense – one will typically only record the battle as such (if newspapers were published every minute the perspective could possibly be changed to the individual soldier). Correspondingly, the event that takes place over a longer time-span will go unrecorded unless it reaches some kind of dramatic climax (the building of a dam goes unnoticed but not its inauguration). Needless to say, this under-reporting of trends is to some extent corrected by publications with a lower frequency. A newspaper may have a habit of producing weekly 'reviews', there are weeklies and monthlies and quarterlies and yearbooks – and there are *ad hoc* publications. If we concentrate on dailies, however, the thesis is probably valid and probably of some heuristic value when other aspects of news communication are to be unravelled.

The second thesis is simply that there is something corresponding to the idea of 'amplitude' for radio waves. What this says is only that the bigger the dam, the more will its inauguration be reported *ceteris paribus*; the more violent the murder the bigger the headlines it will make. It says nothing about what has greater amplitude, the dam or the murder. It can also be put in a more dichotomous form: there is a threshold the event will have to pass before it will be recorded at all.[7] This is a truism, but an important one.

The third hypothesis is also trivial at the radio level but not at the news level. What is 'signal' and what is 'noise' is not inherent; it is a question of convention,[8] as seen clearly when two radio stations are sending on the same frequency. Clarity in this connection must refer to some kind of one-dimensionality, that there is only one or a limited number of meanings in what is received. Thus interpreted the hypothesis says simply the following: the less ambiguity the more the event will be noticed. This is not quite the same as preferring the simple to the complex, but one precization of it rather; an event with a clear interpretation, free from ambiguities in its meaning, is preferred to the highly ambiguous event from which many and inconsistent implications can and will be made.[9]

The fourth hypothesis also deals with meaning but not with its ambiguity. 'Meaningful' has some major interpretations. One of them is 'interpretable within the cultural framework of the listener or reader' and all the thesis says is that actually some measure of *ethnocentrism* will be operative: there has to be *cultural proximity*. That is, the event-scanner will pay particular attention to the familiar, to the culturally similar, and the culturally distant will be passed by more easily and not be noticed. It is somewhat like the North European radio listener in say, Morocco: he will probably pass by the Arab music and speech he can get on his dial as quaint and meaningless and find relief in European music and French talk.

The other dimension of 'meaningful' is in terms of *relevance*: an event may happen in a culturally distant place but still be loaded with meaning in terms of what it may imply for the reader or listener. Thus the culturally remote country may be brought in via a pattern of conflict with one's own group.[10]

The fifth hypothesis links what is selected to the mental pre-image, where the word 'expects' can and should be given both its cognitive interpretation as 'predicts' and its normative interpretation as 'wants'. A person *predicts* that something will happen and this creates a mental matrix for easy reception and registration of the event if it does finally take place. Or he *wants* it to happen and the matrix is even more prepared, so much so that he may distort perceptions he receives and provide himself with images consonant with what he has wanted. In the sense mentioned here 'news' are actually 'olds', because they correspond to what one expects to happen – and if they are too far away from the expectation they will not be registered, according to this hypothesis of consonance.[11]

The sixth hypothesis brings in a corrective to the fourth and fifth. The idea is simply that it is not enough for an event to be culturally meaningful and consonant with what it expected – this defines only a vast set of possible news candidates. Within this set, according to the hypothesis, the more unexpected have the highest chances of being included as news. It is the unexpected *within the meaningful and the consonant* that is brought to one's attention, and by 'unexpected' we simply mean essentially two things: *unexpected* or *rare*. Thus, what is regular and institutionalized, continuing and repetitive at regular and short intervals, does not attract nearly so much attention, *ceteris paribus*, as the unexpected and *ad hoc* – a circumstance that is probably well known to the planners of summit meetings.[12] Events have to be unexpected or rare, or preferably both, to become good news.

The seventh hypothesis is the idea that once something has hit the headlines and been defined as 'news', then it will *continue* to be defined as news for some time even if the amplitude is drastically reduced.[13] The channel has been opened and stays partly open to justify its being opened in the first place, partly because of inertia in the system and partly because what was unexpected has now also become familiar. Thus F_7 is, in a sense, deducible from F_3 and F_6.

The eighth and final hypothesis refers to the *composition* of such units as evening entertainment for the family around the radio set, the front page of a newspaper, the newscast on radio, the newsreel on TV or in the cinema, and so on. The idea is this: imagine the news editor of a broadcasting station has received only news from abroad and only of a certain type. Some minutes before he is on the air he gets some insignificant domestic news and some foreign news of a different kind. The hypothesis is that the threshold value for these news items will be much lower than would otherwise have been the case, because of a desire to present a 'balanced' whole. Correspondingly, if there are already many foreign news items the threshold value for a new item will be increased.

As mentioned, these eight factors are based on fairly simple reasoning about what facilitates and what impedes perception. They are held to be culture-free in the sense that we do not expect them to vary significantly with variations in human culture – they should not depend much on cultural parameters. More particularly, we would not expect them to vary much along the east-west, north-south or centre-periphery axes which we often make use of to structure the world. In particular, these factors should be relatively independent of some other major determinants of the press. A newspaper may vary in the degree to which it caters to mass circulation and a free market economy. If it wants a mass circulation, all steps in the news chain will probably anticipate the reaction of the next step in the chain and accentuate the selection and distortion effects in order to make the material more compatible with their image of what the readers want. Moreover, a newspaper may vary in the degree to which it tries to present many aspects of the situation, or, rather, like the partners in a court case, try to present only the material that is easily compatible with its own political point of view. In the latter case selection and distortion will probably be accentuated and certainly not decrease.

But there is little doubt that there are also culture-bound factors influencing the transition from events to news, and we shall mention four such factors that we deem to be important at least in the north-western corner of the world. They are:

F_9: *The more the event concerns élite nations, the more probable that it will become a news item.*

F_{10}: *The more the event concerns élite people, the more probable that it will become a news item.*

F_{11}: *The more the event can be seen in personal terms, as due to the action of specific individuals, the more probable that it will become a news item.*

F_{12}: *The more negative the event in its consequences, the more probable that it will become a news item.*

Again, some comments are in order.

That news is *élite-centred*, in terms of nations or in terms of people, is hardly strange. The actions of the élite are, at least usually and in short-term perspective, more consequential than the activities of others: this applies to élite nations as well as to élite people. Moreover, as amply demonstrated by the popular magazines found in most countries, the élite can be used in a sense to tell about everybody. A story about how the king celebrates his birthday will contain many elements that could just as well have been told about anybody, but who in particular among ordinary men and women should be picked for the telling of the story? Elite people are available to serve as objects of general identification, not only because of their intrinsic importance. Thus in an élite-centred news communication system ordinary people are not even given the chance of representing themselves. *Mutatis mutandis*, the same should apply to nations.

More problematic is the idea of *personification*. The thesis is that news has a tendency to present events as sentences where there is a subject, a named person or collectivity consisting of a few persons, and the event is then seen as a consequence of the actions of this person or these persons. The alternative would be to present events as the outcome of 'social forces', as structural more than idiosyncratic outcomes of the society which produced them. In a structural presentation the names of the actors would disappear much as they do in sociological analysis and much for the same reason – the thesis is that the presentation actually found is more similar to what one finds in traditional personified historical analysis. To the extent that this is the case the problem is *why*, and we have five different explanations to offer:

1. Personification is an outcome of *cultural idealism* according to which man is the master of his own destiny and events can be seen as the outcome of an act of free will. In a culture with a more materialistic outlook this should not be the case. Structural factors should be emphasized, there will be more events happening to people or with people as instruments than events caused by people.

2. Personification is a consequence of the need for meaning and consequently for *identification*: persons can serve more easily

as objects of positive and negative identification through a combination of projection and empathy.

3. Personification is an outcome of the *frequency-factor*: persons can act during a time-span that fits the frequency of the news media, 'structures' are more difficult to pin down in time and space.

4. Personification can be seen as a direct consequence of the *élite-concentration* but as distinct from it.

5. Personification is more in agreement with modern techniques of news gathering and news presentation. Thus, it is easier to take a photo of a person than of a 'structure' (the latter is better for movies – perhaps), and whereas one interview yields a necessary and sufficient basis for one person-centred news story, a structure-centred news story will require many interviews, observation techniques, data gathering, etc. Obviously, there is an egg-chicken argument implied here since it may also be argued that personification came first and that techniques, the whole structure of news communication, were developed accordingly.

We only offer those explanations without choosing between them; first of all because there is no reason to choose as long as they do not contradict each other, and secondly because we have neither data nor theory that can provide us with a rational basis for a choice. It is our hunch that future research will emphasize that these factors reinforce each other in producing personification.

When we claim that *negative* news will be preferred to positive news we are saying nothing more sophisticated than what most people seem to refer to when they say that 'there is so little to be happy about in the news', etc. But we can offer a number of reasons why this state of affairs appears likely, just as we did for the factor of personification. We shall do so using the other factors relatively systematically:

1. Negative news enters the news channel more easily because it satisfies the *frequency* criterion better. There is a *basic asymmetry* in life between the positive, which is difficult and takes time, and the negative, which is much easier and takes less time – compare the amount of time needed to bring up and socialize an adult person and the amount of time needed to kill him in an accident: the amount of time needed to build a house and to destroy it in a fire, to make an aeroplane and to crash it, and so

on. The positive cannot be too easy, for then it would have low scarcity value. Thus, a negative event can more easily unfold itself completely between two issues of a newspaper and two newscast transmissions – for a positive event this is more difficult and specific. Inaugurating or culminating events are needed. A PR-minded operator will, of course, see to that – but he is not always present.

2. Negative news will more easily be *consensual and unambiguous* in the sense that there will be agreement about the interpretation of the event as negative. A 'positive' event may be positive to some people and not to others and hence not satisfy the criterion of unambiguity. Its meaning will be blurred by other overtones and undertones.

3. Negative news is said to be more *consonant* with at least some dominant pre-images of our time. The idea must be that negative news fulfils some latent or manifest needs and that many people have such needs. Of the many theories in this field we prefer the cognitive dissonance version because it is falsifiable. The theory, however, presupposes a relatively high level of general anxiety to provide a sufficient matrix in which negative news can be embedded with much consonance. This should be the case during crises,[14] so a test of this theory would be that during crises news that is not related to the crisis tends to be more negative and not more positive (as a theory of compensation rather than of dissonance/reduction would predict).

4. Negative news is more *unexpected* than positive news, both in the sense that the events referred to are more rare, and in the sense that they are less predictable. This presupposes a culture where changes to the positive, in other words 'progress', are somehow regarded as the normal and trivial thing that can pass under-reported because it represents nothing new. The negative curls and eddies rather than the steady positive flow will be reported. The test of this theory would be a culture with *regress* as the normal, and in that case one would predict over-reporting of positive news. This is exemplified by news about the illness of an important person: the slightest improvement is over-reported relative to a steady decline.

Again we do not have sufficient theory to make a choice between these possible explanations – nor do we have to do so since they do not exclude each other.

As to these last four factors it was mentioned that they seem to be of particular importance in the northwestern corner of the world. This does not mean that they are not operating in other areas, but one could also imagine other patterns of relationship between the set of events and the set of news. Table I shows some examples:

TABLE I

SOME PATTERNS OF NEWS STRUCTURE

Pattern	F_9 nation	F_{10} people	F_{11} personification	F_{12} negativization
I	élite centred	élite centred	person centred	negative centred
II	élite centred	élite centred	structure centred	positive centred
III	élite centred	élite centred	both	negative centred
IV	non-élite centred	élite centred	person centred	positive centred

Pattern I is the pattern we have described above. Pattern II would, where the last two aspects are concerned, be more in agreement with socialist thinking, and where the first two are concerned, with big-power thinking. It might fit the news structure of the Soviet Union, but with the important proviso that one would probably use Pattern III to describe Western powers. Similarly, a newly independent developing nation might use pattern IV for itself, but also receive pattern III for former colonial powers. But all this is very speculative.[15]

Let us then list systematically the twelve factors we have concentrated on in this analysis; with subfactors:

Events become news to the extent that they satisfy the conditions of

F_1: *frequency*
F_2: *threshold*
$F_{2.1}$: *absolute intensity*
$F_{2.2}$: *intensity increase*
F_3: *unambiguity*
F_4: *meaningfulness*
$F_{4.1}$: *cultural proximity*
$F_{4.2}$: *relevance*

F_5:   *consonance*
$F_{5.1}$: *predictability*
$F_{5.2}$: *demand*
F_6:   *unexpectedness*
$F_{6.1}$: *unpredictability*
$F_{6.2}$: *scarcity*
F_7:   *continuity*
F_8:   *composition*
F_9:   *reference to élite nations*
F_{10}: *reference to élite people*
F_{11}: *reference to persons*
F_{12}: *reference to something negative*

As mentioned, these twelve factors are not independent of each other: there are interesting inter-relations between them. However, we shall not attempt to 'axiomatize' on this meagre basis.

Let us now imagine that all these factors are operating. This means, we hypothesize, three things:

1. *The more events satisfy the criteria mentioned, the more likely that they will be registered as news* (selection).
2. *Once a news item has been selected what makes it newsworthy according to the factors will be accentuated* (distortion).
3. *Both the process of selection and the process of distortion will take place at all steps in the chain from event to reader* (replication).

Thus the longer the chain, the more selection and distortion will take place according to this – but the more material will there also be to select from and to distort if one thinks of the press agencies relative to special correspondents. In other words, we hypothesize that every link in the chain reacts to what it receives fairly much according to the same principles. The journalist scans the phenomena (in practice to a large extent by scanning other newspapers) and selects and distorts, and so does the reader when he gets the finished product, the news pages, and so do all the middle-men. And so do, we assume, people in general when they report something, and, for instance, diplomats when they gather material for a dispatch to their ministry – partly because they are conditioned by their psychology and their culture partly because this is reinforced by the newspapers.

In general this means that the cumulative effects of the factors should be considerable and produce an image of the world different from 'what really happened' – for instance in the ways indicated by Östgaard.[16] However, since we have no base-line in direct reports on 'what really happened' on which this can be tested we shall proceed in a different direction. Our problem is how the factors relate to each other in producing a final outcome.

Imagine that all factors, for the sake of simplicity, are dichotomized so that an event either possesses them or does not possess them. A given event can receive a score from 0–12 according to this system, and we claim that this is as good a score of that elusive concept of 'newsworthiness' as any, in a culture where F_8–F_{12} are valid. This has two theoretical implications that will be spelt out. The first one is almost too simple to mention:

Additivity hypothesis: The higher the total score of an event, the higher the probability that it will become news, and make headlines.

This may be seen as a hypothesis about how journalists work, about how the night editor reacts to incoming news-script or about how the reader reacts when he scans his newspaper for something worth reading. It may be more valid in the first two than in the last case – we do not know. But it is interesting to put down some pairs that should be considered particularly newsworthy:

(9, 10): *news about élite people in élite nations*[17]
(9, 12): *news of a negative nature relating to élite nations – in other words, big power conflict*
(10, 12): *news of a negative nature relating to élite people – in other words, struggle for power etc., at the top of society*
(11. 12): *news of a negative nature relating to persons – in other words, scandals.*

It is hardly necessary to make a content analysis to substantiate the claim that these four categories account for a sizeable fraction of the news presented by newspapers in most parts of the world.

But there is another hypothesis that is less trivial. An event obviously does not have to score 12 to hit the headlines. Imagine the floor level for acceptance is at score 6, which can be obtained in $\binom{12}{6} = 924$ different ways. (This high number, by the way, explains why factors may be operating and still not be noticed by the public: the variety is too great.) The implication of this is only that if the event is low on one dimension or factor *it may compensate for that by being high on another*, and still make the news. For instance, the less an event refers to persons as actors the more negative will it have to be (earthquakes, accidents that are presented in terms of technical errors, not in terms of 'the human factor'). The more culturally close and hence meaningful the event, the less does it have to refer to élite people – and vice versa: the more culturally distant the event, the more should it refer to élite people, *ceteris paribus* (which corresponds to the impression that rank-and-file people are highly under-reported when they live in far away countries). And so on, and so forth: this will be spelt out in section 5 below.

Since we have 12 factors this principle gives rise to $\binom{12}{6} = 66$ hypotheses, all of the following form:

Complementarity hypothesis:
$F_i \dashrightarrow F_j$, $i \neq j$; $i, j = 1, 2, \ldots \ldots \ldots 12$

The reasoning is always the same; if an event is low on F_i, then it will have to be high on some F_j to make news at all. For a low F_i the probability that any F_j is high is greater than for a high F_i – since a high F_i has already contributed towards the total score. According to the additivity hypothesis there will also be news where both are high, and much prominence will be given to them. But events where both are low will not be admitted as news.

Thus, for the simple case of two factors only, F_i and F_j, we have the three kinds of events indicated in Table II:

TABLE II

A TRICHOTOMY OF EVENTS ACCORDING TO NEWSWORTHINESS

	F_i	F_j	Score of newsworthiness
Type 1. Prominent news	high	high	2
Type 2. Ordinary	high	low	1
	low	high	
Type 3. Events, not news	low	low	0

The additivity hypothesis focuses on type 1 and the complementarity hypothesis on type 2 – one might then add the obvious *exclusion hypothesis* that would focus on type 3.

We then turn to the presentation of our data and to a systematic testing and discussion of a selection of the hypotheses mentioned.

3. *The data*

We have selected four Norwegian newspapers, three international crises, and for each crisis a number of variables to use in the content analysis of what the newspapers wrote about the crises. The rationales behind our selections are as follows.

a. *The newspapers.* Newspapers play an important role in Norway[18] and appear in a relatively decentralized pattern. However, when it comes to foreign news only newspapers in the bigger cities would give sufficient coverage to merit a content analysis, and particularly the newspapers in the capital, Oslo. They are 10 in number, and we have selected 4 according to the following design:

TABLE III

THE NEWSPAPERS IN THE SAMPLE
AND THEIR AVERAGE CIRCULATION

	Morning		Afternoon	
	I		II	
Radical	1960	67,494	1960	98,352
	1964	67,000	1964	95,000
	III		IV	
Conservative	1960	21,204	1960	37,040
	1964	16,800	1964	38,000

No. I is the government paper, no. II is the afternoon paper of the widest circulation, no. III a conservative paper and no. IV is a conservative afternoon paper, of tabloid format. Apart from the conservative morning paper, circulation figures have been constant during the period. As usual the morning papers are considered more 'serious', and indeed are, at least in terms of lay-out, use of headlines and vocabulary

– this holds true for the radical as well as for the conservative press. But these political terms are generic terms and do not imply that the papers in the same category follow the same party line.[19]

The reason for this particular choice lies in the experimental design we obtain: by means of the two axes in the Table we get a sufficient dispersion to provide a setting for replication. A finding that holds true for all four papers will receive a higher degree of confirmation when the papers are different than when they are similar.[20]

b. *The crises.* We have selected three crises, and according to a very simple experimental design. We wanted both synchronic and dia-chronic comparisons to check for consistency in the way news was presented in the four Norwegian papers. For that reason two crises were selected that occurred simultaneously and otherwise were roughly comparable: the Congo and Cuba crises in the summer of 1960. In 1964 a third crisis occurred that had some of the same characteristics, viz. the Cyprus crisis, and we decided to give it the same kind of analytical treatment. Obviously none of the three crises have very definite points of initiation and termination, so we had to select more or less arbitrary cutting points. For the Congo and Cuba these cuts were made so as to coincide almost with the month of July 1960, which will be remem-bered as a rather conflict-laden one. For Cyprus the month of March and the first half of April 1964 were included. In three appendices we have given chronological surveys of what happened in the three areas during the periods mentioned, according to *Keesing's Contemporary Archives.* We do not claim that they represent well-defined chapters in the books about these crises – nor is that in any sense essential for our purpose.

It may be objected that these three crises are much too special to give a basis for assessing the structure of foreign news, and we would agree with that assertion. On the other hand, the three crises contain elements of particular interest and relevance in the current world situation. The conflicts are acted out in theatres remote from the élite northwestern corners of the world – but with traditional powers in that corner deeply involved – Belgium, France, the USA, Britain. In all three cases world conflicts, both of the East-West and the North-South variety, are superimposed on local conflicts or vice versa: local conflicts develop from world conflicts. The UN intervened in the Congo and Cyprus conflicts and not in the Cuba conflict. In short, many elements of the contemporary international situation are present. In addition the conflicts are so similar that roughly the same analytical scheme can be used so as to obtain comparability.

c. *The variables.* The *'unit of analysis'* is the press cutting as defined by the newspaper itself when it typographically sets a unit apart from its surroundings, such as a news story, an editorial, an article (reportage, interview) or a letter to the editor – to quote the categories we have used. The *contextual unit* is the newspaper itself, which means that for all units we have two kinds of variables: *contextual variables* referring to the newspaper (its name, party colour, date, etc.), and *proper variables* that refer to the unit itself. These variables may again be subdivided into variables that apply to the cutting as a whole (its presentation in the newspaper, its length, its 'type' as above, the source in terms of press agency, person quoted, etc.) and variables that apply to what is written. As to the latter we have worked with a list of items and coded a unit according to the presence or absence of these items.

More specifically we have been interested in:

1. Nation		underdog (colony)		topdog (motherland)		
2. People	top leader	élite		rank-and-file		no people
3. Perspective	East-West	East-colony	West-colony	motherland-colony	UN-colony	intra-colony
4. Mode	negative		positive	neutral	(both or neither)	
5. Focus	economic		political	social		cultural

We have used the generic terms 'underdog-colony' and 'topdog-motherland' for, respectively, Congo-Cuba-Cyprus (Greek or Turkish) on the one hand and Belgium/France-us-Britain/Greece/Turkey on the other. The terms denote a difference in rank and a dependence relationship that is basic to the crises – and nothing else. As can be seen at a glance the list covers some but certainly not all of the factors we are interested in, according to the theory – nevertheless they can be brought to bear on a number of the hypotheses.

Let us then give in Table IV a brief survey of the nature of our data.

Although it makes little sense to pool the data from the four newspapers – the sample is made for replication and not for estimation – unless they can be shown to be sufficiently homogeneous, it is interesting to see that 91% of the cuttings are news messages in all three cases.

TABLE IV

SURVEY OF THE PRESS CUTTINGS CODED

Paper	Congo			Cuba			Cyprus		
	News	Other	(N)	News	Other	(N)	News	Other	(N)
I	89%	11%	(112)	98%	2%	(37)	96%	4%	(171)
II	96%	4%	(100)	89%	11%	(43)	88%	12%	(178)
III	90%	10%	(103)	88%	12%	(65)	91%	9%	(241)
IV	87%	13%	(108)	93%	7%	(29)	92%	9%	(75)
Total	91%	9%	(423)	91%	9%	(174)	91%	9%	(665)

Thirty-six units were editorials (divided 23–4–9 on the three crises) and there were 58 articles, etc. (divided 25–8–25). But out of a total of 1,262 pieces this means 3% and 5% respectively – and the number of letters to the editor was less than 1% of the total. Although we shall certainly not neglect this 9% in the total picture we nevertheless feel

TABLE V

THE DISTRIBUTION OF THE NEWS MESSAGES
ON THE PRESS AGENCIES*

	Congo	Cuba	Cyprus
Associated Press (AP)	12%	20%	9%
United Press International (UPI)	20%	17%	17%
Reuters	31%	22%	52%
Agence France-Presse (AFP)	19%	15%	24%
Norsk Telegrambyrå (NTB)[22]	28%	20%	54%
Tass	1%	2%	0%
Others	4%	1%	4%
(N)	(382)	(158)	(612)
Own correspondent	2%	1%	7%†

* Percentages do not add up to 100% since items from different agencies are often pooled together in one unit, and sometimes there is no reference to agency.

† 43 cuttings out of which 37 or 86% are due to paper II – it had a correspondent in Cyprus and this accounts for 23% of its coverage.

justified in focusing the analysis of what was written in these four papers on the news items.

And this brings us to our main justification in presenting these data at all, the answer to the obvious 'Who cares about four Norwegian papers in the world? – at most half a million Norwegians'. We are concerned with who has transmitted the news and for each unit we have put down the press agency or agencies quoted as a source:

Table V substantiates what we are after: the sources of the news in these Norwegian newspapers – among the most important politically – are international. 'Own correspondent' is quite insignificant as a category, which is not strange, taking into consideration the economy of Norwegian newspapers and the distance to these particular theatres.

This means, briefly, that foreign press agencies account for about 95% of the news items about these three crises, and the news items account for 91% of the total number of units appearing in these papers about these crises. That, in turn, means that four foreign press agencies take care of 95% of 91% or about 87% of the total – which again means that Norwegians, *in casu*, are rather dependent for their images of how the international system functions on the quality and quantity of news delivered through these agencies.[22]

Consequently our study is a study of a part of the foreign news system, using how it impinges on four Norwegian newspapers in three crises as twelve case studies.

4. *Testing the hypotheses*

We then proceed to tests of the theory of the structure of foreign news with the data we have. All we can do is to exhaust the possibilities our data give for tests of the theory, and we start with:

H_1: *The more distant the nation, the higher the tendency to report élite action.*

If a nation is 'distant', here of course taken in the cultural and not in the geographical sense, identification with rank-and-file people will be correspondingly low. At the same time, to become news events will have to fulfil some other requirements. We shall first test this hypothesis on the Congo and Cuba crises since here what is close and what is distant is so obvious. The data are as in Table VI:

TABLE VI

DISTANCE OF NATION AND RANK OF PEOPLE REPORTED

Crisis	Congo			Cuba		
Nation	Congo	Belgium	% diff.	Cuba	USA	% diff.
Top leader	47%	15%	+32	53%	23%	+30
Elite	50%	40%	+10	47%	39%	+ 8
Common people	30%	35%	− 5	24%	6%	+18
(N)		(158)			(382)	

Reading downwards one would expect decreasing percentage differences according to the hypothesis; each percentage difference should be lower than the preceding ones. This holds in five out of the six cases and gives us a degree of confirmation of 0·84 using that as a criterion. Rank-and-file Americans went under-reported in Cuba – and this is certainly understandable if one compares this with the Congo case. There is a difference between nationalizing industrial enterprises and open conflict: the former is more abstract and does not give rise to the same amount of stories about women and children, for instance.

Let us then turn to the data from Cyprus. They are complicated by two factors. First of all, we do not at all have a clear pattern with two parties to the conflict, as between the Congo and Belgium and between Cuba and the USA in July 1960. At least five parties are involved at three levels of dominance. At the bottom there is the conflict between Greek Cypriots and Turkish Cypriots. Related to either and at an intermediate level is the conflict between Greece and Turkey, partly over Cyprus, partly over anything else that can be added. Above that level again looms Britain and other big powers, but we have concentrated on Britain because of her past as a colonial power in Cyprus and her present as the holder of major air-force bases on the island. Thus, there is no clear bipolar pattern here as in the other two cases, with clear foci of identification.[23]

Secondly, the ethnical dimension is harder to apply. Greeks and Greek Cypriots, Turks and Turkish Cypriots are hardly very different relative to, say, Norwegians, although the Greeks are probably somewhat more familiar. But Britain can be set apart relative to the other four.

The data, in Table VII, are quite interesting and confirm more or less everything we have said, with one important proviso: The British

TABLE VII

DISTANCE OF GROUP AND RANK OF PEOPLE REPORTED, CYPRUS

	Greek Cypriots	Turkish Cypriots	Greeks	Turks	British
Top leader	30%	7%	11%	13%	5%
Elite	4%	4%	6%	5%	12%
Common people	40%	34%	6%	9%	15%
(N)		(612)			

are the only case where there is a clear increase in the percentage of reporting as we move down the social ladder. This is in agreement with the hypothesis of closest identification with the UK since none of the other four percentage-sets have a correspondingly clear and mono-tone pattern. But if we look at the rest an interesting suspicion emerges: that there has been more identification with the Turks than with the Greeks. Although the differences are small they are there: the common people/top leader ratio is 1·3 for the Greek Cypriots and 4·9 for the Turkish Cypriots, 0·6 for the Greeks and 0·8 for the Turks. Of course, the over-reporting of Makarios may be explained on such bases as the fact that he was well known from the fight against the British and that he, not the Turkish minority leader Dr Kutchuk, is the President of Cyprus. Nevertheless, there is the suspicion of differential identifica-tion built into the structure of the news. This is not a part of the hypo-thesis, however, since cultural distance can hardly be said to be a factor here. But it is nevertheless consistent with what was reported by one Norwegian with special insight into the area, as to British and Turkish views and perspectives being favoured in general in the Norwegian press.[24]

A particular way of looking at this hypothesis is by counting the number of times people are *quoted* in the news. To many readers it will be obvious that common people are quoted in only 2 of the 612 cuttings from the Cyprus crisis, to take one example (more frequently in the Congo news where relative identification with the Belgians was stronger). The élite and the top leaders are very frequently quoted and in general the ratio between cuttings where people are mentioned with quotes and mentioned without quotes decreases rapidly with decreasing rank. This, then, is one more factor of identification that favours the élite.

These general findings were checked in further newspapers and stood up against the test — the finding is repeated.

After the relationship between distance of nation and rank of the person reported we turn to the relationship between what we have called 'mode' of reporting and rank of persons reported. We have coded for each cutting whether it reports something 'negative' (something is destroyed, disrupted, torn down) or something 'positive' (something is built up, constructed, put together) and we are interested in knowing, for each of our three rank levels where people are concerned, whether they are seen in a context that is negative or positive (we omit the cuttings where the event-context is coded as 'neutral', 'both' or 'neither'). The obvious hypothesis to be deduced from the complementarity principle is:

H_2: *The lower the rank of the person, the more negative the event.*

We tested this hypothesis not only within each crisis but also for each country or nationality, which gives a total of nine cases (Cuba, the US, the Congo, Belgium, Greek Cypriot, Turkish Cypriot, Greece, Turkey, Britain). For each case we had three ranks (top leader, élite, rank-and-file) and for each rank the event could be either negative or positive since we discarded all cuttings that were not clear. To arrive at a composite measure -1 was given to a negative cutting and $+1$ to a positive one, and the average 'mode' was computed. Thus, with 80 negative cuttings and 35 positive we would get:

$$\frac{-80+35}{80+35} = \frac{-45}{115} = -0.39$$

In general the index ranges from -1 to $+1$, but the limits were hardly attained; the news was almost never completely one-coloured.

The data are as in Table VIII:

Out of the nine cases the hypothesis is clearly confirmed in cases nos. 3, 4, 5, 6, 7, and 9; which means in 6 of the 9 cases. In the other three

TABLE VIII

RANK OF THE PERSON AND MODE OF THE EVENT

	Top leader	Elite people	Common people
1. Cuba	−0·66	−0·51	−0·59
2. USA	−0·91	−0·72	−1·0
3. Congo	−0·39	−0·45	−0·47
4. Belgium	−0·08	−0·33	−0·45
5. Greek Cypriots	+0·16	−0·20	−0·38
6. Turkish Cypriots	+0·13	−0·43	−0·47
7. Greece	+0·21	−0·10	−0·20
8. Turkey	−0·26	−0·18	−0·38
9. Britain	+0·39	−0·20	−0·33

the trend from 'élite' to 'common people' is as it should be, but the three top leaders are seen in a more negative context than one would predict from the theory. Two of these cases, nos. 1 and 2, concern Cuba–US relations which were then in a very critical phase with both top leaders declaring negative actions against one another in an escalating sequence. The third case has to do with the Turkish top leader who in that period used a language characterized by threats and invasion menaces. (See Appendix III.) However, any exception from the rule can always be 'explained' away by invoking some special circumstances, so we shall be satisfied by noticing that out of a total of 27 numerical relationships (three for each case) 23 or 85% are in the expected direction, i.e., increasingly negative with decreasing rank. This is high even though the 27 relationships are not independent.

The general finding was checked for newspaper and for press agency and stood up well against that additional source of variation.

Thus, we have been brought a step forward towards the idea that common people have to appear or be presented in a negative context to make news, much more than is the case for people higher up – relatively speaking. It may well be that the total volume of negative events reported in connection with élite people – whether happening to them or having them as causes – is higher, due to the élite concentration reported above. But the proportion of negative events relative to the total number of contexts is higher the lower down in society the news comes from. Or, in other words, where positive events are reported they will be more likely to occur as contexts for an élite person than as something surrounding the common man.

However, one thing is context, another thing is who is seen as the cause of the event. According to our hypothesis one would expect the same pattern if the news stories are analysed for their tendency to attribute causes to somebody, and this is what we actually get as Table IX shows:

TABLE IX

RANK OF CAUSAL AGENT OF AN EVENT
AND THE MODE OF THE EVENT*

	Yule correlation, Q	Percentage difference	% negative in the news from the group
1. Cuba	1·0	21%	79%
2. USA	1·0	4%	96%
3. Congo	0·47	15%	91%
4. Belgium	0·46	18%	76%
5. Greek Cypriots	0·80	44%	65%
6. Turkish Cypriots	1·0	25%	94%
7. Cypriots, not specified	0·93	51%	87%
8. Greece	0·76	40%	86%
9. Turkey	0·57	18%	90%
10. Britain	0·57	27%	67%

* Top leader and élite have been pooled together.

Thus, the hypothesis is confirmed in 10 out of 10 cases: the lower the rank of the causal agent, the lower also the chance that he is seen in a context of something positive happening.

From here we may turn to the next hypothesis, thus completing the triangle we have made of variables:

H_3: *The more distant the nation, the more negative the event.*

The data in Table IX are relevant for the hypothesis and do not appear to give any clear pattern of confirmation. We have used the data about causal agents only, not the data where a nation may also appear as the victim of a negative act. As can be seen the British, as a total, with the three rank categories pooled together, appear as the causes of negative events less frequently than do the others, with the exception of the Greek Cypriots. Correspondingly, the Belgians are causes of negative events less than the Congolese. But the US are producers of negative acts more than the Cubans. One reason may be that these negative acts were actually not seen as negative by the agencies reporting them, often AP and UPI – but as adequate reactions in a situation of intense conflict.

It should be kept in mind that although the material includes all news from the Congo, Cuba and Cyprus in the periods of analysis, this is not the case with the 'mother countries': Belgium, the USA, the UK, Greece, and Turkey. News from those places which have no relevance to the areas of crisis have appeared in the papers in addition to the coded items. (Just to mention one example: the death and funeral of King Paul of Greece took place in the middle of March, causing Greece to appear quite heavily in the news stories for a week.) In the case of culturally close countries like the UK, the USA and Belgium, a great variety of news stories reaches the papers every day, regardless of major events. This would serve to balance off the negative impression these countries give as partners in the colonial crises analysed. Nevertheless we do not feel that H_3 has been confirmed, although it has not been disconfirmed either.

Another way of looking at these data now is to ask the question: Cuba, the Congo and Cyprus are far away places, they are 'culturally distant' (factor $F_{4.1}$). How do the events come to be represented at all as news? Because they are made 'relevant' (factor $F_{4.2}$). Thus we get the hypothesis:

H_4: *The more culturally distant the theatre, the more relevant must the event appear to be.*

Unfortunately, we do not have data from theatres with a wide range in cultural distance, but we can get some idea about the validity of this hypothesis in Table X from the distribution of the news stories on what might be called the 'perspective': A purely cold-war perspective involving East and West alone has not been made much use of, but

TABLE X

LOCATION OF THE THEATRE AND PERSPECTIVE
OF THE NEWS STORY

	Relations between						
Crisis	East-West	East 'colony'	West 'colony'	Mother-land-'colony'	UN-'colony'	Intra-'colony'	(N)
Cuba	9%	35%	22%	59%	9%	20%	(158)
Congo	9%	20%	20%	52%	41%	36%	(382)
Cyprus	0%	4%	8%	54%	59%	29%	(612)

East and West reappear in their relations with the 'colony', thus increasing relevance by linking the conflict to the East-West system. Most important, of course, is the 'motherland-colony' perspective, appearing in more than half of all the news stories. It may be said that this was what the conflicts were about, but that is not so obvious. There are many ways of presenting an event, and particularly many ways of presenting what to many appeared as fights of independence. Thus, nationalization of industries, independence of a new nation and the fight between a majority and a minority might all have been presented as fairly internal events with local actors only and the 'motherland' appearing more as a constant condition that could be mentioned in, perhaps, 10% of the stories. But this would have presupposed a much higher degree of identification, up to the level one probably had in the newspapers from the Congo, Cuba and Cyprus during those periods. Instead, events are seen as unfolding themselves in the periphery of the 'motherland' with no real local autonomy. The 'colonies' are not causally self-sufficient. News stories that have an 'intra-colony' perspective exist, but there are two simple explanations for that. The first one is in terms of F_{12} – the idea that events will have to be negative – and simply refers to the fact that in both the Congo and Cyprus local conflict is at the root of the 'crisis'. Even under this condition, however, the local conflict is not enough: some familiar groupings, such as the East, the West, the motherland, the UN, have to be added to it to make it really newsworthy. And the other explanation is in terms of F_7: since the theatre is already in the news it will probably remain in the news because an apparatus has been established that requires a certain quantity of news stories to be maintained.

That there are explanations of the *mechanism* underlying this in terms of such factors as the nationality of the press agencies and the training of some of the journalists, whether they are foreign or local by nationality, is obvious. Thus, one would expect the news from Cyprus to be much concerned with events seen as relevant to Britain, since the British agency Reuters appears in connection with 52% of the news stories. One consequence of this is found in the circumstance that Cyprus is seen in its relationship to Britain in 31% of the stories, which is a high percentage if one conceives of the conflict as essentially limited to the Greece-Turkey-Cyprus triangle.

There is another way of testing the hypothesis, taking as in Table XI the focus of the news story as point of departure. The figures are quite

TABLE XI

LOCATION OF THE THEATRE AND FOCUS OF THE
NEWS STORY

	Focus				
Crisis	Economic	Political	Social	Cultural	(N)
Cuba	63%	56%	0%	1%	(158)
Congo	13%	86%	11%	2%	(382)
Cyprus	10%	95%	1%	0%	(612)

clear and tell the kind of story one would predict: the three countries in the world periphery enter by way of variables that link them to the centre part of the world. 'Social' and 'cultural' are more internal and do not have the same immediate ramifications to the topdog nations. The only variation in the focus is from economic to political as one moves from Cuba via the Congo situation to Cyprus, and that corresponds well to most images of 'what really happened'.

Again, the findings hold up against the variation in newspaper and press agency. We let this suffice as an indication of how hypotheses derived from the complementarity theory can be tested.

It may be objected that what we have said is an artefact of the three crises we have picked for our sample. There is no other way of exploring this objection than by means of a new project.

5. Discussion

On the basis of what we have presented we feel that it would be unreasonable not to have some confidence in the general hypothesis. There is probably such a phenomenon as *complementarity of news factors* although much remains to be done in terms of refinement of the hypothesis. Under what conditions will the effect be more pronounced or less pronounced, which pairs of factors tend to produce the strongest (or weakest) effect of complementarity, and how do the factors combine in patterns of three and four, etc.? We leave this for future research, and turn to a discussion of what this implies – under the assumption of the general validity of our thesis.

A discussion of this kind can best be done by selecting out of the 66 possible pairs some crucial pairs that are particularly important in terms of their consequences for the kind of image of the world that they will promote. The numbers refer to the list of twelve factors. These hypotheses are bivariate only, and coming research in this field will have to carry the thinking and the analysis up to, at least, the level of three variables or factors at the same time.

(1,4): *The more distant a nation is, the more will an event have to satisfy the frequency criterion.*
In other words: the distant nation will have to produce events that capture attention particularly easily in order to be recorded. The consequence of this is an abruptness and unconnectedness that the news from such countries will display. Natural disasters and accidents will play an important role, and changes of government. The build-up of events, based on small quantitative changes, will go under-reported – it is only when they lead to the big qualitative changes that they make news. This again may provide readers with an image of these countries as places where things happen all of a sudden and in an unpredictable way – in other words inherently dangerous and inherently different places.

(4,3): *The more distant an event, the less ambiguous will it have to be.*
The remote and the strange will at least have to be simple

if it is to make news – complexities can be taken care of if they are found within one's own culture, but not if they are found at a considerable distance. The implication of that is obvious! The culturally distant acquires a presentation in terms of 'ideal types'; whole nations and continents are described in sweeping terms and this may leave the impression of a uniformity and homogeneity that is not present in the reality of that nation. One's own nation is described in complex terms which will correspond more to the idea most people have of a 'civilized existence'. On the other hand, the phenomenon indicated here will tend to foster the idea of a simple, primitive and more 'human' kind of existence in remote countries.

(4,5): *The more distant the nation, the more consonant will the news have to be.*

For a far away nation to make news it will be particularly necessary that the news should fit a pattern of expectation. Thus the *golpe militar* in Latin America, according to this hypothesis, will make news exactly because that is expected – it is a case of news being 'olds'. The opposite development will not so easily fit the expectation pattern and for that reason less easily be reported, because probably it will, consciously or unconsciously, be registered as a quasi-event that will not last. Any story of sexual extremism from Sweden will receive an *a priori* credibility that will make it pass many filters of news communication, whereas stories or statistics to the opposite effect may be seen as atypical or even fake and propaganda, and not be reported. The consequence of this will be that distant nations appear as essentially unchangeable whereas one's own cultural sphere undergoes real, basic change.

(7,2): *The higher the continuity effect, the lower can the threshold be.*

We only list this hypothesis for the sake of completeness, for it is actually the definition of the continuity effect. Once an event has 'made it' the news channel will be more readily open for the follow-up events, at a lower threshold value. The effect of this will be the creation of 'news strings' that may create artificial continuities just because the channel is open.

(8,2): *The higher the composition effect, the lower can the threshold be.*

This is also listed for the sake of completeness, since it is already included in the definition of the composition effect. The idea is simply that news can enter because of under-representation of categories that should be represented according to some overall judgement – not because they are important by themselves. This, in turn, means that in periods where little else happens abroad the limit defining newsworthiness may be drastically lowered so as to include news items that score relatively low, and this in turn may produce images of discontinuity that do not correspond to the real world.

(1,12): *The less negative the news, the more important the frequency condition.*

This is already referred to in connection with the theory for the negativism of the news. But here it is put in a stronger form: positive events will have to be particularly short of duration to appear as news. This means, essentially, that a premium will be put on the ability to make ceremonies where developments can be telescoped into an event that is reportable. Obviously the more élite people can be added to it the better for the newsworthiness, and this has a double effect. First of all it may contribute to a false image of how positive developments come about, since the amount of planning and painstaking work, mostly and in most cases by non-élite people, goes under-reported. Secondly it forces many people into a kind of activity referred to as PR – public relations – that is often accepted as a part of their work, where one might question the wisdom of the structure of the news communication instead.

(9,4): *The lower the rank of the nation, the lower must the cultural distance be.*

This only means that if a nation is low in terms of rank it must compensate for that in terms of proximity. Or in other words: the topdog nations of the world will each have their own set of underlings that they over-report from, relative to what they report from other low rank nations. For the US it will be Latin America, for France Communauté Française, for Britain the Commonwealth countries, for the Soviet Union the socialist bloc, for China (probably) selected countries in South and Far East Asia. This pattern, in turn, will tend to reinforce existing divisions of the world since reporting will probably make for some kind of identification.

(9,5): *The lower the rank of the nation, the more consonant will the news have to be.*

This is very similar to the hypothesis of the relationship between distance and consonance – but whereas that hypothesis emphasized consonance with what one would expect from more or less stereotyped conceptions of a foreign culture, we are here concerned with stereotypes about low rank. The typical example would be news that emphasizes the difficulties low rank nations have: signs of 'immaturity' in terms of payment crises, political instability, murder at the top of society, etc. The consequences are the same as for hypothesis (4,5) above.

(10,6): *The lower the rank of the person, the more unexpected will the news have to be.*

This has actually been touched upon in different contexts already and the idea is simply that whereas élite people can have their day-to-day routine reported, rank-and-file people will only make news when something happens that stands in a very marked contrast to their ordinary existence. The good examples are sudden acquisitions of wealth and negative actions.

(9,10): *The lower the rank of the nation, the higher will a person have to be placed in that nation to make news.*

This may lead to an image of the world underdog nations as extremely élite-dominated with a non-existing mass of rank-and-file people. In political terms this image will probably tend to reinforce the conditions that make such images warranted. This will also make for poor identification, particularly if élite action in low rank nations is also negative.

(9,12): *The lower the rank of the nation, the more negative will the news from that nation have to be.*

In other words, when something positive and good is happening it will have to be located in a high ranking nation – from the underdog nations of the world, typically, news reports will be overwhelmingly negative. The Latin American proverbial case of the *golpe militar* is one example; all the disaster news from such nations is another. The thesis is that positive things that happen in the underdog countries will go under-reported and this will promote an image of those countries as being unable to govern themselves, and as inherently inferior to the top-dog countries.

(10,12): *The lower the rank of a person, the more negative will his actions have to be.*

In other words, the thesis is that common people must do something negative to make the news, and the lower down the person is, the more negative should it be. At the bottom of society one enters the news pages more easily as a criminal – but sport should of course be mentioned as the big compensating mechanism. It may also be regarded as so important, together with the arts and entertainment, that it actually invalidates the hypothesis. Nevertheless, the kind of positive action the rank-and-file person has it in his power to perform is, perhaps, more likely to be of a kind that will never make the news – not only for the reason mentioned in the hypothesis but because it does not satisfy the criteria of frequency, threshold, unexpectedness and continuity either. If the ordinary man is to enter positively, it will probably have to be in an article, reportage, etc. It may be objected that he enters when he wins in the lottery – but this is not an act of his – it happens to him, like a catastrophe. The implication of all this may easily be a kind of reinforcement of class society in the sense that the top is over-represented with the good and the positive that occurs, and the lower layers of society are portrayed as producers of less fortunate events.

(11,12): *The less personal the news, the more negative will it have to be.*

In other words, when something positive happens it is more likely to be attributed to people, whereas something attributed to non-people will have to be negative to hit the news. In a sense this may also be seen as a reflection of the dominant idea of man as the maker of his own progress against the forces of nature that tend to inundate him with floods, shake him to pieces with earthquakes, etc.

It may be worth while to collect together what has been said about nations that are culturally distant and nations that are low in international rank.[25] We can combine it because what we have said should *a fortiori* be valid when these two criteria – negative for newsworthiness – are superimposed on each other. In short, from such countries news will have to refer to people, preferably top élite, and be preferably negative and unexpected but nevertheless according to a pattern that is consonant with the 'mental pre-image'. It will have to be simple and it should, if possible, provide the reader with some kind of identification – it should refer to him or his nation or group of nations. This will, in turn, facilitate an image of these countries as dangerous, ruled by capricious élites, as unchanging in their basic characteristics, as existing for the benefit of the topdog nations, and in terms of their links to those nations. Events occur, they are sudden, like flashes of lightning, with no build-up and with no let-down after their occurrence – they just occur and more often than not as a part of the machinations of the ruling or opposition élites.

The consequence of all this is an image of the world that gives little autonomy to the periphery but sees it as mainly existing for the sake of the centre – for good or for bad – as a real periphery to the centre of the world. This may also tend to amplify more than at times might seem justified the image of the world's relatedness. Everything's relevance for everything else, particularly for us, is overplayed. Its relevance to itself disappears:

> Mr Mboya complained of the Press (foreign-owned) in Africa behaving and writing as though it were operating in London, Paris or New York 'where the problems and anxieties are entirely different from those current in Africa'. He said these and many other questions kept coming up in the minds of many Africans as they try to figure out what freedom of the press meant in the African context. He was of the view, therefore, that it was important that the Press should concern itself with finding out what goes on in the African mind. The world's verdict on Africa, however, was often reduced from subjective dispatches of foreign journalists paying short visits to the various parts of Africa. The result was that news coming out of Africa was often related to the already biased and prejudiced mind that keeps asking such questions as: 'is this pro-East or pro-West?' but nobody asked: 'is this pro-African?'[26]

This is particularly dramatic in connection with new countries. Their newness, which is probably the major fact for the majority of their inhabitants, is not stressed except as reports from the independence ceremony if there is any (because it satisfies F_1). Instead the news is interpreted in a context of the old, and since all three countries were centres of major events in the periods we have analysed, they have probably for many people come to be defined for some time through these crises. This, in turn, may influence people's behaviour towards the nations in question, and if they are very young nations serve as a kind of imprinting experience,[27] with the consequences that implies for later relationships. It would be interesting to know something more precise about how far behind political independence what one might call causal independence (or auto-causation, causal autonomy) is lagging.

As to the developed countries the general implication of what we have said has already been mentioned: conflict will be emphasized, conciliation not.[28]

6. *Some policy implications*

The policy implications of this article are rather obvious: try to counteract all twelve factors. More specifically, this means:

1. More emphasis on build-up and background material in the total media output. Journalists should be better trained to capture and report on long-term development, and concentrate less on 'events'.

2. Occasional reports on the trivial even if it does not make 'news', to counterbalance the image of the world as composed of strings of dramatic events.

3. More emphasis on complex and ambiguous events, not necessarily with any effort to interpret them.

4. More reports from culturally distant zones even if the content has no immediate relevance for oneself. Experiments with newspapers in different countries exchanging local columns might prove even more interesting than reprinting what was said in the newspaper fifty or a hundred years ago.

5. More emphasis on the dissonant, on that which does not fit stereotypes. Training of journalists to increase their insights into their own stereotypes so as to facilitate their awareness of the consonance factor.

6. More emphasis given to the predictable and frequent, for the same reason as under 2 above.

7. More awareness of the continuity factor – and at the same time more emphasis on follow-ups even if the chain of events has been interrupted for some time. Often one has the impression that one hears about something negative that has happened but not about how it has been counteracted, if the time-span is so long that the continuity has been broken.

8. More awareness of the composition factor in order not to create news artefacts.

9. More coverage of non-élite nations.

10. More coverage of non-élite people.

11. More reference to non-personal causes of events. Special training is probably needed here.

12. More reference to positive events.

These implications work on one factor at a time and would, if implemented, reduce the effects of the factors. However, the combined effects of the factors might still persist even if the effect of any one factor is reduced.

One might say that all or much of this is what the élite paper tries to do, and that is probably true. However, élite papers are probably mainly read by élite people and this may increase the distance between centre and periphery where international perspective is concerned.

Hence one additional need is for a more widely dispersed style of news communication in agreement with these principles. It should be emphasized, however, that the present article hypothesizes rather than demonstrates the presence of these factors, and hypothesizes rather than demonstrates that these factors, if present, have certain effects among the audience.

Appendix I

A short chronological survey of events in Cuba, July 1960. (From *Keesing's Contemporary Archives.*)

29/6   The Cuban Government confiscates Texaco's oil refineries.
1/7   The Cuban Government confiscates Esso's and Shell's oil refineries because all the refineries had refused to refine Soviet crude oil.
5/7   British protest against the confiscation of the Shell refinery.

United States reduces its import of Cuban sugar by 700,000 tons.

6/7   American protest against the confiscation of the Texaco and Esso refineries.

8/7   The Cuban Government refuses to accept the protests, referring to the obligation of the refineries to refine any crude oil. Dr Miro Cardona requests political asylum in the USA.

10/7   The Government of the USSR announces that it will buy 700,000 tons of Cuban sugar in addition to its usual quota.

11/7   The Cuban foreign minister accuses the USA of 'economic aggression', in the UN Security Council.

18–19/7   Debate in the Security Council concerning US–Cuban relations. Decided to hand the matter over to the OAS before any UN steps are taken.

17–21/7   Raoul Castro visits the Soviet Union.

23/7   The Cuban Government confiscates four US sugar refineries. Trade agreement between Cuba and China concerning a yearly sale of 500,000 tons of Cuban sugar for five years.

Appendix II

A short chronological survey of events in the Congo, July 1960. (*From Keesing's Contemporary Archives.*)

30/6–1/7   The Congo independent at midnight. Speeches by King Baudouin, Prime Minister Lumumba and President Kasavubu. Lumumba attacks the Belgian colonial administration.

2/7   Lumumba demands the immediate withdrawal of all Belgian troops from the Congo.

5/7   Mutiny among private Congolese soldiers in Thysville and Leopoldville against their Belgian officers. Lumumba and Kasavubu intervene in order to restore order, but with no great success. The anti-European feelings spread to other provinces.

7/7   Europeans in the Leopoldville province flee to Congo-Brazzaville.

8/7   The Belgian Government announces that troop reinforcements will be sent to the Congo.

10/7   Belgian forces attack Congolese in various places.

11/7   The Congolese Government appeals to UN for assistance. Tshombe declares Katanga an independent state.

14/7   The Security Council adopts a resolution concerning the immediate sending of UN forces to the Congo, and asks Belgium to withdraw its troops. The Congo breaks off diplomatic relations with Belgium.

15/7   The first UN troops arrive in Leopoldville.

17/7   The Congolese Government informs the UN that it will ask for Soviet troops if the UN does not succeed in getting the Belgian troops out of the country within 72 hours.

17/7   Vice-Secretary-General Ralph Bunche reports that an agreement has been reached with the Belgian authorities to withdraw the Belgian troops from Leopoldville.

20/7   Tshombe warns the UN against entering Katanga, states that any support of the central government against Katanga will lead to war between Katanga and the rest of the Congo.

21/7   The Security Council adopts a resolution requesting Belgium to withdraw its troops from the Congo as soon as possible, and which authorizes the Secretary-General to take the necessary steps to execute the resolution. The Belgian Government declares that its troops will stay in the Congo until law and order have been restored.

23/7   Belgian troops entirely withdrawn from Leopoldville.

24/7   Lumumba arrives in New York to confer with Secretary-General Hammarskiöld.

26/7   Hammarskiöld goes to Brussels and Leopoldville.

27/7   Hammarskiöld meets Prime Minister Eyskens and King Baudouin in Brussels. The Congolese Government issues its political programme, stating the wish for cooperation with Belgium and that the foreign policy of the Congolese Government will be characterized by 'positive neutralism'.

28/7   Hammarskiöld arrives in Leopoldville for talks with Kasavubu. The Belgian Government issues a detailed report on atrocities in the Congo. The report estimates the number of raped white women to be 291. Number of killed not given. The number of UN soldiers in the Congo is given as 10,000. The number of refugees from the Congo is officially given in Brussels as 35,000.

29/7   The Belgian Government announces that the withdrawal of some of the troops in the Congo will start at once. No information on when all the troops will be withdrawn.

30/7   Announcement after Hammarskiöld's meeting with the Congolese

Government that agreement had been reached concerning the task of the UN in the Congo.

Appendix III

A short chronology of events in Cyprus, December–April 1964. (From *Keesing's Contemporary Archives.*)

6/12 President Makarios reportedly sends a memorandum to Vice-President Kutchuk concerning his desire to amend certain provisions of the Constitution, such as the separate majority vote on taxation laws, separate courts of justice, separate municipalities and certain other 'unreasonable rights'.

21–26/12 Communal violence in Cyprus, in which 200 Greek and Turkish Cypriots were believed to have been killed.

25–28/12 Turkish military movements, in and outside Cyprus.

26/12 A joint Greek, Turkish and British force, under British command should restore order. This was accepted by all the governments.

27/12 Cypriot representatives in the UN protests to the Security Council.

28/12 The British Colonial Secretary, Mr Duncan Sandys, arrives in Nicosia for talks with the local leaders.

30/12 Vice-President Kutchuk denounces the protest of the Cypriot UN representative, Mr Rossides. Since the fighting the Turkish Cypriot ministers had refused to attend meetings of the Cabinet, which in consequence had become representative only of the Greek Cypriot community.

1/1 The Cypriot Government accepts a proposal that a UN representative should be stationed in Cyprus.

16/1 General Gyani appointed UN representative in Cyprus.

15/1 A conference in London to decide the future government of Cyprus, attended by the Greek and Turkish Foreign Ministers, Greek Cypriot and Turkish Cypriot delegations, and chaired by Mr Duncan Sandys, UK. The conference ended in deadlock towards the end of the month.

31/1 An Anglo-American plan for a NATO emergency force to be placed in Cyprus, including the Greek and Turkish forces already on the island.

1/2 The Greek and Turkish Governments accept the proposals.

2/2   Vice-President Kutchuk accepts the plan in principle.

4/2   President Makarios's Government rejects the plan, while stating that it would accept an international force under the Security Council.

7/2   Premier Khrushchev protests against the planned NATO force.

11–13/2   Heavy fighting in Limassol.

15/2   Requests from the British and Cypriot Governments to the Security Council to consider the situation in Cyprus.

Latter part of February. Greek and Turkish military preparations, threats of intervention.

2/3   Common Turkish-American and Greek navy manœuvres started.

4/3   UN Security Council unanimously approves the formation of an international force and the appointment of a mediator.

4–5/3   Shooting in both Greek-Cypriot and Turkish-Cypriot villages.

6/3   General Gyani appointed leader of the UN forces.

7/3   Secretary-General U Thant asks member governments for voluntary financial contributions to the force.
Hard fighting in the village of Ktima.
Forty-nine Turkish hostages released on Makarios's orders.

8/3   Cease-fire in Ktima after negotiations led by Gyani. Two-hundred-and-twenty-eight Greek hostages released.

9/3   Cease-fire broken.

10/3   Vice-President Kutchuk accuses the Greek-Cypriots of intending to eliminate the Turkish-Cypriot society before the arrival of the UN force.

13/3   About 13,000 Turkish troops embarked at Iskenderun.

14/3   The first part of the Canadian force arrives in Nicosia; the rest to be flown in during the next two weeks.

16/3   A secret meeting of the Turkish Parliament agrees to give the Government permission to start a military intervention in Cyprus if necessary.

25/3   Ambassador Tuomijoja appointed UN mediator in Cyprus.

27/3   The UN force formally established.

31/3   President Makarios informs the Greek and the Turkish Prime Ministers that the formation of a UN force had ended the agreement under which Greek and Turkish military units had served under British command, and requested that these units be withdrawn to their camps.

1/4 Prime Minister Inonu replies that the Turkish troops would not be withdrawn. About £5·3 million of contributions promised.

2/4 Tuomijoja arrives in Nicosia.

4/4 President Makarios informs Prime Minister Inonu that Cyprus has ended the alliance treaty with Turkey.

6/4 The Turkish Prime Minister warns Makarios that the Turkish Government regards the treaty as still valid, and will take all necessary steps in case of aggressive actions intended to prevent the Turkish-Cypriot minority in exercising its rights.

7/4 The British force in Cyprus reduced to 4,500 soldiers.

8/4 U Thant asks Sweden, Ireland and Finland to increase their forces by 300 soldiers each. Sweden and Finland agree to do so.

11/4 President Makarios arrives in Athens for talks with the Greek Government and with General Grivas.

14/4 Makarios returns to Cyprus.

PART FOUR:

Content and Audience

1. Reflections on the Impact
of Broadcasting

Robert Silvey

Those of us who remember the winter of 1939–40 are unlikely to have forgotten the sound of a voice which was, perhaps, as familiar as any at that time. It addressed each of us, evening after evening, as we sat in our blacked-out homes: 'This is Gairmany calling, Gairmany calling Hamburg, Bremen, and DXX in the 49-metre band.' It was, of course, the voice of William Joyce, the reader of Germany's news service for Britain. He had a remarkable following; every evening his broadcasts were listened to by something like one-third of the population of this country. His broadcasts were news-worthy; he got plenty of press publicity. There cannot have been many people at that time who had not heard of, even if they had not actually heard, 'Lord Haw-Haw'.

My department was called upon to study and report on this phenomenon and the results of this enquiry are an instructive illustration of the impact which broadcasting *can* have. We found, as I have said, that his audiences were prodigious. But we also found that he was being listened to most by those who listened most to BBC News and were the most avid readers of the press. We found the incidence of listening to Haw-Haw was greatest among those with most education. Readers of *The Times* and the more serious papers listened to him more than did readers of the tabloid press.

We applied tests designed to show whether his listeners accepted his news as fact. We found that quite often they did; and with the benefit of hindsight we can now say that in these cases his listeners were quite right to do so. Hamburg Radio was shrewd enough to realize that its cause could best be served by intermingling fact with fiction.

But we also studied listeners' attitudes to these broadcasts and these

* First delivered as a BBC public lecture and published as a BBC pamphlet in 1963.

showed a remarkable degree of unanimity: it was fun to listen to Lord Haw-Haw – after all it was a novel experience to be able to listen to the enemy, at a safe distance and in snug comfort, surrounded by your own kind. What was more, you stood a chance of hearing something which 'they', in Whitehall, did not think it would be good for you to know. Besides, this war did seem a bit 'funny', no fighting yet in the west, no bombing as we expected. But of course we would win in the end.

These attitudes may have been jejune and over-confident but that, substantially, is what they were. And there is an interesting postscript to them. Once the phoney war ended with the invasion of Norway and the Low Countries, listening to Hamburg almost ceased. It became distasteful, a bit shabby, 'not done'. It was no longer the time for 'fun', things were too grim. When a man's hands are on your throat you are not interested in what he is saying out of the side of his mouth.

Love/hate relationship

But this is to anticipate. Speculating, at the time, on the Hamburg listening phenomenon, we wondered whether Hamburg radio had indeed made a wise choice, from its own point of view, in selecting William Joyce as its news reader. His voice was distinctive, certainly, and compelling, but what were the associations it conjured up? It seemed to us that these were not, as was implied by the nickname 'Lord Haw-Haw', those of a seedy aristocrat, but those of the wicked squire of barn-storming melodrama, the heavily moustached villain whose designs on the innocent village maiden and whose sticky end could both be foreseen. If we were right, this could go far to explain both his conspicuous success in getting himself listened to, and his equally conspicuous failure to convert his listeners into disciples.

To the extent that listening to Hamburg felt like watching old-time melodrama, it could not fail to be conditioned by the conventions which surrounded a full-blooded performance of *Maria Marten and the Red Barn*. These conventions dictated that you cheered the hero, booed the villain, and wept for his victim – and thoroughly enjoyed every gory detail. You could do so without feeling a trace of guilt because you knew perfectly well that the action took place within a proscenium arch, that it could be seen all over again if you could afford to stay for the second house. It was quite a bargain; you got all the kicks without expending psychological ha'pence. I suggest that the effect of Hamburg's use as a news broadcaster of a man whose voice was reminiscent of the wicked squire ('Sir Jasper' would, I think, have been a more apt nickname than 'Lord Haw-Haw') was to ensure themselves a large audience and at the same time to immunize it against his influence.

The short-lived story of the love/hate relationship between Lord Haw-Haw and the British public is now a part of history. But though it was a brief and exceptional encounter it serves to illustrate that the nature of the impact which broadcasts make is the product of the interaction of a number of elements of which the nature of the communication is only one. Whatever the broadcaster's objective, whether, like Haw-Haw's, it be to demoralize its audience, or whether it be to persuade or enlighten it, to stir its heart or simply to interest or amuse it, the achievement of the objective is only partially within the broadcaster's control. Even if he shows superlative skill, and is recognized to do so by every listener, success in achieving the intended impact will not follow automatically. However good the seed, it will not germinate unless it falls on receptive soil.

Meeting a need

Like all other forms of communication, broadcasts have an impact only in so far as they meet, or seem to the listener to meet, some need in himself. The 'need' may be one of which the listener is unconscious or one which he would find it hard to put into words. It may, or may not, be in the best interests of the individual that his 'need' should be directly gratified; all that one can say of it is that it exists, seeks satisfaction, and will continue until it is satisfied or somehow diverted.

If the communicator sets out to satisfy an innocent and legitimate need and is completely successful in doing so he has every right to be a happy man. Occasionally, of course, a broadcaster may aim at a pigeon and shoot a crow; he may fail completely to meet the need he intended to gratify, while in fact gratifying a need of an entirely different kind. A notorious case in point is the broadcaster who intended, by a word-picture, to satisfy the homebound listener's desire to visualize a Naval Review but who, instead, succeeded triumphantly in satisfying the need to be entertained.

What, then, were the needs which were met by the Hamburg broadcasts in the winter of 1939–40? One might say that the need was for news, and cite in evidence the fact that those whose appetite for news was greatest were the most regular listeners to Hamburg. But the way the audience melted away in the late spring of 1940, even though the need for news was certainly no less, shows this supposition to be inadequate. I believe the need which led people to listen to Hamburg was both deeper and more complex than this. The first winter was aptly named the 'phoney' war; in terms of 1914–18 and of all we had been led to expect, it did not make sense. But one of the basic needs of men is to make sense, or some seeming sense, of their environment. There was a chance that the mystery might at least be lessened if we listened to what the enemy had to say. In addition to this there was the frustration resulting from inaction. We wanted to get this war over with, but all we seemed to be required to do was to sit about and wait. Say, if you like, that we had assumed a posture for combat and no combat had followed – or, perhaps more accurately, that we had ducked to avoid a rain of blows that had not come – either way, we had 'summoned up the blood', or at least the adrenalin, and found no outlet in action. Listening to Haw-Haw offered a substitute, if a mild one.

Whether or not these were the needs which Haw-Haw gratified, he certainly failed to achieve his ultimate objective which was to demoralize us, or at least to soften us up. The 'seed' fell on unreceptive soil; to use a seventeenth-century Quaker phrase, the real intention of the Hamburg broadcasts was not one which 'spoke to our condition'. Had such a campaign been directed at us at the end of a long war in which we had lost faith in our cause, hope of victory, and confidence in our leaders, then indeed it might well have spread alarm and despondency. A people in such circumstances has a 'need' to submit. The Freudians would no doubt describe this as a demand for humiliation and punishment to assuage an intolerable sense of guilt, guilt not necessarily for wrong-doing, but for losing. Be that as it may, the course of our own allied propaganda in both great wars tells the same story. It had little impact so long as the enemy was winning, but it materially accelerated his collapse once the tide had turned.

Communication

'Communication' cannot be said to have taken place unless there is a recipient as well as a communicator and the part played by the recipient is anything but passive. Though the audience at home cannot by its attitude influence the broadcaster at the moment that he is before the microphone, the listener is a very active partner in determining the broadcast's impact. He is, both in the popular and in the scientific sense, one of the variables. (This is apparent whenever one sees, as one often does, two people reacting quite differently to the same broadcast, or recalls how much one's own reactions can vary with one's mood.)

This would not need to be said if it were not so often overlooked. Much popular discussion of the impact of broadcasting seems to be based on the curious assumption that the listener is a *tabula rasa* who will faithfully receive an exact impression of whatever is projected at him. This leads to a concentration on the communicator and what he is saying. If what he is saying is deemed to be vicious, the assumption is that a vicious result will automatically follow, and if it is meritorious, that good results will follow or – equally fallaciously – that ill consequences cannot follow. Were this truly so the task of studying the impact of mass communications would be relatively simple. All that would then be necessary would be an adequate analysis of the content of the output.

Schramm and his colleagues at Stanford University have pointed out in their study *Television in the Lives of Our Children* that the impact of television on children depends as much on what the child brings to it as on what it brings to him. You must ask not merely what television 'does to' children, but what children 'do with' television, before you can hope for a satisfactory answer. And that most certainly goes for adults too.

So let us ask what we, the public, 'do with' broadcasting. Faced with its unending stream, the first thing that we do is to select from it. No one listens to everything, if only because the alternative services are simultaneous. It sometimes happens, of course, that we must suffer what someone in the household has selected. Sometimes we just listen to what is 'on' (but even so someone at some time must have chosen the position at which the dial is set). Even the listeners who have never in their lives tuned to the Third Programme wavelength have, in effect, chosen to exclude it from the range of their day-to-day choice. In short, although the choice may not always be rational, may sometimes indeed be irrational, and is often, I suspect, non-rational (like so many of our day-to-day choices), the choice is made.

But this is only the first option which is open to us. Having chosen, we can still change our minds – we can switch off or switch over. But more than that: without touching the knob we can vary the amount of attention we pay to the broadcast. We may not want it to be more than a background; we may, reluctantly, have to treat it so because the demands of courtesy compel us to give our attention to the garrulous guest: or we may, on the other hand, listen (or view) to the point of being oblivious to all else.

Selective perception

And we have a further option, though this is one which we exercise unconsciously; we can perceive selectively. In practice, we do not have to 'take in' the entirety of the communication before we can decide which aspects of it interest, amuse, or gratify us and which do not. We can, to an important degree, save ourselves that trouble by simply failing to perceive what for any reason we do not want to perceive. And we can do more than this. Without being in the least conscious of doing so, we can distort what our senses report to us so that what reaches our consciousness is what we want to hear. Sometimes we 'tailor' an unacceptable communication so that it becomes acceptable to us. At other times, with apparent perversity, we distort a quite innocent statement in such a way to make it trigger off pet fears and suspicions. (In an earlier lecture of this series my colleague, Donald Edwards, referred to the complaints about BBC news which are based on a mis-hearing of what was in fact said. One wonders how often such mistakes are, if the truth be known, examples of selective perception.) Selective perception can result in our entertaining quite a false impression of what was transmitted and we are all liable to practise it in some degree.

This tendency has a perfectly respectable origin. Our senses are perpetually bombarded with such a wealth and variety of stimuli that if we were to accept them all into consciousness we simply could not cope. We are compelled to classify what we see and hear, to identify objects and events by seeing them as examples of general categories rather than as things-in-themselves. We learn to do this economically by relying on cues. If I am introduced to a man and he proffers me his right hand, I do not wait to take up his references before I accept it. I assume he is friendly and wants to shake my hand – I have relied on two cues; that my friend has introduced me to him and that his right hand is sticking out.

We learn most of our cues without realizing that we are doing so. The whole business of classifying experience becomes 'second nature'. That this is so becomes apparent to us when we are thrown into a totally unfamiliar situation; then we are cue-less, bewildered, and, usually, very uncomfortable. In such a situation we have to pay conscious attention to all the evidence our eyes and ears bring us and try, as fast as we can, to make sense of it.

But there are dangers in this inevitable process. Walter Lippmann called attention to them in his classic work on 'Public Opinion' written forty years ago. We are all too ready to forget that the conclusions we derive from our cues may be wrong; we may have misread them or have failed to appreciate that they are not infallible. But when we have drawn a wrong conclusion we try all too often to put things right by tinkering with the evidence in such a way as to enable us to stick to our first assessment – we try to make the facts fit what Lippmann aptly called the 'stereotype'. Of course we cannot alter the objective facts, but we can alter our perception of them by simply ignoring the inconvenient ones, changing their positions round a bit and perhaps, if we can fool ourselves, throwing in a few which were not there.

The literature of mass communications research abounds in case studies on this theme. To cite one from our own records: we broadcast a television documentary designed to reveal the differing points of view of management and men in industrial disputes, in the hope that this would lead to better mutual understanding. We then measured its impact. Many of its audience, naturally enough, approached the broadcast with a bias in favour of one of the two points of view. But the significant finding was how often the partisans not so much heard and rejected the point of view they opposed, as simply failed to hear it at all. For them it might just as well not have been expressed.

As is true of so many psychological phenomena, this is one which the conventional wisdom has long recognized; 'there are', we say, 'none so blind as those who will not see'. But let me re-emphasize two points. First, that I am talking about something which we ordinarily do quite unconsciously. Secondly, that the world is not divided into those who perceive selectively and those who do not. Some of us are more prone to it than others, that's all.

The answer to the question 'what do we do with broadcasting?' is, then, that we select from it but not merely by choosing certain programmes rather than others and exercising our freedom to switch off what we do not want. We also select by varying the attention we devote to what is before us and, more subtly, by perceiving it selectively.

What we select is, in the last analysis, determined by our needs – the needs we ourselves experience, not what other people think we need; our psychic needs, in short, are what we 'bring to' broadcasting. They correspond to what the economist calls 'demand'.

Preserving the self

Though each of us has his own peculiar needs, there are some which are as universal as is the physical need for sleep, food, and shelter. I have already referred to one – man's need to make sense of his environment – which, at any rate in part, explains the universal appetite for news. But there is another which in my view goes far to explain how people 'use' broadcasting; this is our need to preserve our own personal identity.

Our 'selves' are of paramount importance to each one of us, and this is so even though we may be deluded about ourselves, failing 'to see ourselves as others see us' or as we really are, and even though we may dislike ourselves and wish we were different. Once we lose our self-esteem, our sense of uniqueness, we have lost everything. (There could be no clearer testament to the truth of this than that those who seek absolute power over other men know very well that this can only be achieved by breaking down and destroying the self-esteem of those who would oppose them.)

The 'self' being so precious to us, we are highly sensitive to anything which impinges upon it, and, of course, broadcasting is a very important source from which such impingement may come. It follows that if we are confronted with a broadcast which threatens the 'self', we tend to take avoiding action, or else resist it as best we can. On the other hand, we tend to lend our ears to those broadcast messages which minister to our self-esteem.

The extent to which these tendencies affect a listener's attitude to broadcasting and hence its impact upon him, depends upon how far he is a subjective person. This can vary enormously. At the one extreme are those highly subjective people who, we say, 'take everything personally'. They do not distinguish between what is, and what is not, part of themselves. At the other extreme are those who are highly objective, having achieved the rare but truly creative capacity for taking disinterested interest. Most of us, of course, are somewhere between these two extremes.

The subjective man identified himself with the ideas, values, and institutions which he supports, treating them, not as things outside himself to be judged, accepted, or rejected on their merits, but as extensions of his own individuality. The old school, the football team, the firm, the party, the nation, the race, are obvious examples of groups which can be used in this way or, as we say, which can become 'ego-involved'. But values and ideas can also become 'ego-involved', and it makes little difference whether such ideas are manifest nonsense – such as that any man is the intellectual superior of any woman – or of acknowledged nobility – such as that the strong should defend the weak. Ego-involved values, ideas, and institutions become important to the individual in exactly the same way as his own selfhood is important. As a result, he treats anything which he sees as enhancing *them*, as though it will enhance *him*, and anything which threatens them, as though it threatens him. Thus both a man's support for, and his defence of, the institution, values, and ideas with which he has identified himself tend to become as automatic and as tenacious as if his own personality were at stake.

Before we can attempt to assess the effect of this kind of identification upon the impact of broadcasting in this country we need some estimate of its prevalence. No one, as far as I know, has tried to measure this statistically, so we must rely on impressionistic estimates. I think you will probably agree that most of us indulge in it a great deal more than we like to admit. Perhaps this is not surprising, since in infancy none of us is capable of distinguishing between ourselves and the world around us. Subjectivity is, in the true sense, childish, and 'putting away childish things' is not so easy as it sounds. (One may question whether our culture is sufficiently alive to all that is involved in encouraging children – and adults – to achieve what might be described as psychic maturity.)

The 'other-directed' person

In this connection I would remind you of a passage in one of Professor Carstairs's Reith Lectures. He recalled David Riesman's three types of moral system – the 'tradition-directed', the 'inner-directed', and the 'other-directed'. The 'other-directed' is the one in which 'the individual subordinates his own values to the expectations of other people who surround him'. As a result of this 'feelings of individual insignificance' are encouraged and this inevitably means that the personality is 'impoverished'.

But, normally, the 'other-directed' person does not subordinate his values to those of his neighbours *in order* to experience feelings of individual insignificance. That is the very reverse of what he wants. Like everyone else, he needs desperately to feel himself to be important. The feelings of insignificance which are the unwelcome consequences of his other-directed orientation will therefore impel him to grasp at any available means which seems to offer him hope of psychic self-preservation. The process of identification of which we have been speaking is a ready and easy way out.

If I am right in concluding that the other-directed person is particularly prone to choose this way of compensating for his feelings of insignificance, and if Riesman and Carstairs are right in thinking that 'other-directedness' is growing in our society, then this suggests that the prevalence of identification is on the increase. And since identification represents a ready means by which we can magnify our sense of self-importance and so meet, however spuriously, our need to preserve our personal identity, the effect of this need upon the impact of broadcasting must correspondingly be increasing.

I suspect that this need plays an important part in determining what people listen to and what people like. For example, one of the reasons (though, of course, not the only reason) for the immense popularity of Westerns is that the audience feels safe with them. The viewer, moving within the cosy ambit of the familiar, need have no fear of encountering ideas or values which might challenge those which he has made his own. The same, indeed, could be said of many other popular forms of broadcasting.

On the other hand, if one studies the impact of broadcast drama, one is not infrequently confronted by viewers and listeners who, finding that a play is set in a period or place where they feel 'at sea' or comes to grips with a problem which is outside the range of their experience, do not confine themselves to saying, as well they might, that they found it dull or boring, but react with an outburst of spluttering rage. Where there is anger there is often fear – it is a form of making ugly faces at the threatening enemy – and one suspects that in such cases, little though the listener realizes it, what is behind his fury is fear for the self, engendered by feelings of defencelessness in the face of a mysterious unknown.

The effect of the need to defend the ego is easiest to detect in the realm of what in the BBC we still call 'Talks'. For instance, the people who are most inclined to take avoiding action when ideas are being discussed are precisely those who might benefit most by listening – the people who do not so much think, as rearrange their prejudices. They are least likely to listen, the least likely to pay attention if they do, and the most likely to perceive what they are exposed to in ways which will render any new ideas harmless.

I have dealt at some length with this need, but I would not have you think I regard it as the only need which people bring to broadcasting – far from it. There are many others which it would be fascinating to examine if time allowed. Some of them, indeed, may positively conflict with the need to defend the ego. For example, we all need recreation, and for some of us recreation – or should I pronounce it re-creation – takes place in the act of listening to or viewing material which *does* threaten ego-involved attitudes. In such a case – other things being equal – what we do depends upon which need is the stronger. The Hamburg story is a good illustration of this. These broadcasts undoubtedly threatened ego-involved concepts in a big way – concepts like 'our country' and 'our side' – but at the same time they ministered, as we have seen, to other needs, and these other needs proved the stronger.

A much more topical illustration is *That Was The Week That Was*. Many people can't take it and so don't view. To be sure, the pleasure which some viewers derive from it comes from seeing *other people's* sacred cows assaulted. But there are some who view it and enjoy it even though its barbs threaten their own ego-involved concepts, and here, too, we can only assume that for such a viewer the need to protect the pseudo-self is outweighed by other needs also clamouring for satisfaction.

The power of broadcasting

All the same, I make no apology for stressing the need to assert our personal identity as one of the constellation of needs which, shaping our listening and viewing, ultimately determines the impact which broadcasting makes upon us, for it appears to me to go far to explain one finding about the effects of broadcasting – and indeed of mass communications in general – which has the support of a growing body of empirical research. This is that mass communications, including broadcasting, are much more effective in reinforcing existing values, attitudes, and ideas than in changing them. This may be quite contrary to the broadcaster's intention; it happens because most of us are conservatives with a small 'c'; most of us, most of the time, exercise our freedom of choice to fend off the unfamiliar.

This is why one needs to treat with caution the more extravagant claims about the power of broadcasting to transform society. (Though the opposite assertion, that broadcasting can do no more than reflect the society which it serves, is equally suspect.) As so often happens both thesis and antithesis have a measure of truth; sweeping generalizations are inappropriate.

As has already been pointed out, the impact of broadcasting, and hence its power, is not to be gauged simply by examining what it brings *to* people. It depends as much on what people bring to broadcasting. To the extent that they bring to broadcasting a truly satisfying way of life, confidently and securely grounded in tried and accepted values, the power of broadcasting to change it, assuming it wanted to, would be minimal. But in so far as people bring to broadcasting a way of life which does *not* satisfy them, if they are insecure and bewildered, then they are susceptible to change. There can be little doubt that, whatever other power broadcasting could exercise, its power to effect change would be far less in a closed society, steeped in tradition, than in a society struggling to accomplish in a decade adjustments which elsewhere had taken centuries.

If we would seek to identify those areas within our own society wherein broadcasting is most likely to exercise an influence – indeed where it cannot escape doing so, whether it consciously accepts its responsibilities or not – we should look for them amongst those issues about which there is most perplexity, those values which are most questioned, and those attitudes which are most fluid. Only the purblind could deny that such areas exist. In short, the power of broadcasting to influence people's ideas, attitudes, and values is at its greatest where there is bewilderment and emotional insecurity. This is a sobering thought for those who bear the responsibility.

2. The Effects of the Media Portrayal of Violence and Aggression*

James Halloran

Many people who believe that our society is more violent than ever before are convinced that a major cause of the alleged increase in violence is the frequent portrayal by the mass media of violence and aggression. (No attempt will be made in this paper to distinguish between violence and aggression, and for the most part the terms will be used interchangeably.) Some of these people see media violence as one of the major problems of our time. The media violence is, of course, selectively defined. For example, the portrayal of war and other 'legitimate' uses of violence, even the use of 'extra-legal' violence by the police, are rarely included in the media content which apparently produce the concern and help to nourish the frequent and vociferous protests. There is no recognition that society in its attempts to maintain social control may foster violence by approving or legitimizing certain forms of violent behaviour, and it is not generally understood that not only experiences of, but expectations about, reactions to, and definitions of, violent behaviour can vary from one social group to another within any given society.

There is no doubt that people are concerned about the extent and nature of media violence and it must be admitted that on the surface there are grounds for such concern. It seems likely that the mass media have made it possible for more people to witness more violence (both real and fantasy) than ever before. Unfortunately the public debate on the consequences of this media activity, like that on almost any other aspect of the mass media, does not take place at a very high level. The effects of media consumption or exposure are predicted direct from crude analyses of content, levels of effect are not differentiated, con-

* First published in *Revista Española de la Opinion Publica*, 13 (1968).

314

cepts are not clearly defined, and the influence of mediating factors (e.g., socio-economic background, intelligence, etc.) and the part played by personal relationships and group affiliations in the communication process are not taken into account.

However, despite all this and even though many of those who protest about media violence do not appear (judging from some of their personal, social and political actions) to be aware of or to believe in many aspects of the dangers they denounce, it is still necessary for social scientists to address themselves to this area of concern. They must attempt by a systematic and objective approach to throw some light on the main aspect of the problem, namely, how the nature and incidence of real violence might be affected by exposure to mass media violence.

Not that social scientists have all the answers, in fact they sometimes appear to add to the confusion. Admittedly they can show that such claims as: Violent behaviour must inevitably follow from heavy viewing of ~~conventionally~~ defined violent material – a great deal of delinquent behaviour can be traced directly to the media – there is a causal relationship between increasing media consumption (usually television) on the one hand and increasing delinquency on the other – will not stand up to close analysis. In general they would accept that the media-consumer relationship is a complex one and that what a person brings to the viewing, listening or reading situations (~~predispositions etc.~~) is just as important as the content presented to him. These social scientists do not ask 'What do the media do to people?' but 'What do certain individuals with certain predispositions do with the media?'.

Dr Frederic Wertham, an American psychiatrist who has spent many years studying and writing on the influence of media violence on young children, has little sympathy with 'the so-called scientific methods' employed by the social scientists in studying effects. He claims that the problem is not so complex as the social scientists would have us believe and that his clinical methods have established 'that there is a cumulative effect in all this enormous amount of violence and that this violence is a contributing factor to all kinds of childhood troubles'.

Not all psychiatrists, however, would want Wertham to speak for them. Dr Bruno Bettelheim, Professor of Psychology and Psychiatry at the University of Chicago, is 'convinced that neither comics nor television seduce the innocent'. He calls for a recognition of and an acceptance of violence as 'a normal mode of human behaviour' for only then, he claims, will we be able to deal with it. He criticizes Wertham for attacking the symptoms rather than the disease and for basing his therapy on deprivation and restriction and although he accepts that the media may reinforce delinquent tendencies and provide new delinquent skills, he emphasizes that the root problem is the delinquent tendencies, not the mass media.

This last statement is not far removed from the one traditionally associated with the position of Dr J. T. Klapper, a sociologist and Head of Social Research at the Columbia Broadcasting System in the United States. Klapper was one of the three experts – the other two were Wertham and Dr Leonard Berkowitz, a psychologist from the University of Wisconsin – who made up the experts panel at Governor Rockefeller's Conference on Crime held in New York in 1966, where this whole question was examined.

At this conference, Klapper was clearly not impressed by Wertham's clinical approach and repeated his oft-stated argument that the media reinforce already existing attitudinal and behavioural patterns rather than produce new ones. He feels that time and resources would be better spent studying the children and the problems they bring to the media than attempting to persuade those responsible for programmes to reduce screened violence. It is interesting to note that the 'reinforcement' argument is used by some producers to absolve themselves from responsibility for the effects of their products.

Klapper would claim that he is not attempting to whitewash the media, and readily accepts that reinforcement may strengthen tendencies which are socially unwholesome. He rightly draws attention to the fact that the media is but one set of influences among many, but his general position can be criticized on several counts. In this instance the main one is the apparent overlooking of the role of the media in the early stages of the child's development. Moreover, although reinforcement may be the rule, Klapper himself stated some years ago that in certain conditions (when the mediating factors were not operating or when their influence was in the same direction as the media) the media may operate in a more direct way. However, his recent statements on media violence seem frequently to be made without due attention being given to the operation of these mediating factors.

Berkowitz comes from a different research tradition and his experimental work leads him to suggest that the heavy dosage of violence in the mass media, although not a major determinant of anti-social violent behaviour, heightens the probability that someone in the audience will behave aggressively in a later situation. He accepts that the effect may be short-lived and recognizing that aggressive drive is not the same thing as aggressive behaviour, which is culturally defined, admits that exposure by itself is not enough. Berkowitz states that the effects of observed violence depend upon at least three other types of factors, namely, the readiness to act aggressively, attitudes towards the observed violence, and the 'cue qualities' or the relationship of the victim to the portrayed incident. There are several reasons here which may explain why surveys have not been able to pick up the effect of media violence.

An interesting aspect of this work deals with the possible effects of witnessing violence or aggression which is presented as justified or as socially sanctioned (e.g., the villain getting his just deserts). Justification may operate like a reward or the absence of punishment and some of Berkowitz's work indicates that following exposure to 'justifiable' aggression people are inclined to behave violently towards 'the villains in their own lives'. This is a consideration not normally uppermost in the minds of those who regard media violence as a major problem.

The work of Berkowitz, together with that of other experimentalists such as Bandura and Walters, gives no support to the theory of 'cathartic effect', which suggests a purge or discharge and predicts a decrease in aggressive urges following affective media participation. There is, in fact, very little support for the cathartic model from American research although some recent Italian research does lend some support to the theory. The main reason for this difference would appear to be that in the different experiments the label 'violence' was used to cover different things. This should serve to remind us that our understanding of the problem is not likely to be furthered unless much more attention is given to conceptual clarity in relation to both content and reaction. What sort of material do we label as violent? What is a violent or an aggressive response? Could we include the urge to achieve for example?

Where distinctions have been made both with regard to types of violence portrayed and types of response produced, as in some

Australian work, a 'more subtle form of catharsis' appears to be a possibility.

The child and the adolescent project their personal, even subconscious, problems on to the film and the viewer is provided with the means of expressing and translating his conflicts. 'Catharsis' here results from the conjunction of several mechanisms, some dynamic or expressive, others inhibiting. It also seems possible that the child can develop a perceptual defence to protect himself from the shock and anxiety experienced from violent films.

This work also suggests that children who view crime dramas might acquire an insensitivity and stereotyped reactions to violent events in real life. It confirms that wide generalizations about children in general and violence in general are not likely to be valid and it lends some support to those who stress the importance of taking into account such factors as context, plot and genre in the study of effects.

All experimental laboratory work in this field has several disadvantages and these, together with some specific criticisms of the Berkowitz and Bandura work referred to above, have been set out in considerable detail by Klapper in a summary of a somewhat incomplete and, in the opinion of this writer, partial survey of work in this field which has been produced by Dr R. Hartley. In brief it is argued that the prerequisites (adequate working definitions, samples, controls, design, experimental situation etc.) for extrapolation to real life are missing, and it must be admitted that many of the arguments advanced are not without force.

Commenting on the experimental work an American psychologist, Eleanore Maccoby, writes:

All we may safely assume from the experiments cited is that tendencies toward performing certain actions may be acquired (or augmented) from watching others perform them in the mass media. These tendencies will then enter as one element in the set of behaviour tendencies aroused later in some relevant situation, and whether the particular item of behaviour will actually occur will be a function of the strength of competing responses and the restraints acting upon the media-acquired behaviour. One should seldom expect to find a one-to-one matching of the child's behaviour to that of the movie model. But a child's behaviour may show the effects of exposure all the same, even without direct matching, in the sense that his real-life actions may represent a compromise between the newly acquired element and previously established patterns of behaviour. Furthermore, if the behaviour is of a kind that is usually subject to sanctions, it may require stronger sanctions to suppress it after the film exposure.

The discussion so far has concentrated mainly on more or less direct forms of the media-viewer relationship, and even some of these forms (the role of the media in stimulating or schooling people for violent collective action by reporting or portraying actual collective violence, e.g., news reports of race riots) remain largely unexplored. But there is much more to the relationship than studies on imitation or increased drive can provide. For example an Australian, S. H. Lovibond, claims that his studies have established quite firmly that there is a relationship between exposure to media crime and violence and an endorsement of an ideology which makes use of force in the interest of ego-centric needs the essential content of human relationships. This, so it is claimed, produces a decreased readiness actively to oppose delinquent behaviour and associated systems of ideas.

On another score we are reminded by the Australian psychologist, David Martin, that 'the fascination with overt violence misses the point' – and that the central problem is that of arousing anxiety rather than eliciting violence. Some American research also reports that some delinquent boys were more disturbed and behaved violently after seeing a film where parent-child relationships were central than after seeing a film which portrayed violence. Clearly the problem is a many-faceted one and is unlikely to be solved or fully understood if we confine our work to the more obvious aspects of the direct violent media-violent behaviour relationship.

There are limitations to all of the studies referred to above. From the research so far carried out we know very little about accumulative effects or about long-term effect on attitudes and values, and it seems possible that the research designs so far employed have not been capable of picking up those vital long term 'barely discernible incipient trends'.

All this must be rather confusing and disappointing to the general public, particularly to those like parents and teachers who feel that they have to make important decisions now about the media activities of those in their care.

Two points are worth making in this respect. First, that the social sciences are young and that even if they are unable to provide all the answers they have gone a long way towards completing the vital first stage of asking the right questions. The dialogue (admittedly sometimes a little acrimonious) between researchers on methodological short-comings and alternative strategies although confusing to the layman, is on the whole a healthy sign and absolutely essential if future developments are to be fruitful.

Secondly, one rarely gets out of a subject more than one puts into it. Little of the research referred to in this article has been carried out in Britain. The work at present being carried out, under the auspices of the Television Research Committee, will throw some light on the issues under discussion, but this is only a small beginning; a small part of the total work that will be necessary if we wish to get to grips with the problem. If we take the problem seriously and if we wish to respond to the expressed concern by trying to find the answers to the many questions which have been raised, then we must be prepared to carry out much more research than is at present contemplated.

Although the arguments cannot be fully developed here, an article on the Media and Violence must draw attention to the need to study the media within the wider social setting. On the most obvious level this means looking at the production process as being embedded in an economic, political and social network – at all the influences operating in the production and distribution of violent content in a mass media system. At a rather less obvious level it means opening up the debate so that we can examine the social functions of violence in our society and the role of the media in relation to these functions, and this may involve taking into account a set of values different from the conventional, dominant middle class values which denounce non-legitimized violence.

Lewis Coser, the American sociologist, reminded us several years ago that the social functions of violence could be seen as a danger signal, as a form of achievement for those for whom social status cannot be achieved through normal channels, and as a catalyst.

As far as the catalyst function is concerned, it has been claimed that the use of 'extra-legal' violence by law enforcement agents in Civil Rights disturbances in the United States under the full glare of television cameras and under the observation of newspaper reporters called forth a sense of solidarity against this behaviour. It could be argued that 'all societies depend for their maintenance on a certain amount of dirty work by shady agents of the powers that be', but that 'the usefulness of those doing the dirty work may come to an end when it must be performed in the full view of "good people" '.

The media may also be studied in relation to the function of violence as a danger signal. First by the straightforward reporting of outbreaks of violence such as the recent Detroit disturbances, the media can relay to a wider public the signal indicating a social sickness which requires an immediate remedy if society is not to be destroyed. The signal may thus reach those who have the power to take effective remedial action although it would be unwise to ignore selective exposure, attention, perception and interpretation as possible counter-influences.

Secondly, it is possible to study media violence in a way similar to the one adopted by Professor David Brion Davis in his treatment of the theme 'violence as reality in modern American literature'. He maintains that it can stand for man's spontaneous outrage at oppression, the true nature of the class struggle, the way life really is, the brutality of a world to which one must be resigned, even as a vehicle of unrelieved dehumanization, perhaps all the expressions arising from 'an international disenchantment with the view that life is essentially decent, rational and peaceful'.

Is it possible to say of our media as Professor Davis has said of modern American literature that 'the treatment of violence has grown increasingly ominous for a people who profess to believe in peace and human brotherhood'? If it is and to the degree that media violence represents repudiation and disenchantment then we have a danger signal. But without understanding the role of the media and without wishing to absolve media producers from their responsibilities it could be a danger signal about society as a whole rather than about the media.

A select bibliography will be found in the Notes.

3. The Mass Media and Egyptian Village Life*

Ibrahim Abu-Lughod

The role of the mass media as a shaper of public opinion and as a significant agent of public information and education has experienced tremendous growth in non-western countries in only the past decade. Dramatically apparent is its widespread national exploitation by many of the new states of Asia and Africa.

Egypt, a country of over twenty-five million inhabitants, undergoing a deep social and political revolution, mirrors quite typically the increasing dependence upon the mass media for citizen education. In that country in 1956 there were some 405,000 radio receivers in use; by 1960 that number had swelled to over a million sets.[1] In 1960, radio transmission in Arabic amounted to forty-eight and a half hours per day, as compared with only twelve hours of transmission as recently as 1956.[2] Daily newspaper circulation rose from half a million in 1956 to over 650,000 by the end of 1960.[3]

Gross figures, however, do not reveal the shift in consuming publics which is also taking place, a trend which has a significance at least equal to that of the general increase. The mass media today are reaching the rural areas of the country as never before. The urban centres of Egypt were without doubt the principal consumers of the mass media in former times. While they still continue to dominate the scene, the general improvements in the standard of living in rural areas, the extension of educational opportunities and facilities to these sections of the country, the implementation of compulsory education acts, etc., have all been significant factors in increasing the villagers' consumption of the mass media. This, in turn, is affecting deeply the national

---

* First published in *Social Forces*, 42 (1963), pp. 97–104.

and international 'orientation' of the Egyptian villager who is gradually becoming a 'participant' in modern society.

This increase is reflected in the relatively high degree of exposure to the mass media (press and radio) which was found in the six villages selected for the study. Within these Delta villages, having a combined population of some 14,000 persons, it was found that 156 daily newspapers were regularly sold, and an additional 91 weekly periodicals were in circulation. Within the six villages there was a total of about 135 radio sets. This represents one daily newspaper for every 89 men, women and children and one radio set for every 103 persons.[4] Purchase and ownership figures, however, underestimate the true degree of exposure, since to an extent not paralleled in an industrialized nation, the sharing of the radio and to a lesser degree the newspaper is a common practice which multiplies the audience reached. While exact figures are lacking, the present use of the mass media in these villages does represent a sizeable increase over previous years, as attested by all informants.

Over the past decade, Egypt has undertaken a challenging programme of social and economic development. In its efforts to marshal public support and enthusiasm, the government has quite consciously been utilizing the mass media of communication – over which it holds a virtual monopoly – to inform and educate the public, not only on internal matters but on matters of wider regional and international significance as well. The objective has been to encourage the growth of a more internationally-oriented public, aware of Egypt's involvement in world affairs and willing to support the régime in its diverse activities.

To what extent, however, is the government succeeding in transmitting its messages to the public, particularly to that largely illiterate, formerly totally excluded public which still comprises two-thirds of the entire population, the Egyptian villager? Which elements of mass communication are effective in transmitting the message, and to whom? What is the nature of the communication process, insofar as the Egyptian rural community is concerned?

Near the end of February 1961 the survey of the six Egyptian villages referred to above was conducted, partly to help answer these questions.[5] Since our objective was to measure relative response to the stimulus of the mass media, we utilized the occurrence of a relatively 'important' but not too significant regional event as the object of the probing.[6] On the 26th of February, Cairo Radio in its 10 p.m. broadcast announced the death of King Mohammed V of Morocco, news which was repeated in the early edition of the following morning's newspapers. The King had been treated as an important and respected Arab leader by the Egyptian mass media. One year prior to his death he made an official state visit to Egypt which was widely publicized and photographed by the press. His death was not, however, a matter of vital concern to Egypt. By selecting this particular stimulus, then, we were able to assume that if news of his death could spread in rural areas, certainly more vital events and events affecting the lives of villagers more directly would be even better known and understood.

On the 27th of February a cadre of ten professionally-trained and experienced interviewers who were familiar with the villages and were already known to the villagers interviewed a random sample of 300 heads of households,[7] utilizing a questionnaire which had been previously prepared, except for the specific questions concerning Mohammed V himself, which were added the preceding evening. The analysis of the responses was based on the 272 successfully completed interviews obtained within thirty-six hours of the event.

Results of the study

A surprisingly high percentage of the persons interviewed correctly identified the person of the deceased king; that is, they knew who he was, what country he ruled, and the fact that at some point in the past he had visited Egypt. Some 62 per cent of the sample fell within this category. This was higher than one might expect, considering the fact that the universe was rural and composed chiefly of illiterates and semi-literates with parochial interests, and the fact that the king himself was of no particular consequence to them. This suggests that the mass media in general are quite successful in transmitting news and that the villagers are beginning to develop interests which transcend their local confines.

Only half of these (31 per cent of total sample), however, were aware, within that first day after the event, that the king had died, indicating that they had learned of his death from the radio, the newspaper or from personal word-of-mouth communication. Eighty-five individuals answered 'death' to the very general question of 'Do you know of anything that has happened to him recently?' which was asked *only* of those who had identified him correctly in the first instance. Had the study been conducted several days later, or repeated at different time intervals, this response would undoubtedly have been higher, but these data suggest that news does not necessarily 'travel fast', even in the highly personal society of the village.

The individuals aware of King Mohammed V's death differed significantly in many respects from the uninformed. Before presenting these differences, we might digress somewhat into the question of who consumes the mass media in a typical Egyptian village. Two basically different types of consumers may be distinguished. The first – which in education, function, and general cultural background belongs rather to the more urban and cosmopolitan sector of society – consists of the government officials and representatives. They are the individuals, not necessarily from rural backgrounds, who are assigned to the village to run the schools, collect the taxes, maintain law and order, or extend the various social, health, and agricultural services which are a part of a national programme. They are, by definition, literate, and by occupation, in constant contact with the community outside the village. Socially differentiated from the villagers in all important respects, they tend to remain fairly isolated from the social life of the village community, interacting in limited roles related chiefly to their official functions, and in many cases operating under a shadow of hostility and suspicion inherited from a previous era.

The second group consists of the village community itself, with its fine social and economic distinctions based on property and kinship. This group contains several sub-species. Most easily distinguished are the 'affluent', those individuals who by virtue of extensive land holdings and/or engagement in business have both the means and the need for travelling outside the village community. This outside contact gives them a broader orientation and subjects them to a wider network of influences. While on the whole the group is not literate, its better economic position grants it access to the alternate media, the radio. The remainder of the community, too illiterate to read the press and too poor to purchase a radio, and limited in their contact with the outside world by low mobility, are, in the final analysis, dependent for what they learn on what the two previously noted groups give them.

In the light of this hypothetical typology, let us return now to the differences between informed and uninformed members of the village.

Table I compares the informed with the uninformed respondents according to sex, age distribution, literacy, and occupation.

As can be seen from this table, the person in an Egyptian rural community who is most likely to be informed on events of a non-local nature is male, literate, non-agricultural in occupation, and, as we shall

TABLE I

THE TOTAL SAMPLE, THE INFORMED SUB-SAMPLE,
AND THE UNINFORMED SUB-SAMPLE, BY CHARACTERISTICS*

Characteristics	Total sample		Informed sub-sample		Uninformed sub-sample		Difference between informed and uninformed sub-sample
	No.	%	No.	%	No.	%	
Total	272	100·0	85	31·0	187	69·0	
Sex							
Males	237	87·0	79	33·3	158	66·7	$x^2=3·8051$
Females	35	13·0	6	17·1	29	82·9	Significant at ·05 level
Age							
Under 30	28	10·0	13	46·4	15	53·6	$x^2=8·111$
30–59	203	75·0	54	26·6	149	73·4	Significant at ·02 level
60 plus	41	15·0	18	43·9	23	56·1	
Literacy							
Illiterate	166	61·0	28	16·9	138	84·1	$x^2=40·736$
Literate	106	39·0	57	53·8	49	46·2	Significant at ·001 level
Occupation							
Farmers	181	66·0	45	24·9	136	75·1	$x^2=28·45$
Gov't officials	25	9·0	19	76·1	6	24·0	Significant at ·001 level
Merchants	16	6·0	8	50·0	8	50·0	
Others†	50	18·0	13	26·0	37	74·0	

* Difference between sub-samples based on x^2 test of association. Sex and literacy have 1 d.f. each; age 2 d.f.; occupation 3 d.f.

† This category includes women, itinerant businessmen and those with ill-defined or no occupations.

see, with access to one of the mass media. Of the 85 respondents who knew of the death of Mohammed V, almost 44 per cent had heard the news broadcast over the radio, 21 per cent had read of the event in the newspaper, while 35 per cent had been told of the occurrence by a friend or relative. This latter point is in itself quite significant, since it demonstrates the importance of the 'two-step' flow in extending the influence of the mass media beyond the initial audience.

Leaving aside the self-evident factor of sex and the reasonably significant factor of age, we might explore further the implications of both literacy and occupation, to show their relationship to the hypothetical typology suggested earlier. Both literacy and occupation are important factors, not only in predisposing particular sub-groups to knowledge, but in determining the 'source' of information most effective in reaching each sub-group. Table II presents the source of information utilized by, and the literacy of, the knowers, distinguished by occupation.

One of the most significant facts to emerge from these data is the rather specialized 'audience' of the newspaper. Despite the generally

TABLE II

OCCUPATION OF KNOWERS BY LITERACY AND
SOURCE OF KNOWLEDGE

	Literacy		Source of information		
Occupation	Literate*	Illiterate	Radio	News-paper	Persons
Gov't officials	19	0	2	16	1
Merchants	7	1	6	2	0
Farmers	21	24	27	0	18
Others	10	3	2	0	11
Total (N=85)	57	28	37	18	30

* This includes the barely literate as well as the functionally literate. Actually, there is a wide gap between minimum literacy and the ability to read the fairly complex prose of a normal newspaper. Our hypothesis is that many of the farmers and others who are listed as 'literate' lack sufficient capacity to understand a regular newspaper. This 'barely literate' audience was recognized by the UNESCO Centre which prepared a monthly newspaper *(The Water Wheel)* in large type and simple language for distribution in the neighbouring villages.

high rate of literacy of the informed group, this capacity did not
necessarily predispose respondents to obtain their information from
written sources. Only 18 out of the 57 literate 'knowers' had obtained
their information from the newspaper and, of these, all but two were
government officials. Looking at these same figures from another point
of view, whereas almost all government officials gained their knowledge from the newspaper, only two true members of the community
depended upon this source for their information.

There is no doubt, then, that the 'outsiders' to the village community, i.e. the government officials, are the chief consumers of the
newspaper in the village.[8] They are not only universally literate, but
are also sufficiently literate so that the newspaper presents no reading
difficulties. Actually, their orientation towards the outside world
coupled with their virtual social isolation in the village makes them
almost compulsive consumers of their sole daily link with the non-
village world – the newspaper. They do not even tend to select items in
the newspaper according to interest; rather, they consume it (average
length ten pages) from cover to cover, indiscriminately absorbing its
contents in a manner which they otherwise might not, were they in a
more stimulating environment.

Just as the government officials are almost universally newspaper
readers, the true members of the village community, whether literate
or not, are chiefly radio listeners. This is true even of the merchant
group, despite their high rate of literacy. Of the eight informed merchants, only two read the news in the paper whereas six heard it on the
radio.

To understand the significant role which radio plays in communicating with the merchant group which, because of its pivotal position as
a link between the outside and the village worlds, is a most crucial one,
it is necessary to visualize the 'office' or 'shop' of the village merchant.
Let us take the grocery shop as an example. Small in size, limited in
stock to the very basic staples, presided over by the proprietor assisted
by a young boy, usually a relation, it is open to the street, equipped
with the necessary counter, a few chairs, and a kerosene burner to boil
water for coffee and tea. It inevitably contains a radio in constant operation. This radio is a standard prop not only in the grocery store but in
the offices of the seed merchant, the grain dealer, the cotton agent, etc.
The radio plays constantly not only to entertain the proprietor, for
whom business is always slow, but as a service to his friends and

customers. Those with business to transact, and even those with no pressing business at all, will stop leisurely to listen for a while, discuss the programmes, exchange pleasantries, news, and gossip.

In much the same way that the government official is a 'captive audience' to his newspaper, the merchant and his visitors are equally indiscriminately exposed to the stimulus of the radio. It creates a steady drone of background to the day's activities, interrupted only briefly at the times of prayer and sleep. Therefore, news as well as other content is absorbed almost unconsciously by the hearer. Further, because the merchant's prime business is human conversation, irrespective of his specific economic function, he is likely to 'pick up' and transmit items of interest which would help bolster his image as a sophisticated man of knowledge. That this is indeed the case will be verified below.

As one might suspect, the farmer and the 'others' are least likely to be quickly informed of non-local events. Well informed he may be on questions of local gossip or even governmental programmes having immediate implications for himself,[9] but in the matters concerning the outside world, he is both slower in absorbing facts and more passive in his reception. The newspaper, which requires 'active' pursuit of knowledge, seems to play no real role in his life. None of the farmers nor the persons classified as 'other' learned of the King's death through the newspaper. The somewhat more passive medium of the radio accounted for the knowledge of more than half the farmers and a minimal per cent of the 'others'. Where knowledge did not come from the radio it came from the still more passive source, word-of-mouth conveyance by someone else. Eighteen of the 45 farmers and fully 11 of the 13 'others' were told the news by someone else in the village.

A certain selectivity, however, seems to play a role in determining the persons to whom such news is transmitted orally. It should be noted that even the farmers and others included in the informed sub-sample diverged from the remainder of the sample by virtue of their relatively high literacy. Therefore, while literacy in this group does not seem to contribute to their tendency to gain knowledge through written sources, it does tend to single out these individuals as having 'broader interests' and as having contacts with the consumers of the mass media, both of which lead to their being told news of the outside.

Next to the radio, this personal or 'two-step' flow of communication from the mass media was the most important source of news in the village sample studied.[10] Because it plays such a critical role in transmitting information even about non-local events, it is necessary to investigate more carefully the process whereby word-of-mouth transmission takes place. This can be done through a comparative study of the members of the informed sample who passed their information on to others and those who, while equally informed, did not inform others. Table III compares the 42 persons who told the news to others with the 43 persons who did not transmit their knowledge.

TABLE III

CHARACTERISTICS OF TRANSMITTERS

Characteristics*	Sub-sample of transmitters		Sub-sample of non-transmitters		In-formed total sample	
	No.	%	No.	%	No.	
Sex						
Males	41	51·9	38	48·1	79	$x^2 = 2·7699$
Females	1	16·7	5	83·3	6	Significant at ·10 level
Literacy						
Illiterate	17	60·7	11	39·3	28	$x^2 = 2·1343$
Literate	25	43·9	32	56·1	57	Significant at better than ·20 level
Occupation						
Farmer	23	51·1	22	48·9	45	$x^2 = 3·1741$
Gov't official	8	42·1	11	57·9	19	Significant at ·40 level
Merchant	6	75·0	2	25·0	8	
Other	5	38·5	8	61·5	13	
	42		43			
Source of knowledge						
Radio	29	78·4	8	21·6	37	$x^2 = 27·4900$
Newspaper	9	50·0	9	50·0	18	Significant at ·001 level
Word-of-mouth	4	13·3	26	86·7	30	

* Sex and literacy have 1 d.f. each; occupation 3 d.f.; source 2 d.f.

On the surface, Table III seems to indicate that, of all the variables studied, the source of information – radio, newspaper or word-of-mouth – is the single most important factor determining whether an already informed member of the community will or will not transmit his knowledge to others. Thus, of those who learned of the event through radio listening, four out of five passed on their information to others; among the small sub-sample of newspaper readers, the ratio was only one in two. Least effective of all were those whose knowledge had been gained initially through the passive reception of word-of-mouth knowledge, since only a handful in this sub-sample told others of the event. Neither occupation nor literacy *per se* was significant in determining transmission, and sex had only a minor relationship to transmission.

What accounts for the high degree of association found between source of information and tendency to transmit knowledge to others? Certainly there is no necessary relationship nor element inherent in the media themselves that would lead directly to these results. Intervening variables are probably operating to *select out* certain types of individuals as radio listeners and others as newspaper readers. It was our hypothesis that, although occupation itself was not related significantly to transmission, it was a most important intervening variable in the dynamics of communication in the village setting. This factor, in conjunction with source of information would account for most of the observed variations. Table IV was constructed to test this hypothesis.

TABLE IV

TRANSMITTERS BY OCCUPATION AND SOURCE OF
KNOWLEDGE

Occupation	N	Transmitters knowing from			Non-transmitters knowing from		
		Radio	Paper	Persons	Radio	Paper	Persons
Farmer	45	22	0	1	5	0	17
Gov't official	19	1	7	0	1	9	1
Merchant	8	4	2	0	2	0	0
Other	13	2	0	3	0	0	8
Total	85	29	9	4	8	9	26

This table, comparing transmitters and non-transmitters by both source of information and occupation, is quite suggestive. Note that, among the farmers, almost all who learned of the event through radio transmitted their information to others, while it was only an exceptional farmer hearing from others who passed on his knowledge. This relationship was obscured in Table III. While source of information was exceedingly important among farmers, it was relatively insignificant among both government officials and merchants. Merchants, regardless of source, tended to transmit information, while government officials, again regardless of source, tended to be less effective in spreading news. The fact that the former were more likely to be radio listeners while the latter were more likely to be newspaper readers helps to strengthen the observed connection between source and transmission while obscuring that between occupation and transmission. The miscellaneous category of 'others' tends, in its behaviour, to approximate that of farmers rather than that of the other two groups.

While the totals in each of the critical cells are too small for legitimate conclusions to be drawn from this table, the data hint at hypotheses that might be tested further using a much larger sample. These hypotheses relate directly to the role each occupational group plays in the communication and attitude-formation network within the village community.

The communication network of the village operates *within* the indigenous community. When information is learned by the more informed members of the community, the latter will serve as a connecting link between the outside world and the less-informed members of the community. For the most part, the outside world is brought to these members of the community through the radio. It is almost never brought in through the newspaper, despite increasing literacy. Thus, indigenous members of the community hear news via the radio and, having obtained it from this respected source, are conscientious in passing on their information by word-of-mouth. The passive recipients of their information, however, possibly because they are less concerned and possibly because they occupy lower positions in the power-status hierarchy of the village, fail to perpetuate the chain, and much of the information reaches a dead end with them.

There is a secondary chain of information which operates below its potential because it remains tangential to the indigenous community. This is the chain which connects the outside world to the village via the newspaper. News filters into the village via newspaper, but only to the peculiar sub-sample of readers who are, for the most part, government officials temporarily attached to the village. That half of the sub-sample obtaining their information from this source fail to transmit their knowledge to villagers is a function *not* of the nature of the newspaper as a source but a function of the newspaper reader *at this point in time* being an outsider to the community. In view of the dependence of the government upon these officials for guiding villagers to fuller knowledge and understanding of government policies both at home and abroad, one may merely note that their performance leaves something to be desired.

Conclusions

Exposure to the mass media is increasing in the rural areas of Egypt and, at least in the case studied, seems to be creating an audience receptive to news of non-local significance, even though such news may filter into the rural community more slowly than into the saturated urban community.

In this process, the radio is the most effective medium for reaching villagers, even literate ones. Therefore, for some time to come, even as literacy rates improve in the rural areas, one must depend chiefly on radio to get a message across. The newspaper in the village, while important, addresses a rather specialized set of consumers who are actually marginal to the rural community. It constitutes a link between the urban centres and the urbanized individuals who serve as government officials in rural areas, but is not particularly effective in reaching the indigenous members of the rural community.

Word-of-mouth transmission of news gained originally through the mass media is still an important element in the process of spreading knowledge about the outside world. When the purview of the villager was confined to the local community, this technique of communication was the most important and, essentially, the only one. However, as the horizon of the villagers broadens and non-local events assume a larger place in the world view of the villager, this technique becomes merely a complementary method for transmitting information, secondary in importance to the mass media themselves. This method seems also to become ineffective at the second stage of communication, since persons learning non-local news through word-of-mouth have low potential as transmitters.

4. The Audience for Television Plays*

Denis McQuail

The study described below was initially carried out in order to shed some light on the nature of the mass audience. It was hoped, in particular, that a detailed analysis of response to plays broadcast on television would help to answer questions about the relationship between 'mass' culture and 'minority' culture, about the scope for improvement in levels of popular taste and about the possibility of a 'common culture' developing. Underlying many discussions of mass culture there is a view of the public as culturally stratified in such a way that a small minority appreciate and enjoy what is excellent, and the majority are interested only in what is inferior. The resulting continuum of taste has been aptly described by Kurt Lang as allowing one 'to divide off and speak of a "lowbrow" fare appealing to a mass audience of "lowbrows", and a "highbrow" fare attracting a small and selective group of "highbrows" '.[1]

This widely current view appears to have some support in empirical evidence as well as in common observation. The large-circulation press in Britain is, for example, commonly distinguished from the lower circulation 'quality' press, and many traditionally valued cultural activities – music, painting, opera, theatre have to be supported by subsidy in order to survive, and rely on relatively small patronage groups. The extent to which evidence of this kind can be applied generally to public taste is, however, doubtful. The stratification of the press readership owes much to the needs of advertisers who like their audience to be defined in socio-economic terms, while the lack of public support for much traditionally valued culture may derive from difficulties of access and from differences of habit and circumstance which strongly affect behaviour and attitudes.

There is at least a strong case for enquiring more closely into the

* Not previously published.

reality which underlies the stereotyped image of public taste, especially in the circumstances which may have been altered by the rise of television as a dominant medium of mass communication. There may not be a problem for those who believe like T. S. Eliot[2] that 'it is an essential condition of the quality of culture that it should continue to be a minority culture', or to those who see a hierarchical distribution of 'taste' as simply a reflection of the inequalities of valuation and opportunity maintained by a class-stratified society, and open to alteration only by a social revolution. For anyone who is at all curious about the bases on which tastes and preferences are formed, the notion that inferiority of a cultural object can be recognized principally by its wide appeal is a puzzling one. Unless we believe that the majority actually look out for mediocrity and shoddiness in their cultural fare, we cannot satisfactorily account for the main features of the prevalent model of public taste, with its implied connection between quality of material and quantity of devotees. The many partial explanations which can be put forward do not shed much light on the central question of what people think they are doing when they choose one type of cultural pattern rather than another. The existing pattern is, however, so firmly entrenched as a result of learned habits and values which people cannot easily change and by a fixed pattern of supply, based largely on market considerations, that it is difficult to conceive of an alternative model, even if we believe there to be alternatives. Only by experimenting with the system of provision can the assumption of an inevitable class-related hierarchy of taste be put to the test. At the time this enquiry was carried out, the circumstances of broadcasting in Britain offered at least a modest possibility of doing just this. Both main television networks provided a general public service seeking to combine high standards of production and content with high levels of popularity, an aim facilitated by the near-monopoly control of broadcasting. Very large audiences were drawn to material which included light entertainment, large amounts of news and current affairs and drama of all kinds. The barriers which normally compartmentalize audiences for 'culture' and entertainment, and for 'serious' rather than 'non-serious' content generally are much less effective in the case of television, since habitual and continuous viewing is the norm, and the majority do not or cannot readily take the avoiding action needed to preserve their own patterns of interest. Constraints imposed on the use of other communication media by varying availability, cost, lack of information, habits formed by education and group experience and the efforts of advertisers and media controllers to match content to their own stereotype of the typical consumer are all much less important in the case of television.

Television drama was chosen for the purposes of this study because its audience – especially that drawn to non-serial plays – seems to exemplify this novel situation. 'Single' television plays for adults of an hour or more in length were produced in large numbers (over 300 each year) at the time this study took place; they generally attracted large audiences and included material varying widely in type and quality – established 'classics', serious plays by new dramatists, adaptations of classic novels, along with the general run of straightforward crime plays, comedies and love stories. This diversity stemmed from the absence of a consistent policy in drama broadcasting, of any conscious adherence to a formula of mass appeal and from the large amount of freedom allowed to drama departments, individual producers and writers – a situation which has not fundamentally altered. The intention of the survey was to examine the reactions of a relatively unstructured audience to this very diverse body of material, and to look in particular at the way in which groups differing in social class and educational background reacted to the same material. Probably no other category of television content would have been so suitable, either because variations in quality would not be so well represented, or because few types of content are as universally popular as drama, and therefore as inclined to draw an audience representative of different social groups. The size of the audience for television plays was especially important since the intention of obtaining a sample of the audience for particular plays, sufficiently large to compare the reactions of sub-groups within it, could only be achieved at fairly low cost where the total audience was a large one. While estimates of the size of audience vary, in the period just prior to the survey, the BBC Audience Research Department estimated the size of the audience as ranging between 12% and 26% of the adult population able to receive both BBC and ITV programmes.

The survey of viewer reaction was carried out in Leeds in late 1961 and in spring 1962. It began with the drawing of a stratified random sample of 923 names from the electoral registers. A total of 625 were interviewed, after the elimination of those without television (115) and others who fell out or were not contacted for the usual reasons. The main purpose of the initial interview was to recruit a panel of viewers who would agree to make postal returns of questionnaires concerning television plays which they might subsequently see. After the further elimination of those who did not wish to take part in the panel and a small number who had no interest in television plays, a viewing panel of 551 adults was established. Questionnaires were sent out at three intervals of time, each covering plays broadcast over a three-week period. Eventually, information was obtained about response to 40 plays broadcast on both channels. Although the overall response rate to the postal questionnaire was initially only 70%, and declined subsequently, the average number reporting on any one play was 123. Because of the nature of the sample, the initial elimination and interviewing failures, and the drop-out during the postal stages of the enquiry, the sample cannot be considered representative of the population of the country as a whole, or the town of Leeds, or the viewing public. Even so, the composition of the sample in terms of occupation, age, sex and educational level was reasonably close to that for the United Kingdom as a whole and insofar as comparisons could be made, the relative size of audiences for the plays studied tallied with regional estimates made by the BBC Audience Research Department.

The questionnaires used at the postal stage of the enquiry consisted of booklets naming a series of plays to be broadcast during the subsequent three weeks, and asked for a rating of each play in terms of the degree to which it had been liked and the reasons for this opinion. A reaction scale was provided, with five possible response positions: 'liked – very much; – quite a lot; – moderately; – not very much; – not at all'. Panel members were asked not to alter their normal pattern of viewing, but simply to report on any named play they happened to see. In analysing the results of the survey it was possible to compare plays of different kinds in terms of the reaction received; to compare the response of different groups in the same audience to the same play; and to examine the effect of audience characteristics, especially education and social class, on the response given.

The findings can be considered in two parts – those which emerged as a direct result of the main aims, and those which were reached in the attempt to explain some puzzling features of the evidence. First of all, as had been anticipated, there were wide variations in the extent to which individual plays were liked by their audience. Of the 40 plays studied, only 22 were liked 'very much' by 50% or more of those who saw them, and eight were disliked by a majority. The range of response can be seen from Table I. In order to provide a convenient index of response, the replies to the five point scale were given numerical weights, ranging from 1 for 'liked very much' to 5 for 'not at all liked'. Thus an 'average reaction score' could be calculated for each play from the five-point scale.

TABLE I

DISTRIBUTION OF PLAYS ACCORDING TO OVERALL
LEVEL OF AUDIENCE REACTION

	Average reaction score						
	1·0:1·4	1·5:1·9	2·0:2·4	2·5:2·9	3·0:3·4	3·5:3·9	4·0:4·5
Number of plays	1	13	12	4	3	6	1

A second expectation that was borne out by the evidence was the lack of any strong relationship between the size of the audience and the amount of satisfaction derived. It is especially important, in the case of television, to obtain evidence of the quality of response in addition to that of quantity, since audience size is frequently a function of the time of showing during the evening and the competition available on other channels. The likelihood of a discrepancy between audience size and reaction is heightened in the case of 'single' television plays because there are relatively few clues available in advance to guide the viewer and many plays represent novel or unwelcome experiences to those looking for relaxation and entertainment. This at least is suggested by the low correlation between relative audience size and average audience response indicated by Table II. Figures for BBC and ITV plays are given separately because they have distinct, although overlapping, patronage groups in the audience as a whole and the average audience size for the two groups of plays differed noticeably at the time of the survey. The percentage figures for audience size are based on the number taking part in the postal survey.

These findings serve to confirm an initial assumption that the television audience shows relatively little selectivity in its behaviour and does not differentiate noticeably amongst the content available. They also provide a warning against making inferences about the tastes of

TABLE II

AVERAGE AUDIENCE SIZE AND AVERAGE REACTION SCORE

BBC plays		ITV plays	
Av. audience size	Av. reaction score	Av. audience size	Av. reaction score
35% plus	1·75	55% plus	2·75
30–34%	2·35	45–54%	2·47
Under 30%	2·50	Under 45%	2·76

the audience from the content of what is provided for them and even what they actually see. A related point to emerge, again confirming an assumption which has already been mentioned, was that sample audiences varied little from play to play in terms of their representation of different social class groups. There was a general tendency for the BBC play audience to include significantly more middle class respondents than the ITV play audience; but apart from this, the audiences departed little from the expected pattern, i.e., that of the sample as a whole. Thus, in only six cases out of 40 did the sample audiences significantly (P.=·05) over- or under-represent the more skilled occupation groups, and by the same criterion, only four plays out of 40 differed in terms of the educational background of audience members. It would seem that only exceptionally were decisions to view or not view these television plays affected by education or social class, and that the audience for these plays was indeed generally representative of all social groups.

In seeking to account for the variations in response, the audience for each play was divided up first of all according to educational level and occupational background, and the reactions of sub-groups looked at separately. It emerged very clearly that occupational and educational differences were almost totally unrelated to reactions to any of the plays: in three cases out of 40 there was a small tendency for a play to be preferred by those at higher occupational levels, and two plays were differentially liked by working-class respondents. There was slightly more evidence that educational background played a part, but again the effects were marginal. The plays which appealed more to early school leavers tended to have realistic settings and to deal with contemporary or personal problems, while plays by authors known outside television tended to appeal to those with longer education. It should be emphasized, however, that the great majority of plays received identical levels of response from different social groups, and the variations found contribute almost nothing to an explanation of variations in reaction as a whole. Age and sex differences were, if anything, slightly more influential than occupation or education. As might have been predicted, older viewers responded more favourably to the less violent and disturbing plays, and plays dealing with personal and family relationships seemed to have a greater appeal for women than for men. However, the great majority of the 40 plays studied were liked or disliked to the same extent by all age groups and by men as well as women. It is difficult to convey eloquently the extent of agreement between audience sub-groups, but a statistical measure of the fact can be reported. This is the coefficient of concordance (Kendall's W), which measures the extent of agreement between a number of judges about the ranking of the same set of objects. If we treat audience sub-groups as judges and rank the plays according to the average reaction score received from relevant audience sub-groups, the measure can be applied. The coefficient can range from 0 to 1·0, the latter indicating complete agreement in any comparison of rank orders. The comparison between higher and lower occupational groups produced a coefficient value of 0·973; for the comparison between the under-45 and over-44 age group the value was 0·933 and for that between men and women it was 0·932. These figures, which are all highly significant, demonstrate the great similarity of judgment between different groups.

While it is likely that the reactions of more sharply contrasted groups of middle class and working class respondents than were contained in the sample to carefully chosen types of content could have shown more evidence of different tastes and standard of judgment than these findings reveal, an unexpected problem of interpretation is, nevertheless, posed. The sample of plays studied was in no way homogeneous, except in having been drawn from the output of British television, and the sample, however unrepresentative of any known population, was diverse enough to reflect some at least of the variations in ability and 'brow' level which are believed to matter so much in determining tastes and preferences. How are the large variations in reaction to be explained if the conventional ways of dividing up the audience are so unhelpful?

Three additional pieces of evidence suggest at least a partial answer to this question – evidence of a link between type of content and level of reaction, information available from the written comments of respondents and evidence of an inter-relationship of appeal between certain groups of plays. It was noticed that when the plays were listed in terms of their descending level of popularity, as measured by audience reaction, certain similarities of content became apparent at various levels of response. Broadly speaking, three levels could be distinguished. Those plays with the highest level of response were likely either to be detection or suspense stories, or alternatively comedies with a romantic basis. The plots were either light, amusing or sentimental or they followed a stereotyped pattern of detection and suspense. This could be said of at least 11 of the 14 plays which received an audience reaction score of better than 2·0. Those plays falling between the extremes of approval or disapproval (reaction scores ranging between 2·0 and 3·0) also tended to have some elements in common. They almost all dealt with a social or personal problem in a serious way – representing a play genre which television itself has done much to establish. The plays which were least liked, as a group, seemed to have qualities the reverse of those found amongst the most popular group. They all had some element of unfamiliarity of plot or setting and were found disturbing or controversial by their audiences. The continuum along which plays were judged seems to reflect a movement from the conventional and familiar to the unexpected, violent and morally repugnant.

The claim that meaningful groupings of plays are established by similarities of overall level of response can be supported not only by an analysis of play content but also by reference to the comments of respondents. Thus overall *level* of response is related to the *kind* of reasons actually given for liking and disliking plays. For example, almost all the plays which were found either 'gripping' or 'entertaining' or 'amusing' by a high proportion of respondents were included in the most favourably received group of plays; plays with a middle range reaction score tended to be liked because they were 'true to life' or 'realistic', and where the unpopular plays were liked at all, it was because they were 'unusual' or 'different'. The reasons given for disliking plays also tended to confirm the basic groupings established. The least popular group of plays were regarded as 'far-fetched', 'unreal', 'hard to understand', 'pointless' and the middle range plays were criticized because they were 'boring', 'drawn-out', and 'wordy'. These findings seem to confirm that the degree of popularity can to some extent be predicted from knowledge of content, and that in some sense a 'continuum of taste' does exist. They do not, however, support the view that differences of 'quality', however defined, provide the key to variations in audience preference.

To understand the basis on which audience preferences are formed requires a further examination of the reasons given for liking or disliking the plays included in the survey. An impression then emerges, however hazy, of a distribution of audience expectation from television drama, a set of satisfactions which are looked for, which in turn suggests an underlying pattern of audience needs. Essentially television drama is seen in functional terms, as meeting these needs which range in their salience for each individual and in their importance for the audience as a whole. The evidence for this view emerged only incidentally from an analysis of audience comments, and a study specially designed for the purpose would be required to validate the preceding statement. However, some indication of the nature of audience expectations and their distribution can be given. Television plays are expected by different groups and at different times to hold attention; satisfy curiosity; amuse; entertain and relax; be true to life; be down to earth; be out of the ordinary; have a good moral or meaning; be exciting; be thought-provoking. Clearly these expectations are often incompatible and the provision of one satisfaction to some entails a dissatisfaction to others, a fact which is reflected in the pattern of response to many plays. For example, plays which were *liked* because they were 'interesting', 'had a good meaning' or because they were 'thought-provoking' generally belonged to that middle group of moderately liked plays and were criticized by part of their audience because they were 'slow', 'boring', 'dull' or 'lacking in action'. Similarly, the plays which appealed to some because they were 'unusual' or 'out of the ordinary' were generally not much liked and were criticized by a majority because they were 'far-fetched', 'unreal' or 'hard to follow'. Television plays are especially prone to this conflicting reception because they receive such a large and disparate audience. The point to be stressed here, however, is that the net outcome of audience reaction depends on the varying extent to which the satisfaction offered by the play concerned is looked for by the play audience as a whole. The idea that some expectations occur more frequently than others and are more widely spread amongst the audience is a simple one, but it is crucial to the explanation of audience behaviour which is being presented here.

Of course, the main problem about such a proposition is that of defining and validating the expectations and of assessing their order of importance and frequency of occurrence. A brief indication of their nature has already been given, and some idea of their varying salience can be obtained from what we know of the popularity of different plays studied in the survey. Thus we can group plays according to the main reasons given for liking them and compare the average audience reaction scores for the resulting groups of plays. With this in mind, six groups – each of five plays – were examined, with each group belonging to a different category of audience response and representing a principal type of satisfaction derived by the audience. The groupings, with the average reaction scores, were as follows:

	Principal reason for liking each group of plays	Average audience reaction score for the group*
Group 1	Amusing; entertaining	1·98
„ 2	Gripping; held attention	2·19
„ 3	Credible; realistic	2·16
„ 4	Had a good moral	2·78
„ 5	Interesting	2·85
„ 6	Different; unusual	3·86

* The average reaction score can range from 1.0, representing maximum satisfaction, to 5.0, indicating complete dislike.

The results are somewhat distorted by the widely varying size of the numbers from which a 'like' response was obtained, but even so, the data show a broad progression of popularity from material liked because it is amusing, gripping or realistic to plays which were thought different or unusual, with those believed to 'have a good moral' holding a middle position. At one end of the scale plays which satisfy a majority expectation are widely popular with the kind of unselective audience attracted to television plays, and at the other extreme, plays catering to a minority taste are in these circumstances unpopular. This statement provides the basis on which we can infer something of the relative importance of the different audience expectations. To reiterate an earlier point, the continuum of taste is not based on a differentiation in terms of better or worse, but in terms of differences of content echoed by, and related to, different expressions of interest on the part of audience members. It has been suggested that the distribution of audience expectations in turn reflects an underlying pattern of audience 'needs' which are met by drama content. This further step must remain a modest suggestion, in the absence of any further evidence. Even so, it is difficult to make sense of the reasons which are given for liking or disliking plays, or of the categories of content which have been established, without employing the concept of the function which mass media material serves for its users. A good deal of evidence already exists to show that mass communications are often regarded by those who attend as instrumental in different ways in their daily lives.[3] According to Klapper: 'The audience member selects from the vast supply of media fare the sort of material which serves his immediate needs, and he reacts to that material in accordance with those needs.'[4] The evidence described here suggests that it is mainly in these terms and in terms of the resulting pattern of tastes and preferences that coherence can be given to the variation in response to television plays reported above.

What the evidence does not tell us is the way in which audience expectations vary. Are there separate sub-groups in the audience looking for different types of satisfaction, or is the play audience a relatively homogeneous population which has a persistent demand for material offering suspense and excitement and a less frequently occurring taste for material offering other satisfaction? In the former case we should be able to locate separate groups of individuals, identifiable by the possession of a particular need and, in the latter, with an aggregate of more or less similar individuals whose needs simply vary from one time to another, but who experience some needs more frequently than others. The former image of the audience is closest in spirit to the traditional picture of the stratified audience – consisting of 'highbrows', 'middlebrows' and 'lowbrows'. Although no clear answer can be given to this question, the evidence as a whole does not support the traditionally favoured explanations.

One further source of evidence was provided by examining the inter-association between reactions to plays to see if liking certain plays tended to go with liking other plays. The results served mainly to confirm the findings already presented, since the most noticeable tendency was for the most popular plays to be liked by the same people and the most disliked plays also to have a common appeal to the same small group. This latter finding suggests the existence of a distinct minority taste for plays with a strong element of fantasy and often with an unconventional presentation of violence. There were some other indications that similarity of subject matter could form the basis of appeal to identifiable groups. Common appeal could arise, for example, from an interest in plays about war, or politics, or social problems, or romance. The number of plays was too small to chart these groupings at all fully, but the limited evidence available suggested a need to consider tastes as structured at different *levels* – the most fundamental being related to strongly felt needs, but with aspects of plot and setting becoming important at more superficial levels. A second set of findings relevant to the location of distinct audience sub-groups was available from a separate questionnaire distributed to the panel member, asking them to rate a number of aspects of television plays in terms of their importance. The replies, when inter-correlated, did show a broad dichotomy of response, according to whether respondents were looking for excitement, suspense and action, or alternatively were most interested in plays about ordinary people, everyday life, and the real world. Even so there was a good deal of overlap between these two groups and the differentiation did not seem to have shown itself either in the selection of different kinds of plays or in differences of reaction. This may be due partly to the particular characteristics of the plays studied, which did not lend themselves to any simple categorization in terms of content type or appeal in the way that might have been possible with formula drama productions. It is worth noting, however, that the division of respondents according to these two basic types of preference fits a classification derived previously from a study of children's television viewing behaviour. When Himmelweit, Oppenheim and Vince intercorrelated the replies of children to questions about television programme preferences, they found 'substantial evidence of an underlying pattern of taste'.[5] They isolated 'five fairly distinct clusters of related types of programme': an 'excitement' cluster; a 'social empathy' cluster; a 'mixed social empathy and excitement cluster'; an 'artistic cluster'; and an 'intellectual cluster'. The first two of these seem to bear a broad resemblance to the groupings described above, since the social empathy cluster is based on correlations between 'programmes about ordinary families' and several other programme types, while the excitement cluster derives from correlations between a liking for Westerns, adventure, crime and space fiction programmes. The authors concluded that 'it is not true . . . to suggest that children's preferences are haphazard and idiosyncratic; in the background there is always a regular taste pattern clearly discernible at the age of ten. . . . The taste patterns are in their turn linked with the child's personality and outlook.'[6] The correspondence between these two sets of findings – about children and about adults – suggests that at least some differences of taste are quite fundamental, probably permanent, and possibly related more to personality than to immediate social background.

The main findings of this study – that social class and education play relatively little part in determining response to TV plays – seem at first sight inconsistent with accepted facts about cultural divisions. How are the two to be reconciled? It must first be admitted that the sample studied was quite small, local and incomplete, and thus unrepresentative of the full range of cultural differences. Very few respondents were highly educated or members, in any acceptable sense, of a cultural or educational élite. There are, nevertheless, reasons for believing that the findings of the study are in this matter valid, or at least, that they should not be surprising. First of all, the 'accepted facts' are themselves due for revision, especially since the arrival of television as a dominant mass medium. A good deal of empirical evidence now exists to suggest that both in Britain and the United States, classlessness in media behaviour is more common than has often been supposed. A study, by Wilensky, of leisure patterns, mass media use and occupational differences in an American city showed that the great majority share very much the same cultural tastes and preferences, especially where television is involved.[7] He writes: 'there is little doubt from my data as well as others' that educated strata – even products of graduate and professional schools – are becoming full participants in mass culture', and goes on to say that from a sample of 1,345 only 19 cases could be found of people who 'insulate themselves from mass culture' and who made 'rather heroic efforts to cultivate the best in media'. Of this 19, 16 were by occupation professors. Findings from another survey of the American television audience made at around the same time (1962) and reported by Steiner seem to confirm these results. Differences of socio-economic background were seen to be almost unrelated to differences of behaviour in the use of television, although did affect verbal statements.[8] The tendency for verbal statements of preference for media material to be more strongly affected by education and social background than actual behaviour is not new, and may partly explain why the image of a class-differentiated pattern of taste is so pervasive. An earlier account of the American TV audience had, for example, pointed out that 'while opinion surveys . . . show considerable differences in the programme *preferences* of various population groups, actual audience measurements indicate fewer differences than might be expected in the extent to which various segments of the audience actually view programmes of different types'.[9] Some evidence relating to Britain can also be cited to support these basic findings. On the basis of a sample of over 13,000 adults, Abrams reported in 1959 that almost no differences in media habits could be distinguished between the upper 1% and the remainder.[10] The Granada Viewership Survey, relating to the same year, also showed only very slight differences in the social class composition of the audiences for different categories of television programme.[11]

In assessing the evidence of classlessness in the television play audience it should be recalled that the circumstances of television broadcasting in Britain are peculiarly conducive to the development of similar habits of television viewing on the part of different social groups. Viewing television is a popular leisure pastime at all social levels, governed more by habit and inertia than by conscious choice. The fare available does not vary sufficiently from one channel to another to encourage the fragmentation of the audience into separate and more homogeneous groups, of the kind which make up the readership for some periodicals or the audiences for different BBC radio channels.

An undifferentiated television play audience, in line with the expectation described at the outset, is therefore unsurprising. The unexpected element in the findings of this survey is the similarity of *reaction* of different social groups. An explanation of this fact has, however, already been presented, at least by implication. There is simply no good reason to expect groups, differentiated by class or education, to react differently, since the plays are seen primarily as meeting a set of needs and expectations which do not vary in any consistent way according to social background. We have, at least, no grounds for supposing that the general incidence of a wish for amusement, or relaxation, or excitement, or the satisfaction of curiosity should occur more frequently in one social group rather than another. The link between television drama and its audience is forged by the presence of a set of expectations, varying in their salience over time and in their importance as between individuals. The acceptability or otherwise of any particular play depends not on a judgment of its quality but on the extent to which an identifiable audience expectation is fulfilled.

The categorization of play content in terms of its cultural or aesthetic merit, or of the audience in terms of its level of discrimination or the quality of its taste, is not helpful in understanding response and can be misleading. No doubt differences in these terms can be established, but the behaviour of the great majority of television viewers does not fit such categories and is not illuminated by them. To think primarily in terms of a distinction between 'high' and 'mass' culture or between 'highbrow' and 'lowbrow' taste is to miss the point of television use. It can be described as applying a 'collector' instead of a 'user' model. The response to television plays is not that of the critic or connoisseur, it is an immediate reaction in terms of its meaning to the individual and his feelings and mood at the time. The critic or connoisseur is primarily concerned with judgments of quality according to some 'objective' or external criteria and may regard the views of the 'consumer' as subjective, often ill-informed and irrelevant to his task. The standards applied are in each case quite different and we should not expect a classification in terms of one set to correspond with the other. However, since the predominant orientation of the great majority of television viewers towards what they see is a functional one and they are seeking to satisfy immediate needs, we can understand audience behaviour only in terms of the subjective meanings attached to behaviour by individual audience members, and thus in functional terms.

The evidence for this assertion is so compelling that any expectation of arriving at a common culture in the sense that a majority will come to share and apply the standards of an educated élite would seem to be a non-starter. On the other hand, something of a common culture is represented already by the widely shared interest in certain kinds of mass media content. While it may be argued that the wide common appeal of some kinds of material does no more than reflect the successful imposition by media entrepreneurs of a limited and debased set of tastes and interests, the evidence of this research suggests the explanation to lie in the similarity between individuals in terms of the needs met by art, culture or communication. For those who are or would like to be optimistic about the future for a democratic culture, there are some consoling aspects to this state of affairs, since a real basis does seem to exist for common culture. What is at issue is the level at which it will be set. Two points at least can be made on the basis of this survey. Although in analysing and discussing the results, the regularities of behaviour and response have had to be stressed, and viewer opinion reduced to a somewhat banal level, there was a fair amount of evidence to show that a sizeable, and changing, minority of the play audience had gained something from the experience of viewing particular plays, had been forced to think about serious things, had been moved or disturbed. While the majority do not judge in terms of aesthetic merit, they do apply serious moral standards to the content of television plays. Equally, the 'functions' served by television drama may be acultural but are not necessarily ignoble. Secondly, it can be said that the existence of a common set of needs and interests in the audience for television plays which determines the degree of approval or disapproval need not inhibit experimentation or originality or the attempts to improve quality. The actual distribution of these needs sets limits to what is acceptable, but their presence is not an obstacle to improvement.

These findings apply to the somewhat artificial circumstances imposed by public policy in Britain. The undifferentiated audience for all kinds of television play would be unlikely to persist to the same extent if existing restrictions were removed and viewers had more freedom to align themselves consistently to the kind of drama content they find most congenial most of the time. Eventually this is more likely to happen than not. What lessons can be learned from the present period of constraint on the audience? Evidently a cultural revolution cannot be achieved simply by altering the quality of what is provided. Even so, there is some reason to believe that new developments in taste will have taken place as well as some widening of the range of acceptance for new themes and dramatic forms. A good deal of experience will also have been acquired by writers and producers in communicating to a disparate but widely representative audience and considerable attempts will have been made to bridge the gap between the social and cultural world of the writer and that of most of the audience.

5. Books, Book Readers and Bookshops*

Peter H. Mann

The study of the sociology of mass communications is of relatively recent origin, and interest in it has been greatly heightened by the development of television since the second world war. Studies of written communication have tended to be overshadowed by the emphasis on television, and whilst there have been some studies of newspapers and magazines there has been very little published on books.[1]

This article is about social aspects of book reading and forms a part of a three-year study, begun in September 1967, into book reading, with particular reference to leisure reading. The project is aided by a grant from the Booksellers Association of Great Britain and Ireland, and individual publishing houses have contributed to the grant. The research is aimed at clarifying the social functions of books, learning something about book readers and studying the sources from which books are obtained.

It is estimated that in Britain today there are over 200,000 titles in print, and nearly 30,000 new titles are published each year. Since each book differs from all the others the 'consumption' of books raises interesting, and extremely difficult, analytical problems. The first task, therefore, is to try to get down to basic questions and a useful starting point is to ask – what is a book for? In a pre-literate society communication is by word of mouth and the written record does not exist. As soon as literacy develops, communication expands enormously and the restrictiveness of the purely verbal communication is replaced by the cumulative knowledge which the written word affords. It is essential

* Not previously published. This paper is based on a lecture given to the Annual Conference of the Booksellers Association of Great Britain and Ireland in 1968.

to recognize that the invention of the written word, and its eventual development through printing into the modern book, means a development of communication and therefore a new skill to be learned by the young person growing up in a *literate* society.

Children learn verbal communication very early in their lives, and some learn the skills of verbal communication better than others. Children who are fortunate enough to be born into good communicating families acquire wider vocabularies and a greater ease with words than others. Sociologists, psychologists and educationists have pointed to the great differences to be found within our society in this skill of communication.[2] Not only do vocabularies differ greatly between, say, well educated middle class families and minimally educated working class families, but even more, the ability to use words for conveying ideas of an abstract type may be a skill limited to the more fortunate child.

Oral communication lays the foundation for a child's entry to written communication. Some parents have children who are good communicators, who enjoy playing with words, who at an early age can use abstract concepts, and who easily turn to the written word. If parents are fortunate in this respect they may find it difficult to understand those less fortunate children who do not come from families where *ideas* are discussed; families where communication is limited, where vocabulary is small and the written word is almost superseded by the wireless or television. For these less fortunate children the introduction to reading at school can be an unpleasant experience. The discrepancy between home and school is great, and the child who starts as a 'poor reader' in the infant class may begin to reject the educational values which give prestige to the child who has got to 'Book Ten' whilst poor Willy is still struggling with 'Book Two'.

It is also important to remember that whilst books can give great pleasure to some, they can be great obstacles to be overcome for others. We have found[3] in a number of interviews with school teachers and pupils the fundamental importance of the school in bringing young people to an acceptance of books as a natural and pleasurable part of their lives. But let us not overlook the fact, brought out time and time again in educational research, that no matter what one may do to the educational system to try to get equality of opportunity, the child whose parents care about education, who help the child by taking an interest in what school is trying to do, and so very often, give the child a home with books, almost certainly help him to do better at school than the child whose family does not care and never opens a book from one month to another.[4] The child who cannot read or does not want to read is penalized by the restriction he places on himself in the communication of knowledge.

A classification of books

To try to sort out a classification of books which might help in research we have developed a 'model' for the study of book reading. At the one end we have put what we call *work books*, which are books which people use in their occupations. They are necessities of life, tools of the trade and are not read for any intrinsic satisfactions they give to the reader – their value and purpose lie in giving the reader information which he needs for a further (or extrinsic) purpose, such as arguing a case at law, diagnosing and prescribing for an illness, calculating the stresses and strains on a building, and so on. Student text books of all sorts come in this category too. Here and there a book may be so well written and so fascinatingly compiled that the reader does actually *enjoy* using it, but giving enjoyment is not the book's prime function.

Moving further to the right on the continuum, we have a section of books which are mainly reference works – cookery books, car manuals, travel guides, and so on. Many people who actually *have* books of this sort do not think consciously of themselves as *having* books. But these *are* books, and some cookery books are *genuinely* big sellers (as opposed to the so-called bestsellers of the Sunday paper lists). This section is an important one in the development of our affluent society since with increasing prosperity and expanding leisure interests this *supportive* type of book may well become more important. It is the book which in many ways is a reference book for the practically minded person who is *not* a great reader. This point is borne out by our enquiries in schools where teachers find non-readers prepared to use books for practical projects.

Moving on to the category of *social reading*, we find the non-fiction and fiction which does qualify as real 'literature'.[5] These are the books which get reviewed in the better newspapers; the ones that do appear in the lists of bestsellers; the ones which it is status conferring to have

A SOCIOLOGICAL MODEL FOR THE ANALYSIS OF LEISURE BOOK READING

WORK ← 'UTILITARIAN' READING ← Extrinsic	'SOCIAL' READING Books reviewed and recommended by opinion leaders	'PERSONAL' READING ← LEISURE Intrinsic →
Work books — Texts Manuals Reference books	← Self-improvement → Non-fiction — Fiction History — 'Good' Biography — novels Memoirs Travel	Distraction — Romances Mystery Detective
Home manuals and reference — Cookery Car manuals Guides Hobbies		
For reference only	Status conferring books May be read and re-read	Only inverted status Read once
Buy to have at hand Borrow to extend knowledge Buy good ones previously borrowed Buy as gifts	Buy or borrow for self. Perhaps buy after reading borrowed copy Buy as present if recipient's taste known, but status present anyway Buy as present only if recipient's tastes very well known	Buy paperbacks Borrow from library or friend 'Throwaway' Doubtful as present
	Challenge the reader's attitudes and beliefs	Reinforce the reader's attitudes and beliefs

read – hence the importance of the reviews to indicate *which* ones to read. In the non-fiction part are books which are informative but not practically oriented. It may be very interesting to read books on the first world war, but unless the reader is a general or a politician they are not exactly 'required reading' or 'reference' works. Certainly these books are educative in the broad sense; they are what may be termed 'self-improving', in that they widen the reader's knowledge and impinge directly on his attitudes to life and society. But they do not, in this category, affect his livelihood or have a supportive value; their enjoyment is much more of the intrinsic type. With the fiction in this category one is also dealing with the novel which is seriously reviewed, which is more than just escapism, and which may seriously challenge one's attitudes and values. It is in this region that the battle of the obscene book is fought – it can only be defended on the grounds that it is a contribution to *literature* first and foremost; if it does not get into this category then the obscenity becomes its prime feature. For this reason the obscene book could hardly be defended in our final category, of the escapist or distraction type. Here one has left high culture and challenging of values and one is in the field of the romance, the detective story and the time-filling fiction which offers an escape from a dull world, a vicarious love affair or sexual experience, but no serious challenge to accepted values. Librarians, publishers and booksellers have ambivalent attitudes to this section of books. They form a great part of the paperback market, and many aimed at the male purchaser are sold by the visual appeal of a partially-naked young woman on the cover. What she gets up to inside the book itself may not be exactly what a well brought up young lady ought to do, but the work is rarely actually pornographic. It may be vaguely salacious – often it is downright dull. But books in this category not infrequently are claimed by publishers to have sales of several millions and are sold in plenty by virtually every bookshop.

Yet some of these bookshops do not stock, and assistants do not even know, series of women's romances which are probably the purest and most moral fiction one could wish for. Probably one reason for this interesting form of discrimination is that women's romances carry with them an image of the working-class woman reader who reads these novels but no other books, whilst the 'men's romances' with their sexy covers are regarded as the light-weight reading of the more 'literary' middle classes. We have been able to obtain some data on the readers of women's romances through a postal questionnaire enquiry[6] of women who receive a spring and autumn catalogue from Mills and Boon, a London publishing house, which issues six romantic novels in paperback (published in Canada and the USA as Harlequin Books) and between eight and ten in hard covers each month. A questionnaire was sent out to approximately 9,000 women in the spring of 1968 and 2,788 usable replies were received. Whilst this response clearly raises problems of bias it was possible to discern that the stereotype of such romance readers as being uneducated young factory girls or aged spinsters must be seriously questioned. These romance novels are full 200 page books of 60 to 70,000 words and require a reasonable reading skill to cope with them, no matter how predictable the story itself may be. We found a higher standard of education than expected, and six per cent had been to college or university. It was clear from the survey that these romances appeal greatly to the type of woman who has probably had some office training after leaving school, has had a clerical or secretarial type of job (in which a reasonable standard of literacy is necessary) and who enjoys a good story well told. Many respondents to the questions were younger married women with children at home and the romances were a pleasant form of escapism from housework and children. It was clear in written comments that these women recognize the 'fairy-story' aspect of their reading and enjoy the books because of their unreality. In short, they enjoy a pleasant vicarious experience of being a young and beautiful heroine, wooed by a tall dark handsome hero in a beautiful setting, often against a background of palm trees or beaches. The morality of the stories is unexceptionable and many women noted that these were books which they could leave about the house or lend to their older daughters without any worry. This survey gave an interesting insight into one part of the world of reading about which very little is known. It would be fascinating to carry out a study of a similar type to try to discover what satisfactions are gained by men from their reading of the modern sex and violence spy thrillers, but sampling is a difficult problem in this respect.

Book readers

The next theme of this paper is the book reader, and here it could be said that quite a lot is known about this person but not enough of it leads to an understanding of him. In our research we have found a fair amount of market research into book reading[7] (more on the continent than in Britain), but rather like the descriptions that witnesses give for the identi-kit man to put together, they do not always seem to produce a recognizable human being. Such market research does give a good and accurate measure of things we may only suspect; the main fault is that in these studies 'books' are nearly always undifferentiated. It is rather like treating 'crime' or 'illness' all as one lump.

Let us accept that it is very difficult to gauge accurately how many people really *read books*, largely because it is so difficult to measure reading and to define a book. But the general picture appears to be that about half the British population (perhaps a bit more) can be said, in general terms, to read books, and of those who do there are rather more men than women, more young than old, and larger proportions of higher status people than lower status ones. Most of the statistical tables produced by market research surveys indicate very much the sort of picture one might get from general observations not based on carefully selected national samples. It adds up to the middle class, better educated people being more 'bookish' than the less well educated working class people. Level of education has been suggested by the French sociologist, Dumazedier,[8] as the key factor in book culture and it may well be that recent studies of newspaper readers, in which separate occupational and educational analyses have produced most interesting ideas, could be applied to book readers too.[9]

The general surveys made of book reading are probably best used, not for trying to get an overall picture of book-reading, which is a dubious aim, but rather for picking out points which stimulate further thoughts and questions.

For instance, nearly a third of people in Britain seem to buy books as Christmas presents, and there is a whole category of books which are called 'coffee-table' books which are usually thought of as beautifully illustrated and produced books which make perfect presents and which are not really expected to be 'read' so much as 'looked at'. Clearly books can be status objects in the home, and to give suitable books is status conferring to the giver. This leads also to the thought that many books are owned but never read. There are several publishers' stories which tell of editions of books being put out with several blank pages or pages in wrong order and only a small proportion of such books are returned by the buyers.

Bookshops

Not even the largest bookshop can hope to stock nearly a quarter of a million titles in print and so the bookseller must always be making decisions about his stock on the shelves and this stock must reflect the bookseller's ideas of his customers. Of course many books, especially popular paperbacks, are sold in shops other than booksellers, and departmental stores and newsagents may do quite a good trade in the more popular titles. But the bookshop itself is still the basic institution for the sale of the whole range of books and we therefore decided at the Christmas period of 1967 to conduct a survey of bookshops in England, our field workers being 47 second year students of sociology at Sheffield University. Of course, bookshops are very busy at Christmas time, and often staff are only temporaries. On the other hand, Christmas is a time when many people who may hardly ever go into a bookshop do visit one for present buying. It can thus be argued that from a *consumer* viewpoint Christmas is not too bad a time for a survey, even though it does afford the bookseller some ready excuses for his failings.

The survey covered 115 bookshops from the north of England down to the south-west coast, with a very reasonable geographical spread of shops. It included 52 Charter Group[10] members, 36 non-charter[11] bookshops, 22 branches of Smiths[12] and five book departments of Boots.[13] The students had no knowledge of whether a shop was charter or non-charter, and they did not know that Smiths' shops would be analysed separately so they had no built-in preconceptions about analysis in their observations. We are fully aware that percentaging for such small totals *can* make the results look misleadingly impressive. We realize that 50 per cent sounds better than 11 out of 22, but the percentaging has been done to allow comparisons between the types of shops, no more.

The survey was an attempt to get an appraisal of bookshops as physical environments for the sale of books, and also as social environments in which customers meet people whose job it is to sell books – and of course this includes advising and informing on books. So first of all we wanted to know something reasonably systematic about bookshops themselves. A bookshop is no ordinary shop. In one way it is a repository of knowledge and culture; in another way it is a help-yourself self-service market.

Two-thirds of the shops surveyed were centrally located on main streets of towns and nearly all the rest were in side streets off a town centre. Smiths had by far the best locations, virtually all of them being on main streets. More shops were rated 'moderately' noticeable than 'very' noticeable – and again Smiths came out best. Very few window displays were 'very' eye-catching and a third were 'not' eye-catching; the non-charter shops seemed poorest here. The non-charter shops also got the largest rating of 'bad' for the general level of window display – half being rated bad.

It had been suggested to us that an open door to a bookshop is a welcoming idea, but only about a fifth of the shops had this. The width of the doors was interesting, in that the Smiths shops had 90 per cent doors rated as wide by the observers, as against 29 per cent of the charter group shops and 36 per cent of the non-charter shops. In an overall assessment as to whether the entrance to the shop was inviting, neutral or uninviting, the Smiths shops romped home with 90 per cent rated as inviting against under 50 per cent of the others.

Having entered the shop we wanted to see whether there were adequate signs to help us find various sorts of books. The charter shops came out best here, but even so only just over a third of them were rated as having *plenty* of signs. The non-charters on the whole were the poorest sign-posted.

Face-up presentation of books is regarded by most publishers as an important way of showing books with attractive dust jackets. This form of display was common in just over 40 per cent of the shops surveyed, but in nearly a fifth of bookshops only a few or even no books were displayed in this way. The Smiths shops were best at this (especially with paperbacks) and the non-charter shops poorest.

Finally in this physical section, we had our observers note the bookshelves. Were they wide enough apart for people to be able to get between them? Were there shelves which were too high? Were there shelves which were too low? We had a simple three point rating of good, so-so and poor, and in general the results were good, with the Smiths shops leading in all three aspects.

At their next task observers had to try to find certain sorts of books which we felt should not be too difficult to locate in a bookshop without having to ask for help. Children's books were the easiest to find

(79% easy), then cookery books (60% easy), then hardback fiction was down to 51% easy, dictionaries, bibles and current bestsellers in the 40s in that order; travel books were at 30% and biography lowest at 25% easy. This distribution is interesting, since travel and biography might well be thought of as popular Christmas purchases for gifts, yet taking 'hard to find' and 'not found' together, they came out as the most difficult to locate in the bookshops.

The next part of the survey looked at the bookshops as social environments – places where human beings are employed to sell other human beings books. There are of course some bookshops which remind one of the comedian, Michael Flanders', comment on some British hotels – 'It seems a pity to disturb their privacy' – but on the whole our observers reported three-quarters of bookshop staff as helpful and only 11 per cent unhelpful.

The students were given certain tasks to carry out in the shops to test the assistants' helpfulness and skill. The first task was to ask for a copy of the Pelican book *Tynan on Theatre*, which we knew was out of print, and had been for some time. A third of assistants reported it o.p.; 18 per cent said they would get it for the customer, 7 per cent said they were 'sold out', 5 per cent offered an alternative book. But a third of the students reported the assistants as 'unhelpful' – and at the Smiths branches two-thirds of assistants were rated unhelpful.

The next task was to ask for help in choosing a book on natural history as a present for a girl aged 12. We will leave aside the enterprising female assistant who said they had nothing on natural history and would a book on ancient history do instead? The help given was rated on a five point scale – 'Excellent', 'good', 'fair', 'poor' and 'very poor'. Just over a third were 'excellent' or 'good', exactly a half were 'poor' or 'very poor'. The charter group shops got the most 'excellents', the Smiths shops got the most 'very poor' (43%).

Our observers also asked for 'the Chichester book'[14] which we considered to be an obvious book for a Christmas present. In only 64 per cent of shops was it in stock. Then the men students had to ask for advice on buying a cookery book for a female friend, and the girl students asked for advice on buying a book about car maintenance for a male friend. The rating of help was very similar to that for the book on natural history.

As a final assessment we asked students to record whether they considered they had been dealing with 'booksellers' or 'shop assistants' in their enquiries. Forty-three per cent said booksellers, 57 per cent said shop assistants. The charter group got 57 per cent rated as booksellers, the non-charter shops 53 per cent, the Smiths 9 per cent.

The survey indicates how clearly superior the Smiths shops are in most aspects as *physical* bookshops, but they are not so good as the private bookshop (and especially the charter group shops) when it comes to the social aspects of things. It does seem that the large-scale Smiths capital investment in better looking and better planned shops is making its mark, and their shops are now in many cases more attractive and better planned than many others. But this does not allow all the non-Smiths shops to excuse themselves simply on grounds of lack of money. Window displays need not just look like the overflow from a jumble sale. Bookshelves can be labelled and sections sign-posted without having to raise a new share issue. Too often there is an air of complacency in bookshops and assistants may be too accustomed to their bookshops to think enough about the person who does *not* know their own particular idiosyncrasies in bookshop layout. University sociologists often have to criticize student questionnaires for bad design because the student has thought only about the question he wants to ask and not enough about the answer which his respondent may give. Some bookshops are rather like this – it may suit the book-seller or his assistant to have all the Macmillan's Papermac series to-gether for *their* convenience, but when I cannot find MacIver & Page's *Society* in the 'sociology' section, I am not amused to be told that certain series are on shelves under *publishers*. This goes for an awful lot of cheaper paperbacks, too. I may distinguish a Pelican from other paperbacks, but I do not really distinguish between ordinary fiction according to Penguin, Fontana, Pan and all the rest of the paperback imprints – so I am pleased when a bookseller thinks of *me* – and offers me categories of Westerns, Romances, Detective stories, Thrillers and so on. Perhaps a walk by the bookseller round a good self-service grocer's shop might not come amiss now and then.

On the *personal-social* side of things it is difficult to be fair in criti-cism. It is important to appreciate that the sale of books in the book-shop itself is usually only a part of the bookseller's income, and often not the most lucrative part. Bookselling as a career has not yet been 'sold' to the young, and especially to the better educated. The financial rewards are not good for graduates *as a whole*; that is as a career grade for the many who will not become managers of the very top shops. So the 'professional service' which some booksellers feel they ought to give their customers is in many cases a dream.

Everyone knows this sort of problem, and yet one does really wonder how much this is really *the* problem. Analyses we have made of sales of books in general bookshops indicate clearly that the bread-and-butter trade of the bookshop is a very humdrum steady sale of books on nursing, do-it-yourself, travel guides and cookery and all sorts of non-intellectual, non-literary interests. Is the bookseller kidding himself a bit at times over this business of books as literature? Is he, like the publisher, concerned with his image as what Fredric Warburg called 'an occupation for gentlemen'?[15]

It is fascinating in talking to publishers to find what terribly bad form it seems in publishing to be actually *trying* to make money. Perhaps a bit of this attitude rubs off on to booksellers and this leads to a split-mindedness and indecision about the function of the book-seller and the bookshop. In some bookshops the relationship is looked on more as professional-client than as tradesman-customer. This may be all right in some circumstances, but it may be illusory in many where the actual seller is not professional in training or outlook and the client is not seeking advice. All he wants is a book.

6. Social and Personality Factors Associated with Children's Tastes in Television Viewing*

D. Harper, Joan Munro and Hilde T. Himmelweit

Within a given region, television offers the same menu to its viewers, yet their responses are very different. It is this aspect which interests the social psychologist: the factors which determine how much an individual views, what he views, and how he reacts to what he has seen.

The majority of studies of viewers' reactions have been concerned with two aspects: how much an individual views and what he likes and dislikes. In the case of adults, differences in reactions were related to the social characteristics of the viewers: age, sex, marital, educational and occupational status. In the case of children, research has also considered the child's adjustment and his needs and values. Himmelweit, Oppenheim and Vince in Great Britain and Schramm in the United States have shown that children who view far more than their age group tend to be of below average ability and to be boys rather than girls. When comparative studies of heavy and occasional viewers (matched for age, sex, ability, type of school attended and social background) were made, the heavy viewers were found to be less well adjusted compared with the occasional viewers.

In the realm of taste, preference for fantasy versus reality programmes and, within fictional programmes, preference for programmes depicting violence have also been studied: Schramm, Himmelweit *et al.* and Pearlin have shown that younger and less able children, and in

* This summary of a much longer report was first published in: Television Research Committee, *Second Progress Report and Recommendations* (Leicester University Press, 1969), pp. 55–63.

Schramm's study those from working-class homes, expressed a preference for fantasy rather than reality programmes. Others found a relationship between the child's way of dealing with his own aggression and anxiety and his preference for programmes with high action and violence content.

These studies show that the taste of the young viewer, like his other attitudes, reflects the culture and subculture in which he is being brought up, his age, ability and psychological needs. While much work has been done to find reliable and valid means of assessing attitudes, this has not been attempted in the case of programme preferences.

The present study attempts to do just this. It applies the well established methods of attitude measurement to that of children's taste.

There are three weaknesses in the way programme preferences are traditionally assessed: first, the range of programmes sampled tends to be small; second, each viewer selects from a private unspecified list so that comparative studies cannot be done; and third, the number of individual programmes selected being so large, the categories into which they are placed are those used by producers rather than those which reflect the viewers' perception of programmes. For example, in the eyes of the viewers, there may be more differences within Westerns (depending on whether human relationships are the main focus as in *Bonanza* or violence as in *Whiplash*) than between Westerns and other human serials, and war or crime programmes. The producer's classification emphasizes the geographical and historical setting, while the viewer may respond primarily to the story and the portrayal of characters.

The study reported here has two broad aims: the first was methodological and directed to the development of more systematic techniques of studying viewing tastes; whilst the second was concerned with the feasibility of using these techniques to clarify the psychological and social determinants of patterns of taste in television viewing.

First, on the methodological side, the problem was to develop quantitative measures that would permit viewers to be classified, on the one hand, into those with *generally* positive or negative attitudes to television, and on the other into groups with strong or weak preferences for particular types of programmes. Their groupings were to be determined empirically on the basis of the children's own ratings: the categories or dimensions which they used, to be compared subsequently with the more traditional classifications of favourite programmes. The technique for determining these dimensions was that of factor analysis.

The second stage of the research consisted of relating these programme preferences to characteristics of the viewers, namely to differences in their social background, ability, achievement and personal adjustment.

Most studies on taste have faced another problem – that of having sufficient measures to describe the viewer. The schools are understandably reluctant to give up too many school periods and it takes time to ask the necessary questions about the young person's reactions to viewing.

By hitching our study to one which had been carried out a year earlier by Bruckmann on 196 ten- to eleven-year-old boys in their penultimate year at primary school,[1] we were able to benefit from the measures she had obtained for her study of the complex relation of ability, social background, need achievement and anxiety to school performance and to future school plans.[2]

A year later, we went back to the classes which had taken part in the earlier study and found 121 of the children originally studied. They are now in their last year at primary school. We obtained three further measures of adjustment: measures of fearfulness, of self-esteem and of acceptance or rejection by the other children in the class (sociometrics) and also found out to which type of secondary school the child had been assigned. In addition, the children were asked to name the three programmes they liked best and those they liked least, the television plays they liked and disliked, and any programmes which had kept them awake or worried them.

Those were the traditional methods of obtaining measures of children's preference which we wanted to evaluate against the new measures. To obtain these, the children were presented with a list of 60 programmes and were asked to indicate for each whether or not they had seen the programmes and if they had, to rate each one on a five-point scale from 'It is one of my favourites' to 'I don't care for it'.[3] The programmes were selected on the following basis: as many as possible were to be programmes which were being repeatedly shown before 9.30 p.m.[4] Where individual programmes were included, e.g. *Silas Marner*, they were drawn from those shown in the two weeks before we questioned the children.

Further, as we wanted to use the ratings to see how far the dimensions along which the young person considered programmes agreed with the classification of producers, we selected sufficient programmes for each main type of traditional category. This was not always easy; for example, relatively few detective programmes were shown in that period (certainly compared with the '50s). Instead, there was an abundance of Westerns. As far as the range of programmes shown before 9.30 p.m. permitted, we tried to represent each traditional grouping like Westerns, Variety, etc., by at least four different programmes.

The sample of 121 ten- to eleven-year-old children contained about equal numbers of boys and girls but was above average in intelligence, with over 60% coming from middle-class homes. This lack of representativeness does not matter in this study, which aims at investigating relationships rather than at establishing typical preferences for a given group of viewers.

The analysis

The full report gives details of the measures used and the analyses carried out. Here we shall describe only the dimensions along which the children grouped their preferences and indicate the usefulness of calculating a preference score for each of these dimensions.

The method used for arriving at taste dimensions was that of factor analysis.[5] The factor analysis yielded twelve factors or dimensions, accounting for 66% of the variance. The name we have given each factor was derived from inspecting the content of those programmes which best expressed that factor (i.e., had the highest factor loadings). We arrived at a name for a dimension by looking both at the programmes which had high negative, and at those which had high positive loadings. These constitute the two ends of the dimension. For instance, Factor IX was labelled Serials (Serious and Comedy) because the programmes which expressed this factor at one end (had negative loadings) were *Emergency Ward 10* and *Coronation Street*, while the programme which best expressed it at the other end (had a positive loading) was the *Dick Van Dyke Show*. Where it was difficult to find a label encompassing all programmes, one expressing the majority was chosen. Thus Factor VII was described as Preference for Children's Programmes even though *Candid Camera*, a programme meant to entertain adults, was included. This is a good example of the value of this type of analysis:

it shows that *Candid Camera* is liked by those ten- to eleven-year-olds who also like programmes designed for children younger than themselves. Others care little for it. One wonders whether this is what the producers intended.

Table I gives our description of the programme dimensions together with all the programmes which best expressed that dimension (negatively and positively). The figures next to each programme represent its factor loadings.

The factors labelled Pop Music, Quiz Programmes, Human Interest, Serials and Sport came out clearly, coinciding closely with the traditional categories. Others differed in interesting ways, suggesting that children react more to the flavour or style of a programme rather than to its content.

For instance, two animal programmes, *Zoo Time* and *National Velvet*, formed part of the Western preference area. Not one of the crime or detective programmes did so. This suggests that ten- to eleven-year-old children may react more to the outdoor life and the riding rather than to the violence of the Westerns. The *Children's Programme area* was interesting in that it excluded the two science fiction programmes specifically designed for children, but included *Candid Camera*, a light entertainment programme designed for adults. The children's programmes which were included are predictable, cosy programmes with a regular format well liked by younger children.

The Science Fiction programmes formed a preference area of their own. Once again, exclusion and inclusion of other programmes suggests what their appeal might be. The inclusion of the *Dickie Henderson* programme and the exclusion of any information programme suggests that science fiction programmes do not scare these viewers and are enjoyed, not for their science contents, but as a form of light entertainment.

Much more can be learnt about the appeal of these programmes and the reasons for their groupings by relating the preferences to the social and psychological data we have obtained for the child. To do this, we computed for each child eleven preference measures, one for each area. The scores were derived from the factor analysis. We then correlated the scores with sex, ability, social background, age at which he would like to leave school, ambition, fear, anxiety and sociometric rating. Differences in intelligence, sex and social background were strongly related to differences in taste. At the second stage of analysis, we

TABLE I

TWELVE FACTORS DERIVED FROM A PROMAX FACTOR
ANALYSIS PREFERENCE RATINGS OF 34 TELEVISION
PROGRAMMES BY TEN- TO ELEVEN-YEAR-OLD BOYS
AND GIRLS

(The programmes with the highest factor loadings are given. The
figures in brackets denote the percentage variance accounted for
by that factor)

Description of Factors	Programmes defining the factors	
	Positive factor loadings	Negative factor loadings
I Pop music (14·50)	·78 *Top of the Pops* ·77 *Ready Steady Go* ·76 *Thank Your Lucky Stars* ·64 *Juke Box Jury* ·50 *Sunday Night at the Palladium*	
II Quiz programmes (7·84)	·74 *Take a Letter* ·73 *Junior Criss Cross Quiz* ·61 *University Challenge*	
III Sport (6·77)	·83 *Grandstand* ·76 *Sportsview* ·65 *Telegoons* ·54 *Professional Wrestling*	
IV Science fiction (5·70)	·73 *Dr Who* ·73 *My Favourite Martian* ·42 *Dickie Henderson Show*	
V Westerns (4·73)	·83 *Bonanza* ·78 *Gunsmoke* ·56 *Laramie* ·40 *National Velvet* ·39 *Zoo Time*	
VI Human interest serials (4·55)	·78 *Compact* ·60 *Emergency Ward 10* ·35 *Coronation Street*	
VII Children's Television programmes (4.00)	·71 *Candid Camera* ·62 *Five O'Clock Club* ·55 *Zoo Time* ·47 *National Velvet*	

VIII Light entertainment (3·90)	·62 *Here's Harry* ·49 *Dickie Henderson Show* ·41 *Laramie* ·40 *Just Dennis*	·64 *Tonight*
IX Serials (serious and comedy) (3·85)	·76 *Dick Van Dyke Show*	·39 *Emergency Ward 10* ·39 *Coronation Street*
X Comedy (3·45)	·75 *Morecombe and Wise Show* ·70 *My Three Sons*	
XI Reality and News (3·20)	·41 *Just Dennis* ·68 *News* ·46 *Professional Wrestling*	·36 *Telegoons*
XII (Could not be interpreted) (2·99)	·34 *Tonight* ·76 *Junior Points of View* ·59 *Dr Kildare*	

Total percentage variance accounted for: (65·50).

partialled out their effect to allow the psychological variables to emerge.[6]

Certain preferences could be explained almost exclusively in environmental terms, reflecting the culture of the time of the role differences between boys and girls. Others reflected differences in ability, in drive or ambition; others again were liked by those with high anxiety and fear. To the first category belongs preference for Pop Music. While, ten years ago, preference for music, singing and dancing was the province of girls, in this study, Pop Music was as popular with boys as with girls, and especially liked by those of working-class background who are particularly oriented towards the teenage culture of their neighbourhood rather than to school. (They are going to secondary modern schools and would like to leave school early.) Preference for fantasy as against reality programmes was also related to the social background, with more working-class children preferring fantasy to reality programmes. These findings coincide with those obtained by Schramm and by Johnstone and Katz.

Boys preferred sport and comedy; girls, human interest serials. Duller children liked Westerns and children's programmes more than the intelligent. Background, sex and ability were the factors which correlated significantly with certain of the programmes. With others, the psychological state of the viewer was the important predictor. Thus

Westerns and children's programmes were liked better, not only by those of low ability, but also by those with low need achievement who were fearful and anxious. This suggests that, for this age group, liking for children's programmes and for Westerns is a sign of intellectual and emotional immaturity. The children's programme preference area did not include *Dr Who* and *My Favourite Martian*. Liking for these programmes which are also specifically designed for children was not related to maturity or adjustment. The fearful and worried young viewer preferred serious serials like *Emergency Ward 10* and *Coronation Street* and comedy like *My Three Sons* and *Just Dennis* more than viewers of the same ability who were better adjusted. In line with Riley's findings, those in our sample who were not liked by the others in the class, tended to retreat into a fantasy world, scoring high on the fantasy preference area.

So far we have discussed differences in the enjoyment of various types of programme. Viewers also differ in their enjoyment of the medium as a whole. To measure this, a *Television Attitude Index* was computed for each viewer consisting of his ratings for all the programmes he had seen divided by the number of programmes viewed. The television fan who liked everything he viewed was found equally at all social levels, tended to be a boy rather than a girl and to be intellectually and emotionally immature. In every way the television fan was like the television addict whom we had studied ten years earlier. On that occasion, we measured the amount a child viewed, irrespective of whether he enjoyed what he saw. *It may well be that any excessive involvement with the medium relative to that characteristic of the age group is an indicator of poor adjustment.*

Finally, we compared the new measures of taste with the traditional ones based on the classification of favourite programmes. There was much agreement between the two measures, with two differences. The preference area score for Pop Music showed that boys and girls liked Pop Music equally, though more girls mentioned it as one of their favourite programmes. In the case of science fiction, the preference area scores showed that boys liked these programmes more than girls, yet as many girls named *Dr Who* or *My Favourite Martian* as their favourite. The traditional method is unreliable because of the small sample on which any comparisons are based. No more than 13% of the sample mentioned the same programmes as their favourite when their choice was restricted to three. When they are given free choice to indicate for each of 34 listed programmes whether it is one of their favourites, a more reliable indicator of taste can be constructed. That the measures are more reliable is shown by the greater clarity with which the relation between preference area scores and characteristics of the viewer can be established compared with the traditional approach.

The research gives confidence in the new methods of determining taste. Perhaps the most interesting contribution of this study lies in the establishment of the distinction between liking for programmes that reflected contemporary fashions and those which are liked because they satisfy psychological needs. Such an approach should be useful for cross-cultural comparisons and also for comparison within one society, both of change over a period of time and of preferences of different age groups. It is, for instance, noteworthy that an adult detective programme, *Fabian of the Yard,* was the universal favourite of ten- to eleven-year-olds ten years earlier; today, the favourite is Pop Music. Both preferences reflect the Zeitgeist rather than psychological needs. It may well be that popularity of a programme begins that way, i.e., interests first those for whom it has some kind of message but, once it becomes popular, fashion overshadows such differences.

The study is exploratory; its emphasis methodological. However, the results are encouraging not only because the preferences were satisfactorily assessed, but also because they linked with significant characteristics of the viewer and so helped to increase our understanding of the complex interaction between the viewer and the medium. There is need, of course, for far more searching enquiry than has been possible here to determine the reasons for the child's liking for given programmes. Such study involves both content analysis of the programme themselves and detailed questioning of their viewers.

7. The Design of Investigations into the Effects of Radio and Television Programmes and other Mass Communications*

B. P. Emmett

Introduction

1.1. The mass media – the press, cinema, radio, television, etc. – exert such a steady pressure on us all that it can hardly be doubted that they constantly modify our behaviour, alter our attitudes and opinions, extend the range of our cultural experiences, increase our stock of information (or misinformation) and even affect such personal individual characteristics as our initiative and ambition. Indeed, the general tendency over the centuries seems to have been to attribute practically any change in our society, real or imaginary, to the baleful influence of one or other of the mass media. That the effects have generally been greatly exaggerated is now widely accepted by most of those who have undertaken any research in this field. Nevertheless, it seems likely that the mass media are increasingly potent means of effecting change, and as such measures of the extent of the changes they produce will inevitably be an even more important part of social research in the future than they have been heretofore.

1.2. The statistician's role in such research is, of course, to advise on the research design, on the sampling methods, and on the appropriate analysis and estimation procedures. But whereas efficient designs and analytical methods are readily available in situations where the factors can be manipulated experimentally, they are conspicuously absent in

* First published in *Journal of the Royal Statistical Society*, Vol. 129, Part I (1966), pp. 26–49.

other situations, the thorough treatment given to design of investigations in the best-known textbook (Selltiz *et al.*, 1959), for instance, making no reference to the difficulties facing those engaged in 'observational' rather than 'experimental' studies. The subject has, however, been receiving more attention of late, notably in Cochran's recent contribution to the Society's proceedings, whilst Harris (1963) has edited an admirable collection of a dozen papers all dealing with the measurement of change, which emphasize the complexity of the problem. This paper was in preparation when Cochran's appeared, but was then put aside since much of what might have been included in it was so admirably dealt with by Cochran. However, the subject is so important and so little discussed that it has seemed worth while to continue the debate by drawing attention to a class of problems that was not referred to by Cochran.

1.3. The investigations with which we in the Audience Research Department of the BBC have been concerned have typically consisted of attempting to measure the effects of a single broadcast or of a short series of broadcasts. We have *not* been directly concerned with measuring *general* effects of the mass media, i.e. in providing answers to questions like 'How has broadcasting affected musical taste?' or 'Does television make people less sociable?' etc. Most attention is therefore paid to the measurement of the effect of a single event at a specific point in time, though a note on long-term effects will be found at the end of this paper. The fundamental difficulty in the study of the effects of the mass media is that the disseminators of the messages cannot determine which individuals will receive them; though they may well be able to predict fairly accurately the number and nature of the recipients. Anyone who has access to a radio or television receiver can, if he wishes, watch or listen to the programmes transmitted, and no investigation or experiment that ignores this self-selection feature of the situation can claim to have been a study of 'effects'. This is not to deny the value of the many laboratory studies of communication which have explored the process by which information is acquired and attitudes altered. The results of such research help to determine the conceptual model of the communication process which any mass media effects study must take into account. However, for such work familiar experimental designs are appropriate. For field observation studies they are not.

1.4. An important point to note in connection with mass communication generally is that, in virtually every case, the communication does not set out deliberately to produce a behavioural effect or even an attitudinal one. Many newspaper stories probably tend rather to satisfy idle curiosity than to build up a store of organized knowledge, whilst the majority of radio and television programmes, of cinema films and of books and magazines, aim almost exclusively at entertainment first and last. Nevertheless, whatever the *intention* may be (and often it will be unknown) some effects must inevitably be produced. Indeed, it is not unreasonable to suspect that greater effects are produced by the many broadcasts that do not set out deliberately to produce any than by the few that do. A good example is furnished by *The Archers* which, besides its prime aim of entertaining a large loyal audience composed mainly of urban dwellers, informs and moulds the professional farming community as effectively as do the broadcasts expressly designed for them. A second point of some importance is that very few studies of the effects of specific messages in the mass media appear to have been made, by ourselves or anyone else, and hence little is known of the efficacy in practice of various methods of investigation. The most comprehensive bibliography of investigations into the effects of the mass media is given by Klapper (1960) and this includes only two studies of specific broadcasts. The four studies described in Part II of this paper were selected from a total of only nine made by the Audience Research Department in the course of the past fifteen years. Incidentally, all of them have been studies of informational-type broadcasts, and so have those few, of which I am aware, that have been made by other researchers. There would be no excuse for discussing these few limited researches of ours if it were not for the fact that the problems we encountered are probably not exclusively our own, precisely similar difficulties apparently facing anyone concerned with the effects of any other of the mass media. A critical examination of some of our experiences may perhaps help to fill the gap left by the absence of any theory of 'non-experimental designs'.

Part I. Research designs

2.1. It might appear that there is no problem in designing investigations into the effects of a single event in time, the obvious technique required being to make one observation before the event and another afterwards. Indeed, a number of 'effects studies' have done no more than this, the

'Immunization' enquiry described in Part II of this paper providing one example. In that study a sample of general practitioners and local authority clinics co-operated in keeping records of the numbers of children brought for first immunization in the two weeks before a television broadcast about immunization and in the three weeks following it. Provided the samples on which the observations are based are adequate this method can yield useful results, though it presents the fundamental difficulty of interpretation, viz. 'can one attribute observed changes to the event itself or did some other event(s) contribute?' In 'longitudinal designs', of which this 'before/after' method is the most simple, the question of extraneous influences can never be avoided. More firmly based conclusions can be drawn if a *series* of observations is made both before and after the event. For instance, if weekly admission figures to a museum exist, the effect of a broadcast on attendance can be gauged more reliably than if only two observations, one before and one after the broadcast, are available. The effects of a broadcast on museum attendance were in fact studied by Himmelweit *et al.* (1958, pp. 293–6), but they were inevitably restricted to single 'before' and 'after' measurements since it was children's attendance with which they were concerned and this could only be assessed by observation and interview at the museum. We have never been fortunate enough to have sufficient warning of a request for the investigation of a broadcast to plan a series of observations, but some good examples are quoted by Campbell (Harris, 1963) in a section devoted to what he calls 'the interrupted time series experiment'. As he says: '... this design is particularly appropriate to those institutional settings in which records are regularly kept and thus constitute a natural part of the environment to which one wants to generalize'.

2.2. Series such as these may permit the estimation of a trend term which can then be removed from the 'before/after' comparison. It may also reveal periodicities, such as seasonal variations, and suggest factors, such as the weather, which can then be introduced into the analysis as 'disturbing' variables. The estimated 'after' value based on the trend term can then be compared with the actual observation and the significance of the difference assessed in the light of the residual variance. A fuller discussion of significance testing with this type of design is given by Campbell, who proposes that separate linear trends be fitted to the 'before' and 'after' observations and these compared with a single linear fit for the whole series, significance in such 'linear tests' being regarded as the minimum needed to support the hypothesis that the event had an effect. Intervening variables, if continuous, are probably best dealt with by multiple regression, though for this to be worth doing, a good series of 'before' observations must be available. The existence of a series of observations also highlights a rarely discussed practical problem, viz. when and how often to make the 'after' measurements. How long, for example, should one continue them? After how long a time is it no longer reasonable to ascribe to the event itself differences from the predicted post-event level? Accretions of knowledge can be assumed to occur at the time of the broadcast itself and to decay thereafter, but behaviour patterns directly attributable to the broadcast may occur a very long time afterwards. The timing of the single 'after' observation can thus be seen to be crucial and more than one observation, well separated in time, seems essential. In all our enquiries we have simply made a single observation as soon as possible after the broadcast since 'learning from the broadcast' has always been an important element in the study, but we have recognized that more extensive enquiries would have yielded valuable additional information.

2.3. A problem of a different kind may also bedevil the interpretation of the post-event observations. It is not unknown for the event so to stimulate behaviour that a form of 'queueing' occurs; for instance, when the variable being measured is demand for a particular book at public libraries. In this instance, one essential is clearly to establish the degree of unsatisfied demand both before and after the event. An ingenious scheme designed by Trenaman (1953) to investigate the influence on library demand of the radio dramatizations of three books went some way towards measuring this. He persuaded 64 librarians to add to the books on their shelves a few 'dummy copies' of the three books concerned. The dummies were simply cases resembling books which, on being opened, were found to enclose a note referring the reader to the enquiry desk for a copy of the book itself. To have provided on the shelves a sufficiently large number of copies of the books themselves to cope with increased demand, however large, would not only have been unacceptable to the libraries, but would also have given the books a grotesque artificial prominence. The dummy books were put on the shelves a fortnight before the broadcast serial started and remained there till a fortnight after it had ended. For two of the serials two libraries used the dummy books in alternate weeks only; in the other weeks real books were replaced immediately they were taken off the shelves. The number of borrowings did not differ from week to week under these different methods. Table I records the weekly average demand for the various books during the three periods – the fortnight before the broadcasts, during the broadcasts and during the fortnight after the broadcasts ended.

TABLE I

LIBRARY DEMAND AND BROADCAST SERIALIZATION

Book	Average weekly demand in fortnight before serialization began	Demand while book was being serialized	Demand in fortnight after serial ended
The Silver Spoon	38	61	51
The Last Chronicle of Barset	26·5	43	27
The House in Paris	61	188	56

If, as some have suggested, the listening to a broadcast serial provides a substitute for reading the book, one would expect the demand for the book to fall off for some time after the serial had ended on the ground that listeners who had heard the serial would not wish to read the book itself. Trenaman's investigation was able to contribute some evidence on this point by comparing the issues for the three months before the serialization with those for the three months after it ended. Briefly, demand did *not* fall off, issues remaining at a higher level after the broadcast than before. Though the risk of unsatisfied demand influencing the measurement of behavioural effects may be widespread, this remains the only investigation in which it has been allowed for.

2.4. Only if the effect being studied is behavioural, and not always then, can the effects study be made by measuring or observing behaviour at the moment it occurs, e.g. at the museum entrance or the library counter. Instead the 'before/after' design must usually involve sample surveys, the informant's behaviour being elicited by questioning. The simple 'two-observation' design can still be used and indeed we used it ourselves as part of a study concerned with the television series 'Crime' (see Para. 9.1 *et seq.*), though it requires that ample warning be given of the event so that the complex task of mounting the 'before survey' can be completed sufficiently far ahead of the event, even before publicity about it has begun. The method is clearly rather insensitive as 'before/after' differences will only be distinguishable from sampling errors if they are substantial. The vexed question of which questions to ask does not fall within the scope of this paper, but it is important to remember that in surveys of this kind the measures themselves generally have an inherent unreliability. Given sufficient time for pilot experiments, it should be possible to reduce this un- reliability and to estimate the amount remaining using the test/re-test reliability coefficients familiar in psychometrics, but time normally being the one commodity of which we are short, it is inevitable that unreliability of the measures will be superimposed on the sampling errors, thus reducing the sensitivity of the before/after comparison even further. If one tests the significance of the difference between the before and after sample values by using the convenient V-scale nomo- grams, of Rosenbaum (1959), it is advisable to allow for the unrelia- bility by arbitrarily assuming a substantially lower level of significance than that indicated. A more extensive consideration of the difficulties of estimating 'change' when working with unreliable measures will be found in Lord (Harris, 1963).

Heightened precision can, of course, be achieved by making a series of sample observations, for example, by adding questions to a con- tinuing series of surveys. This is only practicable if one has very con- siderable notice of the event and it will not improve the reliability of the measures, though it may furnish some estimate of the magnitude of their unreliability. The residual variance about the observed trend will, in this case, include both sampling variance and unreliability.

3.1. Clearly the simple 'before/after' design will not often recom- mend itself as a means of measuring effects; and indeed it must be rare for anyone to have to use it in its crude form. However, if one is inter- viewing a sample of the population, the obvious thing to do is to ask the 'after' sample if they saw or heard the broadcast concerned, thus giving three groups: the 'before' sample, and the 'after' sample divided into 'the exposed' and 'the unexposed'. The obvious way to make use of the extra information thus available is (a) to try to discover the influence of extraneous events by examining the 'unexposed group' results and (b) to try to predict the pre-broadcast values of the 'exposed group'. This can only be done, of course, after the groups have been 'matched' in terms of as many relevant characteristics as possible. Matching by methods such as multiple regression will rarely be possible, (a) because the variables usually include some that are categoric as well as others that are continuous and (b) because there will often be far too many variables, some with remarkable distributions, to make the analysis feasible or the results intelligible. But even if it were practicable, the multiple regression approach is not appropriate since it focuses on estimating the effect of a single variable by trying to hold the others constant. In matching, the objective is rather to welcome all the complex interaction of variables in order to explore the combinations of factors that have produced the observed variability.

3.2. The process of empirical matching lies at the very core of most designs for measuring effects. The pioneer work in this field is largely due to Belson (1956, 1959) who evolved an efficient matching technique, using what he calls stable correlates of the variable under study, and a sequential process of successive dichotomization to select the best 'matching composite'. Essentially, the method scans the available matching variables (all dichotomous and all 'stable' in the sense that they could not themselves have been affected by the event) to select the one which appears to account for more of the variance displayed by the dependent variable than do any of the others. The two groups resulting from splitting the original observations by means of this variable are then scanned independently to discover the best ways of splitting each of them, and so on. The object, of course, is to discover groups of observations in which the residual variance is as low as possible, the matching then being performed by reproducing, or weighting, observations so that the numbers in these groups in the two populations to be matched are equalized. Let us suppose that the samples have been divided by the matching composite into cells, the number of individuals in the ith cell being n_i, the mean value of the observed variable for the cell $\bar{y}(\text{o})_i$ and the within-cell variance

$$\frac{1}{n_i} \sum_j \{g(\text{o})_{ij} - \bar{y}(\text{o})_i\}^2_1$$

these variances being as small as possible. The post-broadcast sample values for the equivalent cells can be written $\bar{y}(e)_i$ for those in the cell who saw the broadcast and $\bar{y}(u)_i$ for those in the cell who did not, the

numbers in each case being $m(e)_i$ and $m(u)_i$. The sample estimate for
the exposed group is thus $\sum m(e)_i \bar{y}(e)_i$ and for the unexposed group
$\sum m(u)_i \bar{y}(u)_i$. If the matching composite is a good one and no extraneous influence has been at work, then $\bar{y}(o)_i$ and $\bar{y}(u)_i$ should be
approximately equal for all groups. It is generally found that the matching will have 'worked', in the sense that the pre-broadcast values for a
group constituted as is the unexposed group will resemble that of the
unexposed group itself, i.e. that

$$\sum m(u)_i \bar{y}(o)_i \quad \text{and} \quad \sum m(u)_i \bar{y}(u)_i$$

will be approximately equal. Unfortunately, this may arise simply
because the exposed group is only a small minority of the total sample –
as has normally been the case in our studies – and hence this equality is
an unsatisfactory measure of the absence of extraneous influences. The
strict test of absence of extraneous influence requires the equivalence
of all the cell means themselves.

3.3. The absence of influence on the unexposed group does not
prove that there has been none on the exposed group either, but this
must be assumed to be so if any estimate of effects at all is to be made.
In our investigations this assumption has never seemed unwarranted.
With this assumption the effect on those who chose to view or listen
to the programme, the exposed group, is estimated as

$$\sum m(e)_i \bar{y}(e)_i \sum m-(e)_i \bar{y}(o)_i.$$

The significance of the effects, as given by differences between the
'exposed group' values and those of the re-weighted 'unexposed group'
can be tested on the Rosenbaum nomograms using an 'effective' instead of actual sample size. Effective sample size (N) has been shown
by Quenouille (1964) to be related to actual size (n) as follows:

$$N = \frac{n}{1+c^2} \quad \text{when} \quad c^2 = \frac{1}{\bar{w}^2} \frac{\sum (w_i - \bar{w})^2}{n}$$

and w_i is the weight given to the ith sample value. If there *has* been
some extraneous influence, it can be allowed for by calculating
$\sum m(e)_i \bar{y}(u)_i$ and using this instead of $\sum m(e)_i \bar{y}(o)_i$. We now see that,

if the matching process has been successful, the pre-broadcast observation has little value in assessing the effects of the broadcast on the exposed group, $\bar{y}(o)_i$ and $\bar{y}(u)_i$ being approximately equal for all i. In other words, for the purpose of measuring overall effects, a post-broadcast study in which pre-broadcast values for the exposed group are estimated by means of 'stable correlate matching composites' is likely to prove as efficient as one in which pre-broadcast observations were made. The advantage of having a pre-broadcast measurement, of course, is that it can help to establish what the 'stable correlates' *are* and can act as a check on the presence or absence of disturbing factors. More often than not in practice, pre-broadcast studies have proved to be impossible since they require more time than is usually available. Examples of the use of the 'matching by stable correlate' design are given in Part II.

3.4. There are several unresolved questions for the statistician in this technique. The first concerns the method of selection of the correlates. By advocating the trying out of a very large number of possibles (100 or more) Belson seems to be inviting the intervention of spurious matching variables. Though this will not, in general, bias the estimate of pre-broadcast values of the unexposed group, it will reduce the true effectiveness of the matching. The second question concerns the dichotomizing process itself. Logically there would seem to be no reason why variables that are not naturally dichotomous should be treated as though they were. Since the object is to produce the most efficient way of discovering groups with small within-group variances, the use of the full distribution to split the sample into more than two groups would almost certainly prove to be more efficient than dichotomization. Furthermore, the dichotomizing process leads to other difficulties if the variables are not naturally dichotomous. Continuous variables such as 'age' can be treated as a series of dichotomies, e.g. under/over 30, under/over 65 and so on, but variables that are essentially categorical usually cannot. Though newspaper readership, for example, is a basically categorical variable, it may be possible to impose an order on to the newspapers (ranging them perhaps from 'highbrow' to 'lowbrow') and hence to make the split by grouping adjacent items in the order. 'Industry', on the other hand, is a categorical variable that cannot generally be subjected to any ordering. Thirdly, the sequential dichotomizing process must be stopped at some point and appropriate rules are needed for this. Fourthly, there is the large question of significance to be dealt with. These questions have all been considered (in a different context) by Sonquist and Morgan (1964). These authors have devised a computer programme for analysing sample survey findings by an almost exactly similar method of sequential dichotomization to obtain the greatest reduction in the unexplained sum of squares at each step. They propose arbitrary rules, based on their considerable experience, such as that no group is eligible for splitting unless the within-group sum of squares amounts to at least 2 per cent of the original sum of squares, unless the group contains a minimum of 24–40 observations and unless the best partition of the group that can be made will account for at least 0·5 per cent of the original total sum of squares. Their objective is the same as Belson's, viz. to identify groups whose within-group variance is as small as possible though they do not propose to use the results of the analysis for matching purposes. Their procedure has been demonstrated to have certain optimal properties, but this does not mean that other forms of sub-division of the observations would not produce sub-groups with even small within-group sums of squares. As they say: '. . . the "tree" produced by the algorithm is not necessarily that one which is better than all other possible trees for the data under consideration. It is only optimal under the sequential algorithm used. But the closer one gets to explaining all of the variation, the more likely it is that the sampling variation is being explained. One buys completeness with the coin of instability.' They have also briefly examined the stability of the 'matching composite', or 'tree' as they call it, by dividing samples into two randomly chosen halves and applying their routine to each half. The 'trees' obtained from the two halves have, it seems, generally resembled one another closely.

3.5. Before leaving this design it is opportune to note that results are usually required in terms of effect on special groups rather than in terms of effects on the population as a whole. It is of less importance to know that X per cent of those who chose to view a programme acquired certain information from it than that Y per cent of a particular sub-group did so. For example, the only sub-group of direct interest in our 'Immunization' study was that consisting of mothers of young children who had not already had them immunized. In the consideration of accretions of knowledge, it is the misinformed, or least well-informed, who are usually of primary interest, and so on. Special efforts to ensure the efficient matching of such sub-groups will therefore be advisable. The procedure for matching will be the same as for the total sample, but it can rarely be carried very far since the sub-groups of particular interest will normally be small. Nevertheless, even a little matching should lead to more reliable conclusions than none.

3.6. An example of the wide difference between our investigations and those considered by Cochran (1965) is afforded by a comparison of his treatment of the 'ex post facto' type of study and this 'matching by stable correlates' approach. Following Chapin (1947) he describes the 'ex post facto' study as one in which the strategy is to set up groups that differ in the dependent variable and examine whether they differ in the suspected causal variable. Thus, for example, two groups with differing distributions of attitudes, or two groups whose 'level of information' about the subject differ, would be examined to see if the proportions of the groups who viewed the relevant broadcast differed. The figures in the resulting 2×2 table would then be tested for significance, using a χ^2 test. In studies of the effects of broadcasting it could safely be assumed that a significant value of χ^2 would nearly always emerge, but this would imply nothing as far as effects were concerned, since people naturally tend to select broadcasts or subjects in which they are already interested and about which they already know something. Significant χ^2 would merely confirm that the more interested the viewer, or the better-informed, the more likely he was to view the programme.

4.1. *'Before/After' – Same Sample.* A major variant of the 'before/after' design that is sometimes practicable is one in which both observations are made on the same sample, thus avoiding completely the need to estimate the pre-broadcast values for the exposed and unexposed groups. The advantages are so attractive that this design is nearly always the first to be considered, though in fact we have rarely used it. Even when we have had enough advance notice to use a 'before/after' design, it has not proved easy to obtain a second interview with a satisfactorily high proportion of the original sample; so that, with losses on both occasions, the final sample from whom complete information is obtained may fall below 60 per cent of that originally selected. Furthermore, the risk that the first interview will affect the behaviour and opinions of the sample cannot be discounted. Cochran believed this to be unimportant on the grounds that '. . . an educational programme that cannot improve health practices more than can a single questionnaire is not wrongly considered a failure'. I think he underestimates the influence a questionnaire can have and over-estimates the influence of most educational programmes. In our own experience people have proved not to be easily manipulated so that relatively small changes in attitudes and behaviour are often the most that can be expected from a broadcast. On the other hand, inter-views or mail questionnaires have been known to produce materially larger changes. One ounce of personal involvement may be worth a ton of second-hand exhortation. Many messages in the mass media are no more than substitutes for personal contact – it being easier to address thousands or millions at one time than to approach each one individually. A sample survey, in fact, makes personal contacts. The 'before/after' design using the same sample is thus seen to be far from perfect, and considerable ingenuity may be required to minimize the risk of influence from the initial interview. Assuming the response difficulty can be overcome and the first interview contamination danger eliminated, then a direct comparison of the 'before' and 'after' values for the unexposed group will indicate the possible presence of disturbing variables. If there seem to be none, then the exposed group values can be used directly to measure the effects, though once again only on the unproven hypothesis that the exposed and unexposed groups are similarly unaffected by extraneous events. If some disturbing variable is present, then its likely effect on the exposed group can be assessed in the same way as in Para. 3.3. From this it is seen that matching by sub-groups remains an essential part of the design and that the identification of correlates of the variables under study must still be undertaken.

4.2. An elaboration of the design to include a second sample inter-viewed only after the broadcast is a possibility that we have not yet explored. Under this system we would have six groups as follows:

	First sample		Second sample
	(1) Before	(2) After	(3) After only
	Exposed Unexposed	Exposed Unexposed	Exposed Unexposed

The difference between Columns 2 and 3 would be a measure of the effect of the pre-broadcast interview. If this is found to be negligible and if overall measurements are all that is required it may be sufficient to compare Columns 1 and 3 only, ignoring Column 2, the only purpose of the second interview being to identify those of the sample who had chosen to view the programme. There are, however, two very good reasons why this is often not desirable, viz. that the precision of the comparison is greatly improved if the same samples are used and that 'before/after' measures on the same sample give the opportunity for effects to be studied individual by individual. This second reason is particularly cogent if, as is often the case, the object of the enquiry is to examine attitude changes. The mechanism of attitude formation and change is extremely complex, many different theories having been propounded to account for the diverse results obtained in psychological experiments. The essence of some of these theories is that the self-same experimental treatment will, in various circumstances, produce diametrically opposite changes in attitude. A calculation of total attitude shift may thus grossly underestimate the effect of a broadcast, owing to the cancelling out of shifts in opposite directions. Broadcasts rarely set out to achieve specific effects – except, of course, to give satisfaction to those who choose to have them on – and hence the proper task of our investigation has been not so much to measure overall changes in the population as to explore the complex pattern of individual attitude changes that has occurred. Effects on listeners' and viewers' knowledge of the subject of the broadcast can generally be assumed to operate in one direction only, but effects on behaviour may, as with attitudes, be produced in opposite directions. It is not impossible that the comparatively slight behavioural effects disclosed by some of our enquiries may be due to the fact that the programmes have caused as many people to reduce their frequency of indulging in the activity which the broadcast might have been expected to promote as to increase it.

4.3. Before turning to a completely different type of design, it is perhaps worth noting that repeated measurements on the same sample over a period of time before the broadcast can increase the confidence that changes are genuinely the effect of the broadcast, whilst repeated measurements over time *after* the broadcast will throw light on the subsequent pattern of effects. In other words, observations on a 'panel sample' will be likely to yield more exact measures of effects than any other design so far considered.

5.1. A common device for measuring effects which unfortunately is rarely available to us in the BBC (at least for television broadcasts) is the 'control area method', i.e. the use of an area not covered by the broadcast transmission to provide a control on the one that is. Virtually all BBC television programmes, and a majority of radio programmes, are fully networked, so that, apart from a few isolated localities, the broadcast is equally available everywhere. The adequacy of control depends, of course, on the closeness of correspondence between the two areas, i.e., upon yet another type of matching. As in the above-mentioned designs, 'before/after' and 'after only' methods can be employed. Control area methods are particularly useful for estimating behavioural effects such as attendance at museums, reading of books and so on, *by observation*, i.e., without the benefit of interviews to discover which people have seen or heard the broadcast. The equivalence of the two areas in respect of relevant variables is best gauged by means of a series of 'before' observations, which will also help to detect the existence of any extraneous factors that may be operating at about the same time as the broadcast. A single 'before' observation in the two areas will, of course, be an unsatisfactory basis on which to assess equivalence; though it may on occasions have to suffice. In such cases, and even more in cases in which no prior observation at all can be made, equivalence of the areas must be estimated on the basis of as many other relevant characteristics as can be identified. Amongst the relevant characteristics one would, of course, normally expect to find demographic characteristics such as the age and sex distributions of the populations, and it is clearly desirable also to obtain information about the opportunities in the two areas for the behaviour to manifest itself. Close similarity between the areas in all these respects suggests adequate control, significant differences point to the need for matching.

5.2. When dealing with measures derived from personal interview, the control area method provides a further opportunity for checking on the presence of extraneous influences but, in fact, adds less than might at first be imagined to the precision of the estimates of effect especially if the design employed is that in which the same sample is interviewed before and after the event. It would be unnecessarily tedious to spell out the process involved in performing the matching needed with this design – they closely resemble the use of matching composites described earlier – and this topic of control areas needs no further word than a warning that, in other fields of research where the method has been extensively employed, e.g. marketing new products, finding adequate control areas has generally proved difficult.

5.3. One familiar difficulty that is certainly not unique to audience research work is that since the control areas by definition do not receive the broadcast under study they must necessarily receive another one. The unfortunate fact is that the alternative broadcasts transmitted in the control areas are often similar in subject matter to the one to be studied. For instance, when we wished to study a radio programme for farmers broadcast in a particular region of the country we found that all other regions broadcast their own farming programmes weekly, even if not on the same day or at the same time. A similar situation would be encountered if it were required to measure the effects of one particular newspaper story out of all the variety of treatments of the same story published in the same day's newspapers.

6.1. To end this description of the designs from which we have had to choose in our 'effects studies', I am glad to have the opportunity to commend an ingenious technique, the authorship of which is unknown to me. A sample of the population is interviewed before the broadcast and asked, as persuasively as possible, to do something else at the time of the broadcast, generally to listen to or watch one of the alternative programmes. In so far as the persuasion is successful, this sample becomes an artificially created control group whose knowledge, opinions and behaviour can be contrasted with those of another, similar, sample whose listening and viewing behaviour was not restricted in any way. This is the nearest one can get to the experimental situation of applying a treatment to one population and not to another. We have not had the opportunity to try the method but I look forward to doing so, even though it only yields overall measurements of total effects, not individual-by-individual measurements.

Part II. Some investigations into the effects of broadcasts

7.1. *Bon Voyage.* One of the earliest of the Audience Research Department's studies of the effects of broadcasts concerned the short television series, *Bon Voyage* (August–September 1953), which set out to teach first-time travellers to France a few useful French words and phrases and to help them to overcome any difficulties they might have to face in coping with the journey. The subjects in the enquiry were people who, when interviewed in the course of the Department's continuous Survey of Listening and Viewing, had been found to have viewed the afternoon television programmes of which the *Bon Voyage* series formed a part. The investigation followed the straightforward 'after only' model with matching of viewers and non-viewers by means of Belson's stable correlate technique; though a 'before sample' was used to check on the adequacy of the matching.

7.2. The investigation has been fully described by Belson (1956) so no detailed description will be given here. It should be noted, however, that in this early study he calculated multiple correlations between the matching composite and each of the three variables under study. This was practicable only because there were no more than four correlates in all and only three were used in any one 'matching composite'. The measure most highly correlated with knowledge of the French words and phrases presented in the *Bon Voyage* series was, not surprisingly, knowledge of similar words and phrases *not* presented in the series, the others being educational background, type of occupation and whether or not the subject had ever visited France. Belson (1956) described the way in which the matching of viewers and non-viewers was carried out, showing that a straight comparison of the two groups would have overestimated the learning of words and phrases that had taken place, that it would have overestimated also the learning of other facts presented in the programmes, and that it would have underestimated the attitude change that occurred. The enquiries took place only a few days after the end of the series but, nevertheless, for those who had seen only the early broadcasts in the series some forgetting may well have occurred. How effective the series was in communicating information that was retained for a long time could only have been discovered, if at all, by making further enquiries at intervals later. In any event, the changes were not great. Of 26 French words and phrases presented in the four broadcasts, the mean number 'known' (in the sense that the English equivalent could be given) rose from four before the series to five afterwards, whilst the mean number 'known' (in the sense that the correct English equivalent could be picked out from a number of plausible alternatives) rose from nine to eleven. In passing it may be noted that the attitudinal change occurred in 'the opposite direction from that which might have been expected, viewers of the programmes becoming, it was found, *less* confident of their ability to cope with a visit to France than they have been before the broadcast. It would have been illuminating to see which types of viewers changed their attitudes and in which direction, but this could only have been accomplished by a design in which the same sample provided the information before and after. It seems probable that what the *Bon Voyage* series did was to make vivid the actual situations that would be likely to arise and, in so doing, tended to bring viewers down to earth. It was in this sense that it increased rather than allayed their anxieties, though it would be equally true to say that the series tended to encourage the viewer to see the situation realistically.

7.3. Belson used two 'before samples' in this enquiry, one consisting of people who had recently viewed *Leisure and Pleasure*, the series of afternoon programmes in which *Bon Voyage* was embedded, and the other of people who had not viewed this series but who resembled the non-viewers in such respects as age, sex and social status. When these two samples were matched in respect of the stable correlates used in the main study, the differences between them as far as knowledge of French words and attitudes towards visiting France were concerned were found to be almost entirely eliminated. As he recognized, this procedure provides no direct evidence of the adequacy of the matching or of the precision of the estimates of the pre-broadcast position of those who actually saw the programmes. It at best provides a subjective reassurance. He did not make use of these 'before sample' results to examine possible extraneous influences, mainly, it seems, because the content of the series had not been finally settled at the time the pre-broadcast enquiry had to be made and hence the tests of word knowledge, etc., that were used in the 'before' and 'after' studies could not be exactly the same.

8.1. *Matters of Medicine*. A variety of designs were employed in our researches into the effects of two programmes in a series of five television documentaries in the spring of 1960 entitled *Matters of Medicine*. As has been mentioned earlier, the behavioural effects of one programme in the series, *Immunization*, were studied by examining records kept by a sample of general practitioners and at five local authority immunization clinics. The family doctors were 118 members of the College of General Practitioners (at whose suggestion the study was conducted). Unfortunately, it must be admitted that their practices were somewhat unrepresentative in that a very high proportion of their patients' children had already been immunized and hence there was very little opportunity for the programme to exercise any effect in this respect. The clinics, on the other hand, were deliberately chosen from local authority areas in which the levels of immunization were known to be close to the national average.

8.2. The general practitioners and clinics recorded their immunizations by completing a card for each child (0–15) years coming for first immunization, or coming again after a lapse of more than three months. Questions on the card sought to discover what it was that had prompted the parent to bring her child for immunization and *when* she had finally decided to have it done. The card also asked for the child's age and sex, and the occupation of the father.

8.3. No information was obtained which would suggest whether or not any trend should be allowed for, nor could any extraneous influences be discovered that might affect the 'before/after' comparison. The effects had, therefore, to be assessed simply as the difference between the 'before' and 'after' observations. What happened can be seen from Table II.

The unfortunate fact is that fewer children were immunized in the period immediately after the programme than in the period immediately before it. The difference in the results for the clinics is not significant, but the large reduction in the numbers immunized by the general practitioners considerably exceeds that which would be significant at the 1 per cent level. The most likely explanation for this unexpected result seems to be that the doctors tended in the pre-broadcast period to clear up any arrears of immunizations they may have had and so left few to do in the next few weeks. The method of enquiry makes it impossible to say whether the programme did anything to mitigate what would otherwise have been a greater decrease.

TABLE II

'IMMUNIZATION' TELEVISION PROGRAMME AND
IMMUNIZATION BEHAVIOUR

	Immunizations per week	
	In the 2 weeks before the broadcast	In the 3 weeks after the broadcast
By the 188 general practitioners	209	130
At the 5 clinics	85	79

NOT TO BE USED BEFORE 9TH MARCH 1960
USE A NEW CARD FOR EACH CHILD (0–15)
COMING FOR FIRST INOCULATION

(Please complete the following details, if possible from your records)

Confidential

1. I expect you always intended to have your child immunized, but about how long ago was it that you first really made up your mind to have it done? (Please record approximate time here)
....

Child's sex.........

2. There is quite a lot of publicity and talk about immunization these days, I am trying to find out whether parents see this publicity and how they come to hear about immunization.

In the last few months –

(a) Have you been told about immunization by the Health Visitor? YES/NO

(b) Have you heard about immunization from the Clinic? YES/NO

(c) Have you seen any posters or leaflets advising mothers to have their children immunized? YES/NO

(d) Did you see the recent Television programme on immunization? YES/NO

(e) Were you advised by the hospital to have it done? YES/NO

(f) Have you discussed it with your friends and neighbours? YES/NO

(g) Did your family doctor advise you to have it done? YES/NO

(Please write any other sources of information mentioned by parent here)...

Child's age...yrs...mths.
Child immunized against:

....

....

Mother's age............

Father's occupation............

Date...............

Please return this card to:

Dr John Fry,
36, Croydon Road,
Beckenham, Kent.

3. All the things I have asked you about are printed on this card here. *(Hand white card to Parents.)* Please look through them and say which ones influenced you most in deciding to have your child immunized.

(Please indicate the most influential sources by putting ticks beside the (a), (b), (c), etc. above.)

on 30th March or as soon as possible afterwards.

TABLE III

REPLIES GIVEN TO GENERAL PRACTITIONERS

Sources of information	Before the programme %	After the programme	
		Those who had seen it %	Those who had not seen it %
The family doctor	46·3	53·1	54·2
Friends and neighbours	6·0	6·2	6·6
Posters and leaflets	6·2	4·4	5·5
The health visitor	7·2	15·0	8·4
Clinics	6·5	6·2	11·0
The hospital	1·0	0·9	1·1
The television programme	Not asked	17·7	—

TABLE IV

REPLIES GIVEN AT IMMUNIZATION CLINICS

Sources of information	Before the programme %	After the programme	
		Those who had seen it %	Those who had not seen it %
The family doctor	10·5	8·1	5·6
Friends and neighbours	8·8	4·1	3·7
Posters and leaflets	7·6	9·5	7·4
The health visitor	22·8	28·4	35·8
Clinics	28·7	21·6	27·2
The hospital	0·6	0·0	1·2
The television programme	Not asked	23·0	0·0

8.4. Some additional indication of the effect of the broadcast was obtained by analysing the questionnaire cards. The two most revealing questions were those which asked the parents to say: (a) which source of information about immunization she considered to be very influential in arriving at her decision to have her child immunized and (b) how long ago she first decided to have her child immunized.

There were very few mothers indeed who had not made up their minds long before the broadcast, though many regarded it has having influenced them in their actual decision. The conclusion that must be drawn is that the broadcast at best reminded some mothers already intending to have their children immunized that they still had not done so, but clearly it did not send them in droves to their doctors' surgeries or local clinics as some had feared might happen.

TABLE V

WHEN PARENTS SAID THEY FIRST DECIDED TO HAVE
THEIR CHILDREN IMMUNIZED

| | | After the programme | |
When	Before the programme %	Those who had seen it %	Those who had not seen it %
At the child's birth	59·7	47·6	50·8
Longer ago than 1 year	3·2	4·8	1·8
Within last year	15·5	11·8	14·5
Within last few months	19·2	32·1	26·7
Since television programme	—	1·1	0·7
Not sure or no reply	2·4	2·6	5·5

8.5. The investigation was in fact inadequate in that (i) only a single 'before' observation could be made, (ii) the prior observation may well have affected the comparison and (iii) the long-term effects, which may have been substantial, were not investigated. Other effects of the programme on viewers were investigated by means of a study using a 'before/after' design with the same sample. Between six and nine weeks before the broadcast, 1,216 persons (a high proportion being parents of young children) were questioned, care being exercised to ensure that the purpose of the questioning was well hidden. Three days after the broadcast they were sent a form asking which of a number of recent programmes they had seen and what they thought of them. The form was completed by 93 per cent and those amongst them who said they had seen the *Immunization* programme were invited to attend a further meeting. In fact, when the meetings were held two or three weeks later, no more than 40 per cent of those invited attended. This response, though disappointing, is rather better than is generally achieved from invitations to attend such group meetings. However, on this occasion a much higher 'turn-up' had been hoped for, as those invited had already attended one meeting and they might consequently have been expected to be more strongly motivated than are viewers in general. In addition to suffering from this poor response rate, there was a weakness in the design in that we did not make any 'after' measurement on *non*-viewers of the programme, thus precluding the estimation of the effects, if any, of extraneous influences.

8.6. In the event, few effects of any kind were disclosed by the before/after comparison though an interesting point emerged concerning the timing of the 'after' observation. A quite separate series of group meetings was held at which a tele-recording of the *Immunization* programme was shown to viewers who had not seen it when it was actually broadcast. They completed questionnaires before viewing the recording and another questionnaire, which repeated some but not all of the earlier questions, shortly after viewing. The results cannot be used as a valid measure of the effects of the broadcasts, since the informants did not themselves choose to view the programme and the viewing situation was artificial. Nevertheless, the fact that a considerable swing was observed in the amount of support for the view that 'an unnecessary fuss was made about immunization' (27 per cent before viewing and 11 per cent after) suggests that, had an immediate 'after' measurement been possible in the effects study itself, some change of this kind might have been observed. In fact the effects study gave identical results before and after. The limitation to a single 'after' measurement, and that some weeks after the event, is unfortunate, but even more regrettable is the fact that though 'before' and 'after' measurements were made on the same sample the material was analysed only in overall terms, not individual by individual.

8.7. Less elaborate investigations were made into the effects of another *Matters of Medicine* series, *Coronary Thrombosis*, for which an 'after only' design was used. The matching composite included such things as occupational level, but I can find no detailed record of the matching process or of its efficiency. An unusual feature of the enquiry was that the pre-broadcast results in the *Immunization* enquiry could be used to check some of the estimated pre-broadcast values in this second enquiry, since some of the variables under study were the same, e.g., attitudes towards general practitioners, effect on hypochondria, etc. In every case the estimated attitudes and levels of knowledge arrived at by using the matching composite in the *Coronary Thrombosis* enquiry closely approximated those of the *Immunization* study viewers when they were first interviewed, *before* the broadcast. On the reasonable assumption that those who chose to watch the *Immunization* programme resembled those who chose to watch that on *Coronary Thrombosis*, this agreement suggests that the matching was successful.

9.1. *Crime.* Another occasion on which we made more than one approach to the measurement of effects concerned a series of six weekly television programmes in August–September 1960, entitled *Crime.* In the study a pre-broadcast survey was a requirement, since we had been asked to help in the planning of the series by discovering the extent of public ignorance of certain facts about the amount of crime and the treatment of criminals. The survey, made three months before the series began, was repeated, using a sample of the same size and design, soon after the series had ended, thus providing one measure of the effects of the series. This 'before/after' comparison was as usual elaborated by identifying the viewers of the series in the course of the second interview, though in this instance they were divided into 'regular viewers', who had seen four or more of the six programmes, and 'occasional viewers', who had seen only one, two or three of them. The 'occasional viewer' and 'non-viewer' groups were matched so that they were similar to the 'regular viewer' group in respect of a simple matching composite which involved sex, age and educational background. In order to limit the questions asked in the survey, none were included simply because of their possible value as matching predictors, the choice for matching lying, therefore, between the few standard classification variables such as age and sex. This basic weakness meant that the extent of the matching could not be very great. Furthermore, the matching should, of course, have been undertaken separately for each variable, but in this enquiry the only respect in which it was attempted was 'knowledge' of the subject of the broadcasts. The mean numbers of correct answers out of five, given by non-viewer informants in each of the matching composite cells, together with the variances, were found to be:

	Mean	*Variance*
Age over 50 – semi-skilled or unskilled job	1·1	0·9
Age over 50 – lower professional or skilled job	1·7	1·0
Age under 50 – semi-skilled or unskilled job	1·4	1·1
Age under 50 – lower professional or skilled job	1·8	1·5
Women – professional	3·2	0·7
Men – professional	3·5	1·2
All non-viewers	1·75	1·7

In respect of 'knowledge', these figures indicate that reasonably successful matching was achieved, but it cannot be denied that the effectiveness of the matching in eliminating original differences between the viewer and non-viewer groups in other respects, such as their attitude towards the offender, may be virtually nil.

9.2. This was an enquiry in which extraneous influences had to be expected. Apart from the constant reporting of crime news in the press there were two documentaries about crime on Independent Television a few weeks before the BBC series, and three reports (*Criminal Statistics, The Annual Report of the Prison Commissioners* and *The Annual Report of the Commissioner for Metropolitan Police*) were all issued at about the same time and all received considerable coverage in the newspapers. The examination of the results of the two surveys, however, does not suggest that all this publicity had an appreciable effect. A direct comparison of the answers of the non-viewers of the series interviewed in September and the matched group of people drawn from the sample interviewed in May revealed only two differences out of a possible twenty which exceeded 3 percentage points. The only instance of substantial differences in the whole comparison was in respect of the numbers believing that 'not enough employers are willing to give the ex-prisoner a chance'. Had an overall result of the two surveys been taken as a measure of the effect of the series on the amount of support for this view, they would have suggested a slight fall from 63 per cent to 58 per cent. In fact, study of the September sample shows that the reverse was true, 69 per cent of the regular viewers of *Crime* as compared with only 52 per cent of the non-viewers supporting this point of view. In other words, a substantial reduction due to extraneous influences was largely counterbalanced by an increase due to the television series.

9.3. A few of the results from this enquiry are given in Table VI, the estimated effects of the series being obtained from a comparison of

Columns 1 and 2 and the effects of extraneous influences by a comparison of Columns 2 and 3.

TABLE VI

'CRIME' TELEVISION SERIES AND ITS AUDIENCE

	Regular viewers of *Crime* %	Non-viewers of *Crime* interviewed in September %	Matched sample of population interviewed in May %
Proportions who:			
Correctly nominated minor larceny as the commonest crime	30	18	21
Believed juvenile crime rate to have increased faster than adult	70	72	74
Believed 'broken homes' were most to blame for the increase in juvenile crime	62	46	49
Believed that more police would effectively reduce amount of crime	46	54	56
Regarded 'indecent assault' as the worst crime	22	26	25
Thought that 'all prisons should be severe and strict'	17	22	20
Were in favour of corporal punishment for all committed of violent assault	72	70	74

9.4. More detailed and extensive investigations were undertaken by inviting groups of viewers to meetings at which their opinions about crime and the treatment of offenders could be investigated more intensively than in the surveys. It proved impracticable to hold meetings after each of the six programmes in the series, instead the programmes had to be dealt with in pairs. The first meetings were held soon after the second programme and at these meetings Programmes 1 and 2 were the principal concern. At the next meetings (held shortly after Programme 4) it was the turn of Programmes 3 and 4. At the final meetings, held after the end of the series, Programmes 5 and 6 were dealt with. Though not theoretically ideal, this design fortunately suited the series quite well. Programmes 1 and 2 described the extent of crime and the complexity of the problem; whilst Programmes 3 and 4 explained how criminals were treated in prisons. Programmes 5 and 6 in a sense summed up, the former presenting a typical case history of an habitual offender and the latter some reflections by experts on problems in the reform and after-care of criminals.

Invitations to attend the meetings were distributed by a special team of interviewers on the Wednesday and Thursday following each programme. The interviewers asked their informants to specify all the television programmes they had viewed on the preceding two evenings. The first seven informants saying they had viewed *Crime* were invited and so were the first four who had not viewed it. The letter of invitation asked the informant to bring with him an adult friend or relation if he wished to do so. Of the informants invited 36 per cent attended the meetings, mostly with friends, the total number attending being 387. The interviews did not divulge that the *Crime* series was to be the subject of enquiry at the meetings, nor did the letter of invitation mention it; it was only at the beginnings of the meetings themselves that their purpose was disclosed.

9.5. The effects of each individual programme – or rather pair of programmes – were assessed by comparing the answers of viewers and non-viewers, once again after these two groups of informants had been matched to eliminate as far as possible irrelevant differences between them. These group studies revealed a quite unexpected pattern of effects. By emphasizing the amount of crime, by interviewing the victims and also some of the generally unrepentant perpetrators of the crimes, Programmes 1 and 2 tended to harden viewers' attitudes towards the criminal, making them more ready to advocate heavy sentences and strict prison sentences. Programmes 5 and 6, on the other hand, by presenting a number of people nearly all of whom favoured a non-punitive approach to the treatment of offenders, countered this tendency and reduced viewers' antagonism towards the criminal. This pattern emerged many times in the analysis of the results. For example, the proportions agreeing that 'criminals need our sympathy and help more than anyone else' were as follows:

Viewers of Programmes 1 and/or 2	33%
Non-viewers of either programme	51%
Viewers of Programmes 5 and/or 6	61%
Non-viewers of either programme	41%

Since it is far more common for people to see only some of the programmes in a series than to see all of them, the exploration of the effects of such series requires studies no less elaborate than the one we employed on this occasion. Once again we might have done better to make more than one survey after the series ended, but this was a case in which at most only one group meeting per programme could be held since the next followed on so soon afterwards and inevitably covered some of the same ground.

10.1. *The Death Penalty.* A year after the *Crime* series, another television documentary was broadcast on a similar subject, *The Death Penalty*. This was a single broadcast giving certain facts about the numbers and kinds of murders committed and presenting arguments for and against capital punishment. The design used to study the effects of the programme was a 'before/after' investigation, using the same sample on both occasions, but, unlike the *Immunization* study, all information was obtained by post. A national sample of 6,000 viewers – selected from amongst those already interviewed in the Survey of Listening and Viewing – was sent one questionnaire through the post before the broadcast took place and another after it. The second questionnaire repeated a number of the questions which had appeared in the first. These concerned viewers' interest in a number of television programme topics (including crime and punishment), the extent of their agreement or disagreement with each of six statements about murder and capital punishment and, finally, their knowledge of whether or not the murder rate had increased, of the effect which the abolition of capital punishment had had in some countries, and of the categories of murder still regarded as capital offences in this country. Some additional questions were included in the second questionnaire in an attempt to assess the extent to which viewers were exposed to other influences. These asked viewers to indicate how closely, if at all, they had followed the subject of capital punishment and reports of murders and murder trials in the papers in recent weeks and to write down, in addition, the names of any books, programmes, magazines, etc., in which they had come across any recent mention of this subject. It was hoped in this way to distinguish those who had been exposed to only slight outside influences from those who were more closely involved with the subject, in order to see whether the programme had affected the former more or less markedly than the latter.

10.2. The first questionnaire, which was posted a fortnight before the broadcast, contained no mention of the fact that a second questionnaire would follow. The second questionnaire was sent out immediately after the programme (when it was explained that we had 'been asked to repeat our enquiry about capital punishment').

TABLE VII

Question: 'DO YOU HAPPEN TO KNOW IF THE NUMBER OF MURDERS PER HEAD OF POPULATION HAS INCREASED OR NOT IN BRITAIN IN THE LAST HUNDRED YEARS?'

Answers	'Before' %	'After' %
'I have no idea at all'	10	8
'I think it has increased'	69	59
'I think it has remained about the same'	13	26
'I think it has decreased'	7	6
No reply	1	4
	100	100
Proportion giving unchanged answer	70%	

By this phrase it was hoped to conceal that the main purpose of the enquiry was to examine differences between the responses on the two occasions. In order to stimulate the response rate, the distribution of each questionnaire was followed by two reminder letters to those who so far had failed to reply. In all, 77 per cent returned the first questionnaire before the broadcast took place and, of these 77 per cent, 80 per cent also returned the second questionnaire. The audience for the broadcast, as measured by the Department's Daily Survey of Listening and

Viewing, was about 23 per cent of all adults with television, so that the expected number of viewers of the programme amongst the original 6,000 adults in the sample for this effects study was 1,380. In fact, 1,522 of the 3,700 who returned both questionnaires were found to have viewed the broadcast. It seems probable, therefore, (a) that the pre-broadcast enquiry stimulated at least a small proportion of the sample who would not otherwise have done so to watch the programme, and (b) that a very high proportion of those in the sample who viewed the programme in fact returned both questionnaires. Since interest in the subject matter will be likely to influence both the completion of the questionnaire and the viewing of the programme, the high response from viewers of the programme was perhaps to be expected. The excellence of the response – compared, for instance, with the 40 per cent 'turn-up' at the 'Immunization' group meetings – would seem to recommend this method strongly, but there is a disadvantage in that the number of questions which can be asked in an enquiry made, like this one, through the post, is strictly limited.

10.3. On this occasion, effects were studied individual by individual and the extent of cancelling out can be judged from the following extracts from the results of the enquiry. The tables give straightforward, unweighted comparisons of the 'before' and 'after' answers of the viewers of the programme and show the proportions whose answers were unchanged.

10.4. The magnitude of the proportions changing their answers is so great that the reliability, or rather reproducibility, of the results must be suspect. One way in which this unreliability might have been examined is by comparing the 'before' and 'after' answers of the non-viewers, though such a comparison would not, of course, yield an uncontaminated measure of unreliability since it could not exclude the effect, if any, of extraneous influences. Unfortunately, owing to the pressure of work at the time of the enquiry the replies of non-viewers were never analysed. Some indication of the extent of changes caused by factors other than the broadcast came from the examination of the replies of those viewers of the programme who claimed that they followed such things as murder cases very closely in the papers and those who claimed to have seen very little about such matters recently. In only one respect did their answers differ materially. When asked the question: 'Quite a number of countries have abolished capital punishment. Do you know what effect this has had on the murder rate?'

TABLE VIII

Question: 'PLEASE SAY WHICH OF THE FOLLOWING KINDS
OF MURDER MAY BE PUNISHED BY DEATH'

	Proportions believing offence to be capital murder		Proportions giving unchanged answer
	Before %	After %	%
Murder of police officers*	88	90	96
Murder in the course of furtherance of theft*	66	76	90
Murder while resisting arrest*	61	76	90
Premeditated murder, e.g. systematic poisoning	71	55	70
Murder committed with extreme cruelty	54	47	77
Murder of children	50	43	78
Murder of members of the government	38	40	76
Murder in connection with rape	46	27	56

* Capital murder as stated in the broadcast.

those who attentively followed news of murders, etc., gave more accurate replies in the 'before' enquiry than did those who expressed no interest, whilst in the 'after' enquiry the reverse was true. The extraneous influences bearing on the former group seemed in this instance to have militated against the assimilation of the facts given in the broadcast.

11.4. *Postscript.* None of the four effects studies that have been described was completely successful, nor indeed were any of the others that have *not* been described. The inadequacies stem primarily from the fact that those of us who were responsible for the enquiries did not give sufficient thought to their design. The slow accumulation of the experience from the studies we have made would, I believe, enable us to produce better measurements of the effect of broadcasts in the future. It is a matter of some regret to me that since 1961 we have not been asked to make any.

TABLE IX

THE POST-BROADCAST RE-GROUPING OF VIEWERS HOLDING
DIFFERENT ATTITUDES TOWARDS THE RETENTION
OF THE DEATH PENALTY (AS INDICATED BY
THEIR ANSWERS TO CERTAIN QUESTIONS)

Attitudes after the broadcast:	Attitudes before the broadcast				
	Very strong retentionists %	Strong retentionists %	Retentionists %	Undecided %	Abolitionists %
Very strong retentionists	68	8	1	2	—
Strong retentionists	26	64	12	9	—
Retentionists	5	18	65	28	2
Undecided	—	9	20	54	20
Abolitionists	1	1	2	7	78
	100	100	100	100	100

Part III. A note on the measurement of the general effects of mass communication

12.1. Post-war research into the mass communication process has been largely channelled into studies of the effects of television, more often than not into its effects on children. Whilst it was natural that this obtrusive new medium should absorb the efforts of researchers almost as completely as it did the attention of the general public, the devotion of so much time and effort to the study of the fascinating and newsworthy subject of the changes that television has wrought in our society and way of life has tended to cloud the realization that such changes are inevitable and irrevocable. Printing has been with us for centuries, and though it has undeniably effected enormous social changes, there is nothing to be gained by trying to measure them. A world without books and newspapers is unthinkable. So too is a world without the theatre, the cinema, radio and television. We can no longer decide whether or not we want the mass media – for better or worse we have got them – but we may wish to decide what to do with them. The interesting and profitable question is not 'What effects has this or that medium of mass communication produced?' but 'What changes would be produced by the dissemination of different material?'

12.2. The study of general, long-term effects of the mass media cannot be effected by any design that involves 'before' and 'after' measurements. One possible method is to contrast the knowledge, attitudes and opinions of those who have been widely exposed to the particular form of communication under study with those of others whose exposure has been much more limited. The matching process is, as Belson has pointed out, precisely similar to that involved in the 'after only' method in which viewers and non-viewers of a particular programme are matched to eliminate original differences between them from the comparison. Apart from the difficulty of obtaining accurate information about the amount of exposure, particularly over a lengthy period of time, the major problem is to exclude the effects of other factors. Consider, for example, the question 'Does the broadcasting of *avant-garde* modern music affect its acceptability?' Whilst it is possible to estimate people's *current* level of listening to such music on the radio – and might even be possible to discover their long-term listening pattern – it has been found that substantial listening to broadcast music invariably accompanies considerable listening to music by other means. Whilst it is undeniable that broadcasting brings far greater opportunities for people to listen to music, it is by no means so certain that it materially affects their inclination to take advantage of these opportunities. Most listening to modern music nowadays is undoubtedly to broadcast music, but our researches suggest that this may mean no more than that the enthusiasts have been able to increase their 'intake' whereas the uninterested remain uninterested. If this is so, the prospect of using the attitudes towards modern music of those who infrequently listen to it in order to estimate the likely attitudes of frequent listeners had they not been able to listen so much is clearly extremely remote, though changes in knowledge about it could perhaps be measured by this means.

12.3. An alternative approach is the longitudinal study, in which a panel of informants are repeatedly interviewed over a number of years. The practical difficulties are considerable but, even if they can be overcome, the analysis and interpretation of the findings present pitfalls. Consider once again the question of the effect of listening on musical taste. The very least elaborate study with only two interviews would involve a 4×4 table of the form shown in Table X.

TABLE X

DIAGRAMMATIC ANALYSIS OF A 'REPEAT-INTERVIEW' INVESTIGATION OF THE HYPOTHESES

(A) THAT LISTENING TO AVANT-GARDE MUSIC RESULTS IN LIKING IT AND

(B) THAT LIKING AVANT-GARDE MUSIC RESULTS IN LISTENING TO IT

First interview		Second interview			
		Don't listen		Listen	
		Like	Dislike	Like	Dislike
Don't listen	Like	(i) No change	(ii) Neither hypothesis holds	(iii) Liking causes listening	(iv) Ambiguous
	Dislike	(v) Neither hypothesis holds	(vi) No change	(vii) Ambiguous	(viii) Neither hypothesis holds
Listen	Like	(ix) Neither hypothesis holds	(x) Ambiguous	(xi) No change	(xii) Listening causes dislike
	Dislike	(xiii) Ambiguous	(xiv) Dislike causes non-listening	(xv) Listening causes liking	(xvi) No change

This is an example of Lazarsfeld's sixteen-fold table as described in Lindzey (1954). The attempts to interpret such data in terms of any simple causal hypothesis would be extremely rash. Indeed, it is fairly certain that for some listeners liking will be the cause of increased listening, for others that increased listening will produce liking, whilst for yet others extraneous factors such as changes in circumstances will help to determine changes in listening and at the same time produce changes in attitude.

Along the leading diagonal of the table there is no change either for liking or listening, whilst along the other diagonal both liking and listening change. These eight cells therefore can contribute nothing to the test of the hypothesis that listening affects liking or that liking affects listening. Of four other cells it can be said that another hypothesis is accountable. For example, those who were found to like modern music on both occasions but reduced their listening must have reduced it for some reason other than a change in their attitude. The remaining four cells are the only ones that can be said to yield information about causation, the results being reducible to:

(1) Of all those who used to dislike modern music and now like it only those persons in the fifteenth cell can be unambiguously said to change their views as a result of their listening.

(2) Of those in the twelfth cell the reverse is true, i.e., listening appears to have resulted in dislike.

(3) Of those who used not to listen but now do, those in the third cell can be presumed to do so because of their liking.

(4) Of those who used to listen but now do not, those in the fourteenth cell are the ones who have reduced their listening because of their dislike.

It must be noted that there may well be others for whom one or other of the hypotheses holds, certainly many of those in the diagonal cells running from top right to bottom left must be in this position, but information available does not support one causal interpretation rather than another.

Lazarsfeld suggested calculating an index derived from the numbers in the various cells of the sixteen-fold table to decide whether more credence should be given to the 'liking producing listening' or the 'listening producing liking' hypothesis. The same problem is tackled in a more elaborate form by Campbell, who considers the case of more than two 'waves' of panel interviewing and variables that are not simply dichotomous. He describes his method as 'cross-lagged panel correlation', the correlations being, for example, between 'amount of listening at time t_i' and 'attitude at time t_i+1' and between 'amount of listening at time t_i+1' and 'attitude at time t_i'. Greater credence is given to the 'listening producing liking' hypothesis if the first of these two correlations is greater than the second, though he recognizes the possibility that alternative hypotheses invoking extraneous influences cannot be ruled out. All inferences based on this kind of evidence are hazardous, but such a scheme of analysis does seem to provide a way of exploring the long-term effects of broadcasting various kinds of material. The effort involved in such enquiries would be considerable, but the results might provide some scientifically based evidence in an area in which speculation and prejudice are rife.

(A list of references will be found in the notes.)

PART FIVE:

The Media and Politics

1. Producers' Attitudes Towards Television Coverage of an Election Campaign: A Case Study*

Jay G. Blumler

Voters depend heavily on the mass media, and increasingly on television, for their perceptions of the significant political issues and personalities of the day. Even though initial predispositions help to filter what electors notice, the sheer visibility of issues and events, as determined by media prominence, must also fill out their maps of the political scene.[1] Since (as Campbell, *et al.*, have pointed out) 'the decisions of those who control communication are partial determinants of public awareness . . . more information is needed about them'.[2] The focus of this attempt to collect such information is a set of attitudes which apparently influenced the approach of certain BBC producers to their task of reporting the British General Election of 1966. It is appreciated that the outlook of communicators is only one of a number of influences on the formation of media content. Nevertheless, many of the attitudes revealed in this enquiry are relevant both to certain policy issues and to the conceptual apparatus that sociologists might wish to apply in future investigations of media workings.

This study was made possible by a generous invitation which was extended to the author by the BBC in late February 1966 to attach himself for the period of the forthcoming campaign to the Current Affairs Group (Television). Its central method was direct observation, supplemented by interviews with most of the non-technical staff of the various programme teams in the Group.[3] The author had full access to the production process at programme level, and the resulting data

* First published in *Sociology of Mass Media Communicators, Sociological Review Monograph*, No. 13 (1969).

mainly reflected producers' perspectives (not those, say, of higher BBC executives or of politicians). The Current Affairs Group was responsible at the time for a varied range of campaign programmes, including *Election Forum*, *Panorama*, and *Question Time*, as well as for the tendering of advice and facilities to the political parties for the making of their own election broadcasts. This particular report is largely based, however, on observations of the preparation of *Campaign Report*, 13 editions of which were transmitted within the nightly current affairs vehicle, *24 Hours*.[4]

The attitudes of producers have been grouped for consideration under four headings, each of which corresponds to a major focus of enquiry in the field of the sociology of the communicators. They include the outlook of journalists and broadcasters on: the structure of rules and policies that is supposed to govern their activities; their sources (in this case leading politicians); the needs of their audiences; and the events they are supposed to cover. Although this case study did not originate in any single theoretical orientation, the interpretation of some of the evidence has been shaped by concepts derived from role theory. In addition, an attempt is made at the end of each section to relate the findings to certain normative questions that can be raised about the functions of election television in a political democracy.

Producers and election broadcasting policy

How should the relationship between policy in a communicating organization and its staff communicators be conceived? A common point of view treats the latter as virtually passive recipients and executants of the former. Such an interpretation need not be unsophisticated; it can take account, for example, of instances of deviation from policy. Nevertheless, there is a tendency to regard policy as something that moulds the work of the communicators and not vice-versa. A 'one-way model' of this relationship has affected even some sociological analyses of the position of communicators. It helped to frame, for example, the central question to which Warren Breed addressed his early study of reporters employed by medium-sized newspapers in the United States: 'How is policy maintained, despite the fact that it often contravenes journalistic norms, that staffers often personally disagree with it, and that executives cannot legitimately command that it be followed ?"[5]

On the face of it, a one-way model should be particularly applicable to an analysis of the election-time responsibilities of British broadcasters. This country is noted for its strong tradition of concern for the political impartiality of the electronic media. Elections have always been regarded as exceptionally sensitive occasions for radio and television. It is appreciated that during a campaign the broadcasters must comment upon the personalities and policies of parties to which their organization will ultimately be accountable after the votes have been counted. Consequently, an elaborate structure of rules and policies has been evolved to guide the election activities of television journalists.

There are three main sources of broadcasting policy. First, there is the current state of the law, as it is authoritatively interpreted by the legal advisers of the BBC, the ITA, and the Postmaster General. This obliges the broadcasters (a) to refrain from the expression of editorial opinions of their own on controversial matters, (b) to maintain a balance between the airing of rival views on controversial matters, and (c) to abstain from any activity which could be construed, under Section 63 of the Representation of the People Act, as an expenditure of money to advance the cause of a political candidate. Second, there is a set of understandings which are negotiated in advance of an election by representatives of the three main parties, the BBC, and the ITA, convened in an informal committee. And third, certain policies emanate from the broadcasting authorities themselves. A formative element in BBC policy, for example, has always been a concept of 'fairness' – one expression of which was the erection of safeguards to ensure that no party could exploit radio and television in the final stages of a campaign to win a last-minute advantage that its rivals could not counteract.

One major development in interpretation of the law occurred between the General Elections of 1964 and 1966. In a case brought by a Communist candidate to test the legality of the appearance of Sir Alec Douglas-Home in a Conservative Party broadcast when he was fighting the Kinross and West Perthshire by-election, the courts had decided that the criterion of 'dominant motive' should determine whether a broadcasting organization had contravened Section 63 of the Representation of the People Act. If the broadcasters' intention was to inform the public and not to advance an individual's candidacy they would be safe from legal challenge. This ruling had the effect of legitimating the participation in current affairs programmes of party spokesmen in the role of discussants in interviews and confrontations. But the understandings that emerged from the negotiations of February, 1966, closely followed the pattern that had been set in 1964. The total time allotted to party broadcasts was slightly reduced, but a 5 : 5 : 3 ratio continued to govern their distribution among the three parties. And it was assumed that it would be 'fair' to apply the same ratio to Corporation-produced election programmes.

It was evident from the outset, however, that many producers did not regard themselves merely as executants of these official policies. They shared what may be described as a set of policy objectives of their own. They wished to direct the contributions of television to an election campaign into channels they regarded as fruitful. This concern, which was most noticeable in the early and formative stages of the 1966 campaign, was not necessarily opposed to the official policies the broadcasters were expected to implement. It chiefly reflected the preoccupation of journalists with the relationship between their own freedom and various inhibitions and restraints that were associated with the political parties. It was in that context that a *24 Hours* producer forecast the strategy that would be followed in the preparation of its *Campaign Report*: 'We shall push at the boundaries wherever we can and try to get the rules relaxed by breaking some of the accepted conventions.'

The producers' strategy for strengthening the contribution of television to the 1966 campaign embraced at least four objectives. First, they aimed to encourage party spokesmen to confront each other in face-to-face discussions (and not to appear separately on election programmes without interchange with their opposite numbers). The willingness of politicians to engage in debate was in doubt at first, for the major parties had insisted on separate interviews with the three individuals who were due to take part in the immediate pre-campaign edition of *Panorama*. Their appearance was staged, however, in a manner that underlined the absurdity of the arrangements (the politicians were placed at separate tables, and the programme reporter marched heavily from one table to another to conduct each interview), and in the end so-called mini-confrontations featured in the next two editions of *Panorama* and in five editions of *Campaign Report*.

Second, the producers were keen to help to promote a top-level party-leader debate between the Prime Minister and his Conservative and Liberal counterparts. At a time when the parties were deadlocked over the conditions for putting on a televised confrontation, a member of the Current Affairs Group devised a complex formula, which seemed to meet the stated requirements of each side.[6] Although it eventually proved impossible to arrange such an encounter, the BBC did forward the reporter's proposal to the political parties, and its existence was publicly revealed in an interview on *Campaign Report* with Mr Heath.

Third, the producers were determined to circumvent any attempts by one or another political party to veto the airing of an election issue by refusing to supply a speaker to discuss it on television. In fact difficulties of obtaining party spokesmen were experienced on each of the first four days of Campaign Report's appearance. But by persisting on behalf of chosen topics (though prepared to be tactically flexible), the producers managed to present items on most of the issues they wished to cover. One example arose from the so-called 'Cowley noose trial'. (This concerned a mass meeting – where a noose had been prominently displayed – at which seven members of the Transport and General Workers Union had allegedly been fined for failing to join an unofficial strike.) *Campaign Report* countered the refusal of one of the parties to provide a speaker to discuss this incident by presenting filmed extracts from its press conference on the subject. And after screening a controversial discussion of the prospects for Britain's eventual entry into the Common Market, a member of the *24 Hours* staff concluded that:

> What we've achieved today is to smoke them out – to get them to participate in the programme on an issue they were unwilling to see dealt with. Having persisted in our determination to cover the Common Market, they finally saw they had to put up someone suitable to discuss it.

Finally, the producers wished to ensure that television did not pay more attention to the Liberal Party than it deserved. This objective reflected their judgment that the third party was electorally less relevant to the political situation of 1966 than it had been in the close race of 1964. Although it was found in the end that the Liberal Party had received the full share of broadcasting time to which it was entitled by the 5:5:3 ratio, out of five inter-party confrontations on *Campaign Report*, Liberals participated in only two (although they also appeared in the two debates that *Panorama* staged).

How can the readiness and ability of producers to take these policy initiatives be explained? The answer lies partly in their reactions to a decade of evolution in the role of election television, a two-fold result of which was, first, to break the parties' original monopoly of campaign broadcasting, and, second, to enlarge the scope of the election programmes produced by the television authorities themselves. The determination of the producers to contribute to policy may be traced specifically, then, to their more or less common conviction that the developments which had taken place up to 1966 were (a) desirable and (b) still incomplete. But a full analysis of the sources of their initiatives would have to take account of at least three rather more general influences as well.

1. *The internal role-definitions of their position to which television journalists subscribe.*[7] These appeared to include two expressions of a sense of responsibility. One was to serve the audience adequately. Although opinions differed about some of its political needs, there was a common agreement that in order to present an election interestingly and illuminatingly to viewers, party politicians should be encouraged to debate with each other in a face-to-face context, the contributions of relatively irrelevant forces should be kept to a minimum, and party aspirations to veto the airing of certain issues should be resisted. Second, the television journalists seemed to be moved by a sense of responsibility to the standards of their own profession. These demanded a readiness to exercise their own judgment upon the election issues that mattered instead of a tame acceptance of the parties' own issue priorities. According to Warren Breed, the ethical norms of journalism include, 'such ideals as responsibility, impartiality, accuracy, fair play, and objectivity'.[8] The responses of members of the Current Affairs Group to the challenge of the 1966 campaign suggest that 'freedom to exercise and apply a journalist's professional judgment' should be added to this list.

2. *The character of the existing body of rules and policies.* Some producer initiatives were facilitated by a *policy vacuum*. When representatives of the parties and the broadcasting authorities met to finalize the arrangements for the use of television during the campaign, it seemed to the BBC participants that both the Conservatives and Labour had lost any interest in the staging of a top-level party-leader debate. They assumed that any attempt on their part to raise this subject might be construed as pressure to impose a controversial form of political tele-

vision on the reluctant parties. But because this matter had not been settled one way or the other, the producers were able to take steps of their own to arrange a confrontation between the party leaders. It was also important that *certain policy stipulations had become less specific and more permissive than in recent years*.[9] For example, the prevailing interpretation of the need for balance in political programming had become less literal and more flexible. It was accepted by 1966 that party balance should be sought over a series of broadcasts and need not be achieved in every single political item. This untied the producers' hands about Liberal appearances on television, enabling them to decide exactly when to seek a Liberal speaker so long as the requirements of the 5:5:3 ratio were fulfilled for the campaign period as a whole. The producers also had less reason to fear the exercise of a party veto on the discussion of delicate issues. Once it was decided that a live speaker from one party could be balanced by filmed extracts from the hustings of press conference contributions of its rivals, the producers were free to go ahead with the coverage of issues of their own choosing – despite non-co-operation by one of the parties. Another liberalizing influence was the outcome of the Kinross and West Perthshire by-election case, for the producers could assume thereafter that, so long as their dominant motive was to inform the public, they were unlikely to get the Corporation into legal trouble.

3. *The place of producers in the authority structure of the* BBC. Although information was not systematically collected under this heading, the effects of three influences were noticed. One is the fact that in the normal course of their programme-making duties, the members of the *24 Hours* and *Panorama* teams are accustomed to exercise a high degree of initiative and discretion. It is well-known that the Corporation tends to operate a *post hoc* system of control by review rather than an anticipatory system of censorship in advance,[10] and it would not be surprising if the initiatives taken by producers in the determination of programme content did not occasionally spill over into certain policy areas as well. Second, some producers may have perceived the policy-making authorities of the BBC as rather indifferent to the case for a more vigorous use of television in an election situation. They may have felt that the BBC's contribution to the pre-campaign negotiations with the parties had been unduly cautious and that the Corporation was somewhat compromised by its close contacts with party headquarters. Some producers may have concluded, then, that it was up to them to

strike a blow for journalistic freedom. Finally, their initiatives may have been facilitated by certain processes of reference group formation. In the Current Affairs Group the more experienced members of the production teams served as what has been called 'magnet elements' for the formation of reference groups, which included some of the executives who were responsible for supervising the implementation of policy. Although these executives often provided effective guidance on policy questions, they also shared many of the norms and aspirations of the television journalists – having risen from their ranks and continued to work closely with them. Presumably that is why, so long as existing policies were not flouted, they did not discourage the policy initiatives of the producers.[11]

It is not implausible to suggest that some of these factors could affect production conditions in other spheres of broadcasting or even the activities of workers in other media. If so, the main theoretical lesson of this part of the analysis is the need to avoid an uncritical application of a perspective of situational determinism to the study of communicators. It may be important to examine their contributions to policy as well as their reactions to it.

But how should the attempt of the BBC current affairs producers to contribute to election broadcasting policy in 1966 be evaluated? This observer found it acceptable, for the overriding aim was to use television to achieve a more *revealing* campaign than the political parties were likely to provide through their own unaided efforts. And that is consistent with a function which viewers themselves wish television to discharge in its coverage of an election campaign.[12]

Producers and their politician sources

It is common knowledge that by the end of the 1966 campaign much tension had been generated between BBC producers and certain Labour Party spokesmen. The degree of personal involvement of the various actors in this situation was, no doubt, unequal on both sides. Nevertheless, the general atmosphere was sufficiently highly charged to have provoked comparisons with the worsening of relations between the Corporation and the Conservative Party at the time of the Suez crisis. A point had been reached, in fact, where a number of leading producers perceived themselves to be the targets of a sustained campaign of pressure from the Labour Party. Some phenomena which were interpreted at the time as belonging to this campaign included: the Prime Minister's persistent refusal to be interviewed on *Campaign Report* (despite two appearances on ITN's *Election '66*); informal expressions of Labour's dissatisfaction with the BBC's attempt to promote a party-leader confrontation on television; and informal reactions of surprise and resentment about a number of the election issues that the makers of *Campaign Report* proposed to discuss on the programme.

The author's opportunities to observe the development of this situation were one-sided and incomplete. He could not see it through the politicians' eyes, and he arrived on the scene after much of the tension had already been built up (stoked by a series of explosive incidents between the BBC and the Labour Party which stretched back to late 1964). He was in no position, therefore, to allocate praise and blame, as if in some semi-judicial capacity, to the various participants in the conflict. He felt at the time, however, that allegations of a pro-Conservative bias in the Current Affairs Group were unwarranted. He had been present on several occasions (which would have been invisible to viewers and politicians alike) when the producers had demonstrated a meticulous concern to ensure that Labour would not suffer from any implicit imbalance in programme content.[13] From his vantage point, then, the author was mainly able to observe the responses of the producers – in attitudes and in actions – to a situation of perceived political pressure.

It should be emphasized, first of all, that those responses did not include many visible signs of personal stress. In their professional capacity, the specialist political reporters tended to perceive themselves – despite any troubles of the moment – as capable of sustaining relations of mutual confidence with many individual politicians. And the politically less specialized producers regarded themselves as personally not very involved in the situation – because not so dependent on maintaining the good will of party politicians.

Nevertheless, one attitudinal effect of the seeming exertion of party pressure on organs of news and publicity is to strengthen a tendency for staff communicators to ascribe to politicians *the role of would-be-manipulators* – at the expense of other role orientations through which they could also be perceived (e.g., the roles of statesmen, experienced men of affairs, men of ideas, puppets of fortune, etc.). There

were times during the 1966 campaign when virtually the whole occupational class was considered to be more or less tarred with this manipulative brush, although some politicians were regarded as far more
tainted than others. It is true that the rather special circumstances under
which producers and politicians often meet probably helped to generate
this unfavourable impression. As one producer pointed out, 'We often
see them at their most calculating, trying to project themselves as
effectively as they can, but we rarely see them in situations where they
are developing their own ideas genuinely.' But each seeming attempt
to put pressure on journalists and broadcasters only reinforced this
picture of politicians as would-be manipulators, not only of the
electorate, but also of the mass media themselves. It was sometimes
said, for example, that the typical politician would like to get the mass
media to do his work for him – to show him in flattering situations
and to emphasize the political themes he stands for.

The reverse side of this coin is a part of the television journalist's
own self-image; a tendency to cast himself in *the role of public watchdog*,
the essence of whose position is an ostensible, but to some degree
vulnerable, form of independence. It is not clear how much power the
producers thought the politicians could muster to back up their pressures and thereby threaten journalistic independence itself. Some
believed the bark of politicians was worse than their bite, while others
found their efforts more menacing. They tended to agree, however,
about the line of response that it was appropriate for journalists to
follow on the plane of action.

In fact it seemed that the typical reaction of producers to a situation
of perceived pressure was not accommodation but resistance. Partly
this was because something vital to journalists (their autonomy) was at
stake. But it was also because repeated indications of a party's dis-
pleasure with the broadcasters' activities had helped to translate each
bone of contention, however minor, into an issue of principle – when
to yield to the party's wishes would have symbolized lack of pride,
courage, and self-respect.

The psychology of this situation was especially noticeable when the
first few editions of *Campaign Report* were being prepared. The opening production could have been built, for example, around one of two
political items: a round-table discussion of opinion poll findings; or
an examination of the role of sterling in the election. The latter had
emerged as a campaign issue from Mr Heath's statement in *Election*

Forum that Labour's return to power would endanger the pound (which had been countered in turn by Mr Wilson's plea that sterling should be kept out of the election). Repercussions of this dispute had already spilled over into the columns of financial journalism. In a *Spectator* article Nigel Lawson had expressed certain fears about the future of sterling, to which William Davis had published a highly critical reply in *The Guardian*. It was envisaged, then, that a treatment of sterling on *Campaign Report* would include a confrontation between the opposed journalists as well as interviews with spokesmen of each of the three political parties.

Such an item was far more appealing to most of the producers than the one on 'the pollsters'. It was highly topical, whereas the 'pollsters' would keep for transmission on any night of the campaign. It was expected that Messrs Lawson and Davis would stage what was called 'a bloody good row'. It was believed that their arguments would shed fresh light on an important subject. ('They'll say things about this that the politicians will try to avoid.') Enthusiasm to bring the two columnists before the cameras was also aroused by their reputation as accomplished television performers.[14] Another attraction was the presence of Mr Davis in Zurich at the time. ('I like the idea of the programme being introduced in effect by the announcement, "Here is William Davis from Gnomesville".') And the entire item was expected to help to clarify an important party difference that had emerged early in the campaign.

The makers of the programme also realized, however, that Labour might be offended by the presentation of such an item. One producer reminded his fellows at an early stage that the Prime Minister had 'taken the pound out of politics last night'. And it was pointed out later that Labour might regard a match between Mr Lawson, who was a committed Conservative, and Mr Davis, whose left-wing leanings were less partisan, as unevenly balanced. Nevertheless, the producers of *24 Hours* decided to follow their journalistic stars. The adoption of any other course in the circumstances would have seemed a betrayal of their self-defined journalistic roles and would have jeopardized their self-respect.

Similar problems occasionally arose when the make-up of other editions of *Campaign Report* was being settled. After it was supposed that the Labour Party had tried to prevent an issue from being aired on the programme by withholding a speaker, a producer commented as follows on the decision to proceed with the contentious item:

> We would be very reluctant to let a major party suppose that it can dictate our coverage of subjects by withholding speakers. In fact it is a marginal argument in favour of going ahead with this item that Labour seemed to want to stop us from dealing with it.

And on another occasion one factor in a decision to present a certain election item was said to have been the fact that Labour had apparently responded to it: '. . . in a snide way. We should not let them influence how we are going to cover the campaign – play it way down just because it suits their book to have a low-keyed campaign.'

And yet a stiffening of the broadcasters' will to resist was not an invariable consequence of the voicing of party complaints. After the Conservatives objected that Labour had enjoyed the advantage of a 'last word' on the immediate pre-campaign edition of *Panorama*, it was decided to offer them the chance of closing the next edition of the programme. A Liberal politician's informal complaint late in the campaign that *24 Hours* had paid scant attention to his party led to a decision to screen a longer interview than usual with Mr Grimond. And a decision to arrange a mini-confrontation on housing was probably influenced by Labour's complaint that *Campaign Report* had previously drawn many of its topics from the Conservatives' election locker.

A common feature of these examples, however, was the appeal of a political party to a principle of fairness which the producers themselves regarded as legitimate. In such a case the exertion of pressure helped to remind the broadcasters of a consideration that had been overlooked in the hectic conditions of election programming. What provokes the resistance of producers, then, is not the application of pressure as such but its accompaniment by: accusations of bias (which they regard as unjust); steps that may be construed as threats (which they perceive as attacks on their professional autonomy); or a concerted series of incidents (which they interpret as evidence of a sustained manipulative intent).

When broadcasters suspect that they are targets of such pressures, even the 'geography' of television production fosters resistance. For example, a party's complaints are often received by telephone and promptly relayed by word of mouth to other available producers.

Since the initial recipient of the message cannot see the party spokesman who is addressing him, he may experience difficulty in judging exactly what the latter is trying to convey. Perhaps it is not surprising that on at least two occasions allegedly inflammatory Labour remarks were withdrawn as misinterpretations after their previous circulation through the corridors of Lime Grove. Lack of privacy in television production could also play a part. Since no member of the *24 Hours* staff had an office to himself, the reactions of a receiving producer to telephoned party comments were immediately visible to many of his colleagues. Those responses were inevitably conditioned, then, by the reference group norms of a circle of dedicated television journalists.

It is evident that during the 1966 campaign the relationship between the observed producers and their politician sources amounted at times to virtually a struggle for access to the audience.[15] Is such a situation likely to have any important public consequences? The findings of Walter Gieber's studies of journalist-source relations suggest that it might. In his opinion the function of reporters and sources as gatekeepers in the flow of news and comment is so central that the fate of a typical story is 'not determined by the needs of the community of the mass media audience but by the demands of the reference group of which the communicator is a member or an employee'.[16]

Some commentators regard the existence of tension between journalists and their politician sources as both natural and beneficial. It suggests that the reporters are on their toes – probing the decisions of wielders of power, holding them to account, and helping to curb their excesses. It may also reflect a healthy determination not to be 'absorbed' by their sources. But it is still necessary to ask whether at some pitch of intensity a struggle between television journalists and politicians may not become harmful.

One danger is the loss of clear and mature judgment that may follow when considerations of pride and self-esteem are injected into a conflict. But even more pernicious consequences could ensue if either side approached a state of near-total disenchantment with the other. If such a mood developed among broadcasters, it might either discourage them from paying much attention to politics at all (in order to avoid the painful wrangles and choices associated with attempts at independent political programming), or it might encourage them to present politicians to the electorate more as objects of amusement and derision than as important public servants. Meanwhile, disenchanted politicians could also develop a rather jaundiced outlook of their own on the intentions and interests of broadcasters. They might, for example, regard television journalists as usurpers, as purveyors of entertainment in the guise of pretended serious programming, as superficial jacks-of-all trades, and as ungrateful biters of the hands that feed them.

Perhaps this is all more reminiscent of a pathology than of the relations that should normally prevail between broadcasters and politicians. But it is not entirely far-fetched to suggest that such a pathology played some part in the tussles of the 1966 campaign – or that it influenced the rejection by the House of Commons, in November 1966, of a motion to carry out an experimental televising of the proceedings of Parliament.[17]

Two styles of producer–audience relations: a sacerdotal vs. a pragmatic approach to election coverage

The producers of the Current Affairs Group were not only at odds with their politician sources during the 1966 campaign; they were also divided among themselves about the amount and type of attention that television should pay to an election. This internal conflict was precipitated by the decision to present *Campaign Report* as part of *24 Hours* – a step which effected a temporary marriage of convenience between teams that had previously been responsible for the quite different (and by 1966 defunct) programmes of *Gallery* and *Tonight*. It was mainly the *Gallery* tradition that shaped the original conception of the programme, but compelling reasons had arisen early in 1966 for incorporating it into the format of *Tonight*'s successor.

The Corporation's plans for producing a late-night *Campaign Report* were drawn up in the spring of 1965 after certain critical conclusions had been reached about the causes of its relatively poor performance during the 1964 election. Responsibility for commenting on that campaign had been split between the BBC News Division, which had put out a special late bulletin called *Election Extra*, and the Current Affairs Group, which had presented six editions of *Election Gallery* at 7.00 p.m. It was considered that this division had not helped the BBC to use its available political talent as effectively as possible: relying on standard newsreaders only, *Election Extra* had lacked imagination, but *Election Gallery* had been transmitted at too early an hour to exploit actuality material from the hustings.[18] The favoured solution envisaged an integrated production, which would concertedly apply both news and current affairs resources to the task of reporting the progress of a campaign.

But by the autumn of 1965 *24 Hours* had succeeded *Tonight* in a new and much later time slot (usually 10.15 p.m.), which *Campaign Report* had been expected to fill once an election was held. As the time for a dissolution of Parliament approached, it was appreciated that both programmes could not be presented separately without congesting the schedules with an unacceptable amount of current affairs material. But the makers of *24 Hours* were proud of the growing audience they had been cultivating with signal success and were reluctant to go off the air for the period of the campaign. Even those producers who did not work regularly for *24 Hours* accepted the legitimacy of its team's concern not to lose touch with its newly-won audience for three weeks. It was decided, therefore, to broadcast *Campaign Report* as a part of *24 Hours*.

This unprecedented arrangement was implemented by a series of compromises. It was agreed that *24 Hours* should remain in operation more or less as before the campaign, presenting a mixture of political and non-political stories, but that its regular staff would be augmented by a few producers and reporters with specialist experience in the political field. The senior members of the *24 Hours* team would assume overall editorial responsibility, but the political specialists would have an important voice in the planning of election material. Certain production features would draw attention to the distinctive character of that material – e.g., the use of the separate title, *Campaign Report*, and the introduction of election and non-election items by different anchor men. But many details of the relations between the two elements remained to be settled daily in the light of prevailing circumstances.

Despite its origin in compromise, this combined operation did not lack positive defenders at the start of the campaign. As one individual put the case for what had been worked out:

> After all, their banner is '24 Hours in Britain and in the World', and you get a better perspective on election events if the producers have had to weigh up whether to present an election item or an item, say, from Paraguay.

Nevertheless, the adherents of somewhat opposed philosophies of current affairs broadcasting were compelled by what had been arranged to work together for a concentrated period. It should not be supposed that their approaches to television journalism differed at every conceivable point. They shared an allegiance to many of the same ethical norms of their profession – such as accuracy, impartiality, and reportorial freedom. They respected each other's technical mastery of such skills of their craft as: an ability to write clear, simple, and vivid passages of commentary; an eye for apt and compelling visual material; speed of response to the challenge of fast-moving events; and an ability to steer an interview into interesting channels. And although they differed over the desirability of aiming deliberately to maximize the size of the audience for a political programme, they all felt, as workers in television, the appeal of the medium's power to address, interest, and inform large numbers of viewers. In spite of these areas of common ground, however, one executive admitted, even before the campaign had officially begun, that some members of his assembled team would 'lean one way' while others would 'lean the other way'.

What exactly were the main points of difference between the two camps? There were disputes about the total amount of time that should be devoted to the election and about the relationship that should be forged within the programme between its election and non-election items. But these were merely outcrops of a deeper conflict – one which a BBC official epitomized in the middle of the campaign as a clash between a sacerdotal and a pragmatic approach to election coverage.

On the one hand, the practitioners of the so-called sacerdotal style of campaign programming tended to think of themselves as providing a 'service' and of an election as an intrinsically important event which entitled it to substantial coverage as of right. From this followed their 'audience image'.[19] They expected implicitly to cater either for voters who were already interested in politics or for viewers who could be helped to grasp the political significance of campaign events. The task of television, then, was to meet the needs of such an audience with a coherent, thoughtful, and illuminating body of programme content. In fact, these reporters were concerned largely with political values and rather less with other production values. One of them considered, for example, that three kinds of material belonged in *Campaign Report*: a response to the leading campaign events of each day, 'logging' them, as it were, for the record; an examination of the underlying issues of the election in some depth; and filmed illustrations of various facets of campaign activity. This individual tended to emphasize the information-supplying function of current affairs broadcasting. It was true, he said, that television could operate effectively on an emotional plane:

> You often hear people say after seeing a leader on TV, 'He looked tired', or passing similar remarks. Yet we must remember that viewers already have certain emotions about politics and elections. There is no need to stimulate and arouse them. The important thing is to try to provide information and inject an element of reason into the presentation of an election. This might be difficult at times, but you've got to continue to plug away at it – for that is what democracy is all about.

The more pragmatically disposed producers, on the other hand, denied the intrinsic right of election material to programme prominence and repeatedly asserted that it must 'fight its way in' on its merits. ('We will treat the election as newspapers do – that on most days it will only be the main but not the sole item of home news.') They wished to avoid creating any impression that they felt *obliged* to cover the campaign. ('We do not want to convey the idea that we have received a directive from high up in the BBC that the election ought to be covered and that we are passing that obligation on to the viewer in the way we handle election items.') And instead of beaming the programme at an audience of mainly politically interested viewers, the pragmatists professed a strong dislike of merely:

> . . . talking to the converted. That is just a bore. I would much prefer to aim our mixture of election and non-election items at the relatively uninterested viewer.

Above all else, it was important not to cultivate what one producer called a 'ghetto audience':

> We should not produce an election programme *per se*, nor should we create an election ghetto within the programme. I do not want to have a special election chunk in the programme, for that is the way to reduce the *24 Hours* audience to a ghetto audience. We should try to break it up into five- to seven-minute lumps scattered throughout the programme.

Whereas the political specialists often pressed the claims of various election items for inclusion in the programme, then, a prime aim of the

24 Hours producers was to keep the demands of election material 'under control'. ('We do not want the viewers to form the impression that we have gone absolutely mad on the election.') The members of the *24 Hours* team hoped that viewers would assume that the programme was continuing to operate along its usual lines, an impression that might be strengthened by splitting up the election and non-election items in the order of transmission. They also wanted to ensure that as many election items as possible were presented in a style which was consistent with the general tone of *24 Hours*: its lively pace, its reliance on immediate viewer appeal, and its lack of solemnity and pontificating. It was important, they thought, not to approach the election with an air of 'excessive reverence'. As one producer put it with his tongue in his cheek, 'It's a good idea for politicians to have to take their place after somebody really important – like David McCallum.'

It is convenient to develop a more general theoretical implication of this contrast here. This concerns the part that is played in broadcasters' work by impressions of audience needs and interests. It may be that such impressions are somewhat less important than the 'transactional' view of communicator-audience relations suggests.[20] This is not to deny that broadcasters wish to hold an audience and welcome any evidence that can show they have evoked a favourable response from it. But the key conflicts that were detected in this study did not spring directly from differences of opinion about the kind of election coverage 'the audience' wanted. It is true that producers conceived various images of audience requirements and aimed their wares at different types of viewers. But those differences could almost be regarded as derivative from at least two other sources of cleavage. One was a conflict in the attitudes of producers towards the *topic* they were assigned to cover – some having approached the election from the role orientation of specialists and others having approached it from the role orientation of 'all-rounders' who were proud of their ability to deal with a quite wide range of items. In addition, there was a clash of broadcasting *styles*, which reflected the different relationships that the opposed producers wished to establish between their programme materials and members of the audience. What divided them, in other words, was the manner of their intended impact *on* viewers, not conflicting interpretations of what the audience liked.

But how were the conflicts between these philosophies resolved in the course of the campaign? As might have been expected, most

editions of *24 Hours* bore the imprint of both styles. After the transmission of certain editions, one group of producers seemed rather more
satisfied with the result than the other; on other occasions, the pattern
of feeling was reversed. The collaboration between the two groups
often proceeded fairly smoothly, although on at least three occasions
sharp conflicts arose which had to be settled rather late in the day.
Those disputes typically flared up in the afternoon after one of the
political specialists had learned that little election content was booked
for the evening's programme, had expressed his dismay, and had then
offered a veritable shower of practical suggestions for repairing the
omission.

Although both contributing producer groups achieved and conceded
some of their stated goals, the *24 Hours* team did not realize its objective of treating election material strictly according to its day-to-day
merits, unaffected by any obligation to cover it. Several factors con-
spired to defeat it on this issue of principle. One was the weight of
authority which the political specialists could wield in their own field.
Another was a commitment to present a number of film reports which
had been planned before the campaign began, which could not have
been discarded without considerable waste, and which bulked large in
the output of *Campaign Report* in the latter half of the campaign. In
addition, the last three or four days tended to be overshadowed by
calculations of the amounts of time that had been devoted thus far to
each of the parties, which encouraged the screening of certain political
items at certain lengths in order to help to get the final sums right.
But perhaps the crucial factor emerged from the first of the three main
clashes mentioned above – a conflict which had arisen because on a
seemingly dull campaign day, the *24 Hours* team had assumed that,
'Today of all days we should let the programme build itself naturally
and compel election material to fight its way in.' An affronted political
reporter's response to that proposition was that, 'We can make things
happen' by the interviews and discussions that are arranged in the
programme. And he carried his point by the force of the argument that
special resources had been allocated for election coverage, which
should be used to serve their intended purpose.

Despite that setback, no edition of *24 Hours* was entirely filled with
campaign material, and in some editions the election and non-election
items were inter-leaved. The *24 Hours* team also managed to transmit
some of its raciest non-election stories during the campaign,[21] and the

slant of several election items reflected its characteristic style as well.[22] Similarly, the political specialists could congratulate themselves on having incorporated into the programme a more solid body of election content than the *24 Hours* producers had bargained for – although some items suffered from the rather hasty preparations that were necessitated by the late hour at which decisions in their favour had been reached. There were some muddles, for example, over the tendering of invitations to politicians to appear in the programme. And a late decision to include a compilation item in the last edition of *Campaign Report* (to be built around inter-leaved extracts on selected themes from hustings speeches by Mr Wilson and Mr Heath) left insufficient time to dig out suitable material and to edit it properly.

It is difficult to evaluate the results of the BBC's decision to provide late-night election coverage within a politically less specialized programme vehicle like *24 Hours*. One executive claimed that the mixing of items had provided 'a useful form of flexibility', enabling *Campaign Report* 'to be expanded or contracted as the circumstances dictated', especially 'in the early stages of the campaign when it had been difficult to judge what the political temperature would be like'. There is also some evidence which suggests that the viewers liked what they were offered on *24 Hours* during the 1966 election. The average size of its audience was virtually identical with the viewing figures that were recorded in the preceding non-campaign weeks,[23] and an Audience Research Department survey of the opinions of members of the BBC Viewing Panel failed to locate any important focus of viewer dissatisfaction. Ninety per cent considered that the programme had treated each party fairly. A majority believed that its usual length had been 'about right'. Many more respondents said they 'particularly liked' each of the programme's commentators than did those who expressed a particular dislike of any of them. Moreover, the average Reaction Index (a measure of audience appreciation) was higher for the campaign editions of *24 Hours* than it had been for *Election Gallery* in 1964 (65 compared with a range between 61 and 63).[24] Though slight, this difference stood out against a general trend whereby most election programmes elicited lower Reaction Indices in 1966 than they had in 1964. Finally, the 'vast majority' of the BBC's respondents thought that this form of *24 Hours* should be used again at the next General Election.[25]

But viewer approval is at best an incomplete guide to the evaluation of any programme form. In the sphere of political broadcasting, it is most likely to be taken seriously by those who stress the value of using television to reach a large audience of only mildly interested electors, many of whom may rely on no other important source of political information. Even so, the available evidence does not tell us which particular features of *Campaign Report* were responsible for its favourable reception by viewers. And the respondents could express an opinion only about what they had seen; they were in no position to judge whether something better could have been produced.

Furthermore, even a popular programme form may jeopardize certain values that election broadcasting should uphold. Two examples of such vulnerable political values may be cited. One concerns the need for comprehensiveness and depth in political reporting and analysis. At least one of the political specialists felt that *Campaign Report*'s record had been relatively unsatisfactory when judged by this criterion. If so, perhaps this was due, not so much to the mixing of election and non-election items, but to the firm commitment of a daily programme to topicality in current affairs. In such a production the hectic needs of instant planning afford little time for contributors to sit back and put the emerging issues into some considered perspective. (It was a striking fact that the most widely praised of *Campaign Report*'s five mini-confrontations happened to revolve around the most topical and ephemeral of the election issues of 1966 – 'the Cowley noose trial'.) But the claims of analytical depth may also suffer from the 'all-rounder's' confidence in the validity of his immediate reactions to developing events.

A second value which may be realized or threatened by election broadcasting arrangements concerns the fidelity of what is produced to the events to be covered. This provides the focus of discussion in the next section of this article.

Producers and campaign events

After completing a participant observation study of CBS coverage of the American party conventions of 1964, Herbert Waltzer outlined eight criteria for evaluating television presentations of any political event, of which one, put in the form of a question, was '. . . did the networks arrogate the centre stage at the convention for themselves?'.

Did television help voters to see and hear an important political occasion at first hand, he asked, or did the medium and its reporters become the main objects of attention instead?[26]

A similar criterion was implicit in the already published reactions of one British critic of *Campaign Report*'s coverage of the General Election of 1966. Writing in a Nuffield College volume about the role of radio and television in that election, Martin Harrison maintained that the programme had concentrated so heavily on comment and analysis that straight reporting of the campaign was neglected. It was necessary, he concluded, to resist a confusion of 'the campaign itself with its reflection in the media', and in the 1966 election television had not yet struck 'an ideal balance in communicating the substance of campaign arguments while scrutinizing and advancing them'.[27]

That analysis raises three related questions. First, did *24 Hours* tend to ignore the campaign that the political parties were waging in 1966? Second, if so, how can its lack of interest in that campaign be explained? And third, should such a tendency be deplored?

If the programme's interest in the 'real campaign' is measured by the extent of its use of actuality material from hustings speeches and press conferences, then the first question must be answered affirmatively. Although some material of this kind was presented in each edition of *Campaign Report*, it was usually overshadowed by other items, and it had often been selected to illustrate a particular issue around which it had been decided to build the night's programme. Full attention could be said to have been paid to campaign speeches in their own right in only about two of the 13 editions of *Campaign Report*.[28]

A quantitative impression of the programme's relative neglect of such material is conveyed by the accompanying table. This compares the output of *Campaign Report* and ITN's *Election '66* for the 12 dates on which both late-night campaign news vehicles were on the air, and it is based on a count of the number of lines of recorded transcript that were devoted to each of seven categories of election items. The table suggests that the activities of the BBC production were far more ambitious, adventurous, and varied than those of its rival on the commercial channel. (*Election '66* neglected four of the categories into which a number of BBC items fell, including the screening of mini-confrontations between major party spokesmen. Those debates occupied more lines of *Campaign Report* transcript, in fact, than did any other class of

ELECTION OUTPUT OF 'CAMPAIGN REPORT'
AND 'ELECTION '66' COMPARED

Item Categories	Campaign Report (BBC) %	Election '66 (ITN) %
1. Extracts from politicians' speeches	15	55
2. Reporters' comments on the campaign	16	26
3. Interviews with individual politicians	14	17
4. Confrontations of two or more politicians	22	—
5. Interviews/discussions with non-politicians	6	1
6. Material about opinion poll findings*	10	1
7. Pre-prepared film reports	18	—
	101	100
Total number of lines of transcript=	4,511	2,291

* This category was conceived in order to test the impression that *Campaign Report* had paid considerable attention to the opinion polls' findings. Material in it derived largely, of course, from reporters' comments, although some also occurred in interviews with politicians and in discussions with non-politicians.

item.) But only 15% of the verbal matter of *Campaign Report* was drawn directly from the speeches of campaigning politicians, compared with 55% in the case of *Election '66*.

Why did *Campaign Report* provide such a sketchy coverage of the platform performances of party spokesmen? Its facilities for obtaining outside broadcast material from election meetings were technically first-class, and the case for making full use of them was pressed by at least one political reporter, who consistently argued that, 'We have a wood and trees problem, and we must log the trees in case they later form part of a wood.' But the combined influence of four factors help to explain why this approach played only a minor part in the actual output of the programme.

1. *The lack of a consistently positive orientation towards hard news among 24 Hours producers.* Although two members of the BBC News Division had been seconded to the programme staff, many *24 Hours* producers had been reared in the distinctive style of *Tonight*. And although some individuals interpreted (and welcomed) the changeover from *Tonight* to *24 Hours* as if it had converted a 'magazine' into a

'newspaper', few leading producers felt obliged at the time to build each edition of the programme around the major news stories of the day. Their main concern, they said, was to broadcast a programme that was 'worth watching' and that had something 'to add' to what other communications sources were saying about a topic. In contemplating *Campaign Report*, then, they naturally felt that, 'The logging area was the most tedious in the form that we did it; the trouble was that there was no *attitude* behind it.' This comment reflects the fact that the viability of a typical *24 Hours* item depended partly on the slant, generated from within the production team, that could be applied to a story. And this outlook helped to dampen interest in actuality materials from the campaign in two ways. First, such material was actually said to be 'outside the control' of the programme's producers (which meant, presumably, that it could not be forced into their structuring of the situation). Second, it lacked the emotional potential on which the *24 Hours* style often relied for impact (by highlighting the dramatic, exciting, tragic, comic, or ironic possibilities of a situation). The presentation of long extracts from election speeches could have reflected nothing more than a sense of *obligation* to do justice to what the politicians were saying on public platforms.

2. *A conviction that sufficient attention was being paid to the party campaign elsewhere.* In their own quotas of election broadcasting time, first of all, the parties had access to an important outlet through which to present their arguments to the public. But if a voter wished to find out what the politicians were saying on the hustings, he could turn for enlightenment to his newspaper. One producer emphatically denied that *Campaign Report* should try to 'log' the course of the election as if it was analogous to *The Times*: 'It is at odds with the ephemeral nature of television to regard it as the provider of a permanent record'. But even on television, it was alleged, the hustings campaign was being covered more than adequately in the main evening news bulletins – the duration of which had been extended from 15 to 20 minutes for the election period. There was a strong feeling that the obligation to report campaign events, as such, fell principally on the News Division and that the task of current affairs programming was to go forward from the news, not to repeat it. In addition, a fear was expressed that the compilers of the news bulletins were in a position to 'pinch the best OB material', leaving only more dull passages for *24 Hours* to present later. And finally, there was some anxiety about overcrowding the air waves

with the sound of party argument – from the main news to party broadcast to *Campaign Report*. Sensitive to the signs of any such political congestion, one executive member of the Current Affairs Group expressed the view that a first priority in making plans for coverage of the next General Election should be a closer integration of its activities with those of the News Division.

3. *A perception of the nature of the 1966 campaign.* Many journalists (and not merely those who worked on *24 Hours*) apparently shared a common set of attitudes towards the 1966 election, which they suspected the electorate was finding tedious. Much comment in the press and in the political weeklies developed an ironic contrast between the dull, placid, and almost ritualistic character of the campaign, on the one hand, and the gravity of the real issues that still faced the country, on the other. The boredom of the campaign was ascribed to an exhaustion of the public's capacity for excitement after 17 months of almost continuous political crisis, to Labour's overwhelming opinion poll lead, and to Mr Wilson's election strategy of deliberately keeping the political temperature down. And yet (it was often pointed out) many severe problems still awaited a political solution: the vulnerability of the economy; the persistence of conservative attitudes in many sectors of industry; Britain's isolation from the Common Market; and the difficulty of devising suitable methods of financing improvements in the social services. In the context of this consensus, perhaps it is not surprising that the producers of *24 Hours* assumed that the parties' hustings manoeuvres deserved only scant attention – and that they aimed instead to promote discussion of those issues which they considered important.

4. *The constraints of programme design.* The design of the programme itself left little room for coverage of the 'real campaign'. The cumulative effect of the various constraints can be judged by looking back at the table above. It was natural that the arrangement of mini-confrontations should have assumed a high priority in the producers' strategy for extending the scope of election television (see row 4 in the table). *Campaign Report* was staffed by several able interviewers whose talents deserved to be exercised (row 3). The intimate familiarity of one of the political commentators with opinion poll trends was exploited on several occasions (row 6). Even before the campaign had been officially launched, a group of producers had started to prepare film reports about campaign activities from various perspectives (in marginal and

safe seats, in Northern Ireland, in a constituency with a prominent local issue, from the standpoint of party agents, from the standpoint of the Deputy Leaders of each of the three main parties, etc.). Altogether, 13 such reports were contemplated, and ten eventually reached the screen (row 7). In addition, the concern of the regular *24 Hours* producers to transmit non-election items from both domestic and foreign sources had to be satisfied. (On the average between one and two non-election items were presented each night, and on a few occasions as many as three were screened.) Under these circumstances it simply was not possible to 'log' the course of the 1966 election more fully than *Campaign Report* did.

Does it matter if an election programme subordinates descriptive coverage of a campaign to the presentation of livelier and more penetrating items of comment, discussion, and analysis? If there are other channels through which the substance of party arguments can reach the public, why should a vehicle like *Campaign Report* be expected to air them fully as well? One reason for ensuring that straight reporting is not neglected concerns the contribution that this could make to a smoothing of antagonisms between producers and their politician sources. The near-pathological elements in the politician's image of the broadcaster might be held in check if he had no ground for suspecting that television was ignoring his pet themes. It can also be argued that in the last analysis it is the parties which pose the terms of the choice that the electorate has to make. It may seem to follow from this that those terms should be placed firmly on a programme's agenda before it proceeds to challenge them or to develop other issues.

These considerations undermine the acceptability of the formula of election programming that the BBC applied in 1966 for two reasons. First, in any election there are likely to be some important features of a party's case which cannot be readily expressed within the issue-centred orientation that the makers of *Campaign Report* favoured. The contrast between 13 years of Conservative rule and 17 months of Labour government, which formed a central theme of Labour's propaganda in 1966, for example, could probably have been developed only through the screening of substantial extracts from campaign speeches or by the arrangement of a rather relaxed interview with a prominent party figure. Second, more time would have to be allocated to election material if a greater emphasis on straight reporting was not to encroach on the many other functions of election television that *Campaign Report* aimed to serve. This suggests that, in order to provide a balanced campaign service, the attempt to combine coverage of election and non-election stories within the same format would have to be abandoned.

This conclusion can be avoided only by questioning whether each and every election programme should seek to provide a complete service in itself. The implication would be that *Election '66*'s thorough reporting of the last campaign had released *24 Hours* from an obligation to cover it equally fully. Unfortunately, this presupposes the achievement of a greater measure of deliberate co-operation between the BBC and the ITA than has usually prevailed in British broadcasting. Officially, relations between the two services are governed by competition, not co-ordination, and very few attempts have ever been made to rationalize their respective contributions to the menu of television fare on offer to the viewing audience. But since both the BBC and the ITA are public service agencies, why should they not collaborate over at least such limited exercise as coverage of a campaign?

Three advantages might flow from an attempt to co-ordinate the election activities of the news and current affairs services on the various channels. First, unnecessary duplications of effort could be avoided. Once a rough division of labour was established between the different election programmes, one production team could ignore the constituency campaign, if it wished, knowing that others were reporting it more fully. (Politicians might also be less quick to take offence at some seeming omission, if they knew in advance how each programme intended to contribute to the campaign.) Second, the concern of many broadcasters not to over-tax the average viewer's capacity to absorb political materials could be tackled as a joint problem. And finally, the broadcasting authorities could try to arrange a coherent series of inter-party debates as a major election event on television, thereby safeguarding these important occasions from the mishaps of hasty planning.

A concluding note on the determinants of current affairs programming

One major outcome of this study is an indication that the character of current affairs output is not rigidly governed by an unalterable set of fixed conditions. Much of the end-product seems to be determined by a number of variable factors that are not usually perceptible to viewers or to other outsiders. The coverage by *24 Hours* of the 1966 election partially depended, of course, on the BBC's official policies for campaign broadcasting, on the Corporation's organizational arrangements, on the financial, technical, and human resources that were allocated to the production team, and on certain fundamental programme ideas that were laid down well in advance of the campaign. But we have seen that election programming was shaped, in addition, by the producers' own policy strategies, by the tenor of their daily relations with party representatives, and by rival styles of political coverage thought appropriate for the intended audience. This underlines the need for a further investigation of the sources of producers' internal definitions of their roles – from which many of the influences detected in this study had emanated.

2. The Spiegel Affair and the West German Press: The Initial Phase[*1]

Ronald F. Bunn

Between 8.30 and 9 p.m. on 26th October, 1962, attorneys of the West German Federal Prosecutor's Office, assisted by the Hamburg criminal police and officers of the Security Group of the Federal Criminal Office, converged on the Hamburg and Bonn offices of the news magazine *Der Spiegel*. Three members of the staff were taken into immediate custody. Rudolf Augstein, the publisher, could not be located that evening by the police, but upon learning of the warrant for his arrest he turned himself in to the authorities on the following day. Conrad Ahlers, an associate editor, was vacationing with his wife in Spain. In the early hours of 27th October, 1962, he was taken into 'provisional custody' by Spanish police and returned to West Germany, where he was promptly arrested. In the weeks that followed, additional arrests were made, including those of Colonel Alfred Martin of the Federal Defence Ministry and Colonel Adolf Wicht of the Federal Intelligence Agency (*Bundesnachrichtendienst*). The Hamburg offices of *Der Spiegel* were placed under surveillance, and for some thirty days federal investigators searched the files and archives. On the morning following the raids and initial arrests, the Federal Prosecutor's Office in Karlsruhe announced that the action had been prompted by the publication in *Der Spiegel* of 'state secrets' in such a way as to 'endanger the security of the Federal Republic as well as the safety and freedom of the German people'. Spokesmen for the Federal Prosecutor's Office explained that the suspicion arose primarily from an article written by Conrad Ahlers and appearing in the 10th October, 1962 issue of the magazine.[2] The charges specifically against Ahlers and

* First published in *Public Opinion Quarterly*, 30 (1966), pp. 54–68.

Augstein were 'betrayal of country, treasonable falsification of information, and bribery'.[3]

The Spiegel Affair came to be one of the most consequential political affairs that the West German political system has experienced since its founding in 1949. Within a week after the 26th October raids and arrests, Federal Minister of Justice Wolfgang Stammberger, one of the five Free Democratic Party (FDP) members of the national coalition government headed by Adenauer, offered his resignation. Stammberger claimed that he had not been informed in advance of the 26th October action and that he had thus been placed in the untenable position of having to defend a procedure of which he had no prior knowledge.[4] Shortly thereafter the FDP leadership threatened to withdraw entirely from the coalition, precipitating the first of two cabinet crises that developed during the affair. The three question periods (7th to 9th November, 1962) in the Bundestag concerning various aspects of the action against *Der Spiegel* were among the stormiest in Bonn's experience. On the last day of the debate Franz Josef Strauss, Federal Defence Minister and chairman of the Bavarian Christian Social Union (CSU) admitted personal involvement in the action by having requested through the West German military attaché in Madrid the assistance of the Spanish police in arresting Ahlers.[5] This admission by Strauss produced a second cabinet crisis, as the FDP, which on 5th November, 1962, had agreed to remain in the coalition, withdrew all five of its members from the cabinet.[6] Strauss, plunged into the most serious crisis of his controversial political career, eventually resigned his ministerial position.[7] Unable since 1949 to gain sufficient electoral support to form a national government and occasionally chided even by its supporters as an ineffectual opposition party in the Bundestag, the Social Democratic Party (SPD) was presented with a promising opportunity to prove its skill as an organized critic of the Adenauer government.[8] Before the Spiegel Affair had run its course, Chancellor Adenauer was compelled to firm up his 1961 commitment to relinquish his position in the autumn of 1963.

These and other consequences of the Spiegel Affair developed against the backdrop of an extensive public debate concerning the investigatory action against *Der Spiegel*. Students protested by demonstrating in several West German university communities.[9] Academicians petitioned political leaders, requesting either clarification or repudiation of the techniques employed in the investigation.[10] Journalist and publisher associations wired protests against an alleged threat to the legitimate freedom of the press.[11] More than forty of West Germany's most prominent writers and artists jointly deplored the action against *Der Spiegel* and gave additional impetus to the controversy by declaring that 'in a time when warfare is outmoded and inconceivable, it is not only the right, it is an ethical duty, to reveal so-called state secrets'.[12] The extent to which the affair occupied the attention of the public is suggested by the findings of reliable surveys, which show that within a few weeks a vast majority of the adult population became informed of one or more key aspects of the controversy.[13]

Various approaches may be taken on analysing and interpreting the Spiegel Affair.[14] The abruptness of the raids, the night-time interrogations and arrests, and the exceptional manner in which Ahlers was seized in Spain were to the harshest critics reminiscent of the style of National Socialist Germany. To those critics who resisted the temptation to draw analogies with the Nazi past, the action suggested at least an overzealous law-enforcement procedure that seemed disproportionate to what the circumstances required and insensitive to the role of the press in a constitutional system. A few observers probed deeply into the psychic condition of the West German population in attempting to account for what they perceived to be a significant popular reaction against the public authorities for the action against *Der Spiegel*. To these commentators the public reaction was illustrative of a widespread alienation that persists in West Germany towards the 'Bonn system' and that had found in *Der Spiegel* both a symbol and a spokesman. Other observers, reasoning along different lines, concluded that the charge of treason no longer arouses the public response it might have produced in an earlier era. Charges of 'treason' and 'crimes against the Reich and Volk', so the argument went, had been used too often in the past to mask violations of human decency to permit similar charges now to be accepted at face value. In short, it was asserted that the West German authorities may have misjudged the public mood if they assumed, even during the Cuban crisis, that the charge of treason would justify to the public the drastic measures initiated on the evening of 26th October.

As a case study of the operation of the West German political system, the Spiegel Affair might also be examined functionally. Viewed from this methodological perspective, the affair consisted of three phases: (1) the formative phase, during which the issues were initially framed and projected broadly into the public arena; (2) the bargaining phase, during which the agents most directly involved in negotiating the issues, particularly the party and government leaders, sought either to moderate the controversy or to translate the issues into demands upon the decision processes; and (3) the adjudication phase, during which the remaining issues, or those not amenable to 'political' resolution, were transferred to the judiciary for clarification and/or determination. The demarcation in time among these three functional phases of the affair, of course, is blurred, and all three functions were, at times, occurring simultaneously.[15]

Any interpretation of the Spiegel Affair need not confine itself to one of these phases. The problems involved in an enquiry into one phase are, in one way or another, intertwined with the others. But the particular framework within which the affair is examined will result in different emphases and concentrate on varying aspects of the affair. Whatever the specific focus, no analysis of the Spiegel Affair can ignore the heavy involvement of the West German press in the public controversy initiated by the raids on the magazine's offices and by the charge of treason levied against certain members of its staff. On the basis of a sample of the West German daily newspapers, our purpose here is to indicate both the nature and the scope of editorial reactions of a significant segment of the press community during the initial phase of the Spiegel Affair. It was during the first five days (27th to 31st October, 1962) following the raids that the major West German newspapers framed their responses, projected them into the public arena, and influenced the tone of the controversy that surrounded the Spiegel Affair. By limiting our enquiry to the reactions of the press, we do not deny the important roles of other groups, particularly the political parties and intellectual élites, in the early stages of the Spiegel Affair.

Research design

Variations in formats, news content, editorial policies, and readerships among the West German newspapers warn against neat generalizations. However, at the risk of oversimplification, we can distinguish four categories within which most of the daily newspapers might be classified: (1) 'boulevard sheets', or tabloids, dependent on street sales for their circulation, heavily employing pictures and colour, and generally inclined to 'sensationalize' the news; (2) *Heimatzeitungen*, or 'hometown' newspapers, which have limited circulations (rarely exceeding 10,000) and are essentially preoccupied with the reporting of local events in the smaller towns and communities; (3) the *Generalanzeiger*, or 'advertisers', which usually attempt a limited coverage of national and international news and occasionally editorialize on public issues, although their primary function is that of providing a medium for local advertisers and the reporting of regional news; and (4) a relatively small number of newspapers, frequently described as the 'serious' press, which is neither as sensational as the tabloid press nor as locally oriented in news coverage as the *Generalanzeiger* and *Heimatzeitungen*.[16] Although certain of the tabloids, particularly the *Bild-Zeitung* with a circulation that regularly exceeds three million copies, reach large numbers of readers, these newspapers are too preoccupied with appealing to and stimulating the reading appetites of the mass reading public for any intensive and sustained contribution to an informed discussion of political issues. The *Heimatzeitungen* include a wide variety of the small-town and village newspapers. Some of them are independently owned, operated, and written, but many of them now depend on major newspapers (*Hauptausgaben*) for whatever reports they carry on national and international news and for features, such as fictional serials and literary supplements. Their editorials on matters that transcend local importance are customarily reproductions of editorials carried in the *Hauptausgaben*. The distinction between a *Heimatzeitung* and a *Generalanzeiger* is frequently marginal, as the latter also contain in many instances 'canned' editorials of the major newspapers with which they are affiliated. Moreover, both the *Heimatzeitungen* and the *Generalanzeiger* are heavily dependent on the wire services for national and international news coverage. Within the fourth category are included those newspapers which are generally regarded as 'prestigious'. Although none of them can claim a circulation figure that even approaches that of the *Bild-Zeitung*, several of them have circulations in excess of 150,000 copies.

Each of the thirty-four daily newspapers comprising our sample (see the Appendix, p. 449) falls within either categories 3 or 4, or tends to combine aspects of both groupings. All of these newspapers are regularly clipped by the Press Evaluation Section (*Presseauswertungabteilung*) of the Bundestag Library in Bonn for its own evaluation purposes.[17] It must be stressed that the sample is numerically a small minority of the daily newspapers published in West Germany and cannot be accepted as definitive and representative of the entire West German press.[18] However, it is believed that the sample is sufficiently representative of the most widely circulated and 'prestigious' daily newspapers in West Germany (including West Berlin) to serve as as meaningful index of the editorial responses of an important segment of the press community.

In Table I the newspapers constituting our sample have been distributed among three categories: Critical, Sympathetic, and Unclassifiable. In the first of these categories we have placed those newspapers which in editorials and reportorial commentaries between 27th October and 31st October, 1962, seemed so preoccupied with either alleged procedural or substantive defects in the 26th October action against *Der Spiegel* as to convey the preponderant impression of an essentially hostile or critical attitude towards the public authorities for their undertaking against the magazine and its staff.[19] In the second category are those newspapers in our sample which in their editorials and reportorial commentaries during this period present an impression of supporting the public authorities in their action against *Der Spiegel* in spite of whatever indiscretions or miscalculations may have marred the procedures. Under the rubric 'Unclassifiable' we have included those newspapers within our sample whose editorial and reportorial responses were of such a nature as to prevent our placing them within either of the two other categories.[20] Each of the categories is broadly drawn and within each of them further refinements could be made.[21] In Table II we have classified the newspapers within each of these three categories in terms of their political orientation. Finally, in Table III, we have profiled the Critical newspapers in terms of the asserted reasons for their basic hostility to the *Spiegel* action. Nine specific reasons for criticizing the action were found to be most frequently cited by these newspapers. Indicated by percentages is the extent to which these twenty-one newspapers, as a whole, relied upon each of these complaints in justifying their condemnation of the public authorities.

Findings and discussion

Table I shows that during the first five days following the 26th October raids a clear majority (61·8 per cent) of the sample took an essentially hostile or negative view of the proceedings against *Der Spiegel*. Slightly less than 18 per cent of the sample endorsed the actions against the magazine. Among the Critical segment of our sample were the three best known and most prestigious West German dailies: the *Frankfurter Allgemeine Zeitung, Die Welt*, and the *Süddeutsche Zeitung*.

TABLE I

CLASSIFICATION OF SAMPLE BY EDITORIAL RESPONSE
TO THE SPIEGEL ACTION BETWEEN 27TH
AND 31ST OCTOBER, 1962

Classification	(N)	Newspapers in category*	Per cent
Critical	(21)	2, 3, 4, 7, 9, 10, 11, 12, 14, 17, 18, 20, 22, 25, 26, 28, 29, 30, 31, 32, 33	61·8
Sympathetic	(6)	1, 5, 6, 13, 15, 34	17·6
Unclassifiable	(7)	8, 16, 19, 21, 23, 24, 27	20·6
Total	(34)		100·0

* Newspapers as numbered in Appendix on page 449-51.

Only in a qualified sense does the classification in Table II demonstrate a correlation between editorial response and political orientation of the newspaper. There appears to be a tentative confirmation of the generalization that the 'leftist' oriented papers, as contrasted with the 'rightist' oriented papers, were more likely to be hostile to the actions against *Der Spiegel*. Thus the three pro-SPD newspapers in our sample were all classifiable as Critical; the one nationalist newspaper in our sample was classifiable as Sympathetic. Yet between these two poles in the 'left-right' spectrum, the correlation is less defined. Although one-third of the pro-CDU/CSU newspapers were Sympathetic with the actions against *Der Spiegel*, more than one-half (55·6 per cent) of this group refrained from developing a clearly classifiable position on the action. Also, the two pro-business newspapers, which cannot by any reasonable definition be regarded as 'leftist', took Critical positions. Significantly, the majority of the Critical newspapers in our sample are independent in their political orientation and include a number of prominent newspapers, such as the *Frankfurter Allgemeine Zeitung*, that had generally been supporters of the policies of the Adenauer governments.

The specifics of the *Spiegel* action substantially producing the criticism among the twenty-one Critical newspapers are indicated in Table III. It is apparent from this table that these newspapers were not uniformly agreed during the initial phase as to the reasons for questioning the action against *Der Spiegel*. Only one 'defect', the lapse of more than

TABLE II

DISTRIBUTION OF TABLE I CATEGORIES,
BY POLITICAL ORIENTATION

Political orientation	Critical		Sympathetic		Unclassifiable		Total		Per cent of total sample
	(N)	Per cent	(N)	Per cent	(N)	Per cent	(N)	Per cent	
Pro-CDU/CSU	(1)[a]	11·1	(3)[b]	33·3	(5)[c]	55·6	(9)	100	26·5
Pro-SPD	(3)[d]	100·0					(3)	100	8·8
Pro-business	(2)[e]	100·0					(2)	100	5·8
Nationalist			(1)[f]	100·0			(1)	100	2·9
Independent	(15)[g]	79·0	(2)[h]	10·5	(2)[i]	10·5	(19)	100	55·9

Newspapers in each group as numbered in the Appendix on page 449-51
[a] 22
[b] 1, 6, 15
[c] 8, 19, 21, 23, 27
[d] 9, 11, 31
[e] 10, 12
[f] 13
[g] 2, 3, 4, 7, 14, 17, 18, 20, 25, 26, 28, 29, 30, 32, 33
[h] 5, 34
[i] 16, 24

two weeks between the appearance of the incriminating article and the 26th October raids, was cited between 27th October and 31st October by a majority (52 per cent) of our sample as a primary basis for complaint against the public authorities. Taken as a whole, however, the nine elements listed in Table III and around which the preponderant criticism clustered rested on two distinct, but related, assumptions: (1) precedents were being followed in the *Spiegel* action that might jeopardize in the future the appropriate rights and functions of a free Press, and (2) 'acceptable' norms for the investigation of suspected violations of law appeared to have been sacrificed in favour of a discriminatory and 'politically inspired' investigation of a magazine that had long been a persistent and enterprising critic of certain policies and personalities (especially Franz Josef Strauss) of the successive Adenauer governments. Thus the night-time raids in themselves suggested a type of insensitivity on the part of the public authorities to the importance of the press in a participatory political system, an insensitivity which certain newspapers argued had broader implications involving the parallel between the timing of the raids and the 'midnight' arrests of the Nazi era. The complaint of pre-censorship, specifically forbidden in Article 5 of the Basic Law, stemmed from reports that during the night of 26th October the investigators had temporarily seized for examination the master proofs of the forthcoming issue of *Der Spiegel*. The impounding and searching of the archival material in the Hamburg office of *Der Spiegel* seemed to challenge the presumed privileged source of information for a free press. The temporary police occupation of the Hamburg offices and the provisional police monitoring of the internal and external communications systems of the Hamburg offices appeared by 31st October to be taking the form, intentionally or unintentionally, of a type of economic harassment, resulting in the interference with future operations, which would be financially disastrous for many press media.

But the Critical segment responded also out of a fear that 'political' or 'personal' considerations conditioned both the substance and the procedure of the investigation against *Der Spiegel*. The complaint that was voiced by the greatest percentage of the Critical newspapers – that too much time had elapsed between the appearance of the article and the 26th October action – implied the possibility that the investigation may have been partially intended as a 'retaliation' for the magazine's role in the Fibag Affair.[22] The seizure in Spain of Ahlers

TABLE III

PRIMARY CRITICISMS OF THE SPIEGEL ACTION BY THE
TWENTY-ONE 'CRITICAL' NEWSPAPERS BETWEEN
27TH AND 31ST OCTOBER, 1962

Criticism	Percentage of the twenty-one newspapers which singled out this factor
The lapse of two weeks between the publication of the Foertsch article and the *Spiegel* action	52
The alleged attempt by the investigators on the night of 26th October, 1962, to pre-censor the forthcoming issue (No. 45/1962) of *Der Spiegel*	39
Prolonged and extensive searching and examining of materials and archival data in the Hamburg office of *Der Spiegel*	39
Confusion and questionable legality surrounding the procedures used in securing the arrest in Spain of Conrad Ahlers	35
Failure of the investigators to effect immediate arrests also against possible collaborators of *Der Spiegel* in positions of public responsibility	35
The ambiguity of legal distinctions between freedom of the press and publication of 'state secrets'	26
Staging of the Bonn and Hamburg raids and arrests at night	26
Possibility that Franz Josef Strauss improperly influenced the *Spiegel* investigations	26
Temporary monitoring by public authorities, immediately after the 26th October raids, of telephone and intercom system of *Der Spiegel*'s Hamburg offices	22

suggested collusion on the part of the Spanish and West German authorities that had little regard for the niceties of legal or international practices, particularly when viewed in the context of the extradition agreement between West Germany and Spain, which precluded the rendition of persons accused of political crimes (including treason).

And, aside from the strictly legal question in the Ahlers incident, here was additional basis for suspecting that officials in Bonn had intervened in such a manner as to call into question the essential motivation of the *Spiegel* investigation. Both the West German Foreign Office and the Federal Prosecutor's Office had immediately denied responsibility for the intervention of the Spanish police in securing Ahlers. By 31st October, 1962, when it was known that the West German military attaché in Madrid had requested Spanish assistance in locating Ahlers, the Critical newspapers were no longer willing to discount the possibility of Strauss's personal involvement in the Ahlers incident in such a manner as to exceed his official responsibilities. The failure of the federal prosecution to bring charges promptly against those within the federal government who may have leaked 'state secrets' to *Der Spiegel* aggravated the suspicions among certain newspapers in the Critical category that the investigation was essentially designed to intimidate *Der Spiegel*.

Undoubtedly, the confused and contradictory account the press was receiving from the authorities about the various aspects of the investigation compounded the press criticism of the *Spiegel* action. At best, the official news releases reflected a poorly co-ordinated and hastily conceived investigation against *Der Spiegel*; at worst, the contradictions and omissions in the official releases hinted at a deliberate attempt to avoid answers to some embarrassing questions.[23]

Appendix

THE THIRTY-FOUR NEWSPAPERS CONSTITUTING THE SAMPLE
UPON WHICH TABLES I, II, AND III ARE CONSTRUCTED[a]

Newspaper	Place of publication	Political orientation	Circulation	Primary region of circulation
1. *Aachener Volkszeitung*	Aachen	CDU	79,327	Aachen and environs
2. *Der Abend*	Berlin	Independent-democratic	91,118	West Berlin
3. *Abendzeitung*	Munich	Independent	104,684	Bavaria, especially Munich
4. *Allgemeine Zeitung*	Mainz	Nonpartisan	106,369	Mainz and the 'Rheinhessen' region

5. *Badische Neueste Nachrichten*	Karlsruhe	Independent	130,245	Karlsruhe and environs
6. *Deutsche Tagespost*	Würzburg	Independent-Catholic	14,200	German Federal Republic, West Berlin, abroad
7. *Frankfurter Allgemeine Zeitung*	Frankfurt	Independent-liberal civic foundations	258,554	German Federal Republic, West Berlin, abroad
8. *Frankfurter Neue Presse*	Frankfurt	Independent (pro-CDU)[b]	110,301	German Federal Republic
9. *Frankfurter Rundschau*	Frankfurt	Nonpartisan, liberal (pro-SPD)	114,300[c]	Frankfurt and Rhine-Main area
10. *Handelsblatt*	Düsseldorf	Independent-business	33,500	German Federal Republic, West Berlin, abroad
11. *Hannoversche Presse*	Hanover	Independent (pro-SPD)	146,300[c]	Lower Saxony
12. *Industrie Kurier*[d]	Düsseldorf	Entrepreneurial-antisocialist	26,346	German Federal Republic, West Berlin
13. *Kasseler Post*	Kassel	Middle-class, nationalistic, independent	20,910	Kassel and environs
14. *Kölner Stadt-Anzeiger*	Cologne	Nonpartisan, independent	169,650[c]	Cologne and environs
15. *Kölnische Rundschau*	Cologne	Independent-Christian Democratic	161,067[c]	Cologne and environs
16. *Der Kurier*	Berlin	Independent	23,628	West Berlin
17. *Mannheimer Morgen*	Mannheim	Independent	132,164	Baden-Württemberg and Rhineland-Palatinate
18. *Der Mittag*	Düsseldorf	Independent-nonpartisan	59,300	German Federal Republic and neighbouring countries
19. *Münchener Merkur*	Munich	Independent (pro-CDU)	174,844	Munich and Bavaria
20. *Neue Rhein Zeitung (Neue Ruhr Zeitung)*[e]	Cologne	Independent	231,944	Cologne, Düsseldorf, and Aachen
21. *Rhein Zeitung*	Koblenz	Independent (pro-CDU)	177,898	North Rhineland-Palatinate
22. *Rheinische Post*	Düsseldorf	Christian Democratic	265,064	Düsseldorf and Rhine-Ruhr areas

23. *Ruhr-Nach-richten*	Dortmund	Independent-Christian	187,885	Rhineland, North Rhine-land-Westphalia
24. *Saarbruckener Allgemeine*	Saarbrucken	Independent	36,950	Saarland
25. *Süddeutsche Zeitung*	Munich	Nonpartisan-independent	224,188	Munich, South Bavaria, and German Federal Republic
26. *Stuttgarter Zeitung*	Stuttgart	Independent	143,577	Baden-Württem-burg
27. *Der Tag*	Berlin	Independent-Christian Democratic	24,083	West Berlin
28. *Die Welt*	Hamburg, Essen, Berlin	Independent	267,183	German Federal Republic, Berlin, abroad
29. *Weser Kurier*	Bremen	Independent-nonpartisan	119,321	Bremen and environs
30. *Westdeutsche Allgemeine*	Essen	Independent-nonpartisan	418,482	Ruhr area
31. *Westdeutsche Rundschau*	Wuppertal	Nonpartisan (pro-SPD)	13,180	Wuppertal and environs
32. *Westdeutsches Tagesblatt*	Dortmund	Independent	24,299	Dortmund, Hagen and Münster
33. *Westfälische Rundschau*	Dortmund	Neutral	228,551	Münster, Dort-mund and Arnsberg regions
34. *Wiesbadener Kurier*	Wiesbaden	Nonpartisan	63,378	Wiesbaden and environs

[a] Unless otherwise indicated, the source for the political orientation, circulation figures, and regions of primary circulation distribution is *Die deutsche Presse 1961*, Berlin, Duncker und Humblot, 1961. The 1961 edition was the most recently published edition prior to the Spiegel Affair.

[b] The indication in parentheses of a pro-party orientation suggests a general editorial sympathy with the views of that political party, even though the newspaper does not formally claim a party orientation. Wherever these references appear in this table, they are based on the author's judgment and material contained in *1963 Editor and Publisher Yearbook*, New York, Editor and Publisher Company, 1963, and Walter H. Mallory, ed., *Political Handbook of the World*, New York, Harper, 1961, pp. 78–80 (published for the American Council on Foreign Relations).

[c] Figures based on *Political Handbook of the World*.

[d] Appears four times weekly.

[e] Appears under both titles cited here.

3. The Audience for Election Television*

Jay G. Blumler and Denis McQuail

Introduction

Many different and conflicting images of the audience for political television have been propagated in recent years and vie with each other at present for acceptance. The controversy has arisen partly from the sheer size of the viewing public and its strategic importance for the competing parties and leaders. This has inevitably provoked speculation about the typical viewer's relationship to political materials: the degree of his interest in them and the nature of his response to them. In addition, the politicians and broadcasters who address the television audience cannot speak, as it were, to the empty air. They must sketch out some impression of the interests and capacities of the receivers of their words and pictures – especially since their own personal contacts with ordinary citizens are usually infrequent and unrepresentative.[1]

One image that has been generated by this situation portrays the viewer as a sitting duck – as an isolated component of an anonymous mass audience, the members of which are highly vulnerable to the persuasive torrents unleashed on television.[2] But a quite opposed image of the political viewer depicts him as the inhabitant of a strongly guarded fortress – shielded from influence by attitudes and loyalties that help to convert most messages into agencies for reinforcing whatever position he already holds dear.[3] Yet a third image presents the typical viewer as a heedless hedonist – as someone who uses television mainly to relax and be entertained, and whose indifference to politics dissipates the impact of any propaganda to which he may be exposed.[4] And finally, there still persists the classical notion of the follower of politics,

* Not previously published.

whether on television or elsewhere, as a conscientious democratic citizen – as someone who aims to base his political choices on rational grounds and on sifted informational materials. (Although it was once supposed that the findings of various voting studies had obliterated this last image,[5] it has recently enjoyed a modest revival, even in the writings of tough-minded political scientists.)[6]

It is not very satisfactory to allow speculation and intuition to dominate the discussion of the issues posed by these rival interpretations. Each is associated with allegations of fact which, in principle at least, should be empirically testable. The collection of relevant research evidence should also counteract some of those dangers which frequently accompany attempts to form very general notions of rather remote objects. In this case, for example, it could correct the tendency for different communicators to base their audience images merely on what it *suited* them to believe about the targets of their messages. And it should help to overcome a tendency to lose sight of important distinctions between the orientations and responses to political programming of different types of viewers.

We believe that the work of the Granada Television Research Unit at the University of Leeds[7] shows how research findings can shed light on the character of the audience for a defined body of television output. Major surveys were carried out during the British General Elections of 1959 and 1964, and the results were published in *Television and the Political Image*[8] and in *Television in Politics: Its Uses and Influence*,[9] respectively.

The Leeds Election Study of 1959

The earlier of the two investigations was conceived essentially as an 'effects study'. That is, it was designed to examine the impact on voters of their exposure to election propaganda – both on television and in other media. For this purpose, interviews were conducted before and after the 1959 campaign with a large sample of voters drawn from two Yorkshire constituencies. The research strategy rested on the assumption that influence from a communication source could be inferred when a positive and progressive association was found between some measure of campaign change in the political outlook of electors and some measure of the degree of their exposure to the source concerned.

The study's measures of campaign change were devised with meticulous care. Developments in the respondents' voting intentions played a relatively minor part in the analysis, since it was appreciated in advance that something like three quarters of the electorate would probably remain faithful to their preferred parties throughout the campaign. Consequently, a more discriminating scale of attitudes towards the Conservative and Labour Parties was prepared, which could register opinion shifts less drastic than a switch of votes. The individual items in the scale were chosen by procedures which ensured that they would reflect the criteria voters themselves used when judging the merits of the major parties. In the event, this instrument proved both valid (respondents' attitude scores were very closely associated with the votes they had cast on Polling Day) and sensitive (it succeeded in tapping sample-wide movements of opinion during the campaign). Three other indicators of campaign change were also deployed in the analysis: a knowledge test (which required the respondents to identify the parties that had put forward certain specified election policy proposals); a measure of voters' issue priorities; and a scale of their attitudes to the rival party leaders. But the main focal points of this attempt to examine the role of the mass media in the 1959 campaign were the test of political knowledge and the scale of party attitudes.

In gist, what did investigators find? No noteworthy developments emerged from the voting front as such. Within the body of respondents (amounting to 27 per cent of the sample) who had taken some kind of voting decision during the campaign, each party's gains were more or less cancelled out by its losses. There had been a substantial increase, however, in the average level of political information during the campaign period. Out of eight policies about which the respondents were questioned, for example, an average of 4·1 were correctly identified in the pre-campaign interview, compared with 4·7 after Polling Day. And the measure of party attitudes had registered a definite, though modest, swing of opinion in favour of the Conservative Party. On a scale with a scoring range of +9 to −9, there had been an average pro-Conservative shift of one whole point among the Conservative voters and of half a point among the Labour voters.

And how, if at all, had television, the press, radio, and the local constituency campaigns contributed to these developments? The principal findings and conclusions of the study are set out in the three passages from *Television and the Political Image* which appear below. The first considers how political information is communicated to voters during an election campaign. The second examines the responses of political attitudes to campaign stimuli. And the third outlines the general conclusions which Joseph Trenaman and Denis McQuail reached about the impact of election propaganda on the audience.

Television enlarges political knowledge[10]

The results of this study force us to make a sharp distinction between the cognitive level of perception, at which a person consciously augments his knowledge of political policies and programmes, and the deeper levels of attitude and conviction. . . .

It is important to make this distinction because of the line of demarcation that marks off our findings in the cognitive field from those in the attitude field. The General Election campaign added to the electors' knowledge of the party policies in both constituencies alike, and there is a significant association between these increments and the viewing of political programmes on television. There is a progression in the findings so that the more programmes people viewed the more they learned, and this was true whether we confine the comparison to Party election broadcasts, or to political news bulletins, or the whole output. The link with the Party election broadcasts is a little stronger than with the news bulletins. For the whole sample, the correlation is not large, being slightly more significant among men than women, i.e. ·113 (standard error ·05). Among the 27 per cent of the electors who were classed as 'changers' [in vote intentions], the correlation is ·32, and it is much the same among the sub-samples for each constituency. . . .

What of the other campaign influences, how did they affect changes in knowledge of policies? We could find no significant link with any other factor, either in the whole sample, among men or women, or in the changers. The corresponding correlations were: —·06 between increases in knowledge and exposure to political material on sound radio, ·04 with newspaper reading and ·03 with local participation, none of them anywhere near significant.

How is this difference to be explained? Sound radio was a primary source of news for less than a quarter of Northern electors and this quarter of the population is different from the three-quarters with television, being on the whole, slightly older, poorer and rather less well-educated than the television audience. They would, for those reasons, be less likely to learn quickly, and any effects would be swamped by the majority of the non-listening public. As a further check, we separated off the people without television who relied on sound radio and plotted out their gain in knowledge of policies against their listening to the political programmes on the radio. Again, we could find no significant connection between the two.

The absence of any comparable link with newspaper reading is more difficult to explain. A far greater volume of political news and comment appeared in the Press than in any other medium; nineteen out of every twenty people read a newspaper and in our constituencies 51 per cent read some political news. An analysis of the Press coverage of the campaign . . . shows that, although its mass was great, it included a good deal of personal comment and of sidelights on election affairs which may have served to obscure the real political messages of the parties. A more probable explanation is that an entirely different set of associations surrounds political broadcasting compared with Press campaigning. Thirty-eight years of BBC impartiality in controversial matters, the careful balancing of party representation in the broadcasts and the alternation of programmes between parties, all this lends to the television situation an atmosphere of restrained public debate, very different from the partisan campaigning so often associated with the popular press. This argument is supported by two statistics in our findings which, though small in degree, are of some significance. The people who read about politics in the newspapers tend to be Conservative rather than Labour (the correlation is ·28) partly because people in higher grade jobs read more in the Press and such people are also more inclined to Conservatism. Yet the more they read about the campaign in the newspapers the weaker their loyalty to the Conservative Party became; this was expressed by a negative correlation, consistent in both constituencies, of −·16 and this despite the fact that there was an overall strengthening of Conservative attitudes. The inference is that the average reader was slightly repelled rather than persuaded by what often appeared to be a partisan presentation of political news in the Press. And since pro-Conservative newspapers are in a majority and have a larger readership than pro-Labour papers the reaction was anti-Conservative. The point is underlined by the fact that there was a suggestion of a similar (anti-Labour) reaction among readers of a pro-Labour newspaper.

The effectiveness of the local campaign is sometimes underestimated in these days of pre-occupation with mass persuasion.

... How far the parties succeeded in impressing local aspects of the struggle on their electors we cannot say, for our questions were based on national problems and policies, but so far as these were concerned we could trace no significant impact on attitude changes from local sources.

As a result of this outpouring of political persuasion, people saw more clearly not only what the main policies of the parties were; they gained a better understanding of the nature of the parties, of their attitudes to the public and to public problems. And yet, of all the channels through which this information was conveyed, only television produced a direct and progressive effect.

The insulation of attitudes[11]

Attitudes changed. In all a surprisingly large proportion of the electorate (27 per cent) made some change from their voting intention in September 1959. Although political 'swings' are very small in their net effect, they have been shown ... to conceal quite considerable cross-movements between parties, even in the campaign period. The two major parties, engaged in an all-out struggle, involved the whole of their supporters in a conflict which resulted in the Right pushing back the Left; different aspects of the party and leader images strengthened and weakened under the impact of the barrage of persuasion. The barrage was fired from every public medium and through many private channels until it fell upon nearly every member of the electorate.

With three incidental and slight exceptions, no medium or source of propaganda or combination of sources, had any ascertainable effect upon any attitude changes. And attitude changes were certainly large enough to be susceptible of effect. However one splits the sample or isolates single groups, like changers, or people heavily exposed to the campaign, no direct connection can be traced between the message and the effect. One might argue that it is a mistake to expect changes to be progressively related to exposure; but, even if we consider merely the presence of absence of some sources of persuasion, like the viewing of Party election broadcasts, still no significance emerges. The attitude measures have been rigorously validated against voting behaviour, and found to be extremely sensitive. The campaign measures have been tested against each other, as for instance, television against sound radio exposure, or age and sex against occupation, and found to show the associations which were to be expected in the population as a whole. The absence of any association is, therefore, not the result of inadequate measures. Perhaps electors' memories or the interviewing techniques were at fault? Yet the informants' recollections of political broadcasts viewed over the three-week period produced estimates of audience proportions which correspond very closely to the national estimates published by the BBC. Having examined every possibility of error and every combination of analysis, we have reached the conclusion that within the frame of reference set up in our experiment, political change was neither related to the degree of exposure nor to any particular programmes or argument put forward by the parties.

The three incidental exceptions to this finding are most clearly seen in the group of changers. One slight tendency to react away from the Conservative campaigning of some newspaper editors has already been mentioned. Another effect (a borderline correlation of ·12, but consistent in sub-groups) was a tendency for electors to rate Mr Gaitskell's personal qualities rather higher after the campaign, the more they had participated in local political activities. One cannot say whether they were cause and effect or whether the sort of person who took an interest in what was going on in his own constituency and also, as we know he did, saw more of political television, and read a great deal more than the average elector of the newspaper reports, and heard more of the party broadcasts on sound radio, revised his views as a general consequence of this exposure or for some more remote reason motivating all of these activities. The third exception was also connected with Mr Gaitskell's personal standing and relates it positively but slightly to the viewing of television political broadcasts (again the correlation is only ·12 – of borderline significance but consistent in sub-groups).

It is, perhaps, not easy to see that what is established here is not merely an absence of cause and effect but *a definite and consistent barrier between sources of communication and movements of attitude in the political field at the General Election.* It is not that the causal connections between television or the sources of information and campaign changes were insignificant – rather that the two were persistently and in a highly significant way disconnected. It is not easy to convey the impression made by table after table of statistics of exposure plotted against statistics of change, the two fields varying independently, so that at every level of exposure one finds every variation in degrees of attitude change.

To put this finding thoroughly to the test, a number of combinations of factors were considered. Thinking that it might be the total weight of the barrage rather than the accurate fire of any particular propaganda that might count in the end, we plotted out the total recorded exposure for each elector in the sample against every type of attitude change, counting not only movements towards or away from either major party, but also total change in any direction. Again, no consistent association could be found. Among the changers we distinguished those who moved from support of one party to another over the period of the campaign, and whose interest in politics and exposure to the campaigning were typical of the solid mass of constant voters; in another category are those who remained doubtful or abstained from voting, whose general level of interest was low, and who tended to avoid or, by some means, see less of the arguments of the parties. By taking these two groups together, one appears to have a small measure of association between political change and exposure to propaganda. But it is not found as a factor operating differentially *within* these groups, building up increasing change with increasing exposure. So far as we can see, it is a group difference which does not form any exception to the principle of resistance found in the sample as a whole.

Conclusions[12]

We are, therefore, driven to two conclusions. The first is that political attitudes have some protective device which, once the elector has recognized an election campaign as propaganda aimed at persuading him, can apparently screen off and, at least temporarily, suppress any direct effect. Secondly, behind this protective screen there seems to be an element of independent judgment and free choice at work. Free will, which by definition resists persuasion, is usually the last factor to be considered by social scientists, the authors not excepted, if indeed it is considered at all.

Such independence of thought must operate within limits. The individual is subject to many influences. He has inborn tendencies which dispose him to react to events in a particular way and connect him to his antecedents. He is partly a product of his upbringing, in which his early education and his family background are vital factors. He is partly a product of his work or profession which has disciplined and shaped his capacities and activities. He is partly a member of a community in which he lives and works, and it, too, conditions his responses. He is probably a member of a family unit and there are interactions between members of this close group to which he contributes and which affect him. The relative importance of these different factors must vary from one individual to another and will not remain constant in any one. Beyond these factors and beyond the uniqueness of their combinations in him, how far is the individual a distinctive person with independent judgment? Here, we can only say that the evidence we have quoted points to the operation of some quite important factor which is not included in any of the variables we have tried to assess. Its effect suggests that it may be what, for the want of a more precise term, we call individual judgment. . . .

In so far as the ordinary elector *is* making up his own mind in an election, how does he view the arguments put before him and what is he looking for? . . .

The elector approaches the campaign with an assumption that his political decision, if it has not already been made, is going to be made privately, independently of any persuasion so far as he can manage it. What he is looking for in a political party is a capacity to govern. We see this in the analysis of his attitudes, in listening to his comments on the television broadcasts he saw, from other studies in this field, and from his general approach to the election situation.

He is looking for a whole, coherent policy, for a general picture of what the party as a whole stands for, and it is this general impression, and not particular items of policy, that weigh most with him. This is particularly true of working men and women who are accustomed to look at life in this comprehensive way. Their minds may not be trained to undertake classificatory analysis, as one soon discovers in social studies. They judge situations as a whole, as they judge the merits of a football team or the qualities of the boss or the honesty of a shopkeeper. They look for moral qualities as well as intellectual and they are particularly concerned with the practical working out of any proposals put before them. Their interest in concrete points or particular human illustrations does not contradict this comprehensive view. The concrete items they remember and recount, or fit into an accepted frame of reference. The comprehensive view is an almost involuntary process. . . .

The consequences of this holistic approach is that the election programmes and individual items of the campaign matter less than the general impression created by a party. We found no connection between what electors believed to be particularly important issues, or even changes in emphasis, and voting or attitude movements. After the election, people tended to choose issues to which the parties had devoted a good deal of attention, but, as with their knowledge of policies, this choice had no direct bearing on their attitudes.

It might be objected that the Conservative Party did not unfold many specific policies by which electors could judge their case. Perhaps they did not need to do so since they were claiming no more than the right to carry on as they had done before. People understood this and were evidently sufficiently satisfied not to want to make a change. A party which has been in opposition for eight years or more has a more difficult problem. It has either to make its case by a process of explanation or wait for a situation in which the electorate is so anxious to get rid of the other party that they are prepared to take it on trust. One of the lessons of this study is that any process of explanation might best proceed on the assumption that the matter is more important than the manner, and that the elector is looking for a simple, coherent and united policy not necessarily identified with his own pocket.

The Leeds Election Study of 1964

When in 1964 the authors[13] designed a follow-up to the 1959 survey, we aimed to study the audience for political television from a previously little explored angle. We were not content merely to count the number of election programmes seen by voters and to observe how their attitudes had responded to what they had watched. In addition, we wished to clarify the *point* of political viewing – the reasons why people were prepared to follow a campaign on television and in other media. It is true that the essential elements of the 'effects design' of 1959 were replicated in the 1964 survey, but this was supplemented by, and to some extent integrated with, yet another research orientation: what is sometimes called the 'uses and gratifications approach' to the study of mass communications. In the field of political television this committed us to an attempt to answer such questions as the following: Why do viewers watch or avoid party broadcasts? In what programme forms do they prefer politicians to appear? How do they feel about being the targets of political persuasion? Are they sceptical about what they see and hear through TV, or do they rely on TV to help them to make sense in some way of the claims and counter-claims of party arguments?

At least three fresh perspectives on the audience for election television were opened up by the adoption of this approach. First the distribution within the audience of different types and levels of motivation for following politics on TV could be charted. Second, the connections between measured motivations for political viewing and actual patterns of such viewing could be traced. And third, the role of motivational forces in facilitating or impeding the process of persuasion itself could be examined.

In the British context there was a particular reason for following this third line of analysis. In this country the simultaneous transmission of party broadcasts on all available channels brings election materials to within an easy reach of virtually every citizen. It follows that the body of electors who are heavily exposed to televised propaganda may be quite heterogeneous, consisting both of keen followers of *politics* and of inveterate addicts of *television*. And if political attitudes in these two different parts of the audience were to respond quite differently to the parties' persuasive efforts, it would be vital to try to allow for this when studying the impact of election television. It was in this sense that we expected the uses and gratifications approach to refine our search for television effects.

Why people watch political programmes

The members of the 1964 sample were drawn from the same Yorkshire constituencies in which the 1959 survey had been staged. In the pre-campaign round of interviewing an attempt was made both to establish the respondents' particular reasons for following the election on TV and to measure the strength of their general motivation for doing so. Table I, which presents some of the evidence that was collected about these matters, is based on the responses of the television owners in the sample to (a) a check-list of eight reasons for watching party election broadcasts and (b) a check-list of nine reasons for avoiding them, which could apply to their viewing behaviour during the forthcoming campaign.

An analysis of the patterns of endorsement to the first check-list located four main clusters of reasons for following an election on TV. Two of them stood for motives relating expected viewing to considerations of party allegiance and choice: 'to remind me of my party's strong points' and 'to help make up my mind how to vote'. In the main these items attracted quite different types of electors. The former were

TABLE I

TV OWNERS' REASONS FOR WATCHING AND AVOIDING
PARTY ELECTION BROADCASTS

Reasons for watching*	%	Reasons for avoiding*	%
1. To see what some party will do if it gets into power.	55	1. Because my mind is already made up.	37
2. To keep up with the main issues of the day.	52	2. Because you can't always trust what politicians tell you on television.	35
3. To judge what political leaders are like.	51	3. Because I am not much interested in politics.	26
4. To remind me of my party's strong points.	36	4. Because they hardly ever have anything new to say.	24
5. To judge who is likely to win the election.	31	5. Because I prefer to relax when watching television.	23
6. To help make up my mind how to vote.	26	6. Because some speakers talk over one's head.	20
7. To enjoy the excitement of the election race.	24	7. Because some speakers talk down to the audience.	16
8. To use as ammunition in arguments with others.	10	8. Because I dislike being 'got at' by politicians.	14
		9. Because politics should not intrude into the home and family affairs.	9

N = 677 TV set owners.

* The respondents could endorse more than one reason.

stable and highly partisan supporters of whatever parties they preferred. The latter were more likely to switch allegiance during the campaign and to register lukewarm political feelings on our party attitude scales. The evidence, then, disclosed no overriding tendency for the bulk of voters to seek a reinforcement of their existing loyalties through political viewing. It was apparently a mistake to look for some single standard pattern of electoral motivation on these matters. Instead it was as if the respondents were distributed along a continuum, with a group of staunch reinforcement seekers occupying one pole and a smaller number of vote-guidance seekers located at the opposite pole.

The remaining electors were more likely to be moved by one or both of two other sets of reasons for receiving political materials. One reflected the excitement engendered by the competitive ebb and flow of a campaign. For example, many of those individuals who would watch party broadcasts 'to judge who is likely to win the election' also wanted 'to enjoy the excitement of the election race'. However, this excitement-seeking cluster of motivation also applied to only a minority of the television owners.

The approach of the majority to political viewing was reflected mainly in the endorsements of the first three items on the list of reasons for watching party broadcasts – which were strongly inter-correlated with each other. This pattern seemed to reflect the desire of many voters to use television to undertake what we called a surveillance of the political environment. Such a motive had both a general and a more specific connotation. In the more general sense, watching political television was most analogous to tuning in to the news. It was the kind of thing that an individual might do just to keep in touch with wider trends affecting his country's welfare. But, more specifically, it was also a way of finding out what might be in store for him, his family, or some group he identified with, should one or another party win an election and obtain power.

These findings suggested that a citizen could be motivated to seek information about his political environment, even if he was neither undecided enough to need guidance in voting, nor committed enough to wish to be reminded of his party's strong points. The kernel of sense embedded in this approach to political communications is emphasized in the following passage of *Television in Politics*:

Despite its obvious lack of sophistication, there is a sense in which the approach of these voters to propaganda may be said to be guided by rationality. Apparently, many of them were interested less in judging the competence of the parties (although that was sometimes involved) than in forming some impression of how political developments might affect the tangible circumstances of their own lives in the near future. That is why there was so much concern to find out from political broadcasts what the parties proposed 'to do' – about rents, pensions, schools, mortgages, roads, etc. And if trying to plan one's life in the light of information about the various circumstances that can affect it – including those which result from the measures of government – is rational, then this should count as a rational basis for following political television.

These findings do not conflict with other sources of evidence about the attitudes of the general public towards politics, although they illustrate the need to ensure that the depth and extent of political apathy is not exaggerated. It is one thing to insist that many people engage in their personal affairs to the exclusion of most forms of political activity and another to imply that they perceive little or no *connection* between the world of politics and their immediate concerns. According to our evidence, many citizens recognize that political developments impinge upon their personal circumstances, and they wish to acquire information that might help them to grasp how they are likely to be affected by the connection. After all, if most electors regarded politics as irrelevant to their material needs, it would be difficult to explain why voting behaviour is associated so powerfully with socio-economic status.

We do not claim that the drive of the average citizen to obtain political information is usually strong or intense. Many other pursuits are undoubtedly far more attractive and absorbing. Nevertheless, a moderate degree of interest in surveillance of the political environment does seem to lie behind much exposure to political broadcasting. This may help to explain why many voters actually acquire previously unfamiliar information about party policies through exposure to political television during an election campaign.[14]

The check-list of reasons for avoiding party broadcasts (see the right-hand side of Table I) speaks more or less for itself. Except for a general lack of interest in politics, and the feeling of many electors that they already knew how they would vote, the main sources of hostility to televised propaganda were a mistrust of its unreliability and boredom with its predictability. When both check-lists were considered together, however, they highlighted yet another important feature of the audience's outlook on political broadcasting: its essential ambivalence. Thus, the various satisfactions that viewers derived from following politics on television were counteracted by a number of reservations and misgivings.

It was this mixture that provided the key to our attempt to measure the *strength* of an individual's disposition to receive political materials through television. Conceiving this as an outcome of a set of pulls and pushes, a measure of strength of motivation for following election television was derived from the *ratio* of (a) the total number of reasons for watching party broadcasts that each respondent had endorsed to (b) the total number of reasons for avoiding them that he had endorsed. After calculating this index it was found that the sample could be split into five groups, varying in rated motivation from 'very strong' to 'very weak'.[15] Table II shows how these groups were distributed in the sample, and it also compares their responses to a direct question about their intentions to view party broadcasts during the forthcoming campaign.

TABLE II

LEVELS OF MOTIVATION TO VIEW ELECTION TV
AMONG TELEVISION OWNERS

	Motivation				
	Very strong	Moder-ately strong	Medium	Moder-ately weak	Very weak
Distribution of the groups among TV owners in the sample	18%	25%	28%	15%	15% = 101%
Proportions in each group stating they would 'definitely' view at least one party election broadcast	86%	65%	52%	35%	15%

Political viewing: the links between attitudes and behaviour. Despite their seemingly direct relevance, it could not be taken for granted that viewers' expressed motives for following politics on television would prove on their own to be accurate predictors of the use made of campaign communications or of reactions to them. Discrepancies between measures of interest in certain programmes and actual viewing behaviour frequently crop up in the findings of audience research.[16] In addition, as we have noted earlier, the electors who are highly exposed to TV propaganda are a disparate group, combining the active followers of politics with the heavy users of television sets. To clarify the structuring of the audience for election television and for campaign materials in other media, our analysis concentrated on the role of four dispositional factors, some of which interacted with each other.

First of all, there is the viewer's general propensity to use television as an all-purpose medium – for news, entertainment and enlightenment. For example, a division of the sample into groupings of heavy, medium and light viewers respectively (based on the total number of hours devoted to viewing of any kind in an average week) yielded the following figures for the average number of party election broadcasts seen during the 1964 campaign (out of 13 transmitted): 5·6; 4·9; 3·5.

This tendency for general habits of viewing to determine the degree of exposure to political programmes posed in a very sharp form the issue of the independent influence of a second variable – our measure of strength of motivation to follow election television. In fact it transpired that the relationship between the index of customary weight of all-purpose viewing and the index of strength of motivation was *inverse*: that is, with each step down the motivational scale more habitually heavy viewers were represented. This meant that the two measures could work against each other, so that their effects on the viewing of political material would not only be hard to identify separately but could cancel each other out. Nevertheless, we found that a higher level of motivation did go with higher average levels of political viewing. For example, the average number of party election broadcasts seen had ranged from 5·4 and 5·6 for those rated 'very strong' and 'moderately strong' in motivation, to 4·8 in the 'medium' group, 4·5 among those who were 'moderately weak' in motivation, and to only 3·0 in the 'very weak' group. Table III allows us to see the independent effect of each variable once the other is held constant. As we had originally postulated, a high level of exposure to political TV could be due either to habit or to keenness – factors which, in the political field at least, can be accounted opposites.

A third possible influence on voters' use of political communications stemmed from the distinction in our sample between those individuals who were seeking a reinforcement of existing party loyalties and those who wanted help in deciding how to vote. We detected signs, for example, that some of the so-called reinforcement seekers had taken definite steps to avoid a broadcast put out by a party they opposed. Table IV overleaf shows that in fact these two groups sought their political information from a somewhat different mixture of sources. According to the top row, for example, the vote-guidance seekers had tuned in to party election broadcasts slightly more often than did the reinforcement seekers. Although the difference was not in itself large, its full significance emerged when the other forms of campaign

TABLE III

AVERAGE NUMBER OF PARTY ELECTION BROADCASTS SEEN:
BY CUSTOMARY WEIGHT OF VIEWING AND BY STRENGTH
OF MOTIVATION FOR FOLLOWING ELECTION TELEVISION

Customary weight of viewing	Motivation				
	Very strong	Moderately strong	Medium	Moderately weak	Very weak
Heavy viewers	5·6	6·6	5·3	6·2	3·6
Medium viewers	6·0	5·4	4·8	4·0	2·9
Light viewers	4·0	4·3	3·9	2·6	1·9

TABLE IV

POLITICAL MOTIVES FOR RECEIVING BROADCAST PROPAGANDA
AND EXPOSURE TO THE CAMPAIGN

	Vote guidance seekers %	Reinforcement seekers %
Saw four or more party election broadcasts	65	61
Saw the main news at least three times per week	59	65
Saw late election news bulletins at least three times per week	18	25
Scored three or more for viewing non-party political programmes*	48	52
Scored two or more for exposure to politics in the press†	49	60
N=	109	174

* The range of possible scores was 0–14.
† The range of possible scores was 0–5.

exposure were considered. On each of the other measures of media use, the reinforcement seekers registered higher exposure scores than did the vote-guidance seekers. The difference was most marked for following campaign news in the press. Evidently, those individuals who wished to bolster their already established party preferences were strongly attracted to a medium that could express editorial opinions more freely.

Yet a fourth determinant of voters' reliance on different communication channels emerged when those individuals who thought they were likely to be asked for their political views by their acquaintances, and who had actually discussed the 1964 campaign with somebody, were compared with the main body of the sample who did not qualify as 'opinion leaders' according to these criteria. The results, which appear in Table V, can be interpreted most suitably by distinguishing between less and more specialized sources of political information. The former includes party broadcasts and the main news, exposure to which was influenced only slightly by the role of opinion leadership. Into the latter category must be placed the late election news, non-party election television (programmes that had been put out by the broadcasting authorities themselves) and the press, since each of these had been used quite extensively by the sample's opinion leaders.

TABLE V

OPINION LEADERSHIP AND EXPOSURE TO THE CAMPAIGN

	Opinion leaders %	Not opinion leaders %
Saw four or more party election broadcasts	62	52
Saw the main news at least three times per week	67	57
Saw late election news bulletins at least three times per week	29	19
Scored three or more for viewing non-party political programmes	54	37
Scored two or more for exposure to politics in the press	83	42
N=	79	540

Perhaps one general conclusion can safely be drawn from much of this evidence. The commonly accepted conception of the viewing public as a vast and undifferentiated mass audience must be modified. This point is emphasized in the following passage of *Television in Politics*:

Is the viewing public a mass audience?[17]

... It is true that, so long as present policies of control continue, the composition of audiences for political programmes on television is likely to remain much more representative of the electorate than, say, the readership groups of different newspapers (the major alternative means of communicating political information and comment). Nevertheless, we have found, by focusing on attitudinal parameters, that the television audience does tend to be structured somewhat more than is often supposed – particularly when different kinds of programmes are taken into account. We have seen, for example, that one element in the party broadcast audience is a highly motivated stream of viewers. We have seen that the vote-guidance seekers are differentially dependent on party broadcasts, while the opinion leaders turn more often to the programmes which are originated by the broadcasting authorities themselves. All in all, it appears that the audience for political television, though large and heterogeneous, can be divided in significant ways, the important distinctions relating to interests and motives which have not been given sufficient weight in the past. A fuller appreciation of the degree to which members of the viewing public do have positive expectations, needs, likes and dislikes, which can and do affect their behaviour, must modify any conception of the television audience as simply an undifferentiated mass.

How motivation filters effects. Does the impact of propaganda on a voter's political outlook depend in any way on his reasons for attending to it? This question represented one of the guiding preoccupations of the 1964 investigation. It is worth noting that if we had not injected motivational variables into our analysis of media effects, the basic pattern of the 1959 findings would have simply been repeated. This would have shown that TV had enlarged knowledge but failed to shape attitudes. In 1964 as in 1959, then, average gains in political information had increased with rising levels of exposure to election television.

And although many respondents were more favourably disposed to the Labour Party after the campaign than before (just as their predecessors of 1959 had veered towards the Conservatives), none of our records of exposure to the mass media was significantly related to that particular shift of opinion.

Nevertheless, the 1964 survey did tap two forms of opinion change which had not been detected in 1959. One concerned the issues that people thought the government should tackle with most urgency. There was a striking increase during the campaign in the sample's awareness of the need for economic growth (a prominent theme of Labour propaganda at the time) and a less pronounced increase in the emphasis given to two Conservative issues – those of retaining the nuclear deterrent and maintaining a high standard of living. Our ability to plot a second type of change arose from a decision to ask the respondents to rate the Liberal Party, as well as the two major parties in the field. And the results showed that public attitudes towards the Liberals had improved dramatically between the pre-campaign and post-election interviews.

But could any of these developments be traced to the influence of television or of other campaign sources? It was at this point that the introduction of a motivational distinction into the analysis proved vital. The variable that helped us to pin-point the impact of propaganda was our index of 'strength of motivation to follow election television', and the critical distinction on it was a dichotomy between those who had been rated 'strong' in motivation and those whose motivation had been measured as 'medium' or 'weak'.

When this line was drawn, it was found that the more highly motivated group had been exclusively involved in a complex array of 'effects' which linked (a) changes in issue salience with (b) altered attitudes towards the major parties, and (c) exposure to party broadcasts. For example, those individuals who had become more favourably disposed to the Labour Party had also responded more positively to the issue of economic growth. Contrariwise, those individuals whose party attitudes had shifted in favour of the Conservatives had also become more sensitive to the nuclear deterrent and standard of living issues. Moreover, some of these changes in issue salience were significantly associated in turn with certain measures of exposure to party broadcasts. Those highly motivated respondents who had become more aware of the need for economic growth had also seen an above-average number of Labour broadcasts, while those who had responded to the standard of living issue had seen an above-average number of Conservative broadcasts. And this cluster of associations applied only to the strongly motivated members of the sample; no equivalent relationships emerged when a parallel analysis of the less politically minded respondents was carried out.

An instance of the impact of television on the political attitudes of this larger body of less keen voters had to be sought elsewhere. It was found in the development of their attitudes to the Liberal Party. Their tendency to look more favourably on the Liberals was significantly associated with measures of their exposure to political programmes at the one per cent level (meaning that such a relationship would have occurred by chance only once in a hundred times). And this effect was concentrated exclusively among those viewers whose motivations to follow the campaign had been classified as 'medium' or 'weak'. Table VI presents some figures which illustrate the role of motivation in this finding. The top row of figures, representing the strongly motivated viewers, shows only a random relationship between average shift in Liberal Party attitude score and the number of Liberal broadcasts watched by respondents. But the bottom row records a steady increase in the magnitude of favourable attitude change with each increase in the number of political programmes viewed by the less politically involved electors.[18]

TABLE VI

PRO LIBERAL ATTITUDE SHIFT AND EXPOSURE TO
LIBERAL BROADCASTS BY STRENGTH OF MOTIVATION
TO FOLLOW ELECTION TV

	Number of Liberal election broadcasts seen			
Average scores of pro Liberal attitude change* among those rated:	0	1	2	3
Strong in motivation	+0·23	−0·06	+0·76	+0·20
Medium or weak in motivation	+0·23	+0·72	+0·94	+1·30

* Scores on the Liberal Party attitude scale could range from +5 to −4.

Apparently television was not quite so impotent to influence political attitudes as had been supposed in 1959. But no single effect was common to the entire sample; the strongly motivated voters had responded in one direction and the less keen in another. How could the emergence of this pattern be explained? An attempt to provide an answer appears in the following passage of *Television in Politics*:

Strength of motivation as a condition of communication effects[19]

A prominent feature of the evidence presented in this chapter is the differential role of motivational level in mediating the impact of political communications upon party attitudes. Whereas opinions of the strongly motivated voters were influenced by major party propaganda, the politically less keen electors responded favourably to presentation of the Liberal case.... Clearly, strength of motivation is not related straightforwardly to persuasibility. Why, then, did motivational level act differently in the cases of Liberal shift and [shifting attitudes to the major parties]?

The discovery that the most powerful television effects were experienced by the politically more indifferent electors was consistent with one of the hypotheses that influenced the design of this study. In a situation where much television viewing arises from habit, and where the political content of the medium is suddenly enlarged by the launching of an election campaign, the group most likely to undergo a substantial increase in exposure to political communications will consist of those individuals who would not normally seek out political programmes but who are unwilling to give up viewing television during an election. If our measure of motivation is accurate, almost the whole of this group should be found within the weakly motivated portion of the sample. It could be deduced, moreover, from our major quantitative hypothesis – that a greater degree of exposure will be reflected in a greater degree of attitude change – that the most substantial shifts overall should occur among those for whom the election campaign provides relatively the biggest increase in exposure above the level of political communication previously received. This captive, mildly tolerant, but rather passive audience relies differentially on television for its political impressions, since the positive effort required to seek out campaign materials from the press or elsewhere would be out of character in the case of individuals who have no burning desire for political enlightenment. Consequently, it was mainly television, and only marginally the press and the local campaign, which precipitated the major attitude change that affected the less motivated respondents.

It is not only their distinctive communications habits that explain the responses of the less keen electors to the 1964 campaign. Their prior orientation to politics may have played a part as well. As a consequence of political indifference, they may have been less well-prepared to meet broadcast propaganda with counter-arguments of their own. This source of vulnerability could have been reinforced by the unpurposive political viewing in which they are probably inclined to indulge. As Bernard Berelson has pointed out, when exposure to a communication is accidental rather than deliberate, '. . . defences against new ideas are presumably weaker because preconceptions are not so pervasively present.' Recent research in the United States has underlined this interpretation by indicating that distracted exposure to a communication can enhance its persuasive force by stifling the *sub voce* framing of counter-arguments against its message. Ironically, the successful penetration of our less interested respondents by televised propaganda may have been due in part to the relatively casual attention they paid when their sets were tuned in to party election broadcasts.

But why was the Liberal Party the sole beneficiary of these effects? It may have gained from its central position in what is essentially a two-party system. If major political loyalties are bipolar, it is easier for adherents of the two foci of identification, in so far as their political outlook changes at all, to shift in favour of the middle and neutrally conceived party, than to look more favourably upon their traditional rivals. Social elements in the viewing situation could work in the same direction. A viewer in a Labour household who expressed appreciation of a Conservative broadcast might provoke ridicule that would be withheld if he voiced a similar degree of approval for a Liberal broadcast.

In addition, lukewarm feelings about the major parties among the politically indifferent electors may have facilitated their pro-Liberal responses. In other words, their receptivity to Liberal propaganda may have arisen from mistrust of the dominant forces in British politics, which they found embodied in the Conservative and Labour Parties. Some support for this interpretation is provided in . . . [the fact that when] pre-campaign vote intention is held constant, and the Labour and Conservative Party attitude scores of the less motivated respondents are compared with those of the strongly motivated electors, we find that in every case except one . . . the former are lower on the average than the latter. . . .

It may also be important that between election campaigns the Liberal Party receives less coverage in the mass media (including television) than it does at election time. It follows that in the inter-election period the average citizen, who is not actively seeking political information but taking it as it comes, will find the Liberal Party getting more remote from his thoughts. He will become less aware of its political stance, and his attitudes towards it will become more fluid and in a sense more out of touch. If so, it is understandable that such an elector should be strongly affected when he receives a considerably stepped-up dosage of exposure to the ideas and leaders of the Liberal Party. This happens particularly on television, which, unlike the press, is obliged to devote a definite proportion of its attention to the Liberals during an election campaign.

Some factual evidence in support of this interpretation . . . [is available]. At the pre-election stage, those who were measured as weak or moderate in motivation had lower Liberal Party attitude scores, on the average, than did those who were rated strong in motivation. . . .

During the campaign, however, the gap in ratings of the Liberal Party closed. The average Liberal Party attitude score of the strongly motivated group as a whole moved up by 0·27 of a point [from 0·52] to 0·79, while that of the less motivated group moved up by 0·56 [from 0·25] to 0·81. The effect of the campaign in this case was to bring the less strongly motivated electors into line with the rest of the sample. It should be noted that no such movement affected attitudes towards the major parties. It seems that the campaign – partly because the Liberals were thrust suddenly into the limelight, and partly because the group we are considering found itself watching them on television whether it wanted to or not – gave these viewers a chance to assess the third party afresh and to bring their attitudes up to date.

No part of this structure of interpretation is undermined by the discovery of a connection between exposure to the campaign and partisanship shift in the strongly motivated group of electors. That link was forged with the help of elements which are likely to prove influential only among politically keen voters. It involved an adjustment of party attitudes to the issue content of the 1964 campaign – which presupposes a capacity to grasp and to respond to arguments mounted in such terms. In addition, some of the developments in this group may be interpreted most suitably as reinforcement effects, which tend again to be sought and experienced mainly by those individuals whose political opinions are already rather firm and definite. Change in response to exposure was less pronounced in this group than among the more indifferent electors, because their own political views could be brought into play more readily whenever campaign materials were being received. And perhaps they were impressed less by Liberal propaganda than by the efforts of the Conservative and Labour Parties, because they tend to perceive campaigning itself as an activity in which the major parties expose their differences in terms of defined issues.

A reassessment of images of the audience for political television

How do those different audience images that were outlined in the introduction to this essay stand up in the light of the findings we have reported? Each appears to have taken what was at best a partial truth and elevated it into a vividly dramatic generalization about the mass audience as a whole.

The picture of the political viewer as a 'sitting duck' for party propaganda, for example, is faintly mirrored in the discovery that in 1964 the less keen electors responded favourably to the appearances of Liberal spokesmen on television. But although this points to a definite potential for influence, it can only be interpreted as a susceptibility of certain groups to limited kinds of change under certain conditions. Similarly, while some viewers may be accurately portrayed as the inhabitants of a protective fortress, it is now clear that only the members of a rather special minority, consisting mainly of zealous partisans, actually seek or achieve a reinforcement of their existing beliefs when using the mass media. Comparable reservations apply to the images of viewers as either heedless hedonists or as rational political animals. The very individuals who often give priority to entertainment over current affairs can also appreciate their own stake in political events and wish to be informed about them. Certainly the audience for political broadcasts is not merely an artefact of the high popularity of TV, nor, at election times at least, is indifference to political communication the predominant attitude. As we have argued earlier, there is even a sense in which the public's response to election television may be described as rational in orientation. Yet there are also many dimensions of his political outlook which the average voter will be willing to re-examine in a spirit of calculation only rarely, if at all. It is doubtful, therefore, whether political television can really be said to attract a typical audience member, since the patrons of campaign programmes vary widely in their motives, their interest levels, their readiness to deliberate about what they have seen, and in the kinds of influence to which they are open or resistant.

Moreover, the 'uses and gratifications approach' has highlighted one critical feature of viewers' expectations that each of the available images of the mass audience had completely disregarded. Perhaps the most striking and well founded conclusions we have reached concerns the *ambivalence* of audience attitudes to politics on television. It is not that electors are merely bored, cynical or uninterested, nor even (despite gradations of keenness) that they invariably divide up neatly into the politically-minded and the apathetic. It is rather that the same individual is both attracted by ways in which television can serve his political needs and repelled by elements that seem endemic to the existing system of political communication – the predictability of party positions, the boredom with what is over-familiar or superfluous, the fact of involuntary exposure to politics at certain times when other satisfactions are sought from television, and the difficulty of entering into any real dialogue with politicians.

The viewer's ambivalence, then, reflects the tensions inherent in a situation where an individual is aware, however, dimly, of certain political needs and yet limited in his opportunities to satisfy them. As we have pointed out, those political needs vary from person to person. The evidence suggests that many citizens simply wish in a general way to keep the political scene under review, especially where developments may affect their own lives, while distinct minorities are either concerned to find support for existing loyalties or are genuinely looking for guidance in coming to their voting decisions. For a fulfilment of their requirements, many electors are inclined to turn especially to television. Television politics happens to be readily available as part of almost everyone's normal pattern of media use, and it is usually geared to the capacities of the man in the street. Tension arises, however, from a lack of trust in televised propaganda as a source of the desired information. Many people are suspicious of the manipulative intentions of politicians and uneasy about their own vulnerability. Although research findings suggest that electoral resistance to persuasion is usually strong, the ordinary voter does not yet seem able to share this confidence in the impregnability of his own defences.

Any attempt to conceive a more accurate image of the audience to replace those which have dominated our thinking in the past must take full account of this fact. If there is a typical customer for political television, he is someone who sees himself as reliant on the mass media for meeting varying political needs and yet unsure about how well he is being served and uncertain about how far he can trust what he is told. In fact the element which has so far been noticeably absent from characterizations of the audience is an understanding of how the individual sees his own situation and how he perceives those who address him in it. The later work of the Television Research Unit at the University of Leeds has been concerned to fill this gap.

4. The National Press and Partisan Change*

David Butler and Donald Stokes

The following passage is taken from a chapter on 'The Flow of Political Information' in our book *Political Change in Britain*. This book rests much of its argument on the findings of a nationwide panel study conducted in the mid-'sixties. Over 2,000 electors from all over Britain answered hour-long interviews in the summer of 1963. They were reinterviewed after the General Election in October 1964 and again after the General Election in March 1966. We were very conscious of the difficulties of isolating the impact of specific stimuli in the mass media – in television even more than in the national press. Yet we hope that we have shown some new possibilities of measuring how far the press does or does not exercise a partisan impact on voting behaviour.

Partisan dispositions and the national press

Eight national morning newspapers are available at breakfast time to the overwhelming bulk of British households.[1] In 1964 they provided 92 per cent of the 18 million morning newspapers sold each day and they reached over 80 per cent of households – a higher proportion than in any other country.[2] Because of this centralization, fully established for a couple of generations, Britain has a smaller total of independent morning newspapers than any comparable nation.[3] On the other hand, the individual citizen, with at least eight different papers reaching his locality, has an unusual range of choice. One consequence

* First published in David Butler and Donald Stokes, *Political Change in Britain* (Macmillan, London, 1969), pp. 229–44.

of the centralization of the press is that the market tends to be divided up, each paper angling its presentation to a limited segment of the population. And since each paper has its own independent newsgathering and editorial resources, each manages to be fairly strongly differentiated from its rivals in style and in politics.

The mass circulation papers are all explicit in their partisanship, and all to some degree carry their partisanship from their editorial to their news columns. Though seldom slavish in their party othodoxy, the *Daily Express*, *Daily Mail*, *Daily Telegraph* and *Daily Sketch* are Conservative while the *Daily Mirror* and *Daily Herald/Sun*[4] are Labour. The 'élite' papers, *The Times* and the *Guardian*, are harder to place. In 1964 and 1966 *The Times*, in the end, gave very qualified advice to vote Conservative while the *Guardian* abandoned its traditional Liberalism to ask support for the Labour Party.

A newspaper's readers tend to be remarkably faithful to it. Most people read only one morning newspaper and go on buying it for very long periods. Morning newspaper circulations, despite vast promotion efforts, only edge up or down by, at most, a few per cent a year. In 1964 the circulation of every national daily was within 10 per cent of where it had been four years earlier, apart from the *Daily Sketch* (down 20 per cent) and the *Guardian* (up 20 per cent). Although it is a simple thing to change one's delivery order at the newsagent or pick up a different paper at the station bookstall, few people do so. Less than 4 per cent of our sample admitted to ever having switched morning newspapers. Indeed, over successive interviews only the distribution of characteristics such as age and sex showed greater stability than readership of the morning dailies.

What bearing does the partisanship of a newspaper have on the partisan preferences of its readers? It is clear, to begin with, that the partisan bias of the newspapers is reflected fairly faithfully in the biases of their readers. In every case, as Table I shows, a preponderant group of readers of the mass circulation dailies shared the paper's traditional partisanship – overwhelmingly in the case of the *Telegraph* and the *Sun* and by a substantial margin in every other case except that of the *Guardian* (which has a long Liberal tradition). If only those who had read their paper for ten years or more were considered, the proportion of readers favouring the paper's choice of party was higher in almost every case. The proportion of Conservative-minded *Express* readers rose from 48 per cent to 52 per cent; and for the *Telegraph* from

TABLE I

PARTISANSHIP OF NEWSPAPER READERS, 1963
(in percentages)

Readers' Partisanship	Conservative				Labour		Less committed	
	Telegraph	Sketch	Mail	Express	Mirror*	Herald/Sun	Times	Guardian
Conservative	78	54	48	48	18	9	60	23
Labour	9	29	28	38	66	83	20	33
Liberal	6	13	18	10	11	3	10	37
Other or none	7	4	6	4	5	5	10	7
	100% (n=111)	100% (n=48)	100% (n=190)	100% (n=434)	100% (n=445)	100% (n=128)	100% (n=10)	100% (n=31)

* This figure includes *Daily Record*, the Glasgow version of the *Daily Mirror*.

78 per cent to 82 per cent. The proportion of Labour-inclined *Sun* readers rose from 83% to 86%. The two exceptions are not surprising: the veteran readers of the *Guardian* appeared unpersuaded by the paper's switch to Labour support – even more of them were Liberal. The veteran readers of the *Mirror* were not more Labour-inclined than the new young readers the paper had won in the last ten years.

The combined circulation of the Conservative papers exceeded by half that of the Labour papers. Whether this gave the Conservatives an advantage, and if so whether it was a short-term or a long-term one, are questions which we can answer only by considering the effects of reading a partisan newspaper. It is nonetheless true that more than a fifth of Labour's supporters in 1963 were exposed to a Conservative newspaper, whereas only a tenth of the Conservatives' supporters were exposed to a Labour paper. Because the *Mirror*'s angling towards youth is balanced by the elderly readership bequeathed to the *Sun* by the *Herald*, there is little difference of age between the readership of the two groups of partisan newspapers.

The cross-reading of newspapers favouring the other party is complemented by the phenomenon of people who do not recognize that their newspaper is partisan. We asked readers of each paper which party it supported. Very few gave the 'wrong' party, but, apart from readers of the *Telegraph* and the *Herald*, only a bare majority, if that, named the 'correct' party, as Table II shows. Well over a third of all readers thought that their paper was neutral.

The profiles of reader partisanship in Table I and of attributed party bias in Table II bear obvious resemblances. The papers with the most purely partisan followings, the *Telegraph* and the *Herald/Sun*, are also those whose partisan angle is seen most clearly. The relationship between the reader's own agreement with his paper and his detection of party bias is summarized in Table III, which shows that it is the readers who agree with their newspaper's bias who are most likely to perceive it. But the table also shows that many readers who see clearly what their paper's bias is do not themselves agree with it. Conscious cross-reading is the daily habit of a good many British electors.

All of this scarcely begins to unravel the problem of the press's partisan influence, a problem that is made more difficult by the fact that readership and partisanship may both reach far back into the past. The distinctive partisan colouring of those who read the morning dailies could be taken as evidence of the press's influence only if it is clear that

TABLE II

READER'S RECOGNITION OF HIS NEWSPAPER'S PARTISANSHIP, 1963

(in percentages)

Attributed partisanship	Telegraph	Sketch	Mail	Express	Mirror	Herald/Sun	Times	Guardian
Conservative	72%	25%	52%	44%	1%	—	30%	—
Labour	—	11	2	4	52	76%	—	17%
Liberal	1	2	2	1	—	—	—	37
None	24	54	36	42	34	18	70	43
Don't know	3	8	8	9	13	6	—	3
	100% (n=111)	100% (n=48)	100% (n=191)	100% (n=434)	100% (n=448)	100% (n=127)	100% (n=10)	100% (n=30)

TABLE III

DETECTION OF NEWSPAPER BIAS BY AGREEMENT OF
READER'S PARTISANSHIP WITH HIS NEWSPAPER'S
PARTISANSHIP, 1963

	Reader has partisanship consistent with newspaper's	Reader does not have partisanship consistent with newspaper's
Reader perceives newspaper's partisanship	57%	44%
Reader doesn't perceive newspaper's partisanship	43%	56%
	100% (*n*=812)	100% (*n*=333)

the choice of a newspaper preceded the choice of a party. But it is, of course, quite possible either for a paper to be chosen for its partisanship or for the choice of both paper and party to reflect the influence of a family or class milieu. In such a case, the press might play a role in conserving a party tie; it would not have created it.

These alternative possibilities supply the only plausible explanations for the way in which parents' partisanship is echoed in their children's adult choice of newspaper, as shown by Table IV. The reflection of early family partisanship in newspapers taken by voters from politicized homes casts a new light on the political distinctness of those who read the morning dailies, since the correlation seen here is the work of factors that will also increase this distinctness without any need for newspapers to have influenced their readers. The correlation shown in Table IV cannot result from the voter's family having influenced the paper's editors. And today's editors cannot have influenced the family in the voter's childhood. The correlation is most likely to have been produced by the family's passing on a partisanship which the child has matched by his choice of paper, or by its passing on a more general social location to which both paper and party are appropriate. If the voter's report on his family is accepted, it is clear that newspapers often profit from, rather than shape, their readers' party ties.

TABLE IV

PARTISANSHIP OF PRESENT NEWSPAPER

BY PARTY OF CHILDHOOD FAMILY, 1963

Respondent now reads†	Family was*		
	Conservative	Other	Labour
Conservative newspaper	66%	55%	35%
Labour newspaper	22%	36%	55%
Other	12%	9%	10%
	100%	100%	100%
	(n=393)	(n=589)	(n=405)

*'Conservative' or 'Labour' homes are those in which both parents had this partisanship or one did and the other had none. 'Other' homes are those of mixed, Liberal or no partisanship.

† 'Conservative' or 'Labour' readers are those seeing only newspapers from one partisan group. 'Other' readers are those who see newspapers from both or neither party group.

We should not, however, discount the press's role in conserving partisanship. When the agreement of a child with parent is examined separately for those who read a paper consistent with their parent's party and those who do not, as is done in Table V, we see an impressive difference in the survival of parental partisanship according to the child's current reading habits. Too simple a view ought not to be taken of these findings; once again the adults may have kept or changed his partisan reading habits to accord with his evolving partisan beliefs or his changed social conditions. Nonetheless, it is difficult to think that the conserving and reinforcing effect of the partisan press has nothing to do with these differences.

What is more, the formative role of the press may be somewhat larger in the case of voters whose political legacy from their family was mixed or relatively weak. Table VI divides such people by whether they now read a Conservative or Labour newspaper. The cleavage in the current partisanship of these two groups is at least suggestive of the influence of the press in forming or sustaining a party tie.

The ambiguities which surround the analysis of the press's role in forming and changing party ties are less severe when we turn to short-term movements of partisanship. The chance to dispel some of these

TABLE V

PARTY SUPPORT BY PARTISANSHIP OF RESPONDENT'S FAMILY
AND RESPONDENT'S PRESENT NEWSPAPER, 1963

| Respondent's own party | Family was* | | | |
| | Conservative Respondent's newspaper is† | | Labour Respondent's newspaper is† | |
	Conservative	Labour	Conservative	Labour
Conservative	79%	44%	25%	5%
Labour	13%	42%	62%	86%
Other‡	8%	14%	13%	9%
	100% (n=259)	100% (n=85)	100% (n=141)	100% (n=221)

* See fn. *, Table IV.
† See fn. †, Table IV.
‡ Includes Liberals, other parties and voters without a party.

TABLE VI

PARTY SUPPORT BY PARTISANSHIP OF NEWSPAPER
AMONG PERSONS FROM OTHER THAN CONSERVATIVE
AND LABOUR FAMILIES, 1963

| Respondent's own partisanship | Partisanship of newspaper* | |
	Conservative	Labour
Conservative	48%	14%
Labour	28%	66%
Other†	24%	20%
	100% (n=321)	100% (n=231)

*'Conservative' or 'Labour' readers are those who see no morning paper except one or more from their own partisan group.
†Includes Liberals, other parties and voters without a party.

uncertainties in treating shorter term changes was greatly enhanced by the fact that our study bridged a period when newspaper partisanship fluctuated greatly in intensity if not in direction. In the winter of 1962–3 the national press became unprecedentedly critical of the Conservative Government. Its attacks on the handling of general public issues may have owed something to a particular grievance that had grown up between Fleet Street and Downing Street. Mr Macmillan seems to have felt that he had been hounded by quite unjustified press innuendos into accepting the resignation of Mr Galbraith, a junior minister indirectly involved in the Vassall spy scandal. The Radcliffe tribunal which the Prime Minister set up to enquire into the affair was given terms of reference which were interpreted by much of Fleet Street as a mandate to pillory the press, and in the course of the hearings two reporters were sent to prison for refusing to reveal their sources. Journalistic *amour propre* was involved and it was widely argued that the splash treatment given to the Profumo scandal in June 1963 had some elements of revenge in it. Whether or not that was the case, it is plain that the Conservatives, who could normally rely on reasonably sympathetic coverage in most of the national press, were at an exceptional disadvantage throughout the year 1963.

By 1964 the tide had turned. The Conservative press had, with the disappearance of Mr Macmillan, abandoned any vendetta it may have had against the Government. There is no doubt that those exposed to the mass media in 1964 were receiving substantially less anti-Conservative material than in 1963. The difference can be demonstrated by a tabulation of the tone and number of political lead stories and editorial comments. The results of such a content analysis are presented in Table VII. As the table shows, in Conservative papers the balance of party advantage was not too far from even in 1963, but by 1964, and above all in the month before the election, it was almost as rare to find an article giving comfort to the other side in a Conservative as in a Labour paper. The picture of the Conservative papers rallying to their traditional party attachment is shown graphically in Figure I, which combines the measurements for the four Conservative papers and two Labour papers. The graph makes clear that we have chanced upon a kind of 'natural experiment' under which the readers of Conservative newspapers were exposed to very different political coverage in mid-1963 and in late 1964, whereas readers of Labour papers were treated to an almost perfectly unrelieved pro-Labour view in both periods. Since

TABLE VII

PARTISANSHIP IN FRONT-PAGE ARTICLES AND EDITORIAL COMMENTS*

| | Conservative papers | | | | | | | | Labour papers | | | |
| | Telegraph | | Sketch | | Mail | | Express | | Herald/Sun | | Mirror | |
	Pro govt	Anti govt	Pro govt	Anti govt	Pro govt	Anti govt	Pro govt	Anti govt	Pro govt	Anti govt	Pro govt	Anti govt
Lead story												
March–May 1963	10	3	2	2	4	4	3	8	0	10	1	4
July 15–October 15, 1964	13	4	10	0	6	2	8	1	0	12	1	14
September 15–October 15, 1964	8	0	8	0	4	2	3	1	0	9	1	9
Other front page story												
March–May 1963	7	5	1	3	5	2	0	6	0	6	0	1
July 15–October 15, 1964	19	2	4	0	9	1	8	1	0	7	0	6
September 15–October 15, 1964	11	1	3	0	5	1	6	1	0	4	0	3
Editorial												
March–May 1963	18	3	5	2	8	4	15	16	2	15	3	9
July 15–October 15, 1964	35	0	17	0	18	2	23	3	0	30	0	11
September 15–October 15, 1964	17	0	9	0	14	0	11	2	0	13	0	3

*The figures in this table are for the number of stories of each type which appeared in each paper in each time period. For the purposes of this table only articles with fairly specific party connotations have been counted. Even some which bore on contentious questions but were strictly neutral in tone have been excluded. Articles suggesting that the Government had done something praiseworthy or that contained bad news about the Opposition's fortunes are classed as pro-government. Articles that suggested the reverse are classed as anti-government.

the Conservatives did in fact gain in support during these fifteen months, it is natural to wonder whether this variation in stimulus was not in part responsible.

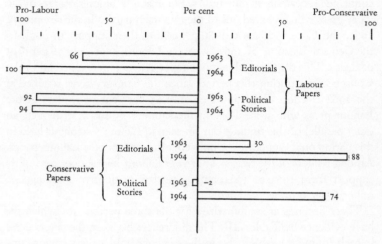

FIGURE I

Direction of partisanship of editorials and news stories
of Labour and Conservative newspapers, 1963 and 1964

Each bar of the figure is formed by subtracting the percentage of editorials or political stories in a given period that was inconsistent with the papers' normal partisanship from the percentage consistent with this partisanship. '1963' refers to the three-month period from 1st March to 31st May, '1964' to the three-month period from 15th July to 15th October. For this figure we have combined 'lead' stories and other front-page political stories.

The press and partisan change

We may assess the short-run influence of the press by examining changes of preference among readers of Tory and Labour papers. These changes give unmistakable evidence of the stronger attraction which a party that is favoured by a given paper has for the paper's readers. Those who already support the party are more likely to remain steadfast; those not already supporters are more likely to become so. The nature of these findings can be suggested by the physical analogy of magnetic force. Readers who are already close to their paper's party will tend to be held close; those at some distance will tend to be pulled towards it.

The tendency of a reader to keep to his newspaper's partisanship is confirmed repeatedly in our studies. For example, among readers of the Tory press who favoured one of the two main parties in the summer of 1963, the Conservatives kept 86 per cent of their support through to the General Election of 1964, whereas Labour kept only 76 per cent of theirs. This difference does not simply reflect a general trend to the Conservatives during this period, since the Conservatives retained at the 1964 election the support of only 63 per cent of readers of the Labour press who were Tory in the summer of 1963. Moreover, an exact parallel of this finding can be seen in Labour's stronger hold in this period on its supporters who were also readers of a Labour paper. Among readers of the *Mirror* or *Herald* Labour kept 84 per cent of its support from 1963 to 1964; among readers of the five Tory papers, only 76 per cent, as we have seen.

These findings are summarized for the three periods for which we have evidence by Table VIII. The differences between the percentages in each row of the table attest to the stronger hold a party has on supporters who read a paper favourable to it. In each of these periods the erosion of the parties' strength was decidedly more marked among supporters who were exposed to papers whose partisanship contradicted their own.

TABLE VIII

STABILITY OF MAJOR PARTY PREFERENCE
BY CONSISTENCY OF OWN AND PAPER'S
PARTISANSHIP

Proportion retaining preference from	Among readers of the partisan press whose initial preferences were	
	Consistent with their paper's	Inconsistent with their paper's
1959 to 1963	83%	63%
1963 to 1964	85%	73%
1964 to 1966	86%	81%

There is equally general evidence of the dynamic attraction a party has for uncommitted electors who read a paper favourable to it. For example, among electors who did not have a major-party preference in the summer of 1963 but who ended up voting for one of the major parties in 1964, the Conservatives won a substantial majority of votes among readers of the Tory press and Labour a substantial majority among readers of the Labour press. And the voter who made a straight switch between the major parties in this period was more likely to have gone from Labour to the Conservatives if he read a Tory paper and from the Conservatives to Labour if he read a Labour paper.

These findings are summarized for the three intervals of change within our studies by Tables IX and X. The entries of the rows of Table IX show that the newly-crystallized party preferences in each of

TABLE IX

CRYSTALLIZATION OF PREFERENCE AMONG READERS
OF PARTISAN PRESS WHO WERE PREVIOUSLY
UNCOMMITTED

Period of crystallization	Moved towards their paper's party	Moved towards opposite party	Totals
1959–63	66%	34%	100%
1963–64	63%	37%	100%
1964–66	73%	27%	100%

TABLE X

MOVEMENTS OF SUPPORT BETWEEN MAJOR
PARTIES AMONG READERS OF THE
PARTISAN PRESS

Proportion switching between major parties	Among major party supporters whose initial preferences were	
	inconsistent with their paper's	consistent with their paper's
1959 to 1963	19%	4%
1963 to 1964	11%	5%
1964 to 1966	10%	3%

these periods tended to follow the party bias of the reader's paper; those who ended one of these periods in a major-party camp, but who began it outside either camp, were more likely to have joined the Conservatives if they read a Tory paper, Labour if they read a Labour paper. The entries of Table X make the complementary point that the likelihood of an elector's leaving one camp for the other was in each of these periods measurably greater if he were moving towards the party supported by his paper rather than away from it. These findings convey a clear sense of the greater pull of a party for the elector whose normal reading practices expose him to a paper favouring it.

On the other hand, these findings do not imply that the readers of each group of partisan papers are moving towards a single, homogeneous preference. In fact, the process of change implied by Tables VIII, IX, and X will be in rough equilibrium when the division of party preference within each group of readers falls a good deal short of homogeneity. To clarify the reasons for this let us divide the readers of papers with a common editorial slant into two groups: those whose preferences agreed with their paper's and those whose preferences did not – either because they supported the other party or the Liberals or because they did not have a preference. Let us denote by m_1 the relative proportion or mass of readers falling in the first of these groups, by m_2 the mass falling into the second. And let us denote by p_1 the probability that a reader who supports his paper's party will move away from it over a given period and by p_2 the probability that a reader who is not aligned with his paper's partisanship will become so over this same period (see Fig. II). In other words, we have reduced a fairly complex set of changes to the simplest kind of process, one involving only two 'states' and two 'transition probabilities' describing the rates of change between these states.

What the evidence of Tables VIII, IX and X tells us is that p_2 tends to exceed p_1, that is, that non-supporters tend to move towards their paper's party at a higher rate than supporters move away from it. This relationship is of course very much prey to the influence of short-run electoral tides, which typically flow in both readership groups at once. Unless there were large-scale and appropriately timed transfers of readers between the newspaper groups themselves, or unless change were to come entirely from non-readers of the party press (ideas that are implausible on their face), swings of party fortune could be achieved only by a raising and lowering of p_1 and p_2, and we shall see that these

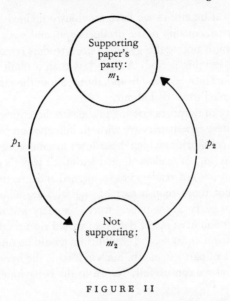

FIGURE II

changes tend to occur in both readership groups together. But these swings do not obscure the underlying tendency of the reader of a partisan newspaper to move towards, rather than away from, his paper's party.

And yet this tendency may not increase the partisan one-sidedness of a readership group at all. The key to this apparent puzzle is that among such a group those who are already aligned with their paper's editorial view are more numerous than those who are not. Hence, a lower *rate* of defection can produce an actual *number* of defectors that is as large as the number of the party's new recruits from readers who were previously not aligned with it. The way such offsetting movements can yield a rough dynamic equilibrium is illustrated by changes of partisanship among readers of the Labour press between the general elections of 1964 and 1966. The chance that a reader who failed to vote Labour in 1964 would support the party in 1966 was almost twice as large as the chance that a reader who voted Labour in 1964 would fail to do so in 1966. And yet, since the readers of the Labour press who were already aligned with the party were twice as numerous as those who were not, the resulting transfers of strength to and from Labour were almost perfectly offsetting. These exchanges are summarized in terms of the statistical quantities we have previously defined by Figure III where the virtual equality of the products p_1m_1 and p_2m_2 indicates that Labour's strength among this group of press readers remained in rough equilibrium over this period. A little less than a tenth of the entire group of readers moved away from Labour; about the same fraction of all readers moved towards Labour.

The equality of numbers flowing in the two directions by no means implies that these newspapers are without influence on party strength. The dynamic equilibrium which these flows sustain is one under which the proportion (m_1) of readers aligned with their paper's party exceeds the proportion (m_2) of readers not so aligned and greatly exceeds the proportion (not more than a part of m_2) who are aligned with the opposite major party. If the papers were to somehow *de*magnetize the parties, the probability (p_1) of defection would rise; there would be a massive flow from m_1 to m_2 and equilibrium would be restored at very different levels of party strength. Such at least is the hypothesis.

It is here that we can usefully return to the behaviour of the Con-

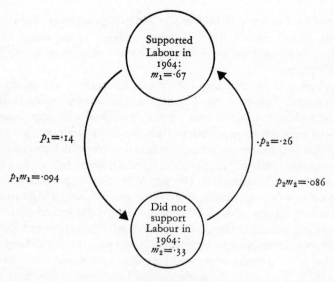

FIGURE III

Transfers of strength to and from Labour Party among readers of Labour newspapers between General Elections of 1964 and 1966

servative press in the dark days of 1963 and examine the flows of party strength in the specific periods for which we have evidence. Is it possible that by 1963 the Tory papers had to some degree 'demagnetized' the parties for their readers, with a consequent loss of Conservative strength? When we reconstruct the partisan shifts of their readers between 1959 and 1963, the deterioration of Tory strength is indeed impressive. To begin with, and quite against the general pattern of the findings we have presented, the rate of defection from the Conservatives was actually higher than the rate of the attraction among readers of the Tory press. As Figure IV shows, the probability that a reader who had supported the party in 1959 would leave it by 1963 was almost half again higher than the probability that a reader who had not supported the Conservatives in 1959 would be ready to do so in 1963. Applied to the preponderant share which the Tories had of such readers in 1959, this desertion rate produced a substantial haemorrhaging of party strength.

Any idea that this was the only portal through which the Conserva-

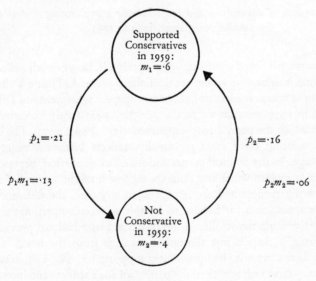

FIGURE IV

Transfers of strength to and from Conservative Party among readers of Conservative newspapers, 1959 to 1963

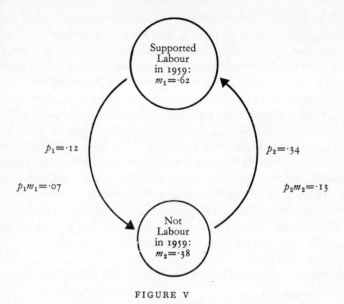

FIGURE V

Transfers of strength to and from Labour Party among readers of
Labour newspapers, 1959 to 1963

tives' strength ebbed away during this period is, however, dispelled by
comparable figures for readers of the Labour press. As Figure V shows,
the rate at which readers of Labour newspapers who were not Labour
voters in 1959 were drawn to the party by 1963 vastly exceeded the
rate at which the party's 1959 supporters were drawn away. The huge
gap separating these rates presumably reflects Labour's 'objective'
advantages in the political events and issues of the period, beyond the
greater attraction which our findings suggest it might 'normally' have
had among readers of Labour papers. In any case, the difference of
rates was sufficient for Labour to be able to recruit many more new
supporters from the smaller group of readers who had not previously
supported it than it lost through defections from the much larger
group of readers who had previously supported it. The Conservative
press may have demagnetized the parties for their readers and increased
the loss of Tory strength. But there was also a parallel gain of Labour
strength among readers of the Labour papers.

We may gain added insight into the effects of the unusually mixed

treatment of politics in the Conservative press by early 1963 if we
compare the rates of change of the 1959–63 period with those of the
1963–4 period. This comparison, as set out in Table XI, does show
a remarkable shift of the rates of Conservative gain and loss among

TABLE XI

RATES OF CHANGE OF PARTY PREFERENCE AMONG
READERS OF THE PARTISAN PRESS

	1959–63	1963–64
Among readers of Conservative papers:		
Probability of Conservatives losing supporter (p_1)	0·21	0·14
Probability of Conservatives gaining supporter (p_2)	0·16	0·21
Among readers of Labour papers:		
Probability of Labour losing supporter (p_1)	0·12	0·15
Probability of Labour gaining supporter (p_2)	0·34	0·30

readers of the Tory press. In the earlier period, as we have seen, the
rate of defection sufficiently exceeded the rate of renewal to produce a
sharp Tory loss. But as the line taken by the Conservative press
hardened over the 1963–4 period there was a dramatic reversal of these
proportions. The rate of gain did not exceed the rate of new loss by
enough in this period to account for the greater number of readers
already aligned with the Conservatives and produce a net gain for the
Tories. Here again, the advantage which a favoured party enjoyed in
terms of rates of change did no more than sustain its strength, and we
shall not find in this group the source of the mild Tory revival before
the 1964 election. And yet the shifting rates of change among readers
of the Conservative papers – contrasting with the more stable rates
among readers of Labour papers – do suggest that the disaffection of
the Tory press somewhat demagnetized the parties for their readers and
permitted a short-term run-off of Conservative support in the middle
years of the 1959 Parliament. The evidence of this particular loss
strengthens the view of the importance which the partisan papers
customarily have in sustaining their party's preponderant support
among their readers.

We may therefore attribute to the press some role in changing the
relative strength of the parties in the short run as well as in forming and

conserving more enduring allegiances. Yet it would be wrong to see most short-term political changes as the product of short-term angling by the press. The parallel movements of party strength among readers of both groups of partisan newspapers suggest that readers are absorbing more than their editor's bias. A great deal of common information flows out to the mass British electorate through media which are heavily overlapping and which are describing political issues and events that they have seldom done anything to shape.

Notes and Sources

Approaches to the Historical Development of Mass Media Studies

1. Bernard Berelson, 'The State of Communications Research', *Public Opinion Quarterly*, Vol. 23 (1959), pp. 1–6. Reprinted in Lewis Anthony Dexter and David Manning White (eds.), *People, Society and Mass Communications* (New York: Free Press, 1964).

2. Paul F. Lazarsfeld, Bernard Berelson and Hazel Gaudet, *The People's Choice* (New York: Columbia University Press, 1944).

3. See Elihu Katz and Paul F. Lazarsfeld, *Personal Influence* (Glencoe: Free Press, 1955), especially Section One, 'Images of the Mass Communications Process'. See also Elihu Katz, 'Communications Research and the Image of Society: Convergence of Two Traditions', *American Journal of Sociology*, Vol. 65 (1960), pp. 435–40. This is reprinted in Dexter and White (eds.), op. cit.

4. David Manning White, 'Mass Communications Research: A View in Perspective', in Dexter and White (eds.), op. cit.

5. Berelson takes 1935 as marking a watershed in the development of public opinion research. See Bernard Berelson, 'The Study of Public Opinion', in Leonard D. White (ed.), *The State of the Social Sciences* (Chicago: University of Chicago Press, 1956). See also Wilbur L. Schramm, 'Twenty Years of Journalism Research', *Public Opinion Quarterly*, Vol. 21 (1957), pp. 91–107.

6. Melvin L. DeFleur, *Theories of Mass Communication* (New York: David McKay, 1966).

7. Terence H. Qualter, *Propaganda and Psychological Warfare* (New York: Random House, 1962), especially Chapter 2, 'The Development of Propaganda'.

8. Edward A. Shils, 'The Study of the Primary Group', in Daniel Lerner and Harold D. Lasswell (eds.), *The Policy Sciences* (Stanford: Stanford University Press, 1951).

9. See the bibliography in Qualter, op. cit. A representative work is A. J. Mackenzie, *Propaganda Boom* (London: Right Book Club, 1938).

10. Some historical notes on the experimental method are given by E. Boring, 'The Nature and History of Experimental Control', *American Journal of Psychology*, Vol. 67 (1954), pp. 573–89. See also R. L. Solomon,

499

'An Extension of Control Group Design', *Psychological Bulletin*, Vol. 46 (1949), pp. 137–50.

11. A representative work is Carl I. Hovland, Arthur A. Lumsdaine and Fred D. Sheffield, *Experiments in Mass Communications* (Princeton: Princeton University Press, 1949). A section from this book is reprinted as 'Short-Time and Long-Time Effects of an Orientation Film', in Bernard Berelson and Morris Janowitz (eds.), *Reader in Public Opinion and Communication* (New York: Free Press, 1966).

12. For a discussion, see Herbert H. Hyman and Paul B. Sheatsley, 'Why Information Campaigns Fail', *Public Opinion Quarterly*, Vol. 11 (1947), pp. 412–23.

13. A brief history of surveys in Great Britain is given in D. Caradoc Jones, *Social Surveys* (London: Hutchinson, 1948).

14. Carl I. Hovland, 'Reconciling Conflicting Results Derived from Experimental and Survey Studies of Attitude Change', *American Psychologist*, Vol. 14 (1959), pp. 8–17. This is reprinted in Berelson and Janowitz (eds.), op. cit.

15. See the attack on the newer empirical methods in C. Wright Mills, *The Sociological Imagination* (New York: Oxford University Press, 1959), especially Chapter 3, 'Abstracted Empiricism'.

16. William Albig, 'Two Decades of Opinion Study, 1936–1956', *Public Opinion Quarterly*, Vol. 21 (1957), pp. 14–22.

17. For another view of commercial survey research, see Charles R. Wright, 'Access to Social Science Data in Commercial Communications Reports', *Public Opinion Quarterly*, Vol. 28 (1964), pp. 573–83.

18. Joseph T. Klapper, *The Effects of Mass Communication* (Glencoe: Free Press, 1960).

19. A relatively early expression of the view is given in Louis Wirth, 'Consensus and Mass Communication', *American Sociological Review*, Vol. 13 (1948), pp. 1–14. This is reprinted in Wilbur L. Schramm (ed.), *Mass Communications* (Urbana: University of Illinois Press, 1960). See also Warren Breed, 'Mass Communication and Sociological Integration', *Social Forces*, Vol. 37 (1958), pp. 109–16. This is reprinted in Dexter and White (eds.), op. cit.

20. For example, analysis of the contents of local newspapers designed to show that accounts of local conflict tend to be suppressed.

21. For his discussion of the general paradigm see Robert K. Merton, *Social Theory and Social Structure* (Glencoe: Free Press, 1957). For applications to the media field, see Charles R. Wright, 'Functional Analysis and Mass Communication', *Public Opinion Quarterly*, Vol. 24 (1960), pp. 605–20. This is reprinted in Dexter and White (eds.), op. cit.

22. Joseph T. Klapper, 'Mass Communication Research: An Old Road

Resurveyed', *Public Opinion Quarterly*, Vol. 27 (1963), pp. 515–27. Some representative studies are reprinted in the section 'Why They Attend to Mass Communication' in Schramm (ed.), *The Process and Effects of Mass Communication* (Urbana: University of Illinois Press, 1960).

23. Merton, op. cit. Part III, 'The Sociology of Knowledge and Mass Communications'.

Mass Communication and Social Change

1. See, for example, Frank Luther Mott, *American Journalism* (New York: The Macmillan Co., 1941); Henry L. Smith and Edwin Emery, *The Press in America* (Englewood Cliffs, New Jersey: Prentice-Hall, 1954); Lewis Jacobs, *The Rise of the American Film* (New York: Harcourt, Brace & Co., 1939); Benjamin Hampton, *A History of the Movies* (New York: Corvici, Friede, 1931); Llewellyn White, *The American Radio* (Chicago: University of Chicago Press, 1947); Meyer Weinberg, *TV in America* (New York: Ballantine Books, 1962).

2. A number of such studies have been summarized in Everett M. Rogers, *Diffusion of Innovations* (New York: The Free Press of Glencoe, 1962).

3. For a summary of early diffusion studies in sociology see Melvin L. DeFleur and Otto N. Larsen, *The Flow of Information* (New York: Harper & Bros., 1958).

4. Bryce Ryan and Neal C. Gross, 'The Diffusion of Hybrid Seed Corn in Two Iowa Communities', *Rural Sociology*, 8 (March 1943), pp. 15–24.

5. Robert K. Merton, *Social Theory and Social Structure* (Glencoe: The Free Press, 1959), pp. 141–9.

6. An excellent example of this usage is contained in Richard Colvard, 'Risk Capital Philanthropy: The Ideological Defense of Innovation', in George K. Zollschan and Water Hirsch (eds.), *Explorations in Social Change* (Boston: Houghton Mifflin Co., 1964), pp. 728–48. The 'risk capital' concept constitutes a new norm or code for philanthropic foundations.

7. The use of adjectives, verbs and nouns, e.g., 'innovation', 'to innovate', and 'innovators' as derivatives of 'innovation' implies this usage. See Herbert Menzel, 'Innovation, Integration and Marginality: A Survey of Physicians', *American Sociological Review*, Vol. 25 (October 1960), pp. 704–13. See also Rogers, op. cit., pp. 193–5.

8. By the term 'analytical' is meant 'based upon the study of elementary units'. If traits are considered as elementary units of culture, then a study of the adoption of or diffusion of a particular trait, or a theory which approaches social change, within such a framework, can be said to be 'analytical' in this sense.

9. Talcott Parsons et al., *Toward a General Theory of Action* (New York: Harper & Row, 1962), p. 7.

10. Rogers, op. cit., p. 154.

11. David Sheppard, *A Survey Among Grassland Farmers* (London: Central Office of Information, Social Survey Number 274).

12. Many of the possible explanations behind such 'diffusion curves' have been discussed in mathematical as well as behavioural terms in pioneering work by Stuart C. Dodd. See, for example, 'Diffusion is Predictable: Testing Probability Models for Laws of Interaction', *American Sociological Review*, Vol. 20 (August 1955), pp. 392–401.

13. For an excellent summary and broad inter-disciplinary overview of this literature, see Elihu Katz, Martin L. Levin, and Herbert Hamilton, 'Traditions of Research on the Diffusion of Innovation', *American Sociological Review*, Vol. 28 (April 1963), pp. 237–52.

14. Rogers, op. cit., p. 76.

15. Parson et al., op. cit., pp. 111–58.

16. Studies of the social and psychological functions of the newspaper indicate that the daily paper satisfies many needs and is probably here to stay, at least for some time. See Bernard Berelson, 'What Missing the Newspaper Means', in Paul Lazarsfeld and Frank Stanton (eds.), *Communication Research 1948-1949* (New York: Harper & Bros., 1949). Also see Penn Kimball, 'People Without Papers', *Public Opinion Quarterly*, Vol. 23 (Fall, 1959), pp. 389–98.

17. See Eliot Freidson's excellent discussion of the way in which movie attendance is related to social interaction within primary groups. 'Communication Research and the Concept of the Mass', *American Sociological Review*, Vol. 18 (June 1953), pp. 313–17.

18. Paul F. Lazarsfeld and Robert K. Merton, 'Mass Communication, Popular Taste and Organized Social Action', in Lyman Bryson (ed.), *The Communication of Ideas* (New York: Harper & Bros., 1948), pp. 95–118.

Film, Communication and Content

1. See George C. Homans, *Sentiments and Activities* (London: Routledge and Kegan Paul, 1962) and *Social Behaviour: Its Elementary Forms* (New York: Harcourt, Brace and World, 1961).

2. Harold D. Lasswell, 'The Structure and Function of Communication in Society', in Bernard Berelson and Morris Janowitz (eds.), *Reader in Public Opinion and Communication* (New York, London: The Free Press, 1966).

3. George A. Huaco, *The Sociology of Film Art* (New York, London: Basic Books, 1965).

4. P. Kendall and K. Wolfe, 'The Analysis of Deviant Cases in Communication Research', in Paul F. Lazarsfeld and Frank Stanton (eds.), *Communications Research, 1948–1949* (New York: Harper, 1949).

5. See G. Mialaret, *The Psychology of the Use of Audio-Visual Aids in Primary Education* (London: Harrap, 1966) for a summary of some of these researches.

6. J. E. Hulett, Jr, 'Estimating the Net Effect of a Commercial Motion Picture upon the Trend of Local Public Opinion', *American Sociological Review*, Vol. 14, 2 (1949). Many other variables have been explored in this context. Examples of experimental studies may be found in Carl Hovland, Arthur Lumsdaine, and Fred D. Sheffield, *Experiments on Mass Communication* (New York: Wiley, 1949). Summaries of research into audience characteristics may be found in Leo A. Handel, *Hollywood Looks at its Audience* (Urbana: University of Illinois Press, 1950).

7. There may be interesting possibilities in this respect arising from Blalock's work on causal models. See Hubert M. Blalock, Jr, *Causal Inferences in Nonexperimental Research* (Chapel Hill: University of North Carolina Press, 1964).

8. See, for example, George A. Huaco, op. cit., and, for a general organizational picture, *The British Film Industry* (London: P.E.P., 1952 and 1958). On the two-step flow hypothesis see Elihu Katz and Paul F. Lazarsfeld, *Personal Influence* (Glencoe: The Free Press, 1955).

9. As just one criticism see George Gerbner, 'On Content Analysis and Critical Research in Mass Communication', in Lewis Anthony Dexter and David Manning White (eds.), *People, Society, and Mass Communications* (New York, London: The Free Press, 1964).

10. The major example of 'media determinism' is the work of McLuhan. See, for example, Marshall McLuhan, *Understanding Media* (London: Sphere Books, 1968).

11. A possible development here would be that derived from semiology, the science of signs. See Peter Wollen, *Signs and Meaning in the Cinema* (London: Secker and Warburg, 1969); Peter Wollen, 'Cinema and Semiology: Some points of Contact', and Frank West, 'Semiology and the Cinema', Peter Wollen (ed.), *Working Papers on the Cinema: Sociology and Semiology* (London: British Film Institute, 1969).

12. Perhaps the best known of such studies is David Riesman with Nathan Glazer and Reuel Denney, *The Lonely Crowd* (New Haven and London: Yale University Press, 1950). For more modern usage see Harold L. Wilensky, 'Mass Society and Mass Culture', in Bernard Berelson and Morris Janowitz, op. cit.

13. See, for example, Daniel Lerner, *The Passing of Traditional Society* (Glencoe: The Free Press, 1958).

14. Martha Wolfenstein and Nathan Leites, *The Movies: A Psychological Study* (Glencoe: The Free Press, 1950); George A. Huaco, op. cit., Siegfried Kracauer, *From Caligari to Hitler* (Princeton: Princeton University Press, 1947); Herbert J. Gans, 'Hollywood Films on British Screens: An Analysis of the Functions of American Popular Culture Abroad', *Social Problems*, Vol. 9, 4 (1961).

15. Parsons has devoted much time to formulating structural categories applicable to social and cultural systems, and to the analysis of their relations. See his contributions on the social and cultural systems in Talcott Parsons, Edward Shils, Kaspar D. Naegele, and Jesse R. Pitts (eds.), *Theories of Society* (New York: The Free Press, 1961). Kavolis has adapted some of Parsons' ideas to apply to art; see V. Kavolis, 'Economic Correlates of Artistic Creativity', *American Journal of Sociology* (1946), as an example. Berger has developed a scheme for the sociology of knowledge and applied it in the sociology of religion; see Peter L. Berger and Thomas Luckmann, *The Social Construction of Reality* (London: Allen Lane, The Penguin Press, 1967), and Peter L. Berger, *The Social Reality of Religion* (London: Faber and Faber, 1969). The concern of the latter with 'plausibility' and 'legitimation' might well provide an interesting approach to macro-sociological analysis of the media.

16. Cf. the discussions of 'levels of meaning' in Terry Lovell, 'An Approach to the Sociology of Film', and Andrew Tudor, 'Sociological Perspectives on Film Aesthetics', both in Peter Wollen (ed.), *Working Papers on the Cinema: Sociology and Semiology*, op. cit.

17. Cf. Cyril Barrett, 'Film as a Means of Communication', *Clergy Review* (December 1967).

18. One of the classic formulations is to be found in Bernard Berelson, *Content Analysis in Communication Research* (Glencoe: The Free Press, 1950). The subject has since become increasingly complex taking its impetus from fields such as information theory and linguistics. For one modern approach see Charles E. Osgood, George J. Suci, and Percy H. Tannenbaum, *The Measurement of Meaning* (Urbana, Chicago, London: University of Illinois Press, 1957).

19. See Sergi M. Eisenstein, *The Film Sense* (London: Faber and Faber, 1948), and *Film Form* (New York: Harcourt, Brace and Co., 1949).

20. George A. Huaco, op. cit. The fact that Huaco's study has been mentioned frequently in this paper should not be taken to imply that it is a particularly good piece of work. For a lengthy criticism see my review in *Views*, 11 (1966).

21. See the collection of readings in James Hodd (ed.), *Psychology and the Visual Arts* (Harmondsworth: Penguin, 1969). For a short summary see Douglas Sandle, 'The Science of Art', *Science Journal* (March 1967).

The Impact of Television on the Audience for National Newspapers, 1945–68

1. The best summaries are contained in Leo Bogart, *The Age of Television* (New York: Frederick Ungar, 1956); W. A. Belson, *The Impact of Television* (London: Crosby Lockwood, 1967) – a book of major importance on the effects of television viewing on attitudes and behaviour; *The Effects of Television on Children and Adolescents* (Paris: UNESCO, 1964); John P. Robinson 'Television and Leisure Time', *Public Opinion Quarterly* (1969). The publication *Sociol. Abstracts* provides useful, but brief, summaries of research conducted in countries such as Mexico and Poland which are not readily available.

2. W. A. Belson, 'Respondent Memory as a Factor in Survey Research', Esomar Conference Paper (1963).

3. Kent Geiger and Robert Sokol, 'Social Norms in Television Watching', *American Journal of Sociology*, No. 65 (1959).

4. Gary Steiner, *The People Look at Television: A Study of Audience Attitudes* (New York: Knopf, 1963).

5. W. A. Belson, *The British Press: A Study of the Public's Attitudes towards the Press, Related to Past and Future Circulation Trends*, Part II (London Press Exchange, 1960).

6. W. A. Belson, *The British Press*, Part II; W. A. Belson, 'Television and the Other Mass Media', *Business Review* (April 1961); W. A. Belson, *The Impact of Television* (London: Crosby Lockwood, 1967). This last provides a more qualified interpretation of the original LPE survey results.

7. 'Thorough Readership' is defined as reading a newspaper item in full.

8. 'National Daily Newspaper Readership Studies: Feature Readership in National Dailies', Odhams Report DH77 (1963). See also other reading and noting studies conducted by Odhams and the International Publishing Corporation, and by Social Surveys (Gallup Poll) Ltd, National Opinion Polls Ltd, Research Services Ltd and Marplan Ltd commissioned by national newspaper publishing companies.

9. W. A. Belson, *The British Press*, Part II.

10. 'News Broadcasting in 1962: A Study of Listening and Viewing and of Public Attitudes towards New Broadcasts', Parts I–V: BBC Audience Research Report LR621586. 'Readership of *Daily Express*: Qualitative Research', *Daily Express*/Research Services Ltd, 1968. For similar findings obtained in the United States see 'The Public's View of Television and Other Media, 1959–64', Elmo Roper and Associates, New York 1965.

11. 'A Study of News Listening and Viewing and of the Public's Attitude Towards the BBC News Service', Parts I–II, BBC Audience Research Report

LR57920 (1957). Cf. Unpublished Research of Israel Institute of Applied Social Research, Jerusalem 1967–9.

12. The most relevant summaries are contained in B. P. Emmett, 'The Television Audience in the United Kingdom', *Journal of the Royal Statistical Society*, Vol. 119 (1956): 'The Public and the Programmes', BBC Audience Research Report VR59332 (1959): Leo Bogart, *The Age of Television* (1956): W. A. Belson, *The Impact of Television* (1967); See also S. Graham, 'Cultural Compatibility in the Adoption of Television', *Social Forces*, No. 33 (1954).

13. H. Zorbaugh and C. W. Mills, 'A Report on the Impact of Television in a Major Metropolitan Market', *Puck the Comic Weekly* (New York, 1952).

14. 'Metropolitan New York Survey 1952', National Broadcasting Company.

15. Same sources as Note 8.

16. 'Changes in Daily Newspaper Reading: Report of a Survey in the Greater London Area' (1962), Odhams Report DH63; 'Readership of *Daily Express*: Qualitative Research', *Daily Express*/Research Services Ltd (1968); 'Starting and Stopping Sunday Newspapers' (1968), International Publishing Corporation (IPC) Report MS. 52.

17. 'The Effect of Recent Price Changes on Sunday Papers', Odhams Report P.R 1 9 (1958). Also sources in Note 16.

18. 'Effects of Television on Children', Ministry of Education, Japan (1959) *Shimbun Kenkyu*, No. 116, 1961.

19. Wilbur Schramm, Jack Lyle and Edwin B. Parker, *Television in the Lives of Our Children* (Stanford, Cal.: Stanford University Press, 1961); Reuben Mehling, 'Television's Value to the American Family Member', *Journal of Broadcasting*, Vol. IV (1960); 'The 1962 Youth Marketing Survey', Market Investigations Ltd (London) *inter al.*

20. W. A. Belson, 'A Technique for Studying the Effects of a Television Broadcast', *Journal of Applied Statistics*, Vol. 5 (1956), and 'Matching and Prediction on the Principle of Biological Classification', *Journal of Applied Statistics*, Vol. 8 (1959), and *The British Press*, Appendix I. It is theoretically possible but extremely unlikely that the behavioural variables adopted in Dr Belson's system of intercorrelations also correlate with the missing variables referred to in the text.

21. 'The Press and its Readers: Preliminary Report' (1947), Mass-Observation Ltd Report L3009; 'A Motivational Study for the Bristol *Evening Post*' (1965), Personnel Administration Ltd/Conrad Jameson Associates.

22. Odhams Survey Reports: '*Daily Herald* Analysis of Readership', DH41 (1957); 'Report on a Survey to Study Attitudes on Daily Newspapers', NR9 (1958); 'Current Attitudes to the *Daily Herald*', DH49 (1960); '*Daily Herald* Analysis of Readership', DH56 (1961); 'Report on a Newspaper

"Product" Test', MS57 (1961); *'Daily Herald* Image – Self-Designation by Social Class', DH60 (1961); *'Daily Herald* Image – Readership of News Stories by Page', DH66 (1962); 'National Daily Newspapers – An Analysis of Readership with Special Reference to the *Daily Herald'*, DH64 (1962); 'Report on Discussion Groups – Daily Newspapers', DH71, PR136, PR137, PR138 (1963); 'National Daily Newspapers: An Analysis of Readership with Special Reference to the *Daily Herald'*, DH75 (1964); 'National Daily Newspaper Readership Studies: II Attitudes to Newspapers and Newspaper Reading', DH7617 (1964).

23. See 'The Relationship Between the Amount Read in Sunday Papers and the Behaviour and Attitudes of Their Readers', International Publishing Corporation Report PRI42 (1966), for the interrelationship not merely between readers' attitudes, and reading intensity but also newspaper duplication, reading frequency and newspaper purchase.

24. Corroborative evidence of the 'identity' relationship between a newspaper and its readership can also be found in other studies which, in dealing with different social groups, would suggest that an 'identity' relationship is, in fact, a general pattern: 'Attitudes of Three Groups [Negroes, Latin Americans and teenagers] Towards Miami Newspapers', *Miami Herald/* Social Research Inc. (Chicago, 1954); 'A Study of Miami Newspapers', *Miami Herald/*Social Research Inc. (Chicago, 1954); 'Survey of Middle Class Readers of Sunday Newspapers', *Observer/*Research Services Ltd (1960) – the findings of this survey are more interesting than the interpretation; 'The Role of In-Home Media', Study conducted by The Institute of Motivational Research Inc. (New York) for The Canadian Daily Newspaper Publishers Association, Toronto (1962); 'Report on a Survey to Study Attitudes on Daily Newspapers', Odhams Report NR9 (1958); 'National Daily Newspaper Readership Studies: II Attitudes to Newspapers and Newspaper Reading', Odhams Report DH 77 (1964); 'Report on Discussion Groups – Daily Newspapers', Odhams Report DH71 (1963); 'Motivational Research into Newspaper Readership', *Financial Times/*Conrad Jameson Associates (1968); 'Marketing Study of the *Financial Times* Readership: Final Report', *Financial Times/*Conrad Jameson Associates (1968); 'Seven Local Weeklies: A First Psychological Study', Weekly Newspaper Advertising Bureau/Research Services Ltd (1968); 'Study of Daily Newspapers', *Daily Express/*Image Research Services Ltd, 1968). The 'identity' relationship, revealed by these studies, would explain divergent responses to identical stimuli mentioned earlier, e.g., divergent responses to newspaper price increases.

25. Quoted in Jeremy Isaacs, 'Television Journalism', *Encounter* (March 1968) , p. 84.

26. Newspaper Proprietors Association Documentary Evidence, *Royal Commission on the Press 1961–2*, Vol. IV (Cmd. 1812–7), p. 32, *cf.* Evidence

of Co-operative Press Ltd. (Cmd. 1812–4), Vol. I, p. 48; News of the World Organisation Ltd., Vol. I, pp. 190–1; The Manchester Guardian and Evening News Ltd, Vol. I, pp. 252, 270; Thompson Newspapers Ltd, Vol. I, p. 249; D. C. Thompson and Co. Ltd and John Leng & Co. Ltd, Vol. II (Cmd. 1812–5), p. 104; Lord Layton (*News Chronicle*) Vol. V (Cmd. 1812–8), pp. 244–5.

27. Clive Irving, 'Newspaper Reading – A Reply', *Encounter* (Mar 1968).

28. Quoted in Claud Cockburn, *I Claud* (Harmondsworth: Penguin Books, 1967), p. 428.

29. Marshall McLuhan, *Understanding Media: The Extensions of Man* (London: Routledge and Kegan Paul, 1964), p. 207.

30. Melvin L. DeFleur, *Theories of Mass Communication* (New York: David McKay, 1966). For earlier and rather different interpretations, based on a correlational analysis, see Harvey J. Levin, 'Competition among the Mass Media and the Public Interest', *Public Opinion Quarterly* (1954), and Leo Bogart, *The Age of Television* (1956).

31. *United Nations Statistical Yearbook* (Annual Report); *World Communications* (Paris: UNESCO, 1950 edition and revised editions 1951, 1956, and 1964); 'The Daily Press: A Survey of the World Situation in 1952', *Reports and Papers on Mass Communications*, No. 7 (Paris: UNESCO, 1953); *Statistics of Newspapers and other Periodicals* (Paris: UNESCO, 1959); *Basic Facts and Figures* (Paris: UNESCO, 1950, 1951, 1956, 1964).

32. National newspapers have been defined as publications with a nation-wide audience (read in all regions as defined by the Registrar General), published regularly either on Sundays or on the other six days of the week, and appealing to a wider audience than an exclusively ethnic or specialist minority. Unless otherwise stated, the statistical tables relate to all national newspapers, except for the transient *New Daily* for which statistical information is lacking. An exception has also been made of the *Daily Record* in Table X due to its inclusion as a national daily in the IPA 'Group Readership Tables', and in Table III to ensure comparability between these two tables. A case can be made, however, for treating the *Daily Record* as an alternative, Scottish edition of a national newspaper (*Daily Mirror*). See Cecil King, *Future of the Press* (London: MacGibbon and Kee, 1967).

33. For pre-war circulation figures, see A. P. Wadsworth, 'Newspaper Circulations 1800–1954' (Manchester Statistical Society, 1955); W. A. Belson, *The British Press*, Part III (1960); *Royal Commission on the Press 1947-9* (HMSO, Cmd. 7700).

34. P. Kimble, *Newspaper Reading in the Third Year of the War* (London: Allen and Unwin, 1942); L. Moss and K. Box, *Newspapers and the Public* (London: Central Office of Information, 1943); also Newspaper Readership

Surveys, Mass-Observation Ltd, 1941, 1942, 1944, and British Institute of Public Opinion (Gallup Poll Ltd, 1944).

35. For estimates of the pre-war level of pagination, see *Royal Commission on the Press 1947–9* (HMSO, Cmd. 7700) and *1961–2* (incl. Cmd. 1811–9).

36. For different estimates of newspaper duplication in the 1930s, see 'Investigated Press Circulations', Repfords Ltd (1932); Institute of Incorporated Practitioners in Advertising (IIPA) Readership Surveys (1930, 1931, 1934, and 1939); Incorporated Society of British Advertisers, 'The Readership of Newspapers and Periodicals in Great Britain' (1936); London Press Exchange Ltd, Readership Surveys (1934 and 1939). For equally discrepant estimates of readership duplication in the 1940s see: Hulton Readership Surveys (1947, 1948, 1949); IIPA, 'Survey of Press Readership' (1947); Attwood Readership Surveys (1947 and 1949); *The Press and its Readers*, Mass-Observation, London, Art and Technics Ltd (1949); Odhams Net Readership Surveys (1945 and 1946), and references in Note 34.

37. The *Daily Herald, Daily Worker, Daily Graphic* and *Sunday Pictorial* have not been included amongst the failed newspapers since they resumed publication under another title.

38. IPA National Readership Survey, Second Supplementary Report, 1960.

39. See: *Royal Commission on the Press 1947–9* (HMSO, Cmd. 7700); N. Kaldor and R. Silverman, *A Statistical Analysis of Advertising Expenditure and the Revenue of the Press* (National Institute of Economic and Social Research/Cambridge University Press, 1948); Marjorie Deane, 'United Kingdom Publishing Statistics', *Journal of the Royal Statistical Society*, Vol. CXIV (1951); J. Edward Gerald, *The British Press under Economic Control* (Mineapolis: University of Minnesota Press, 1956); W. A. Belson, *The British Press*, Part III (London Press Exchange Ltd, 1960); *Royal Commission on the Press 1961–2* (HMSO, Cmd. 1811–18); *Survey of the National Newspaper Industry* (London: Economist Intelligence Unit Ltd, 1966); *Monopolies Commission Report on The Times Newspaper and the Sunday Times Newspaper* (H.C. 273, 1966); National Board for Prices and Incomes, Report No. 43, *Costs and Revenues of National Daily Newspapers* (HMSO, Cmd. 3435, 1967).

40. It is not possible to obtain total consumer expenditure on all the media from the National Income and Expenditure Reports. The print media are defined as newspapers, magazines and books.

41. Defined as expenditure on sugar, preserves and confectionery, alcoholic drink, tobacco, motor cars and cycles, radio, electrical and other durable goods, books, newspapers and magazines, recreational goods and 'other recreational goods', running costs of vehicles, telephones, communications, entertainments, domestic service, 'other services', income in kind, etc.,

consumer expenditure abroad, and 10% of all expenditure on clothing and footwear.

42. Defined as expenditure on travel, post, chemists goods, household textiles, house maintenance, repairs and improvements, beverages, all products and services in the 'luxury' category, and an additional 50% of all expenditure on clothing and footwear.

43. Defined as total consumer expenditure in the United Kingdom, excluding expenditure by foreign tourists.

44. *Royal Commission on the Press 1961–1962 Report*; *Survey of the National Newspaper Industry* (Economist Intelligence Unit Ltd).

45. *Royal Commission on the Press 1961–1962 Report*, Appendix IX; 'A Comparison of Selected Media in the UK, Europe and the USA', International Publishing Corporation Report MS151 (1967).

46. Figures for the 1940s must be treated with caution since they are projected from estimates of average thorough readership for a limited sample of papers. The relatively static level of reading intensity for newspapers in the late 1940s and early 1950s, for which detailed evidence is available, suggests however that these projected estimates are relatively reliable. The basic techniques used in reading and noting studies have also been extensively criticized. See 'Reading and Noting: An Appraisal', London Press Exchange Ltd paper (1967) and, in greater detail, International Publishing Corporation memo – K. M. Vagg (1968) for the best summaries of methodological criticisms of reading and noting methods.

47. Survey Reports on the time spent reading national newspapers would also seem to provide confirmation that *per capita* reading intensity has increased during the post-war period, although it should be noted that not all these reports are strictly comparable in terms of sample and questionnaire design and the number of newspaper publications checked. See '*Daily Herald* and *Daily Mail* Readership Survey', British Institute of Public Opinion (1947); 'Tottenham Book Reading Survey', Mass-Observation Report MO2537 (1947); 'The Press and its Readers: Preliminary Report', Mass-Observation Report N3009 (1948); A. Stuart, 'Reading Habits in Three London Boroughs', *Journal of Documentation*, Vol. 8 (1952); 'Time Spent Reading Daily Newspapers', Odhams Report DH32 (1955); 'Cultural and Intelligence Ratings Report on Supplementary Questions', Odhams Report P16a (1953); 'Housewives Survey', Gallup Poll Ltd (May 1957); 'Reading Popular Sunday Papers and Reading and Viewing on Sunday', IPC Report MS173 (1967); 'Detailed Analysis of Time Spent Reading Sunday Papers On and After Sunday', IPC Report PR16 (1963)/'Newspaper Survey', National Opinion Polls Ltd, 1963.

48. During the period 1947–1968, the total average circulation of the quality press increased by 139%. Yet the time spent reading an average

quality newspaper in 1963, for instance, was 37% greater than it was for an average popular newspaper (calculated from 'Newspaper Survey' National Opinion Poll Ltd, 1963).

49. Strict accuracy of comparison cannot be achieved between Hulton and IPA estimates of readership penetration (Table X), due to differences of survey procedure, and no attempt has been made to weight the results. Averages have been calculated to offset short-term fluctuations in the estimates, arising from the random factor in the sample. During the period for which comparison is possible – i.e., the two periods covered by the Hulton and IPA Readership Surveys respectively – the overall situation remained virtually unchanged.

The JICNARS group readership estimates for 1968 do not significantly differ from the average IPA estimates for 1963–7 and have therefore been incorporated in the summary table reproduced in the text. But it should be noted that the JICNARS methods differed slightly from those of the IPA. See '1967/1968 National Readership Surveys: An Analysis of Differences', JICNARS Paper, August 1969.

50. The sale of television sets has reached 'saturation' level. *Euromonitor* (November 1967.)

51. BBC Audience Research Department.

52. During the period 1965–1968, an increase of only 1·4 p.p. occurred, which is very much less than the possible margin of statistical error. Derived from the annual average of the estimates reported in the BBC Audience Research Bulletins (quarterly reports).

53. During the same four-year period, an increase of only 1 p.p. took place, which again is very much less than the possible margin of statistical error. Calculated as in Note 52.

54. Calculated from JICNAR National Readership computer cards (February–June 1968), relating to persons over 15 years old.

55. Calculated from average percentage viewing figures for BBC/ITV among persons over the age of four (BBC Audience Research Bulletins). This figure has been weighted on the basis of average percentage viewing figures for children aged 5–14 during the period 1961–4, adjusted according to the average percentage change in the subsequent period, to obtain an estimate for average percentage viewing among persons over the age of 14 in 1968.

56. See Readership Surveys commissioned by The Newspaper Society, Evening Newspaper Advertising Bureau (ENAB), Thomson Organization Ltd, Westminster Press Provincial Newspapers Ltd, Provincial Newspapers Ltd, D. C. Thompson Ltd, Eastern Counties Newspapers, *inter al.*

57. Many of the contributory causes are world-wide phenomena – i.e., the immediate post-war shortage of pulp, curtailing the size and price of

newspapers; the absence of major technological advances in newspaper production necessary to counteract sharply rising newsprint, labour and distribution costs; the falling share of small circulation popular newspapers' advertising expenditure due to the rising level of newspaper pagination, competition from new advertising media, and increasing statistical sophistication among advertising agencies; the monopolistic pressures arising from economies of scale and non-price competition, etc.

58. *Understanding Media: Extensions of Man* (London: Routledge and Kegan Paul, 1964); *Medium is the Massage* (London: Penguin Books, 1968).

59. Two reading and noting studies conducted before 1939 are available: 'A Survey of Reader Interest in The National Morning and London Evening Press – 1934', Parts 1–9, London Press Exchange Ltd, 1934; 'A Study of Newspaper Reading', British Institute of Public Opinion (Gallup Poll Ltd, 1933).

60. See references in Notes 22 and 24, *inter al.*

Public Service and Private World

1. This paper is an excerpt from an unpublished report to the BBC based on an enquiry into the Corporation as an occupational milieu.

The main body of interviews on which this report is based were carried out on forty days during the early months of 1963. They were confined to members of the staff of four sections of the Corporation, chosen to give a fairly wide array of people and functions: Technical Operations and Maintenance in Television Centre; Schools Broadcasting (Sound and Television); Staff Administration (including Central Establishment Office); and Light Entertainment.

While these departments differ greatly from each other in many respects, they are not, of course, a representative sample of the Corporation's activities or staff. So that while, to avoid the annoyance of perpetual qualification or periphrasis, I speak of 'the Corporation', or aspects of it, or of 'staff', or categories of staff, it will be borne in mind that the reference is always to the Corporation as it appears in, or to, those departments I got to know and the people I met.

2. Howard Becker, *Outsiders* (London: Collier Macmillan, 1963), p. 7. See also Tom Burns 'Micropolitics', *Administrative Science Quarterly*, Vol. 6 (1961), pp. 257–81.

3. Stuart Hood, *A Survey of Television* (London: Heinemann, 1967), pp. 49–50.

4. I am here omitting a fairly lengthy discussion of the social function of

the mass communication industries in contemporary advanced industrial societies.

5. M. Maruyama, *Thought and Behaviour in Japanese Politics* (London: Oxford University Press, 1963), p. 3.

6. R. Bendix and S. M. Lipset, 'Political Sociology', *Current Sociology*, Vol. VI, No. 2 (Paris: UNESCO, 1957), p. 84.

Newspaper Staff as a Social System

1. See W. Kornhauser, *Scientists in Industry* (Berkeley, 1962) as well as a number of publications by F. Andrews and D. C. Pelz (Institute for Social Research at the University of Michigan). In Poland, too, during the last few years, there have been a number of studies on teams of research workers. See: A. Matejko, *System społeczny zespołu naukowego* [The Social System of the Research Team], Warszawa 1966. All the aforesaid research in Poland was carried out by the Laboratory for Research on the Problems of Scientific Staff, which comes under the Inter-University Centre for Research on Advanced Education in Warsaw (head – Professor Jan Szczepański).

2. In Poland in 1963, for example, a structural-functional analysis was made of one of the theatrical teams, that of the 'Teatr Laboratorium 13-tu Rzędów', which at one time was in Opole but is now in Wrocław.

3. Cf. R. Likert, 'The Nature of Highly Effective Groups', in *New Patterns of Management* (New York, 1961), pp. 162–77; N. R. F. Maier, J. J. Hayes, *Creative Management* (New York, 1962); H. W. Gabriel, *Techniques of Creative Thinking for Management* (Englewood Cliffs, 1961), etc.

4. In the author's view, this analysis should be made on four planes: (i) interorganizational (formal organization – informal organ), (ii) inter-system (interrelationships between the social, technological, administrative, and economic systems), (iii) inter-structural (interrelationships between the various structures of social bonds), (iv) efficiency (the combination of various elements of social behaviour in a harmonious whole).

5. L. G. Rosten, *The Washington Correspondents* (New York, 1937); F. C. Prugger, 'Social Composition and Training of the Milwaukee Journal News Staff', *Journalism Quarterly*, No. 18 (1941); C. F. Swanson, *The Mid-City Daily* (1948, unpublished doctor's thesis).

6. W. Breed, *The Newspaperman, News and Society* (New York: Columbia University, 1952, unpublished doctor's thesis); cf. W. Breed, 'Social Control in the Newsroom. A Functional Analysis', *Social Forces*, Vol. 33 (1955).

7. The detailed results of this survey are given by A. Matejko in *Postawy*

zawodowe dziennikarzy na tle systemu społecznego redakcji [The Occupational Attitudes of Newspapermen against the Background of the Social System of a Newspaper Staff] (Warszawa-Kraków, 1962–1963).

8. There is a fairly sharp difference here between the newspapermen studied by us and the American newspapermen studied by W. Breed. The American ones live in a circle of their own, which restricts their ambitions. The Polish ones live in the professionally mixed environment of intelligentsia and are under the pressure of its traditional values, norms, and patterns.

9. It must be remembered, however, that in the Polish case the newspapermen belonged to some of the leading papers in the country, whereas in America the newspapermen studied by W. Breed worked on average provincial papers somewhere in the north-eastern States.

10. T. Kotarbiński, *Traktat o dobrej robocie* [Treatise on the Good Work] (Łódź, 1955), p. 149. Also cf. Kotarbiński, *Praxiology. An Introduction to the Sciences of Efficient Action* (Oxford–Warsaw, 1965).

11. According to a study made towards the end of 1958 by W. Wesołowski and A. Sarapata on the opinions of Warsaw inhabitants, the newspaperman comes ninth in the list of occupations as regards social prestige and financial rewards (preceded by university professors, physicians, lawyers, cabinet ministers, etc.), but eleventh on the list as regards security of job. See A. Sarapata, W. Wesołowski, 'The Evaluation of Occupations by Warsaw Inhabitants', *American Journal of Sociology*, No. 6 (May 1961).

12. Cf. T. Kupis' study of newspapermen's working conditions and standard of living: *Zawód dziennikarza w Polsce Ludowej* [Journalistic Profession in People's Poland] (Warszawa 1966), and S. Dzięcielska's *Sytuacja społecza dziennikarzy polskich* [The Social Position of Polish Journalists] (Wrocław, 1962).

13. For a discussion of these mechanisms, which act as subsystems in the social system, see D. Katz, R. L. Kahn, *The Social Psychology of Organizations* (New York, 1966); also B. S. Georgopoulos, A Matejko, 'The American General Hospital as a Complex Social System, *Health Services Research*, No. 1 (1967).

14. See A. Matejko, *Społeczne warunki pracy twórczej* [The Social Determinants of Creative Work] (Warszawa, 1965); A. Matejko, 'Status incongruence in the Polish Intelligentsia', *Social Research*, Vol. 33, No. 4 (1966).

Journalism Recruitment and Training: Problems in Professionalization

1. *Royal Commission on the Press 1947–1949* (London: HMSO); *Royal Commission on the Press 1961–1962* (London: HMSO).

2. G. Millerson, *The Qualifying Associations. A Study in Professionalization* (London: Routledge and Kegan Paul, 1964), Chapter 1.

3. Ernest Greenwood, 'The Elements of Professionalization', in H. M. Vollmer and D. L. Mills (eds.), *Professionalization* (Englewood Cliffs, New Jersey: Prentice-Hall, 1966).

4. William Goode, 'The Librarian: From Occupation to Profession?', *The Library Quarterly*, 31, No. 4 (October 1961). Also in Vollmer and Mills (eds.), op. cit.

5. *Report of the Tribunal appointed to Inquire into the Vassall case and Related Matters* (London: HMSO, Cmd. 2009, 1963).

6. By Jeremy Tunstall to whom I am indebted for permission to use this and other comparative data. A 'specialist' is here defined as a newsgathering journalist whose attention is mostly confined to a recognized subject area.

7. H. Phillip Levy, *The Press Council: History, Procedure, Cases* (London: Macmillan, 1967).

8. Millerson, op. cit., p. 9.

9. Joseph Lelyveld, 'Dadaists in Politics', *New York Times Magazine* (2nd October 1966), pp. 32 ff.

10. R. M. Blackburn, *Union Character and Social Class* (London: Batsford, 1967), Chapter 1.

11. Kenneth Prandy, *Professional Employees* (London: Faber and Faber, 1965). For analysis of 'class' and 'status' based employee organizations see Chapters 1 and 2 particularly. Also D. Lockwood, *The Blackcoated Worker* (London: Allen and Unwin, 1958), from which Prandy's study develops.

12. G. Millerson, op cit., p. 10.

13. W. Goode in Vollmer and Mills (eds.), op. cit., pp. 41–2.

14. Jeremy Tunstall, *The Westminster Lobby Correspondents* (London: Routledge and Kegan Paul, 1970).

15. G. Millerson, op. cit., pp. 10–13 ff.

16. The survey was financed by the Leverhulme Trust. It was originally intended to include a graduate course in the survey, but time-tabling arrangements made this impossible.

17. G. Millerson, op. cit., p. 9.

18. W. J. Reader, *Professional Men* (London: Weidenfeld and Nicolson, 1966).

19. A. M. Carr-Saunders and P. A. Wilson, *The Professions* (London: Cass, 1964).

20. The now defunct Kemsley group training scheme was perhaps the best known of these. Other large newspaper groups, such as IPC, the Thomson Organization, and Westminster Press have their own recruitment arrangements, but which are allied with those of NCTJ in training. The NCTJ has attempted to monopolize training. There do exist, however, courses in

communications and correspondence which purport to offer qualifications suitable for entry into journalism, but which are not approved by the NCTJ.

21. The data concerning influence in vocational choice by significant others, and the differences between pre-entries and other groups in this respect is not statistically significant, but important enough to warrant mention.

22. The NCTJ has deliberately sought to raise the proportion of women entering the occupation through its pre-entry course, but has restricted the proportion to around 30%, despite the fact that women applicants for the pre-entry course far outnumber applications from men. About two-thirds of the applicants for the pre-entry course are selected by joint consultation panels, including NCTJ teachers, senior NUJ members and editors. The remainder are recruited by editors. The NUJ made joint-consultation in selection a precondition to allowing a pre-entry course.

23. Guy H. Stewart, 'Journalism Education in Britain Enters a Period of Change', *Journalism Quarterly* (Spring, 1968), p. 106.

24. G. Millerson, op. cit.

25. W. Goode, op. cit.

26. R. L. Jones, 'Journalism Education in the Joyful Sixties', *Journalism Quarterly* (Winter, 1968).

27. M. S. Maclean, et al., 'AEJ Members and Their Attitudes on Journalism Education Issues', *Journalism Quarterly* (Winter, 1965).

28. Eric Oderdahl, 'College Backgrounds of Staffs of American Daily Newspapers', *Journalism Quarterly* (Summer, 1965).

29. Jeremy Tunstall, op. cit.

30. R. Murray Thomas, 'Reinspecting a Structural Position on Occupation Prestige', *American Journal of Sociology* (March, 1962), pp. 561–5.

31. E. Lloyd Sommerlad, 'Journalism Training for a Modern World', in *Reports and Papers on Mass Communication*, No. 45 (UNESCO, 1965), p. 7.

32. Broom and Smith, 'Bridging Occupations', *British Journal of Sociology*, XIV (1963).

33. Compare with medical students: R. K. Merton, et al., *The Student Physician* (Harvard University Press, 1957).

34. J. Tunstall, op. cit.

35. The elements of non-routine, non-conventionality, and sociability run together in most cases. The underlying reason for satisfaction with work experience in this context are those related to individual control over the work-process. Cf. Paul Blumberg, *Industrial Democracy* (London: Constable, 1968), esp. Ch. 5. Nevertheless, this evidence must be placed in the context of figures for 1967 which show the equivalent of 27·9% of the intake in that year *left* journalism from the ranks of juniors. The possibility that this reflected inadequate selection no doubt encourages the NUJ in its support

for experimental selection into pre-entry courses. The figures also reflect, probably, growing concern amongst juniors about their income possibilities after the initial two years.

36. The evidence on time-consumption is based on trainees' own estimates. They should be regarded as only very rough guides.

37. It is difficult to assess in what way the recent Industrial Training Board will affect Journalism training. Uncertainty about this reflects uncertainty amongst those concerned about how the Board will actually operate. But it is apparent that the Board is prepared to keep journalism training distinct from other training procedures in the printing industry. The vocational bias of the ITB may lead those who are examining the need for better non-vocational training to go outside the present NCTJ frames of reference altogether.

Selection and Communication in a Television Production – A Case Study

1. The project was designed and supervised by J. D. Halloran, Director of the Centre for Mass Communication Research. A survey of audience reactions was carried out by R. L. Brown. A full report is in preparation.

2. Apart from the study of the feature film, *The Red Badge of Courage*, by Lillian Ross, exceptions to this generalization have generally been studies of journalists and of decision making within newspapers, and a few autobiographical accounts. See L. Ross, *Picture* (London: Gollancz, 1953), and for an autobiographical account of a television production M. Miller and E. Rhodes, *Only You Dick Daring* (New York: Wm Sloane Assocs, 1964).

3. The author would like to acknowledge the great debt which this study owes to the producer and his team and others in the television organization for their help and cooperation throughout the research.

4. An analysis of some of the different forms which this relationship has been given may be found in M. C. Albrecht, 'The Relationship of Literature and Society', *American Journal of Sociology*, Vol. 59 (1954), pp. 425–36.

5. 'Conventional wisdom' is borrowed from J. K. Galbraith's analysis of contemporary economic theories to draw attention to the diffuse, anecdotal and largely unanalysed nature of opinions about phenomena which are widely disseminated in society. It is not intended as a pejorative term. See J. K. Galbraith, *The Affluent Society* (London: Hamish Hamilton, 1958).

6. One of the most explicit statements of the analogy is to be found in D. McQuail, 'Uncertainty about the Audience and the Organization of Mass Communications' *Sociological Review Monograph* No. 13, 1969, pp. 75–84.

7. See, for example, H. J. Gans, 'The Greater Audience Relationship in

the Mass Media', in B. Rosenberg and D. M. White (eds.), *Mass Culture* (Glencoe: Free Press, 1959).

8. Indeed this forms the starting point for McQuail's argument, op. cit.

9. Although this paragraph sets the situation of the production team within the organization it must be remembered that the study was limited to the level of programme production. It cannot, for example, answer questions about the general planning of programmes and output.

10. The executive producer did intervene in the production of the last two programmes in the series. This intervention does not affect the present argument and is outside the scope of the present paper.

11. This paragraph is based on a pre-production interview with the producer.

12. It must be emphasized that the term 'communication' is not intended to include just a socially purposive message, but any ideas and information about the subject.

13. This included especially a general survey of the field, G. W. Allport, *The Nature of Prejudice* (New York: Addison-Wesley, 1954), and reference to the work on the authoritarian personality as an important controversy in the field. T. W. Adorno, E. Frenkel-Brunswick, D. J. Levinson, and R. N. Sanford, *The Authoritarian Personality* (New York: Harper, 1950).

14. Figures for the use of different visual techniques in all the programmes of the series taken together were:

		%
Studio discussions		53
Original film	Individual interviews	23·5
	'Vox Pop' interviews	1·4
	Research experiments and school locations	4·4
Archive film		3·9
Presenter's links		13·8

The use of stills is not counted separately. They are included with the presenter as they usually illustrated his links.

15. The core production team consisted of the producer, the director, the researcher, the production assistant and the presenter. In formal terms, the producer was responsible for the content of the programmes; the director for their appearance; the researcher collected programme material for the producer; the production assistant handled the administration and the presenter, in addition to appearing on the screen, played a part in script writing especially by reviewing the pieces written as his links.

16. In research generally it seems to have been difficult to make people admit that they themselves hold prejudices. See for example W. W. Daniel, *Racial Discrimination in Britain* (Harmondsworth: Penguin, 1968).

17. This appears to have important implications for such questions as the accommodation of creativity in organizational structures but these cannot be developed in this paper.

18. Programme 1 also included most of the archive film because this was believed to have special impact to attract an audience for the series.

19. Again the implications are outside the scope of the present paper but it is interesting to relate this point to such work as Selznick's study of the Tennessee Valley Authority and Kornhauser's theory that in mass society voluntary associations tend to disappear, leaving the mass available to the élite through the media. The suggestion here is that the media themselves need voluntary organizations as a source of material. This also suggests another reason why the media devote attention to leadership figures, apart from the assured appeal of personalizations. See P. Selznick, TVA *and the Grass Roots* (Berkeley: University of California Press, 1952); W. Kornhauser, *The Politics of Mass Society* (London: Routledge and Kegan Paul, 1960).

20. The production of the programme followed a series of controversial Reith Lectures which had the effect of elevating the Reith lecturer into the select company of 'global thinkers'. These criteria were apparently also in use in other productions. The lecturer turned down a request to come on the programme, because he had already been inundated by other such invitations.

21. The ideal seems to approximate to the image of conversation in an Oxbridge Senior Common Room or an exclusive London Club. In this context it is interesting to compare the style of such early BBC–TV productions as *The Brains Trust*.

22. Another source for the discussion style adopted by the presenter was the interview style used in current affairs programmes. This lays particular stress on the journalist's responsibilities to ask the critical questions which might occur to the viewer, and, if necessary, to play the 'devil's advocate'.

23. The presenter's claim to represent the audience within the production team can be seen as an instance of a general occupational phenomenon. Members of occupations tend to claim special expertise which explicitly or implicitly rejects interference in their work by others who might want to control them. See especially E. C. Hughes, *Men and their Work* (Glencoe: Free Press, 1958).

24. In this context it is interesting that many of the letters received from viewers after the transmission of the programmes were 'fan letters' for the presenter.

25. In fact at the instigation of the guest, not the producer, this discussion was later re-recorded. The guest was afraid that she had devoted too much time to what might appear simply as a dispute between academics.

26. For an introductory survey of such factors see, for example, J. Scupham, *Broadcasting and the Community* (London: Watts, 1967).

27. D. McQuail, op. cit., pp. 80–1.

Books and Their Publishers

1. This is perhaps reflected in changes in new graduate recruitment patterns. Though the aggregate numbers applying for jobs remains roughly constant, three differences exist by comparison with fifteen years ago: (i) women now greatly outnumber men; (ii) there has been a decline in the quality of the academic achievements of applicants; (iii) with the expansion in university numbers, the proportion of graduates wanting to enter publishing has dropped sharply (though other factors are clearly at work here).

2. A. Etzioni, *A Comparative Analysis of Complex Organizations* (Glencoe: Free Press, 1961).

3. M. Weber, *The Methodology of the Social Sciences* (Glencoe: Free Press, 1949).

4. Mann has carried out a survey of the readership of a publisher of this kind. See P. Mann, *The Romantic Novel: A Survey of Reading Habits* (London: Mills and Boon, 1969).

5. D. Glass (ed.), *Social Mobility in Britain* (London: Routledge and Kegan Paul, 1954), Chapter XI, 'Self-Recruitment in Four Professions', by R. K. Kelsall.

6. P. Mann, pp. 351-62 in this volume

7. See, for example, M. J. Lane and K. A. Furness-Lane, *Books Girls Read* (London: Society of Young Publishers, 1967).

Developments in Soviet Radio and Television News Reporting

1. The number of wired radio loudspeakers increased from 13·8 million in 1953 to 33·7 million in 1963. Wave radio sets increased from 3·7 million in 1953 to 35·2 million in 1963. Television sets increased from 0·22 million in 1953 to 11 million in 1963. Note the drastic change in the proportion of wired to wave sets: 3·7 to 1 in 1953, and almost 1 to 1 in 1963. The proportion of wave to wired sets in 1967 is even greater.

2. The increase in the number of wave sets made it easier to hear foreign broadcasts. It is not known exactly how many short-wave sets, which are best for long-distance reception, exist in the USSR; the number is fairly substantial, since in addition to Soviet-produced short-wave sets (which have a limited band of wavelengths) many people adapt their medium- and long-

wave sets to receive short-wave broadcasts from abroad. Jamming of most
foreign broadcasts ceased in 1963.

3. 'In the Party Central Committee; On Improving Soviet Radio Broadcasting and on Further Developing Television', *Partiinaya Zhizn (Party
Life)*, No. 4 (February, 1960), pp. 26–34.

4. T. Boglovskiy and Z. L'vov, *'Posledniye Izvestiya' po Radio ('The
Latest News' on Radio)* (Moscow: State Committee of the Council of
Ministers, ussr, on Radio and Television, Scientific-Methodological
Department, 1963), p. 5.

5. Alex Inkeles, *Public Opinion in Soviet Russia* (Cambridge, Mass.:
Harvard University Press, 1958), p. 140.

6. Boglovskiy, op. cit., p. 6.

7. Ibid., p. 66.

8. 'The Publicizing of High Ideas: All-Union Creative Conference of
Publicists', *Sovietskaya Pechat (Soviet Press)*, No. 7 (July 1964), pp. 1–17.

9. Conducted by the Centre for International Studies, mit, with post-1958
émigrés from the Soviet Union.

10. 'Soviet Television', editorial in *Pravda* (19th August, 1965), p. 1.

The Structure of Foreign News

This is a much revised and extended version of a paper presented at the First
Nordic Conference on Peace Research, Oslo, 4th–8th January, 1963 and as a
guest lecture at Danmarks Journalisthöjskole, Århus, May, 1964, here published as Peace Research Institute, Oslo publication No. 14–2. The authors
wish to express their gratitude to the Institute for Social Research, the
Norwegian Research Council for Science and the Humanities, and the
Norwegian Council for Research on Conflict and Peace for financial support;
to stud.mag.art. Marit Halle and stud.mag.art. Elisabeth Bögh for assistance
with the data-collection and to our friends and colleagues at prio and particularly to Einar Östgaard for stimulating criticism and suggestions.

1. Einar Östgaard, 'Factors Influencing the Flow of News', *Journal of
Peace Research*, No. 1 (1965), pp. 39 ff.

2. For an interesting article making systematic use of these two indicators
of interdependence, see Kaare Svalastoga, 'Technology and Autonomy',
Acta Sociologica, Vol. 5, pp. 91–9.

3. Thus, a completely realistic image of other people's image of oneself
might have a harmful effect on the social adequacy of one's behaviour. Thus,
there is the important finding by Caplow and McGee in *The Academic
Marketplace* (New York: Basic Books, 1958) that members of organizations
are often subject to an Aggrandizement Effect whereby they overestimate

their own organization relative to others in the field. One might argue that if they did not, the consequent drop in self-image would result in lower achievement levels. And this may have a parallel in the field of international affairs: if the news structure was symmetric, giving to each nation its due, relative to how it was estimated by other nations, an important source of self-pride and assertiveness might be too weak to spur effective action.

4. For one way of describing this chain see Johan Galtung and Mari Holmboe Ruge, *Presentasjonen av utenriksnyheter* (Oslo: PRIO stencil No. 14–1, 1962), pp. 71–8.

5. Östgaard, op. cit., pp. 42 f.

6. For an impression of what sociologists can get out of the condition of sleeping see Vilhelm Aubert and Harrison White, 'Sleep: A Sociological Interpretation', *Acta Sociologica*, Vol. 4, No. 2, pp. 46–54 and Vol. 4, No. 3, pp. 1–16.

7. This, of course, is a fundamental idea in the psychology of perception. Actually there are two separate ideas inherent here: the notion of an absolute level that must not be too low, and the notion of the increase needed to be noticed – the 'just noticeable differences' (jnd's). The jnd increases with increasing absolute level; the stronger the amplitude, the more difference is needed to be noticed (whether this is according to Weber's principle or not). This principle probably applies very explicitly to news communication: the more dramatic the news, the more is needed to add to the drama. This may lead to important distortions. The more drama there already is, the more will the news media have to exaggerate to capture new interest, which leads to the hypothesis that there is more exaggeration the more dramatic the event – i.e., the less necessary one might feel it is to exaggerate.

8. N. R. Ashby in *An Introduction to Cybernetics* (New York: Wiley, 1957) defines noise simply as distortion that may create differences in interpretation at the sender and receiver ends of a communication channel. But one may just as well say that the signal distorts the noise as vice versa.

9. B. Berelson and G. A. Steiner in their *Human Behaviour: An Inventory of Scientific Findings* (New York: Harcourt, Brace & World, 1963) mention a number of principles under 'Perceiving', and two of them are (p. 112 and p. 100):

B7:   The greater the ambiguity of the stimulus, the more room and need for interpretation.

B3.3a: There may also be decreased awareness of stimuli if it is important *not* to see (perceptual defence).

What we have been doing is to combine these theorems (but not deductively) into the idea of defence against ambiguity. There are several reasons for this. Modern newspapers are mass media of communication, at least most of them, and publishers may feel (justifiably or not) that increase in ambiguity may decrease the sales. Moreover, to the extent that news shall serve as a basis for action orientation ambiguity will increase rather than reduce the uncertainty and provide a poorer basis for action.

10. The common factor behind both dimensions of what we have called 'meaningfulness' is probably 'identification'.

11. Again, some findings from Berelson and Steiner are useful (op. cit., p. 101 and p. 529):

B3.2: With regard to expectations, other things equal, people are more likely to attend to aspects of the environment they anticipate than to those they do not, and they are more likely to anticipate things they are familiar with.

B3.3: With regard to motives, not only do people look for things they need or want; but the stronger the need, the greater the tendency to ignore irrelevant elements.

A1: People tend to see and hear communications that are favourable to their predispositions; they are more likely to see and hear congenial communications than neutral or hostile ones. And the more interested they are in the subject, the more likely is such selective attention.

12. For a discussion of this see Johan Galtung, 'Summit Meetings and International Relations', *Journal of Peace Research* (1964), pp. 36–54.

13. For a discussion of this factor see Östgaard, op. cit., p. 151.

14. Festinger has a very interesting account of how Indians selected rumours following an earthquake, and consistent with the fear provoked by the earthquake: 'Let us speculate about the content of the cognition of these persons. When the earthquake was over they had this strong, persistent fear reaction but they could see nothing different around them, no destruction, no further threatening things. In short, a situation had been produced where dissonance existed between cognition corresponding to the fear they felt and the knowledge of what they saw around them which, one might say, amounted to the cognition that there was nothing to be afraid of. The vast majority of the rumours which were widely circulated were rumours which, if believed, provided cognition consonant with being afraid. One might even call them "fear-provoking" rumours, although, if our interpretation is correct, they would more properly be called "fear justifying" rumours.' Leon Festinger, 'The Motivating Effect of Cognitive Dissonance', in Gardner Lindzey (Ed.), *Assessment of Human Motives* (New York: Grove Press, 1958), p. 72.

15. As an example some impressions can be given from three months' systematic reading of the Moroccan newspaper *Le Petit Marocain*. In very summarized form: the first page contained news about progress in Morocco, the second about decadence, murder, rape and violence in France – so that

anybody could draw his conclusion. Of course, such things will depend rather heavily on the value-systems of the editorial staff – but we nevertheless postulate the existence of general patterns. Ola Mårtensson, in a mimeographed report (in Swedish) of a content analysis of three major papers in the USSR, indicates both personification and élite concentration. Ola Mårtensson, *Pravda, Izvestija och Krasanaja Zvezda under våren hösten 1964* (Lund: Institute for Political Science, Lund University, Sweden, 1965), 26 pp. mimeo.

16. Östgaard, op. cit., pp. 52 ff.

17. As an example it can be mentioned that in a survey carried out in Norway, November–December 1964, to the question 'What do you think has been the most important event in the news recently?' 53% answered in terms of elections in the US and changes of power in the Soviet Union, i.e., in terms of the top élite people in the top élite nations. The next answer category, 'events in the Congo', made 9%.

18. Norway appears as No. 7 in a list of 125 countries, according to the *UN Statistical Yearbook 1962* (New York: United Nations, 1963). The variable used is daily newspaper circulation per 1,000 population.

19. We omit the names of the papers, not so much out of considerateness, which would be out of order – firstly because we have nothing really inconsiderate to say about them, and secondly because they are public phenomena that might well be subject to public appraisals. The names, however, are of interest to Norwegian readers only and carry many connotations that will not be used in the analysis anyhow.

20. Not included in our sample is the biggest Norwegian newspaper with two daily issues and an average 1964 circulation of 168,000. This paper is the one with the most complete coverage of international events. Its political attitude is moderately conservative. The reason for excluding this paper is not only the considerable extra work of coding that it would imply, etc., but also the fact that we were primarily interested in papers with a very clear political profile that would span the political spectrum better.

21. One thing that should be explained is 'Norsk Telegrambyrå'. Only in some very few cases (nine in all) in connection with Norwegian soldiers recruited for UN service in the Congo does this mean that the Norwegian agency was actually the source of the piece of news. In all other cases NTB actually stands for AFP or Reuters and other Scandinavian agencies, since it acts as an agent for these foreign bureaux in Norway. (UPI and AP have their own offices in Oslo.)

22. With the exception that the two less wealthy conservative papers have chosen one each of the American agencies (III does not subscribe to UPI and IV not to AP), all four papers were subscribers to these agencies in 1960 and 1964. And all four agencies (AP, UPI, Reuters, AFP) have their headquarters

in the three major powers of the world's Northwest – a region where Norway is also located.

23. It should be noted that the time-span covered in the Cyprus crisis is of a somewhat different nature than for the Congo and Cuba. The building up of the Cyprus crisis actually took a long time and only culminated during the winter months of 1963–4. For comparative reasons we still decided to analyse a short period. We chose the weeks immediately prior to and during those in which the UN was actively brought into the conflict, in order to be able to make a comparison with the Congo situation. But this excluded the period in which Greek-Turkish-Cypriot relations were most strained, probably in January–February.

24. Bjarte Kaldhol, 'Norske soldater til Kypros', *Dagbladet*, 12/2 (1964), p. 4.

25. Wilbur Schramm refers in his book, *Mass Media and National Development* (Paris: UNESCO, 1964), p. 64, to an investigation where Indians have commented on the way India is presented in the American press. Four aspects of this particular news communication are resented, and it is claimed that they represent the greater part of the news total: India in the East-West power struggle and communism, American economic aid to India, stories about disasters and hunger, and stories about 'bizarre and outlandish things' in connection with child marriages, untouchability, etc. The first two are typical examples of increased relevance by tying what happens in remote places to one's own country, the third is a clear case of F_{12}, but also of a case where distant countries are presented as victims rather than agents of what happens. The last factor is a case of $F_{5.1}$ – it is consonant in the sense of being predicted from 'knowledge' of Indian culture; it fits stereotypes.

26. *The Indian Express* (11th July, 1962), p. 6.

27. For some comments on the phenomenon of 'imprinting' see Berelson, Steiner, op. cit., pp. 41 and 43.

28. Alan Coddington, in an unpublished paper, *A Study of Policies Advocated in Conflict Situations by British Newspapers*, studies ten national dailies over a period of two weeks (12 days) to find out how the kind of solution they recommend for conflicts in their editorials relates to whether the conflict is domestic or international. He finds quite opposite patterns for domestic and international conflicts: both are relatively low where recommendations in terms of 'external settlement' (mediation and arbitration) are concerned, but whereas domestic issues rank high on 'mutual adjustment' (compromise and reconciliation) and low on 'policies of force' (conquest and containment), the foreign issues show exactly the contrary pattern. This may be very rational and due to the more integrated nature of the domestic social system relative to the international system. But it may also be seen as a natural consequence of the structure of foreign news and as compatible with our hypotheses about the implications of that structure.

The Effects of the Media Portrayal of Violence and Aggression

SELECT BIBLIOGRAPHY

A. Glucksman, 'Report on Research Concerning the Effect on Youth of Scenes of Violence in the Cinema and on Television', *Communications*, No. 7 (Centre d'Etude des Communications de Masse, 1966), pp. 74–119.

J. D. Halloran, *The Effects of Mass Communication with Special Reference to Television*, Working Paper No. 1, Television Research Committee (Leicester University Press, 1964).

J. D. Halloran, 'Television and Violence', *Twentieth Century*, 173, No. 1024 (1965), pp. 61–72.

J. D. Halloran, 'Television Violence', *Censorship*, No. 8 (Autumn, 1966), pp. 15–21.

Otto N. Larsen (Ed.), *Violence and the Mass Media* (New York: Harper and Row, 1968).

Otto N. Larsen, 'Patterns of Violence', *The Annals of the American Academy of Political and Social Science* (March 1966).

Television Research Committee, *Second Progress Report and Recommendations* (Leicester University Press, 1969).

UNESCO, 'The Influence of the Cinema on Children and Adolescents – An annotated international bibliography', *Reports and Papers on Mass Communication*, No. 31 (1961).

UNESCO, 'The Effects of Television on Children and Adolescents', op. cit., No. 43 (1964).

The Mass Media and Egyptian Village Life

The research for this article was conducted when the author was head of the Division of Social Science of UNESCO's Arab States Training Centre for Education for Community Development (Egypt). I am indebted to my former colleague Dr L. K. Meleikeh for assistance in the research and to Mr and Mrs Gene Petersen of the American University (Beirut) for helpful suggestions and criticisms of an earlier draft.

1. The 1956 figure is taken from UNESCO, *World Communications* (Paris, 1956), p. 61. The 1960 figure was obtained by the author directly from the Ministry of Communications of the Egyptian Government which issues a permit for each legally-operated non-transistor receiver. Since a charge is made for the permit and since the number of transistor radios is increasing daily, the 1960 figure errs in underestimating the actual number of sets.

2. Transmission in other languages to Asian, African, European, and South American countries totalled an additional forty hours daily by 1960, representing a similar increase over the previous years. For data on hours of transmission in various languages for the different programmes, see Technical Bureau, Broadcasting Service, UAR, *Annual Report* (Cairo, 1960), in Arabic.

3. UNESCO, op. cit., for 1956 figure. The 1960 figure was obtained by the author from the Distribution Section of the government owned paper, *al-Jumhuriyyah*, which has kept distribution figures for all newspapers in the country since their nationalization.

4. The six villages ('Attar, Hit, Kafr al-Bagur, Mazaydeh, Qalata al-Kubra, and Sangalaf) were all located within the Menoufia Province of Lower Egypt and within a radius of about forty miles of the exclusive centre of the mass media, the metropolis of Cairo. Although exposure to the mass media in these villages was lower than the national average, it is somewhat higher than the norm for villages throughout the country and significantly higher than the villages of Upper Egypt. National averages on radio ownership indicate a ratio of one receiver for every 25 to 26 persons and one newspaper for every 80 persons. Low literacy rates coupled with the relatively high cost of the daily paper (3 cents per day in a country with an average annual *per capita* income of about $100) explain this fact.

5. An earlier survey, differently motivated but with relevant data and conclusions, was conducted in an adjacent area. See Gordon Hirabayashi and F. al-Khatib, 'Social Consciousness and Means of Communication', *Review of Economics, Politics and Business Studies*, Cairo University, Vol. 5, No. 4 (1957), pp. 13–30; and 'Communication and Political Awareness in the Villages of Egypt', *Public Opinion Quarterly*, Vol. 22, No. 3 (1958), pp. 355–63. See also, E. Brunner, 'Rural Communications Behaviour and Attitudes in the Middle East', *Rural Sociology*, Vol. 18, No. 2 (1953), pp. 149–55.

6. For comparative purposes, see Delbert C. Miller, 'A Research Note on Mass Communication', *American Sociological Review*, Vol. 10, No. 5 (1945), pp. 691–4.

7. Complete censuses of the households in all six villages had already been made in connection with another research project. The names of all household heads in the six villages were arranged serially, and the sample selected by applying the Kendall table of random numbers to the known universe.

8. This fact is easily confirmed from an independent source, the newspaper seller. Newspapers in the village are not available on the 'news stand'. Rather the dealer for several villages has standing orders from steady customers, for whom he orders the paper and delivers. No provision is made for excess supply to be sold on impulse or to be returned unsold to the distributor.

9. This fact is confirmed by L. K. Meleikeh, *Patterns of Communication and Influence in a Rural Society: A Sociometric Study* (Sirs el-Layyan, 1960), in Arabic, pp. 24–5.

10. See Elihu Katz and P. F. Lazarsfeld, *Personal Influence: The Part Played by People in the Flow of Mass Communications* (Glencoe, Illinois: The Free Press, 1955); E. Katz, 'The Two-Step Flow of Communication: An Up-To-Date Report on an Hypothesis', *Public Opinion Quarterly*, Vol. 21, No. 1, 1957, pp. 61–78; and Daniel Lerner, *The Passing of Traditional Society: Modernizing the Middle East* (Glencoe, Illinois: The Free Press, 1958).

The Audience for Television Plays

1. K. Lang, 'Mass Appeal and Minority Tastes', in B. Rosenberg and D. M. White, *Mass Culture – The Popular Arts in America* (New York: Free Press, 1957), pp. 379–84.

2. T. S. Eliot, *Notes Towards a Definition of Culture* (London: Faber, 1948), p. 48.

3. Cf. E. Katz, 'Mass Communication Research and the Study of Culture', *Studies in Public Communication*, Vol. 2 (1959), pp. 1–60.

4. J. T. Klapper, *The Effects of Mass Communication* (New York: Free Press, 1960), p. 172.

5. H. T. Himmelweit, R. Oppenheim and P. Vince, *Television and the Child* (London: Oxford University Press, 1959), pp. 142–6.

6. Ibid., p. 150.

7. H. L. Wilensky, 'Mass Society and Mass Culture: Interdependence or Independence?' *American Sociological Review*, 29 (2) (1964), pp. 173–97.

8. G. Steiner, *The People Look at Television* (New York: Alfred Knopf, 1963).

9. L. Bogart, *The Age of Television* (London: Crosby Lockwood, 2nd edition, 1958), p. 91.

10. M. Abrams, 'The Mass Media and Social Class in Great Britain', *Proceedings of the World Congress of Sociology* (1959).

11. Granada Viewership Survey, Granada TV Limited (1959).

Books, Book Readers and Bookshops

1. Useful studies do however include Robert Escarpit, *The Book Revolution* (London: Harrap/UNESCO, 1966); Lester Asheim, *Report on the Conference on Reading Development* (American Book Publishers Council, 1951); and Brewster Porcella's 'A Summary of Research on the Reading Interests

and Habits of College Graduates' (University of Illinois Graduate School of Library Science Occasional Papers, No. 74, December 1964).

2. See, for example, J. Bossard and E. Boll: *The Sociology of Child Development* (1948), and J. Bowlby, *Child Care and the Growth of Love* (1953).

3. In interviews carried out in Sheffield schools by Miss Jacqueline Burgoyne, research assistant in this research project.

4. Particularly the work of J. W. B. Douglas, as in *The Home and the School* (London: MacGibbon & Kee, 1964).

5. Escarpit defines 'literature' as 'any work which is not functional, but an end in itself'. See *The Sociology of Literature*, translated by Ernest Pick (Pairsville, Ohio: Lake Erie College Studies, 1965).

6. See Peter H. Mann, *The Romantic Novel: a Survey of Reading Habits* (London: Mills and Boon, 1969).

7. Many market research reports are duplicated and confidential. Useful published surveys are: Tottenham Public Libraries 'Reading in Tottenham', *Mass Observation* (London, 1952); A. Stuart, 'Reading Habits in Three London Boroughs', *Journal of Documentation*, Vol. 8, No. 1 (1952), and Society of Young Publishers 'Books in London', *Books* (January–February 1959).

8. Joffre Dumazedier, *Towards a Society of Leisure* (London: Collier-Macmillan, 1967).

9. See M. Abrams, 'Education, Social Class and Newspaper Reading', Institute of Practitioners in Advertising (London, 1963).

10. 'Charter Group' booksellers are members of the Booksellers Association who subscribe to the highest standards of bookselling and, amongst other things, lay down minimum training requirements for management and staff. Charter booksellers agree to send their staff to training courses run by the Booksellers Association.

11. 'Non-Charter' bookshops are in virtually every case members of the Booksellers Association but are not members of the Charter Group. Although a small number of reasonably large and progressive bookshops have not joined the Charter Group most non-members are smaller shops who cannot, or do not wish to, undertake the responsibilities required of Charter Group members.

12. W. H. Smith & Son are a large company owning shops and bookstalls all over the country. They are both wholesalers and retailers of newspapers, magazines, books and also sell stationery and some fancy goods such as toys, games, etc.

13. Boots are a national chain of chemists whose larger shops usually include sections selling travel goods, pottery, cameras, stationery, gramophone records and a book section.

14. Sir Francis Chichester's account of his single-handed voyage round

the world, entitled *Gypsy Moth Circles the World*, published in November, 1967.

15. This reference is from Fredric Warburg the publisher's auto-biography *An Occupation for Gentlemen* (London: Hutchinson, 1959). The phrase is taken from a question asked of Fredric Warburg by a fellow guest at a cocktail party: 'Tell me, since you seem to know something about it, is publishing an occupation for gentlemen, or is it a real business?' The questioner was Israel Sieff of Marks and Spencer.

Author's note: For a fuller treatment of this research see Peter H. Mann and Jacqueline L. Burgoyne, *Books and Reading* (London: André Deutsch, 1969).

Social and Personality Factors Associated with Children's Tastes in Television Viewing

1. The children came from three different schools in the North West of London.

2. For this purpose, she obtained for each child a measure of social background, his intelligence, his class results, his placement in class, his job aspirations, the age at which he would like to leave school (were he free to choose) and a projective measure of his need achievement as well as measures of anxiety and strength of conscience.

3. The other points on the scale were: 'I like it very much; I quite like it; I don't mind it.'

4. Our earlier study had shown that ten to eleven-year-olds watch as late as that.

5. Programmes which had been seen by less than 83% of the sample were excluded from the factor analysis: this reduced the number of programmes from 60 to 34. The Promax method of factor analysis, developed by Hendrickson and White, was used.

6. All relationships discussed in this paper were significant at at least the 0·05 level.

The Design of Investigations into the Effects of Radio and Television Programmes and other Mass Communications

REFERENCES

BBC Audience Research, *Bon Voyage* (an unpublished report, 1955).
BBC Audience Research, *Matters of Medicine* (an unpublished report, 1960).

BBC Audience Research, *Crime* (an unpublished report, 1961).

BBC Audience Research, *The Death Penalty* (an unpublished report, 1962).

W. A. Belson, 'A Technique for Studying the Effects of a Television Broadcast', *Applied Statistics*, 5 (1956), pp. 195–202.

W. A. Belson, 'Learning and Attitude Changes Resulting from Viewing a Television Series "Bon Voyage" ', *British Journal of Educational Psychology*, 26, 31 (1956).

W. A. Belson, 'Matching and Prediction on the Principle of Biological Classification', *Applied Statistics*, 8 (1959), pp. 65–75.

F. S. Chapin, *Experimental Designs in Sociological Research* (New York: Harper, 1947).

W. G. Cochran, 'The Planning of Observational Studies of Human Populations', *Journal of the Royal Statistical Society*, A, 128 (1965), pp. 234–66.

C. W. Harris (Ed.), *Problems in Measuring Change* (Madison: University of Wisconsin Press, 1963).

H. T. Himmelweit, A. N. Oppenheim and P. Vince, *Television and the Child* (London: Oxford University Press, 1958).

J. T. Klapper, *The Effects of Mass Communication* (Glencoe: Free Press, 1961).

G. Lindzey (Ed.), *Handbook of Social Psychology* (Reading, Mass.: Addison-Wesley, 1954).

S. Rosenbaum, 'A Significant Chart for Percentages', *Applied Statistics*, 8 (1959), pp. 45–52.

C. Selltiz, M. Jahoda, M. Deutsch and S. W. Cooke, *Research Methods in Social Relations* (New York: Holt, 1959).

J. A. Sonquist and J. N. Morgan, *The Detection of Interaction Effects* (1964).

J. Trenaman, *The Effect of Broadcasting a Serialized Version of a Book on the Reading of the Book* (an unpublished BBC report, 1953).

Producers' Attitudes Towards TV Coverage of an Election Campaign

1. Empirical evidence of the effects of exposure to political materials in the mass media on voters' awareness of election issues is presented in Chapter 10 of Jay G. Blumler and Denis McQuail, *Television in Politics: Its Uses and Influence* (London: Faber and Faber, 1968).

2. Angus Campbell, Philip E. Converse, E. Warren and Donald E. Stokes, *The American Voter* (New York: John Wiley, 1960), p. 60.

3. The author is grateful to Mr John Grist, the then Deputy Head of the Current Affairs Group, for the imaginative initiative which made this study possible. He also wishes to express his appreciation of the candour with which the many members of the Group discussed their work with him.

4. As the only nightly programme produced by the Current Affairs Group, *Campaign Report* was intended to provide the most topical coverage of election developments. The whole of each of three editions of *Panorama* was devoted to a single campaign issue (incomes policy, the Rhodesian crisis, and the financing of the welfare state). *Election Forum* and *Question Time* provided platforms from which politicians answered questions emanating from an independent source (ordinary viewers and working journalists, respectively).

5. Warren Breed, 'Social Control in the Newsroom: A Functional Analysis', *Social Forces*, Vol. XXXII, No. 4 (1955), pp. 326–35.

6. The deadlock arose seemingly from the pitting of Conservative pressure for a debate *à deux* between the major parties' spokesmen (Mr Heath and Mr Wilson) against Labour's insistence that Mr Grimond, the Liberal leader, should also appear in any confrontation. The BBC reporter envisaged a programme in two halves, one part of which would be two-sided and the other three-sided, so timed that a 5:5:3 ratio would govern the shares of attention received by each individual.

7. This passage reflects an acceptance of Levinson's distinction between two meanings of the concept of role. (Cf. D. J. Levinson, 'Role, Personality, and Social Structure in the Organizational Setting', *Journal of Abnormal and Social Psychology*, Vol. LVIII, No. 2 (1959), pp. 170–80). First, a role may be conceived as a set of external, organizationally-given demands on an individual, comprising 'the situational pressures that confront him as the occupant of a given structural position'. But second, the concept of role may stand for an individual's own view of his part in an organization – his inner definition, that is, of what someone in his social position is supposed to think and do about it. It is the latter notion of role that has shaped the author's analysis of certain attitudes of television journalists towards their own profession, their sources, and their audiences.

8. Warren Breed, op. cit.

9. According to Levinson (op. cit.), one of the determinants of a role occupant's degree of autonomy is 'the specificity or narrowness with which the normative requirements [of an externally set role] are defined'. As he puts it, 'the less specific the norms – the greater the area of personal choice for the individual'.

10. Cf. Lord Normanbrook, 'The Functions of the BBC's Governors', Lunch-time Lectures, 4th Series, No. 3 (London: British Broadcasting Corporation, 1965).

11. Breed (op. cit.) discerned quite different effects of the processes of reference group formation in American newspaper offices. He maintained that a new staff reporter was typically socialized to the policy requirements of his employer through his identification with a reference group of execu-

tives and veteran staffers. Perhaps one of the tasks of a sociology of the communicators is to specify those factors which determine whether a reference group linking staff members to higher executives serves primarily as an agency of conformity to official policy or mainly as a support for policy initiatives stemming from the staff level.

12. Cf. Blumler and McQuail, op. cit., Chs. 5 and 6.

13. When the last *Election Forum* was being prepared, for example, the reporters spent much time looking for a suitable final question to put to Mr Wilson. They sought one that would give to the Labour Leader the same opportunity that Mr Heath had enjoyed on the previous night to wind up with a positive and broad-ranging summary of his party's election case. When preparing an item on floating voters for *Campaign Report*, many filmed interviews were inspected before the producers were satisfied that the reason given by a Labour leaner for supporting the Government would seem as convincing as the material they intended to present from a pro-Conservative leaner. And during a *24 Hours* debate on housing, instructions were passed on to the interviewer to steer the discussion into an area of presumed Labour strength (rents and local authority housing), so that it would not be dominated by challenges to other aspects of the Government's record in this field.

14. Some of the qualities sought in discussants on current affairs programmes are suggested by one producer's explanation of his confidence in Messrs Davis and Lawson:

They are both highly professional experts who know how to encapsulate what they want to say in simple terms. They also have a good sense of timing. They adhere, that is, to a sort of Queensberry's rules for the conduct of television rows. They won't interrupt in the wrong places. They won't deliver a monologue. And they won't anticipate in their opening statements something that can be said more effectively later.

15. Walter Gieber has suggested that three possible relationships between reporters and their sources can be envisaged: '(a) the reporters remain independent of their sources; (b) the reporters and the sources find areas of collaboration for their mutual benefit; (c) the sources "absorb" and dominate the reporters, or vice-versa.' But in spite of the seeming completeness of this typology, none of these formulations fits the relations that obtained in 1966 between the BBC journalists and certain politicians. This is because each of the categories refers to a resolved state of affairs, whereas the situation observed by the author was essentially unresolved. Hence it has been characterized in the text as a continuing struggle for access to the public. Cf. Walter Gieber, 'News is What Newspapermen Make It', in Lewis

Anthony Dexter and David Manning White (Eds.), *People, Society, and Mass Communications* (Glencoe: The Free Press, 1964), pp. 173–80.

16. Walter Gieber, 'Two Communicators of the News: A Study of the Roles of Sources and Reporters', *Social Forces*, Vol. XXXIX, No. 1 (1962), pp. 76–83.

17. Cf. Jay G. Blumler, 'Parliament and Political TV', *Encounter* (March 1967), pp. 52–6.

18. According to interview material, one source of this unfavourable judgment was a perception of how a rival service had more successfully reported the same campaign. It was noted that ITN's *Election '64* had won both high audience ratings and critical approval and that it had been able to combine late coverage with comment and interviews by such specialist reporters as Alastair Burnet, George Ffitch, and Robert Kee.

19. The concept of an 'audience image' is defined by Herbert J. Gans in 'The Creator-Audience Relationship in the Mass Media: An Analysis of Movie Making', in Bernard Rosenberg and David Manning White (Eds.), *Mass Culture: The Popular Arts in America* (Glencoe: The Free Press, 1957), pp. 315–24. It is a notion formed by a communicator of the standards that will shape the reactions of an intended audience to his work. In Gans' words, it 'functions as an external observer-judge against which the communicator unconsciously tests his product even while he is creating it'.

20. The transactional model represents one reaction against exaggerated notions of the power of the mass media to shape the opinions and attitudes of audience members. It puts the communicator and the audience on terms of equality – as if each side was engaged in a bargain with the other, giving something so that it may receive something it desires in return. This implies that the communicator is motivated to find out what the members of his audience expect or would welcome from him. An outline of the transactional model has been presented by Raymond A. Bauer in two writings: 'The Communicator and the Audience', *Journal of Conflict Resolution*, Vol. II, No. 1 (1958), pp. 76–77; and 'Communication as Transaction' in Donald E. Payne (Ed.), *The Obstinate Audience* (Ann Arbor, Michigan: Foundation for Research on Human Behaviour, 1965), pp. 3–11.

21. In addition to presenting pieces on Vietnam, Cyprus, Saudi Arabia, and Israel during the campaign, *24 Hours* transmitted a long report on the case of a 'natural father' (who insisted on retaining the custody of his illegitimate child, despite the mother's wish to have him adopted), an item on a Canadian sex/spy scandal, coverage of the climb of Mount Eiger, a profile of the starlet, Miss Racquel Welch, and interviews with David McCallum and Michael Caine.

22. The row between Nigel Lawson and William Davis probably belongs in this category, together with a four-sided confrontation on the 'Cowley

noose trial' (between Quintin Hogg, Ray Gunter, a trade union spokesman, and one of the alleged victims), and an outside broadcast from an unusual pub in which the reactions of many foreigners to a British election were presented.

23. The average audience for 12 editions of *24 Hours* between 14th March and 29th March was 9·4% – compared with 10·6% in the immediately preceding weeks. The somewhat later hour at which the programme was presented during the campaign probably explains the slight decline. (Cf. 'The 1966 General Election', Audience Research Department, British Broadcasting Corporation, April 1966.)

24. The BBC compiles its Reaction Index by asking members of a rotating viewing panel to record their impressions of a broadcast as a whole by ticking one of five scale positions, ranging from exceptional enjoyment to extreme dislike or boredom. These positions are scored 0–4, and the index is expressed as a percentage of the maximum that could have been scored. Thus, it ranges from zero to 100.

25. Cf. 'The 1966 General Election', op. cit.

26. Herbert Waltzer, 'In the Magic Lantern: Television Coverage of the 1964 National Conventions', *Public Opinion Quarterly*, Vol. XXX, No. 1 (1966), pp. 33–53.

27. Martin Harrison, 'Television and Radio' in D. E. Butler and Anthony King, *The British General Election of 1966* (London: Macmillan, 1966), pp. 125-48.

28. On 18th March the programme opened with long extracts from the speeches of rival party figures on the issues of the Common Market, Rhodesia, and whether or not there should be a television confrontation. And in its final edition of 29th March the programme ended with contrasted extracts taken from speeches made earlier in the campaign by Mr Wilson and Mr Heath about housing, the economy, Rhodesia, and the welfare services.

The Spiegel Affair and the West German Press: The Initial Phase

1. This paper focuses on one of several aspects of the Spiegel Affair under investigation by the author. Field research for the entire project was made financially possible through a Fulbright Research Grant and grants from the Research Councils of Louisiana State and University of Texas.

2. 'Strafverfahren gegen das Nachrichtenmagazin "Der Spiegel" ', *Bulletin des Presse-und Informationamtes der Bundesregierung* No. 203 (Bonn, 31st October, 1962), p. 1716. Dated 10th October, 1962, the issue of *Der Spiegel* (Vol. 16, No. 41) in which the article appeared was actually released to the public two days earlier. More than 8,000 words in length, the article is

presented as a cover story, or 'Titelgeschichte', superficially conveying the impression of focusing on the personality and views of the then Inspector-General of the Bundeswehr, General Friedrich Foertsch. In fact, the article is developed around the views of the then Defence Minister Franz Josef Strauss and is a sequel to an article, 'Stärker als 1939?', which was published in the 13th June, 1962 issue (Vol. 16, No. 23). Both articles represented an attempt by *Der Spiegel* to analyse the problems confronting NATO in devising an effective strategy in the event of war initiated in Europe by the Soviet Union and to examine the implications of alternative strategies for the Bundeswehr. The Foertsch article reveals that, as a result of the NATO 1962 fall exercises (code-named Fallex 62), the Bundeswehr was found to be poorly prepared to make a major contribution to an effective resistance by NATO to an attack from the East and thus received the lowest possible rating from the NATO manœuvre judges. More importantly, the article critically discussed the alleged assumption of Strauss that an attack from the East requires an immediate nuclear retaliation from the West. By citing apparently 'inside' information, the article concluded that Strauss, in pursuing his nuclear deterrent policy, had not only opposed the prevailing thinking within NATO but had also rejected the advice of a substantial group of military advisers within his own ministry.

3. Formal charges of treason against Ahlers, Rudolf Augstein, and Colonel Martin were filed on 23rd March, 1963, by the Federal Prosecutor's Office with the Federal High Court (*Bundesgerichtshof*). Some two years later the Third Senate of the High Court dismissed the charges against Ahlers and Augstein on the ground of 'insufficient evidence'. The Court held open the charge against Martin. (*Bundesgerichtshof-Beschluss vom 13. Mai 1965, 6 StE 4/64.*) Formal charges have not been brought against the other persons who were originally detained for investigatory purposes.

4. *Süddeutsche Zeitung* (29th October, 1962), p. 1; *Der Spiegel*, Vol. 16, No. 45 (7th November, 1962), p. 52. The available evidence suggests that Stammberger knew generally that an investigation was under way against *Der Spiegel* but neither his State Secretary (Walter Strauss) nor the Federal Prosecutor's Office alerted him in advance to the particulars of the planned action of the night of 26th October. The failure of Walter Strauss to inform Stammberger, a breach of the relationship that presumably is to exist between a State Secretary and his immediate superior, the Minister, produced a curious sequence of charges and denials. At one point in the episode, the State Secretary (Volkmar Hopf) in the Defence Ministry assumed responsibility for having instructed his counterpart in the Justice Ministry in such a way that the latter assumed he was to keep the planned action secret from the Justice Minister. Later, the circle of responsibility widened to include the Defence Minister Franz Josef Strauss, who in turn added that he had acted

with the approval of Chancellor Adenauer. Adenauer denied that he had authorized anyone to keep the planned action secret from Stammberger. Both Walter Strauss and Volkmar Hopf were temporarily relieved of their positions, but were later returned to active status in other capacities.

5. *Stenographischer Bericht, 47. Sitzung, Bonn, Freitag, den 9. November 1962*, Deutscher Bundestag, pp. 2077–8.

6. The second cabinet crisis ended on 7th December, 1962, when the FDP leadership revealed that it was prepared to re-enter a coalition with the CDU/CSU. Among the assurances received by the FDP were that it would be more fully integrated into the decision processes of the Adenauer government and that Strauss would not be permitted to remain in the cabinet. Stammberger was also dropped from the newly constructed cabinet, and in 1964 he switched his party affiliation from the FDP to the SPD.

7. In a position paper prepared in 1965 by the FDP national leadership for circulation among FDP candidates and *Land* organizations, the prevention of Strauss's return to a ministerial post was presented as a key strategic goal of the party if it were again to help form a government after the 1965 Bundestag election. ('Die Situation der Parteien vor der Bundestagswahl 1965', FDP, mimeographed, no date. Cf. *Die Winterreise der FDP*, Bonn, FDP, 1965, p. 15.)

8. In attempting to clarify and criticize the role of the federal government in the *Spiegel* action, the SPD relied largely upon the questioning techniques available to it in the Bundestag. Without seeking a special parliamentary investigation of the affair, the SPD Bundestag delegation published its own findings in *Bericht der Sozialdemokratische Bundestagsfraktion über die Behandlung der 'Spiegel' Affäre durch die Bundesregierung* (Bonn: Neuer Vorwärts-Verlag, 1963).

9. Demonstrations involving from a few hundred to several thousand students occurred in Frankfurt, Munich, West Berlin, Hamburg, and Bonn. Petitions of protest were circulated among the students of most West German universities and technical colleges.

10. See Jürgen Seifert, 'Die Spiegel Affäre', in Erich Kuby et al., *Franz Josef Strauss, Ein Typus unserer Zeit* (Munich: Verlag Kurt Desch, 1963), pp. 233–314, at p. 313, footnote 155.

11. In addition to various regional associations, the two major national associations were the *Deutscher Journalistenverband* and the *Verband deutscher Zeitschriftenverleger*. On 30th October, 1962, the International Press Institute issued a statement from its Zurich headquarters expressing concern over the action and concluding: 'It would appear that the democratic principle of freedom of the press has been disregarded in the determination to investigate an alleged criminal action by individual journalists' (*Die Welt*, 31st October, 1962, p. 1).

12. Ibid. Most of the signers were prominent members of 'Gruppe 47', a gathering of German writers and intellectuals who began meeting annually in 1947.

13. The *Institut für Demoskopie* found in a survey that by 22nd November, 1962, 91 per cent of the sample 'was informed about the Spiegel Affair'. Erich Peter Neumann, 'Die Spiegel-Affäre in der Öffentlichen Meinung', Allensbach am Bodensee (19th June, 1963), p. 7, offset print. A poll by EMNID· Institute showed that 93 per cent of the male sample and 78 per cent of the female sample 'had heard or read of the arrest of Rudolf Augstein and certain of his co-workers'. *EMNID-Informationen*, No. 8 (18th February, 1963), p. 2.

14. Cf. Seifert, op. cit.; Theodor Eschenburg, *Die Affäre, Eine Analyse* (Hamburg: Broschek, 1962); Martin Löffler, *Der Verfassungsauftrag der Presse, Modellfall Spiegel* (Karlsruhe: Verlag C. F. Muller, 1963); George Bailey, 'The "Spiegel" Affair: A Distorting Mirror', *The Reporter* (6th December, 1962), pp. 29–33; 'The Spiegel Affair: Three Views', *Council for Correspondence Newsletter* (November 1962), pp. 1–6; and Otto Kirchheimer and Constantine Menges, 'A Free Press in a Democratic State?' in Gwendolen M. Carter and Alan F. Westin (Eds.), *Politics in Europe* (New York: Harcourt, Brace, and World, 1965), pp. 87–138. An official version of the procedures used in the investigation is contained in 'Der "Spiegel" Bericht: Darstellung der Vorgänge beim Ermittlungsverfahren gegen Verleger, Redakteure und Informanten des Nachrichtenmagazins "Der Spiegel" ', *Bulletin des Presse-und Informationsamtes der Bundesregierung*, Bonn, No. 23 (5th February, 1963), pp. 195–204.

15. The Spiegel Affair might also be usefully examined in terms of Adenauer's 'equilibrial' system, particularly as he sought during the bargaining stage to reconcile the demands of various groups upon which he was dependent for continued support in the Bundestag. See Peter Merkl, 'Equilibrium, Structure of Interests and Leadership: Adenauer's Survival as Chancellor', *American Political Science Review*, Vol. 56, No. 3 (1962), pp. 634–50, in which one version of this equilibrial system is developed.

16. This typology, in revised form is borrowed from W. Phillips Davison, 'The Mass Media in West German Political Life', in Hans Speier and Davison (Eds.), *West German Leadership and Foreign Policy* (Evanston, Ill.: Row, Peterson, 1957, pp. 242–81, at pp. 244–6.

17. I am indebted to the staff of the *Presseauswertungabteilung* for making available to me their extensive file of newspaper clippings on the Spiegel Affair. None of the staff, of course, is responsible for views expressed in this paper.

18. In the year prior to the Spiegel Affair there were 1,636 newspapers in

the Federal Republic, including West Berlin, with a total circulation of some 20·5 million copies, *Die deutsche Presse 1961* (Berlin: Duncker und Humblot, 1961).

19. In determining the editorial positions of the newspapers, both editorials in the formal sense and commentaries by editorial staff writers have been taken into account. Use of the latter is justified in certain cases because of the tendency of many German newspapers not to distinguish clearly between editorials and interpretative news reports.

20. A few newspapers in the Unclassifiable category simply took no editorial position during the initial stage of the Affair. Most of the Unclassifiable newspapers presented a type of 'balanced' editorial position which could not be classified as either Sympathetic or Critical.

21. A refinement particularly could be attempted in discovering the *intensity* of attitude toward the *Spiegel* action. Certain newspapers in our sample were obviously more critical or more sympathetic than others in the same category.

22. In 1961, and again in 1962, *Der Spiegel* published reports implying that Strauss, improperly and possibly for personal financial gain, had attempted to influence the awarding by the US Defense Department to the 'Fibag' firm *(Finanzbau-Aktiengesellschaft)* of a contract for the construction in West Germany of housing for American military personnel. At the formal request of the SPD delegation, the Bundestag in 1962 established a committee of enquiry to investigate the charges. The committee's first report, submitted orally by the committee chairman on 20th June, 1962, exonerated Strauss of any violations of legal and official responsibilities (Deutscher Bundestag, *Stenographischer Bericht, 37. Sitzung, Bonn, Donnerstag, den 28. Juni 1962*, pp. 1580 ff.). The first report was endorsed by the CDU/CSU and FDP committee members; the SPD members protested the procedures used in developing the first report. At the request of the SPD delegation in the Bundestag, this time supported by the FDP, the committee was asked to continue its investigation and to attempt to clarify and substantiate the evidence developed prior to the first report. The second report was brought before the Bundestag on 25th October, 1962 (ibid., *43. Sitzung, Bonn, Donnerstag, den 25. Oktober 1962*, pp. 1874 ff.). The majority of the committee members (FDP and CDU/CSU) again held that Strauss had not committed a violation of his official competence *(Dienstpflichtverletzung)*; the SPD dissented and found Strauss had done so by endorsing the Fibag firm's efforts to secure the contract without properly determining the capabilities and legal competence of the firm to undertake such a construction project. The Foertsch article appeared in public on 8th October, 1962. The court order permitting the raids against *Der Spiegel* were issued in confidence on 23rd October, 1962. Why, in short, the press complained, had there been a delay both in securing the search and

seizure warrants and in executing them? Were the raids timed to coincide with the 'acquittal' of Strauss by the Bundestag for his role in the Fibag incident?

23. Cf. Seifert, op. cit., pp. 272–81.

The Audience for Election Television

1. For a discussion of the effects of the need of communicators for guidance from images of their audiences, see Denis McQuail, 'Uncertainty about the Audience and the Organization of Mass Communications', *The Sociological Review*, Monograph No. 13 (1969), pp. 75–84.

2. For examples of the assumption that modern techniques of communication place great power in the hands of political propagandists, see Vance Packard, *The Hidden Persuaders* (London: Longmans, Green, 1957) and James M. Perry, *The New Politics* (London: Weidenfeld and Nicolson, 1968). Perry asserts that campaign managers can now 'play upon the voters like virtuosos. They can push a pedal here, strike a chord there. And presumably they can get precisely the response they seek.'

3. The findings of empirical research are often cited in support of this interpretation. It was also furthered by Joseph Klapper's conclusion drawn from an authoritative review of many studies of communications effects, that 'persuasive mass communication functions far more frequently as an agent of reinforcement than as an agent of change'. (Cf. Joseph Klapper, *The Effects of Mass Communication* (Glencoe: The Free Press, 1960).

4. The allegedly faint interest of the general public in following politics has often been used as ammunition in British controversies about the development of political broadcasting. It was cited, for example, as an argument against the televising of Parliament in the Commons debate of 24th November, 1966; cf. Jay G. Blumler, 'Parliament and Political TV', *Encounter* (March 1967). Richard Crossman's recent plea for an extension of specialist political programming, intended to cater for the interests of activists, also rested on a distinction between 'mass viewer demand for easy popular entertainment and the demand of minority groups for programmes with creative qualities'. Cf. Richard Crossman, 'The Politics of Television', in *Three Studies in Modern Communications*, Panther Records No. 7 (London: Panther Books, 1969).

5. Notably Bernard Berelson, Paul F. Lazarsfeld and William N. McPhee, *Voting: A Study of Opinion Formation in an Election Campaign* (University of Chicago Press, 1954).

6. Cf. V. O. Key, Jr, *The Responsible Electorate* (Cambridge, Mass: Harvard University Press, 1966).

7. In 1966 the Television Research Unit was incorporated into an enlarged Centre for Television Research at the University of Leeds.

8. Joseph Trenaman and Denis McQuail, *Television and the Political Image* (London: Methuen, 1961).

9. Jay G. Blumler and Denis McQuail, *Television in Politics: Its Uses and Influence* (London: Faber and Faber, 1968).

10. Taken from pp. 187–90 of *Television and the Political Image*.

11. Ibid., pp. 190–3.

12. Ibid., pp. 203–6.

13. Following the sudden death of Joseph Trenaman in 1962, Jay G. Blumler joined Denis McQuail in the Television Research Unit in 1963. Dr McQuail left Leeds in 1965 and is currently a Lecturer in Sociology at the University of Southampton, while Dr Blumler is the Research Director of the Leeds Centre for Television Research.

14. Taken from *Television in Politics: Its Uses and Influence*, pp. 84–5.

15. For example, the 'very strong' category included all the respondents who had endorsed at least three reasons for watching party broadcasts and no more than one for avoiding them. The 'very weak' category included all the respondents whose number of reasons for avoiding party broadcasts had exceeded their reasons for watching them by two endorsements or more. Full details of the definition of the intermediate categories can be consulted in *Television in Politics*, p. 128.

16. Cf. Leo Bogart, *The Age of Television* (London: Crosby, Lockwood, 1958) and Gary A. Steiner, *The People Look at Television* (New York: Alfred Knopf, 1963).

17. Taken from *Television in Politics: Its Uses and Influence*, pp. 152–3.

18. It should not be concluded from Table VI that only Liberal broadcasts had helped to achieve this result. An even closer association was found between Liberal Party attitude change and exposure to the election news on TV.

19. Taken from *Television in Politics: Its Uses and Influence*, pp. 217–23.

The National Press and Partisan Change

1. There are in fact ten serious national dailies produced in London. But because of their specialist nature and the size of their circulation we do not deal here with the *Financial Times* (150,000) or the *Daily Worker/Morning Star* (65,000).

2. In 1964 there were seventeen provincial morning newspapers (in no case with a circulation of more than 130,000). There were seventy evening

newspapers, with a total circulation of over eight million, which tended to be primarily local in their coverage. There were also eight Sunday morning newspapers, with a total circulation of 24 million. The circulation of newspapers per head of population is 66 per cent greater in Britain than in the United States. For morning newspapers it is three times as great.

3. One reason for our special focus on the morning press in this chapter is that electors give it precedence over the other newspapers. While 60 per cent of our respondents claimed to have followed the campaign in their morning newspaper only 11 per cent mentioned a Sunday paper as a political source and only 6 per cent an evening newspaper.

4. The *Daily Herald* was transmuted into the *Sun* on 15th September, 1964.

Further Reading

There is no truly satisfactory way of producing a list of further reading for a volume such as this. The selected bibliography below follows several (conflicting) criteria:

(1) It is very much a selection.
(2) Preference is given to items which contain good bibliographies.
(3) Preference given to items referred to in the pieces in the volume or the introduction. This involves a bias towards pieces on media organizations and communications – and towards the sociology of journalism, rather than, for instance, entertainment.
(4) Preference given to pieces in the quoted Readers.
(5) But in many cases items which appear in one of these Readers are not listed separately.

The student who is seriously interested in following up the literature in a specialized area must use some other bibliography.

BIBLIOGRAPHIES

The best general bibliography at the time of writing was:

Donald A. Hansen and J. Herschel Parsons, *Mass Communication: A Research Bibliography* (Santa Barbara, California: The Glendessary Press, 1968), paper, 144 pp.

Other bibliographies are:

Joffre Dumazedier and Claire Guinchat, *La Sociologie du Loisir* (Paris: UNESCO in Current Sociology, 1968).

Warren C. Price, *The Literature of Journalism* (University of Minnesota Press, 1959).

Wilbur Schramm, *The Effects of Television on Children and Adults* (Paris: UNESCO, 1964).

William A. Taft, *200 Books on American Journalism* (University of Missouri, 1966, paper).

READERS

Bernard Berelson and Morris Janowitz (Eds.), *Reader in Public Opinion and Communication* (New York: Free Press; London: Collier-Macmillan, 1966)

Lewis Anthony Dexter and David Manning White (Eds.), *People, Society and Mass Communications* (New York: Free Press; London: Collier-Macmillan, 1964).

Wilbur Schramm (Ed.), *Mass Communications* (Urbana: University of Illinois Press, 1960).

Bernard Rosenberg and David Manning White (Eds.), *Mass Culture: The Popular Arts in America* (New York: Free Press, 1957 and 1964, paper).

David Manning White and Richard Averson (Eds.), *Sight, Sound and Society: Motion pictures and Television in America* (Boston: Beacon Press 1968).

INTRODUCTORY TEXTS

A student using this Reader is advised to consult one of several introductory texts, according to his main interest. One very useful introductory text is:

Denis McQuail, *Towards a Sociology of Mass Communications* (London: Collier-Macmillan, 1969), 122 pp. In addition to being a helpful broad introduction to media research in general, and to audience studies in particular, McQuail's short book contains a valuable Annotated Bibliography – which includes brief comments on over 200 items, many of them not listed in this Reader.

Other short introductory texts include:

David Chaney, *The Social Organization of Mass Communications* (London: Macmillan, 1970).

Richard R. Fagen, *Politics and Communication* (Boston: Little, Brown, 1966, paper).

James Halloran (Ed.), *The Effects of Television* (London: Panther, 1970, paper).

Robert E. Lane and David Sears, *Public Opinion* (New York: Prentice-Hall, 1964, paper).

Charles R. Wright, *Mass Communications: a sociological perspective* (New York: Random House, 1959, paper).

Selected Bibliography

The items in the alphabetical bibliography are first listed by authors under the same headings as in the Introduction.

1. *The media: a value-laden subject.* All the 'introductory texts' deal with concepts. For three extremely broad uses of 'Communication' see Deutsch (1963), Doob, and Duncan. For a critical account of 'Mass' see Bramson, for 'Escape' see Katz and Foulkes.

2. *History of media research.* For the Flow of News – International Press Institute (1953); Östgaard. The media and society – Parsons and White; Wright. For the gatekeeper and the opinion leader – White (1950); Katz and Lazarsfeld (1955). Other influential accounts of media studies – Lasswell (1948); Merton (1957); Rose (1962) and Bramson (1961).

3. *Historical study of the media.* Altick, Barnouw (1966 and 1968); Blumler and McQuail (1965); Briggs (1961 and 1965); Cranfield; Edelman; Emery; Gross; Herd; Hower; Mott; Paulu; Political and Economic Planning (1938, 1952 and 1958); Pound and Harmsworth; Siebert; *The Times;* F. Williams (1957 and 1969).

4. *Cross-media patterns.* Belson; Carter and Greenberg; DeFleur (1966); Pinkus; Roper; UNESCO (1964).

5. *Organizational goals and* (6) *Media organizations, communications organizations.* Bensman; Breed (1960); Buckmaster and Moore; Economist Intelligence Unit; Escarpit; Goulden; Janowitz (1952); Nixon and Ward; Park; Stark; Tunstall (1964); Windlesham (1969).

7. *Communicators.* Most of the following deal with journalists: Bensman; Breed (1955 and 1960); Carr-Saunders and Wilson; Cohen; Crawley; Donohew; Gieber; Gill; Hohenberg; International Press Institute (1961 and 1962); Kelley; Kruglak (1955 and 1963); Mansfield; Matthews; Nimmo; Rosten; Samuelson; Stark; Tannenbaum; Tunstall (1964 and 1970); White (1950).

8. *Performers and Stars.* Cornwell; Findlater; Greenberg and Parker; Kraus; Lang and Lang; Love; Lowenthal; Merton (1946); Morin; Morin and Bremond; Rosenberg and Fliegel.

9. *Media content: culture, news, violence.* Batlin; Berelson (1952 and 1964); Friendly and Goldfarb; Hart; Hall and Whannel; Hoggart; Kracauer (1952 and 1960); Lippmann; Lowenthal (1944 and 1961); Lyle; McClelland;

Merrill; Park; Pool (1952 and 1959); Sharf; Shibutani; Wilensky (1964); R. Williams.

10. *Audiences.* Strong bibliographies on certain aspects of the audience are contained in: (a) Knapper and Warr – Perception of persons and media. (b) Belson (1967) – The television audience. (c) Blumler and McQuail (1968) – The political audience. Other references are: DeFleur and DeFleur; Dumazedier; Halloran; Hanson; Himmelweit (1958, and 1962 two); Hovland (1949, 1953 and 1957); Inkeles; Johnson; Katz and Lazarsfeld (1955); Klapper; Larsen, Lazarsfeld et al. (1944); Mann and Burgoyne, McLeod; Merton (1946); Musgrave, Payne; Robinson and Converse; Sainslieu; Schramm et al. (1961); Seldes; Shils and Janowitz; Steiner; TV Research Committee; Wilensky (1964).

11. *Audience research by the media.* Belson (1962 and 1967); Handel; Market Research Society.

12. *Media and politics.* Beith; Berelson et al. (1954); Blumler (1967); Blumler and McQuail (1968); Butler and Stokes; Cater; Cohen; Converse; Dreyer and Rosenbaum; Glaser; Gosnell; Harrison (1964 and 1966); Hart; Kelley; Key; Kraus; Kruglak (1955 and 1963); Lang and Lang; Lazarsfeld et al. (1944); Matthews; Newland; Nimmo; Pickles; Remand and Neuschwander; Rokkan and Torsvik; Rose (1966 and 1967); Rosten; Rubin; Seymour-Ure (1962, 1966 and 1968); Shils and Janowitz; Trenaman and McQuail; Tunstall (1970); Waltzer; Whale; Wilensky (1964 and 1967); Windlesham (1966).

13. *American media dominance.* Beattie; Cooper; Dizard; Kruglak (1963); Maddox; Schiller; White and Leigh; F. Williams (1953).

14. *American media research dominance.* On the Media and Development. Doob; Goody; Lerner (1958); Lerner and Schramm (1967); Pye; Rao; Schramm (1964); Sommerland; Yu (1964). Two studies dealing with Negroes and the media, and Jews and the media, respectively: Myrdal; Sharf.

15. *Public media policy and social research.* Barnouw (1966); Briggs (1961); Chafee; Gerald (1956 and 1963); Hale; Harrison (1964); Henderson; International Press Institute (1959); Levy; Ogilvy-Webb; Rourke; Skornia; Wedell; Wilson.

16. *Theory, ideology and methods.* No attempt will be made here to select from the huge social science literature on theory and methods. Two useful introductions to some theoretical approaches which have been used in relation to the media are: Schramm (Ed.), *The Science of Human Communication* (1963) and DeFleur, *Theories of Mass Communication* (1966).

   Some of the methods which have been used in media research are discussed in: Lazarsfeld and Rosenberg (Eds.), *The Language of Social Research* (1955), Nafziger and White (Eds.), *Introduction to Mass Communication Research*

(1963), and Berelson and Janowitz (Eds.), *Reader in Public Opinion and Communication* (1966), pp. 623–755.

Current developments can be followed in the *Public Opinion Quarterly* and other journals.

Richard D. Altick, *The English Common Reader: a social history of the mass reading public 1800–1900* (University of Chicago Press, 1957; 1963 paper).

Erik Barnouw, *A Tower in Babel: A History of Broadcasting in the United States*, Vol. 1 to 1933 (N.Y.: Oxford University Press, 1966).

Erik Barnouw, *The Golden Web*, Vol. 2 1933 to 1953 (N.Y.: Oxford University Press, 1968).

Robert Batlin, 'San Francisco Newspapers' Campaign Coverage: 1896, 1952', *Journalism Quarterly*, 31 (1954), pp. 297–303.

Earle Beattie, 'In Canada's Centennial Year: US mass media influence probed', *Journalism Quarterly*, 44 (1967), pp. 667–72.

A. J. Beith, 'The Press', Chapter 11 in D. E. Butler and Anthony King, *The British General Election of 1964* (London: Macmillan, 1965).

Bernard Berelson, *Content Analysis as a Tool of Communications Research* (Glencoe: Free Press, 1952).

Bernard Berelson, 'The State of Communication Research' (first published 1959) in Dexter and White (Eds.), *People, Society and Mass Communications*, pp. 501–20.

Bernard Berelson, 'In the Presence of Culture', *Public Opinion Quarterly*, 28 (1964), pp. 1–12.

Bernard Berelson, Paul F. Lazarsfeld and William McPhee, *Voting: A Study of Opinion Formation in a Presidential Campaign* (Chicago University Press, 1954).

William A. Belson, *Studies in Readership* (London: Business Publications for Institute of Practitioners in Advertising, 1962).

William A. Belson, *The Impact of Television: Methods and Findings in Programme Research* (London: Crosby Lockwood, 1967).

Joseph Bensman, 'The Advertising Man and his Work, its Organization, Ethics and Meaning' in *Dollars and Sense* (N.Y.: Macmillan, 1967), pp. 9–68.

A. William Bluem, *Documentary in American Television: Form, Function, Method* (N.Y.: Hastings House, 1965).

Jay G. Blumler, 'British Television – The Outlines of a Research Strategy', *British Journal of Sociology*, 15 (1964), pp. 223–33.

Jay G. Blumler, 'Parliament and Political TV', *Encounter* (March, 1967) pp. 52–6.

Jay G. Blumler and Denis McQuail, 'British Broadcasting – Its Purposes, Structure and Control', *Gazette*, 11 (1965), pp. 166–91.

Jay G. Blumler and Denis McQuail, *Television in Politics: Its Uses and Influence* (London: Faber, 1968).

Jay G. Blumler and John Madge, *Citizenship and Television* (London: Political and Economic Planning, 1967, paper).

Leo Bogart, *The Age of Television* (N.Y.: Frederic Ungar, 1956).

Neil Borden, *The Economic Effects of Advertising* (Chicago: Richard D. Irvin, 1942).

Leon Bramson, *The Political Context of Sociology* (Princeton University Press, 1961).

Warren Breed, 'Newspaper "Opinion Leaders" and Processes of Standardization', *Journalism Quarterly*, 32 (1955), pp. 277–84.

Warren Breed, 'Social Control in the News Room', in Wilbur Schramm (Ed.), *Mass Communications* (1960), pp. 178–94.

Asa Briggs, *The Birth of Broadcasting* (London: Oxford University Press, 1961).

Asa Briggs, *The Golden Age of Wireless* (London: Oxford University Press, 1965).

Asa Briggs, 'Prediction and Control: Historical perspectives', *Sociological Review Monograph*, No. 13 (*The Sociology of Mass Media Communicators*) (1969), pp. 39–52.

British Market Research Bureau, *The GEC Bid for AEI: A Report on Factors Affecting Investment Decisions* (London: J. Walter Thompson, 1968).

Buckmaster and Moore, *International Publishing Corporation* (London: Buckmaster and Moore, Stockbrokers, 1969).

David Butler and Donald Stokes, *Political Change in Britain* (London: Macmillan, 1969).

Antony Buzek, *How the Communist Press Works* (London: Pall Mall, 1964).

A. M. Carr-Saunders and P. A. Wilson, 'Journalists' in *The Professions* (London: Oxford University Press, 1933), pp. 265–70.

Richard F. Carter and Bradley S. Greenberg, 'Newspapers or Television: Which Do You Believe?', *Journalism Quarterly*, 42 (1965), pp. 29–34.

Douglass Cater, *The Fourth Branch of Government* (Boston: Houghton Mifflin, 1959).

Zechariah Chafee, 'Government and Mass Communications' (first published 1947) in Berelson and Janowitz (Eds.), *Reader in Public Opinion and Communication*, pp. 220–32.

Marquis Childs and James Reston, *Walter Lippmann and His Times* (N.Y.: Harcourt Brace, 1959).

James B. Christoph, 'The Press and Politics in Britain and America', *Political Quarterly*, 34 (1963), pp. 137–50.

Bernard C. Cohen, *The Press and Foreign Policy* (Princeton University Press, 1963).

Philip E. Converse, 'Information Flow and the Stability of Partisan Attitudes', Chapter 8 in Angus Campbell et al., *Elections and the Political Order* (N.Y.: John Wiley, 1966).

Kent Cooper, *Barriers Down: The Story of the News Agency Epoch* (N.Y.: Farrar and Rinehart, 1942).

Elmer E. Cornwell, *Presidential Leadership of Public Opinion* (Indiana University Press, 1965).

G. A. Cranfield, *The Development of the Provincial Newspaper 1700–1760* (London: Oxford University Press, 1962).

John Crawley, *The Work of a BBC Foreign Correspondent*, BBC lunch-time lecture (London: BBC, 1964).

Melvin L. DeFleur and O. N. Larsen, *The Flow of Information* (N.Y.: Harper, 1958).

Melvin L. DeFleur, 'Occupational Roles as Portrayed on Television', *Public Opinion Quarterly*, 28 (1964), pp. 57–74.

Melvin L. DeFleur, *Theories of Mass Communication* (N.Y.: McKay, 1966, paper).

Melvin L. DeFleur and Lois B. DeFleur, 'The Relative Contribution of Television as a Learning Source for Children's Occupational Knowledge', *American Sociological Review*, 32 (1967), pp. 777–89.

Karl W. Deutsch, *Nationalism and Social Communication* (Michigan: M.I.T. Press, 1953, 1966 paper).

Karl W. Deutsch, *The Nerves of Government: Models of Political Communication and Control* (N.Y.: Free Press, 1963, 1966 paper).

Wilson P. Dizard, *Television: A World View* (Syracuse University Press, 1966).

Lewis Donohew, 'Newspaper Gatekeepers and Forces in the News Channel', *Public Opinion Quarterly*, 31 (1967), pp. 61–8.

Leonard W. Doob, *Communications in Africa: A Search for Boundaries* (Yale University Press, 1961).

Edward C. Dreyer and Walter A. Rosenbaum (Eds.), *Political Opinion and Electoral Behaviour: Essays and Studies* (Belmont, California: Wadsworth, 1966, paper).

Joffre Dumazedier, *Toward a Society of Leisure* (N.Y.: Free Press, 1967).

Hugh Dalziel Duncan, *Communication and Social Order* (London: Oxford University Press 1962 and 1968 paper).

The Economist Intelligence Unit, *The National Newspaper Industry: A Survey* (London: EIU for the Joint Board for the National Newspaper Industry, 1966).

Maurice Edelman, *The Mirror: A Political History* (London: Hamish Hamilton, 1966).

Edwin Emery, *The Press and America: An Interpretive History of Journalism*

(Englewood Cliffs: Prentice-Hall, 1962 edition).

Walter B. Emery, *Broadcasting and Government: Responsibilities and Regulations* (Michigan University Press, 1961).

R. Escarpit, *The Book Revolution* (London: Harrap/UNESCO, 1966).

Leon Festinger, *A Theory of Cognitive Dissonance* (Evanston, Illinois: Row, Peterson, 1957).

Richard Findlater, *The Book Writers* (London: Society of Authors, 1966, paper).

Alfred Friendly and Ronald Goldfarb, *Crime and Publicity: The Impact of News on the Administration of Justice* (N.Y.: Random House, 1967 and 1968 paper.)

J. Edward Gerald, *The British Press under Government Economic Controls* (University of Minnesota Press, 1956).

J. Edward Gerald, *The Social Responsibility of the Press* (University o Minnesota Press, 1963).

Walter Gieber, 'How the "Gatekeepers" View Local Civil Liberties News', *Journalism Quarterly*, 37 (1960), pp. 199–205.

Rafael E. Gill, 'Press Corps in Israel: Statistical Trends 1955–59', *Gazette*, 7 (1962), pp. 283–90.

William A. Glaser, 'Television and Voting Turnout', *Public Opinion Quarterly*, 29 (1965), pp. 71–86.

Jack Goody (Ed.), *Literacy in Traditional Societies* (Cambridge University Press, 1968).

Harold F. Gosnell, 'Relation of the Press to Voting' in *Machine Politics: Chicago Model* (University of Chicago Press, 1937 and 1968 paper), pp. 156–82.

John Goulden, *Newspaper Management* (London: Heinemann/National Council for the Training of Journalists, 1967).

Bradley S. Greenberg and Edwin B. Parker (Eds.), *The Kennedy Assassination and the American Public* (Stanford University Press, 1965).

John Gross, *The Rise and Fall of the Man of Letters: English Literary Life since 1800* (London: Weidenfeld and Nicolson, 1969).

Oron J. Hale, *The Captive Press of the Third Reich* (Princeton University Press, 1964).

Stuart Hall and P. Whannel, *The Popular Arts* (London: Hutchinson, 1964).

J. D. Halloran, *The Effects of Mass Communication with Special Reference to Television* (Leicester University Press, 1964).

Leo A. Handel, *Hollywood Looks at Its Audience* (University of Illinois Press, 1950).

Derek Hanson, 'Young Radio Listeners', *New Society* (20th February, 1969).

Martin Harrison, 'Government and Press in France During the Algerian War', *American Political Science Review*, 58 (1964), pp. 273–85.

Martin Harrison, 'Television and Radio', Chapter 10 in D. E. Butler and Anthony King, *The British General Election of 1964* (London: Macmillan, 1965).

Martin Harrison, 'Television and Radio', Chapter 7 in D. E. Butler and Anthony King, *The British General Election of 1966* (London: Macmillan, 1966).

Jim A. Hart, 'Election Campaign Coverage in English and US Daily Newspapers', *Journalism Quarterly*, 43 (1966), pp. 443–8.

John W. Henderson, *The United States Information Agency* (N.Y.: Frederick Praeger, 1969).

Harold Herd, *The March of Journalism* (London: Allen and Unwin, 1952).

Hilde T. Himmelweit, A. N. Oppenheim and Pamela Vince, *Television and the Child* (Oxford University Press, 1958).

Hilde T. Himmelweit, 'Television Revisited', *New Society* (1st November, 1962).

Hilde T. Himmelweit, 'A Theoretical Framework for the Consideration of the Effects of Television: A British Report', *Journal of Social Issues*, 18 (1962), pp. 16–28.

Richard Hoggart, *The Uses of Literacy* (London: Penguin, 1958, paper).

John Hohenberg, *Foreign Correspondence: The Great Reporters and Their Times* (Columbia University Press, 1964).

Stuart Hood, *A Survey of Television* (London: Heinemann, 1967).

Carl I. Hovland, Irving L. Janis, and Harold H. Kelley, *Communication and Persuasion* (Yale University Press, 1953 and 1963 paper).

Carl I. Hovland (Ed.), *The Order of Presentation in Persuasion* (Yale University Press, 1957).

Carl I. Hovland, Arthur A. Lumsdaine, and Fred D. Sheffield, *Experiments on Mass Communication* (Princeton University Press, 1949; and N.Y.: John Wiley, 1965 paper).

Ralph M. Hower, *The History of an Advertising Agency* (Harvard University Press, 1949).

Alex Inkeles, *Public Opinion in the Soviet Union: a study in mass persuasion* (Harvard University Press, 1950).

International Press Institute, *The Flow of News* (Zurich: IPI, 1953).

International Press Institute, *The Press in Authoritarian Countries* (Zurich: IPI, 1959).

International Press Institute, *Press Councils and Press Codes* (Zurich: IPI, 1961).

International Press Institute, *Professional Secrecy and the Journalist* (Zurich: IPI, 1962).

Morris Janowitz, *The Community Press in an Urban Setting* (University of Chicago Press, 1952; 1967 paper).

Nicholas Johnson, 'What do Children Learn from War Comics?', *New Society* (7th July, 1966).

Elihu Katz and David Foulkes, 'On the Use of the Mass Media as "Escape": Clarification of a Concept', *Public Opinion Quarterly*, 26 (1962), pp. 377–88.

Elihu Katz and Paul F. Lazarsfeld, *Personal Influence: The Part Played by People in the Flow of Mass Communications* (Glencoe: Free Press, 1955; 1964 paper).

S. Kelley, Jnr, *Professional Public Relations and Political Power* (Baltimore: Johns. Hopkins Press, 1956).

V. O. Key, Jnr, *Public Opinion and American Democracy* (N.Y.: Knopf, 1961).

Chris Knapper and Peter B. Warr, 'The Effect of Position and Layout on the Readership of News Items', *Gazette*, 11 (1965), pp. 323–28.

Siegfried Kracauer, 'The Challenge of Qualitative Content Analysis', *Public Opinion Quarterly*, 16 (1952), pp. 631–42.

Siegfried Kracauer, *Theory of Films, the Redemption of Physical Reality* (N.Y.: Oxford University Press, 1960).

Sidney Kraus (Ed.), *The Great Debates* (Indiana University Press, 1962).

Hillier Krieghbaum, *Science and the Mass Media* (New York University Press, 1967).

T. E. Kruglak, *The Foreign Correspondents* (Geneva: Librairie E. Droz, 1955).

Theodore E. Kruglak, *The Two Faces of Tass* (N.Y.: McGraw-Hill, 1963, paper).

Kurt Lang and Gladys E. Lang, *Politics and Television* (Chicago: Quadrangle, 1968).

Otto N. Larsen, 'Social Effects of Mass Communication' in Robert E. L. Faris (Ed.), *Handbook of Modern Sociology* (Chicago: Rand McNally, 1964), pp. 348–81.

Harold Lasswell, 'The Structure and Function of Communication in Society' (first published 1948) in Berelson and Janowitz, *Reader in Public Opinion and Communication*, pp. 178–90.

Paul F. Lazarsfeld, Bernard Berelson and Hazel Gaudet, *The People's Choice: How the Voter Makes up his Mind in a Presidential Campaign* (Columbia University Press, 1944).

Paul F. Lazarsfeld and Morris Rosenberg, *The Language of Social Research* (N.Y.: Free Press, 1955 and 1965 paper).

Daniel Lerner, *The Passing of Traditional Society: Modernizing the Middle East* (Glencoe: Free Press, 1958).

Daniel Lerner and Wilbur Schramm (Eds.), *Communications and Change in Developing Nations* (Honolulu: East-West Center Press, 1967).

H. Phillip Levy, *The Press Council: History, Procedure and Cases* (London: Macmillan, 1967).

Walter Lippmann, *Public Opinion* (first published in 1922, N.Y.: Free Press, 1965 paper).

Ruth Leeds Love, 'Television and the Kennedy Assassination', *New Society* (13th October, 1966).

Leo Lowenthal, 'Biographies in Popular Magazines', in Paul F. Lazarsfeld and Frank Stanton (Eds.), *Radio Research 1942–43* (Fairlawn N.J.: Essential Books, 1944).

Leo Lowenthal, *Literature, Popular Culture and Society* (Englewood Cliffs N.J.: Prentice-Hall, 1961).

Jack Lyle, *The News in Megalopolis* (San Francisco: Chandler, 1967).

Brenda Maddox, 'The Connections: A Survey of Communications', *The Economist* (9th August, 1969).

Peter Mann and Jacqueline L. Burgoyne, *Books and Reading* (London: Andre Deutsch, 1969).

F. J. Mansfield, *'Gentlemen, The Press': Official History of the National Union of Journalists* (London: W. H. Allen, 1943).

Donald R. Matthews, 'Senators and Reporters', in *US Senators and Their World* (N.Y.: Vintage Books, 1960 paper).

The Market Research Society, *Research in Advertising* (London: MRS and Oakwood Press, 1963).

Donald McLachlan, 'The Press and Public Opinion', *British Journal of Sociology*, 6 (1955), pp. 159–66.

W. D. McClelland, 'Women's Weeklies', *New Society* (31st December, 1964).

Jack McLeod, Scott Ward, and Karen Tancill, 'Alienation and Uses of the Mass Media', *Public Opinion Quarterly*, 29 (1966), pp. 583–94.

Marshall McLuhan, *Understanding Media* (London: Routledge and Kegan Paul, 1964).

Henry Mayer, *The Press in Australia* (London: Angus and Robertson), 1964).

Harold Mendlesohn, *Mass Entertainment* (New Haven: College and University Press, 1966 paper).

John C. Merrill, 'How *Time* Stereotyped Three US Presidents', *Journalism Quarterly*, 42 (1965), pp. 563–70.

Robert K. Merton, *Mass Persuasion* (N.Y.: Harper, 1946).

Robert K. Merton, 'The Sociology of Knowledge and Mass Communications', *Social Theory and Social Structure* (Glencoe: Free Press, 1957 edition), pp. 439–528.

Edgar Morin, *The Stars: An Account of the Star-System in Motion Pictures* (N.Y.: Grove Press, 1960 paper).

Edgar Morin and Claude Bremond, 'An International Survey on the Film Hero', *International Social Science Journal*, 14 (1963), pp. 113–19.

Frank Luther Mott, *American Journalism* (N.Y.: Macmillan, 1962).

P. W. Musgrave, 'How Children Use Television', *New Society* (20th February, 1969).

Gunnar Myrdal, 'The Negro Press' in *An American Dilemma*, Vol. 2. *The Negro Social Structure* (N.Y.: McGraw-Hill, 1944, 1964 paper), pp. 908–24.

Ralph O. Nafziger and David M. White (Eds.), *Introduction to Mass Communications Research* (Louisiana State University Press, 1963 edition).

Chester A. Newland, 'Press Coverage of the United States Supreme Court', *Western Political Quarterly*, 17 (1964), pp. 15–36.

Dan D. Nimmo, *Newsgathering in Washington* (N.Y.: Atherton Press, 1964).

Raymond B. Nixon and Jean Ward, 'Trends in Newspaper Ownership' (first published 1961) in Berelson and Janowitz, *Reader in Public Opinion and Communication*, pp. 193–205.

Marjorie Ogilvy-Webb, *The Government Explains: A Study of the Information Services* (London: Allen and Unwin, 1965).

Einar Östgaard, 'Factors Influencing the Flow of News', *Journal of Peace Research*, 1 (1965), pp. 39–56.

Robert E. Park, *On Social Control and Collective Behavior* (Ed. Ralph H. Turner) (University of Chicago Press, 1967 paper).

Talcott Parsons and W. White, 'The Mass Media and the Structure of American Society', *Journal of Social Issues*, 16 (1960), pp. 67–77.

B. Paulu, *British Broadcasting in Transition* (London: Macmillan, 1961).

D. Payne (Ed.), *The Obstinate Audience* (Ann Arbor, Michigan: Foundation for Research on Human Behavior, 1965).

Theodore Peterson, Jay W. Jensen, and William L. Rivers, *The Mass Media and Modern Society* (N.Y.: Holt, Rhinehart, and Winston, 1965).

William Pickles, 'Political Attitudes in the Television Age', *Political Quarterly*, 30 (1959), pp. 54–66.

Philip Pinkus, *Grub Street Stripped Bare: The Scandalous Lives and Pornographic Works of the Original Grub Street Writers* (London: Constable, 1968).

Political and Economic Planning, *The British Press* (London: PEP, 1938).

Political and Economic Planning, *The British Film Industry* (London: PEP, 1952 and 1958).

Ithiel de Sola Pool, *The 'Prestige Papers': A Survey of their Editorials* (Stanford University Press, 1952).

Ithiel de Sola Pool (Ed.), *Trends in Content Analysis* (University of Illinois Press), 1959).

Reginald Pound and Geoffrey Harmsworth, *Northcliffe* (London: Cassell, 1959).

Hortense Powdermaker, *Hollywood: The Dream Factory* (Boston: Little, Brown, 1950).

Lucian Pye (Ed.), *Communication and Political Development* (Princeton University Press, 1963).

Y. Rao, *Communication and Development: A Study of Two Indian Villages* (University of Minnesota Press, 1966).

Rene Remond and Claude Neuschwander, 'Télévision et Comportement Politique', *Revue Française de Science Politique*, 13 (1963), pp. 325–47.

John W. Riley and Matilda White Riley, 'Mass Communication and the Social System', in Robert K. Merton et al. (Eds.), *Sociology Today* (N.Y.: Basic Books, 1959), pp. 537–78.

John P. Robinson and Philip E. Converse, 'The Impact of Television on Mass Media Usage: A Cross-National Comparison', (Survey Research Center, University of Michigan, duplicated. Paper read at the sixth World Congress of Sociology in Evian, France, 1966).

Stein Rokkan and Per Torsvik, 'The Voter, the Reader and the Party Press: An Analysis of Political Preference and Newspaper Reading in Norway', *Gazette*, 6 (1960), pp. 311–28.

Elmo Roper, 'The Public's View of Television and Other Media', in Edward C. Dreyer and Walter A. Rosenbaum (Eds.), *Political Opinion and Electoral Behavior* (Belmont: Wadsworth, 1966 paper), pp. 309–17.

Arnold Rose, 'The Study of the Influence of the Mass Media on Public Opinion', *Kyklos*, 15 (1962), pp. 465–82.

Richard Rose (Ed.), *Studies in British Politics* (London: Macmillan, 1966), pp. 150–201.

Richard Rose, *Influencing Voters: A Study of Campaign Rationality* (London: Faber, 1967).

Bernard Rosenberg and Norris Fliegel, *The Vanguard Artist: Portrait and Self-Portrait* (Chicago: Quadrangle, 1965).

Leo C. Rosten, *The Washington Correspondents* (N.Y.: Harcourt, Brace, 1937).

Francis E. Rourke, *Secrecy and Publicity: Dilemmas of Democracy* (Baltimore: Johns Hopkins Press, 1961, and 1966 paper).

Bernard Rubin, *Political Television* (Belmont, Cal.: Wadsworth, 1967 paper).

Renaud Sainsaulieu, 'Les Classes Sociales Defavorisées en Face de la Télévision', *Revue Française de Sociologie*, 7 (1966), pp. 201–14.

Merrill Samuelson, 'A Standardized Test to Measure Job Satisfaction in the Newsroom', *Journalism Quarterly*, 39 (1962), pp. 285–91.

Herbert I. Schiller, *Mass Communications and American Empire* (N.Y.: Augustus M. Kelley, 1969).

Wilbur Schramm, *Responsibility in Mass Communication* (N.Y.: Harper, 1957).

Wilbur Schramm, Jack Lyle, and Edwin B. Parker, *Television in the Lives o our Children* (Stanford University Press, 1961).

Wilbur Schramm, Jack Lyle and Ithiel de Sola Pool, *The People Look at Educational Television* (Stanford University Press, 1963).

Wilbur Schramm, *Mass Media and National Development* (Stanford University Press and UNESCO, 1964).

Gilbert Seldes, *The Great Audience* (N.Y.: Viking Press, 1950).

Colin Seymour-Ure, 'The Parliamentary Press Gallery in Ottawa', *Parliamentary Affairs*, 16 (1962), pp. 35–41.

Colin Seymour-Ure, 'The Press', Chapter 8 in D. E. Butler and Anthony King, *The British General Election of 1966* (London: Macmillan, 1966).

Colin Seymour-Ure, *The Press, Politics and the Public* (London: Methuen, 1968).

Andrew Sharf, *The British Press and Jews under Nazi Rule* (London: Oxford University Press – Institute of Race Relations, 1964).

Tamotsu Shibutani, *Improvised News: A Sociological Study of Rumor* (Indianapolis: Bobbs-Merrill, 1966).

Edward A. Shils and Morris Janowitz, 'Cohesion and Disintegration in the Wehrmacht' (first published 1948) in Berelson and Janowitz (Eds.), *Reader in Public Opinion and Communication*, pp. 402–17.

Frederick Seaton Siebert, *Freedom of the Press in England 1476–1776* (University of Illinois Press, 1952; 1965 paper).

Harry J. Skornia, *Television and Society: An Inquest and Agenda for Improvement* (N.Y.: McGraw-Hill, 1965).

E. Sommerland, *The Press in Developing Countries* (Sydney University Press, 1966).

Rodney W. Stark, 'Policy and the Pros: An Organizational Analysis of a Metropolitan Newspaper', *Berkeley Journal of Sociology* (1962), pp. 11–31.

Gary A. Steiner, *The People Look at Television: A Study of Audience Attitudes* (N.Y.: Knopf, 1963).

Norman Swallow, *Factual Television* (London: Focal Press, 1966).

Percy H. Tannenbaum, 'Communication of Science Information', *Science* (10th May, 1963), pp. 579–83.

Television Research Committee, *Second Progress Report and Recommendations* (Leicester University Press, 1969).

The Times, *The History of The Times* (London: *The Times*, 1935 to 1952), 5 volumes.

Joseph Trenaman and Denis McQuail, *Television and the Political Image* (London: Methuen, 1961).

Jeremy Tunstall, *The Advertising Man in London Advertising Agencies* (London: Chapman and Hall, 1964).

Jeremy Tunstall, *The Westminster Lobby Correspondents* (London: Routledge and Kegan Paul, 1970).

UNESCO, *World Communications: Press, radio, television, film* (Paris: UNESCO, 1964).

Herbert Waltzer, 'In the Magic Lantern: Television Coverage of the 1964 National Conventions', *Public Opinion Quarterly*, 30 (1966), pp. 33–53.

Peter B. Warr and Christopher Knapper, *The Perception of People and Events* (London: John Wiley, 1968).

E. G. Wedell, *Broadcasting and Public Policy* (London: Michael Joseph, 1968).

John Whale, *The Half-Shut Eye: Television and Politics in Britain and America* (London: Macmillan, 1967).

Urban G. Whitaker, Jr, (Ed.), *Propaganda and International Relations* (San Francisco: Chandler, 1960, and 1962 paper).

David Manning White, ' "The Gatekeeper": A Case Study in the Selection of News' (1950 first published) in White and Dexter, *People, Society and Mass Communication*, pp. 160–71.

Llewellyn White and Robert D. Leigh, 'The Growth of International Communications' and 'The International News-Gatherers', in Wilbur Schramm, *Mass Communications*, pp. 70–94.

Harold L. Wilensky, 'Mass Society and Mass Culture: Interdependence or Independence?' *American Sociological Review*, 29 (1964), pp. 173–97 (and reprinted in Berelson and Janowitz, *Reader in Public Opinion and Communication*, pp. 293–327).

Harold L. Wilensky, *Organizational Intelligence: Knowledge and Policy in Government and Industry* (N.Y.: Basic Books, 1967).

Francis Williams, *Transmitting World News: A Study of Telecommunications and the Press* (Paris: UNESCO, 1953).

Francis Williams, *Dangerous Estate: The Anatomy of Newspapers* (London: Longmans, 1957).

Francis Williams, *The Right to Know: The Rise of the World Press* (London: Longmans, 1969).

Raymond Williams, *Communications* (London: Penguin, 1962 paper).

H. H. Wilson, *Pressure Group* (London: Secker and Warburg, 1961).

Lord Windlesham, *Communication and Political Power* (London: Jonathan Cape, 1966).

Lord Windlesham, 'Television: Some Problems of Creativity and Control', *Sociological Review Monograph*, No. 13 (*The Sociology of Mass Media Communicators*) 1969, pp. 129–40.

John Playsted Wood, *The Story of Advertising* (N.Y.: Ronald Press, 1958).

Charles R. Wright, 'Functional Analysis and Mass Communication', *Public Opinion Quarterly*, 23 (1960), pp. 605–20.

Frederick C. Yu (Ed.), *Mass Media and the Behavioral Sciences* (N.Y.: Russell Sage, 1968).

Frederick C. Yu, *Mass Persuasion in Communist China* (London: Pall Mall, 1964).

OFFICIAL PUBLICATIONS

Many official publications deal with specialized aspects of the media. In Britain there are reports of specialized Parliamentary Committees (e.g., on Public Accounts, and on Privilege), White Papers, reports on prices and incomes and on monopoly issues, official investigations of printing strikes and so on. The press and broadcasting are the subject of Parliamentary Debates. A much larger number of official publications refer to the media in relation to other subjects of enquiry.

Among major British official publications in the 1960s were:

1. (Pilkington) *Report of the Committee on Broadcasting, 1960*, (London: HMSO, 1962), Cmnd 1753. Plus 2 volumes of evidence (Cmnd 1819).
2. (Shawcross) *Royal Commission on the Press, 1961–62, Report* (London: HMSO), Cmnd 1811. Plus 9 volumes of evidence (Cmnd 1812).
3. Monopolies Commission, *Report on The Times Newspaper and The Sunday Times Newspaper* (London: HMSO, 1966) (H.C. 273).
4. Monopolies Commission, *Films: A Report on the Supply of Films for Exhibition in Cinemas* (London: HMSO, 1966) (H.C. 206).

ANNUAL REPORTS

Reports and Handbooks are published at least annually in London by the British Broadcasting Corporation, the Independent Television Authority, the General Council of the Press. All the major national media organizations (except the BBC) are public companies and publish annual company reports.

List of Contributors

Ibrahim ABU-LUGHOD, Smith College.

Joseph BENSMAN, Department of Sociology and Anthropology, City College, New York.

Jay G. BLUMLER, Centre for Television Research, University of Leeds.

Oliver BOYD-BARRETT, Industrial Sociology Unit, Imperial College, London University.

Roger L. BROWN, Centre for Mass Communication Research, Leicester University.

Ronald F. BUNN, Department of Political Science, University of Houston.

Tom BURNS, Department of Sociology, University of Edinburgh.

David BUTLER, Nuffield College, Oxford University.

James CURRAN, Trinity College, Cambridge University.

B. P. EMMETT, BBC Audience Research.

Melvin L. DEFLEUR, Department of Sociology, Washington State University.

Philip ELLIOTT, Centre for Mass Communication Research, Leicester University.

Winston FLETCHER, MCR Advertising Ltd, London.

Johan GALTUNG, International Peace Research Institute, Oslo.

James HALLORAN, Centre for Mass Communication Research, Leicester University.

D. HARPER, Industrial Sociology Unit, Imperial College, London University.

Hilde T. HIMMELWEIT, Department of Social Psychology, London School of Economics.

Gayle Durham HOLLANDER, School of Social Science, Hampshire College, Amherst, Massachusetts.

Michael LANE, Department of Sociology, University of Essex.

Peter H. MANN, Department of Sociological Studies, University of Sheffield.

Denis MCQUAIL, Department of Sociology, University of Southampton.

Aleksander MATEJKO, Cracow Press Research Centre.

Joan MUNRO, Department of Social Psychology, London School of Economics.

Mari Holmboe RUGE, International Peace Research Institute, Oslo.

Robert SILVEY, formerly head of BBC Audience Research.

Donald STOKES, Department of Political Science, University of Michigan.

Andrew TUDOR, Department of Sociology, University of Essex.

Malcolm WARNER, London Graduate School of Business.

Name Index

Subject Index